INTERNAL CORPORATE INVESTIGATIONS

INTERNAL CORPORATE INVESTIGATIONS

THIRD EDITION

Barry F. McNeil and Brad D. Brian
Editors

Cover design by ABA Publishing.

The materials contained herein represent the opinions and views of the authors and/or the editors, and should not be construed to be the views or opinions of the law firms or companies with whom such persons are in partnership with, associated with, or employed by, nor of the American Bar Association or Section of Litigation, unless adopted pursuant to the bylaws of the Association.

Nothing contained in this book is to be considered as the rendering of legal advice, either generally or in connection with any specific issue or case; nor do these materials purport to explain or interpret any specific bond or policy, or any provisions thereof, issued by any particular franchise company, or to render franchise or other professional advice. Readers are responsible for obtaining advice from their own lawyers or other professionals. This book and any forms and agreements herein are intended for educational and informational purposes only.

© 2007 American Bar Association. All rights reserved.

No part of this publication may be reproduced, stored in a retrieval system, or transmitted in any form or by any means, electronic, mechanical, photocopying, recording, or otherwise, without the prior written permission of the publisher. For permission, contact the ABA Copyrights & Contracts Department at copyright@abanet.org or via fax at 312-988-6030.

Printed in the United States of America

10 09 08 07 5 4 3 2 1

Library of Congress Cataloging-in-Publication Data

Barry F. McNeil and Brad D. Brian, eds.
  Internal Corporate Investigations, 3rd ed.
Library of Congress Cataloging-in-Publication Data is on file.

ISBN 13: 978-1-59031-915-4

Discounts are available for books ordered in bulk. Special consideration is given to state bars, CLE programs, and other bar-related organizations. Inquire at Book Publishing, ABA Publishing, American Bar Association, 321 North Clark Street, Chicago, Illinois 60610-4714.

www.ababooks.org

Contents

About the Editors xiii

About the Contributors xv

CHAPTER 1 Overview: Initiating an Internal Investigation
and Assembling the Investigative Team 1

I. INTRODUCTION 2
   A. The Sarbanes-Oxley Act of 2002 and Its
      Aftermath 3
   B. The McNulty Memo of 2007: Cooperation,
      Waiver and Indemnification 5
II. DIFFERENT TYPES OF INTERNAL
    INVESTIGATIONS 6
III. THE INITIAL MEETING 7
   A. The Starting Point: Identifying the Client and
      Deciding Whether to Conduct an Investigation 7
   B. Defining the Scope of Internal Investigation 9
   C. Applying the Attorney-Client Privilege and
      Work-Product Doctrine 10
   D. Assembling the Investigative Team 11
   E. Agreeing to Lines of Reporting and Supervision 12
   F. Anticipating What Can Go Wrong 13
IV. PRELIMINARY STEPS TO PREPARE FOR
    GOVERNMENT INVESTIGATIONS 14
V. CONCLUSION 16

CHAPTER 2 Implications of the Attorney-Client Privilege
          and Work-Product Doctrine 17
I. INTRODUCTION 18
II. ATTORNEY-CLIENT PRIVILEGE 19
    A. Definition of the Attorney-Client Privilege 19
    B. Elements of Attorney-Client Privilege 21
    C. Practical Problems of Employee Interviews 36
III. WORK PRODUCT PROTECTION 44
    A. Work-Product Doctrine Defined 44
    B. Factual Versus Opinion Work Product 46
    C. Elements of the Work-Product Doctrine 47
    D. Overcoming the Qualified Immunity 56
    E. Protection of a Lawyer's Mental Impressions 57
IV. OVERCOMING THE ATTORNEY-CLIENT
    PRIVILEGE AND WORK-PRODUCT DOCTRINE 60
    A. Waiver 60
    B. The Crime/Fraud Exception 78
    C. Shareholder Litigation 82
V. EFFECT OF THE SARBANES-OXLEY ACT AND
    RECENT SECURITIES EXCHANGE COMMISSION
    AND DEPARTMENT OF JUSTICE POLICIES
    ON THE ATTORNEY-CLIENT PRIVILEGE 86

CHAPTER 3 The Witness Interview Process 93
I. INTRODUCTION 94
II. PREPARING FOR WITNESS INTERVIEWS 95
    A. Initial Concerns 95
    B. Key Principles 98
    C. Before the Interview 100
III. CONDUCTING THE INTERVIEW 102
    A. Mechanics 102
    B. Warnings to Witnesses and the
       Attorney-Client Privilege 103
    C. Conducting the Interview 107
IV. MAKING A RECORD OF THE INTERVIEW 108

V. SPECIAL ISSUES 111
   A. Sarbanes-Oxley and the Responsibilities
      of Counsel 111
   B. Obstruction of Justice 112
   C. Other Typical Problems That Arise during Witness
      Interviews 114
VI. CONCLUSION 116

CHAPTER 4 Perjury and Obstruction of Justice 117
I. INTRODUCTION 117
II. PERJURY AND SUBORNATION OF PERJURY 118
   A. Perjury Under § 1621: Essential Elements 119
   B. Burden of Proof and the Two Witness Rule 121
   C. True Answers and Ambiguous Questions 122
   D. Perjury Under § 1623: Differences 124
   E. Subornation of Perjury 126
III. OBSTRUCTION OF JUSTICE 130
   A. False Statements 131
   B. Witness Tampering 135
   C. Document Destruction 140

CHAPTER 5 Gathering and Organizing Relevant
           Documents: An Essential Task in Any
           Investigation 147
I. INTRODUCTION 148
II. ORGANIZATION AND PLANNING 150
   A. Initial Dialogue with Management 150
   B. Document Retention and Preservation 152
   C. The Investigating Team 152
   D. Initial On-Site Inspection 153
III. DOCUMENT GATHERING 153
   A. Ensuring Comprehensiveness 153
   B. Ensuring Integrity and Control 154
   C. Electronic Document Gathering 155
IV. DOCUMENT PROCESSING 156
   A. Overview 156
   B. Numbering 157

C. Copies 157
D. Review 158
E. Indexing and Coding 159
F. Computer Imaging of Documents 160
G. Inadvertent Waiver of Privilege 161
V. PREPARATION OF INTERNAL SUMMARIES,
CHRONOLOGIES, BINDERS 162
A. Hot Document Chronology 162
B. Summaries 164
VI. PRODUCTION OF DOCUMENTS TO GOVERNMENT
OR CIVIL LITIGANTS 164
A. Advocacy Considerations 164
B. Personal versus Business Records 166
C. Production Abuses 167
D. Destruction of Documents 167
E. Confidentiality Agreements 168
VII. CONCLUSION 169

APPENDIX A 170
APPENDIX B 172
APPENDIX C 173
APPENDIX D 174

CHAPTER 6   The Hydra Effect: Parallel Proceedings
            Accompanying Internal Investigations 175

I. INTRODUCTION 176
II. RECURRING ISSUES IN PARALLEL
    PROCEEDINGS 178
A. Obtaining Civil Stays to Prevent Criminal Prejudice . 178
B. The Fifth Amendment and Adverse Civil
   Inferences 185
C. Criminal and Civil Penalties: Double Jeopardy? ... 188
D. Collateral Estoppel: The Consequences of "Losing" . 193
E. Responding to Employee Misconduct 197
F. *Ex Parte* Contacts by Government Lawyers 200
G. Providing Legal Representation for Employees 210

H. Joint Defense Agreements: Benefits, Limits, and Risks 215
I. Keeping the Government-Disclosure Genie in the Bottle 224
J. The Perils of Parallelism for Government Contractors 231
K. The *Gestalt* of Parallel-Proceedings Resolution ... 234
III. CONCLUSION 240

CHAPTER 7 Disclosure of Results of Internal Investigations to the Government or Other Third Parties 241
I. INTRODUCTION 242
II. REQUIRED DISCLOSURE 243
  A. Common-Law Rule 243
  B. Statutory Disclosure Requirements 245
  C. Problems Arising from Counsel's Knowledge of Criminal Conduct 248
III. VOLUNTARY DISCLOSURE 250
  A. The Benefits 250
  B. The Risks 254
IV. THE MECHANICS OF DISCLOSURE 259
V. CONCLUSION 259

CHAPTER 8 The Special Litigation Committee Investigation: No Undertaking for the Faint of Heart 261
I. THE SETTING 262
II. THE THEORETICAL FOUNDATION FOR A SPECIAL LITIGATION COMMITTEE 263
III. DERIVATIVE PLAINTIFF'S COUNSEL 265
IV. THE TOTAL CONTEXT 265
V. SELECTION OF COUNSEL 266
VI. THE INDEPENDENCE OF THE COMMITTEE 267
VII. THE DILEMMA INHERENT IN THE COMMITTEE'S WORK 269
VIII. IT IS THE COMMITTEE'S INVESTIGATION 270

IX.	COMMITTEE INTERVIEWS	271
X.	MINUTES OF COMMITTEE MEETINGS	271
XI.	RELATIONSHIP WITH OTHER INSIDE AND OUTSIDE COUNSEL	272
XII.	APPEARANCE OF COUNSEL FOR DERIVATIVE PLAINTIFF	273
XIII.	PROTECTING THE PRIVILEGE	274
XIV.	THE INVESTIGATION	277
XV.	CONCLUSION	279

APPENDIX A 280
APPENDIX B 281
APPENDIX C 282

CHAPTER 9 Unique Problems Associated with Internal Investigations in Environmental Cases 283

I.	INTRODUCTION	284
II.	REACTIVE INVESTIGATIONS	285
	A. Search Warrants	285
	B. Agency Demands to Review and Photocopy Documents	288
	C. Notices of Violations	289
	D. Conducting a Reactive Internal Investigation	289
III.	VOLUNTARY ENVIRONMENTAL INTERNAL INVESTIGATIONS	291
	A. Reasons for Environmental Compliance Audits	291
	B. Importance of Periodic Audits by Outside Consultants	292
	C. Problems Posed by Audits	293
	D. Electronic Records	294
	E. Audit Privilege Law	294
IV.	CONCLUSION	295

APPENDIX A 296

CHAPTER 10 Report of the Investigation 301

I.	INTRODUCTION	302
II.	DISCOVERABILITY OF THE INTERNAL INVESTIGATIVE REPORT	304

A. Attorney-Client Privilege 305
B. Work-Product Doctrine: A More Certain Refuge ... 308
C. Expanding the Privilege of Self-Criticism 310
III. PROTECTING THE REPORT: SHAREHOLDER ACTIONS AND DISCLOSURE TO GOVERNMENT AGENCIES 312
A. Shareholder Actions 312
B. Disclosure to Government Agencies 315
IV. LIBEL 319
A. Written Reports May Invite Libel Claims 319
B. Example of Libel Claims against Counsel 321
C. Opinion and Qualified Interest Privileges 322
D. Strategies for Minimizing Liability for Defamation .. 329
V. CONCLUSION 331
A. Summary 331
B. Minimizing Risks 331

CHAPTER 11 Internal Investigations
for Government Contractors 335
I. WHO ARE GOVERNMENT CONTRACTORS? 336
A. Suppliers to the Federal Government 337
B. Health Care 338
C. Other Government Contractors 338
II. BEGINNING OF THE INVESTIGATION 339
A. Subpoenas 340
B. Internal Discovery 342
C. The Qui Tam Telephone Call 342
III. RESPONDING TO A FRAUD INVESTIGATION BASIC PRINCIPLES FOR GOVERNMENT CONTRACTORS 344
A. Unique Features of Fraud Investigations Faced by Government Contractors 344
IV. CONCLUSION 350

CHAPTER 12 No Security: Internal Investigations
into Violations of the Securities Laws 353
I. OVERVIEW OF SECURITIES VIOLATIONS 354

II. DUTIES—AND PRESSURE—TO UNCOVER,
INVESTIGATE, AND REPORT VIOLATIONS 360
   A. Publicly Traded Companies 360
   B. Brokers and Dealers 381
III. CONDUCTING INTERNAL INVESTIGATIONS
AND DEALING WITH RELATED ISSUES
IN THE CONDUCT OF PARALLEL PROCEEDINGS .. 384
   A. Ensuring an Independent Investigation 386
   B. The (Largely) Insoluble Problem of Using
      the Investigation to Assist in Dealing with
      the Government without Waiving the Privilege 389
   C. Fifth Amendment Assertions: The Difficult Choices
      Faced by Individuals in Internal Investigations,
      and the Potential Impact of Those Choices
      on the Company 406
   D. Stays of Parallel Civil and SEC Proceedings 413
   E. Auditors' Involvement in Internal Investigations 417
IV. CONCLUDING LESSONS 420

CHAPTER 13   Internal Investigations in Health Care:
             Unique Enforcement Environment
             and the Dilemma of Disclosure 423

I. INTRODUCTION 424
II. HEALTH CARE ENFORCEMENT ENVIRONMENT ... 424
   A. Civil and Administrative Enforcement 425
   B. Criminal Enforcement 425
III. CORPORATE COMPLIANCE PROGRAMS 427
   A. Federal Sentencing Guidelines 427
   B. The OIG Model Plans 428
   C. Corporate Integrity Agreements 430
IV. SELF-REPORTING: MANDATORY OR VOLUNTARY .. 431
   A. Relevant Statutes 432
   B. Corporate Integrity Agreements and the OIG
      Model Plans 433
   C. The OIG's Provider Self-Disclosure Protocol 434
   D. Risks and Benefits of Voluntary Disclosure 436
V. CONCLUSION 439

CHAPTER 14 An Overview of Internal Investigations
from the In-House Perspective 441
I. INTRODUCTION 441
II. WHEN SHOULD AN INTERNAL INVESTIGATION
BE UNDERTAKEN? 449
III. WHO SHOULD CONDUCT THE INVESTIGATION? ... 450
IV. INITIATING THE INVESTIGATION 452
V. STRUCTURING THE INVESTIGATION 453
    A. Assembling the Investigative Team 453
    B. The Investigative Plan 453
VI. REPORTING THE RESULTS OF THE INVESTIGATION 463
VII. CONCLUSION 464

CHAPTER 15 Internal Investigations in Antitrust Matters .. 467
I. OVERVIEW OF APPLICABLE LAWS
AND ENFORCEMENT LANDSCAPE 467
    A. Federal Enforcement 467
    B. State Enforcement 468
    C. Foreign Enforcement 468
II. UNIQUE CONSIDERATIONS IN ANTITRUST
INTERNAL INVESTIGATIONS 469
    A. Identifying Your Client 469
    B. Investigative Steps 470
    C. Privilege Waiver Issues 471
    D. Reporting Process 471
    E. Relations with Counsel for Other
       Investigated Parties 472
III. CRIMINAL INVESTIGATIONS—WHAT EVERY
PRACTITIONER AND CLIENT MUST KNOW 472
    A. Increasingly High Stakes 473
    B. Investigative Tools 475
    C. Amnesty Under the Corporate Leniency Policy 478
    D. Value of Cooperation When Amnesty
       Is Not Available 485
    E. Assessing Whether Individual Employees
       Need Separate Counsel 486

F. Making a Proffer and Preparing for Interviews
   and Testimony 487
IV. RELATED LITIGATION 488
   A. Types of Civil Actions 488
   B. Parallel Litigation Concerns 489
   C. Benefits in Private Litigation from Amnesty
      Participation 490
V. CONCLUSION 490

CHAPTER 16 SOX It to Me: Internal Investigations
            in a *Sarbanes-Oxley* World 491

I. INTRODUCTION 492
II. BACKGROUND OF THE ACT 493
III. THE ACT'S IMPLICATIONS FOR INTERNAL
    CORPORATE INVESTIGATIONS 496
   A. Provisions of the Act Contributing
      to the Increase of Investigations 496
   B. Preliminary Considerations at the
      Commencement of the Investigation 499
   C. Dealing with the Company's Outside Auditors 505
   D. Disclosure to the Market 509
   E. Remedial Steps 510
IV. CONCLUSION 511

INDEX 513

About the Editors

Brad D. Brian
Mr. Brian, a partner in the Los Angeles firm of Munger, Tolles & Olson LLP, is a Fellow in the American College of Trial Lawyers and is listed in *The Best Lawyers in America* (S. Naifeh & G. Smith) in the business litigation, criminal defense, and bet-the-company categories. Mr. Brian was selected by the *National Law Journal* as one of the top ten trial lawyers of 1994 and has been identified by *California Law Business* every year from 1998 through 2006 as one of the 100 most influential lawyers in California. He has conducted more than 100 internal corporate investigations in the areas of securities regulation, environmental compliance, government contracts, the Foreign Corrupt Practices Act, the False Claims Act, bribery, and other matters, and has lectured regularly about internal investigations and crisis cases. Mr. Brian served as Chair of the American Bar Association Litigation Section in 2005–2006, and has taught trial advocacy at the University of Southern California Law Center, Harvard Law School's trial advocacy program, and the National Institute for Trial Advocacy. Mr. Brian graduated magna cum laude in 1977 from the Harvard Law School, where he served as Managing Editor of the *Harvard Law Review*. He later served as an assistant U.S. attorney in Los Angeles.

Barry F. McNeil
Mr. McNeil, a partner in the Dallas office of Haynes & Boone, LLP, is a Fellow in the American College of Trial Lawyers and a former chair of the Litigation Section of the American Bar Association. For 35 years Mr. McNeil has defended companies and senior officers before juries throughout the country in class actions and in corporate proceedings. Mr. McNeil oversees the 35 lawyer White Collar, Antitrust and Securities Group. He serves as counsel for numerous Special Litigation Committees, audit committees and outside directors, where he advises on issues arising under federal and state securities and antitrust laws, federal criminal statutes and conspiracy and fraud charges. In *The National Law Journal*'s "Biggest Defense Verdict of 1999" (May 22, 2000), Mr. McNeil led the successful defense of a national healthcare provider, winning a "slam-dunk defense verdict."

About the Contributors

Scott N. Auby is Counsel in the Washington, D.C., office of Debevoise & Plimpton LLP.

Nancy E. Barton is a former senior vice president, general counsel, and secretary at General Electric Capital Corporation, Stamford, Connecticut.

Dennis J. Block is a senior partner at Cadwalader, Wickersham & Taft LLP, New York, New York.

Stacy L. Brainin is with Haynes and Boone LLP in Dallas, Texas.

Brad D. Brian is a partner at Munger, Tolles & Olson LLP in Los Angeles, California.

H. Lowell Brown is the former Assistant General Counsel for Compliance at Northrop Grumman Corporation and now practices law in Washington, D.C., where he is counsel to the law firm of Cadwalader, Wickersham and Taft LLP.

Robert B. Buehler is a shareholder at Heller Ehrman LLP.

James Chen is a partner with the Washington, D.C.-based firm of Crowell & Moring, LLP, where he practices environmental and safety regulatory law.

Michele C. Coyle is Campus Counsel, University of California, Riverside, California.

David S. Frankel is engaged in the defense of white collar criminal cases, SEC enforcement actions, and other administrative agency proceedings at Kramer Levin Naftalis & Frankel LLP in New York, New York.

Ada Fernandez Johnson is with the Washington, D.C., office of Debevoise & Plimpton LLP.

Lawrence J. Fox is a partner at Drinker, Biddle & Reath.

xvii

ABOUT THE CONTRIBUTORS

Larry A. Gaydos is a partner in Haynes and Boone LLP in Dallas, Texas, where he is a member of the White Collar Defense and Antitrust Practice Group.

Thomas E. Holliday is a partner in the law firm of Gibson, Dunn & Crutcher in Los Angeles, California, and a member of the firm's Business Crimes and Investigations Group. Mr. Holliday also is a Fellow in the American College of Trial Lawyers.

Barry F. McNeil is a partner at Haynes and Boone LLP in Dallas, Texas.

Mark Miller is with Baker Botts LLP in Washington, D.C.

Bill Morrison is with Haynes and Boone LLP in Dallas, Texas.

Gary P. Naftalis is engaged in the defense of white collar criminal cases, SEC enforcement actions, and other administrative agency proceedings at Kramer Levin Naftalis & Frankel LLP in New York, New York.

Edwin G. Schallert is a partner at Debevoise & Plimpton in New York, New York.

Michael J. Shepard is a shareholder at Heller Ehrman LLP.

Jacqueline K. Shipchandler practices in the area of antitrust and white collar defense at Haynes and Boone LLP in Dallas, Texas.

Charles J. Stevens is a founding partner of Stevens & O'Connell LLP in Sacramento, California, and a former United States Attorney for the Eastern District of California.

Randall J. Turk is with Baker Botts LLP in Washington, D.C.

Michael Waldman is a partner at the firm of Fried, Frank, Harris, Shirver & Jacobson in Washington, D.C. He specializes in representing clients in internal investigations, civil fraud, False Claims Act, and white-collar criminal defense matters.

Gregory J. Weingart is a partner at Munger, Tolles & Olson LLP in Los Angeles, California.

J. Martin Willhite is a partner at Munger, Tolles & Olson LLP in Los Angeles, California.

Natalie R. Williams is Chief of the Civil Rights Bureau of the Office of the New York State Attorney General in New York, New York.

Overview: Initiating an Internal Investigation and Assembling the Investigative Team

Barry F. McNeil and Brad D. Brian

I. INTRODUCTION   2
   A. The Sarbanes-Oxley Act of 2002 and Its Aftermath   3
   B. The McNulty Memo of 2007: Cooperation, Waiver and Indemnification   5
II. DIFFERENT TYPES OF INTERNAL INVESTIGATIONS   6
III. THE INITIAL MEETING   7
   A. The Starting Point: Identifying the Client and Deciding Whether to Conduct an Investigation   7
   B. Defining the Scope of Internal Investigation   9
   C. Applying the Attorney-Client Privilege and Work-Product Doctrine   10
   D. Assembling the Investigative Team   11
   E. Agreeing to Lines of Reporting and Supervision   12
   F. Anticipating What Can Go Wrong   13

Barry F. McNeil is a partner at Haynes and Boone LLP in Dallas, Texas. Brad D. Brian is a partner at Munger, Tolles & Olson LLP in Los Angeles, California.

IV. PRELIMINARY STEPS TO PREPARE FOR GOVERNMENT
   INVESTIGATIONS   14
V. CONCLUSION   16

I. INTRODUCTION

SINCE THE 1990s, the business world has been roiled by one corporate scandal after another, each with its own accompanying corporate investigation. Internal investigations have provoked some scandals and have simply dissected others. But regardless of outcome, corporate investigations remain the single-most effective management tool for uncovering wrongdoing and instituting remedial relief. Today, more and more companies are vesting legal counsel with a broad mandate to investigate conduct, fashion remedies and communicate findings—good or bad—to enforcement authorities.

Internal Corporate Investigations was first published in 1992, a time when there was no Holder Memo (1999), no Seaboard (2001), no Sarbanes-Oxley (2002), no Thompson Memo (2003) and no McNulty Memo (2006).[1] While, in the intervening years, the mechanics of the investigative process have remained largely unchanged, these developments have vastly complicated the investigative process and the role of counsel within it.

For example, most of us thought it rare indeed that an attorney conducting a corporate investigation would himself or herself become a witness in a later criminal trial. Nor would we have envisioned how others would come to regard us as agents of enforcement authorities. And who could have anticipated the dramatic increase in the need for special litigation committees—wholly independent of management—who retain their own counsel and oversee counsel's investigation, threatening longstanding professional relationships and friendships and leading to divisions with unpredictable results? The protection of confidences has undergone real change. There was a time when lawyer and client could be relatively certain confidential communications

---

1. Memorandum from Deputy Attorney General Eric Holder, Jr., Federal Prosecution of Corporations (1999); Report of Investigation Pursuant to Section 21(a) of the Securities Exchange Act of 1934 and Commission Statement on the Relationship of Cooperation to Agency Enforcement Decisions, Securities Exchange Act Release No. 44969 (Oct. 23, 2001), *available at:* http://www.sec.gov/litigation/investreport/34-44969.htm; The Sarbanes-Oxley Act of 2002, Pub. L. No. 107-204, 116 Stat. 745 (2002); Memorandum from Deputy Attorney General Larry D. Thompson, Principles of Federal Prosecution of Business Organizations (2003) and Memorandum from Deputy Attorney General Paul J. McNulty, Principles of Federal Prosecution of Business Organizations (2006).

would remain just that. We now know that the protection of confidences is far less secure. And any discussion of privilege leads directly to the role of the company's external auditors and their demands upon the process. The choice of counsel has taken on enormous added importance. Some companies bear deep scars arising from the selection of lawyer and law firm by the special committee and the ensuing unthinkable cost and unparalleled scope, with little or no comparable benefit.

If we have learned anything over the past two decades, it is that the questions addressed during an internal investigation are far more important—indeed critical—to the future of the company than we ever imagined. From start to finish, legal guidance on matters like scope, document retention, advancing fees and interviewing employees demands skills that allow few if any mistakes of judgment or advice.

Conducting an internal investigation requires scrupulous attention to detail and a full understanding of legal developments and recent experiences of other investigative counsel. These experiences are often chronicled in the public domain and provide keen insights into the process. Before setting out the steps of an internal investigation, we turn to two recent occurrences that without question reshape the task of those involved in conducting internal investigations: the Sarbanes-Oxley Act of 2002 and the McNulty Memo of 2007.

A. The Sarbanes-Oxley Act of 2002 and Its Aftermath

Any discussion of the investigative process must begin with the Sarbanes-Oxley Act of 2002[2] and its dramatic impact in this area of practice. Aimed at eliminating accounting fraud and implemented as an attempt to restore confidence in corporations, the Act has had an immediate effect on public companies in the United States, as well as the accounting, legal and investment banking community.

Sarbanes-Oxley imposes heightened requirements on officers, directors and advisors of corporations to identify material issues before publishing financial statements and requires that they make affirmative representations about the veracity of financial statements and the health of internal corporate controls. In addition to generally increasing the level of scrutiny given to corporate conduct, Sarbanes-Oxley has most affected internal investigations in three ways.[3]

---

2. Pub. L. No. 107-204, 116 Stat. 745 (2002).
3. For a more detailed discussion of the effect of Sarbanes-Oxley on internal investigations, see Chapter 16, "SOX It to Me: Internal Investigations in a Sarbanes-Oxley World."

First, Sarbanes-Oxley and related SEC Rules have increased the number of mechanisms for uncovering allegations of misconduct. Executive officers now publish codes of conduct for their senior financial officers. Each company must report on the health of its internal reporting processes as well as its financial results. Elaborate certification processes have become commonplace to support the CEO and CFO as they certify the company's financial results. The Act also requires audit committees to set up mechanisms for collecting confidential, anonymous "whistleblower" reports. Wrongdoing disclosed to the chief legal officer by counsel through "reporting up" requirements is only discharged once the company make an "appropriate response." Any one of these mechanisms can uncover evidence of potential misconduct sufficient to require an internal investigation. Taken together, the reporting requirements of Sarbanes-Oxley present a mountain of potential issues facing the company each time it publishes its financials.

Second, Sarbanes-Oxley complicates the analysis of who should conduct and who should supervise an internal investigation. Although the Act is short on specific guidance, a company will frequently form a special committee of the Board, and the committee will engage independent counsel to conduct the investigation. The fact that companies have turned to special committees or called upon their independent audit committee is nothing new. What has changed in recent years is the frequency of their investigations. It is not uncommon for the General Counsel to turn to a standing committee like the Audit Committee or to the entire Board to review allegations of misconduct and to determine how those allegations will be investigated. There are times when the investigation must be handled by a Special Litigation Committee whose independence and disinterestedness can withstand any challenge.

Third, Sarbanes-Oxley has widened the constituencies who must ultimately be satisfied with the results of the internal investigations. Sometimes, government agents or the investing public will be apprised of the results of an investigation.[4] More commonly, an internal investigation is conducted under the immediate scrutiny of the company's outside auditors. Because of increasing pressures placed on auditors by Sarbanes-Oxley and other recent regulatory changes, auditors now aggressively seek access to internal investigations, even in the planning stages. When refusing to sign off on financial statements until all issues have been thoroughly run to ground, auditors exercise signifi-

---

4. See Chapter 7, "Disclosure of Results of Internal Investigations to the Government or Other Third Parties;" see also Chapter 12 "No Security: Internal Investigations into Violations of the Securities Laws."

cant power over a corporation's investigation and can turn even the most straightforward investigation into a significant, time-sensitive endeavor.

B. The McNulty Memo of 2007: Cooperation, Waiver and Indemnification

In its 2003 Thompson Memorandum,[5] the Department of Justice redefined traditional notions of cooperation by declaring that, among other factors, waiver of attorney-client privilege and advancement of legal fees could be considered in assessing "cooperation" and thus determining whether a business entity should be criminally charged.

From the outset the Thompson Memo drew sharp criticism from many corners of the bar concerned that the new policy effectively required that every company under investigation waive its attorney-client privilege or risk being labeled non-cooperative. In response, in 2006 the Department published the McNulty Memorandum, creating a two-tiered approach to requesting waiver of privileged information.[6] The new policy requires that prosecutors obtain written authorization from their U.S. Attorney (who must consult the Assistant Attorney General for the Criminal Division) before requesting waiver; the policy also distinguishes between waiver of purely factual information ("Category I") and attorney-client communications or non-factual attorney work product ("Category II").

Like the debate over waiver, the Department's pronouncement that advancement of legal fees is a factor in charging decisions also received criticism from many sources, most notably United States District Judge Lewis A. Kaplan.[7] Noting that state laws grant corporations the power to advance legal fees to employees prior to formal findings of fault, the McNulty Memorandum reversed course and now precludes prosecutors from considering advancement of legal fees, except in "extremely rare cases."[8]

---

5. Memorandum from Deputy Attorney General Larry D. Thompson, Principles of Federal Prosecution of Business Organizations (2003).

6. Memorandum from Deputy Attorney General Paul McNulty, Principles of Federal Prosecution of Business Organizations (2006).

7. *See* United States v. Stein, 435 F. Supp. 2d 330 (S.D.N.Y. 2000). In its investigation of KPMG, the government discouraged KPMG from advancing legal fees to its employees. Judge Kaplan found that the resulting capped advancement of legal fees—conditioned on the employee's waiver of Fifth Amendment rights—violated both the Fifth and Sixth Amendments to the Constitution.

8. McNulty dictates that advancement of fees should only be considered in charging decisions if the totality of the circumstances shows the advancement of fees was made to impede a criminal investigation.

Whether or not McNulty adequately addresses criticisms of Thompson, the new policy will undoubtedly have implications for internal investigations.[9] At the very least, those performing investigations will have to remain cognizant of whether they are discovering (or creating) information that could be subject to waiver as either Category I or Category II information. With respect to advancement of fees, Judge Kaplan's decision is of obvious importance, and the McNulty Memorandum, in reversing earlier policy, is the Department of Justice's attempt to minimize any uncertainty. As with any policy, there are exceptions, and how "extremely rare cases" will be determined throughout the various United States Attorneys' Offices is currently unknown.

II. DIFFERENT TYPES OF INTERNAL INVESTIGATIONS

Internal investigations may arise in a variety of ways and uncover a wide band of problems. Underlying many internal investigations is corporate conduct that can trigger confrontations on a number of fields, each with different opponents, different rules and different referees. A company's illegal conduct may result in federal and state prosecutions, administrative actions, private litigation and, many times, difficult dealings with the news media. A lawyer's failure to recognize this reality at the outset will greatly diminish the overall effectiveness of the investigation.

As a consequence, there are several types of internal investigations. One is purely reactive, arising in response to some external event—for example, a grand jury subpoena, a document request by the Inspector General of a government agency, an administrative audit or a private lawsuit. Another is proactive—the company conducts the internal investigation on its own initiative to determine whether any wrongdoing has occurred and, if so, to take remedial steps. Finally, many internal investigations fit into neither category but are a mixture of both.

Counsel's role in connection with the internal investigation will vary depending on the type of investigation under way. For example, if the investigation is triggered by some government action (e.g., grand jury subpoena or administrative audit), counsel may be retained for one or more of three purposes: first, to conduct the investigation; second, to advise the company of its

---

9. Recent legislation introduced by Senator Arlen Specter, if passed, would forbid government agencies from considering waiver of the attorney-client or work-product privilege in a charging analysis. *See* Attorney-Client Privilege Protection Act of 2007, S. 186, 110th Cong. § 3 (2007).

legal rights and potential liabilities; and third, to represent the company in a lawsuit or other proceeding brought against the company by the government or a private litigant. Having a single counsel perform all three roles can be a prudent (and less costly) decision under many circumstances. However, in other circumstances—for example, where the company is likely to waive the attorney-client privilege otherwise protecting the investigation—the company may be better served by retaining one law firm to conduct the investigation and provide legal advice to the company, and a second firm to conduct all later legal procedures. Importantly, for those companies wishing to rely on its investigation to influence governmental decisions, enforcement authorities will wholly discount its value unless the investigation was conducted by truly disinterested and objective counsel.

III. THE INITIAL MEETING

Experience teaches that a crucial event in an internal investigation is the initial meeting between the client and the lawyer who will conduct the internal investigation. The lawyer learns for the first time the conduct at issue and, together with client, begins exploring the steps involved to marshal the facts and analyze their legal consequences. Decisions must be made in this first session, and the judgments underlying those decisions are ones that both the company and counsel must live with throughout the ensuing inquiry. A modest but acceptable agenda for the initial meeting will include discussion along the following lines:

- The starting point: defining the client and deciding whether to conduct an investigation.
- Defining the scope of the investigation.
- Applying the attorney-client privilege and the attorney work-product doctrine.
- Assembling the investigative team.
- Agreeing to lines of reporting and supervision.
- Anticipating what can go wrong.

A. The Starting Point: Identifying the Client and Deciding Whether to Conduct an Investigation

As mentioned before, the first decision is identifying "the client." Should it be the CEO, the Board or its Chairman, the Audit Committee or a Special Litigation Committee? This judgment must be made at the outset, because it clarifies the attorney-client relationship and identifies the person or entity who will later be called on to address remedial actions and employment decisions and potential negotiations with enforcement authorities.

Once the client has been identified, the question must then be asked: Should the company conduct any investigation at all? Why should the company investigate claims that, if true, will subject the company to criminal or civil lawsuits? This impulse—isn't the company better off not knowing?—is not irrational and should be addressed head-on at the outset.

The predominant factor in deciding whether to conduct an internal investigation is the existence—actual or potential—of a government investigation or private lawsuit. If the Justice Department or other prosecuting agency has served a grand jury subpoena or is otherwise conducting an investigation, the company has no choice but to conduct its own internal investigation. The same reasoning applies if a former employee has complained to the government about allegedly illegal conduct.

The harder question arises when a company has no knowledge of a government inquiry but becomes concerned about possible wrongdoing. Here, management may be tempted not to investigate itself, hoping that the allegations, if material, will never become public. The better course favors an investigation. A company is criminally liable for its employees' illegal conduct if employees acted within the scope of their employment and intended, at least in part, to benefit the corporation.[10] The law's reach alone is enough to compel self-analysis and correction.

Conducting an internal investigation will enable the company to decide whether to disclose to the government the allegations and the company's findings in response to those allegations.[11] Under some circumstances, disclosing the results of an internal investigation will enable the company to avoid an enforcement action—either because the allegations are unfounded or because, as a result of the company's cooperation, the government chooses not to prosecute the company.[12]

Internal investigations provide another significant advantage to the company—that of enabling the company to formulate its defenses at an early

---

10. *See* United States v. Beusch, 596 F.2d 871 (9th Cir. 1979); Standard Oil Co. v. United States, 307 F.2d 120 (5th Cir. 1962).

11. The topic of disclosure is addressed in detail in Chapter 7, "Disclosure of Results of Internal Investigations to the Government or Other Third Parties."

12. Memorandum from Deputy Attorney General Paul McNulty, Principles of Federal Prosecution of Business Organizations (2006).

stage in anticipation of later criminal or civil proceedings. For example, while a corporation generally is liable for its employee's acts, such liability might not attach where the employee has acted for personal benefit contrary to the corporation's diligent efforts to prevent such misconduct.[13] In addition, while a company is legally responsible for some acts of misconduct, it is not necessarily liable for the full scope of employee misconduct. A properly conducted investigation will enable the company and its counsel to place the misconduct in its best light, to assert defenses where appropriate and to argue mitigation.

Finally, although a corporation generally is not required to disclose a prior crime,[14] in many instances disclosure may be the only means of preventing future criminal conduct. For example, in the field of government contracting, companies are often called upon to certify financial statements, to make accurate financial records available for audit or to otherwise represent the company's prior conduct. Under these circumstances, disclosing prior misconduct may be the only practical method of preventing the occurrence of another criminal act that will expose the company—and perhaps its individual officers—to further criminal liability.

B. *Defining the Scope of the Internal Investigation*

In the initial meeting, client and counsel should reach agreement on the scope of the investigation. That scope should correspond to the severity of the matter under investigation. There is a wide difference between suspicion that a bookkeeper has embezzled funds on the one hand, and public allegations of widespread bribery in government procurement procedures on the other.

If the internal investigation results from a recently commenced government inquiry, the scope of the internal investigation is somewhat preordained—one will likely mirror the other. The question of scope becomes more difficult, however, where the allegations of misconduct arise within the company and there is no known government investigation.

There are numerous instances where a company may elect to review internal practices solely for corrective action and not in fear of litigation. For example, a hospital corporation may wish to review and institute new tracking systems in light of recently instituted government regulations; a company

---

13. *See, e.g.,* Beusch, 596 F.2d at 878 (due diligence is a factor to be weighed by the jury in determining whether the individual actor intended to benefit the corporation).

14. See Chapter 7, "Disclosure of Results of Internal Investigations to the Government or Other Third Parties."

may analyze pricing practices in connection with an annual antitrust compliance program; management may be concerned about possible kickbacks by its purchasing department; or a company may suspect drug abuse in the workplace and wish to formulate a remedial plan.

In any of these instances, counsel and management should reach a clear understanding of the scope of the inquiry and should strictly conform all services to the agreed-upon parameters. Such an approach helps to ensure that the results of the investigation are fully protected from unwanted disclosure. If, for example, counsel veers beyond the agreed-upon scope—gathering information and giving advice outside the understood areas of concern—the risk of disclosure increases.[15] Additionally, a clear articulation of the engagement—and thus of counsel's role to obtain facts and render legal advice—makes less likely any challenge to the investigation on grounds that counsel acted as a business advisor, not a lawyer.

The client will want to confirm in writing the scope of the investigation. Whether or not in the form of an engagement letter, the document should state that counsel has been asked to investigate certain allegations; that the investigation is being conducted to enable counsel to advise the company regarding its legal rights, obligations and potential liabilities; and that all communications with counsel are protected by the attorney-client privilege and thus intended to remain confidential. In some cases, it may be wise to circulate this memorandum among the employees to be interviewed.

C. *Applying the Attorney-Client Privilege and Work-Product Doctrine*

There can be no greater risk in commencing an investigation than to treat issues of privilege carelessly. Upon the conclusion of the investigation, the company may decide to disclose the results. Importantly, this decision should be one of choice, not the product of carelessness or ignorance.

Thus, before commencing the investigation, both client and counsel should be versed in fundamental principles of privilege. Under the United States Supreme Court's decision in *Upjohn Co. v. United States*,[16] counsel's communications with company employees will be protected by the com-

---

15. While the attorney-client privilege presumably protects all client communications, the work-product privilege may not attach to the lawyer's efforts outside the scope of the engagement (other than client communications) when those efforts are unrelated to the prospect of future litigation. Third-party interviews are one example of this concern.
16. 449 U.S. 383 (1981).

pany's attorney-client privilege under certain described circumstances.[17] Federal and state laws give added work-product protection if counsel's work is "in anticipation of litigation or for trial."[18]

The initial engagement is important to the question of privilege. When management chooses to investigate its own conduct and no legal proceeding is under way, counsel must carefully consider whether its role—the gathering of data, the analysis, the conclusions—will be protected from later, unwanted disclosure. Is management seeking business advice or legal advice? Is counsel performing an investigative service or a legal service? Are employees clearly informed that their communications with company counsel are intended to remain confidential? The answers to all these questions will affect the degree to which the internal investigation can be protected from unwanted disclosure.

D. *Assembling the Investigative Team*

There may be no more delicate task than reaching agreement on who should conduct the internal investigation. The choice often is between a lawyer and a nonlawyer—for example, in-house security personnel. Except in relatively insignificant matters (e.g., petty theft), lawyers are the better choice to conduct the investigation. This conclusion is arrived at for two reasons.

First, having counsel conduct the internal investigation better enables the company to protect the entire investigation pursuant to the attorney-client privilege and the attorney work-product doctrine. Although an investigation by a nonlawyer may conceivably come within some work-product protection, far greater protection comes where a lawyer has conducted the investigation consistent with all available legal privileges.[19]

Second, the internal investigation inevitably will lead to an analysis of the company's legal rights, obligations and potential liabilities, all issues legal counsel can best address. Although nonlawyers should not supervise the internal investigation, they can perform valuable roles. Many internal investigations deal with complex questions that only specialists can address. Auditors, engineers, or specialized technicians can provide invaluable assistance in these areas. Because many of these individuals can be found within the company,

---

17. *Upjohn* protects these communications if challenged in a federal proceeding; state law, both statutory and common, provides guidance for protection should the assertion be challenged in a state proceeding.

18. FED. R. CIV. P. 26(b)(3). State laws may vary in their protections afforded the lawyer's work product.

19. See Chapter 2, "Attorney-Client Privilege and the Work-Product Doctrine."

their participation will have the added benefit of reducing the cost of the internal investigation.

Once the company decides to have a lawyer conduct the investigation, the next question is whether the lawyer should be a member of the company's law department or outside counsel. There is no simple answer to this question, except to say that it depends upon all the circumstances, including cost. In almost all circumstances, it will be less expensive to have the investigation conducted in-house than to retain outside counsel.

Cost considerations are of obvious importance but should not dominate the determination. Indeed, financial concerns often quickly give way to the more important factor of comparative independence of counsel conducting the investigation. Although the government will not perceive outside counsel as totally independent, outside counsel is presumptively more independent than inside counsel. Inside counsel, after all, has only one client—the company.

This question of independence comes sharply into focus when considering the interview process. If inside counsel both interviews key employees and provides them with legal advice, counsel may find it difficult to approach the investigation with total independence. Additionally, under some circumstances, lawyers employed by the company may themselves be witnesses to the underlying conduct, thus disqualifying them from the role of counsel. This potentiality is certainly not remote and should be examined at the outset to prevent future problems during the investigation.

Moreover, if pertinent employees have previously relied on inside counsel for legal advice, they might regard counsel as their personal lawyer during the course of their interviews. Although all witnesses should be told that the company's counsel does not represent them personally, a prior legal relationship between a witness and an inside lawyer can obscure this admonition and create at least a factual dispute over the witness's understanding at the time of the interview.[20]

E. *Agreeing to Lines of Reporting and Supervision*

Above, we discussed the task of identifying the "client." Who is the "client" and who does the lawyer report to? Will counsel report to the General Counsel? To senior management? To the Chief Executive Officer? To the Chairman of the Board? Or to an Audit or Special Committee?

---

20. See Chapter 3, "The Witness Interview Process," for a more complete discussion of this issue.

These questions involve both practical and political problems. Management is vitally interested in the investigation, its progress and its discoveries. Indeed, it must have *some* information regarding the underlying conduct to meet its responsibilities. Yet what if senior management is itself responsible for the practices under investigation? Steps must be taken, on the one hand, to shield management from unwanted information and, on the other, to insure the integrity of the investigation and its conclusions.

Experience teaches that the best course is to confront this issue early on and resolve it before going forward. Failure to do so only defers these hard questions and makes for a more difficult resolution at later stages in the investigation, when emotions are high (with the possible onset of government action) and objectivity is short.

F. *Anticipating What Can Go Wrong*

Those who follow this area of practice understand full well the perils found within the investigative process. A publicly traded company may learn all too late that the findings of its investigation are splashed on the front page of local and national newspapers. Thus, management's instinctive judgment that an investigation may generate more bad than good is common. Counsel should anticipate this instinct and should use it as an opportunity to educate the client on the value of a company's self-inquiry. But counsel must also alert the client to the fact that in any investigation, however well managed, there will necessarily be unpredictable bumps, some of which may be harsh.

Inadvertent disclosure of the investigation's results is one such serious risk. There are numerous ways in which the privilege can be compromised and confidences disclosed. Even though counsel scrupulously observes privilege considerations, unwanted disclosure is far from theoretical. A sloppy employee interview can create a passel of later problems. Investigative counsel must approach the interview process along carefully drawn lines. Because of its central importance to the investigative process, mistakes made there can severely compromise the ability of the company to defend itself later. Counsel must clearly define their role—whom they represent and whom they do not. They must set out equally clearly the nature of the investigation and the employee's obligation to maintain the confidentiality of the interview. To do otherwise will unnecessarily cause confusion and invite problems later. Investigative counsel must provide the clearest possible instructions to the witness, informing him or her of his or her obligations to the company, the importance of a candid and frank communication and the potential later decision by the "client" to disclose the contents of the interview.

The importance of clear and concise instructions can best be seen by reviewing the indictment in *U.S. v. Singleton*.[21] In that case, a trader for a worldwide energy company was indicted on charges of obstruction of justice, wire fraud and false reporting. The obstruction of justice charge focused on the trader's statements to independent investigative counsel. Investigative counsel interviewed the trader and informed him that the information he provided might at some later point be disclosed to government authorities. The trader chose to participate in the interview and, according to the indictment, gave false and misleading information to outside counsel. These statements later became one of several counts upon which he was indicted. At trial, investigative counsel was subpoenaed by criminal enforcement authorities to testify about the interview, its context in the overall investigation, the questions asked and the answers given.

Defamation actions are far from theoretical in the aftermath of internal investigations. Investigations yield information, and that information must be reported in one form or another within the company and possibly to outsiders. It is often difficult to achieve the proper balance between the company's need to act upon the information and its desire not to incur defamation charges from employees or third parties. This concern is a vital one, however, and should be flagged earlier in the investigation, so that both management and counsel are sensitive to it.

Finally, it is wise to emphasize to the client that during the internal investigation, employees should not create new documents discussing the allegations, except under the strict supervision of counsel. It is also wise to point out that, despite this advice, employees may nevertheless do just that. Clear written instructions to employees at all levels will help to minimize this risk. The instructions can be included in a memorandum setting out the nature of the investigation and the documents sought and providing assistance on responding to any outstanding discovery request.

IV. PRELIMINARY STEPS TO PREPARE FOR GOVERNMENT INVESTIGATIONS

When the internal investigation comes as a result of a criminal inquiry by enforcement authorities, counsel should take immediate steps to prepare management for certain key events that could occur during the course of a crimi-

---

21. United States v. Singleton, No. 4:04-cr-514-1 (S.D.T.X. filed Nov. 17, 2004).

nal investigation. At the outset of an internal investigation, it is impossible to predict each of the issues that will arise in the event of later government investigations, but the following sets out several important cautions.

One increasingly common event is the government's use of search warrants. Not long ago, business litigators had only to concern themselves with the case law surrounding grand jury subpoenas *duces tecum*.[22] Increasingly, federal investigators are making use of search warrants as an alternative method of obtaining documents from a company.

The growing use of warrants poses unique concerns to the company and its counsel. By their very nature, search warrants are sudden and without notice. Also, by using warrants, government agents put themselves in a position (arguably improperly) to obtain statements from employees before they have reviewed any documents, before they have consulted with counsel if they choose to do so and before they understand their legal rights.

Moreover, a well-planned and executed search can be a spectacle. When government agents descend upon a company in the midst of its workday—fully armed—the trauma to the individual employees and the company can be enormous. This procedure can pose enormous costs to the company's treasury and to the employees' morale. Counsel should therefore warn management of the potential use of search warrants and should apprise employees of the procedures to be followed in the event of a search. A written memorandum can prove helpful.

The company should also be warned of potential for government agents' *ex parte* contacts with company employees. The company, and employees thought to be affected, should be apprised of this possibility and of the employees' rights and obligations in the event they are contacted. Employees should *not* be told they cannot speak with government agents. But they can be told what their rights are—they have the right to talk or not to talk, they can consult with counsel before deciding whether to talk and they can have company counsel present at any interview if they choose. Moreover, there is nothing improper in advising employees that, in view of the strict penalties flowing from enforcement of federal criminal laws and in view of the breadth of case law regarding corporate liabilities, management would prefer to have its counsel attend any interviews of company employees. Finally, counsel is well advised to engage government counsel in discussions, hoping to reach agreements that no current employee will be approached without first talking with company counsel.

---

22. Fed. R. Crim. P. 17(c).

V. CONCLUSION

Without doubt, internal investigations pose significant risks to the corporate client. Unexpected turns can occur, mistakes can be made and, more fundamentally, misconduct will be uncovered. Yet, clearly the bias favors commencing the investigation and learning of the underlying activity, for good or bad. How else can the company adequately defend itself in any ensuing civil or criminal proceeding?

Implications of the Attorney-Client Privilege and Work-Product Doctrine

2

Dennis J. Block and Nancy E. Barton

I. INTRODUCTION   18
II. ATTORNEY-CLIENT PRIVILEGE   19
   A. Definition of the Attorney-Client Privilege   19
   B. Elements of Attorney-Client Privilege   21
   C. Practical Problems of Employee Interviews   36
III. WORK PRODUCT PROTECTION   44
   A. Work-Product Doctrine Defined   44
   B. Factual Versus Opinion Work Product   46
   C. Elements of the Work-Product Doctrine   47
   D. Overcoming the Qualified Immunity   56
   E. Protection of a Lawyer's Mental Impressions   57
IV. OVERCOMING THE ATTORNEY-CLIENT PRIVILEGE AND WORK-PRODUCT DOCTRINE   60
   A. Waiver   60
   B. The Crime/Fraud Exception   78
   C. Shareholder Litigation   82

Dennis J. Block is a senior partner at Cadwalader, Wickersham & Taft LLP, New York, New York, and Nancy E. Barton is a former senior vice president, general counsel, and secretary at General Electric Capital Corporation, Stamford, Connecticut.

V. EFFECT OF THE SARBANES-OXLEY ACT AND RECENT SECURITIES EXCHANGE COMMISSION AND DEPARTMENT OF JUSTICE POLICIES ON THE ATTORNEY-CLIENT PRIVILEGE 86

I. INTRODUCTION

AN INTERNAL CORPORATE INVESTIGATION is generally a matter of high intensity, with the significant risk of criminal prosecution, civil litigation, potential bankruptcy, and other serious consequences. The investigative record compiled by outside counsel can be vital for the corporation's board of directors and senior management to understand what happened, what the consequences are, and how to manage the situation from a legal standpoint. One thing is certain: the corporation's adversaries, particularly the government, will eagerly seek this investigative record.

The corporation's principal safeguard against providing a detailed roadmap to its adversaries is the legal protection afforded by the attorney-client privilege and/or the work-product doctrine.[1] As detailed below, the elements

---

[1]. Another privilege, called the "self-critical analysis privilege" or "self-evaluative privilege," possibly could be available to protect the record of corporate internal investigations from discovery. This privilege was first recognized in *Bredice v. Doctor's Hospital, Inc.*, 50 F.R.D. 249 (D.D.C. 1970), *aff'd mem.*, 479 F.2d 920 (D.C. Cir. 1973), in the context of a medical staff's evaluation of potential improvements in procedures. The application of the self-critical analysis privilege requires satisfying the following three criteria:

> First, the information contained in the document must result from an internal investigation or review conducted to evaluate or improve a party's procedures or products; second, the party must originally have intended that the information remain confidential and demonstrate "a strong interest in preserving the free flow of the type of information sought"; finally, the information contained in the documents "must be of a type whose flow would be curtailed if discovery were allowed."

Etienne v. Mitre Corp., 146 F.R.D. 145, 147 (E.D. Va. 1993) (citations omitted). While some courts have discussed the potential applicability of this privilege to corporate internal investigations, few courts have upheld a claim of privilege on this basis. *See, e.g.*, FTC v. TRW, Inc., 628 F.2d 207, 210 (D.C. Cir. 1980) (self-evaluative privilege does not apply in the context of governmental subpoena); Westmoreland v. CBS, Inc., 97 F.R.D. 703, 706 (S.D.N.Y. 1983) (internal study for self-evaluation not protected where relied upon in public statements); Lloyd v. Cessna Aircraft Co., 74 F.R.D. 518, 521 (E.D. Tenn. 1977) (internal problem list not protected by self-evaluative privilege); *but see In re* Crazy Eddie Sec. Litig., 792 F. Supp. 197, 205-06 (E.D.N.Y. 1992) (magistrate's decision denying motion to compel discovery of accounting firm's internal review of its own prior audit). Other courts have entirely rejected the self-critical analysis privilege. *See, e.g.*, Griffith v. Davis, 161 F.R.D. 687, 701 (C.D. Cal. 1995) (the Ninth Circuit does not recognize the privilege of "self-critical analysis"); Aramburu v. Boeing Co., 885 F. Supp. 1434, 1440-41 (D. Kan. 1995) (rejecting "self-critical analysis privilege" in Title VII cases); *see also In re* Application of Federation Internationale de Basketball for Subpoena Pursuant to 28 U.S.C. § 1782, 117 F. Supp. 2d 403, 407 (S.D.N.Y. 2000) (declining to consider whether there is a self-evaluative privilege and noting that the issue has not been decided by the Supreme Court or the Second Circuit).

of these protections have developed over the past twenty-five years, producing a predictable protection for counsel's investigative materials, with well-understood exceptions and limitations.[2]

In the past few years, however, the U.S. Government has shifted the balance decisively against the corporation. The Sarbanes-Oxley Act and several policy statements issued by the Department of Justice and the Securities and Exchange Commission, discussed below, have dramatically increased the risks to the corporation if it does not waive the otherwise applicable privileges.[3]

There are essential differences between the attorney-client privilege and the work-product doctrine. The court in *Scourtes v. Fred W. Albrecht Grocery Co.*[4] distinguished them as follows:

> The purpose of the attorney-client privilege is to encourage full disclosure of information between a lawyer and his client by guaranteeing the inviolability of their confidential communications. The "work product of the attorney," on the other hand, is accorded protection for the purpose of preserving our adversary system of litigation by assuring a lawyer that his private files shall, except in unusual circumstances, remain free from the encroachments of opposing counsel.[5]

Because of the difference in the rationale underlying each doctrine, the protections afforded by the attorney-client privilege and the work-product doctrine may be waived or overridden in different circumstances.[6]

II. ATTORNEY-CLIENT PRIVILEGE

The principal means for preserving the confidentiality of counsel's investigative record is the attorney-client privilege.

A. Definition of the Attorney-Client Privilege

The attorney-client privilege is defined in the often-cited decision in *United States v. United Shoe Machinery Corp.*:[7]

> The privilege applies only if (1) the asserted holder of the privilege is or sought to become a client; (2) the person to whom the communication was made (a) is a member of the bar of a court, or his subordinate and (b) in connection with this communication is acting as a lawyer; (3) the communication relates to a

---

2. *See* Parts II, III, and IV, *infra*.
3. *See* Part V, *infra*.
4. 15 F.R.D. 55, 58 (N.D. Ohio 1953).
5. *Id.*
6. *See* Parts II and III, *infra*.
7. 89 F. Supp. 357 (D. Mass. 1950).

fact of which the attorney was informed (a) by his client (b) without the presence of strangers (c) for the purpose of securing primarily either (i) an opinion on law or (ii) legal services or (iii) assistance in some legal proceeding, and not (d) for the purpose of committing a crime or tort; and (4) the privilege has been (a) claimed and (b) not waived by the client.[8]

The burden of establishing a claim of privilege is on the party claiming it.[9]

The attorney-client privilege is an evidentiary rule.[10] As such, federal courts approach questions including the applicability of the privilege differently depending upon whether the cause of action that is the subject of the litigation arises under federal or state law. Federal Rule of Evidence 501 provides, in relevant part:

> Except as otherwise required by [federal law] ... the privilege of a witness, person, government, State or political subdivision thereof shall be governed by the principles of the common law as they may be interpreted by the courts of the United States in the light of reason and experience. However, in civil actions and proceedings with respect to an element of a claim or defense as to which State law supplies the rule of decision, the privilege of a witness, person, government, State or political subdivision thereof shall be determined in accordance with State law.

In adopting the Federal Rules of Evidence, Congress deleted proposed rule 503, which would have provided a uniform federal definition of the attorney-client privilege. Although the proposed rule was rejected by Congress, some federal courts have relied on the formulation of the proposed rule to define the federal common-law attorney-client privilege under rule 501.[11]

---

8. *Id.* at 358-59.

9. *In re* Grand Jury Proceedings, 219 F.3d 175, 182 (2d Cir. 2000); von Bulow v. von Bulow, 811 F.2d 136, 146 (2d Cir.), *cert. denied sub nom.,* 481 U.S. 1015 (1987).

10. United States v. Rogers, 751 F.2d 1074, 1077 (9th Cir. 1985); United States v. Segal, 313 F. Supp. 2d 774, 779 (N.D. Ill. 2004). The confidentiality of clients' communications with counsel is also mandated by the professional codes governing the practice of law. *See, e.g.,* ABA MODEL RULES OF PROF'L CONDUCT R. 1.6; ABA MODEL CODE OF PROF'L RESPONSIBILITY DR 4-101; Jackson v. Adcock, No. Civ. 03-3369, 2004 WL 1661199, at *3 n.24 (E.D. La. July 22, 2004) (*citing* ABA, BNA LAWYER'S MANUAL ON PROFESSIONAL CONDUCT § 01:301 (ABA/BNA 1991 & Supp. 2004)).

11. *See, e.g.,* Ross v. City of Memphis, 423 F.3d 596, 601 (6th Cir. 2005); *In re* Feldberg, 862 F.2d 622, 626 (7th Cir. 1988); Diversified Indus., Inc. v. Meredith, 572 F.2d 596, 605 n.1, 610 (8th Cir. 1978) (en banc); United States v. McPartlin, 595 F.2d 1321, 1336-37 (7th Cir.), *cert. denied,* 444 U.S. 833 (1979).

Other courts seeking to develop a federal common law of privilege may look to state law for guidance.[12] One court has articulated four factors that should be weighed in determining whether to apply a state privilege rule to a federal claim:

> [F]irst, the federal government's need for the information being sought in enforcing its substantive and procedural policies; second, the importance of the relationship or policy sought to be furthered by the state rule of privilege and the probability that the privilege will advance that relationship or policy; third, in the particular case, the special need for the information sought to be protected; and fourth, in the particular case, the adverse impact on the local policy that would result from non-recognition of the privilege.[13]

Where the claim is based on state law, the privilege is a "substantive" matter to be governed by state law,[14] and many states have statutes governing the privilege. For example, a New York statute provides, in relevant part:

> Unless the client waives the privilege, an attorney or his or her employee, or any person who obtains without the knowledge of the client evidence of a confidential communication made between the attorney or his or her employee and the client in the course of professional employment, shall not disclose, or be allowed to disclose such communication, nor shall the client be compelled to disclose such communication, in any action, disciplinary trial or hearing, or administrative action, proceeding or hearing conducted by or on behalf of any state, municipal or local governmental agency or by the legislature or any committee or body thereof.[15]

B. *Elements of Attorney-Client Privilege*

Simply stated, the elements of the attorney-client privilege are: (1) a client, (2) a lawyer, (3) a retainer for the purpose of rendering legal advice, (4) a

---

12. *See, e.g.,* Wynne v. Loyola Univ. of Chi., No. 97 C 06417, 1999 WL 759401, at *2 (N.D. Ill. Sept. 3, 1999); Los Angeles Mem'l Coliseum Comm'n v. National Football League, 89 F.R.D. 489, 492 (C.D. Cal. 1981).

13. *United States v. King,* 73 F.R.D. 103, 105 (E.D.N.Y. 1976).

14. *DiBella v. Hopkins,* 403 F.3d 102, 121 (2d Cir.), *cert. denied,* 126 S. Ct. 428 (2005); Republic Gear Co. v. Borg-Warner Corp., 381 F.2d 551, 556 n.2 (2d Cir. 1967); *see also* FED. R. EVID. 501.

15. N.Y. C.P.L.R. 4503(a)(1) (McKinney 1992 & Supp. 2006); *see also* CAL. EVID. CODE §§ 950-962 (West 1995 & Supp. 2006); D. I. Chadbourne, Inc. v. Superior Ct. of City & Cty. of San Francisco, 388 P.2d 700, 709-10 (Cal. 1964) (setting forth criteria for applicability of the privilege in the corporate context).

communication between them, and (5) an intent that the communication be confidential.

1. The Client

A client may be an individual or a corporation,[16] and a corporate client may include subsidiaries and affiliates.[17] A lawyer representing a corporation represents the *corporate entity*, not its shareholders, officers, or directors.[18]

It has been long established that a corporate client, like an individual client, may assert the attorney-client privilege.[19] However, since a corporate client can act only through its human constituents, a lawyer communicating with a corporate client must be mindful of which corporate agents sufficiently personify the corporation so their communications with counsel will be privileged.

Prior to the Supreme Court's 1981 decision in *Upjohn Co. v. United States*,[20] the United States Courts of Appeals were divided as to the appropriate test for determining which corporate employee communications with counsel were protected. The Third and Sixth Circuits embraced the so-called "control group" test, which protected only the communications of senior management; the Seventh and Eighth Circuits adopted a broader test, the so-called "subject matter" test, which encompassed certain communications of lower-level employees.

---

16. CFTC v. Weintraub, 471 U.S. 343, 348 (1985) ("[i]t is by now well established . . . that the attorney-client privilege attaches to corporations"); Bell v. Maryland, 378 U.S. 226, 263 (1964) ("[a] corporation, like any other 'client,' is entitled to the attorney-client privilege"); Radiant Burners, Inc. v. American Gas Ass'n, 320 F.2d 314, 322-23 (7th Cir.), *cert. denied,* 375 U.S. 929 (1963); Reed v. Baxter, 134 F.3d 351, 356 (6th Cir.) ("it is now well settled that private corporations and other organizations may constitute clients for purposes of the attorney-client privilege"), *cert. denied,* 525 U.S. 820 (1998); *see also* Berroth v. Kansas Farm Bur. Mut. Ins. Co., 205 F.R.D. 586, 591 (D. Kan. 2002) (same).

17. *See, e.g.,* United States v. United Shoe Mach. Corp., 89 F. Supp. 357, 359 (D. Mass. 1950); Duplan Corp. v. Deering Milliken, Inc., 397 F. Supp. 1146, 1184-85 (D.S.C. 1975); Miller v. IBM, No. C 02-2118 MJJ, 2006 WL 1141090, at *1 (N.D. Cal. May 1, 2006) (corporation did not waive attorney-client privilege by exchanging documents with its subsidiary).

18. Diversified Indus., Inc. v. Meredith, 572 F.2d 596, 611 n.5 (8th Cir. 1978) (en banc); Tuttle v. Combined Ins. Co., 222 F.R.D. 424, 429 (E.D. Cal. 2004) ("Generally, there is no individual attorney-client privilege between a corporation's attorney and individuals within the corporation unless there is a clear showing that the individual consulted the corporate counsel in the officer's individual capacity"); *In re* Bevill, Bresler & Schulman Asset Mgmt. Corp., 805 F.2d 120, 125 (3d Cir. 1986); *see also* ABA MODEL RULES OF PROF'L CONDUCT R. 1.13; ABA MODEL CODE OF PROF'L RESPONSIBILITY EC 5-18.

19. CFTC v. Weintraub, 471 U.S. 343, 348 (1985); Radiant Burners, Inc. v. American Gas Ass'n, 320 F.2d 314, 322-23 (7th Cir.), *cert. denied,* 375 U.S. 929 (1963).

20. 449 U.S. 383 (1981) (discussed *infra*).

The control group test, as articulated in *City of Philadelphia v. Westinghouse Electric Corp.*,[21] requires that the person making the communication be "in a position to control or even to take a substantial part in a decision about any action which the corporation may take upon the advice of the attorney," or be "an authorized member of a body or group which has that authority."[22] This control group test was widely criticized by commentators as too restrictive, particularly when the advice is complex, because the lower-level employees most likely to have detailed factual knowledge are also least likely to be in a control position.[23] As one commentator pointed out, counsel is faced with a difficult choice—required to proceed without benefit of the privilege if full factual development is to be accomplished, or to proceed without necessary factual background if the privilege is to be maintained.[24]

In recognition of the deficiencies of the control group test, a number of courts developed tests that accounted more realistically for the practicalities of corporate existence. The first attempt was made in *Harper & Row Publishers, Inc. v. Decker*,[25] where the Seventh Circuit concluded that communications with counsel by noncontrolling employees are privileged when "the employee makes the communications at the direction of his superiors in the corporation and where the subject matter upon which the attorney's advice is sought by the corporation and dealt with in the communication is the performance by the employee of the duties of his employment."[26]

Subsequent decisions approved in concept the greater flexibility afforded by the *Harper & Row* test, but suggested additional criteria designed to curb its potential abuse, which might occur if employee communications were routinely

---

21. 210 F. Supp. 483 (E.D. Pa.), *mandamus and prohibition denied sub nom.* GE Co. v. Kirkpatrick, 312 F.2d 742 (3d Cir. 1962), *cert. denied,* 372 U.S. 943 (1963).

22. *Id.* at 485.

23. *E.g.,* Dennis J. Block & Nancy E. Barton, *Internal Corporate Investigations: Maintaining the Confidentiality of a Corporate Client's Communications with Investigative Counsel,* 35 BUS. LAW. 5, 13-17 (1979); James B. Kobak, Jr., *The Uneven Application of the Attorney-Client Privilege to Corporations in the Federal Courts,* 6 GA. L. REV. 339, 362-71 (1972); Note, *Privileged Communications—Inroads on the "Control Group" Test in the Corporate Area,* 22 SYR. L. REV. 759, 761-62 (1971); Comment, *The Application in the Federal Courts of the Attorney-Client Privilege to the Corporation,* 39 FORDHAM L. REV. 281, 290-93 (1970); Alan J. Weinschel, *Corporate Employee Interviews and the Attorney-Client Privilege,* 12 B.C. IND. & COMM. L. REV. 873, 875-76 (1970); *but see* Note, *Attorney-Client Privilege for Corporate Clients: The Control Group Test,* 84 HARV. L. REV. 424, 435 (1970).

24. Alan J. Weinschel, *Corporate Employee Interviews and the Attorney-Client Privilege,* 12 B.C. IND. & COMM. L. REV. 873, 876 (1970).

25. 423 F.2d 487 (7th Cir. 1970), *aff'd by an equally divided Court,* 400 U.S. 348 (1971).

26. *Id.* at 491-92.

funneled through counsel. Thus, in *Diversified Industries, Inc. v. Meredith*,[27] the court made explicit a requirement (undoubtedly implicit in *Harper & Row*) that the communications directed by corporate superiors and made by the lower-level employee have been for the purpose of enabling the corporation to secure legal advice.[28]

Notwithstanding the criticisms of the control group test, the Third Circuit in *In re Grand Jury Investigation*[29] and the Sixth Circuit in *United States v. Upjohn Co.*[30] adopted the control group test, explicitly rejecting the more flexible subject matter tests formulated by the Seventh and Eighth Circuits.[31]

In *Upjohn Co. v. United States*,[32] the Supreme Court rejected the strict control group test, but declined to establish a bright-line test of its own. Instead, the Court held that the privilege should be determined on a case-by-case basis.[33] On the facts of *Upjohn*, the Court held that the privilege applied based on the following factors:

- The communications were made by employees to corporate counsel in order for the corporation to secure legal advice.
- The employees were cooperating with corporate counsel at the direction of corporate superiors.
- The communications concerned matters within the employees' scope of employment.
- The information communicated to counsel was not available to counsel from upper-echelon management.[34]

This formulation is remarkably similar to the subject-matter test the Court declined to adopt.[35] In light of *Upjohn*, corporate counsel undertaking an internal investigation should document the fact that the corporation is seeking legal advice from its counsel and that the cooperation of corporate employees, including lower-level personnel, is expressly requested regarding matters within their scope of employment.

---

27. 572 F.2d 596 (8th Cir. 1978) (en banc).
28. *Id.* at 605.
29. 599 F.2d 1224 (3d Cir. 1979).
30. 600 F.2d 1223 (6th Cir. 1979), *rev'd on other grounds*, 449 U.S. 383 (1981).
31. *In re Grand Jury Investigation*, 599 F.2d 1224, 1237 (3d Cir. 1979); United States v. Upjohn Co., 600 F.2d 1223, 1225 (6th Cir. 1979), *rev'd on other grounds*, 449 U.S. 383 (1981).
32. 449 U.S. 383.
33. *Id.* at 396.
34. *Id.* at 394; *see, e.g.*, Sanchez v. Matta, 229 F.R.D. 649, 660 (D.N.M. 2004) (communications made by employees to attorney held privileged because all communications were made confidentially for the purpose of obtaining professional legal services).
35. *See* Upjohn, 449 U.S. at 391-92 (1981).

2. The Attorney

Investigative counsel also should ensure that legal services are rendered only by qualified personnel. When the attorney is admitted to practice in a state or nation, membership in the bar where the services are performed "is not a *sine qua non*."[36] The prevailing view is that membership in the bar where the services are performed is "merely one factor to be considered in determining whether counsel was acting in a legal capacity."[37]

The involvement of the corporation's inside counsel in an internal investigation does not vitiate the privilege, since the attorney-client privilege also applies to a corporation's house counsel:

> [T]he apparent factual differences between these house counsel and outside counsel are that the former are paid annual salaries, occupy offices in the corporation's buildings, and are employees rather than independent contractors. These are not sufficient differences to distinguish the two types of counsel for purposes of the attorney-client privilege. And this is apparent when attention is paid to the realities of modern corporate law practice. The type of service performed by house counsel is substantially like that performed by many members of the large urban law firms. The distinction is chiefly that the house counsel gives advice to one regular client, the outside counsel to several regular clients.[38]

In addition, communications with agents and immediate subordinates working under the direct supervision and control of the lawyer are within the

---

36. Zenith Radio Corp. v. Radio Corp. of Am., 121 F. Supp. 792, 794 (D. Del. 1954) (Bar membership should properly be of the court for the area wherein the services are rendered, but this is not a *sine qua non*, e.g., visiting counsel, long-distance services by correspondence, *pro hac vice* services, "house counsel" who practice law only for the corporate client and its affiliates and not for the public generally, for which local authorities do not insist on admission to the local bar); *but see* United States v. United Shoe Mach. Corp., 89 F. Supp. 357, 360 (D. Mass. 1950) ("The fact that [house patent counsel], though resident of Massachusetts and regularly working here, have never received a license to practice law here shows that these regular employees are not acting as attorneys for United").

37. Paper Converting Mach. Co. v. FMC Corp., 215 F. Supp. 249, 251 (E.D. Wis. 1963); Georgia-Pac. Plywood Co. v. United States Plywood Corp., 18 F.R.D. 463, 466 (S.D.N.Y. 1956); *see, e.g.,* Hanson v. United States Agency for Int'l Dev., 372 F.3d 286, 291 (4th Cir. 2004) (client communications with attorney who was educated as an engineer and who had extensive experience in many facets of the construction industry privileged because "it is clear that [attorney] both advertised himself and was hired by [client] as a lawyer who could bring both his legal skills and construction expertise to the job").

38. United States v. United Shoe Mach. Corp., 89 F. Supp. 357, 360 (D. Mass. 1950); O'Brien v. Board of Educ. of City Sch. Dist. of N.Y., 86 F.R.D. 548, 549 (S.D.N.Y. 1980) (fact that document was authored by in-house counsel rather than by independent counsel was "of no significance"); *see also* Shelton v. American Motors Corp., 805 F.2d 1323, 1326 n.3 (8th Cir. 1986); *but see* United States v. Ackert, 169 F.3d 136, 139 (2d Cir. 1999) (communications between in-house tax counsel and an investment banker regarding an investment proposal for the corporation not privileged).

scope of the attorney-client privilege.[39] Courts have recognized that a lawyer's effectiveness depends on the ability to rely on the assistance of various aides, including "secretaries, file clerks, telephone operators, messengers, clerks not yet admitted to the bar, and aides of other sorts."[40] However, merely denominating persons as "agents" will not necessarily make them so for purposes of preserving the privilege.[41]

The attorney-client privilege has also been found to protect communications to and from outside experts retained to assist the lawyer, such as accountants or private investigators. Statements made to and from these experts are generally considered to be privileged if the communication is made in confidence for the purpose of obtaining legal advice from a lawyer or enabling the lawyer to render legal advice.[42] Thus, "information provided to [an] accountant by the client at the behest of his lawyer for the purposes of the interpretation and analysis" would be protected by the attorney-client privilege "to the extent that it is imparted in connection with the legal representation."[43] Similarly, statements made by a client or lawyer to an investiga-

---

39. Zenith Radio Corp. v. Radio Corp. of Am., 121 F. Supp. 792, 794 (D. Del. 1954); FTC v. TRW, Inc., 479 F. Supp. 160, 163 n.7 (D.D.C. 1979) ("Immediate subordinates" include "the general office clerks and help, law clerks, junior attorneys, and the like who habitually report to and are under the personal supervision of the attorney through whom the privilege passes. However, a privilege available to the attorney-chief of a department or intermediate chief does not, as such, protect everyone in his department or everyone organizationally under him; his privilege, if any, extends only to immediate subordinates as indicated"), *aff'd*, 628 F.2d 207 (D.C. Cir. 1980); *In re* Asousa P'ship, Bankr. No. 01-12295DWS, 2005 WL 3299823, at *4 (Bankr. E.D. Pa. Nov. 17, 2005); Caremark, Inc. v. Affiliated Computer Servs., Inc., 192 F.R.D. 263, 264 (N.D. Ill. 2000) (attorney-client privilege applies to communications between attorney and his agent who has "express authority to coordinate legal review of contracts and service relationships for the purpose of renegotiating its terms").

40. *See, e.g.*, United States v. Kovel, 296 F.2d 918, 921 (2d Cir. 1961).

41. *See* Burlington Indus. v. Exxon Corp., 65 F.R.D. 26, 40 (D. Md. 1974); Cavallaro v. United States, 284 F.3d 236, 247 (1st Cir. 2002) (agency relationship between parties is relevant to inquiry but not dispositive).

42. *See* United States v. Cote, 456 F.2d 142, 144-45 (8th Cir. 1972) (the test is "whether the accountant's services are a necessary aid to the rendering of effective legal services to the client"); *see also* Sanchez v. Matta, 229 F.R.D. 649, 661 (D.N.M. 2004); United States v. Randall, 194 F.R.D. 369, 372 (D. Mass. 1999) (attorney-client privilege "extends to communications made by the client to certain agents of the attorney, including an accountant, hired to assist the attorney in providing legal advice"); Part III, *infra; but see* Cavallaro v. United States, 153 F. Supp. 2d 52, 58 (D. Mass. 2001) (attorney-client privilege does not extend to accountants where the "undisputed evidence" is that accountants were paid for and worked solely for client and its shareholders), *aff'd*, 284 F.3d 236 (1st Cir. 2002).

43. United States v. Schwimmer, 392 F.2d 237, 243 (2d Cir. 1989) (*citing* United States v. Kovel, 296 F.2d 928, 922 (2d Cir. 1961)); *see also* Summit, Ltd. v. Levy, 111 F.R.D. 40, 41

tor hired by a lawyer are protected by the attorney-client privilege if the investigator was assisting the lawyer to provide legal advice.[44]

It should make no difference whether the accountant or other expert or assistant was hired by the lawyer or the client, as long as the accountant's or other expert's role is to assist the lawyer in rendering legal advice; *however*, it may be more difficult as a practical matter to establish the requisites for invocation of the privilege when the expert is retained by the client independent of a request by the lawyer.[45]

Investigative counsel and their clients who retain such outside experts should take appropriate steps to document the fact that the expert is being retained to assist in rendering legal advice.

3. Legal Advice

A central issue for counsel in connection with an internal investigation is whether counsel has been employed to perform legal services. The question of what functions are included under the rubric of "legal advice" is

---

(S.D.N.Y. 1986); *see also* In re Grand Jury Proceedings, 220 F.3d 568, 571 (7th Cir. 2000) ("material transmitted to accountants may fall under the attorney-client privilege if the accountant is acting as an agent of an attorney for the purpose of assisting with the provision of legal advice"); United States v. Ackert, 169 F.3d 136 (2d Cir. 1999) (noting that "*Kovel* recognized that an accountant can play a role analogous to an interpreter in helping the attorney understand financial information passed to the attorney by the client"); *but see* Ampa, Ltd. v. Kentfield Capital LLC, No. 00 Civ. 0508 NRB AJP, 2000 WL 1156300, at *1 (S.D.N.Y. Aug. 16, 2000) (presence of outside accountant, uninvolved in the legal issue discussed, waives privilege); Cavallaro v. United States, 153 F. Supp. 2d 52, 55 (D. Mass. 2001) (no attorney-client privilege where there is no evidence that attorneys hired accountants; nor is there evidence that the accountants were hired to assist in the rendering of legal advice), *aff'd*, 284 F.3d 236 (1st Cir. 2002).

44. Sanchez v. Matta, 229 F.R.D. 649, 660 (D.N.M. 2004).

45. *Compare* United States v. Judson, 322 F.2d 460, 465-66 (9th Cir. 1963) (privilege applied to net worth statement prepared for IRS investigation by accountant hired by client at the request of the lawyer) *with* United States v. Adlman, 68 F.3d 1495, 1500 n.1 (2d Cir. 1995) (attorney-client privilege was inapplicable to written analysis of tax consequences of a proposed corporate reorganization where the analyses were prepared by the company's regular outside accountants, and there was no evidence that the accountants were hired to render legal advice or to assist in-house counsel in rendering legal advice); United States v. Brown, 478 F.2d 1038, 1040 (7th Cir. 1973) (attorney-client privilege inapplicable to accountant's notes of meeting between client and lawyer where the accountant's presence was requested by the client and not the lawyer); *see also* United States v. Adlman, 134 F.3d 1194, 1203 (2d Cir. 1998) (remanding to the district court for a determination as to whether the work product privilege protected the accountant's analysis of the litigation risks of the proposed corporate reorganization; if the district court finds that the analysis "would not have been prepared but for [the company's] anticipation of litigation," it is protected).

governed by some general rules that do not translate readily into principles for the conduct of an internal investigation. In general, for the privilege to apply, the lawyer must have been consulted in a professional legal capacity.[46] Where counsel's activities are "business rather than legal in nature," the resulting communications are not privileged.[47] Where legal and business advice is mixed, the communication is not privileged unless "the communication is designed to meet problems which can fairly be characterized as predominantly legal."[48]

---

46. *See, e.g.,* United States v. Dakota, 197 F.3d 821, 825 (6th Cir. 1999) (because client contacted tribal attorney for individual legal advice not relating to corporate matters, no attorney-client privilege existed); United States v. Frederick, 182 F.3d 496, 500 (7th Cir. 1999) ("Communications from a client that neither reflect the lawyer's thinking nor are made for the purpose of eliciting the lawyer's professional advice or other legal assistance are not privileged"), *cert. denied,* 528 U.S. 1154 (2000); United States v. Randall, 194 F.R.D. 369, 372 (D. Mass. 1999) (communications with an accountant referred by an attorney retained as a tax preparer, not for legal advice, did not trigger attorney-client privilege); *In re Kinoy,* 326 F. Supp. 400, 403-05 (S.D.N.Y. 1970) (communication to attorney-parent not privileged where court concluded communication would have been made even if parent were not a lawyer); Modern Woodmen of Am. v. Watkins, 132 F.2d 352, 354 (5th Cir. 1942) (communication to a lawyer as a personal friend not privileged); United States v. Fisher, 692 F. Supp. 488, 492 (E.D. Pa. 1988) (mere eligibility for prepaid legal services by virtue of union membership is insufficient to establish the attorney-client relationship; the relationship will only arise when legal advice is actually sought); *see also* United States v. Tedder, 801 F.2d 1437, 1442 (4th Cir. 1986) (admissions of perjury made by a lawyer to a colleague who had no professional involvement in the case were not privileged), *cert. denied,* 480 U.S. 938 (1987); *but see* Montgomery Cty. v. MicroVote Corp., 175 F.3d 296, 303 (3d Cir. 1999) (client's mere reference to its attorney as a "consultant" does not render the communications non-privileged); Cavallaro v. United States, 284 F.3d 236, 240 (1st Cir. 2002) (attorney must be retained in order to invoke privilege).

47. E.I. du Pont de Nemours & Co. v. Forma-Pack, Inc., 718 A.2d 1129, 1139 (Md. 1998) (communications between corporation and debt collection agency hired by the corporation's legal department are not privileged because agency was hired for the business of debt collection, not for the purposes of litigation); Atronic Int'l, GMBH v. SAI Semispecialists of Am., Inc., 232 F.RD. 160, 162 (E.D.N.Y. 2005); F. H. Krear & Co. v. 19 Named Trustees, 90 F.R.D. 102, 103 (S.D.N.Y. 1981) (communications with lawyer were business related, not legal in nature, and thus not privileged); *In re* Grand Jury Subpoena Duces Tecum Dated Sept. 15, 1983, 731 F.2d 1032, 1037 (2d Cir. 1984) ("the privilege is triggered only by a client's request for legal, as contrasted with business, advice").

48. *See, e.g.,* Neuder v. Battelle Pac. N.W. Nat'l Lab., 194 F.R.D. 289, 292 (D.D.C. 2000) ("[w]here business and legal advice are intertwined, the legal advice must predominate for the communication to be protected"); United States v. Cohn, 303 F. Supp. 2d 672, 683-84 (D. Md. 2003) ("When the legal advice is merely incidental to business advice, the privilege does not apply"); *see also* Cuno, Inc. v. Pall Corp., 121 F.R.D. 198, 204 (E.D.N.Y. 1988); *see, e.g.,* United States v. United Shoe Mach. Corp., 89 F. Supp. 357, 359 (D. Mass. 1950) ("the privilege of nondisclosure is not lost merely because relevant nonlegal considerations are expressly stated in a communication which also includes legal advice").

Conversely, business advice will not be protected simply because legal considerations are also involved.[49]

Matters that can be handled by laymen as easily as lawyers may not be privileged.[50] Similarly, a lawyer's ministerial or clerical duties may not be privileged.[51] However, when the professional training of a lawyer is necessary, the fact that some tasks might be characterized as nonlegal is not dispositive.[52]

The leading authority on the existence of legal advice in the context of internal investigations is *Diversified Industries, Inc. v. Meredith*,[53] in which

---

49. *See, e.g.,* Neuder v. Battelle Pac. N.W. Nat'l Lab., 194 F.R.D. 289, 292 (D.D.C. 2000) (*citing* Great Plains Mut. Ins. Co. v. Mutual Reins. Bur., 150 F.R.D. 193, 197 (D. Kan. 1993) and stating that the privilege is not triggered where rendering legal advice is incidental to business advice); Georgia-Pac. Corp. v. GAF Roofing Mfg. Corp., No. 93 Civ. 5125, 1996 WL 29392, at *4 (S.D.N.Y. Jan. 25, 1996) (attorney negotiating portion of acquisition agreement was not "exercising a lawyer's traditional function" and thus communications with client were not privileged); United States v. Loften, 518 F. Supp. 839, 846 (S.D.N.Y. 1981) (even if "little bits of legal advice were . . . buried within discussions of primarily business matters" in reports, those communications would not qualify as privileged), *aff'd,* 819 F.2d 1130 (2d Cir. 1987); FSLIC v. Fielding, 343 F. Supp. 537, 546 (D. Nev. 1972) ("When the attorney and the client get in bed together as business partners, their relationship is a business relationship, not a professional one, and their confidences are business confidences unprotected by a professional privilege"); Hardy v. New York News, Inc., 114 F.R.D. 633, 643-44 (S.D.N.Y. 1987).

50. *See, e.g.,* Marsh v. Safir, No. 99 Civ. 8605JGKMHD, 2000 WL 460580, at *12 (S.D.N.Y. Apr. 20, 2000) ("[a]n attorney's performance of a function that is normally performed by a non-attorney is not covered by the attorney-client privilege"); SEC v. Gulf & W. Indus., Inc., 518 F. Supp. 675, 683 (D.D.C. 1981) (lawyer was merely acting as scribe); Bird v. Penn Cent. Co., 61 F.R.D. 43, 46 n.3 (E.D. Pa. 1973) (lawyer acted as a "lay claims investigator"); Merrin Jewelry Co. v. St. Paul Fire & Marine Ins. Co., 49 F.R.D. 54, 57 (S.D.N.Y. 1970) (same); Underwater Storage, Inc. v. United States Rubber Co., 314 F. Supp. 546, 548 (D.D.C. 1970) (noting that communications with attorney dealing exclusively with the solicitation of business advice, or with technical engineering aspects of patent procurement are not privileged) (*citing* Georgia-Pac. Plywood Co. v. United States Plywood Corp., 18 F.R.D. 463, 464 (S.D.N.Y. 1956)).

51. *See, e.g.,* Puerto Rico v. S.S. Zoe Colocotroni, 61 F.R.D. 653, 660 (D.P.R. 1974); Duplan Corp. v. Deering Milliken, Inc., 397 F. Supp. 1146, 1168 (D.S.C. 1975) (lawyer served merely as "conduit" for transmission of patent applications); *see also* United States v. Wilson, 798 F.2d 509, 513 (1st Cir. 1986) (attorney acted as "messenger"); United States v. Palmer, 536 F.2d 1278, 1281 (9th Cir. 1976) (attorney acted as "transfer shipping agent"); Attorney Gen. of United States v. Covington & Burling, 430 F. Supp. 1117, 1121-22 (D.D.C. 1977) (lawyer assisted in nonlegal aspects of contract negotiations); Underwater Storage, Inc. v. United States Rubber Co., 314 F. Supp. 546, 549 (D.D.C. 1970) (attorney who engaged in patent solicitation activities such as determining patentability, drafting patent specifications, and preparing and processing applications did not constitute legal advice because these tasks "could as easily have been done by non-lawyers").

52. *See* Diversified Indus., Inc. v. Meredith, 572 F.2d 596, 610 (8th Cir. 1978) (en banc).

53. *Id.*

the Eighth Circuit (en banc) held that this element was present when counsel had been retained in connection with the investigation of a possible "slush fund" used to bribe potential customers' purchasing agents. Although the majority suggested initially that the retention of "a professional legal adviser" resulted in a *prima facie* assumption that the purpose for the retention was securing legal advice,[54] the remainder of the opinion focused more specifically upon elements that would justify this conclusion. The court described the authorization given to counsel as including the conduct of an investigation, the retention of accounting assistance, and the conduct of interviews of employees with knowledge of the facts. These steps were designed specifically to enable counsel "to analyze the accounting data, to evaluate and draw conclusions as to the propriety of past actions and to make recommendations for possible future courses of action."[55] Thus, counsel was utilizing "the training, skills, and background necessary to make the independent analysis and recommendations that the Board felt essential to the future welfare of the corporation," which could not be provided by accountants or lay investigators.[56]

One judge dissented on the ground that counsel had been retained "to make a factual investigation and business recommendations,"[57] which could just as well have been performed by lay investigators or accountants. In so concluding, the dissenting judge relied in part upon the minutes of the board meeting at which the retention of counsel was authorized as indicating the purpose of the retention was investigative, not legal.[58] The dissent also pointed out that counsel's report of the investigation consisted principally of a description of the investigation and its factual findings, with recommendations that could have been made by lay investigators, accountants, bankers, "or, for that matter, by any person possessing ordinary common sense and business prudence."[59]

The Supreme Court's decision in *Upjohn Co. v. United States*,[60] which involved a fact pattern similar to *Diversified Industries*, accepted without much discussion the premise that the corporation had retained counsel "in order to secure legal advice."[61] The concurring opinion was more explicit in

---

54. *Id.*
55. *Id.*
56. *Id.*
57. *Id.* at 614.
58. *Id.* at 614-15.
59. *Id.*
60. 449 U.S. 383.
61. *Id.* at 394.

defining the legal functions that must underlie the assertion of privilege in this context:

> The attorney must be one authorized by the management to inquire into the subject and must be seeking information to assist counsel in performing any of the following functions: (a) evaluating whether the employee's conduct has bound or would bind the corporation; (b) assessing the legal consequences, if any, of that conduct; or (c) formulating appropriate legal responses to actions that have been or may be taken by others with regard to that conduct.[62]

The New York Court of Appeals has held the attorney-client privilege applicable to a lawyer-conducted internal investigation into allegations of fraud in the business relationship between certain employees of a bank and outside vendors. In *Spectrum Systems International Corp. v. Chemical Bank*,[63] the court reiterated its previous holding in *Rossi v. Blue Cross and Blue Shield of Greater New York*[64] that, in order for the privilege to apply, the communication from lawyer to client must be made "for the purpose of facilitating the rendition of legal advice or services, in the course of a professional relationship." While acknowledging that certain functions of the retained lawyers were "investigative" in nature, the court nevertheless held that the fact "[t]hat non-privileged information is included in an otherwise privileged lawyer's communication to its client—while influencing whether the document would be protected in whole or only in part—does not destroy the immunity."[65] The court recognized that "[i]n transmitting legal advice and furnishing legal services it will often be necessary for a lawyer to refer to nonprivileged matter."[66] The court held that "[t]he critical inquiry is whether, viewing the lawyer's communication in its full content and context, it was made in order to render legal advice or services to the client."[67]

After reviewing the document in question and the undisputed facts in the record, the court found that counsel's report offered "no recommendations for desirable future business procedures or corruption prevention measures, or employee discipline . . . . Rather, the narration relates and integrates the facts with the law firm's assessment of the client's legal position, and evidences the lawyer's motivation to convey legal advice."[68]

---

62. *Id.* at 403 (Burger, C.J., concurring).
63. 581 N.E.2d 1055, 1060 (N.Y. 1991).
64. 540 N.E.2d 703, 706 (N.Y. 1989).
65. Spectrum Sys. Int'l Corp. v. Chemical Bank, 581 N.E.2d 1055, 1060 (N.Y. 1991).
66. *Id.*
67. *Id.* at 1061.
68. *Id.*

The *Spectrum* court further found that the fact that counsel's report may have been "inconclusive, looking toward future discussion" was "without significance," recognizing that "[l]egal advice often begins—and may end—with a preliminary evaluation and a range of options. More than that may not be possible upon an initial investigation." Likewise, the absence of legal research in the lawyer's communication was held "not determinative of privilege, so long as the communication reflects the attorney's professional skills and judgments." The Court of Appeals expressly recognized that "[l]egal advice may be grounded in experience as well as research."[69]

Documentation of the purpose of the retention of investigative counsel should clearly reflect that the intended role is broader than simply ascertaining the relevant facts, since a court may later conclude that such efforts are a layperson's function. Additional purposes commonly identified in the documentation surrounding internal corporate investigations include analyzing and advising with respect to the corporation's potential liabilities; analyzing and advising with respect to the corporation's claims against third parties or, possibly, its own employees; preparing to defend the corporation in litigation likely to ensue from the underlying situation; and making recommendations to the corporation as to other kinds of future actions that are legal in nature, such as improved compliance programs.

4. Communication

The attorney-client privilege protects only the communication between the attorney and the client; it does not protect underlying facts from disclosure. As the Supreme Court stated in *Upjohn Co. v. United States*:[70]

> [T]he protection of the privilege extends only to communications and not to facts. A fact is one thing and a communication concerning that fact is an entirely different thing. The client cannot be compelled to answer the question, "what did you say or write to the attorney?" but may not refuse to disclose any relevant fact within his knowledge merely because he incorporated a statement of such fact into his communication to his attorney.[71]

---

69. *Id.* at 1061-62.
70. 449 U.S. 383 (1981).
71. *Id.* at 395-96 (citations omitted); *see also* United States v. O'Malley, 786 F.2d 786, 794 (7th Cir. 1986). Thus, absent special circumstances, a client's identity, date of consultation, and fee information are not privileged. *See In re* Grand Jury Subpoena Served Upon Doe, 781 F.2d 238, 247 (2d Cir.) (en banc), *cert. denied,* 475 U.S. 1106 (1986); *In re* Grand Jury Subpoena Served Upon Shargel, 742 F.2d 61, 63 & n.3 (2d Cir. 1984). However, "[a] client's identity and the nature of that client's fee arrangements may be privileged where the

The privilege plainly protects communications from the client to the lawyer, and should also protect communications from the lawyer to the client.[72] However, some courts have held that a lawyer's communications to the client will not be privileged unless they are based on or relate to a client's confidences, or would reveal such confidences if disclosed.[73]

This approach has been criticized,[74] and many decisions hold that counsel's advice is privileged, whether or not the advice would tend to disclose a confidence of the client.[75]

Counsel in jurisdictions that do not clearly protect the lawyer's communications to the client should take special care to ensure the confidentiality of their advice, particularly in written materials, by making explicit (rather than implicit) the interrelationship between the client's confidences and the lawyer's advice.

---

person invoking the privilege can show a strong probability that disclosure of such information would implicate that client in the very criminal activity for which legal advice was sought." United States v. Hodge & Zweig, 548 F.2d 1347, 1353 (9th Cir. 1977) (*citing* Baird v. Koerner, 279 F.2d 623, 630 (9th Cir. 1960)). Later Ninth Circuit cases have largely limited the *Baird* exception to its facts. *See, e.g., In re* Grand Jury Subpoena, 803 F.2d 493, 497-98 (9th Cir. 1986), *modified,* 817 F.2d 64 (9th Cir. 1987).

72. *See* Hanson v. United States Agency for Int'l Dev., 372 F.3d 286, 291 (4th Cir. 2004); Allen v. West Point-Pepperell Inc., 848 F. Supp. 423, 431 (S.D.N.Y. 1994) (barring defendants from "inquir[ing] as to the legal advice rendered" by attorney); Spectrum Sys. Int'l Corp. v. Chemical Bank, 581 N.E.2d 1055, 1060 (N.Y. 1991) ("the privilege extends as well to communications from attorney to client"); Natta v. Hogan, 392 F.2d 686, 692-93 (10th Cir. 1968) (same); *see also* Upjohn Co. v. United States, 449 U.S. 389, 390 (1981) ("[t]he privilege exists to protect not only the giving of professional advice to those who can act on it but also the giving of information to the lawyer to enable him to give sound and informed advice").

73. *See, e.g.,* Rehling v. City of Chicago, 207 F.3d 1009, 1019 (7th Cir. 2000) ("statements made by the lawyer to the client will be protected in circumstances where those communications rest on confidential information obtained from the client [citation omitted] or where those communications would reveal the substance of a confidential communication by the client [citation omitted]"); Brinton v. Department of State, 636 F.2d 600, 603 (D.C. Cir. 1980) (stating that communications from attorney to client are privileged to the extent that they reveal client confidences), *cert. denied,* 452 U.S. 905 (1981); *see also* United States v. Motorola, Inc., No. Civ. A. 94-2331TFH/JMF, 1999 WL 552553, at *2 (D.D.C. May 28, 1999) (same); American Standard Inc. v. Pfizer Inc., 828 F.2d 734, 745 (Fed. Cir. 1987) (same).

74. *See In re* LTV Sec. Litig., 89 F.R.D. 595, 601-03 (N.D. Tex. 1981).

75. *See, e.g.,* Spectrum Sys. Int'l Corp. v. Chemical Bank, 581 N.E.2d 1055, 1060 (N.Y. 1991) (rejecting the "cramped view" of the privilege espoused in decisions such as Mead Data Central, Inc. v. United States Department of Air Force, 566 F.2d 242, 254 n.25 (D.C. Cir. 1977); United States v. Amerada Hess Corp., 619 F.2d 980, 986 (3d Cir. 1980); United States v. Ramirez, 608 F.2d 1261, 1268 n.12 (9th Cir. 1979).

Another issue faced by investigative counsel is that documents that do not themselves represent confidential communications to a lawyer do not become privileged merely by transmitting them to a lawyer.[76] Thus, the underlying corporate documents examined by counsel are not themselves protected from discovery, although counsel's own assembly and organization of documents that counsel deemed relevant are probably protected by the work-product doctrine.[77]

In addition, the mere presence of a lawyer at corporate meetings, including meetings of the board of directors, will not render the meetings or the minutes privileged.[78] Communications made during corporate meetings will be considered privileged only where they relate to the request for or rendition of legal advice and are intended to be confidential and privileged.[79] Where the purpose of the meeting, attended only by parties within the attorney-client

---

76. *See, e.g.,* Pfizer Inc. v. Ranbaxy Labs. Ltd., No. 03-209-JJF, 2004 WL 2323135, at *2 (D. Del. Oct. 7, 2004) ("Routine, non-privileged communications between corporate officers and employees do not attain privileged status solely because counsel is copied on the correspondence"); *In re* Gabapentin Patent Litig., 214 F.R.D. 178, 186 (D.N.J. 2003) ("Including an attorney on the distribution list of an interoffice memo, cc'ing numerous people who are ancillary to the discussion, one of whom happens to be an attorney, or forwarding an e-mail several times until it reaches an attorney does not amount to 'attorney-client communication'") (citation omitted); American Med. Sys., Inc. v. National Union Fire Ins. Co. of Pitt., Inc., No. Civ. A. 98-1788, 1999 WL 970341, at *4 (E.D. La. Oct. 22, 1999) ("[l]etters that merely transmit documents to or from an attorney, even at the attorney's request for purposes of rendering legal advice to a client, are neither privileged nor attorney work-product"); United States v. Frederick, 182 F.3d 496, 500 (7th Cir. 1999) (information of the type normally furnished to an accountant does not become privileged merely because an attorney is the tax preparer); *In re* Grand Jury Subpoenas Dated Oct. 22, 1991, & Nov. 1, 1991, 959 F.2d 1158, 1165 (2d Cir. 1992) (law firm in possession of client's telephone bills must produce them to the grand jury because "[d]ocuments created by and received from an unrelated third party and given by the client to his attorney in the course of seeking legal advice do not thereby become privileged"); Fisher v. United States, 425 U.S. 391, 403-04 (1976) ("preexisting documents which could have been obtained by court process from the client when he was in possession may also be obtained from the attorney by similar process following transfer by the client in order to obtain more informed legal advice"); SCM Corp. v. Xerox Corp., 70 F.R.D. 508, 523 (D. Conn.) ("[l]egal departments are not citadels in which public, business or technical information may be placed to defeat discovery and thereby ensure confidentiality"), *appeal dismissed,* 534 F.2d 1031 (2d Cir. 1976); IT & T Corp. v. United Tel. Co. of Fla., 60 F.R.D. 177, 185 (M.D. Fla. 1973); Air-Shield, Inc. v. Air Reduction Co., 46 F.R.D. 96, 97 (N.D. Ill. 1968).
77. *See* Part III, *infra.*
78. *See, e.g.,* Neuder v. Battelle Pac. N.W. Nat'l Lab., 194 F.R.D. 289, 293 (D.D.C. 2000) (attorney's attendance at committee meeting did not render documents produced during the meeting subject to the attorney-client privilege); United States v. Motorola, Inc., No. Civ. A. 94-2331TFH/JMF, 1999 WL 552553, at *4 (D.D.C. May 28, 1999) (ordering production of minutes of meeting of board of directors despite an attorney's presence); Diversified Indus., Inc. v. Meredith, 572 F.2d 596, 611 (8th Cir. 1978) (en banc).
79. *E.g.,* IT & T Corp. v. United Tel. Co. of Fla., 60 F.R.D. 177, 185 (M.D. Fla. 1973).

relationship, is to plan legal strategy, or where disclosure would reveal the contents of privileged communications, that portion of the meeting and minutes may be privileged.[80] Accordingly, the records of corporate meetings, particularly board minutes, should reflect plainly on their face that legal advice has been sought or rendered.

Finally, it is important for counsel to appreciate the fact that a lawyer's own files are not necessarily privileged. As the Supreme Court noted in *Hickman v. Taylor*:[81]

> Nor does [the attorney-client] privilege concern the memoranda, briefs, communications, and other writings prepared by counsel for his own use in prosecuting his client's case; and it is equally unrelated to writings which reflect a lawyer's mental impressions, conclusions, opinions, or legal theories.[82]

A lawyer's internal memorandum may not be a communication directed to anyone for purposes of legal advice, and it does not necessarily reflect either a communication from a client or an intention to communicate confidentially with a client.[83] These documents may constitute work product;[84] however, the work-product doctrine may be overcome by an adversary's showing of substantial need and undue hardship,[85] and therefore it is prudent to ensure that the documents are privileged by expressly intertwining the client's communications with the lawyer's conclusions.

5. Confidentiality

Investigative counsel also should ensure that privileged material is treated with the appropriate degree of confidentiality. The privilege protects only those communications made in confidence, and any information a client gives to a lawyer is presumed to be confidential.[86] However, communications

---

80. *See, e.g.,* Diversified Indus., Inc. v. Meredith, 572 F.2d 596, 611 (8th Cir. 1978) (en banc).
81. 329 U.S. 495 (1947).
82. *Id.* at 508 (dictum).
83. *See* Sneider v. Kimberly-Clark Corp., 91 F.R.D. 1, 6 (N.D. Ill. 1980); *see also* SCM Corp. v. Xerox Corp., 70 F.R.D. 508, 523 (D. Conn.) (lawyer's opinions and legal theories, even if never transmitted to client, may be privileged if they reveal confidences from the client), *appeal dismissed,* 534 F.2d 1031 (2d Cir. 1976); Cedrone v. Unity Sav. Ass'n, 103 F.R.D. 423, 429 (E.D. Pa. 1984) (any oral or written communication between lawyers concerning the representation of a client is protected by the attorney-client privilege as long as it utilizes client confidences).
84. *See* Part III, *infra.*
85. *See* Part III.D, *infra.*
86. Barton v. United States Dist. Ct. for Cent. Dist. of Cal., 410 F.3d 1104, 110 (9th Cir. 2005); *In re* EXDS, Inc., No. C05-0787 PVT, 2005 WL 2043020, at *8 (N.D. Cal. Aug. 24, 2005); Analytica, Inc. v. NPD Research, Inc., 708 F.2d 1263, 1267 (7th Cir. 1983).

made in the presence of others are not deemed to be confidential if the third parties are not part of the attorney-client relationship.[87]

Communications meant to be transmitted to third parties do not ordinarily fall under the protection of the privilege.[88] Generally, information disclosed to a lawyer with the intention that the lawyer draft a document to be released to third parties is protected by the attorney-client privilege.[89] However, most courts hold that the mere intent to disclose the substance of communications between a lawyer and a client does not vitiate the privilege; rather, actual disclosure is required to breach confidentiality.[90] Thus, investigative counsel should exercise caution in the preparation and preservation of drafts of documents such as press releases, SEC filings, and similar papers.

C. *Practical Problems of Employee Interviews*

As difficult as the application of the attorney-client privilege already is in the context of internal corporate investigations, a further layer of complexity is added by the process of conducting employee interviews.

---

87. *See, e.g.,* Johnson v. United States, 542 F.2d 941, 942 (5th Cir. 1976), *cert. denied,* 430 U.S. 934 (1977); Ampa, Ltd. v. Kentfield Capital LLC, No. 00 Civ. 0508 NRB AJP, 2000 WL 1156860, at *1 (S.D.N.Y. Aug. 16, 2000) (privilege waived with respect to minutes of board meeting at which an accountant, unrelated to the legal issue discussed, was present); Atronic Int'l, GMBH v. SAI Semispecialists of Am., Inc., 232 F.R.D. 160, 163 (E.D.N.Y. 2005) (finding that arguably privileged e-mails sent to legal counsel by corporate employee that were originally produced by the plaintiff in 2003 as part of initial disclosures and again produced to the defendant in 2005 as a binder of exhibits that the plaintiff intended to use at a subsequent deposition were not privileged due to plaintiff's carelessness and the resulting prejudice to defendant if immunity were to be restored).

88. Lorenz v. Valley Forge Ins. Co., 815 F.2d 1095, 1098 (7th Cir. 1987); United States v. Aronson, 781 F.2d 1580, 1581 (11th Cir. 1986); Radio Corp. of Am. v. Rauland Corp., 18 F.R.D. 440, 443 (N.D. Ill. 1955); Rediker v. Warfield, 11 F.R.D. 125, 128 (S.D.N.Y. 1951) (no privilege exists if the communication is made "with the understanding that it is to be imparted to a third party").

89. *In re* Grand Jury Subpoena, 341 F.3d 331, 336 (4th Cir. 2003) ("The underlying communications between Counsel and [client] regarding his submission . . . are privileged, regardless of the fact that those communications may have assisted him in answering questions in a public document"), *cert. denied sub nom.,* 541 U.S. 982 (2004); IMC Chems., Inc. v. Niro Inc., No. Civ. A. 98-2348-JTM, 2000 WL 1466495, at *9 (D. Kan. July 19, 2000) (The attorney-client privilege protects "'any communication from an attorney to his client made in the course of giving legal advice . . . without the qualification that the communication must contain confidential matters revealed by the client earlier to the attorney'") (citation omitted).

90. *In re* Grand Jury Subpoena Duces Tecum Dated Sept. 15, 1983, 731 F.2d 1032, 1037 (2d Cir. 1984) ("although some of the documents appear to be drafts of communications the final version of which might eventually be sent to other persons, and as distributed would not be privileged, we see no basis in the record for inferring that [appellant] did not intend that

1. Potential Conflicts of Interest Warnings to Employees

A lawyer representing a corporation represents the corporate entity, not its employees.[91] In conducting an internal corporate investigation, counsel runs the risk that corporate personnel may mistakenly believe corporate counsel represents the employees individually, in addition to the corporation. If this occurs, counsel may face the possibility of disqualification in a later litigation against an employee.

One former federal judge dubbed the introductory advice to corporate employees as "Adnarim" warnings ("Miranda" spelled backward), and set them forth, in stark terms, as follows:

> I am not your lawyer, I represent the corporation. It is the corporation's interests I have been retained to serve. You are entitled to have your own lawyer. If you cannot afford a lawyer, the corporation may, or may not, pay his fee. You may wish to consult with him before you confer with me. Among other things, you may wish to claim the privilege against self-incrimination. You may wish not to talk to me at all.
>
> What you tell me, if it relates to the performance of your duties, and is confidential, will be privileged. The privilege, however, requires explanation. It is not your privilege to claim. It is the corporation's privilege. Thus, not only can I tell, I must tell, others in the corporation what you have told me, if it is necessary to enable me to provide the legal services to the corporation it has retained me to provide.
>
> Moreover, the corporation can waive its privilege and thus, the president, or I, or someone else, can disclose to the authorities what you tell me if the corporation decides to waive its privilege.
>
> Also, if I find wrongdoing, I am under certain obligations to report it to the Board of Directors and perhaps the stockholders.
>
> Finally, the fact that our conversation is privileged does not mean that what you did, or said, is protected from disclosure just because you tell me about it. You may be subpoenaed, for example, and required to tell what you did, or said or observed, even though you told me about it.
>
> Do you understand?[92]

---

the drafts . . . be confidential . . . . We see no indication that a waiver has yet occurred"); *see also* United States v. Schlegel, 313 F. Supp. 177, 179 (D. Neb. 1970) (the client intends only as much information to be conveyed to third parties as is actually conveyed; all other information remains privileged); *but see In re* Grand Jury Proceedings, 727 F.2d 1352, 1356 (4th Cir. 1984) (statements made by a client to an attorney with the intention that they be communicated to a third party are not privileged even if the intended publication does not occur).

91. ABA MODEL RULES OF PROF'L CONDUCT R. 1.13; ABA MODEL CODE OF PROF'L RESPONSIBILITY EC 5-18.

92. Remarks by Frederick B. Lacey, formerly a U.S. district judge for the District of New Jersey (reprinted with permission).

While so dire a warning is likely to frighten an employee, and thus to be counterproductive, it is necessary that employees are provided enough information, in a clear enough manner, to understand that corporate investigative counsel does not represent the employee.

ABA Model Rule 1.13(f) provides some guidance on this issue, stating that "[i]n dealing with an organization's directors, officers [and] employees ... a lawyer shall explain the identity of the client when the lawyer knows or reasonably should know that the organization's interests are adverse to those of the [organization's] constituents with whom the lawyer is dealing."[93] Further, the comment to this Model Rule suggests that

> [c]are must be taken to assure that the individual understands that, when there is such adversity of interest, the lawyer for the organization cannot provide legal representation for that constituent individual, and that discussions between the lawyer for the organization and the individual may not be privileged. Whether such a warning should be given by the lawyer for the organization to any constituent individual may turn on the facts of each case.[94]

Apart from professional considerations, the impetus to provide appropriate disclosure to employees may be found in a seminal decision, *E. F. Hutton & Co. v. Brown*,[95] in which corporate counsel was disqualified as a result of a corporate officer's lack of understanding of counsel's role. In *Brown*, counsel for Hutton conducted an internal investigation, which included interviewing various Hutton personnel regarding certain transactions. Shortly thereafter, Hutton's lawyer accompanied one of Hutton's officers to two hearings regarding those transactions. During both hearings, the employee informed the judge that he was represented by the counsel for the corporation, and counsel did not take any action to correct this mistake.[96]

In a subsequent litigation by Hutton against the officer arising out of the same transactions, Hutton's counsel was disqualified. The court concluded that the corporate officer reasonably believed that both he and Hutton were jointly represented by Hutton's counsel. The court stated that a lawyer's appearance on behalf of a corporate employee individually at a judicial proceeding raises a presumption of individual representation, which the corporation did

---

93. ABA Model Rules of Prof'l Conduct R. 1.13(F).
94. *Id.* at cmts. 10-11.
95. 305 F. Supp. 371 (S.D. Tex. 1969).
96. *Id.* at 390-91.

not overcome.[97] Consequently, because of the subsequent conflicting interests between the employee and the corporation, the court required the lawyer to withdraw from the litigation.[98]

The court was careful to note that "not all corporate counsel appearing with corporate officers who are called to testify will risk disqualification. Only those counsel who permit the officer to believe that they represent him individually will disable themselves from appearing in subsequent litigation. And it is eminently proper to disqualify these, for they are persons who are in a position, and have the obligation to ensure that there is no misunderstanding by the officer."[99]

2. Counsel's Communications with Former Employees

It is not unusual for investigative counsel to need to interview former employees of the corporation. The opinion of the Court in *Upjohn* did not address the issue of whether the attorney-client privilege extends to communications between counsel and former employees. However, in his concurring opinion, Chief Justice Burger noted his approval of a rule that would treat communications between counsel and former employees as privileged in situations where "a former employee speaks at the direction of the management with an attorney regarding conduct or proposed conduct within the scope of employment."[100]

The extension of the attorney-client privilege to include former employees serves to promote honest communication between the former employees

---

97. *Id.* at 391.
98. *Id.*
99. *Id.* at 398. Another case, United States v. Keplinger, 776 F.2d 678 (7th Cir. 1985), *cert. denied*, 476 U.S. 1183 (1986), followed the same type of analysis as *Brown,* but reached the opposite conclusion, holding that the individual corporate employees were not represented by the corporate counsel. The court based its conclusion on the fact that defendants did not seek individual legal advice, did not inquire regarding individual representation, and did not indicate to defendants their belief that such a relationship existed. Moreover, the mere fact that the corporation's lawyer accompanied one of the defendants to a meeting did not support a finding that the defendant had a reasonable basis for believing that he was being represented individually. *Id.* at 700; *see also* Tuttle v. Combined Ins. Co., 222 F.R.D. 424, 429 (E.D. Cal. 2004) (there is no individual attorney-client privilege between a corporation's attorney and individuals within the corporation unless there is a clear showing that the individual consulted the corporate counsel in the officer's individual capacity).
100. 449 U.S. 383, 402 (Burger, C.J., concurring).

and corporate counsel. Accordingly, most courts have adhered to the view that these communications are privileged.[101]

3. Adversary's Communications with Current or Former Employees

Assuming that counsel's interview with a current or former employee was privileged at the time it was held, it is important to caution the employee not to discuss the interview with anyone else. The traditional waiver problems inherent in the employee's discussions with third parties[102] are exacerbated by the developing law in some jurisdictions that an adversary's counsel may interview current and former corporate employees without notifying the corporation's counsel.[103]

The ABA Code of Professional Responsibility provides that "[d]uring the course of his representation of a client a lawyer shall not . . . communicate or cause another to communicate on the subject of the representation with a party he knows to be represented by a lawyer in that matter unless he has the

---

101. *See In re* Coordinated Pretrial Proceedings in Petroleum Prods. Antitrust Litig., 658 F.2d 1355, 1361 n.7 (9th Cir. 1981) ("Former employees, as well as current employees, may possess the relevant information needed by corporate counsel to advise the client with respect to actual or potential difficulties"), *cert. denied*, 455 U.S. 990 (1982); Command Transp., Inc. v. Y.S. Line (USA) Corp., 116 F.R.D. 94, 97 (D. Mass. 1987) ("a formalistic distinction based solely on the timing of the interview cannot make a difference if the goals of the privilege outlined in *Upjohn* are to be achieved"); *see also* Admiral Ins. Co. v. United States Dist. Ct. for Dist. of Ariz., 881 F.2d 1486, 1493 (9th Cir. 1989) (communications between former employees and corporate counsel would be privileged if the employee possesses information critical to the representation of the corporation and the communications concern matters within the scope of employment); Connolly Data Sys., Inc. v. Victor Techs., Inc., 114 F.R.D. 89, 92 (S.D. Cal. 1987); *but see* Barrett Indus. Trucks, Inc. v. Old Republic Ins. Co., 129 F.R.D. 515, 517 (N.D. Ill. 1990) (refusing to extend the attorney-client privilege to former employees).

102. *See* Part IV.A, *infra*.

103. *See, e.g.*, United States ex rel. O'Keefe v. McDonnell Douglas Corp., 961 F. Supp. 1288, 1295 (E.D. Mo. 1997) (holding that counsel can interview former unrepresented employee of opposing party), *aff'd*, 132 F.3d 1252 (8th Cir. 1998); Thorn v. Sunstrand Corp., No. 95 C 50099, 1997 WL 627607, at **2-3 (N.D. Ill. Oct. 10, 1997) (plaintiff's counsel was permitted to interview a management employee of the corporate defendant who had retired subsequent to being deposed in the litigation and finding that the retiree's statements could no longer bind the company); H.B.A. Mgmt., Inc. v. Estate of Schwartz, 693 So. 2d 541, 544-45 (Fla. 1997) (holding that attorney may engage in ex parte communications with former employees of the defendant-employer); *see also* FleetBoston Robertson Stephens, Inc. v. Innovex, Inc., 172 F. Supp. 2d 1190, 1193 (D. Minn. 2001) (noting that the majority of courts who have considered this matter have reached the same result and citing authorities).

prior consent of the lawyer representing such other party or is authorized by law to do so."[104] The ABA Model Rules of Professional Conduct contain a similar provision.[105]

In the context of a corporate client, it may be difficult to determine which corporate employees are considered to be a party with whom *ex parte* communication by opposing counsel is prohibited. Some courts have taken the view that the term "party" in litigation involving corporations includes only employees who have the legal authority to bind the corporation.[106] The New York Court of Appeals has added that the prohibition also includes "the corporate employees responsible for actually effectuating the advice of counsel in the matter."[107] Finally, the comments to the ABA Model Rules state that the prohibition against *ex parte* contact applies to communications with an employee who "supervises, directs or regularly consults with the organization's lawyer concerning the matter or has authority to obligate the organization with respect to the matter or whose act or omission in connection with the matter may be imputed to the organization for purposes of civil or criminal liability.[108]

At least one court has taken a different approach. In *Mompoint v. Lotus Development Corp.*,[109] the court permitted the plaintiff's counsel to hold *ex parte* interviews with corporate employees in the context of a sexual harassment suit, but only after inquiry into whether the interview would deal with questions within the scope of the employee's employment, and therefore be likely to result in evidence admissible against the corporation. In addition, the court held that it was necessary to consider the need, according to the circumstances of each case, for the corporation to have its counsel present to ensure "effective representation" of the corporation.[110]

The Committee on Professional Ethics of the Association of the Bar of the City of New York reached an even broader conclusion, determining that the "corporation's right to effective representation can be guarded adequately only by viewing all present employees of a corporation as 'parties' for purposes of DR 7-104 where the proposed interview concerns matters within the

---

104. ABA MODEL CODE OF PROF'L RESPONSIBILITY DR 7-104(A)(1).
105. ABA MODEL RULES OF PROF'L CONDUCT R. 4.2.
106. *See Wright ex rel.* Wright v. Group Health Hosp., 691 P.2d 564, 569 (Wash. 1984); Niesig v. Team I, 558 N.E.2d 1030, 1035 (N.Y. 1990).
107. Niesig v. Team I, 558 N.E.2d 1030, 1035 (N.Y. 1990).
108. ABA MODEL RULES OF PROF'L CONDUCT R. 4.2 cmt. 7.
109. 110 F.R.D. 414 (D. Mass. 1986).
110. *Id.* at 418.

scope of the employees' employment."[111] The Massachusetts Bar Association has also adopted this approach.[112]

The authorities seem to be in agreement that the ethical rules do not restrain counsel opposing the corporation from communication with former employees.[113] One court has noted, however, that former employees "are 'barred from discussing privileged information to which they are privy.'"[114]

The application of these ethical rules to federal prosecutors is unclear. In *United States v. Hammad*,[115] the Second Circuit ruled that DR 7-104(A)(1) was applicable to criminal prosecutions,[116] but left open the possibility that certain investigative techniques, particularly those involving informants, may be permissible, even though these techniques would involve the prosecutor's indirect communication with an adverse party represented by counsel.[117] The Attorney General has issued an instruction to Justice Department lawyers that

---

111. Opinion 80-46 of the Committee on Professional Ethics of the Association of the Bar of the City of New York.

112. Committee of Professional Ethics of the Massachusetts Bar Formal Opinion No. 82-7; *but see* Alabama Bar Opinion No. 2002-03 (contact between counsel and employees of opposing party who are nonmanagerial, who are not responsible for act for which opposing party could be liable, and who have no authority to make decisions about the litigation is permitted); State Bar of Nevada Standing Committee on Ethics and Professional Responsibility Formal Advisory Opinion 27 (2005) (same).

113. *See, e.g.,* Davidson Supply Co. v. P.P.E., Inc., 986 F. Supp. 956, 957-58 (D. Md. 1997) (ethical rules did not prohibit plaintiff's counsel from contacting a former employee); Thorn v. Sunstrand Corp., No. 95 C 50099, 1997 WL 627607, at *3 (N.D. Ill. Oct. 10, 1997) (Rule 4.2 of the Rules of Professional Conduct for the Northern District of Illinois does not prohibit contact with a former manager); *but see* Camden v. Maryland, 910 F. Supp. 1115, 1123 (D. Md. 1996) (plaintiff's contact with the former employee who conducted the internal corporate investigation into plaintiff's discrimination claims was prohibited by Rule 4.2); Zachair, Ltd. v. Driggs, 965 F. Supp. 741, 754 (D. Md. 1997) (contact with former in-house counsel was prohibited by Rule 4.2), *aff'd,* 141 F.3d 1162 (4th Cir. 1998); Niesig v. Team I, 558 N.E.2d 1030, 1035-36 (N.Y. 1990); *see also* Utah State Bar Ethics Advisory Opinion No. 04-04; D.C. Bar Op.

114. Thorn v. Sunstrand Corp., No. 95 C 50099, 1997 WL 627607, at *3 (N.D. Ill. Oct. 10, 1997) (finding that a retired management employee of a corporate defendant had not disclosed any privileged information to plaintiff and approving of plaintiff's warning to the retiree at the beginning of the interview not to disclose privileged information) (*citing* Orlowski v. Dominick's Finer Foods, Inc., 937 F. Supp. 723, 728 (N.D. Ill. 1996)).

115. 858 F.2d 834 (2d Cir. 1988), *cert. denied,* 498 U.S. 871 (1990).

116. *Id.* at 837-38.

117. *Id.* at 838-40.

"contact with a represented individual in the course of authorized law enforcement does not violate DR 7-104."[118] The Attorney General relies on the Supremacy Clause as mandating that the federal interest in maintaining effective investigation is paramount to the state interests in regulating the legal profession.[119] However, it is far from clear whether the "guideline" issued by the Attorney General can supersede the Second Circuit's contrary ruling.

The Attorney General also promulgated a rule that provides that "[a] communication with a current employee [of a represented party] shall be considered to be a communication with the organization . . . only if the employee is a controlling individual."[120] The rule defines "controlling individual" as "a current high level employee who is known by the government to be participating as a decision maker in the determination of the organization's legal position in the proceeding or investigation of the subject matter."[121]

The Eighth Circuit, in *United States ex rel. O'Keeffe v. McDonnell Douglas Corp.*,[122] held that the above-quoted rule was invalid because there was no statutory authority for the Attorney General to promulgate such a rule.[123] The Eighth Circuit affirmed the district court's holding that the government was barred from having *ex parte* communications with current employees under Missouri Supreme Court Rule 4-4.2, which prohibits, inter alia, *ex parte* communications with "persons having the managerial responsibility on behalf of the organization, and with any other person whose act or omission in connection with that matter may be imputed to the organization . . . or whose statement may constitute an admission on the part of the organization," when the organization is represented by counsel and such counsel's consent to the contact has not been obtained.[124]

---

118. Memorandum From Office of the Attorney General to All Justice Department Litigators (June 8, 1989).
119. *Id.*
120. 28 C.F.R. § 77.10(a).
121. *Id.*
122. 132 F.3d 1252 (8th Cir. 1998).
123. *Id.* at 1252-56.
124. *Id.* at 1252; *see also* Missouri ex rel. Pitts v. Roberts, 857 S.W.2d 200, 202 (Mo. 1993) (en banc) (adopting the above-quoted language as part of Missouri's ethical rules).

Since both current and former employees may have privileged information—including what they discussed with investigative counsel—the cases permitting *ex parte* contact with these employees and the Attorney General's position create an enormous potential hole in the attorney-client privilege. Accordingly, investigative counsel would be wise to request that employees refrain from cooperating with adversaries, at least until investigative counsel can be present to protect the corporation's interests.[125]

III. WORK PRODUCT PROTECTION

A related but independent basis for potentially preserving the confidentiality of counsel's investigative record is the work-product doctrine.

A. *Work-Product Doctrine Defined*

Rule 26(b)(3) of the Federal Rules of Civil Procedure provides, in relevant part:

> Subject to the provisions of subdivision (b)(4) of this rule, a party may obtain discovery of documents and tangible things otherwise discoverable under subdivision (b)(1) of this rule and prepared in anticipation of litigation or for trial by or for another party or by or for that other party's representative (including the other party's attorney, consultant, surety, indemnitor, ensurer, or agent) only upon a showing that the party seeking discovery has substantial need of the materials in the preparation of the party's case and that the party is unable without undue hardship to obtain the substantial equivalent of the materials by other means. In ordering discovery of such materials when the required showing has been made, the court shall protect against disclosure of the mental impressions, conclusions, opinions, or legal theories of a lawyer or other representative of a party concerning the litigation.[126]

Similarly, Rule 16(b)(2) of the Federal Rules of Criminal Procedure provides, in relevant part:

---

125. Such a request is permissible under ABA Model Rule 3.4(f), where the person so requested is an employee or other agent of the corporation and "the lawyer reasonably believes that the person's interests will not be adversely affected by refraining from giving such information." ABA MODEL RULES OF PROF'L CONDUCT R. 3.4(F).

126. FED. R. CIV. P. 26(b)(3).

Except as to scientific or medical reports, this subdivision does not authorize the discovery or inspection of reports, memoranda, or other internal defense documents made by the defendant, or the defendant's attorneys or agents in connection with the investigation or defense of the case, or of statements made by the defendant, or by government or defense witnesses, or by prospective government or defense witnesses, to the defendant, the defendant's agents or attorneys.[127]

These federal rules are a codification of the United States Supreme Court's definition of attorney work product set forth in the seminal case of *Hickman v. Taylor*.[128]

The promulgation of rule 26(b)(3) of the Federal Rules of Civil Procedure resolved varying judicial interpretations of *Hickman* by protecting all materials, including legal theories, research, and factual materials prepared in anticipation of trial, whether prepared by a lawyer, a party, or an agent of a party.[129] Work product protection is available in both civil actions and criminal actions, including grand jury proceedings.[130] The work-product doctrine

---

127. FED. R. CRIM. P. 16(b)(2).
128. 329 U.S. 495 (1947).
129. *See, e.g.,* Stewart v. Falley's Inc., No. 00-1124-WEB, 2001 WL 1318371, at *2 n.3 (D. Kan. Feb. 14, 2001) (research reveals few cases since the 1970 amendments to Rule 26 where the absence of an attorney was even raised as an issue in determining whether material was entitled to work product protection); United States v. Skeddle, 989 F. Supp. 912, 914-15 (N.D. Ohio 1997) (in criminal action against certain officers, corporation had standing to assert the work product privilege over materials obtained by a firm hired to investigate misconduct by the corporation's officers); Hawkins v. District Ct. In & For Fourth Jud. Dist., 638 P.2d 1372, 1376-77 (Colo. 1982) (en banc) (Rule 26(b)(3) does not draw a distinction between trial preparation materials compiled by an attorney and those created by another agent of a party).
130. United States v. Jacques Dessange, Inc., No. S2 99 CR 1182 DLC, 2000 WL 310345, at *3 (S.D.N.Y. Mar. 27, 2000) (noting that the same principles are generally applicable regardless of whether the litigation is civil or criminal); *In re Doe,* 662 F.2d 1073, 1078 (4th Cir. 1981) ("[a]lthough expressed in the Federal Rules in terms of discoverability of relevant material in civil cases, the work product principle also applies to criminal trials and grand jury proceedings"), *cert. denied,* 455 U.S. 1000 (1982); United States v. Skeddle, 989 F. Supp. 912, 914 (N.D. Ohio 1997) (work product protection raised in criminal case); *see also* United States v. Nobles, 422 U.S. 225, 236 (1975) (criminal trials); *In re* Grand Jury Proceedings, 473 F.2d 840, 842-43 (8th Cir. 1975) (grand jury proceedings).

does not protect discovery of the underlying facts of a dispute as opposed to the attorney's mental impressions, conclusions, opinions, or legal theories.[131]

In contrast with the frequent applicability of state law to questions raising the attorney-client privilege, federal courts resolve questions involving the work-product doctrine by reference to Federal Rules of Civil Procedure and federal common law.[132] Many states also have enacted statutes protecting attorney work product—these statutes can differ significantly from the federal rule, and the practitioner is cautioned to consult the appropriate state's law.[133]

B. *Factual Versus Opinion Work Product*

The federal rules and common law distinguish between "factual" and "opinion" work product.[134] Factual work product encompasses documents or

---

131. *See* Moore U.S.A. Inc. v. Standard Register Co., No. 98-CV-485C(F), 2000 WL 876884, at *6 (W.D.N.Y. May 26, 2000) (work-product doctrine does not protect the identity of the people who provided information to counsel that led to the initiation of suit); Thomas & Betts Corp. v. Panduit Corp., No. 93 C 4017, 1997 WL 603880, at *6 (N.D. Ill. Sept. 23, 1997) (identity of distributors contacted during plaintiff corporation's internal investigation into defendant's misappropriation of plaintiff's confidential business information was not protected by the work-product doctrine); *but see In re* Grand Casinos, Inc., 181 F.R.D. 615, 622 (D. Minn. 1998) (where lawyer prepared documents that collated or categorized facts, such documents were held privileged because they "properly reflected their counsel's thought processes or mental impressions").

132. *See, e.g.,* Baker v. GM Corp., 209 F.3d 1051, 1053-54 (8th Cir. 2000) ("In this diversity case, we apply federal law to resolve work product claims and state law to resolve attorney-client privilege claims"); Estate of Chopper v. R.J. Reynolds Tobacco Co., 195 F.R.D. 648, 650 (N.D. Iowa 2000) (court applies federal law to resolve work-product claims in diversity case); Railroad Salvage of Conn., Inc. v. Japan Freight Consolidators (U.S.A.) Inc., 97 F.R.D. 37, 40-41 (E.D.N.Y. 1983) (defendant's work product claim is governed by Fed. R. Civ. P. 26(b)(3)).

133. *See, e.g.,* N.Y. C.P.L.R. 3101 (McKinney 2004 & Supp. 2006); CAL. CIV. PROC. CODE § 2018.010 *et seq.* (West 2004 & Supp. 2006).

134. *See* Upjohn, 449 U.S. 383 at 399, 401 ("opinion" work product that reveals an attorney's mental impressions and legal theories must receive a higher standard of protection); *In re* Grand Jury Subpoena, 220 F.R.D. 130, 144 (D. Mass. 2004) ("Most courts distinguish between 'opinion' work product, which includes 'materials that contain the mental impressions, conclusions, opinions, or legal theories of an attorney,' and 'ordinary' work product, which includes everything else that is eligible for protection as work product, and accord greater protection to the former") (citation omitted); United States v. Jacques Dessange, Inc., No. S2 99 CR 1182 DLC, 2000 WL 310345, at *2 (S.D.N.Y. Mar. 27, 2000) (attorney work

exhibits prepared in anticipation of litigation, while opinion work product includes mental impressions, opinions, or legal theories.[135] There is also a distinction between written statements prepared by witnesses and oral statements made by witnesses to the lawyer:

> But as to oral statements made by witnesses to [the attorney], whether presently in the form of his mental impressions or memoranda, we do not believe that any showing of necessity can be made under the circumstances of this case so as to justify production.[136]

While non-opinion work product may be discovered upon the requisite showing of substantial need and undue hardship, "[i]n ordering discovery of such [work product] materials when the required showing has been made, the court shall protect against disclosure of the mental impressions, conclusions, opinions, or legal theories of a lawyer or other representative of a party concerning the litigation."[137]

C. Elements of the Work-Product Doctrine

Whether the work product is classified as ordinary or opinion, it is necessary that it be prepared in anticipation of litigation or for trial by a lawyer, a party, or a party's representative.[138] As with the attorney-client privilege, the underlying facts incorporated into the work product are not protected from discovery.[139]

---

product can be divided into two classes: "that which recited factual matters and that which reflects the attorney's opinions, conclusions, mental impressions or legal theories"); United States v. Adlman, 134 F.3d 1194, 1197 (2d Cir. 1998) ("Special treatment for opinion work product is justified because at its core, the work-product doctrine shelters the mental processes of the attorney, providing a privileged area within which he can analyze and prepare his client's case'") (*quoting* United States v. Nobles, 422 U.S. 225, 236 (1975)).

135. *See Hickman v. Taylor,* 329 U.S. 495, 508 (1947).
136. *Id.* at 512-13.
137. FED. R. CIV. P. 26(b)(3).
138. *Id.*
139. *See, e.g., In re* International Sys. & Controls Corp. Sec. Litig., 91 F.R.D. 552, 561 (S.D. Tex. 1981) ("It has consistently been held that the work product privilege does not shield from discovery the underlying facts the party's representative learned, the persons from who he learned such facts, or the existence of certain documents"), *vacated on other grounds,* 693 F.2d 1235 (5th Cir. 1982).

1. Anticipation of Litigation

The attorney work-product doctrine attaches only to materials prepared for use in a pending litigation or in contemplation of future litigation.[140] For material to be considered prepared "in anticipation of litigation," the prospect of litigation must be identifiable, though litigation need not have already commenced.[141] Some articulable claim must exist,[142] however, and a remote possibility of litigation is insufficient.[143]

---

140. FED. R. CIV. P. 26(b)(3); *see* United States v. Adlman, 134 F.3d 1194, 1196-202 (2d Cir. 1998) (interpreting "in anticipation of litigation" to mean "if 'in light of the nature of the document and the factual situation in the particular case, the document can fairly be said to have been prepared or obtained *because of* the prospect of litigation'") (citation omitted); Hertzberg v. Veneman, 273 F. Supp. 2d 67, 75 (D.D.C. 2003) ("[W]hile litigation need not be imminent or certain in order to satisfy the anticipation-of-litigation prong of the test, this circuit has held that 'at the very least some actionable claim, likely to lead to litigation, must have arisen, such that litigation was 'fairly foreseeable at the time' the materials were prepared'") (*quoting* Coastal States Gas Corp. v. Department of Energy, 617 F.2d 854, 865 (D.C. Cir. 1980)); Cellco P'ship v. Certain Underwriters at Lloyd's London, C.A. No. 05-3158, 2006 WL 1320067, at *5 (D.N.J. May 12, 2006) (documents discussing legal advice by plaintiff's in-house counsel that were prepared in anticipation of litigation protected from disclosure by the work-product doctrine); Garrett v. Metropolitan Life Ins. Co., No. 95 Civ. 2406, 1996 WL 325725, at *3 (S.D.N.Y. June 12, 1996) ("Regulatory investigations by outside agencies present more than a mere possibility of future litigation, and provide reasonable grounds for anticipating litigation"); Martin v. Monfort, Inc., 150 F.R.D. 172, 173 (D. Colo. 1993) (investigation by the Department of Labor "presents more than a remote prospect of future litigation, and provides reasonable grounds for anticipating litigation sufficient to trigger application of the work-product doctrine"); GE Capital Corp. v. DirecTV, Inc., No. 3:97 CV 1901 PCD, 1998 WL 849389, at *9 (D. Conn. July 30, 1998) (drafts of audit report are prepared in anticipation of litigation when the first sentence of the report provides that the audit is being conducted pursuant to requests from attorneys); Prebena Wire Bending Mach. Co. v. Transit Worldwide Corp., No. 97 Civ. 9336 KMW HBP, 1999 WL 1063216, at *2 (S.D.N.Y. Nov. 23, 1999) ("The Court of Appeals for the Second Circuit has explained that the second element of this test does not limit the doctrine to documents prepared primarily or exclusively to assist in litigation . . . . Nothing in the Rule states or suggests that documents prepared 'in anticipation of litigation' with the purpose of assisting in the making of a business decision do not fall within its scope"); Jaroslawicz v. Englehard Corp., 115 F.R.D. 515, 517 (D.N.J. 1987) (the compilation of documents for an SEC investigation is sufficient to constitute preparation for litigation).

141. *In re* Grand Jury Subpoenas Dated Oct. 22, 1991, & Nov. 1, 1991, 959 F.2d 1158, 1166 (2d Cir. 1992); Panter v. Marshall Field & Co., 80 F.R.D. 718, 725 n.6 (N.D. Ill. 1978); Stix Prods., Inc. v. United Merchants & Mfrs., Inc., 47 F.R.D. 334, 338 (S.D.N.Y. 1969); *accord* Hercules, Inc. v. Exxon Corp., 434 F. Supp. 136, 151 (D. Del. 1977).

142. Coastal States Gas Corp. v. Department of Energy, 617 F.2d 854, 864-65 (D.C. Cir. 1980); Garfinkle v. Arcata Nat'l Corp., 64 F.R.D. 688, 690 (S.D.N.Y. 1974).

143. *See, e.g.,* Garfinkle v. Arcata Nat'l Corp., 64 F.R.D. 688, 690 (S.D.N.Y. 1974).

The Second Circuit, in *United States v. Adlman*,[144] addressed the appropriate test for the phrase "in anticipation of litigation" under Rule 26(b)(3) of the Federal Rules of Civil Procedure. Specifically, the Second Circuit addressed the issue of "whether Rule 26(b)(3) is inapplicable to a litigation analysis prepared by a party or its representative in order to inform a business decision which turns on the party's assessment of the likely outcome of litigation expected to result from the transaction."[145]

Adlman involved the preparation of a memorandum by an Arthur Andersen & Co. accountant and lawyer that contained a detailed legal analysis of likely IRS challenges, defenses to an IRS action, and alternatives to the corporation's proposed reorganization and merger of two of its wholly owned subsidiaries.[146] The reorganization resulted in the company being able to claim a tax refund, which the IRS challenged. The IRS served a subpoena on the accountant/lawyer, seeking the memorandum. The corporation objected to its production, claiming that the memorandum was protected by the attorney-client and work product privileges.[147] The district court first held that the memorandum was not protected by the attorney-client privilege, finding that the corporation had not consulted the accountant in order to obtain legal advice.[148] The Second Circuit affirmed the district court's first holding, but remanded for a determination as to whether the memorandum was protected from disclosure to the IRS under the work-product doctrine.[149] On remand, the district court rejected the work product claim.[150]

The corporation appealed the district court's second decision. The Second Circuit first noted that some courts, in following a line of Fifth Circuit decisions,[151] had interpreted the phrase "in anticipation of litigation" to mean

---

144. 134 F.3d 1194 (2d Cir. 1998).
145. *Id.* at 1197.
146. *Id.* at 1195
147. *Id.* at 1195-96
148. United States v. Adlman, No. M-18-304, 1994 WL 191869, at *2 (S.D.N.Y. May 16, 1994), *aff'd in part, vacated in part,* 68 F.3d 1495 (2d Cir. 1995).
149. United States v. Adlman, 68 F.3d 1495, 1501 (2d Cir. 1995).
150. United States v. Adlman, No. M-18-304, 1996 WL 84502, at *1 (S.D.N.Y. Feb. 27, 1996), *vacated,* 134 F.3d 1194 (2d Cir. 1998).
151. *See* United States v. Davis, 636 F.2d 1028, 1039-40 (5th Cir.) (holding that documents created during the course of preparing tax returns were not protected by the work-product doctrine), *cert. denied,* 454 U.S. 862 (1981); United States v. El Paso Co., 682 U.S. 530, 542-43 (5th Cir. 1982) (holding that documents prepared to establish and justify reserves on the company's financial statements were not protected by the work-product doctrine), *cert. denied,* 466 U.S. 944 (1984).

"'primarily or exclusively to assist in litigation'—a formulation that would potentially exclude documents containing analysis of expected litigation, if their primary, ultimate, or exclusive purpose is to assist in making a business decision."[152] In the Second Circuit's view, "[n]othing in the Rule [26(b)(3)] states or suggests that documents prepared 'in anticipation of litigation' with the purpose of assisting in the making of a business decision do not fall within its scope."[153] Further, Rule 26(b)(3) "takes pains to grant special protection to the type of materials at issue in this case—documents setting forth legal analysis."[154] Specifically, Rule 26(b)(3) "generally withholds protection for documents prepared in anticipation of litigation" where the adverse party

---

152. United States v. Adlman, 134 F.3d 1194, 1196-200 (2d Cir. 1998) (collecting cases).

153. Id. at 1199; see In re Grand Jury Proceedings, 604 F.2d 798, 803 (3d Cir. 1979) (Prudent parties anticipate litigation and begin preparation prior to the time suit is formally commenced. Thus, the test should be whether in light of the nature of the document and the factual situation in the particular case, the document can fairly be said to have been prepared or obtained because of the prospect of litigation'") (citation omitted); National Union Fire Ins. Co. of Pitt., Pa. v. Murray Sheet Metal Co., 967 F.2d 980, 984 (4th Cir. 1992) ("The document must be prepared because of the prospect of litigation when the preparer faces an actual claim or a potential claim following an actual event or series of events that reasonably could result in litigation. Thus, we have held that materials prepared in the ordinary course of business or pursuant to regulatory requirements or for other non-litigation purposes are not documents prepared in anticipation of litigation within the meaning of Rule 26(b)(3) .... Determining the driving force behind the preparation of each requested document is therefore required in resolving a work product immunity question"); Binks Mfg. Co. v. National Presto Indus., Inc., 709 F.2d 1109, 1118-19 (7th Cir. 1983) ("The fact that a defendant anticipates the contingency of litigation resulting from an accident or event does not automatically qualify an 'in house' report as work product .... A more or less routine investigation of a possibly resistable claim is not sufficient to immunize an investigative report developed in the ordinary course of business .... While litigation need not be imminent, the primary motivating purpose behind the creation of a document or investigative report must be to aid in possible future litigation"); Simon v. G.D. Searle & Co., 816 F.2d 397, 401 (8th Cir.) (risk management documents are business planning documents even if the business is litigation and so are not entitled to work product protection because made in ordinary course and not in anticipation of litigation), *cert. denied,* 484 U.S. 917 (1987); Senate of P.R. ex rel. Judiciary Comm. v. United States Dep't of Justice, 823 F.2d 574, 586 n.42 (D.C. Cir. 1987) ("We do not mean to suggest that documents prepared while no active investigations were underway are necessarily unprotected by the work-product doctrine .... The presence, or, as in this case, the absence of an ongoing investigation is but one aspect of the relevant "factual situation" a court must consider in evaluating an agency's work-product claim"); *see also In re* Grand Jury Subpoena, 220 F.R.D. 130, 148 (D. Mass. 2004) ("[T]he lawyer must at least have had a subjective belief that litigation was a real possibility, and that belief must have been objectively reasonable") (*quoting In re* Sealed Case, 146 F.3d 881, 884 (D.C. Cir. 1998)); *see also* 8 CHARLES A. WRIGHT, ET AL., FEDERAL PRACTICE & PROCEDURE § 2024 at 343 (1994).

154. United States v. Adlman, 134 F.3d 1194, 1198 (2d Cir. 1998).

demonstrates a "substantial need" for the documents; but Rule 23(b)(3) also "directs that 'the court shall protect against disclosure of the mental impressions, conclusions, opinions or legal theories'" of a party or its representative concerning the litigation.[155] According to the Second Circuit, given this special level of protection accorded to lawyers' thought processes, opinions, and legal theories, "it would oddly undermine [Rule 26(b)(3)'s] purposes if such documents were excluded from protection merely because they were prepared to assist in the making of a business decision expected to result in the litigation."[156] The Second Circuit found that "a document created because of anticipated litigation, which tends to reveal mental impressions, conclusions, opinions or theories concerning the litigation, does not lose work product protection merely because it is intended to assist in the making of a business decision influenced by the likely outcome of the anticipated litigation."[157]

Other courts, the Second Circuit observed, "ask whether the documents were "prepared 'because of' existing or expected litigation—a formulation that would include such documents."[158] The Second Circuit determined that the "because of" formulation conforms to the plain language of Rule 26(b)(3) and the purposes underlying the work product rule. The Second Circuit concluded that "[t]he fact that a document's purpose is business related appears irrelevant to the question of whether it should be protected under Rule 26(b)(3)."[159] "Conversely, it should be emphasized that the 'because of' formulation... withholds protection from documents that are prepared in the ordinary course of business or that would have been created in essentially similar form irrespective of the litigation."[160] However, a document created for a dual purpose may be considered to have been created in anticipation

---

155. *Id.* (*quoting* FED. R. CIV. P. 26(b)(3) (emphasis in original)).
156. *Id.*
157. *Id.* at 1194; *see also* Granite Partners, L.P. v. Bear, Stearns & Co., 184 F.R.D. 49, 52 (S.D.N.Y. 1999).
158. United States v. Adlman, 134 F.3d 1194, 1201-02.
159. *Id.* at 1200.
160. *Id.* at 1202; Tayler v. Travelers Ins. Co., 183 F.R.D. 67, 69-70 (N.D.N.Y. 1998) ("there is no work product immunity for documents prepared in the ordinary course of business prior to the commencement of litigation"); United States v. Ernstoff, 183 F.R.D. 148, 156 (D.N.J. 1998) (same); Simon v. G.D. Searle & Co., 816 F.2d 397, 401 (8th Cir.) (same), *cert. denied,* 484 U.S. 917 (1987); CBS Corp. v. Northrop Grumman Corp., No. 98 Civ. 3029, 1999 WL 4931, at *1 (S.D.N.Y. Jan. 5, 1999) (memorandum that provides business advice and calculates credits under various business scenarios does not remotely contemplate any litigation and thus is not protected under work product doctrine); *see also* FED. R. CIV. P. 26(b)(3), ADV. COMM. NOTE (1970).

of litigation when the litigation purpose cannot be separated from the non-litigation purpose.[161]

The Second Circuit provided the following hypothetical scenarios in rejecting the "primarily or exclusively to assist in litigation" and adopting the "because of" formulation:

> (i) "A company contemplating a transaction recognizes that the transaction will result in litigation; whether to undertake the transaction and, if so, how to proceed with the transaction may well be influenced by the company's evaluation of the likelihood of success in litigation. Thus, a memorandum may be prepared in expectation of litigation with the primary purpose of helping the company decide whether to undertake the contemplated transaction. An example would be a publisher contemplating publication of a book where the publisher has received a threat of suit from a competitor purporting to hold exclusive publication rights. The publisher commissions its attorneys to prepare an evaluation of the likelihood of success in the litigation, which includes the attorneys' evaluation of various legal strategies that might be pursued. If the publisher decides to go ahead with the publication and is sued, under the "primarily to assist in litigation" formulation the study will likely be disclosed to the opposing lawyers because its principal purpose was not to assist in litigation but to inform the business decision whether to publish. We can see no reason under the words or policies of the Rule why such a document should not be protected."
>
> (ii) "A company is engaged in, or contemplates, some kind of partnership, merger, joint undertaking, or business association with another company; the other company reasonably requests that the company furnish a candid assessment by the company's attorneys of its likelihood of success in existing litigations. For instance, the company's bank may request such a report from the company's attorneys concerning its likelihood of success in an important litigation to inform its lending policy toward the company. Or a securities underwriter contemplating a public offering of the company's securities may wish to see such a study to decide whether to go ahead with the offering without waiting for the termination of the litigation. Such a study would be created to inform the judgment of the business associate concerning its business decisions. No part of its purpose would be to aid in the conduct of the litigation. Nonetheless it would reveal the attorneys' most intimate strategies and assessments concerning the litigation. We can see no reason why, under the Rule, the litigation adversary should have access to it. But under the Fifth Circuit's "to assist" test, it would likely be discoverable by the litigation adversary."

---

161. *In re* Grand Jury Subpoena (Torf/Torf Envtl. Mgmt.), 357 F.3d 900, 909-10 (9th Cir. 2004) (dual purpose documents fall within protection of work-product doctrine when the litigation purpose "permeates" the non-litigation purpose so that the two purposes cannot be separated).

(iii) "A business entity prepares financial statements to assist its executives, stockholders, prospective investors, business partners, and others in evaluating future courses of action. Financial statements include reserves for projected litigation. The company's independent auditor requests a memorandum prepared by the company's attorneys estimating the likelihood of success in litigation and an accompanying analysis of the company's legal strategies and options to assist it in estimating what should be reserved for litigation losses."[162]

The Second Circuit concluded that the work product protection should be accorded to each of the reports described above.[163] Notably, the Second Circuit did not address whether the corporation may have waived the work product protection by producing the documents described in hypotheticals (ii) and (iii) to other companies, banks, underwriters, or accountants.

The Second Circuit remanded the action to the district court for a determination of whether the work product privilege protected the Arthur Andersen memorandum with the following instructions:

If the district court concludes that substantially the same Memorandum would have been prepared in any event—as part of the ordinary course of business of undertaking the restructuring—then the court should conclude the Memorandum was not prepared because of expected litigation and should adhere to its prior ruling denying the protection of the rule.

On the other hand, if the court finds the Memorandum would not have been prepared but for [the corporation's] anticipation of litigation with the IRS over losses generated by the restructuring, then judgment should be entered in favor of [the corporation].[164]

The Second Circuit further concluded that the IRS had not made a sufficient showing of substantial need and unavailability of the information in order to overcome the work product protection.[165]

In dissent, Judge Kearse disagreed with "the majority's expansion of the work product privilege to afford protections to documents not prepared in anticipation of litigation but instead prepared in order to permit the client to determine whether to undertake a business transaction, where there will be no anticipation of litigation unless the transaction is undertaken."[166]

The Second Circuit's decision in *Adlman* with its broader standard calls into question a number of decisions by courts in the Southern District of New

---

162. United States v. Adlman, 134 F.3d 1194, 1199-200.
163. *Id.* at 1200, 1202.
164. *Id.* at 1204.
165. *Id.*
166. *Id.* at 1205 (Kearse, J., dissenting).

York holding that to invoke the work product privilege, the "primary motivating purpose" in creating the materials must be to assist in pending or impending litigation.[167] However, some post-*Adlman* decisions still use a stricter test when determining if the work product doctrine applies.[168]

2. Subsequent Litigation

A split exists among the circuits, and even among certain district courts within the same circuit, regarding whether the protections afforded by

---

167. *See, e.g., In re* Subpoena Duces Tecum Served on Willkie Farr & Gallagher, No. M8-85, 1997 WL 118369, at *2 (S.D.N.Y. Mar. 14, 1997) (counsel's report of internal corporate investigation held not to constitute work product even though shareholder suit had been filed and the SEC had begun an informal inquiry, since litigation must be the "primary motivation" for retaining counsel and creating the report; here, the court found that the company had commissioned the investigation to address its accounting practices, a potential "business problem," and to obtain a clean bill of health from its auditors); Garrett v. Metropolitan Life Ins. Co., No. 95 Civ. 2406, 1996 WL 325725, at *4 (S.D.N.Y. June 12, 1996) ("work product applies if the 'primary motivating purpose' behind the performance of the work was to assist in the pending or impending litigation'") (citation omitted); *In re* Kidder Peabody Sec. Litig., No. 94 Civ. 3954, 1996 WL 263030 at **5, 6 (S.D.N.Y. May 16, 1996) ("inapplicability of the work product rule follows . . . from the existence of pressing non-litigation reasons for the creation of the interview documents" and noting that it was "painfully evident that the Jett scandal presented Kidder not only with a serious legal problem, but also a major business crisis"; holding the internal investigation was not protected by the work-product doctrine, as it constituted "a crucial aspect of Kidder's public relations strategy . . . [that] would have been undertaken regardless of whether litigation was threatened"); Sackman v. Liggett Grp., Inc., 920 F. Supp. 357, 366 (to receive work product protection, the "primary motivating purpose" in creating the materials must be to assist in pending or impending litigation), *vacated on other grounds,* 167 F.R.D. 6 (E.D.N.Y. 1996); *In re* Leslie Fay Cos. Sec. Litig., 161 F.R.D. 274, 280-81 (S.D.N.Y. 1995) (investigation and report used to make decisions on firing responsible personnel, to implement new internal controls, and to reassure creditors was not work product because conducted primarily for business reasons, and "[t]herefore the ancillary existence of ongoing litigation does not shield their investigatory documentation from discovery"); *In re* Woolworth Corp. Sec. Class Action Litig., No. 94 Civ. 2217, 1996 WL 306576, at *3 (S.D.N.Y. June 7, 1996) (affording work product protection to internal investigation report where "a distinction between 'anticipation of litigation' and 'business purposes' is in this case artificial, unrealistic and the line between is here essentially blurred to oblivion") (citation omitted); Stout v. Illinois Farmers Ins. Co., 150 F.R.D. 594, 604 (S.D. Ind. 1993) ("[i]f a document or thing would have been created for non-litigation uses regardless of its intended use in litigation preparation, it should not be accorded work product protection"), *aff'd,* 852 F. Supp. 704 (S.D. Ind. 1994).

168. *See, e.g.,* Carroll v. Bayerische Landesbank, No. 99 Civ. 2892, 2000 WL 1708178, at *1 (S.D.N.Y. Nov. 14, 2000) (Magistrate Judge held tape recordings made by plaintiffs prior to hiring an attorney not entitled to protection).

the work product doctrine lapse once a litigation ends.[169] Some courts have held that the protection applies only if the materials were prepared in anticipation of the suit before the court, and the documents prepared for one case are freely discoverable in another.[170] Other courts have held that work product from a terminated action retains its qualified immunity from disclosure even in subsequent unrelated litigation, and that documents prepared in one case may never be disclosed in a subsequent case.[171] The third, intermediate approach extends work product protection to subsequent cases only where a close relationship exists between the parties or issues in the two actions.[172] The intermediate approach has been criticized because, as noted by the Eighth Circuit, "[t]he unrelatedness of the subsequent litigation provides an insufficient basis for disregarding the privilege articulated in *Hickman* and incorporated in rule 26(b)(3)."[173]

---

169. *In re* Grand Jury Subpoena, 220 F.R.D. 130, 149-50 (D. Mass. 2004) (surveying positions taken by the Circuits); Levingston v. Allis-Chalmers Corp., 109 F.R.D. 546, 552 (S.D. Miss. 1985) (outlining the three views); *see also* Frontier Ref'g, Inc. v. Gorman-Rupp Co., 136 F.3d 695, 703 (10th Cir. 1998) (declining to decide whether subsequent litigation must be closely related to action for which protected material was prepared).

170. *See, e.g.*, United States v. IBM Corp., 66 F.R.D. 154, 178 (S.D.N.Y. 1974); Honeywell, Inc. v. Piper Aircraft Corp., 50 F.R.D. 117, 119 (M.D. Pa. 1970); Hanover Shoe, Inc. v. United Shoe Mach. Corp., 207 F. Supp. 407, 410 (M.D. Pa. 1962); Gulf Constr. Co. v. St. Joe Paper Co., 24 F.R.D. 411, 415 (S.D. Tex. 1959); Tobacco & Allied Stocks, Inc. v. Transamerica Corp., 16 F.R.D. 534, 537 (D. Del. 1954).

171. *See, e.g., In re* Murphy, 560 F.2d 326, 334 (8th Cir. 1977); Duplan Corp. v. Moulinage et Retorderie de Chavanoz, 487 F.2d 480, 484-85 (4th Cir. 1973); *accord In re* International Sys. & Controls Corp. Sec. Litig., 91 F.R.D. 552, 557 (S.D. Tex. 1981), *vacated on other grounds,* 693 F.2d 1235 (5th Cir. 1982); SCM Corp. v. Xerox Corp., 70 F.R.D. 508, 523 (D. Conn.), *appeal dismissed,* 534 F.2d 1031 (2d Cir. 1976); Burlington Indus. v. Exxon Corp., 65 F.R.D. 26, 43 (D. Md. 1974).

172. 4 JAMES WM. MOORE, MOORE'S FEDERAL PRACTICE § 26-70[3] at 26-217-18 (3d ed. 2006); *see, e.g.,* Garrett v. Metropolitan Life Ins. Co., No. 95 Civ. 2406, 1996 WL 325725, at *4 (S.D.N.Y. June 12, 1996) ("[d]ocuments prepared for one litigation that would have been shielded retain the protection in a second litigation if the two actions are closely related in parties or subject matter"); *In re* Grand Jury Proceedings, 604 F.2d 798, 803 (3d Cir. 1979) (identity of subject matter and temporal connection found to exist, no decision on whether relatedness required); Levingston v. Allis-Chalmers Corp., 109 F.R.D. 546, 552 (S.D. Miss. 1985) (documents generated for prior, terminated and wholly unrelated case not subject to work product privilege); Hercules, Inc. v. Exxon Corp., 434 F. Supp. 136, 153 (D. Del. 1977) (parties or subject matter must be closely related); Puerto Rico v. S.S. Zoe Colocotroni, 61 F.R.D. 653, 659 (D.P.R. 1974) (confined work product from previous litigation to where first action not completed or bears a substantial relationship with present litigation, or in which same counsel exists on either side).

173. *In re* Murphy, 560 F.2d 326, 335 (8th Cir. 1977).

Although the United States Supreme Court has not directly addressed the issue, the Court has indicated, in dictum, that as long as the material was initially prepared by a party in anticipation of litigation, it remains privileged in subsequent litigations.[174]

3. Materials Prepared by Corporate Employees

There is no distinction between material prepared by lawyers and material prepared by nonlawyers. Rule 26(b)(3) explicitly extends the work product protection to materials prepared "by or for another party or by or for that other party's representative." As the Advisory Committee Note to rule 26(b)(3) explains, the rule "reflects the trend of the cases by requiring a special showing not merely as to materials prepared by a lawyer, but also as to the materials prepared . . . by or for a party or any representative acting on his behalf."[175] Both opinion and factual work product are protected.[176] Although it is not necessary for an attorney to participate in order to trigger the work product protection from discovery, attorney involvement with non-attorneys helps to defend against assertions that the investigation was conducted in the normal course and thus is discoverable.

D. *Overcoming the Qualified Immunity*

Rule 26(b)(3) provides that a party may obtain discovery of work product materials only (1) upon a showing that the party seeking discovery has substantial need of the materials in the preparation of the party's case, and

---

174. FTC v. Grolier, Inc., 462 U.S. 19, 25 (1983) ("the literal language of [Rule 26(b)(3)] protects material for any litigation or trial as long as they were prepared by or for a party to the subsequent litigation") (dictum) (emphasis by the Court); Walsh v. Seaboard Sur. Co., 184 F.R.D. 494, 497 (D. Conn. 1999) (Rule 26(b)(3) "protects materials prepared for any litigation or trial as long as they were prepared by or for a party to the subsequent litigation"); Sharonda B. v. Herrick, No. 97 C 1225, 1998 WL 341801, at *6 (N.D. Ill. June 11, 1998) (the emerging majority view is that work product privilege extends to subsequent litigation).

175. Fed. R. Civ. P. 26(b)(3), Adv. Comm. Note (1970); *see also* Atlantic Richfield Co. v. Current Controls, Inc., No. 93-CV-0950E(H), 1997 WL 538576, at *3 (W.D.N.Y. Aug. 21, 1997) ("it is of no consequence that most of the subject documents were prepared by non-attorneys . . . the work product privilege applies also to documents prepared by a 'party' and 'representatives' of that party, including consultants, sureties, indemnitors, insurers and agents") (collecting cases); 4 James Wm. Moore, Moore's Federal Practice § 26-70[4] at 26-217-18 (3d ed. 2006) (studies ordered by an attorney to prepare for trial are protected by the work product doctrine, as are reports prepared by agents of the party or the party's attorney).

176. Duplan Corp. v. Deering Milliken, Inc., 540 F.2d 1215, 1219 (4th Cir. 1976) ("opinion work product immunity now applies equally to lawyers and nonlawyers alike").

(2) that the party is unable without undue hardship to obtain the substantial equivalent of the materials by other means.

In *Hickman v. Taylor*,[177] the Court wrote that "[w]here relevant and non-privileged facts remain hidden in a lawyer's file and where production of those facts is essential to the preparation of one's case, discovery may properly be had."[178] The Court added that the "burden rests on the one who would invade that privacy to establish adequate reasons to justify production through a subpoena or court order."[179] The clearest case for ordering production of non-opinion work product is when crucial information is in the exclusive control of the opposing party.[180] In *Hickman v. Taylor*, Justice Murphy indicated that written statements within the work-product doctrine might be discovered if it appeared that "the witnesses [were] no longer available or [could] be reached only with difficulty."[181] The published decisions show considerable variation in the circumstances under which lower courts will determine that sufficient "difficulty" exists and thus will grant motions to compel production.[182]

E. *Protection of a Lawyer's Mental Impressions*

The decision in *Hickman v. Taylor* is based in large measure on protecting the thought processes of counsel:

> Historically, a lawyer is an officer of the court and is bound to work for the advancement of justice while faithfully protecting the rightful interests of his

---

177. 329 U.S. 495 (1947).
178. *Id.* at 511.
179. *Id.* at 512; *see also In re* Sealed Case, 676 F.2d 793, 809 (D.C. Cir. 1982); *In re* Murphy, 560 F.2d 326, 334 (8th Cir. 1977).
180. *See, e.g.,* Loctite Corp. v. Fel-Pro, Inc., 667 F.2d 577, 582 (7th Cir. 1981); Puerto Rico v. S.S. Zoe Colocotroni, 61 F.R.D. 653, 658-59 (D.P.R. 1974).
181. 329 U.S. 495, 511 (1947).
182. *See, e.g.,* Breon v. Coca-Cola Bottling Co. of New England, 232 F.R.D. 49, 54 (D. Conn. 2005) (for fact work-product, the party seeking discovery must meet the "substantial burden" and "undue hardship" tests of Rule 26); *In re* Grand Jury Proceedings #5 Empanelled Jan. 28, 2004, 401 F.3d 247, 250 (4th Cir. 2005) (fact work product can be discovered upon showing of both substantial need and inability to secure substantial equivalent of materials by other means without undue hardship); Loctite Corp. v. Fel-Pro, Inc., 667 F.2d 577, 582-83 (7th Cir. 1981) (ordering production of non-opinion work product when crucial information is in the exclusive control of the opposing party); *see also* United States v. Skeddle, 989 F. Supp. 912, 916 (N.D. Ohio 1997) (ordering production of interview notes of interviews of individuals whom the government would be calling at trial on the grounds that "[o]nce such individual has been called as a witness, his or her version of the pertinent facts becomes publicly known; as a result, there is little reason to protect fact work product").

clients. In performing his various duties, however, it is essential that a lawyer work with a certain degree of privacy, free from unnecessary intrusion by opposing parties and their counsel. Proper preparation of a client's case demands that he assemble information, sift what he considers to be the relevant from the irrelevant facts, prepare his legal theories, and plan his strategy without undue and needless interference. That is the historical and the necessary way in which lawyers act within the framework of our system of jurisprudence to promote justice and protect their clients' interests.[183]

With this rationale in mind, courts have protected the mental impressions and legal theories of a lawyer.[184]

In *Upjohn Co. v. United States*,[185] the Court stated that the draftsmen of rule 26(b)(3) regarded opinion work product as deserving special protection.[186] However, the Court expressly declined to specify what, if any, showing of necessity would be sufficient to compel disclosure.[187]

Rule 26(b)(3) also recognizes that ordinary or factual work product may contain opinion work product. Thus, the rule provides that even when a court finds substantial need and undue hardship sufficient to require discovery of ordinary work product, "the court shall protect against disclosure of the mental impressions, conclusions, opinions, or legal theories of a lawyer or other representative of a party concerning the litigation."[188] There is some disagreement among the courts as to whether opinion work product is absolutely priv-

---

183. Hickman v. Taylor, 329 U.S. 495, 510-11 (1947).

184. *See, e.g., In re* EchoStar Communc'ns Corp., 448 F.3d 1294, 1299 (Fed. Cir. 2006) (Rule allowing discovery of certain types of work product only allows discovery of factual or non-opinion work product and requires the court to protect against the disclosure of an attorney's mental impressions, conclusions, opinions, or legal theories); Nguyen v. Excel Corp., 197 F.3d 200, 210 (5th Cir. 1999); Dade Eng'g Corp. v. Reese, No. 2005/149, 2006 WL 1222221, at *5 (D.V.I. Apr. 13, 2006) (Rule 26 provides a nearly absolute protection against discovery of opinion work product, which consists of "the mental impressions, conclusions, opinions, or legal theories of an attorney or other representative of a party concerning the litigation"); Reliance Ins. Co. v. Keybank U.S.A., No. 1:01 CV 62, 2006 WL 543129 (N.D. Ohio Mar. 3, 2006) (Absent waiver, a party may not obtain the opinion work product of an adversary); Duplan Corp. v. Moulinage et Retorderie de Chavanoz, 509 F.2d 730, 734-35 (4th Cir. 1974), *cert. denied*, 420 U.S. 997 (1975).

185. 449 U.S. 383 (1981).

186. *Id.* at 400.

187. *Id.* at 401.

188. FED. R. CIV. P. 26(b)(3).

ileged,[189] or whether the party seeking discovery of these materials simply must meet a higher burden.[190]

In light of the high-level protection afforded to opinion work product, investigative counsel can maximize the likelihood the work-product doctrine will apply by making explicit the mental impressions and legal theories that ordinarily are implicit in many documents relating to the investigation. In particular, investigative counsel should carefully consider the benefits and detriments of the several ways of eliciting information from corporate employees and others. The use of questionnaires or other written witness statements may be more efficient when there are numerous witnesses involved, but these documents are more likely to be classified as factual work product, subject to discovery upon the requisite showing of substantial need and undue hardship.[191] The conduct of oral interviews and preparation of extensive file memoranda is far more time-consuming, but is more likely to generate documents that

---

189. *See, e.g.,* Duplan Corp. v. Moulinage et Retorderie de Chavanoz, 509 F.2d 730, 734-35 (4th Cir. 1974), *cert. denied,* 420 U.S. 997 (1975) (absolutely immune in subsequent litigation); *In re* Grand Jury Proceedings, 473 F.2d 840, 848 (8th Cir. 1975) (absolute protection).

190. *See, e.g.,* Lugosch v. Congel, No. Civ. 1:00-CV-0784, 2006 WL 931687, at *16 (N.D.N.Y. Mar. 7, 2006) (opinion work product requires a higher protection in that the requesting party has to demonstrate extraordinary justification before the court will allow its release); Baker v. GM Corp., 209 F.3d 1051, 1054 (8th Cir. 2000) (opinion work product can be discovered only in very rare and extraordinary circumstances); Office of Thrift Supervision v. Vinson & Elkins, LLP, 124 F.3d 1304, 1307-08 (1st Cir. 1997) ("[o]pinion work product . . . is virtually undiscoverable" and holding that the OTS had not demonstrated a "substantial need" for lawyers' notes of employee interviews where the OTS had obtained notes from the FDIC's lawyers of those same interviews); City of Springfield v. Rexnord Corp., 196 F.R.D. 7, 10 (D. Mass. 2000) (noting that opinion work product afforded special protection); *In re* Circle K Corp., 199 B.R. 92, 98 (Bankr. S.D.N.Y. 1996) (opinion work product receives higher protection and party seeking discovery must show extraordinary justification), *aff'd,* Nos. 96 Civ. 5801, 6479, 1997 WL 31197 (S.D.N.Y. Jan. 28, 1997); *In re* Sealed Case, 676 F.2d 793, 809-10 (D.C. Cir. 1982) (document not discoverable unless extraordinary showing made); *In re* Grand Jury Investigation, 599 F.2d 1224, 1231 (3d Cir. 1979) (memorandum summarizing oral interview not absolutely protected, but is discoverable only in a "rare situation"); *but see* Donovan v. Fitzsimmons, 90 F.R.D. 583, 588 (N.D. Ill. 1981) (no showing beyond the substantial need/undue hardship standard required to discover opinion work product).

191. *See* Hickman v. Taylor, 329 U.S. 495, 511 (1947); *In re* John Doe Corp., 675 F.2d 482, 492 (2d Cir. 1982); *In re* Grand Jury Investigation, 599 F.2d 1224, 1230-32 (3d Cir. 1979); Connelly v. Dun & Bradstreet, Inc., 96 F.R.D. 339, 342-43 (D. Mass. 1982).

will be classified as opinion work product.[192] Of course, a personal interview is a far preferable method for eliciting complete and candid information, apart from work product considerations. In a complex investigation involving numerous witnesses, a cost/benefit analysis may result in the use of questionnaires for less significant witnesses, while the key personnel are interviewed personally.

IV. OVERCOMING THE ATTORNEY-CLIENT PRIVILEGE AND WORK-PRODUCT DOCTRINE

The corporation and its investigative counsel must be cognizant of the fact that, despite their best efforts, the investigative record may still be subject to discovery. One way otherwise protected materials become discoverable is through waiver, intentional or otherwise.[193] In addition, exceptions to the attorney-client privilege and the work-product doctrine may come into play when a crime or fraud is involved or in connection with shareholder litigation.[194] Thus, investigative counsel should take care in the preparation of documents, even if they are intended to be privileged or work product, because they may become discoverable.

A. *Waiver*

Investigative counsel must take steps to ensure that the attorney-client privilege and the work-product doctrine are not inadvertently waived. Because the attorney-client privilege and the work-product doctrine derive from separate and distinct policies, the actions that will result in waiver are also distinct.

1. Waiver of the Attorney-Client Privilege

An essential element of the attorney-client privilege is the confidentiality of the communication.[195] If a communication ordinarily within the privilege is not intended to be confidential, or the "cloak of confidence" has been lifted, the privilege is waived.[196] The attorney-client privilege may be waived

---

192. *See* Upjohn, 449 U.S. at 400 (1981).
193. *See* Part IV.A, *infra*
194. *See* Parts IV.B and IV.C, *infra*.
195. United States v. Kelsey-Hayes Wheel Co., 15 F.R.D. 461, 464 (E.D. Mich. 1954).
196. *Id.* at 465, *see also In re* McKesson HBOC, Inc. Sec. Litig., No. 99-CV-20743, 2005 WL 934331, at *4 (N.D. Cal. Mar. 31, 2005) (communications found not to be protected by attorney-client privilege because plaintiff agreed to disclose communication to third parties before communications at issue occurred).

intentionally; in addition, through various actions by the client, the privilege may be waived by implication. In the context of internal investigations and the legal proceedings that typically ensue, waiver of privilege is an ever-present concern.

a. Voluntary Disclosure and Disclosure to Government Authorities.

The principal waiver issue faced by the corporation is disclosure to government authorities, which may be required, as a practical matter, to obtain leniency in criminal or other government enforcement actions.[197] As a general matter, the voluntary disclosure of a communication to a third party usually waives the attorney-client privilege.[198] This waiver applies to all communications on the same subject matter.[199]

The attorney-client privilege, and the option to waive it, belongs to the client.[200] When the client is a corporation, the power to waive the corporation's privilege rests with the corporate decision maker at the time the waiver determination is made,[201] whether it be the corporation's management,[202] its board of directors,[203] or a trustee or other successor to the corporation.[204] Thus, the attorney generally is not entitled to waive the privilege without the consent of the client or the permission of the court. However, where a client is

---

197. *See* Part V, *infra*.

198. *See, e.g.,* United States v. Dakota, 197 F.3d 821, 825 (6th Cir. 1999) (corporation may waive attorney-client privilege via voluntary disclosure to third parties); National Educ. Training Corp. v. Skillsoft Corp., No. M8-85, 1999 WL 378337, at *3 (S.D.N.Y. June 10, 1999) (same); *In re* John Doe Corp., 675 F.2d 482, 489 (2d Cir. 1982); Bower v. Weisman, 669 F. Supp. 602, 604 (S.D.N.Y. 1987); Eigenheim Bank v. Halpern, 598 F. Supp. 988, 991 (S.D.N.Y. 1984); Teachers Ins. & Annuity Ass'n v. Shamrock Broad. Co., 521 F. Supp. 638, 641 (S.D.N.Y. 1981).

199. United States v. Workman, 138 F.3d 1261, 1263 (8th Cir. 1998); *In re* Columbia Healthcare/HCA Healthcare Corp. Billing Practices Litig., 293 F.3d 289, 304 (6th Cir. 2002), *cert. denied sub nom.,* 539 U.S. 977 (2003); *In re* Syncor ERISA Litig., 229 F.R.D. 636, 646 (C.D. Cal. 2005).

200. *See* ABA MODEL RULES OF PROF'L CONDUCT R. 1.6 and ABA MODEL CODE OF PROFESSIONAL RESPONSIBILITY DR 4-101, delineating the circumstances in which counsel may unilaterally disclose otherwise privileged communications.

201. Normally, the corporate decision-maker will be a person or group of people who are part of the "control group," despite the fact that lower-level employees may act for the corporate client sufficiently to invoke the privilege in the first instance.

202. *See* CFTC v. Weintraub, 471 U.S. 343, 349 (1985); *In re* Columbia Healthcare/HCA Healthcare Corp. Billing Practices Litig., 293 F.3d 289, 302 (6th Cir. 2002), *cert. denied sub nom.,* 539 U.S. 977 (2003).

203. *See* United States v. De Lillo, 448 F. Supp. 840, 842-43 (E.D.N.Y. 1978).

204. *See In re* Bevill, Bresler & Schulman Asset Mgmt. Corp., 805 F.2d 120, 124-25 (3d Cir. 1986).

aware that the attorney intends to disclose confidential communications, the client must take affirmative action to preserve the confidentiality of the communications to retain the privilege.[205]

While the government focuses on the waiver of privilege as to the government, the corporation has a broader problem. Traditionally, disclosure of privileged communications to a government agency, in the course of an investigation or proceeding by the agency, was held to be a waiver of the privilege for all future cases or proceedings regarding all communications on the same subject matter.[206] Although several courts have recognized a "limited" or "selective" waiver due to policy considerations such as "facilitating the settlement of litigation, permitting full cooperation among joint defendants, expediting discovery, and encouraging voluntary disclosure to regulatory agencies," [207] this type

---

205. *Id.*

206. *See, e.g., In re* Syncor ERISA Litig., 229 F.R.D. 636, 647 (C.D. Cal. 2005) (*quoting In re* Columbia Healthcare/HCA Healthcare Corp. Billing Practices Litig., 293 F.3d 289, 302 (6th Cir. 2002), *cert. denied sub nom.*, 539 U.S. 977 (2003)); *In re* Lupron Mktg. & Sales Practices Litig., 313 F. Supp. 2d 8, 11 (D. Mass. 2004); *In re* Sealed Case, 676 F.2d 793, 824 (D.C. Cir. 1982) (privilege waived where company voluntarily submitted report of investigative counsel to SEC); *In re* Subpoena Duces Tecum, 738 F.2d 1367, 1370 (D.C. Cir. 1984) (privilege waived where client willingly sacrificed confidentiality by voluntarily disclosing the material to the SEC in an effort to convince it that a formal investigation was not warranted); Neal v. Honeywell, Inc., No. 93 Civ. 1143, 1995 WL 591461 at *7 n.2 (N.D. Ill. Oct. 4, 1995) (collecting cases); Teachers Ins. & Annuity Ass'n v. Shamrock Broad. Co., 521 F. Supp. 638, 646 (S.D.N.Y. 1981) (no limited waiver absent an express reservation of rights, stipulation, or protective order).

207. *See* United States v. Upjohn Co., 600 F.2d 1223, 1227 n.12 (6th Cir. 1979), *rev'd on other grounds,* 449 U.S. 383 (1981); Diversified Indus., Inc. v. Meredith, 572 F.2d 596, 611 (8th Cir. 1978) (en banc); Nutramax Labs., Inc. v. Twin Labs., Inc. 183 F.R.D. 458, 467 (D. Md. 1998) (documents consisting of opinion work product, which were put to testimonial use in litigation, were subject to a limited waiver of the documents themselves, but not to a broad subject matter waiver); *In re* Syncor ERISA Litig., 229 F.R.D. 636, 645 (C.D. Cal. 2005) (finding that language of a confidentiality agreement between company and government which gives the sole discretion to the government to destroy any confidentiality waived the attorney-client and work-product privileges); *see, e.g., id.* at 647 (declining to apply the selective waiver doctrine because "there is absolutely no evidence demonstrating that the disallowance of selective waiver would impede the voluntary cooperation of a corporation with the Government"); United States v. MIT, 129 F.3d 681, 685 (1st Cir. 1997) (rejecting the reasoning of the Eighth Circuit in *Diversified* that selective waiver doctrine encourages "the frank exchange between attorney and client in future cases"); *but see* Diversified Indus., Inc. v. Meredith, 572 F.2d 596, 611 (8th Cir. 1978) (en banc) (voluntary compliance with a subpoena issued by a government agency does not constitute a waiver as to subsequent civil litigation); *see generally* Dennis J. Block & Jonathan M. Hoff, *Selective Waiver of Attorney-Client Privilege,* N.Y. L.J., May 19, 1994, at 5, col.1; Dennis J. Block & Nancy E. Barton, *Waiver of the Attorney-Client Privilege by Disclosure to the SEC,* 10 SEC. REG. L.J. 170 (1982); *In re* Martin Marietta Corp., 856 F.2d 619, 623 (4th Cir. 1988), *cert. denied sub nom.*, 490 U.S. 1011 (1989).

of waiver in which a party may "pick and choose" when and to whom it will disclose confidential communications is strongly disfavored in nearly every circuit.[208] As discussed in more detail below, even a "confidentiality agreement" between a corporation and the government might not ensure that the communications remain confidential from other parties.[209]

Voluntary disclosure of an investigative report to a government agency may result in waiver of the attorney-client and work product privileges over not only the report, but the underlying interview notes and memoranda as well. Therefore, in situations where a company discloses an investigative report which is based in part on privileged documents and/or communications in connection with an internal investigation, courts still must determine whether such disclosures of the report also result in a waiver of privilege regarding the documents referred to in the report and/or the entire investigative file. The Supreme Court, in *Upjohn Co. v. United States*,[210] held that employees' responses to a questionnaire designed to investigate an allegation of certain questionable payments to government officials and notes reflecting these payments were communications protected by the attorney-client privilege because these communications "were made by Upjohn employees to counsel for Upjohn acting as such, at the direction of corporate superiors in order to secure legal advice from counsel."[211] Also relevant to the Court's treatment of these questionnaires as privileged was that the questionnaires inquired about matters within the scope of the employee's corporate duties; the questionnaires were accompanied by a statement which "clearly indicated" the purpose of the investigation; and the communications were treated as "highly confidential" when made and continued to remain confidential.[212]

---

208. Indeed, every Circuit Court, except for the Eighth Circuit, that has addressed the issue has held that voluntary disclosures to the government with regard to an enforcement proceeding waives the attorney-client privilege. *See* United States v. MIT, 129 F.3d 681, 685-86 (1st Cir. 1997); *In re* Steinhardt Partners, L.P., 9 F.3d 230, 235 (2d Cir. 1993); Westinghouse Elec. Corp. v. Republic of the Phil., 951 F.2d 1414, 1424-26 (3d Cir. 1991); *In re* Martin Marietta Corp., 856 F.2d 619, 623-24 (4th Cir. 1988), *cert. denied sub nom.*, 490 U.S. 1011 (1989); *In re* Columbia Healthcare/HCA Healthcare Corp. Billing Practices Litig., 293 F.3d 289, 304 (6th Cir. 2002), *cert. denied sub nom.*, 539 U.S. 977 (2003); *In re* Qwest Commc'ns Int'l, Inc. Sec. Litig., 450 F.3d 1179, 1181 (10th Cir. 2006); *but see* Diversified Indus., Inc. v. Meredith, 572 F.2d 596, 611 (8th Cir. 1978) (en banc) (holding that selective waiver is permitted). The Ninth Circuit has not yet determined whether selective waiver of the attorney-client privilege or work-product protection is available. United States v. Bergonzi, 216 F.R.D. 487, 494 n.8 (N.D. Cal. 2003).
209. *See* Part IV.A.1.d, *infra*.
210. 449 U.S. 383 (1981).
211. *Id.* at 396.
212. *Id.* at 394-97.

The Court also held that in-house counsel's notes and memoranda of employees' oral statements during interviews were protected by the work-product doctrine.[213] However, if a corporation does not specify to its employees that a questionnaire must be completed in order for the corporation to obtain legal advice, such documents have been held not to be privileged.[214]

For example, *In re Kidder Peabody Securities Litigation*[215] involved improper trading practices by an employee of Kidder Peabody. The court concluded that where Kidder had made repeated affirmative use in several litigations and agency proceedings and investigations of a report prepared by counsel that summarized the factual findings and recommendations of counsel's internal investigation to show that Kidder was the victim and the employee was the wrongdoer, Kidder had waived the attorney-client privilege for those portions of the underlying interview documents that contain the substance of any of the statements used in the final report.[216]

The court in *In re the Leslie Fay Cos. Securities Litigation*[217] adopted a similar approach. The court there held that, where the final investigative report was disclosed to the SEC and the findings of the report were being used by the company's bankruptcy trustee in the class-action litigation to establish the liability of the company's outside auditors and co-defendants, any privilege covering the subject matters discussed in the report was waived and withholding such information would prejudice the co-defendant auditors.[218] The court held, however, that "an equitable piercing of the attorney-client privilege should be narrowly tailored to address the potential prejudice to the party attacking the privilege" and, thus, concluded that the waiving party was entitled to withhold from discovery any documents containing "legal advice or advice not contained or discussed in" the report.[219]

---

213. *Id.* at 401.
214. Deel v. Bank of Am., N.A., 227 F.R.D. 456, 458 (W.D. Va. 2005) (declining to apply the attorney-client privilege to questionnaires completed by bank's employees in the course of an internal investigation because the bank did not specify to the employees that it needed the information to obtain legal advice).
215. 168 F.R.D. 459 (S.D.N.Y. 1996).
216. *Id.* at 474. In Kidder, the report had been disclosed to the SEC and also used affirmatively by Kidder in pending lawsuits and arbitrations. *Id.*
217. 161 F.R.D. 274 (S.D.N.Y. 1995).
218. *Id.* at 284.
219. *Id.; see also* Peterson v. Wallace Computer Servs., Inc., 984 F. Supp. 821, 824-26 (D. Vt. 1997) (where corporate defendant asserted as a defense that it had conducted an adequate internal investigation into plaintiff's hostile work environment claim, and had agreed that the director of human resources and other employees would testify to the scope and substance of the investigation, the court held that the company waived the attorney-client privilege over the

A contrary result was reached in *In re Woolworth Corp. Securities Class Action Litigation.*[220] In refusing to order the production of interview notes and other memoranda used to prepare an internal investigation report that the company had published and produced to the class-action plaintiffs, the *Woolworth* court rejected the subject matter waiver argument on public policy grounds because "[a] finding that publication of an internal investigative report constitutes waiver [over underlying notes and memoranda] might well discourage corporations from taking the responsible step of employing outside counsel to conduct an investigation when wrongdoing is suspected."[221] The *Woolworth* court rejected plaintiffs' contention that the company was using the assertion of attorney-client privilege over the underlying notes and memoranda of outside counsel as both a "sword and a shield" because "[p]laintiffs are free to depose all of the employees [who] Paul, Weiss interviewed (and plaintiffs had, to a large extent, done so) in order to glean facts not sufficiently set forth in the [r]eport."[222]

b. Placing the Attorney-Client Privilege at Issue. Another circumstance that dictates waiver of the attorney-client privilege is where a party places its privileged communications at issue. The privilege is "intended as a shield, not a sword."[223] Thus, where a party raises an issue to which an effective rebuttal would require inquiry into privileged communications, such as asserting a claim or affirmative defense based upon "advice of counsel" or testifying as to only certain (presumably helpful) portions of the attorney-client communication, the privilege may be deemed waived.[224] Although the mere

---

underlying investigative notes and memoranda even if information not contained in the final report and that plaintiff had demonstrated a substantial need for such material necessary to overcome the work product privilege).

220. *In re* Woolworth Corp. Sec. Class Action Litig., No. 94 Civ. 2217, 1996 WL 306576, at *2 (S.D.N.Y. June 7, 1996).

221. *Id.*

222. *Id.* at *2.

223. 8 JOHN HENRY WIGMORE, WIGMORE ON EVIDENCE § 2327 at 638 (McNaughton rev. ed. 1961).

224. *See, e.g.,* United States v. Cohn, 303 F. Supp. 2d 672, 681 (D. Md. 2003) (corporation waived its attorney-client privilege when its counsel raised "advice of counsel" as a defense in his opening statement to the jury); Robinson v. Time Warner, Inc., 187 F.R.D. 144, 146 (S.D.N.Y. 1999) (attorney-client privilege may be waived where a defendant places privileged matters at issue); Sealy v. Gruntal & Co., No. 94 Civ. 7948, 1998 WL 698357, at *5 (S.D.N.Y. Oct. 7, 1998) (affirmative defense based upon the findings of an internal corporate investigation of a civil rights claim will result in waiver of the privilege); Gorzegno v. Maguire, 62 F.R.D. 617, 621-22 (S.D.N.Y. 1973); *but see* Baker v. GM Corp., 209 F.3d 1051, 1055 (8th Cir. 2000) (declining to extend "at issue waiver" where "a party has used witness testimony and made factual representations that were allegedly contrary to what the privileged documents will reveal").

filing of a complaint or answer will not be deemed a waiver,[225] there may be cases where the opposing party cannot defend itself without inquiry into privileged matters.[226]

(1) *Reliance on advice of counsel.* In the context of internal investigations, the otherwise privileged communications between counsel and the client may be placed at issue by asserting a claim or affirmative defense based on "advice of counsel."[227] For example, a client's assertion of an affirmative defense based upon its reliance on an internal corporate investigation of allegations of discrimination waives attorney-client privilege with respect to communications and documents associated with the investigation.[228] Similarly, when the party holding the privilege seeks to demonstrate good-faith reliance on the advice of counsel, the issue of whether counsel was fully informed of all relevant facts, and was unbiased and competent, may also become rele-

---

225. *See* Mendenhall v. Barber-Greene Co., 531 F. Supp. 948, 950 (N.D. Ill. 1981).

226. *See generally* Hearn v. Rhay, 68 F.R.D. 574, 581 (E.D. Wash. 1975); *see, e.g.,* United States v. Exxon Corp., 94 F.R.D. 246, 247-49 (D.D.C. 1981) (good faith); Sedco Int'l, S.A. v. Cory, 683 F.2d 1201, 1206 (8th Cir.) (estoppel or equitable reliance), *cert. denied,* 459 U.S. 1017 (1982); Russell v. Curtin Matheson Scientific, Inc., 493 F. Supp. 456, 458 (S.D. Tex. 1980) (equitable tolling of the statute of limitations); Pitney-Bowes, Inc. v. Mestre, 86 F.R.D. 444, 447 (S.D. Fla. 1980) (intent of the parties to a contract).

227. *See, e.g.,* Garfinkle v. Arcata Nat'l Corp., 64 F.R.D. 688, 689 (S.D.N.Y. 1974) (defendant's assertion of a defense based on its reliance on an opinion letter drafted by its attorney waived any privileged information relating to the circumstances surrounding the issuance of the letter).

228. *See* Sealy v. Gruntal & Co., No. 94 Civ. 7948, 1998 WL 698257, at *5 (S.D.N.Y. Oct. 7, 1998); *In re* EchoStar Communc'ns Corp., 448 F.3d 1294, 1299 (Fed. Cir. 2006) (when a party waives the attorney-client privilege by asserting an advice of counsel defense, the privilege is waived for all communications on the same subject matter); Handgards, Inc. v. Johnson & Johnson, 413 F. Supp. 926, 929 (N.D. Cal. 1976) (plaintiffs waived attorney-client privilege relating to the subject of good-faith prosecution of patent actions by calling attorneys to the witness stand to demonstrate that prior lawsuits were pursued on the basis of competent legal advice and were, therefore, brought in good faith), *remanded,* 601 F.2d 986 (9th Cir. 1979), *cert. denied,* 444 U.S. 1025 (1980).

229. Axler v. Scientific Ecology Grp., Inc., 196 F.R.D. 210, 212 (D. Mass. 2000) (in order to pursue its statute of limitations defense, "defendants are entitled to discovery from plaintiffs' counsel concerning what investigation they conducted, what information they received, and when they received it"); *In re* Imperial Corp. of Am., 179 F.R.D. 286, 290 (S.D. Cal. 1998) ("party alleging reliance on his attorney's investigation to discover certain causes of action and overcome the statute of limitations bar, impliedly waived the attorney-client privilege and work-product protection that might apply regarding the investigation and its findings and conclusions"); SEC v. Scott, 565 F. Supp. 1513, 1534 (S.D.N.Y. 1983), *aff'd sub nom.* SEC v. Cayman Islands Reins. Corp., 734 F.2d 118 (2d Cir. 1984); United States v. Stirling, 571 F.2d 708, 735 (2d Cir.), *cert. denied,* 439 U.S. 824 (1978) (party relying on advice of

vant.²²⁹ In this situation, the mental processes of counsel would then become a discoverable issue in the case.²³⁰ The assertion of this defense may also waive the attorney's work-product privilege for the document relied upon.²³¹

(2) *Testimony.* Generally, a client may testify in his or her own behalf without waiving the attorney-client privilege.²³² But where the client testifies regarding the substance of privileged communications, or fails to object to such testimony by others, the privilege is waived.²³³

Using a privileged document to refresh the recollection of a witness may present special problems. If a witness uses a writing to refresh memory either before or while testifying, the court may allow the adverse party "to have the writing produced at the hearing, to inspect it, to cross-examine the witness thereon, and to introduce in evidence those portions which relate to the

---

counsel defense was not entitled to jury instruction that its attorneys, auditors, and labor experts failed to ask them sufficiently probing questions).

230. Handgards, Inc. v. Johnson & Johnson, 413 F. Supp. 926, 932 (N.D. Cal. 1976) ("While an attorney's private thoughts are most certainly deserving of special protections, I believe that the concern for a lawyer's privacy must give way when the advice of counsel is directly at issue"), *remanded,* 601 F.2d 986 (9th Cir. 1979), *cert. denied,* 444 U.S. 1025 (1980).

231. Panter v. Marshall Field & Co., 80 F.R.D. 718, 721-22 (N.D. Ill. 1978).

232. *See* New York v. Shapiro, 126 N.E.2d 559, 562 (N.Y. 1955).

233. *See, e.g., In re* Powerhouse Licensing, *LLC,* 441 F.3d 467, 472 (6th Cir. 2006) (When a client offers his or her attorney's testimony as to a specific communication to the attorney, "the privilege is waived as to all communications to the attorney on the same matter"); United States v. Titchell, 261 F.3d 348, 352 (3d Cir. 2001) (calling one's attorney as a fact witness in a prior proceeding constitutes a waiver of the attorney-client privilege, at least regarding the subject of the testimony adduced in the prior proceeding); IMC Chems., Inc. v. Niro Inc., No. Civ. A. 98-2348-JTM, 2000 WL 1466495, at *16 (D. Kan. July 19, 2000) ("When a party or its attorney discloses privileged communications upon deposition, fairness generally dictates that the privilege is waived as to all communications related to the disclosed matters"); Ampa, Ltd. v. Kentfield Capital LLC, No. 00 Civ. 0508 NRB AJP, 2000 WL 1156860, at *1 (S.D.N.Y. Aug. 16, 2000) (where counsel marked a document as an exhibit and asked a question about it during deposition, privilege was waived); United States v. Skeddle, 989 F. Supp. 912, 915-16 (N.D. Ohio 1997) (where the corporation's lawyer testified as to communications with management concerning negotiations with respect to outsourcing the company's computer department, sale of certain gas wells, and an agreement to lease robotics equipment, the attorney-client privilege was waived as to communications regarding those transactions; the in-house counsel's testimony, however, did not waive the attorney-client privilege as to communications during the corporation's internal investigations into the alleged wrongdoing in connection with such underlying transactions); Perrignon v. Bergen Brunswig Corp., 77 F.R.D. 455, 460 (N.D. Cal. 1978); United States v. Gurtner, 474 F.2d 297, 299 (9th Cir. 1973).

testimony of the witness."[234] The rule applies not only to witnesses at trial, but also to testimony at a deposition.[235]

Some courts have assumed that any material consulted by a witness prior to testifying loses its privileged status—*i.e.*, that it is always necessary, "in the interests of justice," to require production.[236] Acceptance of an unqualified rule requiring production whenever a privileged document has been used to refresh recollection, however, has not been universal. A leading commentator has criticized as theoretically unsound a rule imputing waiver whenever a witness uses a privileged document to refresh his recollection.[237]

Some courts have adopted a middle course, holding that the discoverability of privileged material used before testifying is subject to the discretion of the court.[238] Even where privileged information is used to refresh recollection while testifying, the waiver may be limited to only those documents actually used to refresh recollection.[239]

---

234. FED. R. EVID. 612.
235. *See, e.g.*, S & A Painting Co. v. O.W.B. Corp., 103 F.R.D. 407, 409 (W.D. Pa. 1984); IMC Chems., Inc. v. Niro Inc., No. Civ. A. 98-2348-JTM, 2000 WL 1466495, at *16 (D. Kan. July 19, 2000); Nutramax Labs., Inc. v. Twin Labs., Inc. 183 F.R.D. 458, 467 (D. Md. 1998) (applying Rule 612 in the context of a deposition).
236. *See, e.g.*, Marshall v. United States Postal Serv., 88 F.R.D. 348, 350 (D.D.C. 1980) ("once a document is used to refresh the recollection of a witness, privileges as to that document have been waived"); Wheeling-Pitt. Steel Corp. v. Underwriters Labs., Inc., 81 F.R.D. 8, 9 (N.D. Ill. 1978); Berkey Photo, Inc. v. Eastman Kodak Co., 74 F.R.D. 613, 616 (S.D.N.Y. 1977); R. J. Hereley & Son Co. v. Stotler & Co., 87 F.R.D. 358, 359 (N.D. Ill. 1980); Bailey v. Meister Brau, Inc. 57 F.R.D. 11, 13 (N.D. Ill. 1972); *see also* James Julian, Inc. v. Raytheon Co., 93 F.R.D. 138, 145 (D. Del. 1982); *but see* Joseph Schlitz Brewing Co. v. Muller & Phipps (Haw.), Ltd., 85 F.R.D. 118, 120 (W.D. Mo. 1980) (where deponent testified that he had "looked at" his correspondence file of 39 documents prior to testifying, court held that actual use of any of the documents had not been established to invoke Rule 612).
237. 4 JACK B. WEINSTEIN & MARGARET A. BERGER, WEINSTEIN'S EVIDENCE ¶ 612(04) (1997).
238. *See, e.g.*, Smith & Wesson Div. of Bangor Punta Corp. v. United States, 782 F.2d 1074, 1083 (1st Cir. 1986) (no abuse of discretion where trial court ruled that disclosure of an unredacted copy of a report was not necessary "in the interests of justice") (*citing* United States v. Massachusetts Maritime Academy, 762 F.2d 142, 157 (1st Cir. 1985)); Derderian v. Polaroid Corp., 121 F.R.D. 13, 15 (D. Mass. 1988) (personal notes kept by employment discrimination plaintiff were protected from discovery by attorney-client privilege and work-product doctrine, even though the employee reviewed the notes before the deposition, absent showing that disclosure of the notes was necessary in the interests of justice; employer had full access to agents or employees in order to obtain evidence about meetings or communications allegedly recorded in notes, employer had knowledge of the dispute since its inception, and the lapse of time was not great between making of the notes and plaintiff's deposition).
239. *See, e.g.*, S & A Painting Co. v. O.W.B. Corp., 103 F.R.D. 407, 409 (W.D. Pa. 1984).

c. **Inadvertent Disclosure.** Clients traditionally bear the risk of waiver based upon inadvertent disclosure of otherwise privileged communications because "the means of preserving secrecy of communications are entirely in the client's hands and since the privilege is a derogation from the general testimonial duty and should be strictly construed."[240] The courts are in agreement that the privilege may be lost when otherwise privileged documents are accessible to third persons,[241] or where they are indiscriminately mingled with other documents.[242]

Courts are split on what inadvertent acts and circumstances constitute a "waiver" of the privilege. Some courts have held that the privilege is destroyed whenever communications have been intercepted, *i.e.*, by eavesdroppers, or where privileged documents have been lost or stolen.[243] This approach has been criticized, and the current trend is to examine whether the client took reasonable precautions to ensure the confidentiality of the communications.[244]

---

240. 8 JOHN HENRY WIGMORE, WIGMORE ON EVIDENCE § 2326 (McNaughton rev. ed. 1961).

241. *See, e.g.,* Tse v. UBS Fin. Servs., Inc., No. 03 Civ. 6234, 2005 WL 1473815, at *1 (S.D.N.Y. June 21, 2005) (waiver of privilege did not apply to inadvertent disclosure of letter to attorney requesting legal advice that was stored out of sight, on a disk, inside a file folder in plaintiff's work area); *In re Victor,* 422 F. Supp. 475, 476 (S.D.N.Y. 1976) (documents found in public hallway outside lawyer's office "destroyed" privilege).

242. *See In re* Horowitz, 482 F.2d 72, 81-82 (2d Cir.), *cert. denied,* 414 U.S. 867 (1973); Chase v. City of Portsmouth, No. Civ. 2:05CV446, 2006 WL 1096368, at *5 (E.D. Va. Apr. 20, 2006) (disclosure of letter waived privilege because party did not take reasonable measures to ensure its confidentiality); *but see* James Julian, Inc. v. Raytheon Co., 93 F.R.D. 138, 142 (D. Del. 1982) (filing of documents in general file did not destroy privilege because it was impractical to have separate files and screen each employee requiring access).

243. *See, e.g.,* Suburban Sew 'n Sweep, Inc. v. Swiss-Bernina, Inc., 91 F.R.D. 254, 258 (N.D. Ill. 1981) (citing cases).

244. *See* Lava Trading, Inc. v. Hartford Fire Ins. Co., No. 03 Civ. 7037 PKC MHD, 2005 WL 66892, at *2 (S.D.N.Y. Jan. 11, 2005) (to determine if inadvertent disclosure results in waiver, courts will balance four relevant factors: (1) the reasonableness of the precautions taken by the producing party to prevent inadvertent disclosure of privileged documents; (2) the volume of discovery versus the extent of the specific disclosure at issue; (3) the length of time taken by the producing party to rectify the disclosure; and (4) the overarching issue of fairness); American Dental Ass'n v. Khorrami, No. CV 02-3853 DT, 2003 WL 24141019, at *9 (C.D. Cal. July 14, 2003) (applying the "reasonableness test" and finding that defendant impliedly waived his right to assert privilege). In United States v. Zolin, 809 F.2d 1411, 1417 (9th Cir. 1987), *aff'd in part, vacated in part,* 491 U.S. 554 (1989), the court held that, where an agent of the holder of the privilege erroneously discloses privileged material, such disclosure will not amount to a waiver of the privilege. *But see* Transonic Sys., Inc. v. Non-Invasive Medical Tech., 192 F.R.D. 710, 715-16 (D. Utah 2000) (stating that the voluntary production, during discovery, of a document labeled "attorneys' eyes only" did not constitute inadvertent disclosure).

These federal courts follow the "Wigmore rule:" "the risk of insufficient precautions [against unintended disclosure of privileged material] is upon the client," and "[t]here is always the objective consideration that when [a privileged person's] conduct touches a certain point of disclosure, fairness requires that his immunity shall cease whether he intended that result or not."[245] These courts have held that the simple act of disclosure waives the privilege.[246]

Other courts have held that an evidentiary privilege is not waived absent some intention to waive.[247] For example, in *Manufacturers & Traders Trust Co. v. Servotronics, Inc.*,[248] the New York Appellate Division expressly rejected the Wigmore rule, noting that no New York state court had previously addressed the question of waiver with respect to inadvertent disclosure of documents. The court stated that "[i]ntent must be the primary component of any waiver test," but held that a party would be required to demonstrate its intent by objective evidence.[249] In the case before it, the court found that the party asserting the privilege demonstrated its intent to keep the documents in question confidential, despite the documents' inadvertent disclosure during discovery. Reasonable precautions had been taken to ensure their confidentiality, including, inter alia, the precaution of having qualified personnel screen the documents before producing them.[250] One of the factors used by the *Servotronics* court to assess whether an inadvertent disclosure would waive the attorney-client privilege was whether the client promptly objected to the disclosure after discovering it, the court noting that "[a]n objection entered promptly upon learning of a disclosure suggests that a genuine intent to pre-

---

245. 8 JOHN HENRY WIGMORE, WIGMORE ON EVIDENCE §§ 2325, 2327 (McNaughton rev. ed. 1961).

246. *See, e.g., In re* Grand Jury Investigation of Ocean Transp., 604 F.2d 672, 674-75 (D.C. Cir.), *cert. denied sub nom.*, 444 U.S. 915 (1979); Underwater Storage, Inc. v. United States Rubber Co., 314 F. Supp. 546, 549 (D.D.C. 1970) (document inadvertently produced pursuant to consent order "entered the public domain" and destroyed basis for privilege); Thomas v. Pansy Ellen Prods., Inc., 672 F. Supp. 237, 243 (W.D.N.C. 1987) ("voluntary production, even where inadvertent, effects a waiver of privilege"); *accord* Duplan Corp. v. Deering Milliken, Inc., 397 F. Supp. 1146, 1162 (D.S.C. 1975).

247. *See, e.g.,* Dunn Chem. Co. v. Sybron Corp., Misc. No. 8-85, 1975 WL 970, at *5 (S.D.N.Y. Oct. 9, 1975); Connecticut Mut. Life Ins. Co. v. Shields, 18 F.R.D. 448, 451 (S.D.N.Y. 1955).

248. 522 N.Y.S.2d 999 (N.Y. 4th Dep't 1987).

249. *Id.* at 1004.

250. *Id.; see* Bras v. Atlas Constr. Corp., 153 A.D.2d 914, 915, 545 N.Y.S.2d 723, 724 (2d Dep't 1989) (privilege waived where screening procedure utilized by attorney prior to production of documents was "not reasonably designed or executed so as to prevent the inadvertent disclosure").

serve confidentiality existed before disclosure."[251] Other courts have also declined to find waiver when the disclosure was found to be "inadvertent" under the circumstances.[252]

Courts in the Second Circuit, for example, apply a "flexible approach" to determine whether an inadvertent disclosure of otherwise privileged information results in waiver.[253] Courts applying this approach must balance four factors: "(1) the reasonableness of the precautions taken by the producing party to prevent inadvertent disclosure of privileged documents; (2) the volume of discovery versus the extent of the specific disclosure issue; (3) the length of time taken by the producing party to rectify the disclosure, and (4) the overarching issue of fairness."[254] Even where the initial production may have been inadvertent, a delay in claiming the privilege can result in a waiver.[255] While a single act of disclosure may not destroy the privilege, that disclosure may compromise a client's position should there be an inadvertent disclosure in the future.[256]

---

251. Manufacturers & Traders Trust Co. v. Servotronics, Inc., 522 N.Y.S.2d 999, 1005 (N.Y. 4th Dep't 1987); *see also* AFA Protective Sys., Inc. v. City of New York, 788 N.Y.S.2d 128, 129-30 (N.Y. 2d Dep't 2004).

252. *See* United States v. United Techs. Corp., 979 F. Supp. 108, 116 (D. Conn. 1997) (setting forth five factors to consider when determining whether inadvertent waiver constituted an irrevocable waiver of the attorney-client privilege and holding that no waiver had occurred where the company had "made a reasonable effort to sift through a huge volume of documents" to withhold privileged documents; only one privileged document was inadvertently disclosed; the company had listed the document on its privilege log; and the company immediately demanded the document's return); Lois Sportswear, U.S.A., Inc. v. Levi Strauss & Co., 104 F.R.D. 103, 105 (S.D.N.Y. 1985) (no waiver when 22 documents out of 16,000 were inadvertently disclosed); Standard Chartered Bank PLC v. Ayala Int'l Holdings (U.S.), Inc., 111 F.R.D. 76, 85 (S.D.N.Y. 1986) (same, regarding one sentence in a five-page document produced among over 1,000 pages and where counsel took care to withhold all other allegedly privileged documents); Eisenberg v. Gagnon, 766 F.2d 770, 778 (3d Cir.), (the privilege was not waived when information came into the hands of opposing counsel where the party divulging the information believed the disclosure to be in camera), *cert. denied sub nom.,* 474 U.S. 946 (1985).

253. Atronic Int'l, GMBH v. SAI Semispecialists of Am., Inc., 232 F.R.D. 160, 164 (E.D.N.Y. 2005).

254. United States v. Rigas, 281 F. Supp. 2d 733, 738 (S.D.N.Y. 2003); *see also* Atronic Int'l, GMBH v. SAI Semispecialists of Am., Inc., 232 F.R.D. 160, 164 (E.D.N.Y. 2005).

255. Baxter Travenol Labs., Inc. v. Abbott Labs., 117 F.R.D. 119, 121 (N.D. Ill. 1987) (unfair and unrealistic to uphold the privilege where documents have been examined and used by the opposing party prior to assertion of the privilege); *In re* Grand Jury Investigation of Ocean Transp., 604 F.2d 672, 674-75 (D.C. Cir.), *cert. denied sub nom.,* 444 U.S. 915 (1979) (same).

256. *See* Eigenheim Bank v. Halpern, 598 F. Supp. 988, 991-92 (S.D.N.Y. 1984) (after second "inadvertent" disclosure, privilege found waived due to inadequate procedures followed to maintain confidentiality of documents).

d. Non-Waiver Stipulations. The voluntary surrender of potentially privileged documents in exchange for a non-waiver stipulation may not be consistent with an intent to preserve properly the confidentiality of those documents. Several courts have held that the voluntary disclosure of documents pursuant to a non-waiver agreement in a previous litigation effected a waiver of the attorney-client privilege. In *Chubb Integrated Systems Ltd. v. National Bank of Washington*,[257] the court characterized this agreement as "merely a contract between two parties to refrain from raising the issue of waiver or from otherwise utilizing the information disclosed."[258] Noting that "[c]onfidentiality is the dispositive factor in deciding whether a communication is privileged,"[259] the court rejected the argument that the privilege should still attach, inasmuch as "[p]laintiff has no genuine claim of confidentiality to the documents it produced" in the previous litigation.[260]

Even a litigant who discloses documents to its adversary pursuant to a court-ordered non-waiver stipulation may find that another court will refuse to accept the inadvertent waiver position adopted by the previous judge. In *United States v. IBM Corp.*,[261] the government challenged IBM's claim of privilege, arguing that IBM had waived any privilege it might have claimed by previously disclosing the documents in question to the Control Data Cor-

---

257. 103 F.R.D. 52 (D.D.C. 1984).
258. *Id.* at 67-68.
259. *Id.* at 67.
260. *Id.* at 68; *see also In re* Qwest Commc'ns Int'l, Inc. Sec. Litig., 450 F.3d 1179, 1194 (10th Cir. 2006) (confidentiality agreements with SEC and DOJ did not protect company against disclosure of documents in subsequent litigation in part because the DOJ "was not required to 'segregate material obtained from [company], file it under seal, keep records of its use, or otherwise deal with the information in any special way,' and had made no effort to determine what information had been disseminated to third parties") (citations omitted); Republic of Phil. v. Westinghouse Elec. Corp., 132 F.R.D. 384, 390 (D.N.J. 1990) ("once information is disclosed to an adversary . . . a future adversary in a related proceeding may have access to the information"), *mandamus denied in part,* 951 F.2d 1414 (3d Cir. 1991); Republic Gear Co. v. Borg-Warner Corp., 381 F.2d 551, 558 n.5 (2d Cir. 1967) (an "estoppel certificate" offered by plaintiff agreeing not to use any privileged information against any of the nonparty foreign clients was characterized as "illusory," insofar as the court might not have the jurisdiction to interfere in other future litigation).
261. 60 F.R.D. 658 (S.D.N.Y.), *appeal dismissed,* 493 F.2d 112 (2d Cir. 1973), *cert. denied,* 416 U.S. 995 (1974).

poration in other antitrust litigation in Minnesota.²⁶² The New York court ordered IBM to produce the documents, despite IBM's arguments that (1) the earlier disclosure was made under compulsion of discovery orders issued by the Minnesota district court, (2) the documents were produced under what IBM believed to be a non-waiver order expressly protecting the right of its privilege in the documents, and (3) any disclosure of privileged information was "inadvertent."²⁶³

By contrast, in *Transamerica Computer Co. v. IBM Corp.*,²⁶⁴ the court affirmed the district court's denial of the plaintiff's motion to compel IBM to disclose those very same documents produced to Control Data in the Minnesota litigation. The *Transamerica* court characterized IBM's court-ordered production in Minnesota as "compelled," not voluntary, and found that no waiver had occurred.²⁶⁵

e. Joint Defense Agreements. Communications between joint defendants and their respective counsel do not necessarily result in loss of the attorney-client or work product privileges merely by reason of the presence of those persons.²⁶⁶ In a "proper case," the privilege may apply to joint

---

262. *See* United States v. IBM Corp., 471 F.2d 507, 508-11 (2d Cir. 1972), *rev'd on jurisdictional grounds,* 480 F.2d 293 (2d Cir. 1973) (en banc), *cert. denied,* 416 U.S. 979, 980 (1974).

263. *See id.* at 508 (*quoting* Pretrial Order No. 5).

264. 573 F.2d 646 (9th Cir. 1978).

265. *Id.* at 651.

266. Lugosch v. Congel, 219 F.R.D. 220, 238 (N.D.N.Y. 2003) ("The essential benefit of [a joint defense agreement] is that a member of the common legal enterprise cannot reveal the contents of the shared communications without the consent of all the parties"); United States v. McPartlin, 595 F.2d 1321, 1336-37 (7th Cir.), *cert. denied,* 444 U.S. 833 (1979); Hunydee v. United States, 355 F.2d 183, 185 (9th Cir. 1965); Continental Oil Co. v. United States, 330 F.2d 347, 350 (9th Cir. 1964); *see also* United States v. United Techs. Corp., 979 F. Supp. 108, 111-12 (D. Conn. 1997) ("the attorney-client privilege, as extended by the common interest rule, protects from disclosure" all of the documents containing the legal advice of counsel to members of a consortium) (collecting cases); IBJ Whitehall Bank & Trust Co. v. Cory & Assocs., Inc., No. Civ. A. 97 C 5827, 1999 WL 617842, at *3 (N.D. Ill. Aug. 12, 1999); United States v. Henke, 222 F.3d 633, 637 (9th Cir. 2000); *see also* discussion of the requirement that communications be confidential in order for the attorney-client privilege to apply, Part III.C.5, *supra.*

consultations even where the parties are not immediately anticipating litigation.[267] Under the joint defense doctrine, when two or more parties have a common interest, communications by one party to a lawyer in the presence of the other party are not discoverable by third parties; however, in a subsequent dispute between the two parties, either can compel the disclosure of the confidential communications that passed between them and their respective lawyers.[268]

The decision to enter into a joint defense agreement requires careful consideration, because it may restrict the corporation's later options, including the possible disclosure of the investigation's results and underlying documentation to the government in exchange for leniency.[269] Moreover, a corporation and its counsel conducting the internal investigation should not assume automatically that a "joint defense" privilege will protect communications with the alleged wrongdoers or their counsel. On the contrary, the actual or potential conflicts of interest between the corporation and these persons may preclude the assertion of a "common interest."[270]

---

267. United States v. Furst, 886 F.2d 558, 578 (3d Cir. 1989), *cert. denied,* 493 U.S. 1662 (1990); United Coal Cos. v. Powell Constr. Co., 839 F.2d 958, 965 (3d Cir. 1988); SCM Corp. v. Xerox Corp., 70 F.R.D. 508, 513 (D. Conn.) (dicta) (discussions among joint venturers negotiating terms among themselves were not protected, but privilege might apply to protect discussions aimed at exploiting common interest in patents), *appeal dismissed,* 534 F.2d 1031 (2d Cir. 1976); *see also* Burlington Indus. v. Exxon Corp., 65 F.R.D. 26, 43-45 (D. Md. 1974) (privilege applied to confidences shared among joint licensors of patents) (citing cases). More than one court has held that the privilege applies only to an identical legal, not commercial, interest. *See* Sneider v. Kimberly-Clark Corp., 91 F.R.D. 1, 8 (N.D. Ill. 1980); *In re* Eastern Transmission Corp. PCB Contamination Ins. Coverage Litig., MDL No. 764, 1990 WL 139403, at *2 (E.D. Pa. Sept. 19, 1990); Minebea Co., Ltd. v. Papst, 228 F.R.D. 13, 16 (D.D.C. 2005) ("If a joint defense agreement has been proved to exist and the scope of the agreement is clear, the party seeking to claim privilege still must demonstrate that the specific communications at issue were designed to facilitate a common legal interest; a business or commercial interest will not suffice").

268. *See* SIPC v. Stratton Oakmont, Inc., 213 B.R. 433, 439 (S.D.N.Y. Bankr. 1997) (in connection with an action by the SEC, a brokerage firm and its individual officers who were represented by counsel separate from the broker's counsel entered into a joint defense agreement and exchanged information protected by the attorney-client and work product privileges; the bankruptcy court held that in the liquidation proceedings of the broker, the trustee became an adversary to the individual officers and the privilege was waived as to material previously exchanged under the joint defense agreement); Medcom Holding Co. v. Baxter Travenol Labs., 689 F. Supp. 841, 844 (N.D. Ill.1988); CHARLES T. MCCORMICK, MCCORMICK ON EVIDENCE § 91 at 190-91 (Cleary ed., 1972). Similarly, a lawyer who represents two parties with respect to a single matter may not assert the privilege in a later dispute between the clients. Quintel Corp., N.V. v. Citibank, *N.A.,* 567 F. Supp. 1357, 1364 (S.D.N.Y. 1983).

269. *See* Part V, *infra.*

270. *See, e.g., In re* Grand Jury Subpoena: Under Seal, 415 F.3d 333, 341 (4th Cir. 2005) (joint defense privilege did not apply against grand jury subpoenas seeking documents relat-

2. Waiver of the Work-Product Doctrine

Like the attorney-client privilege, work product protection can be waived.[271] However, because protecting client confidences is not the primary purpose of the work-product doctrine, disclosures to a third party do not automatically waive the protection. Rather, the general test is whether the materials at issue have been disclosed in a manner inconsistent with maintaining their secrecy vis-à-vis the adversary.[272]

---

ing to company's internal investigation because at time of internal investigation, agreement was not yet in effect and interviews that were conducted by inside and outside counsel were not for purpose of formulating joint defense), *cert. denied sub nom.*, 126 S. Ct. 1114 (2006); United States v. Sawyer, 878 F. Supp. 295, 297 (D. Mass. 1995) (declining to apply the joint defense doctrine to exclude communications between employee and in-house counsel after finding that in-house counsel "met with [employee] not to promote a joint defense, but as part of an internal investigation to discover facts relevant to [employee's purportedly illegal] expenditures," and that employee met with in-house counsel "to fulfill his duties and obligations to report to his employer" not to pursue a joint-defense).

271. *See, e.g.*, United States v. Nobles, 422 U.S. 225, 239 (1975) (protection waived as to portion of investigator's report when defense decided to present him as witness); Shields v. Sturm, Ruger & Co., 864 F.2d 379, 382 (5th Cir. 1989) (work product protection waived when lawyer requests the witness to disclose the information, or when the lawyer discloses the information to the court voluntarily or makes no objection when it is offered) (*citing* Fox v. Taylor Diving & Salvage Co., 694 F.2d 1349, 1356 (5th Cir. 1983)); Grumman Aerospace Corp. v. Titanium Metals Corp. of Am., 91 F.R.D. 84, 89 (E.D.N.Y. 1981) (disclosure of report to defendant, although in hopes of settlement, waived work product protection); Electronic Memories & Magnetics Corp. v. Control Data Corp., 20 Fed. R. Serv. 2d 705, 706 (N.D. Ill. 1975) (work product waived where attorney himself is witness).

272. *See, e.g., In re* Steinhardt Partners, L.P., 9 F.3d 230, 236 (2d Cir. 1993) (refusing to adopt "a *per se* rule that all voluntary disclosures to the government waive work product protection; crafting rules relating to privilege in matters of governmental investigations must be done on a case-by-case basis"); *see also In re* Grand Jury Proceedings, 219 F.3d 175, 185 (2d Cir. 2000) ("since fairness depends on context," per se rule for implied waiver analysis is not prudent and district court should consider the circumstances surrounding alleged waiver by the corporation's founder's grand jury testimony in deciding whether such testimony created a waiver); United States v. AT & T Co., 642 F.2d 1285, 1299 (D.C. Cir. 1980) (no waiver by producing document to government because government was not an adversary in that particular litigation); *In re* Qwest Commc'ns Int'l, Inc. Sec. Litig., 450 F.3d 1179, 1192 (10th Cir. 2006) (declining to adopt a *per se* rule regarding whether the "selective waiver" doctrine applies in the context of work-product protection but holding that the record in the instant case "is not sufficient to justify adoption of a selective waiver doctrine as an exception to the general rules of waiver upon disclosure of protected material"); Merrill Lynch & Co. v. Allegheny Energy, Inc., 229 F.R.D. 441, 448-49 (S.D.N.Y. 2004) (corporation's disclosure of internal investigative reports to an independent auditor did not constitute a waiver of work product protection because auditor was not in tangible adversarial relationship with corporation and no public revelation of the report was contemplated other than, in the worst case scenario, a general statement by the auditor pertaining to its inability to evaluate the Company's financial statements, noting that "these cases turn on their facts" and so a per se rule is inappropriate;

In *In re Steinhardt Partners, L.P.*,[273] the Second Circuit held that voluntary production to the SEC of an investigation report waived the work product protection with respect to the report in subsequent litigation.[274] The *Steinhardt* court, however, "decline[d] to adopt a *per se* rule that all voluntary disclosures to the government waive work product protection" and noted that "[e]stablishing a rigid rule would fail to anticipate situations in which the disclosing party and the government may share a common interest in developing legal theories and analyzing information, or situations in which the SEC and the disclosing party have entered into an explicit agreement that the SEC will maintain the confidentiality of the disclosed materials."[275]

"[m]oreover, to construe a company's auditor as an adversary under a blanket rule of waiver of the applicable work product privilege under these circumstances could very well discourage corporations from conducting a critical self-analysis and sharing the fruits of such an inquiry with the appropriate actors"); American S.S. Owners Mut. Protection & Indem. Ass'n v. Alcoa S.S. Co., No. 04 Civ. 4309 LAKJCF, 2006 WL 278131, at **1-2 (S.D.N.Y. Feb. 2, 2006) (work product protection not waived when attorney opinion letters disclosed to outside actuary); Bank of Am., N.A. v. Terra Nova Ins. Co., 212 F.R.D. 166, 170-73 (S.D.N.Y. 2002) (reviewing relevant authorities and holding that reinsurer waived "fact" work product protection when it voluntarily disclosed protected factual information to New York State Insurance Department in the hope that a suit would be instituted against an adversary because such selective disclosure is not in pursuit of trial preparation); Peralta v. Cendant Corp., 190 F.R.D. 38, 40 (D. Conn. 1999) (communication with defendant's counsel relating to "former employee's conduct or knowledge" during his or her employment may be protected work product); Gucci Am., Inc. v. Costco Cos., No. 98 Civ. 5613 RLC FM, 2000 WL 60209, at *4 (S.D.N.Y. Jan. 24, 2000) (fact that attorney discussed interview with employees does not constitute waiver because "it did not substantially increase the likelihood that [plaintiff] would secure the [privileged] information"); B.C.F. Oil Ref'g, Inc. v. Consolidated Edison Co., 168 F.R.D. 161, 166 (S.D.N.Y. 1996) (sending a written transcript of internal investigation interview to employee interviewed does not constitute waiver); *In re* International Sys. & Controls Corp. Sec. Litig., 91 F.R.D. 552, 556 (S.D. Tex. 1981), *vacated on other grounds,* 693 F.2d 1235 (5th Cir. 1982); Burlington Indus. v. Exxon Corp., 65 F.R.D. 26, 46 (D. Md. 1974).

273. 9 F.3d 230 (2d Cir. 1993).

274. *Id.* at 236; Information Resources, Inc. v. Dun & Bradstreet Corp., 999 F. Supp. 591, 593 (S.D.N.Y. 1998).

275. *In re* Steinhardt Partners, L.P., 9 F.3d 230, 236 (2d Cir. 1993); *see also In re* Leslie Fay Cos. Sec. Litig., 161 F.R.D. 274, 284 (S.D.N.Y. 1995) (finding no waiver because "the disclosure of privileged information to the government may not constitute a waiver if the government agrees to maintain the confidentiality of the disclosed materials"); *but see In re* Columbia Healthcare/HCA Healthcare Corp. Billing Practices Litig., 293 F.3d 289, 306 (6th Cir. 2002) ("preserving the traditional confines of the rule affords both an ease of judicial administration as well as a reduction of uncertainty for parties faced with such a decision") (*citing* Westinghouse Elec. Corp. v. Republic of the Phil., 951 F.2d 1414, 1431 (3d Cir. 1991)), *cert. denied sub nom.,* 539 U.S. 977 (2003). In *In re* Columbia/HCA, the Sixth Circuit rejected selective waiver in the work product context when plaintiffs in an action against a

The broad subject matter waiver of the attorney-client privilege, requiring the production of all related privileged materials, may not be fully applicable to the work-product doctrine, especially in the context of opinion work-product.[276] More than one court has declined to impose a broad subject matter waiver in the context of an inadvertent waiver relating to opinion work-product.[277] Another court has held that the voluntary disclosure of factual work product for testimonial use resulted in a subject matter waiver, but, as to opinion work-product, the waiver would be limited only to the documents actually disclosed.[278]

Under Federal Rule of Evidence 612, work product protection may be waived where otherwise protected material is used to refresh a witness's recollection and disclosure is necessary "in the interests of justice."[279] Finally, with respect to the interaction between opinion work product under Rule 26(b)(3), also referred to as core attorney work product, and expert disclosure

---

health services provider moved to compel production of documents previously provided to federal government agencies including the Department of Justice and found a waiver despite the existence of a confidentiality agreement with the government. 293 F.3d at 292-93, 302.

276. *In re* Qwest Commc'ns Int'l, Inc. Sec. Litig., 450 F.3d 1179, 1196 (10th Cir. 2006) (noting that "[i]n the context of non-opinion work product, no circuit has adopted selective waiver and five circuits have rejected the doctrine").

277. *See* Duplan Corp. v. Deering Milliken, Inc., 540 F.2d 1215, 1222-23 (4th Cir. 1976) (court noting the "harsh results" of applying a broad waiver to Rule 26(b)(3), including the reluctance of lawyers to produce work product, especially where opinion work product was involved and the waiver was inadvertent); *In re* United Mine Workers of Am. Empl. Ben. Plans Litig., 159 F.R.D. 307, 310-12 (D.D.C. 1994) (finding no subject matter waiver and reasoning that "complete subject-matter waiver would probably yield additional attorney work product that would provide the defendants with a substantial strategic windfall" and such a waiver would undermine the adversary system); Exotica Botanicals, Inc. v. E. I. du Pont de Nemours & Co., 612 N.W.2d 801, 807-809 (Iowa 2000) (collecting cases) (limited disclosure of documents in another case was not subject matter waiver of work product privilege).

278. *In re* Martin Marietta Corp., 856 F.2d 619, 624-26 (4th Cir. 1988), *cert. denied sub nom.*, 490 U.S. 1011 (1989).

279. *See, e.g.,* James Julian, Inc. v. Raytheon Co., 93 F.R.D. 138, 145-46 (D. Del. 1982); Bailey v. Meister Brau, Inc. 57 F.R.D. 11, 13 (N.D. Ill. 1972); Berkey Photo, Inc. v. Eastman Kodak Co., 74 F.R.D. 613, 616 (S.D.N.Y. 1977); *In re* Comair Air Disaster Litig., 100 F.R.D. 350, 353 (E.D. Ky. 1983) (where material is used to refresh recollection, "[FED. R. EVID.] 612 weighs the balance in favor of finding that the 'substantial need' exists [under FED. R. CIV. P. 26(b)(3)], because of the policy in favor of effective cross-examination"); *but see* Bogosian v. Gulf Oil Corp., 738 F.2d 587, 595 n.3 (3d Cir. 1984) ("Rule 612 ... does not displace the protections of FED. R. CIV. P. 26(b)(3)," suggesting that Rule 612 should be construed narrowly in order to respect the protections of work product material embodied in Rule 26(b)(3)).

pursuant to Rule 26(b)(4), courts disagree whether to allow discovery of such work product materials that have been considered by an expert.[280]

B. *The Crime/Fraud Exception*

Another important issue that arises in connection with internal investigations is whether it may later be alleged that the attorney-client privilege or the work-product doctrine is pierced by the crime/fraud exception. The crime/fraud exception to the attorney-client privilege and the work-product doctrine allows discovery of materials that would otherwise be protected where the communication or document involves the furtherance of criminal or fraudulent activity. Several significant differences exist in the application of this exception to the two doctrines.

1. Application to the Attorney-Client Privilege

The attorney-client privilege does not protect communications made "in furtherance of contemplated or ongoing criminal or fraudulent conduct."[281] The crime or fraud need not have occurred for this exception to

---

280. *Compare* Suskind v. Home Depot Corp., No. Civ. A. 99-10575-NG, 2001 WL 92183, at *5 (D. Mass. Jan 2, 2001) (discussing interaction between work product doctrine codified in FED. R. CIV. P. 26(b)(3) and expert disclosure required by FED. R. CIV. P. 26(b)(4) after the 1993 amendments to Rule 26, and opining that the interpretation of the Rule in *Bogosian* that discovery pursuant to Rule 26(b)(4) is limited by Rule 26(b)(3) was rejected by the 1993 amendments (collecting cases); Karn v. Ingersoll-Rand Co., 168 F.R.D. 633, 639 (N.D. Ind. 1996) (not following Bogosian in light of the 1993 amendments and holding that the expert disclosure requirements of the new Rule 26 trump work product protection); Synthes Spine Co., L.P. v. Walden, 232 F.R.D. 460, 463-64 (E.D. Pa. 2005); Manufacturing Admin. & Mgmt. Sys., Inc. v. ICT Grp., Inc., 212 F.R.D. 110, 116 (E.D.N.Y. 2002) (Rule 26 provides and prudence counsels for mandatory disclosure of attorney work product communicated to a testifying expert) *with* Haworth, Inc. v. Herman Miller, Inc., 162 F.R.D. 289, 294-95 (W.D. Mich. 1995) (Advisory Committee Note to new Rule 26 only requires disclosure of factual and not opinion material and does not override work product privilege); Magee v. Paul Revere Life Ins. Co., 172 F.R.D. 627, 642-43 (E.D.N.Y. 1997) (Rule 26(a) should not be construed to vitiate the attorney work product privilege and only the factual materials considered by the expert need to be disclosed); Smith v. Transducer Tech., Inc., 197 F.R.D. 260, 262 (D.V.I. 2000) (discussing Karn and Bogosian and the diverging views on waiver of core work product protection and holding that plaintiff was entitled only to the fact work product provided to the expert witnesses); Krisa v. Equitable Life Assur. Soc'y, 196 F.R.D. 254, 260 (M.D. Pa. 2000).

281. *In re* Grand Jury Subpoena Duces Tecum Dated Sept. 15, 1983, 731 F.2d 1032, 1038 (2d Cir. 1984); *see also In re* John Doe Corp., 675 F.2d 482, 491-92 (2d Cir. 1982); United States v. Lentz, 419 F. Supp. 2d 820, 830 (E.D. Va. 2005) (crime/fraud exception only applies to communications about ongoing or future activities).

apply; it need only have been the objective of the client's communication.[282] The crime/fraud exception also applies where there has been a prior attorney-client relationship and the communication at issue was made in the context of that relationship.[283] The exception will apply even if the lawyer is unaware that advice is sought in furtherance of such an improper purpose.[284]

Mere allegations of fraud are not sufficient to pierce the privilege.[285] Corporate documents are not discoverable under the crime/fraud exception merely upon a showing that the client corporation communicated with counsel while the client was engaged in criminal activity. Rather, the party seeking discovery must establish probable cause to believe that the communication was intended, in some way, to facilitate or conceal the criminal activity.[286]

Courts apply a two-prong test to establish whether the crime/fraud exception applies. First, there must be a prima facie showing that the client was engaged in or planning criminal or fraudulent activities when the advice of counsel was sought, or that the client committed a fraud or crime subsequent to obtaining counsel's advice.[287] Second, there must be a showing that the lawyer's assistance was obtained in furtherance of the criminal or fraudulent act, or was closely related to it.[288]

In *United States v. Zolin*,[289] the Supreme Court rejected a long line of decisions requiring that a prima facie showing of the existence of the crime/fraud exception be established by evidence independent of the contested communication. The Court also held that in appropriate circumstances, in camera review of allegedly privileged attorney-client communications may

---

282. *In re* Grand Jury Subpoena Duces Tecum Dated Sept. 15, 1983, 731 F.2d 1032, 1039 (2d Cir. 1984).

283. *In re* Grand Jury Investigation, 445 F.3d 266, 274 (3d Cir. 2006) (upholding district court's decision to enforce the subpoena to attorney).

284. *Id.;* United States v. Laurins, 857 F.2d 529, 540 (9th Cir. 1988), *cert. denied,* 4902 U.S. 906 (1989); *In re* Omicron Grp., Inc. Sec. Litig., 233 F.R.D. 400, 404 (S.D.N.Y. 2006) ("pertinent intent is that of the client, not the attorney").

285. Ward v. Succession of Freeman, 854 F.2d 780, 790 (5th Cir. 1988), *cert. denied,* 490 U.S. 1065 (1989).

286. *In re* Grand Jury Subpoenas Duces Tecum, 798 F.2d 32, 34 (2d Cir. 1986); SEC v. Beacon Hill Asset Mgmt., LLC, 231 F.R.D. 134, 143 n.5 (S.D.N.Y. 2004); United States v. Cohn, 303 F. Supp. 2d 672, 681 (D. Md. 2003) (alleged crime or fraud need not be proved beyond a reasonable doubt before the privilege is lost).

287. *In re* Grand Jury Investigation, 842 F.2d 1223, 1226 (11th Cir. 1987); *In re* Grand Jury Proceedings #5 Empanelled Jan. 28, 2004, 401 F.3d 247, 251 (4th Cir. 2005).

288. *Id.*

289. 491 U.S. 554 (1989).

be used to determine whether the communications fall within the crime/fraud exception.[290] Such in camera review is not automatic; before a district court may engage in an in camera review at the request of the party opposing the privilege, that party must present evidence sufficient to support a reasonable belief that the review may reveal evidence that establishes the exception's applicability.[291] The party opposing the privilege may use any relevant non-privileged evidence, lawfully obtained, to counter that threshold showing, even if its evidence is not "independent" of the contested communications.[292]

2. Application to the Work-Product Doctrine

The crime/fraud exception also applies to the work-product doctrine.[293] The crime/fraud exception applies not only to factual work product but also to opinion work product.[294]

For factual work product, as with the attorney-client privilege, the attorney's knowledge of the client's activities or motive is irrelevant, and ongoing criminal or fraudulent activity by the client results in a waiver of work product protection for facts recorded by the lawyer.[295] This showing is less than that required for discovery of opinion work product.

---

290. *Id.* at 574.

291. *Id.* at 574-75; *see also* United States ex rel. Mayman v. Martin Marietta Corp., 886 F. Supp. 1243, 1246-47 (D. Md. 1995); IMC Chems., Inc. v. Niro Inc., No. Civ. A. 98-2348-JTM, 2000 WL 1466495, at *26 (D. Kan. July 19, 2000); First Union Nat'l Bank of Fla. v. Whitener, 715 So. 2d 979, 984 (Fla. Dist. Ct. App. June 12, 1998), *review denied,* 727 So. 2d 915 (Fla. 1999).

292. United States v. Zolin, 491 U.S. 554, 574 (1989).

293. *See, e.g.,* United States v. Ruhbayan, 406 F.3d 292, 299 (4th Cir.) (trial court did not abuse discretion in ruling that evidence fell within crime-fraud exception to attorney-client and work product privileges), *cert. denied,* 126 S. Ct. 291 (2005); *In re* International Sys. & Controls Corp. Sec. Litig., 693 F.2d 1235, 1242 (5th Cir. 1982); *In re* Sealed Case, 676 F.2d 793, 812 (D.C. Cir. 1982); *In re* John Doe Corp., 675 F.2d 482, 489 (2d Cir. 1982); *In re* Grand Jury Proceedings, 604 F.2d 798, 802-03 (3d Cir. 1979); Hercules, Inc. v. Exxon Corp., 434 F. Supp. 136, 155 (D. Del. 1977); Olson v. Accessory Controls & Equip. Corp., 757 A.2d 14, 30 (Conn. 1999).

294. *See In re* Doe, 662 F.2d 1073, 1080-81 (4th Cir. 1981) (extraordinary circumstances mandating disclosure may permit piercing the work product doctrine with respect to opinion work product; government must show a greater need for opinion work product than for fact work product), *cert. denied,* 455 U.S. 1000 (1982); *In re* Sealed Case, 676 F.2d 793, 812 (D.C. Cir. 1982) (not necessary to show extraordinary necessity when crime/fraud exception being applied to opinion work product).

295. *In re* Antitrust Grand Jury, 805 F.2d 155, 163 (6th Cir. 1986).

To obtain discovery of opinion work product, the party seeking discovery must establish that (1) the client was engaged in or planning a criminal or fraudulent scheme when seeking the advice of counsel to further the scheme, and (2) the documents containing the lawyer's opinion work product must bear a close relationship to the client's existing or future scheme to commit a crime.[296] In cases where the fraud is that of the client, the retention of the immunity to protect the lawyer's privacy may be appropriate, and the party seeking discovery of the lawyer's mental impressions or other opinion work product may be required to make a prima facie showing that the lawyer knowingly participated in the crime or fraud.[297] However, some courts hold that a guilty client should not be able to assert the work product immunity of an innocent lawyer.[298] Nor should the lawyer be permitted to invoke the immunity to cover the lawyer's own crime or fraud.[299]

---

296. *See, e.g.,* United States v. Ruhbayan, 406 F.3d 292, 299 (4th Cir.) (evidence on crime-fraud point supported trial court's finding that defendant used the attorney to dupe the court and jury at his first trial and so trial court did not err in finding that evidence fell within crime-fraud exception), *cert. denied,* 126 S. Ct. 291 (2005); United States v. Paz, Nos. 04-1156, 04-1809, 2005 WL 548198, at *2 (3d Cir. Mar. 8, 2005) (government met the two-part showing required for invoking the crime-fraud exception to work-product protection); *In re* Murphy, 560 F.2d 326, 338 (8th Cir. 1977); *In re* Sealed Case, 676 F.2d 793, 814-15 (D.C. Cir. 1982); *In re* Grand Jury Proceedings, 604 F.2d 798, 803 (3d Cir. 1979); Hercules, Inc. v. Exxon Corp., 434 F. Supp. 136, 155-56 (D. Del. 1977).

297. *See, e.g.,* Berroth v. Farm Bur. Mut. Ins. Co., C. A. Nos. 01-2095-CM, 01-2096-CM, 2002 WL 1774055 (D. Kan. July 17, 2002) (denying disclosure because plaintiffs failed to provide evidence sufficient to make a prima facie showing that attorney participated in crime); *In re* International Sys. & Controls Corp. Sec. Litig., 91 F.R.D. 552, 559-60 (S.D. Tex. 1981), *vacated on other grounds,* 693 F.2d 1235 (5th Cir. 1982); *In re* Grand Jury Proceedings, 604 F.2d 798, 801 (3d Cir. 1981); *In re* Special Sept. 1978 Grand Jury (II), 640 F.2d 49, 63 (7th Cir. 1980).

298. *See In re* Sealed Case, 676 F.2d 793, 812 (D.C. Cir. 1982) ("[T]here is no need to accord a guilty client standing to assert the claims of its innocent attorney"); *but see In re* Grand Jury Subpoena, 220 F.R.D. 130, 152 (D. Mass. 2004) ("It is the client's state of mind that controls; the exception applies even if the attorney was entirely innocent").

299. *See, e.g., In re* Richard Roe, Inc., 168 F.3d 69, 71 (2d Cir. 1999) (Where the litigation itself is alleged to be in furtherance of a fraud, the party seeking disclosure of material subject to the work product privilege, under the crime-fraud exception, must show probable cause that the litigation or an aspect thereof had little or no legal or factual basis and was carried on substantially in order to further the crime or fraud); *In re* Doe, 662 F.2d 1073, 1078 (4th Cir. 1981) ("No court construing [Rule 26], however, has held that an attorney committing a crime could, by invoking the work product doctrine, insulate himself from criminal prosecution for abusing the system he is sworn to protect"), *cert. denied,* 455 U.S. 1000 (1982).

3. Application to Internal Corporate Investigations

An internal investigation frequently deals with underlying conduct that may be characterized as criminal or fraudulent. In addition, one aspect of an internal investigation may be to determine whether, and to what extent, the underlying conduct must be disclosed, either publicly or to an adversely affected third party, a determination that itself carries overtones of ongoing fraudulent conduct. Accordingly, investigative counsel must remain vigilant concerning the client's conduct and apparent intentions to ensure that counsel does not become enmeshed in criminal or fraudulent conduct of the client and thereby jeopardize the attorney-client privilege and work-product doctrine (or suffer more serious consequences).

C. *Shareholder Litigation*

Public disclosure of the existence of an internal corporate investigation, or the results of such an investigation, frequently gives rise to shareholder litigation. Ironically, it is this predictable consequence of investigative activity that renders the attorney-client privilege most vulnerable. This weakness is created by the *Garner* rule,[300] pursuant to which otherwise privileged communications between counsel and their corporate clients may be discovered by plaintiffs in shareholder actions upon a showing of good cause. The *Garner* rule rests on the principle that a corporation owes a fiduciary duty to its shareholders and therefore should not be allowed to assert the attorney-client privilege against its "beneficiaries."[301]

The court in *Garner* enumerated certain "indicia" of good cause:

> [1] the number of shareholders [calling for the information] and the percentage of stock they represent; [2] the bona fides of the shareholders; [3] the nature of [the] claim and whether it is obviously colorable; [4] the apparent necessity or desirability of the shareholders having the information and the availability of it from other sources; [5] whether, if the shareholders' claim is of wrongful action by the corporation, it is of action criminal, or illegal but not criminal, or of doubtful legality; [6] whether the communication related to past or to prospective actions; [7] whether the communication is advice concerning the litiga-

---

300. *See* Garner v. Wolfinbarger, 430 F.2d 1093, 1103-04 (5th Cir. 1970), *cert. denied*, 401 U.S. 974 (1971).

301. *Id.* at 1101-02. The *Garner* rule is not limited to the corporate arena; it has been applied to various fiduciary relationships. *See, e.g.,* Aquinaga v. John Morrell & Co., 112 F.R.D. 671, 680-82 (D. Kan. 1986) (Garner doctrine applied to union members and officers); Quintel Corp., N.V. v. Citibank, N.A., 567 F. Supp. 1357, 1363 (S.D.N.Y. 1983) (Garner rule applied to investment advisor in real estate transaction); Donovan v. Fitzsimmons, 90 F.R.D. 583, 586-87 (N.D. Ill. 1981) (Garner rationale applied to pension fund trustee).

tion itself; [8] the extent to which the communication is identified versus the extent to which the shareholders are blindly fishing; and [9] the risk of revelation of trade secrets or other information in whose confidentiality the corporation has an interest for independent reasons.[302]

The *Garner* doctrine has been followed in numerous cases, although in most of these decisions the courts denied the discovery sought on the ground that the plaintiff had failed to demonstrate good cause.[303] Some courts, however, have squarely rejected the *Garner* rule and held that there is "no extraordinary avenue ... available to [shareholders] to pierce the [corporation's] privilege."[304]

The rationale for the *Garner* rule rests upon the "joint defense" doctrine,[305] and should thus be limited to derivative actions, where the interests of the corporation and its shareholders are theoretically the same. However, many courts have applied the *Garner* rule in shareholder class actions as well as derivative actions,[306] although the interests of the plaintiff shareholder (sometimes a former shareholder) and the defendant corporation are unquestionably inconsistent.

Some courts have limited the *Garner* doctrine to discovery of the legal advice preceding the allegedly wrongful conduct, while protecting discussions between the corporation and its counsel after the alleged wrongdoing or in connection with subsequent litigation.[307] Since communications with investigative

---

302. Garner v. Wolfinbarger, 430 F.2d 1093, 1104 (5th Cir. 1970), *cert. denied*, 401 U.S. 974 (1971).

303. *See, e.g.*, Cohen v. Uniroyal, Inc., 80 F.R.D. 480, 484-85 (E.D. Pa. 1978); *In re* Transocean Tender Offer Sec. Litig., 78 F.R.D. 692, 696-97 (N.D. Ill. 1978); *but see* Sandberg v. Virginia Bankshares, Inc., 979 F.2d 332, 351-54 (4th Cir. 1992) (plaintiffs did not show good cause), *vacated and remanded*, Nos. 91-1873(L), CA-88-299-A, 91-1874, CA-88-1020-A, 1993 WL 524680 (4th Cir. Apr. 7, 1993); *In re* Bairnco Corp. Sec. Litig., 148 F.R.D. 91, 99 (S.D.N.Y. 1993); Quintel Corp., N.V. v. Citibank, *N.A.*, 567 F. Supp. 1357, 1374 (S.D.N.Y. 1983) (plaintiff did show good cause).

304. *See* Milroy v. Hanson, 875 F. Supp. 646, 651-52 (D. Neb. 1995); Tail of the Pup, Inc. v. Webb, 528 So. 2d 506, 507 (Fla. Dist. Ct. App. 1988); Lefkowitz v. Duquesne Light Co., 1988 WL 169273, at **5-6 (W.D. Pa. June 14, 1988); Shirvani v. Capital Investing Corp., 112 F.R.D. 389, 391 (D. Conn. 1986); *see generally* Dennis J. Block & H. Adam Prussin, *After Upjohn, the Garner Rule Still Creates Uncertainty in the Area of Corporate Attorney-Client Privilege*, 3 BUS. ADVOC. 5 (Spring 1981).

305. *See* Part II.B.5, *supra*.

306. *See, e.g., In re* Transocean Tender Offer Sec. Litig., 78 F.R.D. 692, 696-97 (N.D. Ill. 1978); Bailey v. Meister Brau, Inc., 55 F.R.D. 211, 214 (N.D. Ill. 1972); *but see* Weil v. Investment/Indicators, Research & Mgmt., Inc., 647 F.2d 18, 23 (9th Cir. 1981) (holding that Garner rule was inapplicable to class-action suit by former shareholders).

307. *In re* LTV Sec. Litig., 89 F.R.D. 595, 606-08 (N.D. Tex. 1981); Panter v. Marshall Field & Co., 80 F.R.D. 718, 723-24 (N.D. Ill. 1978).

counsel normally occur in the period following the alleged wrongdoing, this line of cases should protect the investigative report from discovery under the *Garner* rule. Moreover, some courts have held that the *Garner* rule does not apply to materials protected by the work-product doctrine, because the rules for disclosure of work product are contained in the Federal Rules of Civil Procedure, which reject a good cause standard in favor of the substantial need/undue hardship test.[308]

The Sixth Circuit's decision in *In re Perrigo Co.*[309] addressed the issue of disclosure of an investigation report in parallel shareholder derivative and class actions. The report in *Perrigo* was prepared with the assistance of outside counsel after a four-month investigation undertaken following a demand by the shareholders in the derivative action that *Perrigo* sue certain officers and directors. The report concluded that maintenance of the derivative action was not in *Perrigo*'s best interests.[310] A shareholder class action was filed alleging violations of the securities laws based on substantially the same facts and against the same defendants as alleged in the derivative action.[311]

Defendants moved to dismiss the derivative action pursuant to a Michigan statute that provides in relevant part that the court "shall dismiss a derivative proceeding if ... the court finds that" "all disinterested independent directors" "have made a determination in good faith after conducting a reasonable investigation ... that the maintenance of the derivative proceeding is not in the best interests of the corporation" and "the plaintiff shall have the burden of proving that the determination was not made in good faith or that the investigation was not reasonable."[312] *Perrigo* did not use the report or disclose any of its contents in its motion to dismiss and claimed that the attorney-client and work product privileges protected the report from disclosure.[313]

The district court held that the derivative plaintiffs had demonstrated substantial need and undue hardship in obtaining the information in the report from other sources and compelled defendants to produce the report.[314] Specif-

---

308. *See In re* Celotex Corp., 196 B.R. 596, 600 n.3 (M.D. Fla. Bankr. 1996) ("Garner decision does not apply to material protected by the work-product doctrine"); *In re* International Sys. & Controls Corp. Sec. Litig., 693 F.2d 1235, 1240 (5th Cir. 1982); *In re* Dayco Corp. Sec. Litig., 99 F.R.D. 616, 620-21 (S.D. Ohio 1983); *see also* Part III.D, *supra*.
309. 128 F.3d 430 (6th Cir. 1997).
310. *Id.* at 433.
311. *Id.* at 432.
312. MICH. COMP. LAWS ANN. § 450.1495 (West 2002 & Supp. 2006).
313. *In re* Perrigo Co., 128 F.3d 430, 438 (6th Cir. 1997).
314. Kearney v. Jandernoa, 949 F. Supp. 510, 511 (W.D. Mich. 1996).

ically, because the derivative plaintiffs bear the burden under the Michigan statute to demonstrate that the independent directors' decision was not in good faith and the investigation was not reasonable, the court concluded that the derivative plaintiffs should be given access to the report.[315]

The district court held in the class action, however, that plaintiffs had not demonstrated a substantial need or undue hardship and thus were not entitled to the report.[316] The district court entered a protective order prohibiting disclosure of the report, but to the extent either party to the derivative action used any portion of the report in its papers "to induce the court's reliance," the report would become a part of the publicly available record.[317]

The Sixth Circuit upheld the district court's ruling that Perrigo would be compelled to produce the report to the derivative plaintiffs, but not to the class-action plaintiffs, because, "[a]s a matter of fairness and practicality, the derivative plaintiffs (unlike the class action plaintiffs) will need the report in order" to rebut the presumption that the independent directors acted in good faith.[318] With respect to the protective order, the Sixth Circuit upheld that portion of the district court's order that prohibited general disclosure of the report, on the ground that Perrigo had not "utterly waived its privilege" and that "fairness considerations simply do not require public disclosure."[319]

The Sixth Circuit granted mandamus, however, to reverse the district court's order allowing public disclosure of any portions of the report that might be filed in connection with court proceedings.[320] The Sixth Circuit observed that as a result of the district court's decisions, "Perrigo was faced with the choice of waiving the protection of the Report or withdrawing its motion to dismiss" in the derivative action, and held that "such a result would be contrary to Michigan law, which holds that 'it is not within the power of

---

315. *Id.*
316. Picard Chem. Inc. Profit Sharing Plan v. Perrigo Co., 951 F. Supp. 679, 687 (W.D. Mich. 1996); *but see* nonderivative cases in which courts have compelled disclosure of protected information, albeit with a heightened burden on plaintiffs to show the "good cause" required by Garner: Fausek v. White, 965 F.2d 126, 130 (6th Cir.), *cert. denied,* 506 U.S. 1034 (1992); Ward v. Succession of Freeman, 854 F.2d 780, 786 (5th Cir. 1988), *cert. denied sub nom.,* 490 U.S. 1065 (1989); Miller v. Genesco, Inc., No. 93 Civ. 0096, 1994 WL 698287, at *1 (S.D.N.Y. Dec. 13, 1994).
317. Picard Chem. Inc. Profit Sharing Plan v. Perrigo Co., 951 F. Supp. 679, 691 (W.D. Mich. 1996).
318. *In re* Perrigo Co., 128 F.3d 430, 438 (6th Cir. 1997).
319. *Id.* at 439.
320. *Id.* at 440.

the court or any party to waive the privilege for [the client].'"[321] The district court was directed to conduct an in camera review of the report and "weigh the interests of Perrigo in maintaining its privilege" against the interests of the public to inspect judicial records before unsealing the report.[322]

The *Garner* doctrine poses potential problems for a corporation and its counsel in the context of an internal investigation. The matters giving rise to an investigation frequently engender both shareholder derivative actions on behalf of the corporation and shareholder class or individual actions against the corporation—often framed alternatively in the same complaint or joined in consolidated actions. At the same time, the corporation may be subject to civil or criminal claims by government authorities. In these circumstances, the preservation of the corporation's attorney-client privilege may be critical. *Perrigo* poses one solution, although not without flaws: that the internal investigation be kept under court-ordered seal.

V. EFFECT OF THE SARBANES-OXLEY ACT AND RECENT SECURITIES EXCHANGE COMMISSION AND DEPARTMENT OF JUSTICE POLICIES ON THE ATTORNEY-CLIENT PRIVILEGE

Since the 1970s when the Securities Exchange Commission (SEC) announced its "voluntary disclosure program," corporations have felt increased pressure to self-regulate and cooperate with the SEC and Department of Justice in exchange for leniency with regard to formal investigations, lesser penalties, and in the case of criminal prosecution of corporate officers, decreased prison sentences. Whether a corporation is willing to waive its attorney-client privilege during the course of an SEC or Department of Justice investigation has, and continues to be, an important factor considered by these authorities when investigating and prosecuting alleged violations of the federal securities laws. Over the past five years, both the SEC and Department of Justice have announced policies formalizing the details and effects of such cooperation. Congress' passage of the Sarbanes-Oxley Act in 2002 has further shaped this

---

321. *Id.* at 438, 440 (citation omitted).
322. *Id.* at 438.

landscape and has provided attorneys representing corporations under investigation much to ponder when considering if the attorney-client privilege should be waived.[323]

In 2001, the SEC issued its *Report of Investigation Pursuant to Section 21(a) of the Securities Exchange Act of 1934 and Commission Statement on the Relationship of Cooperation to Agency Enforcement Decisions*, commonly referred to as the "Seaboard Report," which memorialized "some of the criteria [the SEC] will consider in determining whether, and how much, to credit self-policing, self-reporting, remediation and cooperation—from the extraordinary step of taking no enforcement action to bringing reduced charges, seeking lighter sanctions, or including mitigating language in documents [used] to announce and resolve enforcement actions."[324] An important factor in this determination is the corporation's cooperation with and voluntary disclosure of "possibly violative conduct" and other potentially incriminating information to the SEC.[325] While recognizing the importance of the attorney-client privilege, the SEC also noted when considering a corporation's cooperation with its investigation, the SEC "does not view a company's waiver of a privilege as an end in itself, but only as a means (where necessary) to provide relevant and sometimes critical information to the Commission staff."[326]

In July 2002, Congress passed the Sarbanes-Oxley Act (the Act) in response to corporate scandals such as those involving Enron and WorldCom.[327] In passing the Act, Congress granted the SEC additional enforcement powers including the ability to issue professional rules of conduct that would, among other things, require an attorney representing issuers to follow an intra-corporate reporting mechanism and potentially withdraw as counsel upon his or

---

323. *See generally* Joseph F. Savage, Jr. & David S. Schumacher, *Attorney-Client Privilege on the Rebound?*, 20 No. 9 ANDREWS WHITE-COLLAR CRIME LITIG. REP. 2 (May 31, 2006); William R. McLucas, *et al., The Decline of the Attorney-Client Privilege in the Corporate Setting*, 96 J. CRIM. L. & CRIMINOLOGY 621 (2006).

324. SEC Rel. No. 34-44969 at 2 (Oct. 23, 2001) (the "Seaboard Release"), *available at* http://www.sec.gov/litigation/investreport/34-44969.htm.

325. *Id.* at 3-4.

326. *Id.* at 4 n.3.

327. Pub. L. No. 107-204, 116 Stat. 745 (2002) (codified in scattered sections of the U.S.C.).

her belief that the intra-corporate report has not been appropriately addressed.[328] The Sarbanes-Oxley Act also contains a number of criminal provisions.[329]

Since the passage of the Act, the SEC and Department of Justice have increasingly pursued enforcement of the federal securities laws. An attorney undertaking an internal corporate investigation in connection with a government

---

328. In November 2002, the SEC issued proposed rules of attorney professional conduct, commonly referred to as the "up the ladder," and "noisy withdrawal" provisions. *See* Proposed Rule: Implementation of Standards of Professional Conduct for Attorneys, SEC Rel. Nos. 33-8150, 34-46868 (Nov. 21, 2002), *available at* http://www.sec.gov/rules/proposed/33-8150.htm. The "up the ladder" requirement is an intra-corporate reporting mechanism that requires an attorney to report to either the chief executive officer ("CEO") or chief legal officer ("CLO") any "evidence" of a "material violation" of the "securities laws or breach of fiduciary duty." 17 C.F.R. § 205.3(b)(1). If the CEO or CLO has not attended to the issue and, in the attorney's opinion, it "would be unreasonable, under the circumstances, for a prudent and competent attorney not to conclude that it is reasonably likely that a material violation has occurred, is ongoing, or is about to occur," the attorney is authorized to report to either the corporation's committee of independent directors or, if no such committee exists, to the board of the directors. 17 C.F.R. § 205.3(b)(i)-(iii); *see also* Susan J. Stabile, *Sarbanes-Oxley's Rules of Professional Responsibility Viewed Through a Sextonian Lens,* 60 N.Y.U. ANN. SURV. AM. L. 31, 40 (2004). If the CEO or CLO or committee believes that the evidence submitted does not comprise of a "material violation" of the law, the reporting attorney need not take other steps. The "noisy withdrawal" rule, which has not yet been finalized, concerns an attorney's duty to act upon his or her belief that the initial report to intra-corporate officials of a material violation of applicable securities laws or a breach of fiduciary duty had not been "appropriately responded to." 17 C.F.R. § 205.2(b). In its original form, the noisy withdrawal rule required the attorney to effectively withdraw from representation of the issuer and report such withdrawal to the SEC. *See* Proposed Rule: Implementation of Standards of Professional Conduct for Attorneys, SEC Rel. Nos. 33-8150, 34-46868 (Nov. 21, 2002), *available at* http://www.sec.gov/rules/proposed/33-8150.htm. However, this type of reporting requirement raised serious concerns for attorney-client privilege and has been the source of many comments opposing the proposed rule. *See* Letter from Seventy-seven Law Firms to Jonathan G. Katz, Secretary, Securities and Exchange Commission (Dec. 18, 2002), *available at* http://www.sec.gov/rules/proposed/s74502/77lawfirms1.htm; Final Rule: Implementation of Standards of Professional Conduct for Attorneys, SEC Rel. Nos. 33-8185, 34-47276, *available at* http://www.sec.gov/rules/final/33-8185.htm; Susan J. Stabile, *Sarbanes-Oxley's Rules of Professional Responsibility Viewed Through a Sextonian Lens,* 60 N.Y.U. ANN. SURV. AM. L. 31, 39 (2004); Proposed Rule: Implementation of Standards of Professional Conduct for Attorneys, SEC Rel. Nos. 33-8186, 34-47282, *available at* http://www.sec.gov/rules/proposed/33-8186.htm. In any event, despite the lack of finality with respect to the noisy withdrawal rule, attorneys should remain aware of the crime/fraud exception to the attorney-client privilege, which permits an attorney to unilaterally withdraw from representation to the extent the communication is made in furtherance of contemplated or ongoing criminal or fraudulent conduct. *See* Part IV.A.1.a.-e, *supra;* Susan J. Stabile, *Sarbanes-Oxley's Rules of Professional Responsibility Viewed Through a Sextonian Lens,* 60 N.Y.U. ANN. SURV. AM. L. 31, 37-43 (2004).

329. These criminal provisions include the prohibition on an issuer from, among other things, improperly influencing its auditors for the purpose of rendering its financial statements

investigation must be aware of the effect of an issuer's assertion of attorney-client privilege on the government's decision of whether to prosecute an alleged violation of the criminal securities fraud statutes.[330] Specifically, a 2003 Department of Justice memorandum emphasized that the corporation's "timely and voluntary disclosure of wrongdoing and its willingness to cooperate in the investigation of its agents, including, if necessary, the waiver of corporate attorney-client and work product protection" is one of the nine factors prosecutors will consider when determining whether to bring charges and negotiate plea arrangements.[331]

On December 12, 2006, the Justice Department issued a revision of its 2003 guidelines.[332] The new memorandum largely reaffirms the previously issued guidelines, but also creates a new process which prosecutors must follow before they seek waiver of the attorney-client or attorney work-product privileges in the course of a corporation's cooperation with a government

---

materially misleading; retaliating against whistleblowers; altering, destroying, mutilating, or concealing a document or record with the intent to impair its integrity or availability of use in an official proceeding or with the intent to impede, obstruct, or influence any federal investigation; and knowingly executing or attempting to execute a scheme to defraud any person in connection with securities of an issuer, or falsely or fraudulently obtaining any money or property in connection with the purchase or sale of its securities. Pub. L. No. 107-204, § 807, 116 Stat. 745, 804 (2002) (codified at 18 U.S.C. § 1348).

330. The SEC rules also contain provisions for sanctions for those attorneys who were required to report under the circumstances described above but failed to do so. 17 C.F.R. § 205.6. An attorney may be subject to "civil penalties and remedies for a violation of the federal securities laws" in an action brought by the Commission against the attorney. *Id.* In addition, the attorney may be "subject to the disciplinary authority of the Commission, regardless of whether the attorney may also be subject to discipline for the same conduct in a jurisdiction where the attorney is admitted or practices," which may result in "censure, or being temporarily or permanently denied privilege of appearing or practicing before the Commission." *Id.*

331. Memorandum from Deputy Attorney General Larry Thompson to Heads of Department Components and U.S. Attorneys, Principles of Federal Prosecution of Business Organizations (Jan. 20, 2003), *available at* http://www.usdoj.gov/dag/cftf/corporate_guidelines.htm ("Thompson Memorandum"). The Thompson Memorandum also explained that "[s]uch waivers permit the government to obtain statements of possible witnesses, subjects, and targets, without having to negotiate individual cooperation or immunity agreements. In addition, they are often critical in enabling the government to evaluate the completeness of a corporation's voluntary disclosure and cooperation. Prosecutors may, therefore, request a waiver in appropriate circumstances." *Id.* at § VI; *see also* Memorandum from former Deputy Attorney General Eric H. Holder, Jr. to All Component Heads and U.S. Attorneys, Bringing Criminal Charges Against Corporations (June 16, 1999), *available at* http://www.usdoj.gov/criminal/fraud/policy/Chargingcorps.html.

332. Memorandum from Paul J. McNulty, Deputy Attorney General, Department of Justice, to Heads of Department Components and United States Attorneys (December 12, 2006) (available at http://ww.usdoj.gov/dag/speech/2006/mcnulty_memo.pdf).

investigation. Specifically, prosecutors may only request waiver of attorney-client privilege or work-product protection when there is a legitimate need for the privileged information to fulfill their law enforcement obligations.[333]

The memo also creates a two-tiered classification of the types of information for which prosecutors can seek waiver and establishes a procedural and record-keeping mechanism for such requests. In essence, the memo generally defines the first category of information as purely factual information ("Category I") and the second category of information as more traditionally protected information such as the mental thoughts and impressions of attorneys ("Category II").

Category II information is the only type of protected information that a corporation can decline to provide to the Justice Department without fear that a prosecutor would hold the declination against the corporation in making a charging decision. On the other hand, the memo reiterates that a "[p]rosecutor may always favorably consider a corporation's acquiescence to the government's waiver request in determining whether a corporation has cooperated in the government's investigation." (*Id.* at 10.)

Interestingly, the McNulty memo provides no process or approval requirements for a corporation's purely voluntary production of material. Because "credit" for cooperation will be given to a company that produces investigative material, the pressure to waive is as high as ever, despite the McNulty memo.

Likewise, in early 2006, the SEC announced that a corporation's cooperation with law enforcement agencies is a factor it will consider in determining the appropriate penalty to impose in connection with violations of the federal securities laws.[334]

The emphasis placed by the SEC and Department of Justice on a corporation's decision to waive the attorney-client privilege is not without its

---

333. Whether there is a legitimate need depends on:
   • the likelihood and degree to which the privileged information will benefit the government's investigation;
   • whether the information sought can be obtained in a timely and complete fashion by using alternative means that do not require a waiver;
   • the completeness of the voluntary disclosure already provided; and
   • the collateral consequences to a corporation of a waiver.

334. *See* Statement of the U.S. Securities and Exchange Comm'n Concerning Financial Penalties, SEC Press Rel. 2006-4 (Jan. 4, 2006), *available at* http://www.sec.gov/news/press/2006-4.htm.

critics.³³⁵ Presumably in response to the concern that recent policies of the SEC and Department of Justice are increasingly eroding the protections provided by the attorney-client privilege, the Federal Sentencing Guidelines have been amended. Until recently, Comment 12 to Section 8C2.5(g) of the U.S. Sentencing Guidelines provided that a corporation was not eligible for a reduced sentence if it refused to waive the attorney-client privilege during the government's investigation.³³⁶ After soliciting comments and holding public hearings, the Sentencing Commission voted to remove from Comment 12 this prohibition on reduced sentences, thus, effective May 1, 2006, a corporation may be eligible for a reduction in sentence whether or not it waives the attorney-client privilege.³³⁷ Nevertheless, despite this recent amendment to the Federal Sentencing Guidelines, an attorney representing a corporation must still consider whether or not it would prove beneficial to the corporation to waive the attorney-client privilege in connection with a government criminal investigation.

---

335. *See* Press Release, U.S. Chamber of Commerce, Chamber Calls on SEC to Appoint Advisory Committee to Examine Enforcement Practices; Enforcement is 'Increasingly Punitive and Adversarial,' Chamber Study Finds (Mar. 9, 2006), *available at* http://www.uschamber.com/press/releases/2006/march/06-42.htm. Among the "punitive and adversarial" practices are "the intense pressure on public companies to waive attorney-client privilege and work product protection during SEC investigations; the imposition of large penalties on public companies as opposed to individual wrongdoers; and 'industry sweeps,' whereby corporations in a targeted industry must respond to broad information requests without an indication of wrongdoing." *Id.; see also* ABA Task Force on the Attorney-Client Privilege, Report to the ABA House of Delegates (May 18, 2005), *available at* http://www.abanet.org/buslaw/attorneyclient/materials/hod/report.pdf; U.S. Chamber of Commerce, Report on the Current Enforcement Program of the Securities and Exchange Commission (Mar. 2006), *available at* http://www.uschamber.com/publications/reports/0603sec.htm.

336. U.S. Sentencing Guidelines Man. § 8C2.5(g) cmt. 12 (2004 & Supp. 2006).

337. U.S. Sentencing Commission, Amendments to the Sentencing Guidelines, Policy Statements and Official Commentary 29-30 (May 1, 2006), available at http://www.ussc.gov.

The Witness Interview Process 3

Randall J. Turk and Mark Miller

I. INTRODUCTION 94
II. PREPARING FOR WITNESS INTERVIEWS 95
    A. Initial Concerns 95
    B. Key Principles 98
    C. Before the Interview 100
III. CONDUCTING THE INTERVIEW 102
    A. Mechanics 102
    B. Warnings to Witnesses and the Attorney-Client Privilege 103
    C. Conducting the Interview 107
IV. MAKING A RECORD OF THE INTERVIEW 108
V. SPECIAL ISSUES 111
    A. Sarbanes-Oxley and the Responsibilities of Counsel 111
    B. Obstruction of Justice 112
    C. Other Typical Problems That Arise during Witness Interviews 114
VI. CONCLUSION 116

Randall J. Turk and Mark Miller are with Baker Botts LLP in Washington, D.C.

I. INTRODUCTION

WITNESS INTERVIEWS CAN be the most significant part of an internal investigation. They are one of the most important tools in the investigating lawyer's arsenal—and one of the most powerful. On a basic level, witness interviews provide an opportunity to discover facts about possible wrongdoing or defenses that cannot be gleaned from documents or physical evidence. They enable the lawyer to lay the foundation for the attorney-client privilege and work-product doctrine and their application to the entire investigation. On a deeper level, witness interviews allow counsel to assess the credibility of the individuals who could be the most significant witnesses for or against the company in any later litigation or government investigation.

But if witness interviews can be the most interesting and important aspect of corporate investigations, they can also create the most risk for the integrity of the process:

- Witness interviews can contaminate other witnesses' recollections or "cross-pollinate" them with the recollections of others.
- Heavy-handed lawyers can chill a client's business atmosphere or frighten potentially important witnesses into ending their cooperation or seeking separate counsel.
- An unprepared or inattentive lawyer can miss the significance of certain witness statements or fail to take appropriate follow-up steps (under Sarbanes-Oxley, for example).
- Witness interviews can reveal the interests or theories of the lawyers investigating the case, which could allow wrongdoers to shape their testimony.
- At their worst, witness interviews can provide opportunities for careless (or unscrupulous) counsel to shape the testimony of witnesses or to obstruct justice.

In the current enforcement climate, when the government is more willing than ever to question the conduct of companies and their lawyers in internal investigations, lawyers need to pay particular attention to best practices in witness interviews in order to steer clear of these and other hazards.

This chapter provides advice on preparing for and conducting witness interviews—from assessing the purposes of the investigation, to preparing for and conducting the interview and making a record—and it explains how to navigate some of the potential hazards that exist.

II. PREPARING FOR WITNESS INTERVIEWS

The key to good witness interviews is preparation. Although witness interviews are ordinarily less formal than civil depositions because no oath is administered, no opposing counsel is present and no verbatim transcript is made, the interviewing lawyer should still engage in the same level of preparation. Just as no careful lawyer would conduct a discovery deposition before fully considering the key factual and legal issues in the case and without understanding the relevant documentary evidence, the lawyer should not think about conducting witness interviews without similar preparation. The better prepared the lawyer is in advance of the interview, the more productive the interview will be.

A. *Initial Concerns*

The circumstances giving rise to an investigation will affect how the witness interviews should be conducted, in what order, how broadly they need to reach, and how quickly they should be done. By the time an investigation has moved into the witness interview phase, the lawyers conducting the investigation should have a firm sense of the answers to such questions as these:

- What is the purpose of the investigation—is it to determine whether discipline is appropriate for particular employees, to generate defenses to perceived legal problems, to determine the likelihood of civil litigation, to determine whether corrective or remedial action is necessary, or to respond to an actual or potential government investigation? Have subpoenas been issued?
- What legal questions are at issue and what sorts of conclusions will need to be drawn at the end of the investigation? Is this a situation, for example, where there is a possibility of receiving amnesty if prompt self-reporting is made to the government?
- What are the potential uses of the investigation's findings? Will they be shared with management or the board of directors—or with the government?
- Is there a risk that information about the investigation could be leaked and trigger litigation against the company by competitors, employees, shareholders, or the government?
- Is the potential wrongdoing believed to be contained among a narrow group of employees, or is there a possibility that it could be more widespread?

The answers to these types of questions will influence how the interviewing lawyer will plan the pace, structure, content, and scope of witness interviews. If the government has issued subpoenas to employees, for example, or if the legal issue is one for which the government provides amnesty or leniency in exchange for prompt self-reporting, witness interviews may need to proceed much more quickly than if they are being conducted in response to some relatively minor employee misconduct. In the former situation, the order of witness interviews may be determined by the order in which the government seeks to interview employees, or the order in which subpoenas were served. In the latter situation, where fewer external pressures exist, the lawyer conducting the internal investigation will have more control over the sequence and pace of the interviews.

Lawyers should also be aware of other issues that could affect the conduct of witness interviews, such as the risk that the investigation itself might prompt employees or others to initiate litigation against the company. Such a risk can influence the scope of the investigation, the number of employees interviewed, and whether former employees—who might be disgruntled or working for competitors—should be interviewed at all. Any decision to limit the scope of the investigation should, of course, be made by whatever person or entity within the client is directing the investigation—the general counsel, senior management, or the board—and not by the lawyer retained to conduct the investigation. But the lawyer should be aware of the risks in order to provide advice upon which management can make such decisions.

The answers to these questions can vary greatly depending upon the circumstances of each case and the type of investigation that is being conducted. Most internal investigations fall into one of the following categories.

Minor Compliance Problems. Minor compliance problems can involve such matters as violations of a company's code of business conduct or other improper conduct committed by individual employees. Many companies address such matters by having someone in-house—often but not always a lawyer—interview the relevant employees and review relevant documents. Frequently, no record of the inquiry is made, or the record does not go beyond what may be called for by the company's disciplinary rules or human resources procedures. Because the purpose of this inquiry is usually to guide a management decision, often at levels below that of senior management, the order of witness interviews is usually less important, and the interviews are usually less structured than would be the case in a more formal investigation. It is important for lawyers conducting such inquiries, however, to recognize when a simple breach of company rules (for example, when pornographic materials are discovered on an employee's computer drive) becomes a serious law-enforcement matter (for example, when the materials contain child pornography).

Routine Internal Investigations. For more significant compliance problems, companies generally need a probing investigation of facts and formalized procedures for recording and reporting results. The stakes are higher in these types of investigations, and the possibility of litigation against the company increases. For these reasons, investigations of this type are usually handled by outside counsel using systematic procedures for document collection and witness interviews. It is important to consider with care who should be interviewed and in what sequence, and to employ skilled techniques in preparing for, conducting, and memorializing the interviews.

Major Investigations. Full-scale investigations are most frequently triggered by serious compliance concerns that affect a company broadly, or by threatened shareholder action addressed to possible management misfeasance. Here, the stakes can be much higher as the results are often newsworthy and can have significant effects on stock price or overall company health. These investigations are usually undertaken by outside counsel, who maintain a record of their inquiry and present a formal report. Again, it is important to conduct the interviews in the proper sequence and to use skilled interviewing and recordkeeping techniques.

Major investigations can include those that are triggered by government enforcement actions, and investigations of this type are generally on a fast track. Counsel often will not have the luxury of arranging witness interviews in the most productive way, *i.e.*, after completing document collection, review, and analysis and in the sequence that would produce the most orderly discovery of facts. It is still important, however, for the interviewing lawyers to be as prepared as possible within the time limits available. In situations where interviews must be done quickly, it is often productive for counsel to use some of the interview time asking the witness to provide and explain any relevant documents that might be in his or her possession.

Another situation that can put witness interviews on a fast track is where prompt disclosure to the government can result in amnesty (e.g., criminal antitrust matters) or significant leniency. In these situations, companies generally need to self-report the conduct before the government learns of it through co-conspirators, competitors, whistleblowers, or other means. If the company is too slow, then the benefits of the disclosure can be completely lost. Often this means that counsel will need to conduct an initial round of interviews quickly to get a rough idea of the facts and to determine whether self-reporting is necessary or worthwhile before the information comes to light through other means. After the initial disclosure is made, the pressure is usually relaxed and the government provides time to conduct a full-scale investigation.

B. *Key Principles*

Organizing a set of witness interviews requires careful thought and planning. It is all too easy to imagine situations in which a lawyer's conduct during the witness interview phase of an investigation could be second-guessed by the client or scrutinized by plaintiffs' lawyers or even by governmental authorities. For this reason, investigating lawyers and everyone on the investigating team should adopt a disciplined approach that is applied consistently throughout the investigation. There are several key principles that can guide the planning at this stage.

First, make a written plan setting forth the order and sequence of witness interviews. This information should be included in the overall work plan for the investigation, and going through the exercise will give the investigating lawyers an opportunity to consider the factors affecting that decision: What individuals should be interviewed? Where are they located? How accessible is each one? In what sequence should they be interviewed for a logical unfolding of the facts? How quickly must they be interviewed? When will the team be collecting their documents? The interview plan will almost certainly change as the investigation proceeds—by definition, a lawyer will not have all the relevant facts at the beginning of an investigation and thus will not necessarily know which individuals will ultimately prove to be the most significant witnesses. The investigating team will need to stay flexible to account for the fact that documents and witness interviews will suggest the need for additional interviews, or that some planned interviews may turn out to be less important than previously believed. From the outset, though, the investigating lawyer should have a preliminary idea about the sequence in which the interviews will unfold.

Second, if time allows, postpone witness interviews until after the document collection and review are complete. Familiarity with the relevant documents can assist an interviewing lawyer in many ways. It provides a road map that helps lay out the sequence of events in advance, which results in more effective and productive questioning. Documents can provide structure and organization to an interview; they can be used to refresh a witness's recollection and help determine whether a witness is being truthful. It is also useful to question witnesses about certain documents and have them explain statements or apparent ambiguities in the documents. Another reason for reviewing documents prior to an interview is that a lawyer may only have one opportunity to question a particular witness, and the lawyer should make the most of that opportunity by being as prepared as possible.

Investigating lawyers do not always have the luxury of conducting a leisurely document review prior to interviewing witnesses, however. The need to decide about self-reporting or to comply with subpoena return dates can create time pressures that truncate the time available for preparation. In major investigations where the document-collection effort will be large and cumbersome, it may not be possible for the team to mobilize quickly enough to complete the process before proceeding to witness interviews. Also, it is often impossible to complete the document-collection process without talking to individual employees first, at least to discuss the existence and location of any relevant documents. In situations where it is not possible to complete the document review prior to witness interviews, the lawyer should proceed with the interviews anyway, and then conduct follow-up interviews as necessary after the document review is complete.

Third, the investigating team should interview witnesses before the government or an adverse party is able to do so. When a witness's recollection is refreshed after being interviewed, it is often difficult to correct the record or an erroneous statement with maximum credibility. Witnesses are understandably reluctant to change their testimony even if they become aware of additional facts later that reveal an error in a prior statement. This is especially true if the first interview was with the government. Contacting individual employees before they are approached by the other side also gives the company's counsel an opportunity to alert the individuals to the possibility of contact and to inform the employee of their right to decide whether to submit to an interview or to have counsel present.

Fourth, again if time permits, interview lower-level employees first and then work up to higher-level employees, or begin with interviews that will help provide general background—to help identify key witnesses or documents, frame the issues, and provide overall context. This sequence often leads to the most logical development of facts and the most productive use of interview time. It allows the investigating lawyer to understand the business, the corporate structure, and the significant background events prior to interviewing the individuals who may have been responsible for or who were closest to the conduct that is the subject of the investigation. Such a sequence will not always be possible. External time pressures or simple difficulties of scheduling may require the investigating lawyer to go directly to the employees thought to know the most about the potential conduct. It could also be the case that the investigators will want to interview those crucial employees early if there is a danger that, once the investigation becomes more generally known throughout the company, they may later refuse to be interviewed.

Fifth, witnesses with knowledge of the same aspect of a transaction or subject of inquiry should be interviewed by the same person or persons. While a memorandum can summarize the witness's statements and the facts gathered in an interview, they rarely communicate all the facts, and they are inadequate to convey important information about a witness's affect, demeanor, personality, and credibility, which can be significant factors in the ultimate conclusions drawn in an investigation. Participating in the entire interview process allows the lawyers conducting the interviews to develop a knowledge base that is better than what can be gleaned from interview memos—which means that using the same interviewers for the same subjects will ordinarily result in the most efficient and effective questioning.

Sixth, and finally, witness interviews should always be seen as opportunities to obtain genuine information, not merely as a way of "going through the motions." No one's interests will be served by interviews that are cursory or superficial or that allow witnesses too much leeway, and such interviews could ultimately harm the company if the government ever has occasion to make a charging decision. Under the principles of the Thompson Memo, the DOJ takes into account whether the company appears to be protecting its officers and employees, and whether the company has made a full disclosure of information to the government.[1] Witness interviews that in hindsight appear to have been less than probing could ultimately hamper the company's ability to affect the government's charging decisions in a positive direction.

C. *Before the Interview*

There are certain substantive steps the investigating lawyer needs to take to prepare for witness interviews.

Legal research. It is essential for the interviewing lawyer to understand the legal questions at issue in advance of the interview. Otherwise, the interviews themselves are likely to lose focus or to focus on only one side of an issue, finding fault without assessing defenses or documenting defenses with-

---

1. Principles of Federal Prosecution of Business Organizations, Office of the Deputy Attorney General, U.S. Department of Justice (January 20, 2003), at VI ("Charging a Corporation: Cooperation and Voluntary Disclosure").

out adequately assessing vulnerabilities. The more the interviewer knows at the outset about what the possible vulnerabilities and legal defenses are, the more useful the interviews will be.

Document review. The importance of documents in witness interviews has already been addressed, but it is worth emphasizing again. Lawyers preparing for interviews should assemble the set of documents to be used in each interview, review those documents in advance, and have a plan for how the documents are to be used in each interview. The documents should be organized and easily accessible during the interviews.

Outlining the interview. A written outline is useful in structuring the interview and making sure that key points are covered. A lawyer may want to prepare the same sort of outline for a witness interview as for a civil discovery deposition. A checklist of key topics is generally better than a list of detailed questions or a script. Such rigid lists of questions can cause an interviewer to focus more on the next question than on the witness's answers. Lists of key topics, by contrast, encourage the interviewer to listen to witnesses' answers and formulate follow-up questions that are appropriate to the situation.

Informing employees. It is often a good idea for a company to notify employees in advance that they may be asked to submit to a witness interview. Such notification can either be oral or in writing. Either way, the notification should state that the company's outside counsel may wish to interview them and that the company requests the employee's cooperation if the lawyer contacts them directly. The notification should also inform the prospective witnesses that the lawyers need information from the witness in order to provide legal advice based upon an accurate understanding of the facts. Any communication should state clearly that the outside lawyers represent the company and not the individual employee. The notification to employees can also be used to remind employees not to discard or destroy any relevant documents, and that all normal document-retention policies are suspended. From a practical standpoint, the notification should come from the general counsel or some other representative of company management with authority to request the employee's cooperation.

Whether the communication is written or oral, it must avoid any suggestion that the company is seeking to influence the testimony or recollections of potential witnesses. Good practice dictates that any written notification to employees be maintained in the investigative file, and any oral notification be done according to a standardized script that is likewise kept in the file. Investigating lawyers must always keep in mind that the conduct of the witness interviews might come under scrutiny at some later time, and they need to protect against the possibility that, in hindsight, any communications with witnesses might appear obstructive, misleading, or otherwise improper.

If a government investigation is under way, the company should notify employees that government investigators may seek to interview them. Again, counsel needs to tread very carefully here and maintain accurate records of such employee notifications. The company may advise employees that their cooperation with government investigators is voluntary, that they have the right to decide whether or not to agree to a government interview request, and that they have a right to have counsel present or seek legal advice before deciding. The company may recommend that the employee speak to company counsel prior to any government interview, but the company should make it clear that such consultation is not required. The company should *never* instruct its employees *not* to be interviewed by the government, and it should remind employees that if they do agree to a government interview, their responses should be completely truthful. The company may request that employees alert the company to any contacts by the government related to the investigation, even if the employee does not intend to seek assistance from the company's counsel. If the company intends to advance attorney fees to employees for the purpose of government interviews, the notification can inform the employees of that fact and instruct them whom to contact in the company for more information or assistance.

III. CONDUCTING THE INTERVIEW

A. *Mechanics*

Witness interviews should generally be conducted by two lawyers: one who leads the questioning and the other who is responsible for taking notes and drafting a memorandum of the interview. (In order to avoid any inconsistencies, the best practice is for only one of the lawyers to draft a memorandum.) Another benefit of having a second lawyer present is for that person to serve as a witness in the event the interviewee ever attempts to back away from any testimony given during the interview. Both lawyers should be familiar with the documents and with other interviews in the case.

Some commentators have suggested using a court reporter to make a verbatim transcript of witness interviews, but it is not common practice to do so. While there may be benefits in making a transcript—such a record is likely to reflect the witness's statements more accurately than a memo would, and it will be harder for a witness to back away from any statements made on the transcript—there are severe downsides as well. Foremost among these are the fact that a transcript would not be entitled to any work product protection and it would likely be subject to production as a "Reverse Jencks" statement of the witness if the investigation proceeded to trial.[2]

Interviews should be conducted in quiet, comfortable surroundings, usually apart from the employee's own office, work space, or home in order to eliminate the distractions of ringing telephones, e-mail messages, and other interruptions. The interview should occur in a setting that both puts the witness at ease and encourages complete attention on the questions of counsel. All relevant documents should be easily accessible. A conference room at the employee's place of business can be ideal, but other locations can work as well.

Throughout the interview process and the investigation itself, the lawyers need to take steps to maintain all applicable privileges. In the area of witness interviews, all personnel engaged in the interview process—whether corporate employees, outside auditors, law firm staff, or third-party vendors—should take their instructions from and report only to counsel responsible for the inquiry. Where responsibility for an inquiry is assigned to a nonlawyer, that person must operate under counsel's direction and report to counsel.[3]

B. Warnings to Witnesses and the Attorney-Client Privilege

At the start of any interview, the lawyer needs to advise the employee-witness of the ground rules that will govern the interview and to make clear where the attorney-client relationships lie and how the privilege applies. This warning should include several main points.

First, the lawyer should explain to the witness that the lawyer represents the company, not the individual employee. If the employee ever becomes the subject of a government enforcement action that proceeds to trial, he or she may seek to suppress any statements made to counsel in the interview on the basis of a putative attorney-client privilege. This can result in problems not only for the witness, but also for the lawyer if the employee seeks to disqualify him or her from representing the company. This warning about individual representation is a necessary step in rebutting claims by an employee that an attorney-client relationship existed between the employee and the company's lawyer.

---

2. *See* FED. R. CRIM. P. 26.2.

3. *See In re* John Doe Corp., 675 F.2d 482 (2d Cir. 1982) (investigation by accounting firm as part of its audit not privileged); *In re* Grand Jury Subpoena, 599 F.2d 504, 510 (2d Cir. 1979) (investigation conducted by management not privileged).

Second, the lawyer should explain that the purpose of the interview is to obtain facts necessary to provide legal advice to the company in anticipation of litigation. This is particularly important for informal internal reviews, especially those conducted by in-house counsel or by nonlawyers. Such investigations may be held to be unprotected by the work-product doctrine because they are not carried out in anticipation of litigation.[4] This warning helps to lay the predicate for the application of the company's attorney-client privilege.

Third, the employee should be told that the interview is subject to the attorney-client privilege but that the privilege belongs to the company and the company has the sole discretion to waive the privilege without first consulting the employee or obtaining the employee's consent. If the company is already cooperating with the government or intends to self-report, the lawyer should also inform the witness that the company will likely instruct the lawyer to waive the privilege with respect to the interview and to produce a copy of the interview memo to the government. This warning is simply a matter of full disclosure for an unrepresented witness: making sure the employee understands that whatever occurs in the interview may be turned over to the government. It can rebut a later claim by a witness that he or she was misled by counsel.

Fourth, the employee should be cautioned not to talk to anyone, including coworkers or supervisors, about the substance of the interview. There are three reasons for this warning: (1) it protects the privileged nature of the interview; (2) it protects the company by maintaining the integrity of each individual's knowledge and rebutting any suggestion of collusion; and (3) it protects the employee from any later suggestion of collusion. In the same vein, the lawyer should not provide the witness with information about others in the company who have been interviewed or will be interviewed or what those other witnesses have said.

At the end of the warnings, the lawyer should ask the witness if he or she understands and whether the witness has any questions or would like to discuss the issues further. The lawyer should obtain the employee's verbal indication that he or she understands the warnings, and the note-taker should make sure the memorandum reflects both the warnings and the employee's affirmative understanding of them. Some companies even require that written admonitions be provided to and acknowledged in writing by the witness.

---

4. *In re* Grand Jury Subpoena, 599 F.2d at 510; Shulton, Inc. v. Optel Corp., No. 85-2925, 1987 U.S. Dist. LEXIS 10097 (D.N.J. Nov. 4, 1987).

The following is an example of introductory remarks designed to advise employees of the interviewer's representation of the company and of the company's attorney-client privilege.

> As you know, the company has asked you to meet with us as part of our inquiry into [the matter].
>
> We are lawyers with the firm of [ ] and we represent the company. We do not represent you or any other employee personally. The purpose of our meeting is to gather the factual information that we need, as counsel, to develop the legal advice that the company has sought and to prepare for possible litigation involving this matter.
>
> This interview is subject to the attorney-client privilege, which means that no one can force you or me to disclose in court what we say to each other today. You should understand, though, that the privilege belongs to the company, not to you personally, and the company may decide to waive the privilege at some point in the future. You cannot waive the attorney-client privilege as applied to this interview. If the company decides to waive its attorney-client privilege, it can do so without getting your consent and without even consulting with you. [You should also understand that the company is cooperating with the government's investigation, and the company has been instructing us to produce memorandums of witness interviews to the government. There is every reason to believe that the company will instruct us to produce the memorandum of this interview to the government as well.]
>
> To allow the company to maintain the privileged nature of the information we gather, it is important that you not discuss the substance of this interview with anyone. It will also protect you in the event the government ever decides to interview you in connection with this matter.
>
> Do you have any questions about any of this before we begin? If you have questions about it at any time during the interview, please let me know and we can discuss your concerns.

In order to secure the work product protection, it is wise to describe the matter broadly enough to encompass a range of consequences—for example, government investigation, parallel civil litigation, suit by a competitor, etc.—so the interview notes will be protected in a wide range of resulting litigation. It may also be useful to confirm these warnings at the end of the interview.

There will always be some tension between the lawyer's desire to encourage complete openness on the part of witnesses and the obligation to warn witnesses about the ground rules of the interview and the possible consequences of cooperation—which could easily chill the employee's willingness to speak freely with company counsel. Despite these conflicting goals, there is general agreement that the warnings must be given to employees at the outset of the interviews. There is some debate, however, about whether the interviewer is obligated to go one step further and either warn the witness that his statements may be used against him or advise the witness to retain separate counsel. One former U.S. district judge, Judge Frederick B. Lacey, has recommended that witnesses be given full "Adnarim" warnings prior to being interviewed ("Adnarim" is "Miranda" spelled backwards). According to Judge Lacey, employees should be told that they have a right to their own lawyers and that they may decide not to talk to the company's counsel.

We do not believe that existing case law requires these additional warnings. Indeed, advising employees that they need not speak with company counsel may conflict with the employees' duty to cooperate, implicit in the employee's duty of loyalty found in some case law.[5] Although there surely are occasions where employees should be advised to retain counsel, company counsel should not assume this additional responsibility in every instance, particularly in advance of interviewing the employee to ascertain what he or she knows and whether retention of separate counsel is either required or advisable.[6] The best course is for counsel to assess the employee's situation following an initial interview, which will provide the factual basis for an opinion.

A related ethical issue that frequently arises in internal investigations relates to the representation by counsel that the witness's statement is protected by the corporation's attorney-client privilege. Model Rule of Professional Conduct 4.1(a) prohibits counsel from knowingly making a false statement of material fact. If the company has a statutory or other obligation to

---

5. *See, e.g.,* Goth v. Loft, Inc., 5 A.2d 503 (Del. Ch. 1939).

6. A constitutional obligation to warn that statements can be used against the employee would arise only if the employer's investigation could be construed as government action.

With respect to the question of separate counsel, the Model Rules of Professional Conduct, which have now been adopted in some form in most jurisdictions, discuss the corporate lawyer's obligation when handling a corporate employee. Model Rule of Professional Conduct 1.13(f) provides:

> In dealing with an organization's directors, officers, employees, members, shareholders or other constituents, a lawyer shall explain the identity of the client when the lawyer knows or reasonably should know that the organization's interests are adverse to those of the constituents with whom the lawyer is dealing.

The annotations to that rule note that a "failure to clarify the nature of [the lawyer's] role in representing the organization may lead a constituent dealing with the lawyer to conclude that the lawyer jointly represents the constituent as well as the organization." AMERICAN BAR ASSOCIATION, ANNOTATED MODEL RULES OF PROF'L CONDUCT at 210 (3d ed. 1996). The Model Rules go on to state that, "When the lawyer knows or reasonably should know that the unrepresented person misunderstands the lawyer's role in the matter, the lawyer shall make reasonable efforts to correct the misunderstanding." Model Rule 4.3 ("Dealing with Unrepresented Person"). For this reason, a lawyer must be sensitive to the circumstances in which an employee could believe that the lawyer represents the employee personally and attempt to correct any misunderstandings.

disclose to the government the substance of the interview—for example, where there is a commitment to make a voluntary disclosure of the witness's statement or where there are allegations falling within the Anti-Kickback Act or the various mandatory reporting requirements found in the federal environmental laws—the employee should be informed of these obligations or the likelihood that the privilege will be waived. Otherwise, the witness might be left with the erroneous impression that the company intends to protect the interview by asserting the company's attorney-client privilege.

C. *Conducting the Interview*

The lawyer's primary goal in conducting a witness interview should be to obtain all of the witness's relevant knowledge regarding any subject relating to the investigation, in the most logical way, so that the lawyer understands what the witness knows and what the witness will say if questioned by a third party. There are as many interviewing techniques and styles as there are interviewers, and many different types of witness demeanors and attitudes that a lawyer will have to deal with, but there are certain fundamental kinds of information that the lawyer must elicit. The interviewer should first gain an understanding of each witness's background and where he or she stands in the company—education and job history, current and former job titles and duties, and reporting responsibilities. This information will help in understanding the context of the witness's relationship to the company and co-workers, and it will ultimately help the lawyer in assessing the employee's role in the subject matter of the investigation.

The interviewer should also ask all of the who, what, where, when, why, and how questions regarding the subjects of the investigation. During this part of the questioning, the lawyer should act as a facilitator for the witness in getting his or her own story out. The questions should be designed both to encourage the witness to tell that story and to recall details: Was anyone else at the meeting? How many times did you meet? Did you take notes? What happened next? Most interviews are structured with these sorts of open-ended, nondirective questions coming first. There are many advantages to doing so. Such questions are noncontentious, which helps the interviewer develop some rapport and put the witness at ease. They help the witness explain his recollection of the events in an unfettered manner and allow the lawyer to draw that story out in a logical sequence. The nondirective questioning can be followed by more pointed or challenging review of details, with or without documents. Such open-ended questioning can also be effective when used in conjunction with appropriate leading questions whose purpose is to make sure the questioner has an accurate understanding of the witness's answers. At all points along the way, it will be important for the interviewer to elicit the basis for the witness's statements—i.e., how the witness came to know what he or she is talking about: is it first-hand knowledge, second-hand hearsay, rumors heard at the water cooler, or after-the-fact reconstruction of what "must" have happened?

Throughout the process, the interviewer should treat the witness with respect, regardless of the conduct at issue or the attitude of the witness. The goals of the interview will not be furthered by arguing with a witness, discussing the matters under investigation, or instructing the witness how he or she should have handled the situation at issue in the investigation. The lawyer is there first and foremost to obtain information, not to argue a case.

Effective interviewing, like effective cross-examination, requires the pursuit of two occasionally inconsistent goals: ensuring that the witness has answered the questions asked, and following up on leads provided by the witness's responses to questions. Rigid pursuit of the first goal can cause the interviewer to miss key pieces of information mentioned by the witness but not directly responsive to the question. Failure to pursue the second goal will undermine a comprehensive understanding of the critical facts. The interviewer must listen to the answers and pursue leads offered by the witness, but always ensure that the witness has responded to the immediate question.

IV. MAKING A RECORD OF THE INTERVIEW

In most instances, the lawyer will want to create a record of each witness interview. A written record helps the lawyer share information within the investigative team and with the client, and it assists in drawing ultimate conclusions at the end of an investigation.[7] Typically the record takes the form of a memorandum drafted by the second lawyer present at the interview. Lawyers must pay particular attention to best practices in creating interview memorandums. There should be no after-the-fact shaping or recasting of a witness's responses. It is all too easy for those memos and the circumstances of their creation to be second-guessed by opposing parties or government authorities—with all the distorting effects that hindsight can provide—and the motives of the lawyers preparing the memo should never be allowed to become an issue, even if those motives are innocent.

---

7. There are circumstances where counsel might recommend *not* creating written records of witness interviews, such as when the danger of disclosure to the government or an opposing party in litigation is great and the client prefers not to provide a road map for the other side.

Creating good interview memorandums often involves two occasionally conflicting goals: the record needs to reflect the witness's recollections as accurately as possible while preserving the application of the work product doctrine to the memo. If the memorandum contains a verbatim transcript of the witness's statements, then the memo will be more difficult to protect because such material will not contain the mental impressions of counsel.

It is relatively easy to establish work product protection for witness interview memorandums. The work product of counsel produced in anticipation of litigation is protected from forced disclosure during discovery.[8] It is important to state on the face of any memorandum that litigation is anticipated. This is made more difficult—though not impossible—when the investigation is handled in-house because in-house counsel have business responsibilities in addition to legal ones, and the dividing line is not always clear.[9] The written record should establish the potential for litigation and, particularly, that all nonlawyer work in the investigation is performed at the direction of counsel in contemplation of litigation.[10] Work product protection has been denied where the anticipated litigation has been found to be too remote.[11]

Work product protection will protect interview notes.[12] Because courts give the greatest protection to work product reflecting the impressions, analysis, and opinions of counsel, the interview memorandum should contain those things to the extent possible.[13] Interview memorandums should also include a statement that they reflect the thoughts, impressions, and opinions of counsel.

---

8. *See* FED. R. CIV. P. 26.

9. *See In re* Sealed Case (Tesoro Petroleum), 676 F.2d 793 (D.C. Cir. 1982); *In re* John Doe Corp. (Southland), 675 F.2d 482 (2d Cir. 1982).

10. *Compare* Southern Bell Tel. & Tel. Co. v. Deason, 632 So. 2d 1377, 1384-85 (Fla. 1994) (internal audits conducted by company employees at the request of counsel are work product) *with* United States v. Rosenthal, 142 F.R.D. 389, 392 (S.D.N.Y. 1992) (accounting firm's report not protected work product where engagement letter ambiguous as to whether work was related to the seeking of legal advice).

11. *See* Diversified Indus., Inc. v. Meredith, 572 F.2d 596, 604 (8th Cir. 1977).

12. *In re* Grand Jury Subpoena, 478 F. Supp. 368, 374 (E.D. Wis. 1979), *In re* Woolworth Corp. Sec. Litig., No. 94 Civ. 2217, 1996 U.S. Dist. LEXIS 7773 at *10 (S.D.N.Y. 1996).

13. *See* Upjohn Co. v. United States, 449 U.S. 383, 400 (1981) (noting that FED. R. CIV. P. 26 accords "special protection" to work product revealing the attorney's mental processes); Hickman v. Taylor, 329 U.S. 495, 511-13 (1947); *In re* Sealed Case (Foster), 124 F.3d 230, 236-37 (D.C. Cir. 1997) (recognizing principle that portions of interview memorandum that are "purely factual" afforded less protection under the work-product doctrine than those reflecting counsel's mental impressions), *overruled on other grounds by* Swidler & Berlin v. United States, 524 U.S. 399 (1998); *In re* Martin Marietta Corp. (United States v. Pollard), 856 F.2d 619 (4th Cir. 1988), *cert. denied*, 490 U.S. 1011 (1989) (finding waiver of work product protection in attorneys' notes other than those reflecting pure opinion).

For the greatest protection, statements of fact should always be interspersed with statements of counsel's mental impressions and strategies. If there is a possibility, however, that the client will voluntarily share interview memos with the government or otherwise waive the privilege, counsel may want to *avoid* including mental impressions and opinions in the interview memorandums in an attempt to limit the scope of the waiver to factual material.

Again, tape recordings and verbatim transcripts are not ordinarily a part of witness interviews, unless the witness is potentially adverse, and then these recording methods should only be used with caution. Verbatim records may not qualify as work product, and under the "Reverse Jencks" rule applicable to criminal cases, the government may later be able to obtain their discovery.[14] This rule arguably extends to counsel's notes of witness interviews if they are "substantially verbatim" statements. Under this rule, if a witness other than the defendant is called by the defense, all prior statements—including a statement "adopted" or signed by the witness, or a "substantially verbatim recital" contemporaneously transcribed—must be made available to the government. This also creates a risk for witnesses who are allowed to review the memorandums of their interviews: if they approve or sign the memo, then a court may later determine that the witness "adopted" the memo as a statement for purposes of Reverse Jencks.

Unless the witness is someone who may not later be available or who may be adverse, the benefits of a verbatim statement are usually outweighed by the vulnerability to discovery of these statements. When there is a witness whose testimony must be "locked in," however, a written statement or transcript may be appropriate. A great deal of thought and preparation must go into this document because it may take on a life of its own,[15] and because the circumstances of its creation frequently become an issue.

The interview memo should always reflect the warnings to the witness that provide the underpinning for the attorney-client privilege. Specifically, the memorandum should reflect that the witness was told the company has sought legal advice and the witness's testimony is necessary for counsel to have a factual basis upon which to render advice.[16] The memorandum should

---

14. Fed. R. Crim. P. 26.2; *see* United States v. Nobles, 422 U.S. 225, 230-32 (1975).

15. Such a document or recording can be especially problematic if the witness's testimony changes later after recollection has been refreshed by facts developed after the original verbatim statement was given.

16. *See* Independent Petrochem. Corp. v. Aetna Cas. & Surety Co., 654 F. Supp. 1334, 1364-65, *reconsideration denied,* 672 F. Supp. 1 (D.D.C. 1986).

further reflect the other warnings to witnesses regarding attorney-client privilege, representation of the company, and the need for maintaining confidentiality; the memo should also state that the witness understood these issues, had no questions, and agreed to the terms.

Interview memos should contain some variation of the following legend at the top or bottom of each page: "Privileged and confidential, Attorney-client communication, Attorney work product, Contains mental impressions of counsel/Prepared in anticipation of litigation." If the interview is conducted by in-house counsel, the memo should state that the inquiry is pursuant to the lawyer's legal responsibilities, rather than business responsibilities, and it should lay a factual predicate for the statement.[17] To minimize the danger of waiver regarding witness interviews, interview memorandums should not be distributed to anyone outside the core group to whom the lawyer is reporting. The disclosure of specific facts memorialized in those memorandums should similarly be limited.[18]

From a practical standpoint, the lead lawyer conducting an investigation should prescribe the interviewing and record-keeping practices that will be followed consistently by each member of the team. Counsel cannot afford to have questions raised about the circumstances surrounding the creation of an interview memo. Memos should be as straightforward as possible. Counsel should not selectively omit statements made by the witness, and only individuals present for a particular witness interview should review the draft memo for accuracy and completeness. Counsel must protect against any second-guessing later on.

V. SPECIAL ISSUES

A. *Sarbanes-Oxley and the Responsibilities of Counsel*

The Sarbanes-Oxley Act of 2002 and the SEC's regulations implementing it impose new requirements on counsel conducting internal investigations for public companies, and lawyers conducting witness interviews must be particularly sensitive to these requirements.[19] While this chapter is not the place for a comprehensive explanation of the Sarbanes-Oxley regime, it is important to

---

17. Spectrum Sys. Int'l Corp. v. Chemical Bank, 157 A.D.2d 444, 558 N.Y.S.2d 486 (1990). *Accord, In re* Grand Jury Subpoena, 599 F.2d 504, 510-11 (2d Cir. 1979).

18. *See In re* Sealed Case, 676 F.2d at 823.

19. 15 U.S.C. § 7201 *et seq.*

understand how certain provisions of Sarbanes-Oxley and SEC Rule 205 affect witness interviews and counsel's response to what may be discovered in those interviews.

The new rules impose an obligation on counsel practicing before the Commission to report to a company's chief legal officer, chief executive officer, or board if he or she becomes aware of "evidence of a material violation" of federal or state securities laws or fiduciary duties or "similar material violations" by an issuer client or by any of its officers, directors or employees.[20] With respect to witness interviews, one significant issue that counsel needs to understand is: What types of information can trigger the duty to report?

The duty to report is triggered by "evidence of a material violation," which is defined as "credible evidence, based upon which it would be unreasonable, under the circumstances, for a prudent and competent attorney not to conclude that it is reasonably likely that a material violation has occurred, is ongoing, or is about to occur."[21] A "material violation" means the violation of any federal or state securities law, any fiduciary duty arising under federal or state law, or any similar federal or state law.[22] The SEC rule creates an objective standard by which the evidence is to be evaluated; the lawyer does not need to "know" that a material violation has occurred or be in a position to "conclude" that such a violation has occurred. There is still room for the lawyer to exercise judgment, however, on such questions as whether the evidence is credible and whether the client's response was appropriate. These are the judgment calls that the interviewing lawyer must be prepared to make.

Lawyers must be alert to the fact that, in the course of an interview, information subject to the Sarbanes-Oxley reporting requirement could be discovered that relates to other possible violations of law, separate from the subject of the investigation itself. The interviewer needs to remain flexible enough in the questioning—and alert enough in the listening—to follow the witness's testimony wherever it leads and to evaluate *everything* a witness says, even if it does not appear to relate directly to the subject of the investigation.

B. *Obstruction of Justice*

Dangers for Counsel. In the current enforcement climate, when the government is more inclined than ever before to take a hard look at the conduct

---

20. 17 C.F.R. §§ 205.3(b)(1), 205.2(i).
21. 17 C.F.R. § 205.2(e).
22. 17 C.F.R. § 205.2(i).

of outside counsel in internal investigations, lawyers conducting witness interviews must be extremely sensitive to practices that in hindsight could seem obstructive to a government investigator. One of the touchstones here will be whether the lawyer's methods of conducting the interviews affected the substance or shape of the witness's testimony. An unscrupulous lawyer has many ways of creating such a result, but an unwitting lawyer can stumble into this trap as well. Lawyers need to take care to avoid any false or misleading conduct, and they must also be alert to how different methods of questioning can suggest answers to witnesses and improperly shape testimony. The lawyer needs to be able to facilitate and encourage the witness to tell his or her story, but not to affect the substance or flavor of that story in any way.

There are four federal statutes relating to obstruction; the one with the most significance to witness interviews is 18 U.S.C. § 1512, which prohibits engaging in "misleading conduct" with intent to influence the testimony of a person in an official proceeding.[23] The statute contains no requirement of corrupt intent. While Section 1512 provides for an affirmative defense when the defendant's actions "consisted solely of lawful conduct" and the "sole intent was to cause truthful testimony" to be given, that defense must be supported by a preponderance of the evidence.

There are numerous ways in which even a lawyer acting with good intentions can fall afoul of this statute. For example, in interviewing a witness prior to the witness's grand jury appearance, a lawyer may attempt to test the witness's memory or to refresh the witness's recollection with documents or other facts. The lawyer's suggestion to the witness of an alternative, non-incriminating interpretation of a transaction or document could subject the lawyer to liability because "misleading conduct" is broadly defined to include concealing a material fact or making a false statement.[24] The burden would then be on the lawyer to establish the affirmative defense of a lack of corrupt intent. Thus, in conducting witness interviews, the lawyer can seek to refresh the witness's recollection or ask about various interpretations (though the lawyer should be careful here not to omit other more incriminating accounts

---

23. The other three statutes are 18 U.S.C. §§ 1503 (Influencing or injuring officer or juror generally), 1505 (Obstruction of proceedings before departments, agencies, and committees), and 1519 (Destruction, alteration, or falsification of records).

24. *See* United States v. Gabriel, 125 F.3d 89, 102 (2d Cir. 1997) (defendant violated § 1512 by attempting to mislead a prospective grand jury witness by providing him with the defendant's recollection of key events).

of the same transaction) but a lawyer should avoid conduct that has the appearance of suggesting facts or other testimony to the witness.

Dangers for Witnesses: The "Computer Associates" Problem. A recent high-profile prosecution suggests that individual employees face new risks in submitting to witness interviews when their company is cooperating with the government. In an accounting practices investigation of Computer Associates International, the company's chief executive officer and its head of worldwide sales were charged with obstruction of justice under Section 1512(c)(2) based in part on misleading statements made in witness interviews.[25] The two pleaded guilty to the charges in 2006. The significant aspect of this prosecution is that the Department of Justice now appears willing to prosecute witnesses for misleading statements made not to government investigators but to *outside counsel* in internal investigations.

A similar charge under Section 1512(c)(2) was recently brought against a Texas-based energy trader in *United States v. Singleton*.[26] The obstruction charge there was based solely on a witness interview conducted by the company's outside counsel in which the defendant allegedly "did not disclose, falsely denied, and otherwise concealed" material facts relevant to ongoing government investigations while believing that the company's outside lawyers would inform government agencies of his statements during the interviews.[27]

Although the court in *Singleton* granted a motion for judgment of acquittal on the obstruction count at trial, that case and *Kumar* raise the stakes significantly for individuals who agree to be interviewed by outside counsel. The cases also raise the stakes for counsel as well, by creating another way in which the conduct of witness interviews may ultimately come under scrutiny by courts or the government. For this reason, counsel must take extra care to conduct witness interviews in a professional manner using the best practices possible.

C. *Other Typical Problems That Arise during Witness Interviews*

A number of situations may arise during the interview that require the interviewer to proceed with caution.

---

25. *See* United States v. Kumar *et al.*, Cr. No. 04-846 (E.D.N.Y. Filed May 17, 2005), Superseding Indictment (Counts Six and Seven); *see also id.* at ¶¶ 58-61.

26. *See* No. 4:06-cr-080 (S.D. Tex. Filed March 3, 2006); *see also* Timothy P. Harkness & Darren LaVerne, *Private Lies May Lead to Prosecution,* NAT'L L.J. S-1 (July 24, 2006).

27. Singleton, Indictment, Count Ten at ¶ A.14.

The Employee Who Asks for Legal Advice. Even when employees have been given the warnings discussed above, it is not uncommon for them to request legal advice or to otherwise suggest that they are looking to the interviewer as personal legal counsel. These situations must be dealt with quickly and clearly. The interviewer must repeat that he or she is representing the company and cannot provide the employee with any legal advice. The employee should be instructed to direct all such questions to the company's general counsel. The lawyer must not move on until the employee has a clear understanding of this issue. If the interview is memorialized, the memorandum should state that the interviewer repeated the warnings and that the employee understood them.

The Reluctant Employee. It is not uncommon for an employee to express a desire not to be interviewed. Even if the employee has a duty to cooperate with the internal investigation, an outside lawyer may certainly court trouble by appearing to bully the employee into agreeing to an interview.[28] In such situations, counsel should consult with the company on the need for the employee's cooperation and weigh that need against the potential exposure from forcing the employee to cooperate. If the interview is essential, the client may very well conclude that it is appropriate to commence disciplinary proceedings against the employee if he or she refuses to cooperate. In any event, such decisions are ultimately for the client to make.

The Employee Who Places Conditions on the Interview. An employee may also insist that an interview take place under certain conditions. These typically include (1) the participation of employee's counsel; (2) the interview is recorded or transcribed; (3) certain topics are avoided; or (4) the company will not disclose the content of the interview without the employee's consent.

This situation also requires counsel and management to weigh the need for the information possessed by the employee against the burdens imposed by the proposed conditions. In those situations where the employee's testimony is essential, counsel may very well recommend that the company agree to the conditions. If so, the understanding between the company and the

---

28. *See* Shepherd v. American Broadcasting Cos., Inc., 62 F.3d 1469, 1483-84 (D.C. Cir. 1995) (reversing district court finding that outside counsel had harassed company employee by attempting to interview her at the company's offices after she had refused to be interviewed); Department of Veterans Affairs Med. Ctr. v. Federal Labor Relations Auth., 16 F.3d 1526, 1534-36 (9th Cir. 1994) (hospital committed unfair labor practice under the Federal Service Labor-Management Relations Statute by failing to inform interviewee that she could refuse to be interviewed without fear of reprisal).

employee should be reduced to writing and signed by all parties. In those situations where counsel has in effect waived any claim of privilege that might otherwise have attached to the interview, counsel must proceed on the assumption that every question and document used during the interview will be made public by the interviewee and conduct the interview accordingly.

Interviewing Former Company Employees. In *Upjohn Co. v. United States*,[29] the Supreme Court declined to address whether the attorney-client privilege protects communications between corporate counsel and a former employee, but the logic of *Upjohn* suggests no meaningful distinction between current and former employees.[30] As with interviews of current employees, management should request the former employee's assistance, explaining that the purpose of the interview is to secure legal advice for the company and asking that the interview be kept confidential. The former employee should also be told that the interviewer represents the company, not the former employee personally. Every effort should be made to ensure that the interview memorandum is protected work product.

VI. CONCLUSION

Like many things in the practice of law, witness interviews are often more art than science, but all artists must begin with a grounding in the basics. For witness interviews, that means preparation. A lawyer cannot afford to go into witness interviews unprepared because, in today's enforcement climate, mistakes can have more significant consequences than ever. But with the right preparation, a lawyer can easily steer around the risks and make effective use of this powerful investigative tool.

---

29. 449 U.S. at 394 n.3.
30. *See In re* Coordinated Pretrial Proceedings in Petroleum Prods. Antitrust Litig., 658 F.2d 1355, 1361 (9th Cir. 1981), *cert. denied,* California v. Standard Oil Co., 455 U.S. 990 (1982); *but see In re* Grand Jury Subpoena Dated July 13, 1979, 478 F. Supp. 368, 374-75 (E.D. Wis. 1979).

Perjury and Obstruction of Justice

4

Gary P. Naftalis and David S. Frankel

I. INTRODUCTION   117
II. PERJURY AND SUBORNATION OF PERJURY   118
   A. Perjury Under § 1621: Essential Elements   119
   B. Burden of Proof and the Two Witness Rule   121
   C. True Answers and Ambiguous Questions   122
   D. Perjury Under § 1623: Differences   124
   E. Subornation of Perjury   126
III. OBSTRUCTION OF JUSTICE   130
   A. False Statements   131
   B. Witness Tampering   135
   C. Document Destruction   140

I. INTRODUCTION

LAWYERS CONDUCTING internal investigations must be aware of the federal criminal statutes that potentially apply to interviewing

---

Gary P. Naftalis and David S. Frankel are engaged in the defense of white collar criminal cases, SEC enforcement actions, and other administrative agency proceedings at Kramer Levin Naftalis & Frankel LLP in New York, New York. Darren LaVerne, an associate at KLNF, assisted in the preparation of this chapter.

and preparing witnesses. These statutes include those covering perjury and subornation of perjury, misprision of felony, and obstruction of justice. Although these statutes are most important when the internal investigation is in response to a government investigation, their terms and prohibitions should be examined in conducting any internal investigation.

In the pages that follow, we review the statutory elements and controlling judicial interpretations of each statute, and then suggest some of the principles that might guide counsel in the course of an internal company investigation. Of special concern are the obstruction of justice provisions enacted as part of Sarbanes-Oxley in 2002, in the wake of the Enron and Arthur Andersen prosecutions. While there are as yet few court decisions construing these provisions, it is likely that they will substantially enhance the government's ability to prosecute obstruction of justice crimes, including those predicated on false statements and document destruction. They will thus influence the advice counsel offers to a client under government scrutiny, and the manner in which counsel negotiates the difficult legal and ethical issues that can arise should it become necessary to conduct an internal investigation.

II. PERJURY AND SUBORNATION OF PERJURY

Perjury is covered by two sections of the criminal code, 18 U.S.C. §§ 1621 and 1623. Section 1621 is the older and more general perjury statute, proscribing willfully false testimony given under oath "in any case in which a law of the United States authorizes an oath to be administered." Section 1623 applies only to false declarations made in proceedings either "before or ancillary to any court or grand jury."[1] However, § 1623 contains provisions designed to relax the government's evidentiary burden by eliminating certain proof requirements applicable in § 1621 prosecutions.[2]

Section 1622 is the federal subornation of perjury statute, which makes it a crime to "procure[ ] another to commit any perjury."

---

1. The Supreme Court has construed the term "ancillary proceeding" to mean pretrial depositions in criminal cases as authorized by FED. R. CRIM. P. 15 and 18 U.S.C. § 3503. Dunn v. United States, 442 U.S. 100, 107-13 (1979).

2. *See, e.g.,* United States v. Bacani, 236 F.3d 857, 859 (7th Cir. 2001) (holding that § 1623 does not require determination of falsehood among irreconcilable statements).

A. Perjury Under § 1621: Essential Elements

In a prosecution for perjury under § 1621, the government must prove that the defendant knowingly and willfully made a material false statement.[3] In addition to perjurious assertions of fact, a witness' materially false avowal of not remembering may be punished as an act of perjury.[4]

The requirement that the false testimony be willfully, as well as knowingly, false is sometimes construed to mean that the defendant must have acted corruptly or with intent to deceive the tribunal.[5] More typically, the dual *mens rea* requirements are considered without any real differentiation.[6] The inquiry reduces to whether the defendant "subjectively knew that [the] statements were false."[7] Implicit in this analysis is the notion that false statements

---

3. *E.g.,* United States v. Markiewicz, 978 F.2d 786 (2d Cir. 1992); United States v. Lighte, 782 F.2d 367 (2d Cir. 1986); United States v. Makris, 483 F.2d 1082 (5th Cir. 1973), *cert. denied,* 415 U.S. 914 (1974); Vitello v. United States, 425 F.2d 416 (9th Cir.), *cert. denied,* 400 U.S. 822 (1970). Section 1621 provides in its entirety:

Whoever—

(1) having taken an oath before a competent tribunal, officer or person, in any case in which a law of the United States authorizes an oath to be administered, that he will testify, declare, depose, or certify truly, or that any written testimony, declaration, deposition, or certificate by him subscribed, is true, willfully and contrary to such oath states or subscribes any material matter which he does not believe to be true; or

(2) in any declaration, certificate, verification, or statement under penalty of perjury as permitted under section 1746 of title 28, United States Code, willfully subscribes as true any material matter which he does not believe to be true; is guilty of perjury and shall, except as otherwise expressly provided by law, be fined not more than $2,000 or imprisoned not more than five years, or both. This section is applicable whether the statement or subscription is made within or without the United States.

18 U.S.C. § 1621 (2000). Thus, as a threshold matter, the government must also prove either (1) that the false statement was made under a properly administered oath, or (2) that the false statement was made in a writing under penalty of perjury as permitted pursuant to 28 U.S.C. § 1746.

4. *In re* Battaglia, 653 F.2d 419 (9th Cir. 1981).

5. *See, e.g.,* United States v. DeZarn, 157 F.3d 1042 (6th Cir. 1998); United States v. Gougen, 723 F.2d 1012 (1st Cir. 1983); United States v. Laurelli, 187 F. Supp. 30 (M.D. Pa. 1960), *aff'd,* 293 F.2d 830 (3d Cir. 1961), *cert. denied,* 368 U.S. 961 (1962); United States v. Rose, 215 F.2d 617 (3d Cir. 1954).

6. *See, e.g.,* United States v. Sweig, 441 F.2d 114, 117 (2d Cir.), *cert. denied,* 403 U.S. 932 (1971) (rejecting contention, in prosecution under § 1621, that government had failed to prove "essential element of knowledge or willfulness").

7. *Id.*

made knowingly are, by definition, not the product of accident or negligence. In that sense, they are "willfully"—that is, purposely or intentionally—made.[8]

The element of "materiality" is broadly defined. In the case of perjury before the grand jury, it is sufficient under one frequently cited formulation that the false statement have the "natural effect or tendency ... to influence, impede or dissuade further investigation," and that the "further investigation" is itself material to the grand jury's task. That is, if a truthful answer had been given, it "would have been of sufficient probative importance to the inquiry so that, at a minimum, further fruitful investigation would have occurred."[9]

Other cases describe the materiality requirement in similar fashion. For example, in *United States v. Berardi*, the Second Circuit stated that materiality is established "if the question posed is such that a truthful answer could help the inquiry, or a false response hinder it, and these effects are weighed in terms of potentiality rather than probability."[10] In *United States v. Makris*,[11] the Fifth Circuit stated:

> The test of materiality is whether the false statement was capable of influencing the tribunal on the issue, or whether the false testimony would have the natural effect or tendency to influence, impede, or dissuade [the investigatory body] from pursuing its investigation.[12]

---

8. *See* United States v. Canova, 412 F.3d 331 (2d Cir. 2005) (citing United States v. Dunnigan, 507 U.S. 87 (1993)); *see also* United States v. Norris, 300 U.S. 564 (1937). In *Norris* the Court rejected the claim that recantation on the day following the false testimony, while the proceedings were still pending, constituted a defense to a perjury charge. The Court defined perjury as "the telling of a deliberate lie by a witness," as distinguished from "an innocent mistake." *Id.* at 576. The requisite *mens rea* was described by the Court as the "willful intent to swear falsely." A "corrupt" state of mind is an element of certain obstruction of justice statutes discussed *infra*.

9. United States v. Freedman, 445 F.2d 1220, 1226-27 (2d Cir. 1971).

10. 629 F.2d 723, 728 (2d Cir. 1980), *cert. denied,* 449 U.S. 995 (1980); *see also* United States v. Gribben, 984 F.2d 47, *rev'd on other grounds,* 515 U.S. 506 (1995).

11. 483 F.2d 1082 (5th Cir. 1973), *cert. denied,* 415 U.S. 914 (1974).

12. *Id.* at 1088 (citations omitted). *Accord* United States v. Regan, 103 F.3d 1072 (2d Cir. 1997); United States v. Wesson, 478 F.2d 1180, 1181 (7th Cir. 1973). Materiality does appear to be somewhat more difficult to establish outside the grand jury context. *See, e.g.,* United States v. Martinez, 837 F.2d 900 (9th Cir. 1988) (use of alias under which defendant had been living for seven years not material to hearing where only issue was financial eligibility for appointment of counsel); United States v. Qaisi, 779 F.2d 346 (6th Cir. 1985) (false statement regarding future viability of marriage immaterial in visa application hearing where validity of marriage at its inception had some bearing on outcome).

For the element of materiality to be satisfied, the allegedly perjurious statement need not relate to the central subject before the tribunal.[13] Nor must the false answer actually impede the investigation for it to be material.[14] In fact, a false answer to a grand jury that knows the witness is lying may still be material.[15]

B. *Burden of Proof and the Two Witness Rule*

Courts traditionally have recognized the potential unfairness in permitting a perjury conviction on the basis of a single witness' uncorroborated testimony.[16] This has led some courts to state that perjury must be made out by a quantum of proof greater than the reasonable doubt standard usually mandated in criminal cases.[17]

---

13. *See, e.g.,* United States v. Silveira, 426 F.3d 514 (1st Cir. 2005); United States v. Blanton, 281 F.3d 771 (8th Cir. 2002); United States v. Wesson, 478 F.2d 1180 (7th Cir. 1973).

14. Silveria, 426 F.3d 514; United States v. Lee, 359 F.3d 412 (6th Cir. 2004); United States v. Gordon, 844 F.2d 1397 (9th Cir. 1988); United States v. McComb, 744 F.2d 555 (7th Cir. 1984); United States v. Wesson, 478 F.2d 1180 (7th Cir. 1973).

15. United States v. Lee, 509 F.2d 645 (2d Cir.), *cert. denied,* 422 U.S. 1044 (1975). Until the Supreme Court's decision in United States v. Gaudin, 515 U.S. 506 (1995), courts had usually deemed materiality to be an issue for the court. In *Gaudin,* the Court ruled that the trial court's refusal to submit the question of materiality to the jury violated the Fifth and Sixth Amendments. It is thus now clear that the materiality element is for the jury.

Gaudin involved a conviction under the federal false statement statute, 18 U.S.C. § 1001. However, courts have generally found that the analysis is the same under the federal perjury statutes and § 1001 regarding the defendant's right to have the jury decide the issue of materiality. *See, e.g.,* United States v. Littleton, 76 F.3d 614, 617 (4th Cir. 1996) (in a § 1623 prosecution, the defendant is entitled to a jury determination on the issue of the materiality of the allegedly false statement, and the government must prove the element of materiality beyond a reasonable doubt); *see generally* J. Shifer, *Perjury,* 43 AM. CRIM. L. REV. 799, 812 (2006); *see also* Johnson v. United States, 520 U.S. 461 (1997) (requiring that the jury determine the materiality of an alleged false statement beyond a reasonable doubt).

16. *See* Weiler v. United States, 323 U.S. 606 (1945) (discussing the need "to protect honest witnesses from hasty and spiteful retaliation in the form of unfounded perjury prosecutions," and the possibility that "equally honest witnesses may well have differing recollections of the same event").

17. *See* LaRocca v. United States, 337 F.2d 39 (8th Cir. 1964) ("substantial evidence excluding every other hypothesis than that of guilt;" "clear, convincing and direct evidence to a moral certainty and beyond a reasonable doubt that the defendant committed willful and corrupt perjury"); United States v. Brandyberry, 438 F.2d 226 (9th Cir.), *cert. denied,* 404 U.S. 842 (1971) (same).

In practice, however, this stricter standard of proof has meant only that the government must prove the falsity of testimony in a perjury case under § 1621 either by the testimony of two witnesses or by the testimony of one witness plus independent corroborative evidence.[18] In LaRocca v. United States, for example, the court found no error in the use of a standard reasonable doubt jury charge, because other instructions were given to the effect that the jury could not convict unless it found independent evidence corroborating the testimony of the government's chief witness.[19] Similarly, in United States v. Makris, the court recited the supposed "moral certainty" burden of proof,[20] and then upheld perjury convictions because the proof was sufficient beyond a reasonable doubt.[21]

The corroborative evidence must be inconsistent with the innocence of the defendant, although it need not, standing alone, be sufficient to support a conviction.[22] Instead, "such evidence must tend to substantiate ... the testimony of the principal prosecution witness...."[23]

C. *True Answers and Ambiguous Questions*

In Bronston v. United States,[24] the Supreme Court held that the general perjury statute does not reach a literally true but nonresponsive answer, even

---

18. *E.g.,* Hammer v. United States, 271 U.S. 620 (1926); United States v. Collins, 272 F.2d 650 (2d Cir. 1959); United States v. Neff, 212 F.2d 297 (3d Cir. 1954); *see also* United States v. Chestman, 903 F.2d 75 (2d Cir. 1990), *vacated en banc on other grounds,* 947 F.2d 551 (2d Cir. 1991), *cert. denied,* 503 U.S. 1004 (1992) ("The two-witness rule 'does not literally require the direct testimony of two separate witnesses, but rather may be satisfied by the direct testimony of one witness and sufficient corroborative evidence.'" (quoting United States v. Diggs, 560 F.2d 266, 269 (7th Cir.), *cert. denied,* 434 U.S. 925 (1977))).
19. 337 F.2d at 43-44.
20. 483 F.2d at 1085.
21. *Id.* at 1087-88.
22. United States v. Stewart, 433 F.3d 273, 315 (2d Cir. 2006).
23. United States v. Weiner, 479 F.2d 923, 927-28 (2d Cir. 1973); *accord* United States v. Brandyberry, 438 F.2d 226 (9th Cir.), *cert. denied,* 404 U.S. 842 (1971) (numerous phone records and other documentary evidence tending to suggest defendant knew or had met with various persons, contrary to his denials in the grand jury); Arena v. United States, 226 F.2d 227, 236 (9th Cir. 1955), *cert. denied,* 350 U.S. 954 (1956) (corroborative evidence sufficient if it "tends to establish the defendant's guilt, and if such evidence together with the direct evidence is 'inconsistent with the innocence of the defendant'"); United States v. Neff, 212 F.2d at 307 (evidence that defendant was member of Communist Party and paid Party dues that were collected at her place of employment neither proves nor tends to prove that she ever attended a Party meeting).
24. 409 U.S. 352 (1973).

one that was arguably misleading by negative implication.[25] Bronston had testified as a witness at a bankruptcy hearing and had been asked first whether he had any bank accounts in Swiss banks, to which he answered, truthfully, "No, sir." He was then asked whether he had ever had any Swiss bank accounts. He answered that his "company had an account there for about six months, in Zurich."[26] Bronston did not disclose that he had had a personal Swiss bank account also, for a period of about five years, in the early 1960s.

The government claimed that the answer regarding the corporate account was perjurious because it was designed to mislead the questioner, especially in light of the immediately preceding question and answer, by implying that Bronston, unlike his company, had not ever had a Swiss account. The Supreme Court rejected this argument:

> Beyond question, [Bronston's] answer to the crucial question was not responsive if we assume, as we do, that the first question was directed at personal bank accounts [rather than corporate accounts, or both corporate and personal accounts]. There is, indeed, an implication in the answer to the second question that there was never a personal bank account; in casual conversation this interpretation might reasonably be drawn. But we are not dealing with casual conversation and the statute does not make it a criminal act for a witness to willfully state any material matter that implies any material matter that he does not believe to be true.[27]

Any incompleteness in the witness's answer, which might be wholly innocent, or even purposeful evasion, is thus to be remedied by additional questioning by the lawyer.[28] As long as the answer is literally true, however, there can

---

25. *Bronston* has since been held to apply to prosecutions under § 1623 also. *See, e.g.,* United States v. Boone, 951 F.2d 1526, 1536 (9th Cir. 1991) (literally true statement not actionable under § 1623); United States v. Reveron Martinez, 836 F.2d 684, 689 (1st Cir. 1988); United States v. Tonelli, 577 F.2d 194, 198 (3d Cir. 1978); United States v. Kehoe, 562 F.2d 65, 68 (1st Cir. 1977). It also applies to 18 U.S.C. § 1001 (false material statements to an agency or department of the United States). *See, e.g.,* United States v. Mandanici, 729 F.2d 914, 921 (2d Cir. 1984); s*ee also* United States v. Attick, 649 F.2d 61, 63 (1st Cir.), *cert. denied,* 454 U.S. 861 (1981) (one cannot be convicted under 18 U.S.C. § 1014, prohibiting material false statements to a federally insured bank, "if the statement claimed to be false is, in fact, literally true").

26. *Id.* at 354.

27. *Id.* at 357-58.

28. *Id.* at 358-59.

be no perjury.[29] On the other hand, where an answer is both responsive—therefore not signalling the need for further questioning—and materially false in context, it is perjurious "even if [it] could be literally true in isolation."[30]

Whether an answer is literally true is an issue of fact for the jury, provided the questions put to the witness were fairly susceptible of only one interpretation.[31] However, if a line of questioning is so vague that it is "fundamentally ambiguous," then the issue becomes one of legal sufficiency and a perjury conviction may not be permitted to stand.[32]

D. *Perjury Under § 1623: Differences*

Section 1623 applies only to false material declarations made in a proceeding before, or ancillary to, a federal court or grand jury.[33] This limitation would appear to mean that SEC depositions, conducted pursuant to a private formal order of investigation issued by the Commission, or other administra-

---

29. *See, e.g.,* United States v. Hairston, 46 F.3d 361, 375 (4th Cir. 1995) (conviction for violation of § 1623 cannot be based on evasive answers or even misleading answers so long as such answers are literally true); United States v. Dean, 55 F.3d 640, 662 (D.C. Cir. 1995) (misleading but literally true statement does not constitute perjury as defined in § 1621); United States v. Chaplin, 25 F.3d 1373, 1380 (7th Cir. 1994) (literal truth of statement is complete defense to § 1621 perjury charge); United States v. Reveron Martinez, 836 F.2d 684, 689 (1st Cir. 1988) (reversing conviction based on plainly nonresponsive but literally true answer not further explored by questioner).

30. United States v. Shafrick, 871 F.2d 300, 304 (2d Cir. 1989).

31. United States v. Culliton, 328 F.3d 1074, 1078 (9th Cir. 2003); United States v. Yasak, 884 F.2d 996, 1000-01 (7th Cir. 1989); United States v. Lighte, 782 F.2d 367, 372-73 (2d Cir. 1986).

32. *See, e.g.,* United States v. Ryan, 828 F.2d 1010 (3d Cir. 1987) (credit card application form asking for "PREVIOUS ADDRESS (Last 5 Years)" fundamentally ambiguous because term "address" might equally well refer to domicile or residence or mailing address, and because question could be read to call for one or more than one previous address—or even no previous address if the applicant did not live there within the last five years); United States v. Bell, 623 F.2d 1132 (5th Cir. 1980) (question of grand jury witness whether he had records that were requested in subpoena could have meant "whether he had brought the records with him [to the grand jury] that day," just as plausibly as whether he had the records in his possession "at his office or anywhere else in the world"). *Compare Lighte,* 782 F.2d at 375-76 (reversing conviction because undefined use of the pronoun "you" made it impossible for witness to know whether questioned in a personal capacity or as trustee of trust bank account; in effect, the answers were necessarily literally true) *with* United States v. Glantz, 847 F.2d 1 (1st Cir. 1988) (literal truth defense not available where testimony read as a whole made it clear who was meant by "them" in question "did you ever tell anyone that money was passed on to them," and evidence established falsity of defendant's answer "absolutely not").

33. Section 1623 applies not only to false oral and written testimony, but also to the use of documentary evidence containing a false declaration. Specifically, 18 U.S.C. § 1623(a) provides:

tive agency cannot give rise to a perjury prosecution under § 1623. On the other hand, interviews conducted in the prosecutor's office, under oath, may come within the meaning of the term "ancillary proceeding."[34]

Whether § 1623 is available to a prosecutor contemplating a perjury case can have significant ramifications. Section 1623 was enacted in 1970 "to facilitate perjury prosecutions."[35] The statute eliminates several of the strict common law evidentiary requirements for establishing falsity, which remain applicable in a prosecution under § 1621:

- The two witness (or direct corroboration) rule is abolished, and proof beyond a reasonable doubt "is sufficient for conviction."[36] The two witness rule remains applicable in § 1621 prosecutions.[37]

> Whoever under oath (or in any declaration, certificate, verification, or statement under penalty of perjury as permitted under section 1746 of title 28, United States Code) in any proceeding before or ancillary to any court or grand jury of the United States knowingly makes any false material declaration or makes or uses any other information, including any book, paper, document, record, recording, or other material, knowing the same to contain any false material declaration, shall be fined not more than $10,000 or imprisoned not more than five years, or both.

18 U.S.C. § 1623(a) (2000). At least one court has affirmed a § 1623(a) conviction based upon supplying false and forged documents to the grand jury in response to a subpoena, and then identifying those documents before the grand jury (although the opinion does not make clear what the defendants said in "merely [identifying]" the documents as business records). United States v. Norton, 755 F.2d 1428, 1431 (11th Cir. 1985) (internal quotation marks omitted). The court stated that "each document, which defendants had affirmatively presented to the Grand Jury, was displayed to them during their testimony. These documents were falsely identified as business records .... when they were not actual business records .... The false documents were identified as depicting events and records that were in reality nonexistent." *Id.* at 1430-31.

34. United States v. Krogh, 366 F. Supp. 1255, 1256 (D.D.C. 1973) (holding that sworn deposition taken in the office of an Assistant United States Attorney General was a proceeding ancillary to a grand jury investigation). *But see* Dunn v. United States, 442 U.S. 100, 111 n.10 (1979) (distinguishing interview in private lawyer's office from situation in *Krogh*, without commenting on whether *Krogh* was rightly decided). Under one reading of *Dunn*, only testimony taken by deposition would come within the term "ancillary proceeding." *See* 442 U.S. at 109-13 (arguably suggesting that sworn affidavits and certifications are not statements accompanied by sufficient procedural safeguards ever to be regarded as possessing the "'degree of formality' required by § 1623").

35. Dunn v. United States, 442 U.S. at 107.

36. 18 U.S.C. § 1623(e).

37. United States v. Diggs, 560 F.2d 266 (7th Cir. 1977), *cert. denied,* 434 U.S. 925 (1977); United States v. Ruggiero, 472 F.2d 599 (2d Cir. 1973), *cert. denied,* 412 U.S. 939 (1973). A prosecutor's election to proceed under § 1623 rather than § 1621, where both are available, is not an equal protection violation. *Id.* at 606.

- Where the defendant has testified inconsistently in more than one proceeding, "to the degree that one of [his declarations] is necessarily false," the government need not allege or prove the falsity of either. Both declarations must be "material to the point in question," and the government must prove that they are "irreconcilably contradictory."[38]
- The *mens rea* requirement under § 1623 is "knowingly," rather than the willfulness standard of § 1621, although as described above this may have little practical effect.

E. *Subornation of Perjury*

18 U.S.C. § 1622 provides:

Whoever procures another to commit any perjury is guilty of subornation of perjury, and shall be fined not more than $2,000 or imprisoned not more than five years, or both.

---

38. 18 U.S.C. § 1623(c) (2000). Apparently recognizing that with the passage of time a witness's understanding of the true facts might change, Congress explicitly made it a defense in a § 1623 prosecution based on inconsistent declarations "that the defendant at the time he made each declaration believed the declaration was true." *Id.*

Section 1623 also specifically makes recantation a defense. The recantation must occur in "the same continuous court or grand jury proceeding in which [the false] declaration is made," and it must occur before the perjury has "substantially affected the proceeding" and before it "become[s] manifest [to the perjurer] that [the perjury] has been or will be exposed." 18 U.S.C. § 1623(d). *See* United States v. Denison, 663 F.2d 611 (5th Cir. 1981); United States v. Moore, 613 F.2d 1029 (D.C. Cir. 1979), *cert. denied,* 446 U.S. 954 (1980). The elimination of the common law rule that recantation is not a defense to perjury is the only respect in which § 1623 is more lenient toward defendants than § 1621. However, it appears that unless recantation is immediate or nearly so, the government may well succeed in a claim that the original perjury was already manifest or had substantially affected the proceeding. *See* United States v. McAfee, 8 F.3d 1010, 1016 (5th Cir. 1993) (recantation by witness during a second deposition of testimony provided during a prior deposition held not to satisfy § 1623(d) because the false testimony and recantation did not take place in the same proceeding); *see also* United States v. Tucker, 495 F. Supp. 607, 613-14 (E.D.N.Y. 1980). Moreover, the adequacy of the recantation defense has been held to be a question of law for the Court to decide. *See* United States v. Fornaro, 894 F.2d 508, 511 (2d Cir. 1990); United States v. Goguen, 723 F.2d 1012, 1017 (1st Cir. 1983) ("the issue whether an effective and timely recantation has been made is one of law to be decided by the court"). Additionally, a valid recantation may only be found in those instances where both an outright retraction and repudiation has occurred. *See, e.g.,* United States v. Sebaggala, 256 F.3d 59 (1st Cir. 2001) (mere

"Procuring" means inducing or instigating in any fashion.[39] In a prosecution under § 1622, the perjury must be proved to have occurred, and all the essential elements of the perjury must be proved as well as its "procurement."[40] This means that subornation of a § 1621 perjury requires proof of the perjury by two witnesses or one witness plus direct corroboration. In a prosecution for subornation of perjury before a court or grand jury, on the other hand, the two witness rule is abrogated.[41] In any event, proof of the inducement to testify perjuriously may come from a single uncorroborated witness.[42]

Most of the reported decisions under § 1622 involve obvious misbehavior by the defendant—usually telling the witness to lie or, worse, to conceal their joint wrongdoing, which has become the subject of investigation.[43] These cases, even though they involve extreme circumstances, do provide some guidance on the type of conduct that should be avoided in interviewing and preparing witnesses in the course of an internal investigation.

In United States v. Sarantos,[44] the defendant Sarantos was a lawyer convicted of aiding and abetting the making of false statements to the Immigration and Naturalization Service (INS) in connection with a sham marriage scheme designed to obtain permanent U.S. residence for male Greek aliens.[45] Sarantos was not involved in arranging the sham marriages; his role was to assist in the filing of a petition with the INS stating that the parties were living together as husband and wife. He also instructed wives who were called

---

implicit admission of false testimony not sufficient to recant under § 1623; outright retraction and repudiation of prior false testimony is required).

39. *E.g.,* Petite v. United States, 262 F.2d 788 (4th Cir. 1959).

40. *E.g.,* United States v. Brumley, 560 F.2d 1268 (5th Cir. 1977); United States v. Tanner, 471 F.2d 128 (7th Cir. 1972), *cert. denied,* 409 U.S. 949 (1972).

41. United States v. Gross, 511 F.2d 910 (3d Cir. 1975), *cert denied,* 423 U.S. 924 (1975).

42. United States v. Cravero, 530 F.2d 666 (5th Cir. 1976).

43. One circuit court has held, however, that a jury could reasonably infer that the gesture of a nod of the head by the defendant toward a witness who was testifying during a hearing was sufficient to conclude the defendant was encouraging the witness to commit perjury in violation of § 1622. *See* United States v. Flint, 993 F.2d 885 (9th Cir. 1993) (unpublished opinion).

44. 455 F.2d 877 (2d Cir. 1972).

45. Sarantos was convicted of aiding and abetting a violation of 18 U.S.C. § 1001 (false statements to government agency), rather than subornation of perjury, but the principles are analogous.

before the INS to say that they were living with their husbands, but not to mention that they had received payment for agreeing to marry.[46]

The government offered no evidence that Sarantos was ever specifically told the couples were not living together. It did, however, present powerful circumstantial evidence that Sarantos must have known that to be the case. For example, the government proved that the couples sometimes required an interpreter because they shared no common language, and that divorce papers were sometimes executed "simultaneously with immigration papers."[47]

Sarantos objected to the trial court's jury charge, which permitted a conviction for aiding and abetting the making of materially false statements if "he knew ... [the statements] were false and ... willfully and knowingly participated in furthering the conduct." In defining "knowingly and willfully," the judge further charged:

> [I]f you find that Mr. Sarantos acted with reckless disregard of whether the statements made were true or with a conscious effort to avoid learning the truth, this requirement is satisfied, even though you may find that he was not specifically aware of the facts which would establish the falsity of the statements.[48]

On appeal, Sarantos argued that when a lawyer is charged with aiding and abetting a false statement, the standard of scienter must be higher than reckless disregard of falsity. Otherwise, Sarantos contended, the attorney-client relationship would be "radically alter[ed]," as the lawyer effectively would be made "an investigative arm of the government."[49]

The Second Circuit rejected this argument, noting that the purpose of construing the term "knowingly" to include willful blindness to the existence of a fact "[i]s to prevent an individual like Sarantos from circumventing criminal sanctions merely by deliberately closing his eyes to the obvious risk that he is engaging in unlawful conduct." As for the claim that such a rule unduly infringes on the lawyer's role, the court stated:

---

46. *Id.* at 879-80.
47. *Id.* at 880.
48. *Id.*
49. *Id.* at 880-81.

We have not held, as appellant contends, that a lawyer must investigate the truth of his client's assertions or risk going to jail. We have held, and continue to hold, that he cannot counsel others to make statements in the face of obvious indications of which he is aware that those assertions are not true.[50]

In *In re Grand Jury Subpoena (Legal Services Center)*,[51] the court was asked to enforce subpoenas calling for production of a lawyer's legal files relating to representation of clients before the INS. The government's theory was the same as in *Sarantos*: that "by 'turning a blind eye' to what the government considers obvious indications of the fraudulent character of their clients' marriages, [the attorneys] committed offenses against the United States including aiding and abetting, 18 U.S.C. § 2; suborning perjury, 18 U.S.C. § 1622; and conspiracy to commit an offense or defraud the United States, 18 U.S.C. § 371."[52]

The court quashed the subpoenas, finding that the government had failed to make a sufficient showing that the lawyers were in possession of information clearly establishing their clients' fraud. The court noted the tension between a lawyer's obligation of zealous representation and any requirement that a lawyer investigate the truth or falsity of a client's assertions. In an effort to accommodate both interests, the court concluded that "[s]o long as the attorney does not have obvious indications of the client's fraud or perjury, the attorney is not obligated to undertake an independent determination before advancing his client's position."[53]

The lawyers in *Sarantos* and *In re Grand Jury Subpoena* were representing individuals and, at least in the latter case, arguably did not have access to information beyond what their clients told them. By contrast, counsel conducting an internal investigation normally will have interviewed a number of employees and reviewed corporate documents, providing additional perspective into whether an employee's proposed testimony is truthful. This means, in many cases, that counsel will have an independent basis for judging the testimony. To the extent there is good reason to mistrust the employee's version

---

50. *Id.* at 881.
51. 615 F. Supp. 958 (D. Mass. 1985).
52. *Id.* at 967.
53. *Id.* at 969.

of the events, at least corporate counsel may not encourage the employee to testify to them.[54] Depending on the circumstances, it may also be appropriate for the employee to be separately represented.[55]

III. OBSTRUCTION OF JUSTICE

In this section, we survey the obstruction of justice laws, with particular attention to several recent amendments and court decisions that raise important issues for counsel conducting an internal investigation. The obstruction laws are codified in a series of statutes at 18 U.S.C. §§ 1501 through 1520, dealing with a wide range of conduct, from the murder of potential witnesses to document

---

54. *See also* Tedesco v. Mishkin, 629 F. Supp. 1474, 1479-80 (S.D.N.Y. 1986) (lawyer violated 18 U.S.C. § 1622 by failing to advise a witness, after hearing proposed testimony and knowing it to be false, against testifying in that manner; under all the circumstances, including repeated prior statements by lawyer indicating harmfulness of truthful testimony, witness understood lawyer's silence to signify agreement that witness should give proposed perjurious testimony).

55. During the course of an internal investigation, counsel may become aware of a crime previously committed. If so, counsel should be sensitive to the federal misprision of felony statute, 18 U.S.C. § 4. The essential elements of 18 U.S.C. § 4 are as follows: (i) the principal committed and completed the felony alleged; (ii) the defendant had full knowledge of that fact; (iii) the defendant failed to notify the authorities; and (iv) the defendant took an affirmative step to conceal the crime. United States v. Ciambrone, 750 F.2d 1416 (9th Cir. 1984); United States v. Baez, 732 F.2d 780 (10th Cir. 1984); United States v. Bolden, 277 F. Supp. 2d 999, 1010-11 (E.D. Ark. 2003).

Mere silence, without some affirmative act of concealment, does not make out misprision of a felony. *See, e.g.,* United States v. Daddano, 432 F.2d 1119 (7th Cir. 1970), *cert. denied,* 402 U.S. 905 (1971). Misprision of felony, like subornation of perjury, should raise few concerns for the lawyer conducting an internal investigation, as long as there is no solicitation of false testimony or suppression of evidence. However, in some cases counsel conducting the internal investigation might be asked whether the company can destroy records apparently evidencing a crime. Destruction of documentary evidence can, under some circumstances, meet the affirmative concealment element of 18 U.S.C. § 4. Although we have found no reported cases directly on point, the applicability of 18 U.S.C. § 4 may depend upon whether the documents are destroyed pursuant to the company's normal practice of retaining records for a certain time period or whether the documents are being destroyed to conceal the earlier crime. The former situation would seem not to violate 18 U.S.C. § 4, but the latter clearly does.

Similarly, in the government contracting industry, findings in an internal company investigation may lead the company to adjust its accounting records in order to repay money owed to the government (e.g., by adjusting the company's overhead account). Corporate counsel, if asked to review this adjustment, should ensure that the adjustment accurately reflects the necessary change and that it is not designed to conceal any prior misconduct.

destruction and preservation of audit records. In an effort both to broaden and to clarify the scope of obstruction of justice crimes, Congress amended the statutes in 1982 (the Victim and Witness Protection Act), 1989 (the Financial Institution Reform, Recovery, and Enforcement Act), and most recently, in 2002 following the collapse of Enron (the Corporate and Criminal Fraud Accountability Act). We will focus on the current state of the law in three areas in particular: (i) false statements; (ii) witness tampering; and (iii) document destruction.

A. *False Statements*

Although there are other laws, including the perjury statutes, *see supra*, and the false-statement statute, 18 U.S.C. § 1001, that criminalize false statements made during sworn testimony or to a federal officer, the obstruction statutes apply in a broader set of circumstances, creating a wider potential for criminal liability. The primary obstruction statute, 18 U.S.C. § 1503, entitled "Influencing or injuring officer or juror generally," contains an omnibus provision that reaches more categories of conduct than the title might suggest. Under § 1503, it is unlawful to "corruptly . . . endeavor[ ], to influence, obstruct, or impede, the due administration of justice. . . ." In general, the case law holds that to prove a crime under the statute, the government must show that (i) there was a pending judicial proceeding; (ii) the defendant was aware of that proceeding; and (iii) the defendant corruptly intended to impede the administration of that proceeding.[56] To satisfy the intent element, the government must demonstrate that the defendant knew that the "natural and probable effect" of his actions would be to impede a judicial proceeding.[57]

In the case law, the term "judicial proceeding" is most often defined narrowly, as a proceeding before a court or, more typically in this context, a grand jury.[58] A law-enforcement investigation is not, by itself, such a proceeding, and courts have generally found that statements made to the FBI, for instance,

---

56. *See* United States v. Macari, 453 F.3d 926, 936 (7th Cir. 2006); United States v. Quattrone, 441 F.3d 153, 170 (2d Cir. 2006); United States v. Fassnacht, 332 F.3d 440, 447 (7th Cir. 2003). *But see* United States v. Vaghela, 169 F.3d 729, 734 (11th Cir. 1999) (holding that no judicial proceeding need be pending to obtain a conviction under § 1503).

57. *See* United States v. Aguilar, 515 U.S. 593, 599 (1995); Quattrone, 441 F.3d at 171; United States v. Schwarz, 283 F.3d 76, 109 (2d Cir. 2002).

58. *See* United States v. Davis, 183 F.3d 231, 239-41 (3d Cir. 1999); United States v. Brown, 688 F.2d 596, 598 (9th Cir. 1982); United States v. Simmons, 591 F.2d 206, 208 (3d Cir. 1979).

without specific knowledge that those statements will be passed on to a grand jury sitting at the time the statements were made, cannot form the basis for a conviction under § 1503.[59] That said, counsel should be aware that an individual who makes false statements, knowing that those statements will have the natural and probable effect of impeding a pending grand jury, or other court, proceeding (and thus interfering with the "due administration of justice"), will be subject to criminal prosecution under § 1503—whether or not that individual is testifying under oath.[60]

The requirement that an individual know that the "natural and probable effect" of his statement will be to impede a judicial proceeding has done much to limit the reach of § 1503. This "nexus" requirement is not self-evident on the face of the statute, but is instead a creature of the case law. In *United States v. Aguilar*, the Supreme Court reversed a conviction under § 1503 of a defendant who had made false statements to an FBI agent conducting an investigation independent from that of the grand jury also investigating the matter.[61] The defendant's statements were not encompassed by § 1503, the Court found, even though the defendant was aware that a grand jury was sitting, and even if the defendant had *intended* that his statements be passed on to the grand jury by the agent. What mattered was that the defendant "lack[ed] knowledge that his actions [were] *likely to affect* the [grand jury] proceeding."[62]

---

59. *See* Aguilar, 515 U.S. at 601; Schwarz, 283 F.3d at 105.

60. A parallel provision, 18 U.S.C. § 1505, criminalizes the obstruction of agency or Congressional proceedings. It applies to anyone who "corruptly . . . impedes or endeavors to influence, obstruct, or impede the due and proper administration of the law under which any pending proceeding is being had before any department or agency of the United States [or investigation before Congress]." The term "proceeding" under § 1505 is generally read broadly, to include an agency investigation that might lead to a civil or criminal proceeding. *See* United States v. Technic Servs., Inc., 314 F.2d 1031, 1044 (9th Cir. 2002); *see also* United States v. Leo, 941 F.3d 181, 198-99 (3d Cir. 1991); United States v. Fruchtman, 421 F.2d 1019, 1021 (6th Cir. 1970). *But see* United States v. Higgins, 511 F. Supp. 453, 456 (W.D. Ky. 1981) ("[T]he meaning of 'proceeding' in § 1505 must be limited to actions of an agency which relate to some matter within the scope of the rulemaking or adjudicative power vested in the agency by law."). While several courts have held that § 1503's nexus requirement, discussed *infra*, applies to § 1505 as well 1503, *see* Quattrone, 441 F.3d at 174; United States v. Senffner, 280 F.3d 755, 762 (7th Cir. 2002), the Ninth Circuit holds that it does not, *see* United States v. Bhagat, 436 F.3d 1140, 1147-48 (9th Cir. 2006).

61. 515 U.S. 593 (1995).

62. *Id.* at 599 (emphasis added). For cases applying *Aguilar*'s nexus requirement, see United States v. Macari, 453 F.3d 926 (7th Cir. 2006); United States v. Fassnacht, 332 F.3d 440 (7th Cir. 2003); United States v. Schwarz, 283 F.3d 76, 109 (2d Cir. 2002); United States v. Triumph Capital Group, Inc., 260 F. Supp. 2d 470 (D. Conn. 2003).

In 2002, Congress, stirred to action by the Enron scandal and allegations of document destruction by Enron's auditor Arthur Andersen, moved to strengthen the obstruction of justice laws. Considering the nexus requirement of § 1503 and other "burdensome proof requirements" in the obstruction statutes to be "shortcoming[s] in the law,"[63] Congress decided to create an entirely new obstruction provision dealing with document destruction in particular, but using language that suggests the statute may reach false statements as well. The Corporate and Criminal Fraud Accountability Act, enacted as Title VIII of the Sarbanes-Oxley Act, amended what had formerly been a statute that dealt exclusively with witness tampering, 18 U.S.C. § 1512.[64] The new § 1512(c) has two subsections. The first of these, § 1512(c)(1), criminalizes "corruptly" destroying, or attempting to destroy, a document or other object "with the intent to impair the object's integrity or availability for use in an official proceeding." The second, § 1512(c)(2), criminalizes what is arguably a much broader category of activity: any corrupt act that "otherwise obstructs, influences, or impedes any official proceeding [or any corrupt attempt to obstruct such a proceeding]." An "official proceeding" is defined for these purposes as, *inter alia*, "a proceeding before . . . a Federal grand jury . . . [or] a proceeding before a Federal Government agency which is authorized by law. . . ."[65] While there is as yet little case law construing subsection (c)(2), the Department of Justice has already used it to prosecute false statements alleged to have impeded grand jury and agency investigations, arguing that the statute is effectively an omnibus provision, and should not be construed to reach only document destruction. At least one court has agreed that subsection (c)(2), by its express terms, encompasses false statements.[66]

---

63. S. Rep. No. 107-146, 2002 WL 32054437 (2002).
64. Pub. L. No. 107-204 (2002).
65. 18 U.S.C. §§ 1515(a)(1)(A) & (C).
66. *See* Order Denying Motion to Dismiss Counts Six and Seven of the Superseding Indictment as to Sanjay Kumar, Stephen Richards, United States v. Kumar, No. 04-cr-846 (ILG) (E.D.N.Y. Feb. 21, 2006) (dkt. no. 149); *see also* United States v. Hey, 2005 WL 1039388 (E.D. Mich. April 29, 2005) (finding that there was sufficient evidence at trial to convict defendant under § 1512(c)(2) where defendant provided false testimony to grand jury). *Cf.* United States v. Singleton, 2006 WL 1984467, at *3 (S.D. Tex. July 14, 2006) (holding that "to violate § 1512(c)(2), the charged conduct must have some reasonable nexus to a record, document or tangible object").

The use of § 1512(c)(2) to reach false statements raises a series of other issues that have yet to be addressed by the courts. It remains unclear, for instance, whether a nexus requirement akin to that of § 1503—linking the defendant's statements with an official proceeding—applies to § 1512(c)(2). Unlike § 1503, § 1512 provides that "an official proceeding need not be pending or about to be instituted at the time of the offense. . . ."[67] Despite this provision, the Supreme Court, in the Arthur Andersen case brought by the DOJ's Enron Task Force, found the nexus requirement applicable to another part of § 1512, subsections (b)(2)(A) and (B).[68] In so doing, the Court rejected the government's argument that Congress' specific direction that there be no pending-official-proceeding requirement under § 1512 implies the absence of a nexus requirement, as well. Nonetheless, courts have yet to squarely address the nexus issue with respect to subsection (c)(2), and until the question is settled the government can be expected to contend that the nexus requirement imposed by *Aguilar* is among the "burdensome proof requirements" that Congress intended to eliminate in enacting the statute. If the courts ultimately agree, it appears that the government, rather than having to show that a defendant knew that the natural and probable result of a statement would be to obstruct an official proceeding, would have to show simply that the defendant acted "corruptly" in making statements that had the effect of obstructing an official proceeding. The *mens rea* standard "corruptly" has no settled meaning in the obstruction context; it has been construed to require a range of mental states, including specific intent, general consciousness of wrongdoing, and even a negligence-like standard of reasonable forseeability.[69] Without a nexus requirement to limit the reach of § 1512(c)(2), the statute might apply quite broadly.[70]

Just how broadly is suggested by two recent prosecutions under § 1512(c)(2) of individuals accused of lying *not* to the government but to private counsel retained by the company during the course of an internal investigation.[71] In

---

67. 18 U.S.C. § 1512(f)(1).

68. *See* Arthur Andersen, LLP v. United States, 544 U.S. 696 (2005).

69. *See* Kimberley A. Schaefer & John S. Schowengerdt, Obstruction of Justice, 43 AM. CRIM. L. REV. 763, 770-771 (2006) (citing cases).

70. *See generally*, Daniel A. Shtob, Note, Corruption of a Term: The Problematic Nature of 18 U.S.C. 1512(c), 57 VAND. L. REV. 1429, 1433 (2004); *see also* United States v. Reich, 420 F. Supp. 2d 75, 84 (E.D.N.Y. 2006) (denying motion for judgment of acquittal following trial and conviction under subsection (c)(2), where evidence showed that defendant's actions "could reasonably be expected to influence a court proceeding").

71. *See* United States v. Singleton, No. H-04-cr-514-SS (S.D. Tex. filed March 8, 2006); United States v. Kumar, No. 04-cr-846 (S-2) (E.D.N.Y. filed June 28, 2005).

both cases, the government alleged that the individuals—employees of the companies conducting the investigations—*knew* that their statements to company counsel would ultimately be passed on to the grand jury and federal regulatory agencies (at whose behest the companies were conducting the investigations). Yet in at least one of these cases, the government argued that such an allegation of nexus was not required to sustain a conviction under § 1512(c)(2).[72] If the Department of Justice ultimately prevails on this argument, it will have greatly expanded the jeopardy employees face in speaking with counsel retained by a company to discover wrongdoing. The standard admonitions supplied by internal investigation counsel to witnesses (e.g., that counsel does not represent the witness and that the attorney-client privilege belongs not to the witness but to the entity) may need to be expanded to explain the position taken by the DOJ and perhaps by other government agencies in this respect. And it may be that employees will conclude they are better off withholding cooperation from counsel altogether than risking prosecution for statements later judged to have been false.[73]

B. *Witness Tampering*

In addition to being aware of the liability that a client company's employees face in the course of an internal investigation, counsel must also remain vigilant that her own conduct does not cross the line between legitimate advocacy and obstruction of justice. The witness tampering provisions of 18 U.S.C. § 1512, added in substantial part by the Victim and Witness Protection Act in 1982, proscribe conduct that is far subtler than the physical force and threats that are commonly associated with the term "witness tampering." Counsel should thus take care that her interaction with potential witnesses does not run afoul of its provisions.

---

72. The government made this argument in response to a pre-trial motion to dismiss the § 1512(c)(2) count in United States v. Kumar, *supra* n.71. The district court did not reach the issue in deciding the motion, however, and the case was eventually disposed of by guilty plea. For a summary of the obstruction of justice issues raised by the *Kumar* and *Singleton* cases, see Timothy Harkness & Darren LaVerne, *Private Lies May Lead to Prosecution*, NAT'L L.J. (July 24, 2006).

73. Also of potential relevance in this context is § 1512(b)(3), found in the witness tampering portion of the obstruction statutes, *see infra,* which makes it a crime to engage in misleading conduct toward another with the intent to "hinder, delay, or prevent the communication to a law enforcement officer or judge of the United States of information relating to the commission ... of a Federal offense...." 18 U.S.C. § 1512(b)(3). While the language of § 1512(b)(3) is broad, we are not aware of any effort by the government to use this statute to prosecute employees for statements made to counsel in the course of an internal investigation.

Under §§ 1512(b)(1) and (2), for instance, it is a crime to "engage[ ] in misleading conduct toward another person,"[74] with the intent to "influence, delay, or prevent" a witness' testimony, or to "cause or induce any person" to "withhold" testimony or documents from an official proceeding.[75] Unlike a prosecution under either § 1503 or § 1505, the government need only prove the defendant acted knowingly with intent to bring about one of the enumerated results, and not specifically with the intent to obstruct justice.[76] Moreover, once the government has established the defendant's intent under § 1512(b), the defendant has the burden of proving, by way of affirmative defense, that his "conduct consisted solely of lawful conduct and that [his] sole intention was to encourage, induce, or cause the other person to testify truthfully."[77] Section 1515(c), part of the statute's definitional provision, provides that § 1512 "does not prohibit or punish the providing of lawful, bona fide, legal representation services in connection with or anticipation of an official proceeding." This provision—which has also been held to be an affirmative defense[78]—of course begs the question as to what "lawful, bona fide, legal representation services" are.

---

74. Courts have interpreted the term "person" to include potential witnesses, United States v. Romero, 54 F.3d 56, 62 (2d Cir. 1995), cert. denied, 517 U.S. 1449 (1996); grand jury witnesses, United States v. Schmidt, 935 F.2d 1440, 1452 (4th Cir. 1991); and excused witnesses, United States v. Risken, 788 F.2d 1361, 1369 (8th Cir. 1986).

75. *See also* 18 U.S.C. § 1512(b)(3), *supra* n.73 (criminalizing misleading conduct intended to "hinder, delay, or prevent the communication to a law enforcement officer or judge of the United States of information relating to the commission . . . of a Federal offense. . . .")

76. *See also* United States v. Bailey, 405 F.3d 102, 108-09 (1st Cir. 2005) (statute does not require that there be an existing or imminent federal investigation at the time of the defendant's misleading conduct).

77. 18 U.S.C. § 1512(e). The Second Circuit has rejected an argument that the affirmative defense provision is a nullity on the grounds that a defendant cannot both possess the intent to cause a witness to withhold evidence and the "sole intent" to encourage truthful testimony. United States v. Johnson, 968 F.2d 208, 213 (2d Cir.), cert. denied, 506 U.S. 964 (1992). The court held that once the government met its burden of proof beyond a reasonable doubt that the defendant intended to cause the witness to withhold testimony, the intent prong of the affirmative defense to section 1512 could still be satisfied by proving, by a preponderance of the evidence, that the testimony that he wanted the witness to withhold was false. *Id.* Such a reading of section 1512(e) was deemed by the court to comport with the Senate Judiciary Committee's view of the affirmative defense as being "intended primarily to avoid the possibility that a [judge or other officer of the court] would violate this statute by threatening a witness or potential witness with a perjury or false statement prosecution if he testifies falsely." *Id.* (quoting S. Rep. No. 532, 97th Cong., 2d Sess. 9, *reprinted in* 1982 U.S. Code Cong. & Admin. News 2515, 2525).

78. *See* United States v. Kloess, 251 F.3d 941, 944 (11th Cir. 2001).

"Misleading conduct" is defined in 18 U.S.C. § 1515(a)(3) as follows:

(A) knowingly making a false statement; (B) intentionally omitting information from a statement and thereby causing a portion of such statement to be misleading, or intentionally concealing a material fact, and thereby creating a false impression by such statement; (C) with intent to mislead, knowingly submitting or inviting reliance on a writing or recording that is false, forged, altered, or otherwise lacking in authenticity; (D) with intent to mislead, knowingly submitting or inviting reliance on a sample, specimen, map, photograph, boundary mark, or other object that is misleading in a material respect; or (E) knowingly using a trick, scheme, or device with intent to mislead.

Before enactment of § 1512(b), a lawyer could reasonably have assumed his behavior was within the bounds of legitimate advocacy as long as it did not go beyond urging the persuasiveness of a witness's innocent explanation and seek to have the witness testify falsely.[79] There was some question in *United States v. Brand* whether the defendants first attempted to have the witness sign a false statement exculpating them. But, the court concluded there was a sufficient basis for defendants to believe that the first proffered statement was true, and "[w]hen finally advised by [the witness] that he would refuse to sign the requested statement, [the defendants] accepted as an alternative the true statement signed by [the witness]."[80] Moreover, the defendants "made [no] effort to alter [the witness's] testimony, or influence it in any manner."[81] Endeavoring *corruptly* to persuade a witness to invoke the privilege against self-incrimination, or not to testify, also was, and is, punishable as obstruction of justice under § 1503.[82] But, § 1512, by its terms, punishes

---

79. *See, e.g.,* United States v. Brand, 775 F.2d 1460 (11th Cir. 1985) (reversing section 1503 conviction based on attempt to secure statement from witness to convince government to dismiss indictment).

80. 775 F.2d at 1469.

81. *Id.; see also* Hall v. United States, 419 F.2d 582, 584-85 (5th Cir. 1969) (no basis for section 1503 witness tampering charge where defendant believed potential government witness would exonerate him, and so visited the witness to try to persuade him to testify truthfully at trial); Cole v. United States, 329 F.2d 437, 439 (9th Cir.), *cert. denied,* 377 U.S. 954 (1964) (section 1503 "cannot proscribe criminal acts consistent with the due administration of justice, such as influencing a witness to tell the truth"); *cf.* United States v. St. Clair, 552 F.2d 57, 58 (2d Cir.), *cert. denied,* 433 U.S. 909 (1977) (18 U.S.C. § 1510 violated "whenever an individual induces or attempts to induce another person to make a material misrepresentation to a criminal investigator").

82. *See, e.g.,* United States v. Gotti, 459 F.3d 296 (2d Cir. 2006); United States v. Capo, 791 F.2d 1054 (2d Cir. 1986); United States v. Cioffi, 493 F.2d 1111, 1119 (2d Cir.), *cert. denied,* 419 U.S. 917 (1974).

misleading conduct that merely seeks to "influence" testimony, and eliminates the requirement that the government prove a corrupt purpose to obstruct justice, as is required under §§ 1503 and 1512(c), *supra*. That language conceivably could reach conduct that does not intuitively seem criminal.

Perhaps the most troubling part of the statute for counsel conducting an internal investigation is § 1515(a)(3)(B), defining "misleading conduct" to include an intentional omission of information that causes a statement to be misleading. Especially in the early stages of an investigation, counsel may not have learned all relevant facts, and will not be in a position to share them in witness interviews. Later, with the benefit of hindsight and a fuller record, the government could conceivably claim that counsel had been acting intentionally in omitting information from a statement to a prospective witness.

More significantly, counsel may have legitimate reason to omit or conceal information in the course of employee interviews. From the corporation's point of view—and this is true not only at the outset but throughout the investigation—it is usually counterproductive to divulge all the facts to each potential witness. After all, the basic purpose of the internal investigation is to uncover possible or suspected wrongdoing. Some employees who are interviewed may be guilty of wrongdoing, or of a subpar job performance, which they wish to conceal. Counsel will want an opportunity to test their statements against those of other witnesses (and against the government's version of the facts, to the extent it is known), without first describing what everyone has so far said. This is true even where the employee being interviewed is not suspected of any misbehavior. Lawyers know that witnesses tend to take their cue in describing events from the lawyer doing the questioning. Thus, there is a risk—especially where a lawyer is acting on behalf of the witness' employer in a criminal or administrative investigation—that innocent employees will tailor their testimony (wittingly or otherwise) to provide what they believe are the *right* answers.

Moreover, if some of the information gleaned in the course of the investigation is harmful to the corporation, counsel will not want to add to the number of witnesses who know the information. Although the corporation has no Fifth Amendment right against self-incrimination, it and its counsel also have no duty to reveal incriminating evidence learned in the course of an internal review. Depending on the extent of its understanding of the conduct under investigation, the government might or might not know enough to seek to question employees who do possess evidence of possible wrongdoing. Requiring counsel, in interviewing and preparing witnesses, to reveal inculpatory information they have learned, or face potential prosecution under § 1512, would unfairly undercut counsel's ability to protect the client.

We do not believe that Congress intended §§ 1512(b) and 1515(a)(3)(B) to require counsel, in conducting internal interviews, to disclose all relevant facts or risk criminal prosecution. Such a rigidly literal interpretation is contrary to the public policy underlying the statutory amendment. That public policy, although designed to expand the prosecutor's arsenal against obstruction of justice, was not intended to curtail a company's internal fact-gathering even in response to a government investigation.

And indeed, we have found no reported cases applying § 1512 to the activities of lawyers in circumstances where there is no corrupt endeavor to obstruct justice. The reported cases under § 1512(b), in fact, generally involve the same kind of culpable behavior previously prosecuted using 18 U.S.C. § 1503.[83]

This may reflect a narrower, and we believe more correct, interpretation of § 1512 than its own language might suggest, or it may reflect a sensitivity on the part of prosecutors to the dangers of interfering with the lawyer-witness relationship, absent a clear and corrupt effort to impede the judicial process. Or, it may simply result from the fact that much of what goes on between lawyer and witness is protected by privilege or otherwise not readily available to the prosecutor.

Nonetheless, there are a number of cautions that a lawyer should consider implementing to further minimize risk of the behavior being challenged under § 1512. Certainly, counsel may not say or intimate—although this was true under prior law—that anything adverse will occur if the witness tells the story a certain way. To the contrary, it is important to emphasize that the employee's duty to cooperate with corporate counsel conducting an internal investigation implies nothing more than an obligation to be candid, and if the witness ultimately testifies, the truth must be told.

The employee should be advised that counsel is representing the corporation, not the employee, and the scope of the company's attorney-client privilege should be explained. Under some circumstances, it may be appropriate to

---

83. *See e.g.,* United States v. Maggitt, 784 F.2d 590 (5th Cir. 1986) (threat to murder witness); United States v. Rodolitz, 786 F.2d 77 (2d Cir.), *cert. denied,* 479 U.S. 826 (1986) (upholding conviction under "misleading conduct" provision of 18 U.S.C. § 1512 where defendant lied to witness in order to persuade witness that giving grand jury testimony that they both knew to be false was justified).

refer to the possibility of separate representation. If counsel requests that the employee not discuss the investigation or the interview with others, counsel should state clearly that this is not meant to suggest that the employee will be precluded from testifying fully and honestly at some later point. To ensure against potential misunderstandings, counsel should have another lawyer or paralegal present as a witness to the interview.

C. *Document Destruction*

Over the last twenty-five years, the advent of the computer, e-mail, and the Internet in the workplace has dramatically increased the amount of tangible evidence available in an investigation. The advance of technology has accordingly enhanced the government's ability to build a case charging a violation of one of the growing number of statutes and rules designed to regulate conduct in the white-collar workplace. Of course, as technology has expanded the kind and amount of evidence available to prosecutors, it has also made destruction of that evidence both easier to accomplish and more common. In conducting an internal investigation, counsel should always be alert to the possibility that a company's management or employees, in an effort to cover up conduct that prompted the initial inquiry, will expose themselves or the company to an additional charge based on the destruction or alteration of documents.

1. Before Sarbanes-Oxley

Until Sarbanes-Oxley, the obstruction laws lacked a provision that dealt directly with document destruction. To bring a case based on destruction or alteration of documents, the government had to rely on the omnibus provision in § 1503, *see supra*, or, following the Victim and Witness Protection Act in 1982, §§ 1512(b)(2)(A) and (B). The latter statute provides:

> Whoever knowingly uses intimidation, threatens, or corruptly persuades another person, or attempts to do so, or engages in misleading conduct toward another person, with intent to ... cause or induce any person to (A) ... withhold a record, document, or other object, from an official proceeding; [or] (B) alter, destroy, mutilate, or conceal an object with intent to impair the object's integrity or availability for use in an official proceeding [shall be fined or imprisoned not more that ten years, or both].

While subsections 1512(b)(2)(A) and (B) deal with document destruction, they do so indirectly, by prohibiting acts that would cause *another* person to withhold, destroy, or alter documents. These statutes do not address the situation where an individual has himself shredded documents or deleted e-mails sought by the government.

Further limits on subsections (b)(2)(A) and (B) were recently established by the Supreme Court in *Arthur Andersen, LLP v. United States*, a case arising from the investigation into fraud at Enron.[84] Andersen, Enron's accounting firm, was convicted of obstruction under § 1512(b)(2) based on directions from senior Andersen staff that instructed employees to "follow the company's document policy"—and thus to destroy a large number of accounting records—after it became clear that the SEC was investigating Enron's accounting policies, but before Andersen itself had received a subpoena. The district court had charged the jury that "[t]he word 'corruptly' means having an improper purpose. An improper purpose, for this case, is an intent to subvert, undermine, or impede the fact-finding ability of an official proceeding."[85] It further instructed that the jury could convict Andersen under subsections (b)(2)(A) and (B) "even if [Andersen] honestly and sincerely believed that its conduct was lawful."[86] The conviction was upheld in the Court of Appeals, but the Supreme Court found the trial court's instructions erroneous because they did not adequately account for the language in § 1512(b) that requires a defendant to have "knowingly . . . corruptly persuade[d]" another in order to be convicted under the statute. Giving particular weight to the modifier "knowingly," the Court held that to prove guilt, the government must demonstrate that a defendant was conscious of wrongdoing when he directed another to destroy or withhold documents.[87]

The *Andersen* decision limited the scope of subsections 1512(b)(2)(A) and (B) in another way, as well. The Court found that that the nexus requirement it had endorsed in *Aguilar* with respect to § 1503, *see supra*, also applied in the context of the government's prosecution of Andersen under § 1512.[88] In other words, unless the government could prove that Andersen knew that the natural and probable effect of the directions to its employees would be to withhold documents from or impair their use in an "official proceeding" (as defined by 18 U.S.C. § 1515, *see supra*), the company could not

---

84. 544 U.S. 696 (2005).
85. United States v. Arthur Andersen, LLP, 374 F.3d 281, 293 (5th Cir. 2004), *rev'd,* 544 U.S. 696 (2005) (emphasis omitted).
86. 544 U.S. at 706.
87. *Id.*
88. *Id.* at 707–08.

be convicted under the statute. Without commenting on whether the evidence at trial established the requisite nexus, the Court pointed to the trial court's failure to give any instruction at all on nexus as another basis for reversal.[89]

2. Section 1512(c)(1)

As described above, even before the Supreme Court's decision in *Andersen*, Congress had decided to include significant changes to the obstruction of justice laws in the context of the Sarbanes-Oxley Act. Title VIII of the Act added three new statutes, §§ 1512(c), 1519, and 1520, all of which address the problem of document destruction. We have already noted that § 1512(c)(1) criminalizes "corruptly" altering, destroying, mutilating, or concealing a record, document, or other object (or attempting to do so), "with the intent to impair the object's integrity or availability for use in an official proceeding." Subsection (c)(1) thus redresses one perceived "shortcoming" with § 1512(b)(2): It punishes the person who actually destroys documents, not just the "corrupt persuader."

As is the case with subsection (c)(2), however, *see supra*, it remains unclear whether a nexus requirement applies to subsection (c)(1). If it does, one could argue that the statute does not punish a significantly broader range of acts than those that are already criminal under §§ 1503 and 1505.[90]

---

89. *Id.; see also* United States v. Quattrone, 441 F.3d 153 (2d Cir. 2006). In *Quattrone*, the Second Circuit applied the Supreme Court's holdings in *Aguilar* and *Andersen* regarding nexus to vacate the conviction of an investment banker under §§ 1503, 1505, and 1512(b)(2). All three counts of conviction were predicated on the defendant's sending of an e-mail to the bank's employees that underscored the need to dispose of documents in accordance with the bank's document policy. Although the court found that there was sufficient evidence before the jury to support a finding of nexus (including evidence that the defendant knew that the bank had received a grand jury subpoena that covered the kinds of documents referred to in his e-mail), it held that the trial court's jury instruction insufficiently conveyed that to be found guilty the defendant had to have known that "his actions were likely to affect" the grand jury or SEC proceedings. *Id.* at 178-79. Because it could not say that the trial court's error was harmless beyond a reasonable doubt, the court vacated the convictions.

90. Counsel should bear in mind, however, that § 1512(c)(1) applies to acts intended to impair the integrity of a document or object for use in an "official proceeding" (as defined by § 1515(a)(1), discussed *supra*, to include "a proceeding before a Federal Government agency which is authorized by law"), not simply acts of document destruction that impede the "due administration of justice" (the term used in § 1503, generally defined as proceedings before a court or grand jury, *see supra*). An "official proceeding," moreover, need not be pending when the document destruction occurs. *See* 18 U.S.C. § 1512(f)(1).

Regardless, given that subsection (c)(1) specifically requires that the government prove an intent to impair a document's "integrity or availability for use in an official proceeding," the absence of a nexus element would not, presumably, broaden the reach of the statute as drastically as it might in the case of subsection (c)(2), which, again, is limited only by the term "corruptly." Indeed, the one decision we have found that explicitly holds that subsection (c)(1) has no nexus requirement points out that the presence of a specific intent element mitigates the concerns that led the Supreme Court to require nexus in the context of § 1503.[91]

3. Section 1519

Seemingly broader than § 1512(c)(1) is new § 1519, a "general anti-shredding provision."[92] It prohibits the destruction, alteration, or falsification of records or documents with the intent to impede, obstruct, or influence (1) the investigation or proper administration of any matter within the jurisdiction of any department or agency of the United States, or (2) any case filed under title 11.[93]

Although there is not yet case law interpreting § 1519, there is some indication as to the intended breadth of the statute in the legislative history. In advocating for its enactment, Senator Leahy explained:

> [T]his section would create a new 20-year felony which could be effectively used in a wide array of cases where a person destroys or creates evidence with the intent to obstruct an investigation or matter that is, as a factual matter,

---

91. *See* United States v. Ortiz, 367 F. Supp. 2d 536, 541 (S.D.N.Y. 2005). *Ortiz* relied on the presence of a specific intent element in § 1512(c)(1) and the absence of a requirement that an official proceeding be pending, *see* § 1512(f)(1), to find that the no showing of nexus was necessary. *See id.* at 542. As both of these conditions are also true of § 1512(b)(2)(B)—which, following *Andersen,* does have a nexus element—the continued viability of *Ortiz* is in doubt.

92. 148 CONG. REC. S7418, 2002 WL 1731002 (daily ed. July 26, 2002) (statement of Sen. Leahy), at S7419.

93. In its entirety, § 1519 provides:

> Whoever knowingly alters, destroys, mutilates, conceals, covers up, falsifies, or makes a false entry in any record, document, or tangible object with the intent to impede, obstruct, or influence the investigation or proper administration of any matter within the jurisdiction of any department or agency of the United States or any case filed under title 11, or in relation to or contemplation of any such matter or case, shall be fined under this title, imprisoned not more than 20 years, or both.

Id.

within the jurisdiction of any federal agency or any bankruptcy. It also covers acts either in contemplation of or in relation to such matters.... It is also meant to do away with the distinctions, which some courts have read into obstruction statutes, between court proceedings, investigations, regulatory or administrative proceedings (whether formal or not), and less formal government inquiries, regardless of their title.... [T]he intent of the provision is simple; people should not be destroying, altering, or falsifying documents to obstruct any government function.[94]

Because there are no cases defining the limits of § 1519, it is difficult to know how broadly the provision might be applied. It is conceivable, for instance, that the statute could be used to prosecute document destruction that occurs before an investigation has even begun. For now, in light of the statute's language (and its twenty-year maximum penalty), counsel conducting internal investigations should be particularly conservative when advising clients on these issues. Certainly, any destruction that occurs after the specter of impropriety has been raised should be viewed with concern.

4. Section 1520

Section 1520 is a more targeted provision, applying only to accountants. The statute requires accountants who conduct audits of companies that have issued securities covered by section 10(a) of the Securities Exchange Act to maintain certain audit records and work papers for a period of five

---

94. 148 CONG. REC. S7418–S7419, 2002 WL 1731002 (daily ed. July 26, 2002) (statement of Sen. Leahy); *see also* Gary G. Gindler & Jason A. Jones, *Please Step Away from the Shredder and the "Delete" Key: §§ 802 and 1102 of the Sarbanes-Oxley Act,* 41 AM. CRIM. L. REV. 67, 68 (2004) ("Whereas previous laws criminalized both the 'corrupt persuasion' of others to destroy documents in connection with an 'official proceeding,' and the obstruction of pending judicial and federal agency proceedings, the new document destruction provision of §§ 802 (codified at 18 U.S.C. §§ 1519 & 1520) and 1102 (amending 18 U.S.C. § 1512(b)) cast a wider net, reaching persons who shred documents even where a proceeding or investigation does not yet exist.").

Some senators expressed concern that § 1519 might be interpreted too broadly. *See* S. Rep. No. 107-146, 2002 WL 32054437 (2002) (views of Senators Hatch, Thurmond, Grassley, Kyl, DeWine, Sessions, Brownback, and McConnell) ("In our view, section 1519 should be used to prosecute only those individuals who destroy evidence with the specific intent to impede or obstruct a pending or future criminal investigation, a formal administrative proceeding, or bankruptcy case. It should not cover the destruction of documents in the ordinary course of business, even where the individual may have reason to believe that the documents may tangentially relate to some future matter within the conceivable jurisdiction of an arm of the federal bureaucracy.")

years from the end of the fiscal period in which the audit was concluded.[95] Only knowing and willful violations of the statute are punishable as a crime.[96] The legislative history explains that the "idea behind the statute is not only to provide for prosecution of those who obstruct justice, but to ensure that important financial evidence is retained so that law enforcement officials, regulators, and victims can assess whether the law was broken to begin with and, if so, whether or not such was done intentionally, or with or without the knowledge or assistance of an auditor."[97]

---

95. 18 U.S.C § 1520.
96. 18 U.S.C. § 1520(b).
97. 148 CONG. REC. S7419.

Gathering and Organizing Relevant Documents: An Essential Task in Any Investigation

5

Larry A. Gaydos

I. INTRODUCTION   148
II. ORGANIZATION AND PLANNING   150
    A. Initial Dialogue with Management   150
    B. Document Retention and Preservation   152
    C. The Investigating Team   152
    D. Initial On-Site Inspection   153
III. DOCUMENT GATHERING   153
    A. Ensuring Comprehensiveness   153
    B. Ensuring Integrity and Control   154
    C. Electronic Document Gathering   155
IV. DOCUMENT PROCESSING   156
    A. Overview   156
    B. Numbering   157
    C. Copies   157
    D. Review   158

Larry A. Gaydos is a partner in Haynes & Boone LLP in Dallas, Texas, where he is a member of the White Collar Defense and Antitrust Practice Group.

E. Indexing and Coding　159
　　F. Computer Imaging of Documents　160
　　G. Inadvertent Waiver of Privilege　161
V. PREPARATION OF INTERNAL SUMMARIES, CHRONOLOGIES, BINDERS　162
　　A. Hot Document Chronology　162
　　B. Summaries　164
VI. PRODUCTION OF DOCUMENTS TO GOVERNMENT OR CIVIL LITIGANTS　164
　　A. Advocacy Considerations　164
　　B. Personal versus Business Records　166
　　C. Production Abuses　167
　　D. Destruction of Documents　167
　　E. Confidentiality Agreements　168
VII. CONCLUSION　169

APPENDIX A　170
APPENDIX B　172
APPENDIX C　173
APPENDIX D　174

I. INTRODUCTION

THIS CHAPTER FOCUSES on document gathering, processing, and review, one of the least glamorous aspects of legal practice. Although tedious and time-consuming, the identification and review of corporate records remain the keystone of every successful internal investigation. Documents are a window to the past—often the best window, sometimes the only window.

The facts underlying an internal inquiry cannot be reconstructed through employee interviews alone. Witnesses are reluctant to supply information voluntarily, especially when it implicates their own misconduct or that of a co-worker. Thus, selective use of key records is often the only means of achieving an effective interview. Similarly, poor memories can often be refreshed through the use of key documents. Finally, because scienter is a component of virtually all government prosecutions, motive, knowledge, and intent can be established, or defeated, by turning to company files.

Thus, investigative counsel is advised to regard this phase of the undertaking with considerable attention and advance planning. Documents may or may not reflect reality, but routinely they are the best available means of attempting to understand reality (through historical reconstruction), occasionally themselves becoming reality when examined in the artificial light of an adversary proceeding.

Before setting out proper procedures for document retention and review, the reader is reminded of the extreme perils of sloppy performance and inadequate organization in the document stage of the investigation: pleadings stricken for failure to comply with required disclosures or productions;[1] waiver of attorney-client privilege or work product protection because of an inadvertently produced document;[2] spoliation sanctions for failure to preserve documents;[3] and individuals convicted of obstructing justice because of alteration or concealment of documents under subpoena.[4]

At the outset of any internal investigation, the learning curve is great, and thousands of documents may have potential relevance. Ultimately, this curve must be mastered through education or through reasonable assumptions, or both. Once this is done, the universe of relevant documents can often be reduced to no more than several binders of "hot documents." These "hot documents" will include records essential to an understanding of past events and those critical to presenting an affirmative case for the company. And, inevitably, this binder

---

1. *See* FED. R. CIV. P. 37(c)(1) (Rule 26 disclosures); FED. R. CIV. P. 37(b)(2)(C) (discovery).

2. *See* Fort James Corp. v. Solo Cup Co., 412 F.3d 1340 (Fed. Cir. 2005) (court followed traditional view that careless disclosure results in waiver of all other communications relating to the same subject matter); Amgen Inc. v. Hoechst Marion Roussel, Inc., 190 F.R.D. 287 (D. Mass. 2000); *In re* Sealed Case, 877 F.2d 976, 980 (D.C. Cir. 1989) (the traditional view is that the privilege is lost as to particular documents or even as to the whole subject matter without analysis of the client's intent); Suburban Sew 'N' Sweep, Inc. v. Swiss Bernina, Inc., 91 F.R.D. 254, 260 (N.D. Ill. 1981) (waiver found where the client threw documents into the trash and a snooping adversary recovered them); *but see In re* Cooper Market Antitrust Litig., 200 F.R.D. 213 (S.D.N.Y. 2001) (finding no waiver in a large document production when request for return of the privileged document was made in less than one week). Some jurisdictions have codified this "claw back" procedure. *See, e.g.,* TEX. R. CIV. P. 193.3(d). *See also* Mendenhall v. Barber-Greene Co., 531 F. Supp. 951, 955 (N.D. Ill. 1982) (holding that the client had not waived the attorney-client privilege where disclosure was the result of lawyer's negligence and not the client's). Other courts have found a good cause exception to the rule in extensive document production schedules provided reasonable precautions were taken to preserve the privilege. *See* Kansas-Nebraska Natural Gas Co. v. Marathon Oil Co., 109 F.R.D. 12, 21 (D. Neb. 1985). For recent Rules regarding inadvertent disclosure of privilege in the production of electronically stored information *see* FED. R. CIV. P. 26(b)(5)(B).

3. *See, e.g.,* U.S. v. Koch Indus., 197 F.R.D. 463 (1998) (sanctions for negligent failure to allow destruction of computer files relevant to the litigation); Carmen Thompson v. U.S. Department of Housing and Urban Development, 219 F.R.D. 93 (D.C. Maryland 2003).

4. *See* 18 U.S.C. § 1512(b)(2)(B) (West 2006); 18 U.S.C. § 1519 (West 2006).

will contain "bad documents," which are either problematic or susceptible to a problematic interpretation. Most every organization, no matter how moral, ethical, well-managed, or careful, will have bad documents in its files, and counsel should never assume otherwise.

The challenges of identifying and gathering relevant documents continue to grow in complexity and difficulty with the proliferation of electronic data storage mediums, the technical sophistication of electronic communications, and the reliance on electronic data as the preferred, and many times exclusive, vehicle for business communications.

Investigative counsel will find that the major objectives of the document portion of the internal investigation are to:

- preserve the original integrity of all documents;
- protect all applicable privileges, confidences, and proprietary secrets;
- ensure a comprehensive review;
- work with minimal disruption of a client's business and maximum cost efficiency; and
- avoid unnecessary duplication of effort in the event the investigation ends in criminal or civil litigation, or parallel or subsequent governmental investigations.

With these objectives in mind, the six typical phases of the documentary portion of the internal investigation are:

- organization and planning;
- implementation of document retention policy;
- gathering;
- processing and review;
- preparation of internal summaries, chronologies, binders; and
- production of documents to government or civil litigants.

II. ORGANIZATION AND PLANNING

A. *Initial Dialogue with Management*

Some clients tend to view document review as costly, intrusive, and, at least to some extent, unnecessary. They appreciate neither the organization nor planning required to orchestrate an efficient and comprehensive document review, nor the importance of the effort.

Thus, counsel must, throughout all strategy sessions, explain the importance of this phase of the investigation to key management personnel.

A checklist for the initial organizational meeting would look something like this:

- discuss the basics of investigative procedure;
- learn the company's organization and recordkeeping system;
- discuss the scope of the investigation;
- discuss the steps necessary to preserve privilege;
- discuss document retention/destruction policies;
- agree on the ground rules for dealing with lower-level employees necessarily involved in the document-gathering process;
- agree on the best way to go about locating all relevant hard copy documents; and
- agree on scope and protocols for securing and searching electronically stored documents.

Another initial issue is the extent to which client personnel will participate in the document gathering, review, or processing. There are many factors to consider, and there is no single, correct approach.[5] When the internal investigation parallels a criminal investigation, control and integrity of documents take on added importance. Company counsel often find it beneficial to have an outside lawyer fully control the process and thereby serve as the corporate witness on subpoena compliance.[6]

If the internal investigation is likely to lead to disclosures to, and cooperation with, government enforcement agencies company counsel will usually want outside counsel to coordinate that effort. Outside counsel will need to be in a position to accurately represent the scope and thoroughness of the document collection process.

If the internal investigation is being conducted by the Audit Committee or Board of Directors and the independence of the investigation is an issue, the independent counsel conducting the investigation will still necessarily work

---

5. The factors include relative cost savings, ability of client personnel to be available to counsel without impairing the business operation, the expertise client personnel can lend to the process (especially in highly technical areas), the degree to which the independence of the investigation could be called into question, the ability to preserve privilege, relative efficiency or inefficiency of client personnel in dealing with documents, and finally, the context of the investigation.

6. In large document productions pursuant to government subpoena, the investigating authority will usually want assurances that the company has complied with the terms of the subpoena. These assurances typically involve either sworn witness testimony before the investigating body or a sworn certification of compliance.

with management to coordinate the document review process, but the independent counsel will ultimately be accountable to the Audit Committee, Board of Directors, outside auditors, and/or any government enforcement agency for certifying the scope and thoroughness of the entire investigative process.

B. *Document Retention and Preservation*

At the very earliest stage of any internal investigation, it is critical that counsel and management agree on the procedures necessary to modify the company's routine document destruction procedures and affirmatively act to preserve relevant documents. The scope of this effort will vary depending on the context of the investigation, but counsel may need to address autodeletion procedures for electronic data, computer imaging of personal laptops used for business purposes, imaging of computers used by terminated or departing employees, preserving back-up tapes for company servers and downloading or forwarding individual pda e-mail files to company servers, as well as the traditional suspension of hard copy document destruction.

C. *The Investigating Team*

The composition of the investigating team reflects the scope of the possible misconduct, but large inquiries will often be staffed by the partner in charge of the overall investigation; a junior partner or senior associate in charge of the document gathering, processing, and review; a number of junior associates for gathering, reviewing, and processing; a legal assistant in charge of gathering documents and client coordination; a legal assistant in charge of processing documents and support services coordination; and additional legal assistants or case clerks as needed for indexing, copying, numbering, data entry, and privilege logs.

It is important to have *one* lawyer who oversees the production, making decisions regarding privilege, and testifying if necessary on the production methodology and steps taken to preserve the integrity of the documents.

Also, when two or more teams are proceeding simultaneously, it is necessary to have an on-site gathering team, as well as a centralized processing and review team. Time-sensitive investigations permit only a general on-site review, targeting, but not closely reviewing, relevant files. The more detailed review occurs at the central location.

In any document management process, the value of talented legal assistants cannot be overstated. Throughout the investigation, they will coordinate support services, handle client inquiries, and respond to client requests for documents.

Finally, counsel should determine whether outside consultants are needed to lend nonlegal expertise in areas such as accounting, economic analysis, or electronic data management. Even if the company or the investigating firm has information systems expertise, it may be advisable to retain outside experts to reconstruct obsolete databases or protect the integrity of electronic data from inadvertent destruction.

D. *Initial On-Site Inspection*

Since corporate-level managers often do not know the location, state, or condition of many relevant documents, counsel should consider an early series of brief visits to each field location to speak with on-site managers for guidance in collecting documents. Thus, at the initial management meeting, these on-site points of contact will be identified, an agenda developed, and an understanding reached concerning how much lower level employees should be told regarding the investigation.

The initial field trips should often be seen as an opportunity, not to gather all pertinent documents, but to learn of their likely locations. The visit can also prepare company employees for the next phase—the gathering of pertinent documents. To the extent counsel will need documents used daily by employees, the initial visit is an excellent opportunity to begin the process of seeking copies of these documents without disrupting ongoing business activities. Documents typically falling in this category are calendars, appointment books, telephone/address books, daily activity logs, rolodexes, business card collections, current customer correspondence files, current customer or supplier files, and current year operational reports. During the initial inspection, counsel should coordinate with company information system specialists to gain an understanding of the company's history of electronic data systems, storage procedures, and back-up policies.

III. DOCUMENT GATHERING

A. *Ensuring Comprehensiveness*

There is an art to document gathering, and the methodology chosen varies with the level of comfort desired concerning the completeness of the search process. Depending on the complexity of the investigation and its overall significance to the company, here are several tips on maximizing the likelihood of locating the full range of requested documents.

- Provide employees with a *written*, understandable description of relevant documents broken down into well-defined categories.
- When practical, talk with each employee about the request, and show them examples of responsive documents.
- Discuss each employee's personal practices with regard to electronic data, including document filing and storage, and procedures for handling and retaining e-mail.
- Identify mobile electronic data storage devices such as laptops, cell phones, and personal digital assistants (pda's).
- In certain instances, counsel may wish to review and pull documents directly from the location—for example, each desk drawer, file cabinet, storage box, closet, and so forth. Additionally, counsel may want to download, copy, or image important electronic files on the spot.

Although this latter approach may seem overreaching, the fact remains that many employees simply forget archived locations and often do not know that responsive documents still exist. Experienced counsel have heard numerous instances of "I forgot I had those files"; "I didn't realize we kept those back-up tapes"; "I've been looking for that"; "I didn't know my secretary kept those old calendars"; "I didn't realize you wanted those"; and "I don't think you're going to find anything useful in there, just old drafts." These remarks, while benign, occur all too often and, if not dealt with, make for problems later on down the line.

B. *Ensuring Integrity and Control*

To standardize and memorialize the gathering of documents, counsel should prepare a search checklist and an index and have them available throughout the process. The checklist should be prepared for each location, listing the categories of documents, the key points of inquiry, and the topics to discuss with each employee. Appendix A is an example of a checklist used in an antitrust compliance investigation.

Where large amounts of documents are collected, the gathering phase should be separate from the review phase. Certainly, an on-site review and culling is necessary, but the focus is at the *file* level rather than on individual documents, thus minimizing disruption of business activity.

Because original files are collected and sent off site, a strictly enforced system must be in place for the comfort of the client and counsel. Each file (though not necessarily each document) should be assigned a number and indexed on site, contemporaneous with the gathering, to ensure the source location is preserved. Although counsel will wish to control the dissemination of the index, it may be appropriate to leave a copy with the document custodian to memorialize the files removed and aid in responding to the client's future requests for copies of selected documents. A sample index can be found at the end of this chapter as Appendix B.

After relevant documents are identified and numbered, the original index should be supplemented to reflect the numbered documents coming from each file. Ideally, documents required for day-to-day business should be identified in advance, so that working copies can be made and retained. If this is not practical, essential documents can be copied during the gathering process or copies can be made and returned to the client. The index should reflect the files that are retained, or copied and returned, in the event it becomes necessary to reinspect files for some reason in the future—for example, subsequent document request in litigation or grand jury subpoena *duces tecum*. A sample of this index is included at the end of this chapter as Appendix C.

The files that are gathered should be boxed as they are indexed. To ensure proper delivery and prevent inadvertent loss of documents, the on-site team should tape the boxes, apply preprinted shipping labels, and arrange for prompt shipment by a reliable service.

C. *Electronic Document Gathering*

Integrity and control of documents is equally important when gathering electronic documents. There should be a well-thought-out search methodology and search results must be documented, to include tracking of the custodian from whom the electronic file was obtained. This is important not only for follow-up questioning, but also to document the scope and thoroughness of the investigation.

Electronic copies of documents can contain important data not contained on a hard copy, including "metadata" indicating filenames, updates, when the information was accessed, and who most recently accessed the information.[7]

---

7. *See* Jay E. Grenig & William C. Gleisner III, eDISCOVERY & DIGITAL EVIDENCE, §§ 1:4-1:5 (2005); *see also* Michele C.S. Lange & Kristin M. Nimsger, ELECTRONIC EVIDENCE AND DISCOVERY: WHAT EVERY LAWYER SHOULD KNOW (2004); Hon. Schira A. Scheindlin & Jeffrey Rabkin, *Electronic Discovery in Federal Civil Litigation: Is Rule 34 Up to the Task?*, 41 B.C. L. REV. 327, 335–39 (2000).

Information stored on an electronic medium is more easily managed than information in hard copy and may actually be the preferred choice by lawyers who may want the documents in a searchable form.[8]

Finally, to ensure comprehensiveness when gathering electronic documents, counsel must remain mindful that information may automatically be backed up on a default directory or permanently archived on an electronic medium even if the author or receiver of the information believes it has been deleted.[9]

IV. DOCUMENT PROCESSING

A. *Overview*

There are five separate functions that logically fit under the rubric "document processing": (1) numbering; (2) copying; (3) reviewing for producible, privileged, and "hot documents"; (4) indexing; and (5) coding/creation of a database. The sequential order of these steps may vary depending on the circumstances.

The first three functions are mandatory in *every* investigation. The last two—indexing and coding—may or may not occur, depending on the nature of the investigation and cost considerations. Although numbering and copying can be costly, they are necessary to maintain the integrity of the documents. In an investigation of significance, proper numbering, copying, and review must take place under controlled procedures. The real question should not be *if*, but rather *when* and *by whom*.

There are many commercial services available to assist in the processing of documents. These litigation support companies provide basic services such as numbering and copying, as well as the more sophisticated indexing, coding, or computerization. Most large law firms now have a comparable capability. Commercial litigation support services may have greater efficiencies and thus a preferable cost structure, but with them there is some loss of control. Some investigations are highly sensitive, and the client may prefer that document review and processing take place solely within the law firm, especially if the commercial service outsources these functions to operations located in a foreign country.

---

8. *See* Grenig & Gleisner, *supra* note 7, at §§ 7:1–7:3.
9. *Id.* at § 1:4.

B. Numbering

Numbering can be done at a low level on a cost-efficient basis, as long as appropriate supervision is available. The numbers must be legible and consistent in their placement (generally the bottom-right corner), and must not obscure any of the document's content.

Bates stamping was the traditional method used, but in the last several years it has given way to more advanced forms such as preprinted labels, reproduction machines with automatic numbering, bar codes, or computer-generated numbers. The Bates stamp can create user fatigue and is limited to alphanumeric codes. Labels can be removable or non-removable. Removable labels are more versatile and faster (a skilled clerk can number 700-800 pages per hour). In addition, removable labels allow easy correction of mistakes, documents to be renumbered for subsequent productions, and important original documents to be returned to their original condition.

In large document cases, it will usually be preferable to use programmable reproduction machines, which can number copies (but not originals) as they are being reproduced. Technological advances now allow "numbering" by placing bar codes on each page (or each document), which allow the investigators to retrieve information about a document simply by scanning the code.

When Bates numbers are used, alphanumeric codes are preferable to a simple numerical sequence. Often, a three-letter prefix tied to the geographic source of the document can facilitate interview preparation. For example, DAL 00246 indicates the document came from the client's Dallas office. Similarly, alphabetic or numeric prefixes can be linked to the subject matter or type of document. For example, DAL 30000 can refer to Dallas location documents regarding Contract X and DAL 40000 documents can refer to Dallas location documents regarding Contract Y. Alphanumeric codes likewise disclose information to adversaries, but this disadvantage is often outweighed by the convenience to the producing party. This coding is also useful when documents must subsequently be organized by category, rather than as maintained in the ordinary course of business. If the documents are likely to be produced to third parties, it may be preferable to simply use an abbreviation of the clients' name as the alphabetic prefix.

C. Copies

How many copies are enough? The answer, it seems, is never enough, particularly when criminal and civil litigation await an internal investigation.

At a minimum, every investigation should generate four distinct groups of documents: (1) the original files that may contain either numbered or unnumbered documents, or both; (2) a working set of all numbered documents; (3) a set of privileged documents; and (4) a set of "hot documents." If portions of the gathered files are subsequently produced in litigation, or to the government, counsel should retain a copy of the production set and possibly a working copy of the production set.

Needless to say, the copying process should be closely supervised. Despite the best of efforts, pages will be missed, some documents mistakenly copied, and so forth. To minimize embarrassing and compromising incidents, quality controls should include a page-by-page check of returned copies to ensure that instructions were followed, privileged documents not placed in production sets, and all pages legibly copied. Use of electronic processing platforms can eliminate some types of human error, but can also sometimes give rise to coding errors that are difficult to identify.

D. *Review*

During the document review stage, the real challenge is to identify the crucial documents early on, for rarely will investigative counsel have the luxury of a comprehensive document review before undertaking the interview phase.

Several steps can be taken to help meet this challenge.

- The document review should take place in a central location to allow a full sharing of information and thus mutual education of the reviewing team.
- Precede the review process by thorough briefings to the review team of the key issues in the investigation, the client's organization, the definition of "hot documents," and expected areas of privileged documents.
- Provide the review team with organization charts, names likely to appear in privileged documents, a chronology of key events, and a priority list indicating the order in which documents should be reviewed.
- Supervise the review closely for the first several days. The supervising lawyer should conduct frequent status meetings to ensure consistency, answer unanticipated questions, share important document discoveries, and help prevent the "forest for the trees" myopia that can develop in the drudgery of reviewing thousands of documents.

E. Indexing and Coding

In every investigation some means of prompt retrieval must be available. The form may be nothing more than the annotated index created during the document-gathering process (see Appendix C), and the preparation of a "hot document" binder. The binder simply collects, by subject, by date, or by some other indicator, the important documents that counsel refers to time and again throughout the inquiry and wants to have at each witness interview. Indeed, the binder may well be the single most important tool at trial, for both direct and cross-examination.

In complex investigations, a more detailed index is often required, and many times a database must be created that allows for automated and sophisticated search techniques. Creation of a database requires standardized "coding," and is often an expensive process. Before rushing headlong into a costly process that may have only marginal returns, counsel should consider other alternatives.

When automated retrieval becomes necessary, counsel should consider the following suggestions:

- Defer the coding process until the document universe is known and key issues are best understood.
- Do not delegate coding to legal assistants without extensive lawyer input and supervision.
- Active lawyer involvement is essential to create a meaningful database.

Issue coding can, of course, be multidimensional and extremely sophisticated. Appendix D at the end of this chapter provides one example of an issue coding sheet.

Finally, counsel must take certain steps to ensure that any database created by counsel is protected from pretrial discovery.[10] To gain such protection under the work-product doctrine, counsel should primarily, or solely, control the database.[11] Courts are more inclined to protect computer databases from

---

10. *See* Devin Murphy, *The Discovery of Electronic Data in Litigation: What Practitioners and Their Clients Need to Know,* 27 WM. MITCHELL L. REV. 1825, 1846-50 (2001); Philip J. Schworer, *Problems Arising from the Creation of a Computer-Based Litigation Support System,* 14 N. KY. L. REV. 263, 265 (1987).

11. *See* Murphy *supra* n.10, at 1846-50; Schworer, *supra.* n.10, at 266; *see also* Fauteck v. Montgomery Ward Co.*,* 91 F.R.D. 393 (N.D. Ill. 1980) (court ordered discovery of database created by testifying experts).

discovery if the database organizes information in a way that reveals the thought processes of the creating attorneys.[12]

F. Computer Imaging of Documents

As a companion to indexing and coding, computer imaging of documents can be an easy and cost-effective way to organize a large-scale document production. Imaging entails copying or scanning documents onto an electronic medium so that the documents can be accessed by computer.[13]

Computer-imaged documents on an electronic medium allow counsel to search the documents more accurately through the use of particular words and phrases or certain characteristics and then immediately review the responsive documents directly on the computer or retrieve a hard copy.[14] It is usually more cost-effective to copy and transport documents when they are imaged.[15] Bar codes and Bates labels can be avoided, since the computer can automatically add consecutive bar codes to the imaged documents.[16] Duplicate sets of photocopies can also be avoided, since the documents can be provided on CD-ROM disks.

Disadvantages of computer imaging include the possibility of working with lawyers who are uncomfortable with new technology and who may require special assistance in accessing the computer imaging system. Counsel must use special computer programs to group or organize the documents into files and show the beginning and end of a document.[17] The more reviewers involved, the greater the risks of coding errors and inconsistencies among reviews, which are difficult to monitor and correct. Tracking which reviewer has reviewed which portions of the database makes it easier to identify documents that need to be re-coded in the event coding errors or inconsistencies surface. Finally, cross-checking an image with the original document requires numbering the original to match the imaged documents.[18]

---

12. *Id.; see also* Santiago v. Miles, 121 F.R.D. 636 (W.D.N.Y. 1988); James H.A. Pooley & David M. Shaw, *The Emerging Law of Computer Networks: Finding Out What's There: Technical and Legal Aspects of Discovery,* 4 TEX. INTELL. PROP. L.J. 57, 68 (1995).

13. *See* Robert L. Haig & Steven P. Caley, *Does a Good Result Beat a Cheap Legal Fee?* 1996 WL 595744.

14. *Id.*

15. *See* Mariam J. Naini, *Cost-Effective Technology in the Management of Complex Litigation: A Stage-by-Stage Review,* 11 No. 5 INSIDE LITIG. 12, 13 (1997).

16. *Id.*

17. *Id.*

18. *Id.*

G. Inadvertent Waiver of Privilege

Throughout the document-processing phase, counsel must keep uppermost in mind that these same documents may later be produced in adversarial proceedings. Counsel must therefore avoid at all costs waiver of privilege because of inadvertent production, a subject given uneven treatment by the courts. Some courts allow continued assertion of privilege after an inadvertent production, in order to avoid a drastic result.[19] Other courts take a balancing approach and weigh different factors in determining whether a party has waived the attorney-client privilege or work-product immunity doctrine.[20] Many courts, however, adopt a harsher stance and find waiver where a mistaken production, made without objection, has provided a windfall of privileged material to the opponent.[21] These courts reason that once a document has been produced, it enters the "public domain" and confidentiality is destroyed.[22] *Parkway Gallery*[23] is particularly instructive to illustrate the harshness awaiting negligent counsel. In that case, the defendants produced 12,000 pages of documents at their offices for the plaintiff's review. For two weeks before the production, a lawyer and three assistants checked all files for questionable material. During the actual production itself, lead counsel for the defendants was hospitalized and unable to attend. Despite all precautions, the plaintiff obtained twenty privileged, inadvertently produced documents. At a later hearing, the court found that the defendants simply failed to protect the attorney-client privilege and therefore waived it, stating that "mere inadvertence, standing alone, is not sufficient to counter the strong policy that disclosure constitutes waiver."[24]

---

19. *See, e.g.,* Deere & Co. v. Mtd Prods. Inc., 2003 WL 21921265, at *2 (S.D.N.Y. Aug. 1, 2003); Kansas-Nebraska Natural Gas v. Marathon Oil Co., 109 F.R.D. 12, 21 (D. Neb. 1985).

20. In determining whether inadvertent disclosure should be considered a waiver of the attorney-client privilege or work product protection, courts generally take into account four factors: (1) the reasonableness of the precautions taken to prevent inadvertent disclosure, (2) the time taken to rectify the error, (3) the scope of discovery and the extent of the disclosure, and (4) overarching issues of fairness. Deere & Co. v. Mtd Prods., Inc., 2003 WL 21921265, at *2 (S.D.N.Y. Aug. 1, 2003) (citing Lois Sportswear, U.S.A., Inc. v. Levi Strauss & Co., 104 F.R.D. 103, 105 (S.D.N.Y. 1985)).

21. Fort James Corp. v. Solo Cup Co., 412 F.3d 1340 (Fed. Cir. 2005); Amgen Inc. v. Hoechst Marion Roussell, Inc., 190 F.R.D. 287 (D. Mass. 2000) (finding waiver where attorneys failed to take adequate precautions against inadvertent production).

22. *See, e.g.,* New York v. Microsoft Corp., 2002 WL 649492, at *2 (D.D.C. Apr. 8, 2002); Underwater Storage, Inc. v. United States Rubber Co., 314 F. Supp. 546, 549 (D.D.C. 1970).

23. 116 F.R.D. 46 (M.D.N.C. 1987).

24. *Id.* at 51.

To make matters worse, some courts treat waiver of privileged information broadly and hold that all materials and information dealing with the same subject matter as the mistakenly produced material must also be provided in discovery once the privilege has been breached.[25]

In view of these bitter consequences, counsel may wish to reach an agreement with opposing counsel that inadvertent production of a privileged document will not be asserted as grounds to argue complete subject matter waiver. Such an agreement benefits both parties, facilitates expeditious production of documents, and avoids overly broad assertions of privilege. These agreements may require return of inadvertently produced privileged documents and a stipulation of nonuse. Attorneys should not overlook the possibility that ethical considerations may require counsel to return inadvertently produced documents.[26] A few courts have even disqualified or considered disqualifying attorneys who have received privileged materials from an adverse party.[27]

V. PREPARATION OF INTERNAL SUMMARIES, CHRONOLOGIES, BINDERS

Important information contained in key documents must be organized into a useful, accessible form, regardless of the size and scope of the inquiry, and regardless of the sophistication or simplicity of the indexing system chosen by counsel. Although there are many ways to approach this, the most common tools are the hot document binder and the hot document chronology.

A. *Hot Document Chronology*

Arranging the hot documents in chronological order and creating a standardized summary is a valuable process separate and apart from the usefulness

---

25. *See, e.g.,* Sinclair Oil Corp. v. Texaco, Inc., 208 F.R.D. 329 (D. Okla. 2002); Smith v. Alyeska Pipeline Service Co., 538 F. Supp. 977, 980-82 (D. Del. 1982), *aff'd,* 758 F.2d 668 (D.C. Cir. 1984); *but see In re* Grand Jury Proceeding, 78 F.3d 251 (6th. Cir. 1996) (the "same subject matter" test should be construed narrowly, but a party should not be permitted to use privilege selectively as a shield and sword); Koch Materials Co. v. Shore Slurry Seal, Inc., 208 F.R.D. 109, 120 (D.N.J. 2002).

26. *See* ABA Comm. on Ethics and Prof'l Responsibility, Formal Op. 382 (1994) (discusses receiving privileged material belonging to adverse party intentionally sent from an unauthorized source); ABA Comm. on Ethics and Prof'l Responsibility, Formal Op. 368 (1992) (discusses inadvertently receiving privileged material belonging to adverse party).

27. *See* Milford Power Ltd. v. New England Power Co., 896 F. Supp. 53 (D. Mass. 1995); Resolution Trust Corp. v. First of America Bank, 868 F. Supp. 217 (W.D. Mich. 1994); Conley, Lott, Nichols Mach. Co. v. Brooks, 948 S.W.2d 345 (Tex. Ct. App. 1997).

of the end product. Thinking sequentially about events while familiarizing oneself with the body of facts is the best available substitute for reenactment of the conduct in question.

A chronology is a living document; as more facts emerge, the document will be supplemented and annotated, for example, with excerpts of key witness testimony. Below is a sample page from a hot document chronology.

98/06/20   DE-159—Exhibit 188—Jones memo to Sam Wilson (Pres. CEO) (cc: Jim Neal, Leo King, Jerry Johnson) re: tests of product produced by Wexlar system; duplication of formula was developed by careful trial and error and analysis
- Duplication of the competitor's formula has been developed by careful trial and error:
- Used Wexlar testing (disclosed in European patent) *Mills Deposition*
— Sandi Samuels was responsible for Wexlar testing

98/06/27   Exhibit 6445—Patent Searchers & Co. letter to Ramsey re: Patent Study; confirms Ramsey instruction to take no further action re: inspecting Patent No. 4,222,111

98/06/28   DE-183—Exhibit 287—Sam Wilson memo to distribution (Neal, King, others) (cc: Samuels, Johnson) re: revised critical paths for product X to be distributed on need-to-know basis
- Market date scheduled for third week of September *Wilson Deposition*
— Had settled on process going to use but not necessarily formulation, some refining work to be done (Wilson, Vol. II, p. 112)

There are four points to note about this sample. First, it is best to have a standard format for similar entries. This sample follows the format "date, document number, author(s), document type, recipient, copies, subject." Key points from the document are bullet points under the identifier entries and interview or testimony excerpts are placed below the key points.

Second, several copies of each document included in the chronology should be put into a separate folder. The folders should be prominently labeled and placed in chronological order. This will greatly facilitate interviews. Third, special attention should be paid to handwritten notes, so authenticity can be part of each interview. Finally, even in complex cases, a hot document chronology can ordinarily be captured in less than 100 pages, making for a manageable tool to use when preparing for and conducting interviews.

Often the columnar format and sorting capabilities of spreadsheets make them the best vehicles for creating chronologies.

B. *Summaries*

Investigations that are not amenable to chronological organization require more creative organizational approaches along issue lines. This approach is effective only if there are several clearly identifiable issues or a manageable universe of documents.

VI. PRODUCTION OF DOCUMENTS TO GOVERNMENT OR CIVIL LITIGANTS

A. *Advocacy Considerations*

While abusive tactics are generally counterproductive, there are legitimate advocacy considerations involved in deciding the methodology for producing documents.

1. Ordinary Course versus Extraordinary Measures

Recipients of document requests from civil litigants or the government are accustomed to lengthy introductory paragraphs containing procedural "guidance" about how the documents must be produced. Most of these directives are properly viewed as requests for extraordinary measures that generally are not compelled by any court or reviewing authority. In 1980, Federal Rule of Civil Procedure 34(b) was amended to permit the party producing documents for inspection to make them available either "as they are kept in the usual course of business" or "organized and labeled to correspond with the categories in the request." This amendment was aimed at forestalling discovery abuses such as the deliberate shuffling of documents or hiding important documents in a mass of irrelevant ones.[28] The parties seeking discovery may elect one of the two methods in which the documents are to be produced. Some experts argue that rule 34(b) as amended is ambiguous and should not be read as giving the responding party an absolute option to produce records as they are kept in the usual course of business. Wright and Miller argue that the producing party "should be required to produce them in a form that will make reasonable use of them possible."[29]

---

28. *See, e.g.,* Board of Educ. v. Admiral Heating & Ventilating, Inc., 104 F.R.D. 23, 36 (N.D. Ill. 1984).

29. *See* 8 Charles Alan Wright, Arthur R. Miller & Richard L. Marcus, FEDERAL PRACTICE AND PROCEDURE § 2213 (2d ed. 1991).

2. Overloading the Opposition versus Narrowing Scope of Request

Document requests are often broadly worded, so a reasonable interpretation could lead to a production of most, if not all, documents within the organization's control. One common reaction is to produce everything asked for, again on tactical grounds. While this strategy may occasionally work, it must not be undertaken lightly, and without regard to the types of documents maintained by the client.

More times than not, this tactic will be unsuccessful and generate unnecessary expense. A client with 200 boxes of inventory records or old computer printouts that are of marginal relevance gains nothing by piling them on top of the production of otherwise relevant documents. To the extent these boxes of documents can be readily identified, they also can be quickly ignored and discarded by the opposition. A more reasonable approach is to negotiate the request in an attempt to narrow its scope. The process of narrowing not only saves cost in the copying and processing phases, but also starts a dialogue that can lead to information about the opposition's case, strategies, and goals.

3. On-Site Inspection versus Production of Complete Set

Another important consideration is whether an on-site inspection should be permitted, or demanded. One advantage is that it may provide important insights about the opponent's case and objectives. An on-site inspection may impose actual or psychological pressures, causing the opponent to overlook important records. Additionally, cost-conscious opponents will not copy irrelevant documents, and costs for both sides may be reduced. In fact, prohibitive cost may be the overriding factor in requesting an on-site inspection of documents.[30] Companies that have been involved in recurring litigation on the same or similar issues may have the universe of potentially relevant documents centrally assembled.

In these cases on-site inspection may be the only reasonable approach. If a client allows an on-site inspection at its facility, the documents should be segregated in an area away from employees, and steps should be taken to ensure that the adversary is not given the opportunity to gain otherwise unavailable information. On-site inspections must always be closely supervised.

By producing a complete set of documents without an inspection, the opponent remains away from the client's facility and the risk of snooping is

---

30. *See* Petruska v. Johns-Manville, 83 F.R.D. 32, 36 (E.D. Pa. 1979).

eliminated. Additionally, if a set of documents is provided, the opponent may never give a proper, thorough review of the documents. An on-site inspection may promote an early intensive focus on your documents.

B. *Personal versus Business Records*

The distinction between a "personal" document and a "corporate" one often is important in federal cases, particularly in the context of a witness or defendant in a criminal case asserting a Fifth Amendment privilege against self-incrimination. The importance of this distinction stems from a line of Supreme Court cases holding that the privilege against self-incrimination protects a person from producing his personal papers, but not from producing corporate documents held in a representative capacity, even if the production is personally incriminating.[31] The rationale for this holding is that the privilege against self-incrimination is "purely a personal one," applicable only to "natural individuals."[32] The privilege against self-incrimination cannot be invoked by a corporation or other collective entity.[33] Despite the importance of the "personal-corporate" distinction, there is relatively little judicial interpretation of these terms. The courts that have addressed the issue generally have considered similar factors, including who produced the document in question and for what purpose, the nature of its contents, who has possession of and access to the document, and whether the document was necessary to or helpful in the conduct of the corporation's business.[34] Courts also consider whether the party resisting production holds the documents in an individual or representative capacity.[35]

The Supreme Court has held that a person cannot claim the Fifth Amendment's protection on the basis of the content of the items demanded.[36] These rulings indicate that the distinction between personal and corporate documents may become less important in coming years.[37] The Supreme Court has

---

31. *See, e.g.,* Hale v. Henkel, 201 U.S. 43 (1901); Wilson v. United States, 221 U.S. 361, 382 (1911).
32. *See* United States v. White, 322 U.S. 694, 698-99 (1944).
33. *Id..* at 699.
34. *See* Wilson, 221 U.S. at 380; *see also In re* Grand Jury Subpoena Duces Tecum Dated April 23, 1981, 522 F. Supp. 977, 984 (S.D.N.Y. 1981).
35. *See* Bellis v. United States, 417 U.S. 85, 92 (1974).
36. *See* Fisher v. United States, 425 U.S. 391 (1976); *see also* United States v. Doe, 465 U.S. 605 (1984).
37. *See* Baltimore City Dep't of Social Servs. v. Bouknight, 493 U.S. 549 (1990).

apparently shifted to a new framework of analysis for documentary subpoenas, under which the validity of a subpoena no longer turns on the contents of the documents demanded, but rather on whether the act of producing them entails testimonial self-incrimination.[38] The most recent analysis under this new framework holds that "a person may not claim the [Fifth] Amendment's protections based upon the incrimination that may result from the contents or nature of the thing demanded."[39]

C. *Production Abuses*

Litigation lore is filled with stories about document productions on hot summer days in rat-infested warehouses without benefit of chairs, desks, or air conditioning. While this scenario may be more fiction than fact, document productions do bring out the worst behavior in some trial lawyers, all in the name of tactical advantage. More courts are moving to sanction abuses, such as "shuffling" documents before production, burying important documents amid a mass of irrelevant material, or actual spoliation of documents.[40] Certainly any counsel or client who attempts such tactics when responding to a government agency's subpoena *duces tecum* risks loss of credibility at a minimum, and possibly severe sanctions, including obstruction of justice charges.[41]

D. *Destruction of Documents*

When incriminating documents are uncovered in the midst of investigation, and there is no ongoing criminal or civil proceeding, counsel may be asked

---

38. *See* Fisher, 452 U.S. at 399, *In re* Three Grand Jury Subpoenas Duces Tecum Dated January 29, 1999, 191 F.3d 173, 178 (2d Cir. 1999).
39. *Bouknight,* 493 U.S. at 555.
40. *See, e.g.,* United States v. Philip Morris, 327 F. Supp. 2d 21 (D.D.C. 2004); Stevenson v. Union Pac. R.R., 204 F.R.D. 425 (E.D. Ark. 2001).
41. FED. R. CIV. P. 37; 18 U.S.C. § 1512(b)(2)(B) (West 2006); 18 U.S.C. § 1519 (West 2006); United States v. Laurins, 857 F.2d 529 (9th Cir. 1988) (concealing documents falls within definition of specific intent required for obstruction of justice); United States v. Gravely, 840 F.2d 1156 (4th Cir. 1988) (stating that in order for defendant to be convicted of obstructing justice for destroying documents, the documents do not have to be under subpoena, if the defendant is aware that a grand jury will likely seek the documents in its investigation); *but see* Richmark Corp. v. Timber Falling Consultants, Inc., 730 F. Supp. 1525 (D. Or. 1990) (holding that "obstruction of justice" did not include alleged concealment or withholding of discovery documents in a civil case).

whether the documents can be destroyed. There are at least four important considerations that bear on this decision:

- Local ethics rules, statutes, or procedural rules may preclude destruction.[42]
- Destruction of *all* copies of any document may be impossible in this age of word-processing disks and reproduction machines.
- It is often less difficult to explain a "bad" document than to justify its destruction later. Destruction carries with it the blackest presumption imaginable.
- Criminal obstruction of justice statutes were broadened in the Sarbanes-Oxley legislation and the full extent of their application has not yet been fully developed by the courts.

Accordingly, the presumption will likely be against destroying problematic documents.

E. *Confidentiality Agreements*

Counsel must consider not only the process of discovery, but the nature of the information produced and the need to retain the confidentiality of certain information. Confidentiality agreements, or agreed protective orders, are essential in civil litigation where sensitive information—operational or financial—will likely be disclosed during the course of litigation. This order can have multiple levels of confidentiality, depending on the nature of the information and the persons viewing it. Confidentiality orders and agreements can take many forms, but items typically addressed include:

- Definition of "confidential information." In some cases it may be appropriate to have "confidential," "highly confidential," and perhaps other designations for extremely sensitive documents, with each classification having its own restrictions concerning who is "qualified" to have access to the information.

---

42. *See, e.g.,* TEX. DISCIPLINARY R. PROF'L CONDUCT 3.04(a), *reprinted in* TEX. GOV'T CODE ANN. tit. 2, subtit. G app. A (Vernon Supp. 2005) (TEX. STATE BAR R. art. X § 9). A lawyer shall not . . . unlawfully obstruct another party's access to evidence; in anticipation of a dispute unlawfully alter, destroy, or conceal a document or other material that a competent lawyer would believe has potential or actual evidentiary value, or counsel or assist another person to do any such act.

- Definition of "qualified persons" to have access to sensitive information. This can be as narrow or broad as needed depending on the sensitivity of the information reviewed. Persons qualified to review the information should be specifically defined by group.
- "Qualified persons" may include outside counsel and their employees, general counsel, or designated associate general counsel for a party, consultants, expert witnesses, or investigators.
- Whether information disclosed at a deposition can be designated as "confidential information" by indicating on the record that the testimony is so designated and subject to the provisions of the order. The portions of the deposition containing confidential information can be separately bound.
- Procedures for introducing confidential information at any hearing conducted in the litigation. For example, prior notification, exclusion of nonqualified personnel from the hearing, and designation of the hearing transcript as "confidential."
- Procedures for disclosing confidential information to a deponent or prospective trial witness, such as requiring prior written agreement to be bound by the terms of the confidentiality order.
- Restrictions on attendance at depositions where confidential information is disclosed.
- Whether inadvertent disclosure of confidential information constitutes waiver of any confidentiality claim.
- Procedures for sealing affidavits, briefs, memoranda of law or other papers containing confidential information that are filed in court.
- Notification procedures in the event a nonparty demands confidential information by subpoena or other legal process.
- Disposition of confidential documents at the conclusion of the litigation (and appeals).

VII. CONCLUSION

Despite the lack of glamour and inescapable drudgery, document gathering, processing, and review are the foundations of internal investigations and complex litigation. Cases may not be won at this stage of a proceeding, but cases *can* be lost if serious missteps occur. Like most other legal endeavors, the keys to success are early planning, organization, attention to detail, and follow-through.

APPENDIX A

Document Review Checklist

Date: _____

Name: _____

Location: _____

I. Preliminary
- ❏ Represent the company, not the individual
- ❏ Purpose and status of investigation
- ❏ Purpose and procedures regarding document gathering
- ❏ Must review all files
- ❏ Will be indexed and preserved (retrievable)
- ❏ Let us know if need copies now
- ❏ Let us know if privileged documents in files
- ❏ No altering or destroying documents

II. Walk-through
- ❏ Show us files and generally describe
- ❏ Any archived or storage documents
- ❏ Computer databases
- ❏ Secretary files

III. Documents
- ❏ Calendars   2006   2005   2004   2003
- ❏ Telephone/Address lists _____
- ❏ Daily planners/notebooks _____
- ❏ Mileage logs, travel and expense reports _____
- ❏ Price lists _____
- ❏ Competitor files _____
- ❏ Marketing information _____

Gathering and Organizing Relevant Documents: An Essential Task **171**

    ❑ Customer files _____
    ❑ Correspondence/Reading files _____
    ❑ Customer entertainment files _____
    ❑ Inventory files _____
    ❑ Bid files _____
    ❑ Other _____

IV. Areas Inspected
    ❑ Desk _____
    ❑ Credenza _____
    ❑ Bookshelves _____
    ❑ File cabinets _____
    ❑ Closet _____
    ❑ Briefcase _____
    ❑ Secretary area _____
    ❑ Other _____

V. Final Remarks
    ❑ Provide business card
    ❑ Limit discussion about investigation
    ❑ Procedure if need document returned/copied
    ❑ Let us know if contacted, hear anything
    ❑ Optional—provide copy of index

APPENDIX B

File Control #	Location	Custodian	File Title or Description	Comments
DAL 0001	Dallas Area Office Mgr file cabinet	Sarah Jones	Profit Plans - 2003	Copies made and left in files
DAL 0002	Dallas Area Office Secretary desk	Sarah Jones	Appointment book - Jan	
DAL 0003	Dallas Area Office Secretary desk	Sarah Jones	Appointment book - Jan Jones; 2003	Original retained; copy made for investigation
AUS 0001	Austin District Office Bill Smith's desk	Bill Smith	Sales reports - FW2003	Hot documents
AUS 0002	Austin District Office hall closet #2	Bob Walker	Telephone/ address book (Betty Brown - 2004)	Storage - former employee files
AUS 0003	Austin District Office main file cabinet	Jim Stanley	Sales Meetings 2002-2004	Copies made and left in files *Hot documents

APPENDIX C

File Control #	Location	Custodian	File Title or Description	Comments
DAL 0001 0001-0084	Dallas Area Office Mgr file cabinet	Sarah Jones	Profit Plans - 2003	Copies made and left in files
DAL 0002 0085-0593	Dallas Area Office Secretary desk	Sarah Jones	Appointment book - Jan Jones; 2002	
DAL 0003 0514-1139	Dallas Area Office Secretary desk	Sarah Jones	Appointment book - Jan Jones; 2003	Original retained; copy made for investigation
AUS 0001 1140-1444	Austin District Office Bill Smith's desk	Bill Smith	Sales reports - FW2003	Hot documents
AUS 0002 Not produced	Austin District Office hall closet #2	Bob Walker	Telephone/ address book (Betty Brown - 2004)	Storage - former employee files
AUS 0003 1445-2218	Austin District Office main file cabinet	Jim Stanley	Sales Meetings 2002–2004	Copies made and left in files *Hot documents

APPENDIX D

ABC Equipment v. Jones Enterprises

CONFIDENTIAL & PRIVILEGED—PREPARED BY AND FOR COUNSEL

DOCUMENT NO.: _____ - _____ REVIEWED BY: _____
                     Beginning   Ending   Attorney Legal Assistant

DOC. DATE: _____ FILE NAME: _____ SOURCE: _____

DOCUMENT TYPE: [Circle appropriate letter(s)]

B Bond	H Handwritten notes	M Memo
E Exhibit (other proceeding)	L Letter	P Pleading
Hot Document: ❏ Yes ❏ No	Marginalia: ❏ Yes ❏ No	❏ Other

Attachments: _____

KEY ISSUES: [Circle Appropriate Number(s)]

01	ABC Negotiations	10	Jones Negotiations
02	ABC Computer Procedures	11	Jones Agreement
03	ABC Bankruptcy Approval	12	Jones Scheduling
04	ABC Schedule	13	Jones Startup
05	ABC Startup	14	Jones Contract Services
06	ABC Agreement	15	Jones Pricing
07	ABC Marketing	16	Jones Performance
08	ABC Expansion	17	Jones Competition
09	ABC Contract Services	18	JoneslNE Computer Services

Other: _____ _____ _____

AUTHOR(S): (1) _____ (2) _____ (3) _____

RECIPIENTS	COPIES	MENTIONED
_____	_____	_____
_____	_____	_____
_____	_____	_____

INTERNAL CORPORATE INVESTIGATION

Description: _____
_____
_____
_____

The Hydra Effect: Parallel Proceedings Accompanying Internal Investigations

6

Scott N. Auby and Ada Fernandez Johnson

I. INTRODUCTION 176
II. RECURRING ISSUES IN PARALLEL PROCEEDINGS 178
   A. Obtaining Civil Stays to Prevent Criminal Prejudice 178
   B. The Fifth Amendment and Adverse Civil Inferences 185
   C. Criminal and Civil Penalties: Double Jeopardy? 188
   D. Collateral Estoppel: The Consequences of "Losing" 193

Scott N. Auby is Counsel in the Washington, D.C., office of Debevoise & Plimpton LLP. Ada Fernandez Johnson is his colleague in that office. The authors are forever indebted to Judah Best, who conceived this chapter and was the principal author of its previous iterations (most recently, Judah Best & Scott N. Auby, *The Practitioner's Guide to Parallel Proceedings, in* INTERNAL CORPORATE INVESTIGATIONS (2d ed., ABA 2003)). This chapter draws heavily not only from Mr. Best's prior work, but also from his guidance and example. The authors also wish to thank Debevoise associates Mark J. Jacoby and Kenya Davis for their substantial contributions to this chapter.

E. Responding to Employee Misconduct   197
F. *Ex Parte* Contacts by Government Lawyers   200
G. Providing Legal Representation for Employees   210
H. Joint Defense Agreements: Benefits, Limits, and Risks   215
I. Keeping the Government-Disclosure Genie in the Bottle   224
J. The Perils of Parallelism for Government Contractors   231
K. The *Gestalt* of Parallel-Proceedings Resolution   234
III. CONCLUSION   240

I. INTRODUCTION

The Hydra had the body of a serpent and many heads. . . . [I]f any of the other heads were severed another would grow in its place. . . . [1]

COUNSEL REPRESENTING corporations in the wake of an announced restatement of financials, an earnings miss, or disclosure of alleged employee misconduct often feel as if they are battling the mythological hydra. When one of the beast's heads is dealt a seemingly fatal blow, its other heads rear in their full terror—and another head seems to sprout in the slain head's place. If only the hydra had been attacked at the outset for the unitary beast it is.

This chapter focuses on the multiple legal actions—so-called parallel proceedings—that corporations almost inevitably face upon the discovery and disclosure of what we will call "bad news." Given the focus of this book, one can assume that the bad news disclosed suggests the presence of improper and potentially unlawful activity within the corporation's employee ranks. Given the vast and ever-increasing network of local, state, federal, and even international legislation and regulation to which companies' operations are subject, it is not surprising that a violation of one normative standard of conduct can lead to the institution of numerous proceedings by various governmental authorities at home and abroad, as well as by private individuals or—more frequently—classes of individuals.

To provide a hypothetical variation on what is by now a familiar theme, assume a corporation that relies on state and federal government contracts for its profitability has discovered an internal control breakdown that calls the

---

1. Ron Leadbetter, *Hydra*, ENCYCLOPEDIA MYTHICA (available at www.pantheon.org/articles/h/hydra.html) (September 2006).

accuracy of its previous public disclosures into question. As is meet and right, the company's audit committee conducts a thorough internal investigation with the assistance of able counsel. Counsel's conclusions are less than flattering. In its eagerness to demonstrate to the company's various constituents—regulators, shareholders, business partners, and customers—that it is a conscientious and responsible corporate citizen, the company's board publicly accepts not only the audit committee's findings, but also the resignations of its most senior managers. The company's press release states that the problem has been addressed, and implores all concerned to move forward.

Not so fast. The disclosure of the audit committee's findings merely serves as the corporation's entrée into the confounding world of parallel proceedings. Disclosure of the report of investigation gives birth to the mythical hydra, whose many heads include:

- A federal criminal investigation of the company and its senior management, with the looming prospect of a grand jury investigation, a criminal indictment, and a lengthy and very public trial;
- A formal SEC investigation, with the threat of SEC administrative and civil actions and accompanying penalties;
- Parallel criminal and civil investigations by the relevant state authorities;
- Multiple class-action lawsuits under the federal securities laws that ultimately will be consolidated into a single case, in which the impact of the company's disclosure on its stock price will be multiplied by investors' class-period purchases, yielding an imposing financial threat;
- Follow-on ERISA class actions seeking recovery from the corporation and its senior management, ostensibly as fiduciaries of the company's U.S. pension plans, for failing to alert the company's shareholder-employees that investing in their employer was a bad deal;
- Shareholder derivative actions, in which a handful of shareholders label the board too interested and dependent to decide whether the company should file its claims against its senior management (and perhaps board members);
- Suspension and debarment proceedings by both state and federal procurement agencies that, if unfavorably resolved, could literally close the company's doors.

There are many other examples where simultaneous, or seriatim, proceedings flow from what one might consider a single "problem." Those coming quickly to mind include proceedings related to violations of federal procurement laws, antitrust laws, environmental laws, and banking laws. In each instance, a single "problem" can result in multiple federal and state criminal prosecutions, civil damage suits, and injunctive actions, as well as local, state, federal, and even international administrative proceedings.

Of course, each substantive area has its own distinct considerations and body of law. Because of the enormous stakes involved in defending corporate interests in multiple arenas, it is of utmost importance that company counsel have a fundamental understanding of the existence of, and interplay among, the federal and state laws and regulations pertinent to the particular circumstances faced by the corporate client accused of misconduct. With this said, parallel proceedings present legal questions and strategic implications that cut across contexts. In any situation where a single "problem" spawns multiple legal proceedings, the outcome of any single proceeding can dramatically impact not only a company's well being, but also its prospects for success in other proceedings.

In the following pages, some of the more important issues confronting the practitioner involved in parallel proceedings are set out and discussed. Each issue is a subject unto itself, and deserves a far more detailed discussion than this already lengthy chapter permits. But in this context, issue identification and characterization are half the battle. It is hoped that this chapter will enable corporate counsel better to anticipate and advise its client through the landmines that lay in the path to a successful resolution of multiple, parallel proceedings.

II. RECURRING ISSUES IN PARALLEL PROCEEDINGS

A. *Obtaining Civil Stays to Prevent Criminal Prejudice*

When civil proceedings are accompanied by an ongoing criminal investigation, evidence obtained in the civil proceeding may be incriminating in the criminal action. This risk typically will not suffice to defer or delay proceedings in the civil case. The Supreme Court has long recognized the government's right to pursue criminal and civil proceedings "simultaneously or successively" based on the same underlying set of facts.[2] Even where private

---

2. Standard Sanitary Mfg. Co. v. United States, 226 U.S. 20, 52 (1912); *see also* United States v. Kordel, 397 U.S. 1, 11 (1970) ("It would stultify enforcement of federal law to require a governmental agency ... to choose either to forgo recommendation of a criminal prosecution once it seeks civil relief, or to defer civil proceedings pending the ultimate outcome of a criminal trial.").

litigation may yield incriminating evidence, a civil court normally will not stay its hand while the criminal matter works its way to completion.[3]

For example, in *SEC v. Dresser Industries, Inc.*,[4] the D.C. Circuit affirmed a district court order compelling Dresser to comply with an SEC subpoena. The court rejected Dresser's argument that compliance would impermissibly allow the government to use information gained during civil discovery to promote the criminal case, concluding that:

> Effective enforcement of the securities laws requires that the SEC and Justice be able to investigate possible violations simultaneously.... The SEC cannot always wait for Justice to complete the criminal proceedings if it is to obtain the necessary prompt civil remedy; neither can Justice always await the conclusion of the civil proceeding without endangering its criminal case.[5]

According to the *Dresser* court, only "special circumstances" could justify blocking concurrent, parallel investigations by the SEC and federal prosecutors.[6]

What, then, are the "special circumstances" that would permit a stay of a civil proceeding until after the completion of a companion criminal proceeding? The *Dresser* court noted in dicta that if a party is under indictment for a serious offense and is required simultaneously to defend against a civil action involving the same underlying issues, the non-criminal proceeding, if not deferred, could, *inter alia*, undermine the party's Fifth Amendment privilege against self-incrimination and effectively abrogate the limits on criminal discovery set forth in Fed. R. Crim. P. 16(b). The court cautioned, however, that

---

3. *See* Sterling Nat'l Bank v. A-1 Hotels Int'l, Inc., 175 F. Supp. 2d 573, 576 (S.D.N.Y. 2001) (noting that it is "well understood" that a "stay is not constitutionally required whenever a litigant finds himself facing the dilemmas inherent in pursuing a civil litigation while being the subject of a related criminal investigation"); *see also* Metzler v. Bennett, No. 97-CV-0148 (RSP/GJD), 1998 U.S. Dist. LEXIS 5441, at *17 (N.D.N.Y. Apr. 15, 1998) (noting that staying a civil case "is an extraordinary remedy"); *In re* Par Pharm., Inc. Secs. Litig., 133 F.R.D. 12, 13 (S.D.N.Y. 1990) (same).

4. SEC v. Dresser Indus., Inc., 628 F.2d 1368, 1377 (D.C. Cir. 1980).

5. *Id.* at 1377; *see also* Gellis v. Casey, 338 F. Supp. 651, 653 (S.D.N.Y. 1972), (denying stay of SEC administrative action when the same transactions were the subject of a potential grand jury investigation, noting that "the SEC, as the agency charged with administering the Securities Acts to protect investors, is merely conducting an ordinary and proper administrative proceeding in good faith").

6. Dresser, 628 F.2d at 1375-76.

delaying the civil proceeding would be appropriate only to the extent it would not seriously injure the public interest.[7]

The progeny of *Dresser* has not been particularly kind to those facing parallel civil and criminal proceedings. Courts often begin their analysis of requests for a civil stay by noting that whether to grant or deny the stay is a matter committed to judicial discretion.[8] In balancing the varying interests implicated by a stay request,[9] courts have been far more vigilant guardians of the ostensible concerns of private plaintiffs[10] and the public[11] than of defendants' Fifth Amendment rights and interests in orderly criminal procedure.

---

7. *Id.; see also* Kordel, 397 U.S. at 11 (suggesting in dicta that a stay may be appropriate if (i) the government pursues the civil action solely to obtain evidence for a criminal prosecution, (ii) the government fails to inform the defendant in the civil case that it plans further criminal proceedings, or (iii) the defendant lacks counsel or reasonably fears prejudice from adverse pretrial publicity or other unfair injury); Afro-Lecon, Inc. v. United States, 820 F.2d 1198, 1203 (Fed. Cir. 1987) (recognizing that "parallel proceedings may result in the abuse of discovery" by impermissibly expanding the scope of "highly restricted" criminal discovery to the broad scope of civil discovery).

8. *See, e.g.,* Federal Sav. & Loan Ins. Corp. v. Molinaro, 889 F.2d 899, 902 (9th Cir. 1989); *In re* CFS-Related Sec. Fraud Litig., 256 F. Supp. 2d 1227, 1236 (N.D. Okla. 2003) (stating that whether to stay civil proceedings pending conclusion of a criminal matter is "entirely discretionary with the Court").

9. *See* Landis v. North Am. Co., 299 U.S. 248, 254-55 (1936) (stating that a request for a stay of proceedings requires a court to balance the competing interests involved).

10. *See, e.g.,* United States v. Int'l Brotherhood of Teamsters et al., 247 F.3d 370, 388 (2d Cir. 2001) (denying request for stay of civil Independent Review Board proceedings pending resolution of criminal action; "the need for the union to proceed with the hearing was particularly urgent because the union was faced with the need to purge itself of corruption at its highest levels"); Wilson v. Olathe Bank, No. 97-2458-KHV, 1998 U.S. Dist. LEXIS 5509, at *22 (D. Kan. Mar. 2, 1998) (stay of class action denied due to risk of "substantial prejudice to the . . . named plaintiffs and the class"); Transatlantic Reins. Co. v. Ditrapani, No. 90 Civ. 2240 (CSH), 1991 U.S. Dist. LEXIS 872, at *10 (S.D.N.Y. Jan. 28, 1991) ("that defendants' conduct also resulted in a criminal charge . . . should not be availed of by [them] as a shield against a civil suit and prevent plaintiffs from expeditiously advancing [their] claim") (quotation omitted); Arden Way Assocs. v. Boesky, 660 F. Supp. 1494, 1497 (S.D.N.Y. 1987) ("It is plainly ludicrous for Mr. Boesky to argue that it is 'unfair' to compel him to face the civil law suits against him which are the creations of his own alleged misconduct. . . . Surely it would be anomalous to suspend plaintiffs' rights in these civil litigations because they deal with Mr. Boesky's misconduct."); Fidelity Bankers Life Ins. Co. v. Wedco, Inc., 586 F. Supp. 1123, 1126 (D. Nev. 1984) ("The long period remaining before the statute of limitations will expire, and any criminal prosecution will be terminated, together with the need by Fidelity for an expeditious resolution of the issues . . . outweigh the impairment of the . . . defendants' ability to put on as complete a defense as they might but for their apprehension of self-incrimination.").

11. *See, e.g.,* SEC v. First Fin. Group of Tex., 659 F.2d 660, 667 (5th Cir. 1981) ("Protection of the efficient operation of the securities markets and the financial holdings of investors

Stays generally have been granted only if a defendant can convince the civil court that its proceeding involves substantially the same facts as those in an ongoing criminal matter,[12] and that a stay will not unduly burden the interests of the public or private plaintiffs.

Brock v. Tolkow[13] is an illustrative and frequently cited case. In *Brock*, the district court entered a protective order staying "all discovery" in a Department of Labor ERISA civil suit pending the outcome of a parallel criminal investigation.[14] The court accepted the defendants' contention that "the criminal prosecution may be based on the same facts as the complaint in the [civil] case"[15] and noted that the defendants were not seeking to stay the entire case, but rather sought only to have discovery deferred pending the outcome of the criminal investigation.[16] Finally, the *Brock* court opined that a civil stay would not unduly prejudice the public interest because "[p]ossible mismanagement

---

... may require prompt civil enforcement which cannot await the outcome of a criminal investigation.") (*citing* Dresser, 628 F.2d at 1375); SEC v. Rivelli, No. 05-CV-1039 (RPM), 2005 WL 2789317, at *1 (D. Colo., Oct. 26, 2005) (denying requested stay of SEC civil enforcement action pending resolution of criminal investigation into the same facts because "resolution of the claims would be in the best interest" of the company, its shareholders, and the public); Sterling Nat'l Bank, 175 F. Supp. 2d at 580 (denying stay of civil RICO case because the interests of nonparties and the public favored prompt resolution).

12. *See* Koester v. American Republic Invs., Inc., 11 F.3d 818, 823 (8th Cir. 1993) ("to warrant a stay, defendant must make a strong showing . . . that the two proceedings are so interrelated that he cannot protect himself at the civil trial by selectively invoking the Fifth Amendment privilege") (citation omitted); Harbour Town Yacht Club Boat Slip Owners Assoc. v. Safe Berth Mgmt., Inc., 411 F. Supp. 2d 641, 644-43 (D.S.C. 2005) ("Absent this relatedness [between the civil and criminal matters], the myriad of tangible concerns in favor of a stay, including the protection of a defendant's Fifth Amendment interest and the deleterious effect of civil discovery on the prosecution or defense, dissipates."); United States v. Eberhard, No. 03-CR-562, 2004 WL 616122, at *4-5 (S.D.N.Y., Mar. 30, 2004) (denying request for a stay of NASD arbitration pending resolution of a criminal investigation where it was unclear that the issues overlapped); Bennett, 1998 U.S. Dist. LEXIS 5441, at *18 ("If there is no overlap [between the issues in the civil and criminal proceedings], then there would be no danger of self-incrimination and no need for a stay."); Trustees of the Plumbers & Pipefitters Nat'l Pension Fund v. Transworld Mechanical, Inc., 886 F. Supp. 1134, 1139 (S.D.N.Y. 1995) ("The first question to be resolved is the extent to which the issues in the criminal case overlap with those present in the civil case, since self-incrimination is more likely if there is a significant overlap.") (citations omitted).

13. 109 F.R.D. 116 (E.D.N.Y. 1985).

14. *Id.* at 121.

15. *Id.* at 118.

16. *Id.* at 119-20 ("Rather, they ask only that discovery therein be deferred pending the outcome of the criminal investigation; in all other respects the civil case will go forward.") (footnote omitted).

of a pension fund simply does not present the same danger to the public interest as violations that other courts have found to warrant denial of a motion for a stay."[17] Unlike *Dresser*, where delaying the civil proceeding would have prejudiced the public's interest in timely regulation of the securities markets, and *Kordel*, where granting the stay would have impeded the government's efforts to stop distribution of mislabeled drugs, the *Brock* court found little or no risk that the pension fund's ability ultimately to meet its obligations to its beneficiaries would be endangered by a stay of discovery.[18]

The *Brock* court's decision to grant the stay seems largely based on its view that doing so would not substantially harm the public interest, which still could be effectively served despite the delay. Whether a post-Enron/WorldCom court would take a similar view of the public interest in preventing pension mismanagement is debatable. But the critical weight given by the *Brock* court to considerations of the public interest remains the cornerstone of the stay analysis. The fact that a stay would not be adverse to the public interest has been crucial to most cases in which a stay of a parallel civil proceeding has been granted.[19]

Counsel should note that a defendant's odds of obtaining a stay of civil proceedings are typically greater after a formal indictment has been issued. Granted, in *Brock*, the defendants had received grand jury subpoenas, but had not been indicted.[20] Still, courts have deemed the case for a pre-indictment stay "'a far weaker one,'"[21] and generally have refused to grant such stays.[22] In particular, courts appear more sympathetic to private plaintiffs' interests before

---

17. *Id.* at 120.

18. *Id.* ("[The Dresser and Kordel] cases, unlike the present one, involve a tangible threat of immediate and serious harm to the public at large. While the allegations in this case are indeed serious, there is no indication that plan beneficiaries are suffering or will suffer any irreparable injury if civil discovery is stayed.").

19. *See, e.g.*, United States v. Armada Petroleum Corp., 700 F.2d 706, 709 (Temp. Emer. Ct. App. 1983); United States v. U.S. Currency, 626 F.2d 11, 17 (6th Cir. 1980); United States v. $557,933.89, More or Less, in U.S. Funds, No. 95-CV-3978 (JG), 1998 U.S. Dist. LEXIS 22252, at *12 (E.D.N.Y. Mar. 9, 1998); United States v. Certain Real Prop. & Premises, 751 F. Supp. 1060 (E.D.N.Y. 1989).

20. Brock, 109 F.R.D. at 119 n.2 (noting that lack of an indictment "may be a factor counseling against a stay of civil proceedings," but "does not make consideration of the stay motion any less appropriate").

21. Molinaro, 889 F.2d at 903 (quoting Dresser, 628 F.2d at 1376).

22. *See, e.g.*, Trustees of Plumbers Pension Fund, 886 F. Supp. at 1139 ("stays will generally not be granted before an indictment is issued"); Rivelli, 2005 WL 2789317, at *1 (denying stay of SEC civil enforcement action where criminal investigation had not produced indictment); Sterling Nat'l Bank, 175 F. Supp. 2d at 576-77 (noting a "practical rule of thumb" that courts are more open to granting a stay after the defendant has been indicted).

indictment, perhaps because of uncertainty about whether and when an indictment might be returned.[23] Some courts have gone so far as to deem the absence of an indictment dispositive (although this is far from the majority view).[24]

Notably, the stay calculus can be altered dramatically where the court believes the government has acted in bad faith.[25] For example, in *SEC v. Healthsouth Corp.*, the court granted a pre-indictment stay of an SEC civil enforcement action largely "[b]ecause this is a case where the government has undoubtedly manipulated simultaneous criminal and civil proceedings, both of which it controls. . . ."[26] The court found that this presented "a special danger that the government can effectively undermine the rights that would exist in a criminal investigation by conducting a de facto criminal investigation using normal civil means."[27] The government's conduct so moved the court that it reasoned the stay would actually *benefit* the SEC (which opposed the stay), by allowing the FBI to continue gathering evidence that might be of use in the SEC's civil case.[28]

Taken together, the post-*Dresser* cases provide helpful guidance to defense counsel seeking a stay of a parallel civil proceeding. Short of establishing government misconduct in connection with simultaneous civil and criminal prosecutions, the cases suggest that the prospects for a stay improve if (i) an indictment has been returned against the defendant seeking the stay; (ii) the civil and criminal cases involve substantially the same facts; (iii) the

---

23. *See, e.g.,* JHW Greentree Capital, L.P. v. Whittier Trust Co., No. 05-Civ-2985, 2005, WL 1705244, at *1 (S.D.N.Y., July 22, 2005) (denying pre-indictment stay because it would frustrate a speedy resolution of the civil action and potentially affect the plaintiff's ability to collect on any future judgment given potential costs of criminal defense); Fidelity Bankers Life, 586 F. Supp. at 1125-26 ("Delay of these proceedings [for as much as three years] would be unfair to the other parties . . . [who] cannot control the timing of any criminal proceedings.").

24. *See* United States v. Private Sanitation Indus. Ass'n, 811 F. Supp. 802, 805 (E.D.N.Y. 1992) (holding that "since [the defendant] has yet to be indicted by any grand jury, his motion to stay may be denied on that ground alone"); *In re* Par Pharm., 133 F.R.D. at 13 ("[C]ourts will stay a civil proceeding when the criminal investigation has ripened into an indictment . . . but will deny a stay of the civil proceeding where no indictment has issued.") (collecting cases, citations omitted). *But see* Walsh Secs. Inc. v. Crisco Property Management Ltd., 7 F. Supp. 2d 523, 527 (D.N.J. 1998) (stating that stay can be granted although an indictment has not yet been returned, and granting stay in such a case); $557,933.89, More or Less, in U.S. Funds, 1998 U.S. Dist. LEXIS 22252, at *12-*13 (granting stay despite lack of indictment); Wilson, 1998 U.S. Dist. LEXIS 5509, at *21 ("While the lack of any ongoing criminal proceedings is a factor for the Court to consider, it is not determinative.").

25. *See, e.g.,* Kordel, 397 U.S. at 10-11; Dresser, 628 F.2d at 1375.

26. 261 F. Supp. 2d 1298, 1326 (N.D. Ala. 2003).

27. *Id.* (internal quotation marks omitted).

28. *Id.* at 1327.

public interests at issue can be described as less than fundamental, or as sufficiently vindicated despite the stay; (iv) the relief requested is carefully circumscribed, involving only postponing civil discovery to some parties for a limited time, rather than staying an entire civil action;[29] and (v) the two actions involve the same statutory or regulatory scheme and will vindicate the same or substantially the same public interests.[30] Unless most of these factors are present, obtaining a stay in the civil case will be an uphill battle.[31] And even if most factors are present, the absence of only one—adequate vindication of the public interest—still may tip the scales against the requested stay.[32]

Even if the court rejects a stay, it may be open to entering a protective order to keep arguably incriminating testimony from being used against the defendant in a criminal proceeding.[33] But today's protective order can be

---

29. Courts are generally hesitant to grant a "total stay" of a parallel civil proceeding. *See, e.g.,* Golden Quality Ice Cream Co., Inc. v. Deerfield Specialty Papers, Inc., 87 F.R.D. 53, 58-59 (E.D. Pa. 1980); *see also* Weil v. Markowitz, 829 F.2d 166, 175 n.17 (D.C. Cir. 1987) ("A total stay of civil discovery pending the outcome of related criminal matters is an extraordinary remedy appropriate for extraordinary circumstances."). The more common result is a stay that is narrowly tailored to protecting the legitimate interests of the defendant. *See, e.g.,* Sidari v. Orleans County, 180 F.R.D. 226, 231 (W.D.N.Y. 1997) (staying civil discovery as to issues on which criminal and civil cases overlapped but refusing to stay entire civil matter); SEC v. Rehtorik, 755 F. Supp. 1018, 1019 (S.D. Fla. 1990) (granting stay only as to accounting procedure which arguably raised Fifth Amendment concerns).

30. *See In re* Par Pharm., 133 F.R.D. at 14 (denying stay because indictments had not been returned and distinguishing *Brock* as involving civil and criminal charges that "arise from the same remedial statute" and were brought for "vindication of the same or substantially the same public interest," making the grant of a pre-indictment stay "particularly appropriate"). Courts are also more inclined to grant a stay if the individual would face default or automatic summary judgment in the civil proceedings by invoking the Fifth Amendment. *See* United States v. Lot 5, 23 F.3d 359, 364 (11th Cir. 1994); Vardi Trading Co. v. Overseas Diamond Corp., No. 85 Civ. 2240 (CSH), 1987 WL 17662, at *2 (S.D.N.Y. Sept. 23, 1987).

31. *See also* Keating v. Office of Thrift Supervision, 45 F.3d 322, 325 (9th Cir. 1995) (identifying the following five factors in connection with consideration of a motion to stay: "(1) the interest of the plaintiffs in proceeding expeditiously with this civil litigation or any particular aspect of it, and the potential prejudice to plaintiffs of a delay; (2) the burden which any particular aspect of the proceedings may impose on defendants; (3) the convenience of the court in the management of its cases, and the efficient use of judicial resources; (4) the interests of persons not parties to the civil litigation; and (5) the interest of the public in the pending civil and criminal litigation"); Private Sanitation Indus. Ass'n, 811 F. Supp. at 805 (same); Golden Quality Ice Cream, 87 F.R.D. at 56 (same).

32. *See In re* Phillips, Beckwith & Hall, 896 F. Supp. 553, 559 (E.D. Va. 1995) (lifting stay after government established prejudice, holding that "[a] party is not entitled to delay resolution of a civil action, even to accommodate her Fifth Amendment interests, if her adversary's case will deteriorate as a result of the stay").

33. *See, e.g.,* Dresser, 628 F.2d at 1376; Digital Equip. Corp. v. Currie Enters., 142 F.R.D. 8, 12 (D. Mass. 1991); Waldbaum v. Worldvision Enters., Inc., 84 F.R.D. 95, 97-98 (S.D.N.Y.

modified or abrogated tomorrow. Thus, there can be no guarantee that testimony provided pursuant to a protective order will not ultimately find its way to the government for use in a criminal prosecution.[34]

Even if obtaining a stay of parallel civil proceedings is unlikely, strong consideration should be given to seeking it. Even if the effort is unsuccessful, the mere fact that the effort was made helps preserve a defendant's right to appeal a subsequent criminal conviction based on incriminating statements made during discovery in the civil litigation.[35] Thus, losing the "battle" over the stay request in the civil proceeding may provide ammunition in the "war" against criminal conviction and its potentially dire consequences.

B. *The Fifth Amendment and Adverse Civil Inferences*

If the civil proceeding is not stayed, and civil discovery goes forward, the defendant's next line of defense is an invocation of the Fifth Amendment's right against self-incrimination.[36] Whether to do so poses a difficult dilemma. If the defendant provides civil testimony, her statements can be used against her in a parallel criminal case. If, on the other hand, the defendant "takes the Fifth," courts permit the civil finder of fact to "infer by such refusal that the answers would have been adverse to the witness' interest."[37] The same result obtains even if the plaintiff in the civil action is the government.[38] The reason

---

1979); *see also In re* CFS-Related Sec. Fraud Litig., 256 F. Supp. 2d at 1240-41 (permitting defendant's civil deposition but ordering it sealed and directing that it not be used for any collateral purpose except impeachment or perjury charge).

34. *See In re* Grand Jury, 286 F.3d 153, 159 (3d Cir. 2002) ("Absent exceptional circumstances, protective orders should not serve to interfere with the unique and essential mechanism of a grand jury investigation."); Andover Data Servs. v. Statistical Tabulating Corp., 876 F.2d 1080, 1083 (2d Cir. 1989); *see generally* Ajit V. Pai, Comment, *Should a Grand Jury Subpoena Override a District Court's Protective Order?*, 64 U. CHI. L. REV. 317 (1997) (discussing the varying approaches taken by the federal circuits in determining whether a grand jury subpoena overrides a civil court's protective order).

35. *See* Mid-America's Process Serv. v. Ellison, 767 F.2d 684, 686 (10th Cir. 1985) ("We believe that by seeking postponement or a protective order from the district court supervising the civil proceeding, on the basis of a reasonable fear of self-incrimination, [the defendants] have adequately preserved their right to object to a subsequent criminal conviction based on their own incriminating statements made during civil discovery.").

36. "No person . . . shall be compelled in any criminal case to be a witness against himself. . . ." U.S. CONST. amend. V.

37. Brink's Inc. v. City of New York, 717 F.2d 700, 707 (2d Cir. 1983) (quoting district court's jury instruction); *see* Baxter v. Palmigiano, 425 U.S. 308 (1976); SEC v. Graystone Nash, Inc., 25 F.3d 187, 190 (3d Cir. 1994); *see also* National Acceptance Co. v. Bathalter, 705 F.2d 924, 929 (7th Cir. 1983) ("After *Baxter* there is no longer any doubt that at trial a civil defendant's silence may be used against him, even if that silence is an exercise of his constitutional privilege against self-incrimination.").

38. *See, e.g.,* SEC v. Tome, 638 F. Supp. 629, 632 (S.D.N.Y. 1986).

for this rule is clear: assertion of the privilege impedes the fact-finding process and blocks potentially useful evidence from the defendant's civil adversary.[39]

There are limits to the impact that "taking the Fifth" can have on a civil proceeding. It is well established that civil liability cannot be imposed based solely upon a defendant's assertion of the Fifth Amendment privilege.[40] Nor can a civil plaintiff defeat a motion for summary judgment simply by pointing to an invocation of the privilege.[41] The adverse inference's impact on a jury, however, is usually powerful—and can be devastating.[42]

The courts have not been particularly sympathetic to defendants stuck between the Scylla of providing civil testimony and the Charybdis of invoking the Fifth Amendment.[43] As one court noted, "the choice may be unpleasant, but it is not illegal and must be faced."[44]

---

39. *See* Doe v. Glanzer, 232 F.3d 1258, 1264 (9th Cir. 2000) ("Not allowing the negative inference to be drawn 'poses substantial problems for an adverse party who is deprived of a source of information that might conceivably be determinative, in a search for the truth.'") (*quoting* Graystone, 25 F.3d at 190).

40. *See* Baxter, 425 U.S. at 317; Lefkowitz v. Cunningham, 431 U.S. 801, 809 n.5 (1977); *see also* LaSalle Bank Lake View v. Seguban, 54 F.3d 387, 390 (7th Cir. 1995) ("Silence is a relevant factor to be considered in light of the proffered evidence, but the direct inference of guilt from silence is forbidden."). This is also true when a civil defendant asserts the Fifth Amendment as the basis for refusing even to deny the allegations in a civil complaint. *See* Bathalter, 705 F.2d at 932 ("It is our best judgment, in the light of *Baxter,* that even in a civil case a judgment imposing liability cannot rest solely upon a privileged refusal to admit or deny at the pleading stage."). Similarly, punitive damages may not be premised solely upon a defendant's invocation of the Fifth Amendment. *See* Koester v. American Republic Invs., Inc., 11 F.3d 818, 823-24 (8th Cir. 1993).

41. Seguban, 54 F.3d at 394; Garrish v. United Auto., Aerospace, and Agric. Implement Workers of Am., 284 F. Supp. 2d 782, 797-98 (E.D. Mich. 2003); Mount Airy Ins. Co. v. Millstein, 928 F. Supp. 171, 174 (D. Conn. 1996). *But see* United States v. Rylander, 460 U.S. 752, 761 (1983) (stating that an invocation of the Fifth Amendment "is not a substitute for relevant evidence"); United States v. 4003-4005 5th Ave., 55 F.3d 78, 83 (2d Cir. 1995) ("[A] claim of privilege will not prevent an adverse finding or even summary judgment if the litigant does not present sufficient evidence to satisfy the usual evidentiary burdens in the litigation.").

42. Indeed, even subsequent acquittal in a criminal case involving the same facts will not invalidate an adverse inference based upon the assertion of the Fifth Amendment privilege in a civil case. *See* Pagel, Inc. v. SEC, 803 F.2d 942, 947 (8th Cir. 1986) (refusing to invalidate retroactively adverse inference in SEC administrative action after a defendant testified at a criminal trial and was acquitted).

43. *See, e.g.,* SEC v. Grossman, 121 F.R.D. 207, 210 (S.D.N.Y. 1987) (refusing to grant a stay of a civil action by defendants who feared that negative inferences would be drawn against them if they asserted their Fifth Amendment privilege in civil litigation).

44. SEC v. Musella, No. 83-Civ-342, 1983 WL 1297, at *2 (April 4, 1983 S.D.N.Y.); *see also* Keating, 45 F.3d at 326 ("A defendant has no absolute right not to be forced to choose between testifying in a civil matter and asserting his Fifth Amendment privilege.").

Corporations, of course, have no Fifth Amendment privilege against self-incrimination,[45] so one might reasonably assume that they would be spared the horns of the adverse inference dilemma. Ironically, however, the choices a corporation's employees make in this regard can have particularly nettlesome consequences for the corporation itself. A leading case, *Brink's, Inc. v. City of New York*,[46] illustrates the problem well. In *Brink's*, company employees asserted their Fifth Amendment privilege at trial and declined to testify; the jury found for the City of New York after being instructed by the trial judge that it was permissible to assume that had the employees testified, their testimony would have been unfavorable to their employer.[47]

This problem is compounded by the fact that not only present employees can create it. Even if a corporation dismisses an employee it finds to have violated the law, if parallel criminal and civil proceedings ensue, and the former employee "takes the Fifth" in civil discovery involving the corporation, the trier of fact is permitted to draw an adverse inference against the corporation.[48] Not surprisingly, some have questioned the appropriateness of an adverse-inference instruction where "the employee was fired or departed on unfriendly terms."[49] Nonetheless, courts have held that admitting a former employee's invocation of the Fifth Amendment as evidence is not *per se*

---

45. Curcio v. United States, 354 U.S. 118, 122 (1957) ("It is settled that a corporation is not protected by the constitutional privilege against self-incrimination"); *In re* Two Grand Jury Subpoenae Duces Tecum, 769 F.2d 52, 57 (2d Cir. 1985) ("There simply is no situation in which the Fifth Amendment would prevent a corporation from producing corporate records, for the corporation itself has no Fifth Amendment privilege."); *In re* Plastics Additives Antitrust Litig., No. Civ. A. 03-2038, 2004 WL 2743591, at *6 (E.D. Pa., Nov. 29, 2004) ("As corporations, defendants will not be able to invoke the privilege against self-incrimination.").

46. 717 F.2d 700 (2d Cir. 1983).

47. *Id.* at 707; *see also, e.g.,* Chariot Plastics, Inc. v. United States, 28 F. Supp. 2d 874, 877 n.1 (S.D.N.Y. 1998) ("An officer's or directors' invocation of the Fifth Amendment is admissible as an adverse inference against the corporation."). There must be a nexus, however, between the inference to be drawn against the corporation and the subject matter to which the employee's invocation of the Fifth Amendment relates. *See* Veranda Beach Club Ltd. Partnership v. Western Surety Co., 936 F.2d 1364, 1374 (1st Cir. 1991); Data General Corp. v. Grumman Sys. Support Corp., 825 F. Supp. 340, 352 (D. Mass. 1993), *aff'd and remanded on other grounds,* 36 F.3d 1147 (1st Cir. 1994).

48. *See In re* High Fructose Corn Syrup Antitrust Litig., 295 F.3d 651, 663-64 (7th Cir. 2002); Rad Servs. Inc. v. Aetna Cas. & Sur. Co., 808 F.2d 271 (3d Cir. 1986); *see also* Federal Deposit Ins. Corp. v. Fidelity & Deposit Co., 45 F.3d 969, 978 (5th Cir. 1995) (permitting adverse inference against an employment fidelity bond surety from invocations by witnesses who had relationships with an allegedly fraudulent employee of the insured).

49. *See* Rad Servs., 808 F.2d at 275 (*quoting Adverse Inferences Based on Non-Party Invocations: The Real Magic Trick in Fifth Amendment Civil Cases,* 60 NOTRE DAME L. REV. 370, 386 (1985)).

reversible error.[50] Indeed, it may be reversible error *not* to admit the invocation as evidence.[51]

Counsel to the corporation may argue that assertions of privilege by nonparties should not be allowed as admissible evidence. As the dissent in *Brinks* observed, the silence that results from the invocation may (i) lack any real probity under Federal Rule of Evidence 403 because no reliable "answer" may be inferred from it (i.e., the unanswered question becomes the evidence)[52] and (ii) leave the corporate defendant with no effective ability to cross-examine the employee asserting the privilege.[53] The courts, however, generally have been unreceptive to these arguments.[54] Rather, if the adverse inference that a trier of fact could draw from the employee's invocation is found "trustworthy under all of the circumstances and will advance the search for the truth," the adverse inference likely will be permitted.[55]

C. *Criminal and Civil Penalties: Double Jeopardy?*

The Double Jeopardy Clause provides that "[n]o person shall . . . be subject for the same offense to be twice put in jeopardy of life or limb."[56] Corporations, of course, do not have "lives" or "limbs," at least not in the biological sense of those terms. But they are unquestionably legal persons subject to governmental sanction, and as such are entitled to protection against Double Jeopardy. Indeed, in a time gone by, there was scope for corporations to argue successfully that prior criminal sanctions against them precluded the government from imposing civil penalties for the same underlying conduct (and vice versa). In all but the rarest of contexts, that time has passed.

---

50. *Id.* at 277; *cf.* Cerro Gordo Charity v. Fireman's Fund Am. Life Ins. Co., 819 F.2d 1471, 1481 (8th Cir. 1987) ("[W]e find that the fact that [defendant] may not be presently involved with [the trust] in an official capacity presents no bar to requiring him assert [sic] the privilege before the jury.").

51. *See In re* High Fructose Corn Syrup Antitrust Litig., 295 F.3d at 663-64 (holding that the district court should have permitted introduction of former executives' invocation of Fifth Amendment as "one more piece of evidence" against ADM).

52. Brink's, 717 F.2d at 715 (Winter, J., dissenting).

53. *Id.* at 716.

54. *See, e.g.,* Cerro Gordo Charity, 819 F.2d at 1482.

55. LiButti v. United States, 107 F.3d 110, 123-24 (2d Cir. 1997) (stating that non-exclusive factors to be considered are (i) the nature of the relevant relationships, (ii) the degree of control of the party over the nonparty witness, (iii) the compatibility of their interests in the litigation's outcome, and (iv) the role of the nonparty witness in the litigation).

56. U.S. Const. amend. V.

In its 1989 *United States v. Halper* decision,[57] the Supreme Court had provided defense counsel with solid, but narrow, support for arguing that contemporaneous or successive governmental civil and criminal actions that both resulted in sanctions offended the Double Jeopardy Clause. In *Halper*, the Court ruled that the federal government could not collect a civil penalty in an action for Medicare fraud after having obtained a criminal conviction of the defendant (and imprisonment and fine) based on the same subject matter. The Court noted the enormous disparity between the government's actual loss and the civil fines assessed against the defendant, and concluded that "[t]he Government may not criminally prosecute a defendant, impose a criminal penalty upon him, and then bring a separate civil action based on the same conduct and receive a judgment that is not rationally related to the goal of making the Government whole."[58] As a practical matter, the Court's holding provided defense counsel with the ability—albeit highly circumscribed[59]—to argue that there were limits to the government's right to impose civil penalties that could be characterized as "punishment" against a defendant already sanctioned under the criminal law. The line drawn by *Halper*: "remedial" civil sanctions did not implicate Double Jeopardy concerns, but "deterrent" or "retributive" civil sanctions did.[60]

In 1997, the Supreme Court's opinion in *Hudson v. United States*[61] "'put the *Halper* genie back in the bottle.'"[62] In 1989, the Office of the Comptroller of the Currency (OCC) had brought administrative charges against the *Hudson* defendants for alleged violations of the federal banking laws. In October of that year, the defendants entered into a consent order with the OCC that resolved the administrative charges in exchange for the defendants' agreement to payment of fines and debarment from the banking industry.[63] In August 1992,

---

57. United States v. Halper, 490 U.S. 435 (1989).
58. *Id.* at 451.
59. *See id.* at 449 ("What we announce now is a rule for the rare case . . . where a fixed-penalty provision subjects a prolific but small-gauge offender to a sanction overwhelmingly disproportionate to the damages he has caused.")
60. *See also id.* at 448-49 ("We therefore hold that under the Double Jeopardy Clause a defendant who already has been punished in a criminal prosecution may not be subjected to an additional civil sanction to the extent that the second sanction may not fairly be characterized as remedial, but only as a deterrent or retribution.")
61. 522 U.S. 93 (1997).
62. *Id.* at 106 (Scalia, J., concurring).
63. *Id.* at 97.

nearly three years later, the defendants were indicted on charges of conspiracy, misapplication of bank funds, and making false bank entries based on the same transactions that formed the basis for the 1989 consent order. The defendants challenged their indictment, arguing that it violated their right not to be placed in jeopardy twice for the same offense.[64]

The Supreme Court held that the Double Jeopardy Clause did not prohibit the defendants' criminal prosecution because the administrative proceedings were civil, not criminal.[65] In so doing, the Court refocused the double jeopardy analysis by stating that the Double Jeopardy Clause "does not prohibit the imposition of any additional sanction that could, 'in common parlance,' be described as punishment"; rather, only multiple *criminal* punishments for the same offense are constitutionally proscribed.[66] In this regard, the Court noted that its analysis in *Halper* had improperly "bypassed the threshold question" of whether a successive punishment was a *criminal* punishment and proceeded directly to determining whether the civil sanction "was so grossly disproportionate to the harm caused as to constitute 'punishment.'"[67]

The *Hudson* Court provided fairly clear guidance to lower courts faced with determining whether civil penalties may be said to be "criminal punishments" that implicate double jeopardy concerns. First, "[w]hether a particular punishment is criminal or civil is, at least initially, a matter of statutory construction. . . . A court must first ask whether the legislature, 'in establishing the penalizing mechanism, indicated either expressly or impliedly a preference for one label or the other.'"[68] Second, even where the legislature indicates its intention that a penalty be civil, courts are to inquire further "whether the statutory scheme [is] so punitive either in purpose or effect . . . as to transform what was clearly intended as a civil remedy into a criminal penalty."[69] The Court stated that the following factors, set forth in its decision in *Kennedy v. Mendoza-Martinez*,[70] "provide useful guideposts" in performing this latter analysis:

> (i) whether the sanction involves an affirmative disability or restraint; (ii) whether it has historically been regarded as a punishment; (iii) whether it comes into play only on a finding of scienter; (iv) whether its operation will

---

64. *Id.* at 97-98.
65. *Id.* at 96.
66. *Id.* at 98-99.
67. *Id.* at 101.
68. *Id.* at 98-99 (citations omitted).
69. *Id.* at 99 (citations omitted).
70. 372 U.S. 144, 168-69 (1963).

promote the traditional aims of punishment-retribution and deterrence; (v) whether the behavior to which it applies is already a crime; (vi) whether an alternative purpose to which it may rationally be connected is assignable for it; and (vii) whether it appears excessive in relation to the alternative purpose assigned.[71]

The Court, however, placed two significant restrictions on use of the *Kennedy* factors to override legislative intent: (i) "these factors must be considered in relation to the *statute on its face*"; and (ii) "*only the clearest proof* will suffice to override legislative intent and transform what has been denominated a civil remedy into a criminal penalty."[72]

Applying these principles to the case before it, the Court held that criminal prosecution of the defendants would not violate the Double Jeopardy Clause.[73] The Court found it "evident" that Congress intended the OCC monetary and debarment sanctions to be civil in nature.[74] As for the *Kennedy* factors, the Court found "little evidence, much less the clearest proof that we require, suggesting that either OCC money penalties or debarment sanctions are 'so punitive in form and effect as to render them criminal despite Congress' intent to the contrary.'"[75] In particular, the Court stated that neither form of penalty had been viewed historically as punishment; that the penalties did not involve imprisonment, so as to impose on the defendants an "affirmative disability or restraint"; that neither sanction required a finding of scienter; that the fact that the conduct for which the OCC sanctions were imposed may also be criminal was insufficient to render the sanctions criminally punitive; and that the mere fact that the sanctions could serve deterrence goals did not alter their civil nature.[76] In short, the Double Jeopardy Clause presented no obstacle to trying the defendants criminally.[77]

---

71. Hudson, 522 U.S. at 99-100.

72. *Id.* at 100 (emphasis added, internal quotation marks omitted). The Court criticized the *Halper* decision for addressing the nature and effect of the actual sanctions imposed rather than limiting the inquiry to the statute on its face. *Id.* at 101. In a concurrence joined by Justice Ginsberg, Justice Breyer opined that inquiring beyond the face of the statute to determine the effect of the sanctions on the individual defendant might be appropriate in some circumstances, and disagreed with the notion that "only the clearest proof" could transform a civil remedy into criminal punishment. *Id.* at 115-17 (Breyer, J., concurring).

73. *Id.* at 103.

74. *Id.*

75. *Id.* at 104.

76. *Id.* at 104-05.

77. *Id.* at 105. Justice Stevens concurred in the result but disagreed with the Court's abandonment of Halper. *Id.* at 106-07 (Stevens, J., concurring).

By criticizing *Halper* as a "deviation from longstanding double jeopardy principles [that] was ill-considered," and as having articulated a test that "proved unworkable,"[78] the *Hudson* decision effectively returned the law to its pre-*Halper* state.[79] Indeed, the lower courts have read *Hudson* to mean precisely what it says: Absent the "clearest proof" of extreme punitiveness under the *Kennedy* factors, a remedial scheme designated as "civil" by the legislature will not implicate the Double Jeopardy Clause. Accordingly, SEC civil fines and disgorgements have been held not to trigger double-jeopardy rights,[80] as have IRS civil penalties and tax additions,[81] broker application denials and debarment orders of the CFTC,[82] "instance-by-instance" administrative fines under OSHA,[83] civil forfeiture proceedings following convictions for false statements to customs officials,[84] civil penalties for violations of the Food Stamp Act,[85] FDIC civil proceedings requesting punitive damages,[86] and permanent occupational debarment under the Generic Drug Enforcement Act.[87]

While it may be tempting to view *Hudson* as a seismic shift in the legal landscape surrounding contemporaneous or successive governmental civil and criminal prosecutions, this would overstate the case for *Halper's* prior efficacy as a defense tool. Although the *Hudson* court granted certiorari "because of concerns about the wide variety of novel double jeopardy claims spawned

---

78. *Id.* at 101-02.
79. *Cf. id.* at 106 (Scalia, J., concurring) (stating that the Court's opinion "return[s] the law to its state immediately prior to *Halper*").
80. United States v. Perry, 152 F.3d 900, 903-04 (8th Cir. 1998); *see also* SEC v. Palmisano, 135 F.3d 860, 864-86 (2d Cir. 1998) (noting the fact that scienter is required to prove a violation of the securities laws is not dispositive under *Hudson*).
81. Louis v. Commissioner, 170 F.3d 1232, 1234-35 (9th Cir. 1999) (additions to tax for fraud); Bickham Lincoln-Mercury, Inc. v. United States, 168 F.3d 790, 794-95 (5th Cir. 1999) (civil penalties).
82. Vercillo v. Commodity Futures Trading Comm'n, 147 F.3d 548, 558 (7th Cir. 1998) (citing Ryan v. Commodity Futures Trading Comm'n, 145 F.3d 910, 913-14 (7th Cir. 1998); Cox v. Commodity Futures Trading Comm'n, 138 F.3d 268, 274 (7th Cir. 1998); LaCrosse v. Commodity Futures Trading Comm'n, 137 F.3d 925, 932 (7th Cir. 1998); Grossfeld v. Commodity Futures Trading Comm'n, 137 F.3d 1300, 1302-03 (11th Cir. 1998)).
83. S.A. Healy Co. v. Occupational Safety & Health Review Comm'n, 138 F.3d 686, 687-88 (7th Cir. 1998).
84. United States v. $273,969.04 U.S. Currency, 164 F.3d 462, 465 (9th Cir. 1999).
85. Traficanti v. United States, 227 F.3d 170, 177 (4th Cir. 2000).
86. United States v. Ely, 142 F.3d 1113, 1122 (9th Cir. 1997).
87. Bhutani v. Food & Drug Admin., 161 Fed. Appx. 589, 592 (7th Cir. 2006).

in the wake of *Halper*,"[88] as a practical matter, *Halper* had provided relatively little assistance to the practitioner seeking to bar a criminal prosecution based on an earlier civil sanction (or vice versa).[89] In addition, it should be noted that more traditional modes of constitutional attack on the propriety of civil penalties—due process, equal protection, and the Eighth Amendment's proscription against excessive civil fines and forfeitures—survive *Hudson* intact.[90]

D. *Collateral Estoppel: The Consequences of "Losing"*

Under the doctrine of collateral estoppel, or issue preclusion, "a final judgment on the merits in a prior suit precludes subsequent relitigation of issues actually litigated and determined in the prior suit, regardless of whether the subsequent suit is based on the same cause of action."[91] This doctrine can present a minefield for counsel facing actual or potential parallel proceedings, be they criminal or civil. Pursuing one course of action in one proceeding can have significant, and adverse, consequences in others.[92]

For example, a criminal judgment against a defendant will operate as an estoppel in any subsequent civil and administrative proceedings as to the

---

88. Hudson, 522 U.S. at 98 & n.4 (collecting cases).
89. *Id.* at 108-09 (Stevens, J., concurring).
90. *Id.* at 102-03.
91. I.A.M. Nat'l Pension Fund v. Industrial Gear Mfg. Co., 723 F.2d 944, 947 (D.C. Cir. 1983); *see also* Parklane Hosiery Co. v. Shore, 439 U.S. 322, 327 n.5 (1979) ("Under the doctrine of collateral estoppel, . . . the judgment in the prior suit precludes relitigation of issues actually litigated and necessary to the outcome of the first action.").
92. Under the broader doctrine of res judicata, or "claim preclusion," "a final judgment on the merits bars further claims by parties or their privies based on the same cause of action." Montana v. United States, 440 U.S. 147, 153 (1979). Claim preclusion has little applicability in the context of parallel proceedings involving governmental civil or criminal prosecutions. First, courts have typically rejected the argument that claim preclusion bars the government from bringing, in a subsequent civil proceeding, claims that arguably could have been pursued in a prior criminal prosecution. *See, e.g.,* United States v. Barnette, 10 F.3d 1553, 1561 (11th Cir. 1994); United States v. Moffitt, Zwerling & Kemler, P.C., 875 F. Supp. 1190, 1196 (E.D. Va. 1995), *rev'd in part on other grounds,* 83 F.3d 660 (4th Cir. 1996); *see also* 47 AM. JUR. 2D Judgments § 732 (1999) ("[A] judgment in a criminal proceeding has no res judicata effect."). Second, since res judicata only bars "parties and their privies" from relitigating claims that could have been pursued, the government typically is not barred from pursuing causes of action against a corporation that were previously pursued by a private party (and vice versa). *See* Montana, 440 U.S. at 153.

specific issues resolved as part of the criminal prosecution.[93] Thus, the government has long been able to use a criminal conviction to collaterally estop defendants from relitigating their guilt, and thus their liability, in subsequent civil proceedings.[94] In addition, a criminal conviction can adversely impact the disposition of private lawsuits involving the same subject matter as the criminal conviction. This is because issue preclusion does not require "mutuality of parties"—that is, it is not necessary that the party attempting to estop the opponent from raising or contesting an issue (previously decided against the opponent) be a party to the prior proceeding.[95] A criminal conviction of the corporation, therefore, may be used offensively in subsequent civil actions by strangers to the prosecution.[96]

Under federal law, a guilty plea in a criminal action is generally accorded the same preclusive effect in a subsequent civil action as a criminal conviction.[97] A party may, however, be able to escape the collateral effect of a guilty plea

---

93. *See, e.g.,* Gelb v. Royal Globe Ins. Co., 798 F.2d 38, 43 (2d Cir. 1986); SEC v. Namer, No. 97-Civ.-2085, 2004 WL 2199471, at *1 (S.D.N.Y., Sept. 30, 2004); *see also* United States v. Uzzell, 648 F. Supp. 1362, 1363-65 (D.D.C. 1986) (criminal conviction of conspiracy after trial operates as estoppel on all underlying facts). A criminal conviction can operate as an estoppel even if the conviction is on appeal. *See* United States v. International Bhd. of Teamsters, 905 F.2d 610, 621 (2d Cir. 1990); *see also In re* Lynch, 315 B.R. 173, 177 (D. Colo. 2004) ("[P]endency of appeal does not alter the finality of a judgment for purposes of collateral estoppel or res judicata, unless the appeal removes the entire case to the appellate court and constitutes a proceeding de novo.").

94. *See* Emich Motors Corp. v. General Motors Corp., 340 U.S. 558, 568 (1951) ("It is well established that a prior criminal conviction may work an estoppel in favor of the Government in a subsequent civil proceeding."); United States v. Killough, 848 F.2d 1523, 1528 (11th Cir. 1988).

95. *See* Parklane Hosiery, 439 U.S. at 322; McLaughlin v. Bradlee, 803 F.2d 1197, 1201 (D.C. Cir. 1986); *In re* Lynch, 315 F.R. at 181. Notably, however, nonmutual offensive collateral estoppel may not be utilized to preclude the federal government from litigating an issue on which it has previously been unsuccessful. *See* United States v. Mendoza, 464 U.S. 154 (1984). Neither are state governments subject to nonmutual offensive collateral estoppel. *See* Hercules Carriers, Inc. v. Florida, 768 F.2d 1558, 1579 (11th Cir. 1985); *see also* Coeur D'Alene Tribe of Idaho v. Hammond, 384 F.3d 674, 689-90 (9th Cir. 2004) (state agency not precluded from relitigating in federal court a legal issue previously determined by a state court); *see also* Petchem, Inc. v. Canaveral Port Auth., No. 6: 04-CV-10800RL28KRS, 2005 WL 1862412, at *3 (M.D. Fla., Aug. 2, 2005) (port authority, as a governmental entity, not subject to nonmutual offensive collateral estoppel).

96. Gelb, 798 F.2d at 43-44; Wolfson v. Baker, 623 F.2d 1074, 1080 (5th Cir. 1980).

97. United States v. Podell, 572 F.2d 31, 35 (2d Cir. 1978) ("It is well-settled that a criminal conviction, whether by jury verdict or guilty plea, constitutes estoppel in favor of the United States in a subsequent civil proceeding.") (citations omitted); *see also* McCarthy v. United

by pleading *nolo contendere* instead.[98] By its terms, a plea of *nolo contendere* applies only to the case in which it is entered and cannot be used in any subsequent civil lawsuit based on the same conduct.[99] Of course, whether a *nolo contendere* plea will be available to the corporation will lie within the discretion of the trial judge, and the prosecutor may well argue that such a plea deprives the public of its interest in a definitive resolution of the criminal matter.[100] In addition, the corporation's *nolo contendere* plea may be admissible for purposes other than showing its guilt or liability.[101]

Can court findings during the sentencing phase of a criminal matter have preclusive effect in parallel civil proceedings? According to the Second Circuit, at least, the answer in most cases should be no. In *SEC v. Monarch Funding Corp.*,[102] the SEC sought to collaterally estop a defendant in a civil case from litigating its liability for violations of the federal securities laws, based on sentencing findings in a criminal matter in which the defendant was found liable for obstruction of justice.[103] The district court applied collateral estoppel and granted the SEC a permanent injunction against future violations.[104]

The Second Circuit reversed. It declined to "adopt a per se rule against extending the doctrine of offensive collateral estoppel to sentencing findings,"[105]

States, 394 U.S. 459, 466 (1969) ("[A] guilty plea is an admission of all the elements of a formal criminal charge."); United States v. 415 E. Mitchell Ave., 149 F.3d 472, 476 (6th Cir. 1998) (affirming application of collateral estoppel in civil forfeiture proceeding based on defendant's guilty plea). *But see* 47 AM. JUR. 2d Judgments § 734 (1999) (collecting cases holding that a guilty plea may not serve as the basis for collateral estoppel in a subsequent civil action).

98. *See* FED. R. CRIM. P. 11(b) & Advisory Comm. Note (1974 amends.) ("Unlike a plea of guilty, . . . [a *nolo contendere* plea] cannot be used against a defendant . . . in a subsequent criminal or civil case."); FED. R. EVID. 410 (with limited exceptions, *nolo contendere* plea inadmissible against defendant who made the plea); Doherty v. American Motors Corp., 728 F.2d 334, 337 (6th Cir. 1984).

99. FED. R. CRIM. P. 11(b) & Advisory Comm. Note (1974 amends.); Ranke v. United States, 873 F.2d 1033, 1037 n.7 (7th Cir. 1989).

100. FED. R. CRIM. P. 11(b) ("Such a plea shall be accepted by the court only after due consideration of the views of the parties and the interest of the public in the effective administration of justice") & Advisory Comm. Note (1974 amends.).

101. United States v. Adedoyin, 369 F.3d 337, 344-45 (3d Cir. 2004) (in a trial for unlawful alien entry into the U.S., prior state court conviction based on *nolo contendere* plea was inadmissible to show guilt, but admissible to show prior felony conviction); United States v. Fredrickson, 601 F.2d 1358, 1365 n.10 (8th Cir. 1979) (finding nolo contendere plea admissible as "other crimes" evidence under Federal Rule of Evidence 404).

102. 192 F.3d 295 (2d Cir. 1999).
103. *Id.* at 298.
104. *Id.*
105. *Id.* at 303.

but held that "precluding relitigation on the basis of such findings should be presumed improper."[106] In particular, the court found that applying estoppel in the case before it would be neither fair nor efficient. Unlike other contexts, where determinations that can be inferred from necessary findings can form the basis of an estoppel, fairness required that the sentencing finding sought to be used be "legally necessary to the final sentence."[107] As to the efficiency of giving preclusive effect to sentencing findings, the court noted that the district court's examination of the collateral estoppel issue "required considerable effort—in all probability more effort than would have been required for a summary adjudication . . . or even for a trial."[108] The court concluded with the following guidance:

> [I]n determining whether to apply collateral estoppel to sentencing findings in the future, district courts should start by making a threshold assessment of whether it will be efficient to do so. Given the potential unfairness associated with extending collateral estoppel to sentencing findings generally, if the court reasonably determines that the doctrine will not promote efficiency, it should feel free to deny preclusion for that reason alone.[109]

Civil judgments and findings can also produce collateral estoppel consequences in simultaneous or subsequent civil and administrative proceedings in which the corporation is involved. Of course, in certain instances, the corporation may be able to argue successfully that its victory in a prior civil lawsuit is entitled to preclusive effect in a subsequent civil case. These instances are effectively limited, however, to actions where the party against whom the estoppel is sought was also a party (or privy to a party) in the prior proceeding, for the simple and obvious reason that nonparties to the prior action cannot be deprived of a "full and fair opportunity to litigate" the issues previously decided in the corporation's favor.[110] In addition, if the corporation

---

106. *Id.* at 306.
107. *Id.* at 307.
108. *Id.* at 310.
109. *Id.; see also* United States v. U.S. Currency in the Amount of $119,984.00, More or Less, 304 F.3d 165, 173 (2d Cir. 2002) (applying *Monarch's* "strong presumption against application of collateral estoppel based on sentencing findings" to vacate district court's application of collateral estoppel to findings in forfeiture sentencing proceeding, where estoppel was neither efficient nor fair).
110. *See* Resolution Trust Corp. v. Keating, 186 F.3d 1110, 1114 (9th Cir. 1999) (stating that the following are necessary elements of nonmutual offensive collateral estoppel against a party: (i) the party was afforded a full and fair opportunity to litigate the issue in the prior action; (ii) the issue was actually litigated and necessary to support the judgment; (iii) the issue was decided against the party in a final judgment; and (iv) the party was a party, or a privy to a party, in the prior proceeding).

litigates an issue in a civil case and loses, the principle of collateral estoppel will permit foreigners to the case to utilize the determination offensively in a separate action involving the corporation.[111]

Unlike collateral use of criminal convictions in subsequent civil proceedings, however, a judgment rendered against a corporation in a civil or administrative proceeding will not produce collateral estoppel effects in an ongoing or subsequent criminal prosecution brought against the company. This is chiefly because of the different levels of proof required in these proceedings—an ultimate finding "by a preponderance of the evidence" that certain acts had occurred does not conclusively establish that the conduct could have been proven "beyond a reasonable doubt" in a criminal case.[112]

Application of the doctrine of collateral estoppel to preclude a defendant from relitigating an issue requires courts to determine exactly what was decided in the prior action.[113] Accordingly, courts deciding the collateral estoppel effects of a prior judgment will examine the totality of the record in the prior proceeding, including pleadings, evidence submitted, jury instructions, and any court opinions, to determine whether an issue on which preclusion is sought was "directly put in issue and directly determined" in the prior suit.[114]

This fact should be kept in mind by counsel for the corporation facing parallel proceedings in which a resolution short of trial in one action has the potential for collateral consequences in another. To the maximum extent possible, civil settlement agreements with both private plaintiffs and governmental agencies should state explicitly that the underlying facts have not been litigated and that no liability or wrongdoing is admitted. It may be possible to structure the terms of any plea agreement in a manner that corrals the issues precluded, or to clarify in the record the basis (preferably limited) for a resulting criminal conviction.

E. *Responding to Employee Misconduct*

In the course of an internal investigation or subsequent proceedings that follow, a corporation may form the view that certain of its employees have

---

111. *See* Parklane Hosiery, 439 U.S. at 331-32.
112. *See* United States v. Meza-Soria, 935 F.2d 166, 169 (9th Cir. 1991); United States v. General Dynamics Corp., 828 F.2d 1356, 1361 n.5 (9th Cir. 1987); United States v. Beery, 678 F.2d 856, 868 n.10 (10th Cir. 1982); United States v. Konovsky, 202 F.2d 721, 726-27 (7th Cir. 1953).
113. *See* Brown v. Felsen, 442 U.S. 127, 139 n.10 (1979) ("[C]ollateral estoppel treats as final only those questions actually and necessarily decided in a prior suit.").
114. *See* Uzzell, 648 F. Supp. at 1363-64 (*citing* Emich Motors Corp., 340 U.S. at 569).

engaged in conduct that transgresses company policy, or even state or federal law. When this happens, management and counsel must squarely confront the issue of employee discipline.

The company's determinations on this issue should not be made lightly. Depending on the context and the reasons provided for disciplining an employee, the fact that an employee—and especially a very senior one—has been disciplined may be subsequently used by adversaries as strong evidence of corporate misconduct. A somewhat more subtle concern is that sanctions of differing severity can provide useful and otherwise unavailable insights into the company's own analysis of the misconduct. On the other hand, the consequences of failing to respond effectively to known employee misconduct can be severe. The government does not look kindly upon corporations that claim to be cooperative and responsible citizens, but that do not react promptly and appropriately to evidence of employee misconduct within their ranks.[115] And swift action to terminate, suspend, or transfer an employee responsible for ongoing misconduct can stop the misconduct and thereby prevent further harm to the company.[116]

For the company that carefully has considered all the implications and chooses to embark upon disciplining select employees, several suggestions are in order. *First*, to provide maximum possible protection for this decision and action, corporate counsel should undertake the task of notifying the employee of the punishment and explaining the ramifications of the employee's conduct underlying the sanctions. Management should resist the temptation to assign this unpleasant task of discipline to the personnel department. A delegation of this nature virtually ensures that no claim of confidentiality will be successful. While counsel may consider explaining, in writing, the basis

---

115. *See* Memorandum from Deputy Attorney Paul J. McNulty, U.S. Dep't of Justice, to Heads of Department Components, *Principles of Federal Prosecution of Business Organizations* (December 12, 2006), at http://www.usdof.gov/speech/2006/mcnulty_memo.pdf. The McNulty Memorandum supersedes and replaces the guidance previously established in the Memorandum from Deputy Attorney General Larry Thompson (Jan. 20, 2003) ("Thompson Memorandum"). *See also* Report of Investigation Pursuant to Section 21(a) of the Securities Exchange Act of 1934 and Commission Statement on the Relationship of Cooperation to Agency Enforcement Decisions, Exchange Act Release No. 44969 (the "Seaboard Report").

116. The SEC has encouraged companies to take "immediate and decisive corrective action" to head off ongoing misconduct. *See In re* Cooper Cos., Exchange Act Release No. 35,082, 58 SEC Docket 591, 596 (Dec. 12, 1994) (investigation report) (criticizing the directors for failing to act swiftly to protect the shareholders in the face of serious indications of management fraud by high-ranking corporate officers).

for its decision, these memorializations should be written as though they will be quoted on page one of *The New York Times*.

Second, thought must be given to the question of disclosure of the disciplinary actions taken. This question is particularly relevant for public companies. In some instances, such as disciplinary action resulting in the resignation of a director, SEC rules may require disclosure of the action taken.[117] Even if public disclosure of disciplinary action is not required by law, it may be a practical necessity in some cases. Particularly where senior managers are implicated, public companies often have little real choice but to take appropriate disciplinary action promptly after discovery and to disclose that action taken.[118] This action can benefit the corporate entity by defusing regulatory hostility and restoring public confidence in company leadership.

Third, counsel should remember that a lawyer's involvement in the disciplinary process does not necessarily "place a cloak of secrecy around all the incidents of such transaction."[119] The mere fact that it was counsel who recommended the sanctions or who notified the employee of them does not automatically render the event privileged. Rather, in assessing the availability of privilege, all facts and circumstances surrounding the sanctions and notification will be considered. All else being equal, a decision to discipline an employee premised upon the advice of counsel provides a more legitimate basis for corporate officials to refuse to answer questions regarding the process, the deliberations, and the results.[120]

Fourth, corporations considering discipline of an employee who has disclosed the existence of improper or illegal conduct to authorities should proceed with great caution. Such employees are protected by state and federal

---

117. *See* SEC Form 8-K, Item 6 ("Resignations of Registrant's Directors"); *see also* SEC Rule 12b-20 ("Additional Information"), 17 C.F.R. § 240.12b-20.

118. Such disclosure may subject the company to a defamation lawsuit by the disciplined employee. *See, e.g.,* Pearce v. E.F. Hutton Group, Inc., 664 F. Supp. 1490 (D.D.C. 1987) (a former employee who was implicated of wrongdoing in an internal investigation report prepared by outside investigatory counsel sued both outside counsel and his former employer for libel).

119. United States v. Freeman, 619 F.2d 1112, 1119-20 (5th Cir. 1980) (*quoting In re* Fischel, 557 F.2d 209, 212 (9th Cir. 1977)); *accord In re* Grand Jury Subpoenas, 803 F.2d 493, 496 (9th Cir. 1986), *corrected by* 817 F.2d 64 (9th Cir. 1987).

120. *See* F.C. Cycles Int'l, Inc. v. Fila Sports, S.p.A, 184 F.R.D. 64, 71 (D. Md. 1998); *In re* Grand Jury Subpoena Duces Tecum, 731 F.2d 1032, 1036-38 (2d Cir. 1984); SCM Corp. v. Xerox Corp., 70 F.R.D. 508, 516-17 (D. Conn. 1976), *appeal dismissed,* 534 F.2d 1031 (2d Cir. 1976).

"whistle-blower" statutes, such as those contained in the False Claims Act[121] and in the Victim and Witness Protection Act of 1982.[122] These statutes and regulations are intended to protect individuals who alert the government to potential wrongdoing and any discipline may be considered retaliation, which can be penalized.

F. Ex Parte *Contacts by Government Lawyers*

Government investigators may seek to gain relevant information about the corporation through *ex parte* contacts with present or former corporate employees. Company counsel should be aware of this possibility and, to the extent possible, formulate official policies and procedures to control these contacts. In so doing, counsel will find support both in case law and in applicable disciplinary rules.

Rule 4.2 of the ABA Model Rules of Professional Conduct (Model Rule 4.2) limits the circumstances when a lawyer ethically can communicate with parties represented by another lawyer. A lawyer may not communicate with persons known to be represented by counsel in a matter concerning the subject of the representation. By contrast, Rule 4.2 authorizes communications where counsel representing the opposing party permits, where "authorized by law," or where authorized by "a court order." State bars across the country have enacted no-contact provisions modeled either on Rule 4.2, or on its predecessor Disciplinary Rule 7-104(A)(1) of the American Bar Association (DR 7-104(A)(1)).

The extent to which prosecutors are subject to these rules has been a source of considerable historical debate between DOJ and the defense bar. The opening salvo in this debate came in the form of a 1989 DOJ internal memorandum, dubbed the "Thornburgh Memorandum." In the memorandum, DOJ took the position that *ex parte* interviews are not improper when conducted during the investigatory phase of a criminal or civil case.[123] The Thornburgh memorandum asserted that defense lawyers had broadly interpreted the no-contact rules "in an effort to prohibit communications by law enforcement personnel with the target of a criminal investigation, whether

---

121. *See* 31 U.S.C. § 3729.

122. *See* 18 U.S.C. § 1512 (codification of Victim and Witness Protection Act of 1982).

123. Memorandum from Richard Thornburgh, Attorney General, to All Justice Department Litigators, dated June 8, 1989 (*reprinted in* In the Matter of John Doe, 801 F. Supp. 478 (D.N.M. 1992)).

or not a constitutional right to counsel has attached."[124] The Memorandum stated:

> It is the clear policy of the Department that in the course of a criminal investigation, an attorney for the government is authorized to direct and supervise the use of undercover law enforcement agents, informants, and other cooperating individuals to gather evidence *by communicating with any person who has not been made the subject of formal federal criminal adversarial proceedings arising from that investigation, regardless of whether the person is known to be represented by counsel.* . . . Routine contacts with witnesses, even when not done undercover, are an integral part of federal law enforcement, even where a lawyer may represent the witness. Traditionally, local bar rules have not been thought to prohibit such contact, and any attempt to use the rules in this way runs afoul of the Supremacy Clause.[125]

Although the Memorandum focused on the applicability of the anti-contact rules in pre-indictment situations, it contained sweeping (and, in the defense bar's mind, inflammatory) language that at the least implied that DOJ attorneys were not constrained by state or court-adopted ethical rules against *ex parte* contacts, even in *post*-indictment situations. In particular, the Memorandum stated:

> In sum, it is the Department's position that contact with a represented individual *in the course of authorized law enforcement activity* does not violate DR 7-104. The Department will resist, on Supremacy Clause grounds, local attempts to curb legitimate federal law enforcement techniques. . . . [A]n attorney employed by the Department, and any individual acting at the direction of that attorney, is authorized to contact or communicate with any individual *in the course of an investigation or prosecution* unless the contact or communication is prohibited by the Constitution, statute, Executive Order, or applicable federal regulation.[126]

The response of the courts to this position was, to say the least, unreceptive. For example, in *United States v. Lopez*, DOJ attempted to rely on the Thornburgh Memorandum to exempt a prosecutor who engaged in post-indictment contacts with a represented party from court-adopted no-contact rules.[127] The prosecutor had conducted *ex parte* meetings with a criminal defendant, and concealed those contacts from the defendant's lawyer in an effort to reach a plea bargain and cooperation agreement with the defendant and a co-defendant

---

124. John Doe, 801 F. Supp. at 489.
125. *Id.* at 492 (emphasis added).
126. *Id.* at 493 (emphasis added).
127. 765 F. Supp. 1433 (N.D. Cal. 1991).

(the co-defendant's lawyer did participate in the meetings).[128] The district court flatly rejected the policy set forth in the Thornburg Memorandum, noting that "[e]ven a cursory examination of the authority cited by the Attorney General reveals that the cases do not support the policy articulated in the Memorandum."[129] In fact, the court was unable to find any authority supporting the proposition that the ethical rules against *ex parte* contacts do not apply to a government lawyer who communicates with a represented individual under indictment.[130] Based upon the long-standing ethical norm prohibiting communications with represented parties and the courts' consistent rulings that the prohibition applies to prosecutors, the court held that "[t]o the extent that the Memorandum purports to authorize DOJ attorneys to disregard an ethical rule which has been adopted by this court pursuant to its Local Rules, the Memorandum instructs federal prosecutors to violate federal law."[131] The court dismissed the indictment, relying upon its supervisory powers.[132] Although the Ninth Circuit reversed the dismissal as an improper remedy, it endorsed the district court's rejection of DOJ's attempt to use the Thornburgh Memorandum to support its conduct.[133]

In 1994, after the Ninth Circuit's opinion in *Lopez*, DOJ largely codified its Thornburgh Memorandum position in regulations contained at 28 C.F.R. § 77.1-12. According to the regulations:

> Except as otherwise provided in this part, an attorney for the government may communicate, or cause another to communicate, with a represented person in the process of conducting an investigation, including, but not limited to, an undercover investigation.[134]
>
> Communications with represented parties and represented persons pursuant to this part are intended to constitute communications that are 'authorized by law' within the meaning of Rule 4.2 . . . [and] DR 7-104(A)(1) . . . In addition, this part is intended to preempt and supersede the application of state laws and rules and local federal court rules to the extent that they relate to contacts by attorneys for the government, and those acting at their direction or under their supervision, with represented parties or represented persons in criminal or civil law enforcement investigations or proceedings; it is designed to preempt the entire field of rules concerning such contacts.[135]

---

128. *Id.* at 1438-44.
129. *Id.* at 1446.
130. *Id.* at 1447.
131. *Id.* at 1450.
132. *Id.* at 1464.
133. United States v. Lopez, 4 F.3d 1455, 1458-61 (9th Cir. 1993).
134. 28 C.F.R. § 77.7 (1994) (repealed).
135. *Id.* § 77.12 (1994) (repealed).

In 1998, the Eighth Circuit considered and rejected these regulations as outside the scope of DOJ's rulemaking authority.[136] In *United States v. McDonnell Douglas Corp.*, the government appealed the district court's order directing DOJ to cease *ex parte* contacts with employees of McDonnell Douglas and provide discovery of information already obtained from such contacts. The government contended that its regulations superseded the local rules of the district court (which incorporated Missouri's anti-contact rule), or, in the alternative, that *ex parte* contacts by government attorneys and agents fall within the "authorized by law" exception of Rule 4.2.[137] The Eighth Circuit upheld the district court order and affirmed the district court's holding that the DOJ's regulations, and specifically section 77.10(a),[138] were beyond the statutory authority of the Attorney General to enact. In addition, the court refused to adopt the DOJ's position that its regulations preempted local court rules.[139]

In October 1998, Congress entered the fray by enacting the Citizen's Protection Act of 1998 (also known as the McDade Amendment).[140] The Act, which became effective in April 1999 despite the vigorous efforts of the Justice Department to delay its implementation or eliminate it altogether,[141] provides that attorneys for the federal government are subject to the ethical rules of the states and courts in which they engage in their duties, and "to the same extent and in the same manner" as other attorneys.[142]

As was required by the Act, the Justice Department scrapped its regulations modeled on the Thornburgh Memorandum, and issued the implementing regulations that are on the books today. Those regulations provide that:

> In all criminal investigations and prosecutions, in all civil investigations and litigation (affirmative and defensive), and in all civil law enforcement investigations and proceedings, attorneys for the government shall conform their conduct and activities to the state rules and laws, and federal local court rules,

---

136. *See* United States v. McDonnell Douglas Corp., 132 F.3d 1252 (8th Cir. 1998).

137. *Id.* at 1254.

138. "A communication with a current employee of an organization that qualifies as a represented party or represented person shall be considered to be a communication with the organization for purposes of this part only if the employee is a controlling individual. A 'controlling individual' is a current high-level employee who is known by the government to be participating as a decision maker in the determination of the organization's legal position in the proceeding or investigation of the subject matter." *Id.* (quoting 28 C.F.R. § 77.10(a) (1994) (repealed)).

139. *Id.* at 1257 & n.4.

140. Congress Enacts Statute that Subjects Federal Prosecutors to State Laws and Rules, 64 CRIM. L. REP. (BNA) 70 (Oct. 28, 1998).

141. *See* Bill Moushey, Justice, Hatch Fight Law Aimed at Overzealous Prosecutors, PITTSBURGH POST-GAZETTE, Mar. 26, 1999, at A-1.

142. 28 U.S.C. § 530B(a).

governing attorneys in each State where such attorney engages in that attorney's duties, to the same extent and in the same manner as the other attorneys in that State....[143]

Notably, the regulations subject government attorneys to state and court ethics rules regardless of whether a matter has ripened into a formal proceeding,[144] and do not conceive of an exception where application of the rules would merely conflict with federal law enforcement policy.[145] In addition, Justice Department attorneys are instructed not to direct investigative agents acting under their supervision to engage in conduct that would violate their own ethical obligations (although good faith provision of legal advice or guidance on request is not prohibited).[146] Finally, to determine which state or states government attorneys may be deemed to be "engaged in their duties," the regulations look to whether a case is pending. If a case has been instituted, government attorneys are subject to the rules of the state or federal court in which the case is pending; alternatively, where there is no case pending, government attorneys are subject to the rules of their states of licensure.[147]

The gravamen of all this for the corporate client is that whether a government lawyer's *ex parte* contacts with corporate employees will run afoul of ethical constraints will be determined by reference to the state or court ethical rules applicable to the attorney's conduct, and which set of rules applies will depend on whether a proceeding has been instituted.[148] For this reason, attention to detail in reviewing the various aspects of the ethical rules of the pertinent jurisdiction or jurisdictions will become critical in any attempt to challenge prosecutorial conduct in this regard. Such a review is beyond the scope of this chapter, but several key considerations should be kept in mind.

First, which employees of an organization are "off limits" to government lawyers?[149] The official comment to Model Rule 4.2, as restated in February

---

143. 28 C.F.R. § 77.3.

144. *Id.* & § 77.2(c).

145. *See id.* § 77.1(b) (28 U.S.C. § 530B "should not be construed in any way to alter federal substantive, procedural, or evidentiary law or to interfere with the Attorney General's authority to send Department attorneys into any court in the United States").

146. *Id.* § 77.4(f).

147. *Id.* § 77.2(j)(1).

148. *See, e.g.*, United States v. Colorado Supreme Court, 189 F.3d 1281, 1284 (10th Cir. 1999) (holding state ethical rule restricting ability of prosecutors to subpoena attorneys for information about clients in criminal proceedings applicable to federal prosecutors, as "the McDade Act ... conclusively establish[es] that a state rule governing attorney conduct is applicable to federal attorneys practicing in the state").

149. It is clear that the no-contact rule does not prevent *ex parte* contacts with *all* company employees. *See* ABA, Formal Op. 95-396 ("[A] lawyer representing the organization

2002, makes it clear that when a company is the client, opposing counsel shall not communicate with:

> A constituent of the organization who supervises, directs or regularly consults with the organization's lawyer concerning the matter or has authority to obligate the organization with respect to the matter or whose act or omission in connection with the matter may be imputed to the organization for purposes of civil or criminal liability. Consent of the organization's lawyer is not required for communication with a former constituent.[150]

In interpreting the no-contact rules adopted in various jurisdictions, the vast majority of courts have taken the position that current upper management and some, but probably not all, low- and mid-level employees are within the reach of the rule. Currently, there are no fewer than five schools of thought on which employees are covered by the no-contact rule:[151]

- Most stringent is the so-called "control-group" test, which in one formulation limits the no-contact rule to employees "responsible for, or significantly involved in, the determination of the organization's legal position in the matter,"[152] and in another limits the rule to "managerial employees with authority to commit the organization to a position regarding the subject matter of the representation."[153]
- The so-called "party-opponent admission" test proscribes contacts with any employee whose statement might be admissible as a company admission—a potentially broad category, given the possibility that any employee speaking within the scope of employment could bind the company.[154]
- The so-called "managing-speaking agent test" limits the no-contact rule to those employees with "managing authority sufficient to give

---

cannot insulate all employees from contacts with opposing lawyers by asserting a blanket representation of the organization."). Indeed, it may be ethically problematic for company counsel to take this position. *See* Op. 2005-3, Ohio S. Ct. Bd. of Comm'rs on Grievances & Discipline (Feb. 4, 2005) (calling counsel's claim to represent the corporation and all its employees "bluster" and "inappropriate," and noting that "such blanket representation . . . would in many instances be fraught with impermissible conflicts of interest for the corporate lawyer").

150. MODEL RULES OF PROF'L CONDUCT R. 4.2 cmt. 6 (Feb. 2002).

151. *See* Snider v. Superior Court, 113 Cal. App. 4th 1187, 1205-1207 (2003) (summarizing the various formulations of the no-contact rule and collecting cases).

152. Michaels v. Woodland, 988 F. Supp. 468, 471 (D.N.J. 1997).

153. Johnson v. Cadillac Plastic Group, Inc., 930 F. Supp. 1437, 1442 (D. Colo. 1996).

154. *See* Palmer v. Pioneer Inn Assocs., Ltd., 59 P.3d 1237, 1243 (Nev. 2002). This view has been criticized as inconsistent with the original intent of the Model Rule 4.2 comments' past use of the phrase "whose statement may constitute an admission on the part of the organization"—a phrase eliminated from the comments in 2002. *Id.* at 1242.

them the right to speak for, and bind, the corporation" on the matters to which the representation relates.[155]
- The so-called "alter ego" test limits the no-contact rule to those employees whose acts or omissions in the matter are binding on or imputed to the corporation for liability purposes, or employees implementing the advice of counsel.[156]
- Finally, some courts have engaged in a so-called "case-by-case balancing" test to determine what *ex parte* contacts should be allowed in the specific case, considering the claims at issue, the employee's position and duties, the interests of the employer in protecting itself and the alternatives available to the opponent to obtain the information sought.[157]

Due to the diversity of approaches employed to decide whether and which current employees are within the scope of the no-contact rule, counsel is advised to study the precedents from the relevant jurisdiction(s) carefully. Moreover, due to the complexity of these approaches and the unsettled nature of the case law, counsel should expect that the applicability of the rule to the facts presented will be a matter of *ex post* interpretation—with resulting *ex ante* unpredictability for both sides on the subject of who may be contacted.

Second, do the ethical rules proscribe *ex parte* contacts with former as well as current employees? Although defense counsel representing a corporate employer can argue persuasively that the no-contact rules apply to communications with certain *present* employees, it is more difficult for counsel to argue that prosecutors and their investigative agents should not be permitted to communicate *ex parte* with *former* employees of the corporation.[158] The majority of courts have held that consent of company counsel is not required

---

155. *E.g.,* Wright v. Group Health Hosp., 691 P.2d 564, 568-69 (Wash. 1984).
156. *E.g.,* Niesig v. Team I, 558 N.E.2d 1030, 1035 (N.Y. 1990). Under the "alter ego" interpretation, the no-contact rule would cover (for example) a truck driver whose involvement in an accident led to a lawsuit against his employer. The truck driver is not a manager, nor is he authorized to speak on behalf of the company. However, his admission of fault would create *respondeat superior* liability for the company. *See* 2 GEOFFREY C. HAZARD JR. & W. WILLIAM HODES, THE LAW OF LAWYERING: A HANDBOOK ON THE MODEL RULES OF PROFESSIONAL CONDUCT § 4.2:105, at 740 (2d ed. Supp. 1998).
157. *E.g.,* Baisley v. Missisquoi Cemetery Ass'n, 708 A.2d 924, 933 (Vt. 1998).
158. *See* Aiken v. Business & Indus. Health Group, 885 F. Supp. 1474, 1477 (D. Kan. 1995) ("Notwithstanding some case law to the contrary, the clear majority of courts interpreting Rule 4.2 have held . . . that [it] does not apply to communication with former employees of an organizational party who no longer have any relationship with the organization") (collecting cases); *see also* U.S. v. W.R. Grace, 401 F. Supp. 2d 1065, 1068-69 (D. Mont. 2005) ("Neither the text nor the comments of Model Rule 4.2 make any effort to distinguish

to contact an unrepresented former employee, at least where nonprivileged information is all that is discussed.[159] This view finds support in a 1991 opinion of the American Bar Association Standing Committee on Ethics and Professional Responsibility,[160] and in the official comments to the February 2002 amendments to Model Rule 4.2.[161]

Critical steps can and should be taken, however, to protect the corporation's interest in the testimony of its former employees. Upon discovery of or notice that an investigation may commence, company counsel immediately should identify and locate all former employees who may be witnesses. Counsel should then seek to conduct face-to-face interviews with the potential witnesses and memorialize their recollection of relevant events. While actual

---

between former managerial employees and former 'lower echelon' employees. Under the current version of Model Rule 4.2, as incorporated in Local Rule 83.13, the government does not violate the ethical standards of this Court by initiating *ex parte* contact with former Grace employees."); Smith v. Kalamazoo Ophthalmology, 322 F. Supp. 2d 883, 888-89 (W.D. Mich. 2004) (holding that Rule 4.2 of the Michigan Rules of Professional Responsibility do not bar *ex parte* communication with former employees who are not themselves represented in the matter); H.B.A. Mgmt., Inc. v. Estate of Schwartz, 693 So. 2d 541, 546 (Fla. 1997) (holding that Florida's version of Model Rule 4.2 "neither contemplates nor prohibits an attorney's *ex parte* communications with former employees of a defendant-employer."); Terra Int'l, Inc. v. Mississippi Chem. Corp., 913 F. Supp. at 1315 (only barring *ex parte* contact with former employees still represented by former employer's counsel); Hanntz v. Shiley, Inc., 766 F. Supp. 258, 265 (D.N.J. 1991) ("Ordinarily, it cannot be assumed the corporation's counsel represents the former employees.") (citations omitted). *But see* Olson v. Snap Prods., Inc., 183 F.R.D. 539, 544-45 (D. Minn. 1998) (rejecting a per se rule permitting contacts with former employees in favor of a "flexible approach" that assesses the likelihood that the contact will invade the corporation's attorney-client privilege).

159. *See, e.g.,* Smith v. Kalamazoo Ophthalmology, 322 F. Supp. 2d at 888-91 (collecting cases).

160. ABA Standing Comm. on Ethics and Professional Responsibility, Formal Op. 91-359 (1991) (opining that counsel to a party adverse to a corporation may communicate about the subject matter of the representation with a former employee without the consent of the corporation's counsel, so long as the former employee is not separately represented).

161. MODEL RULES OF PROF'L CONDUCT R. 4.2, cmt. 6 (Feb. 2002) ("Consent of the organization's lawyer is not required for communications with a former constituent.") *But see id.,* Reporter's Observations, cmt. 6 ("Rule 4.4 precludes the use of methods of obtaining evidence that violate the legal rights of the organization."); LaPoint v. AmerisourceBergen Corp., No. Civ. A. 327-N, 2006 WL 2105862, at *3 (Del. Ch. Ct. July 18, 2006) (*ex parte* communications with former manager permitted "as long as the attorney is seeking only key non-privileged facts, and makes the former employee aware that she cannot divulge any communications she may have had with the adverse party's attorneys, or any other privileged information"); Op. 2005-3, Ohio S. Ct. Bd. of Comm'rs on Grievances & Discipline (Feb. 4, 2005) (attorney "must inform the former employee not to divulge any communications that the former employee may have had with corporate or other counsel").

or potential conflicts of interest may prevent company counsel from also representing individual former employees, counsel can inform the former employees of the investigation and assist them in retaining separate counsel if they desire to do so.[162] Representation of former employees by capable counsel is often the best means of ensuring that the rights of both the corporation and its employees are not compromised by aggressive government investigators. Finally, it may be possible to obtain court-imposed conditions on governmental contacts with former employees, including requiring the government to maintain lists of the former employees contacted and to make all memorandums prepared as a result of those contacts available for inspection upon request.[163]

Third, to what extent are government lawyers subject to no-contact rules in the investigative phase of a matter—that is, prior to a criminal indictment or the initiation of formal civil proceedings? The official comment to Model Rule 4.2 states that the Rule applies to "any person who is represented by counsel concerning the matter to which the communication relates."[164] A broad interpretation of Rule 4.2 would prohibit *ex parte* contacts by government prosecutors regardless of whether a formal criminal proceeding is under way. Enthusiasm for such a broad reading must be tempered by the official comment's additional statement that "[c]ommunications authorized by law may . . . include investigative activities of lawyers representing governmental entities, directly or through investigative agents, prior to the commencement of criminal or civil enforcement proceedings."[165]

Courts have generally concluded that the ethical prohibition against contacts with represented defendants is co-extensive with the Sixth Amendment right to counsel and, therefore, does not constrain noncustodial prosecutorial contacts prior to a criminal indictment.[166] The line is drawn based on the exis-

---

162. State corporate law and the corporation's bylaws may require the company to indemnify employees for their legal fees or even to advance legal fees prior to a decision respecting indemnification. *See, e.g.,* DEL. CODE ANN. tit. 8, § 145. The costs involved can be substantial. It therefore is generally in the corporation's best interests for company counsel to be involved from the outset in the selection and retention of separate counsel for employees and, where possible, to suggest multiple representation as a cost-saving measure.

163. *See, e.g.,* U.S. ex rel. O'Keefe v. McDonnell Douglas Corp., 132 F.3d 1252, 1257-58 (8th Cir. 1998) (upholding district court's imposition of these restrictions).

164. MODEL RULES OF PROF'L CONDUCT R. 4.2, cmt. 2 (Feb. 2002).

165. *Id.* cmt. 5.

166. *See, e.g.,* United States v. Balter, 91 F.3d 427, 436 (3d Cir. 1996); United States v. Powe, 9 F.3d 68, 69 (9th Cir. 1993); United States v. Heinz, 983 F.2d 609, 614 (5th Cir. 1993)

tence or nonexistence of an indictment; that a grand jury is actively considering indictment of the defendant does not seem to alter the calculus.[167] Notably, however, the Second Circuit has held that the anti-contact rules may apply in certain pre-indictment situations, principally because tying the application of ethical proscriptions to the timing of an indictment simply places too much power in a prosecutor's hands.[168] In particular, where the same prosecutor has already commenced a civil action on the same underlying facts, the court may hesitate to exalt form over substance by permitting *ex parte* contacts simply because no criminal indictment has yet been returned.[169]

In light of the complexity of this area of the law, and of the multiple jurisdictions whose law may be in play under the Citizen's Protection Act and the implementing regulations, it is highly recommended that counsel check the most recent decisions involving multiple representation, conflicts, and *ex parte* communications prior to advising their clients. Forming a strategy for communicating with current and former employees on this subject is impossible without a precise and detailed understanding of the ethical rules by which counsel—both for the government and for the corporation—will be governed.

("The dullest imagination can comprehend the devastating effect that [a rule limiting pre-indictment contacts] would have on undercover operations."); United States v. Ryans, 903 F.2d 731, 740 (10th Cir. 1990); United States v. Sutton, 801 F.2d 1346, 1366 (D.C. Cir. 1986); United States v. Dobbs, 711 F.2d 84, 86 (8th Cir. 1983); *see also* United States v. Grass, 239 F. Supp. 2d 535, 541 (M.D. Pa. 2003) ("With the exception of the Second Circuit, every other court has held that the no-contact rule does not prevent non-custodial pre-indictment communications by undercover agents with represented parties which occur in the course of legitimate criminal investigations.");

167. *See* United States v. Talao, 222 F.3d 1133, 1137-39 (9th Cir. 2000) (analyzing whether prosecutor's *ex parte* communications with employee immediately prior to grand-jury testimony violated state ethics rules; fact that grand jury was investigating employer not considered).

168. United States v. Hammad, 858 F.2d 834, 838-40 (2d Cir. 1988) (only extending rule to pre-indictment stage based on "egregious misconduct" by the prosecutor and "urg[ing] restraint in applying the rule to [pre-indictment] criminal investigations"). *But see* Grievance Comm. v. Simels, 48 F.3d 640, 649 (2d Cir. 1995) ("It is significant that since *Hammad*, neither this Court nor any reported district court decision considering an alleged violation of DR 7-104(A)(1) has found that the Rule had been violated."); United States v. Joseph Binder Schweizer Emblem Co., 167 F. Supp. 2d 862 (E.D.N.C. 2001) ("[N]o district court in the Second Circuit applying *Hammad* appears to have found a violation of the disciplinary rule.") (citations omitted).

169. *See* United States v. Bowman, 277 F. Supp. 2d 1239, 1244 (N.D. Ala. 2003) (suppressing pre-indictment statements made by represented defendants to agent of the prosecutor who already had commenced civil forfeiture proceedings), *vacated on other grounds,* No. CR-03-C-0056-E, 2003 WL 23272667, at *1 (N.D. Ala. Sept. 12, 2003).

G. *Providing Legal Representation for Employees*

A company can properly provide legal representation for those employees called as witnesses or named as defendants in the course of parallel proceedings.[170] Payment of attorneys' fees by the employer does not create a per se conflict of interest or require disqualification of counsel who has accepted such a fee arrangement.[171] Indeed, most state business codes expressly authorize employers to indemnify employees and/or advance fees and expenses incurred in connection with legal proceedings, and many companies include provisions in their bylaws authorizing advancement and indemnification to the full extent permitted by the law of their chartering states.[172]

Up until the December 2006 release of the McNulty Memorandum, companies had to be conscious that, pursuant to the Thompson Memorandum, paying for employees' legal representation was one of several factors that federal prosecutors considered when determining whether to charge a company. The McNulty Memorandum, however, now makes it clear that prosecutors considering a corporate criminal charge "should not take into account whether a corporation is advancing attorneys' fees to employees or agents under investigation and indictment."[173] The McNulty Memorandum reasons that many state indemnification statutes grant corporations the right to advance legal fees and that, in many cases, corporations are contractually bound to advance attorneys' fees through provisions in their corporate charters, bylaws, or employment agreements.[174] Accordingly, the McNulty Memorandum pro-

---

170. *See, e.g.*, United States v. Smith, 186 F.3d 290, 295 (3d Cir. 1999) (no conflict found where employer paid for employee's counsel), *abrogation by rule on other grounds recognized by* United States v. Diaz, 245 F.3d 294 (3d Cir. 2001); Bucuvalas v. United States, 98 F.3d 652, 656-57 (1st Cir. 1996) (same).

171. *Smith*, 186 F.3d at 295; Bucuvalas, 98 F.3d at 656-57. There is, however, a potential for conflict of interest in this situation. *See* Wood v. Georgia, 450 U.S. 261, 268-69 (1981) ("Courts and commentators have recognized the inherent dangers that arise when a criminal defendant is represented by a lawyer hired and paid by a third party, particularly when the third party is the operator of the alleged criminal enterprise."); *see also* MODEL RULES OF PROF'L CONDUCT R. 1.8(f) (A "lawyer shall not accept compensation for representing a client from one other than the client unless: (1) the client gives informed consent; (2) there is no interference with the lawyer's independence of professional judgment or with the client-lawyer relationship; and (3) information relating to representation of a client is protected as required by Rule 1.6.").

172. *See, e.g.*, DEL. CODE ANN. tit. 8, § 145.

173. *See* McNulty Memorandum, *supra* n. 115, at 11.

174. *Id.*

vides that "a corporation's compliance with governing state law and its contractual obligations cannot be considered a failure to cooperate."[175]

This seismic shift in DOJ policy is welcome news for corporations and employees facing governmental investigations. It is attributable in no small measure to widespread and vocal criticism of, and calls for amendment to, previous DOJ policy as set out in the Thompson Memorandum.[176] Perhaps the most notable (and influential) criticism came from Judge Kaplan of the Southern District of New York who, just months prior to the release of the McNulty Memorandum, ruled that a federal prosecutor's application of the principles set out in the Thompson Memorandum to discourage KPMG from paying its employees' attorneys' fees violated the employees' Fifth and Sixth Amendment rights.[177] The decision was a ringing endorsement of the common (and, in some cases, required) corporate practice of advancing attorneys' fees[178]—and a rather scathing indictment of the Thompson Memorandum.[179] That indictment seems to have struck the final necessary chord with DOJ to prompt a much-needed change in its policy.

In some cases, the company may consider permitting its employees to be represented by its own counsel.[180] Corporations often prefer one law firm to represent all interested parties because it can significantly lessen the amount of legal fees. Additionally, it usually leads to more efficient representation. Both defense counsel and the company benefit from the centralization of information and the natural advantages flowing from one counsel having

---

175. *Id.*
176. *See, e.g.*, Letter from ABA President Michael S. Greco to U.S. Attorney Alberto Gonzales, *Proposal for Revising Department of Justice Attorney-Client Privilege and Work Product Doctrine Waiver Policy*, dated May 2, 2006, *available at* http://www.abanet.org/poladv/acprivgonz5206.pdf; *see also* Marcia Coyle, *Battle on waivers expanding*, NAT'L L. J., May 15, 2006 (discussing potential Congressional efforts to address Thompson Memorandum's privilege-waiver provisions).
177. *See* United States v. Stein, 435 F. Supp. 2d 330, 335-36 (S.D.N.Y. 2006).
178. *Id.* at 335 (stating that an employee's right to have legal expenses paid if sued as a result of job performance "is as much a part of the bargain between employer and employee as salary or wages").
179. *Id.* at 336 ("KPMG refused to pay because the government held the proverbial gun to its head. . . . The government . . . has let its zeal get in the way of its judgment. It has violated the Constitution it is sworn to defend.").
180. *See, e.g.*, United States v. Finlay, 55 F.3d 1410, 1415 (9th Cir. 1995) (no conflict of interest found where corporation and chief executive officer of corporation were represented by the same attorney).

overall responsibility for the case. Counterproductive debates over defense strategy are often avoided when the company and its employees are jointly represented. Joint representation also avoids the tension that inevitably results from an employee having separate counsel. Moreover, the company retains greater control over the proceedings when only one law firm is retained.[181]

Counsel for the company should note, however, that the DOJ frowns upon joint-defense agreements with potentially culpable employees that might result in the sharing of information about the government's investigation. The McNulty Memorandum (like its predecessor, the Thompson Memorandum) instructs prosecutors to consider any such arrangement "in weighing the extent and value of a corporation's cooperation."[182]

Joint representation also can create a significant potential for conflict of interest. This potential can mature into claims of noncompliance with professional ethics rules, the prospect of disqualification at various stages of the proceeding, exposure to claims of ineffective assistance of counsel, and the possible appearance of impropriety. Model Rule of Professional Conduct 1.7(b) generally prohibits the representation of clients with a "concurrent conflict of interest," either because the representation of one client will be directly adverse to the other, or because there is significant risk that the lawyer's ability to represent one client will be materially limited by responsibilities to the other.[183] So long as the lawyer does not represent one client in asserting a claim against the other in the same proceeding, however, joint representation of clients with a "concurrent conflict of interest" is permissible if "the lawyer reasonably believes that the lawyer will be able to provide competent and diligent representation to each affected client [and] each affected client gives informed consent, confirmed in writing."[184] Thus, the Model Rules require the lawyer to make an objective evaluation of the potential for conflict of interest, and to obtain each client's informed consent in writing to the arrangement.[185] While impermissible conflict of interest is a serious risk

---

181. For an analysis of the advantages and disadvantages of multiple representation, *see* Teresa Stanton Collett, *The Promise and Perils of Multiple Representation,* 16 REV. OF LITIG. 567 (Summer 1997).
182. *See* McNulty Memorandum, *supra* n.115.
183. MODEL RULES OF PROF'L CONDUCT R. 1.7(b).
184. *Id.*
185. According to the comments to Rule 1.7(b), "some conflicts are nonconsentable, meaning that the lawyer involved cannot properly ask for such agreement or provide representation on the basis of the client's consent." Whether this is the case "is typically determined by con-

inherent in joint representation in any type of legal proceeding,[186] the commentary to Rule 1.7(b) notes that in criminal proceedings, the "potential for conflict of interest ... is so grave that ordinarily a lawyer should decline to represent more than one codefendant."[187]

Even if a lawyer determines that joint representation is appropriate under the applicable professional ethics rules, he or she may still be subject to disqualification at various stages of the proceeding on grounds of conflict of interest.[188] Courts have broad discretion to disqualify attorneys on the grounds of actual, or even serious potential, conflict,[189] although the conflict must be

---

sidering whether the interests of the clients will be adequately protected if the clients are permitted to give their informed consent to representation burdened by a conflict of interest. Thus, ... representation is prohibited if in the circumstances the lawyer cannot reasonably conclude that the lawyer will be able to provide competent and diligent representation."

186. The comments to Rule 1.7(b) list some examples of situations in which an impermissible conflict of interest might arise: where there is a "substantial discrepancy in the parties' testimony," where there is "incompatibility in positions in relation to an opposing party," or when "there are substantially different possibilities of settlement of the claims or liabilities in question." *Id.* Furthermore, an obvious conflict of interest exists if the lawyer's judgment may be influenced by concern over future employment by the corporation. *See* United States v. Rodriguez, 929 F.2d 747, 749 (1st Cir. 1991); United States v. Allen, 831 F.2d 1487, 1496-97 (9th Cir. 1988); United States v. Bernstein, 533 F.2d 775, 788 (2d Cir. 1976).

187. *See also* Cuyler v. Sullivan, 446 U.S. 335, 348 (1980) (noting that a "possible conflict inheres in almost every instance of multiple representation").

188. *See* United States v. Malpiedi, 62 F.3d 465, 470 (2d Cir. 1995) ("The government can itself seek to disqualify defense counsel because of a conflict. Indeed, it frequently does so.") (citations omitted). This is true even though disqualification proceedings may be subject to tactical manipulation. *See* United States v. Register, 182 F.3d 820, 833 (11th Cir. 1999) (although "[s]trategic maneuvering by the government to disqualify defense attorneys" is a possibility, district court still given broad discretion to decide the issue).

189. Wheat v. United States, 486 U.S. 153, 164 (1988) (although "[t]he District Court must recognize a presumption in favor of petitioner's counsel of choice, ... that presumption may be overcome not only by a demonstration of actual conflict but by a showing of a serious potential conflict"). This standard applies to both the pre-indictment and post-indictment stages of a proceeding. *See, e.g., id.* at 162 (post-indictment); United States v. Moscony, 927 F.2d 742, 750 (3d Cir. 1991) (same); *In re* Grand Jury Proceedings, 859 F.2d 1021, 1024 (1st Cir. 1988) ("Although *Wheat* involved the Sixth Amendment rights of a criminal defendant, we believe that the standards enunciated in *Wheat* may also apply in the grand jury context, at least to some extent. ... The showing that must be made in order to burden a grand jury witness's right to choose certain counsel need be no greater than when the question is one of restricting the Sixth Amendment rights possessed by criminal defendants.") (citation omitted, emphasis added); *In re* Feb. 1977 Grand Jury, 581 F.2d 1262, 1264 (7th Cir. 1978) ("[I]n the context of a grand jury proceeding, a disqualification motion may be granted without proof of the existence of an actual conflict of interest ... when the possibility of a conflict becomes great enough. ... ").

explicit and specific to justify disqualification[190] and the government bears a "heavy burden" in this regard.[191] Furthermore, disqualification may occur even where a client has knowingly waived the right to conflict-free counsel.[192] As the Supreme Court has stated, "the district court must be allowed substantial latitude in refusing waivers of conflict of interest not only in those rare cases where an actual conflict may be demonstrated before trial, but in the more common cases where a potential for conflict exists which may or may not burgeon into an actual conflict as the trial progresses."[193] Finally, in the post-indictment context, Fed. R. Crim. P. 44(c) requires the District Court to make an independent inquiry into the possibility of a conflict of interest in cases of joint representation and to "take appropriate measures to protect each defendant's right to counsel,"[194] including, where necessary, ordering that co-defendants be separately represented.[195]

Even if an attorney is not disqualified, it should be kept in mind that multiple representation may be the basis for later claims of ineffective assistance of counsel under the Sixth Amendment.[196] Although multiple representation normally should not violate the defendant's Sixth Amendment right to effective assistance of counsel, a defendant may make an ineffective assistance of counsel claim where, for example, similar concessions are achieved for all clients, even though some clients are less culpable than others.[197]

---

190. *See In re* Grand Jury Proceedings, 859 F.2d at 1026 (reversing district court's disqualification order where the court "did not identify any specific conflict, actual or potential. . . . Our concern is that . . . a court could make the requisite *Wheat* finding solely on tenuous inferential relationships. We believe that this is contrary to the holding in *Wheat,* and that generally there must be a direct link between the clients of an attorney—or at least some concrete evidence that one client . . . has information about another client . . .—before the right to counsel of choice is barred by disqualification.") (emphasis in original). *But see* United States v. Lanoue, 137 F.3d 656, 664 (1st Cir. 1998) ("Although the facts of this case may well reach the outer limits of 'potential conflict,' the potential for conflict is a matter that is uniquely factual and presents a special dilemma for trial courts.").

191. *In re* Grand Jury, 859 F.2d at 1026.

192. *See, e.g.,* Wheat, 486 U.S. at 162; United States v. Coleman, 997 F.2d 1101, 1104 (5th Cir. 1993); Moscony, 927 F.2d at 750.

193. Wheat, 486 U.S. at 163.

194. FED. R. CRIM. P. 44(c). The Advisory Committee Notes to Rule 44(c) state that the inquiry is necessary even though attorneys are ethically required to make an independent and objective evaluation of the conflict issues.

195. *See* Wheat, 486 U.S. at 161.

196. Holloway v. Arkansas, 435 U.S. 475, 482-83 (1978).

197. *See, e.g.,* United States v. Swartz, 975 F.2d 1042, 1046 (4th Cir. 1992) (actual conflict of interest existed where defense counsel argued at sentencing hearing that both clients

Furthermore, prosecutors typically are mistrustful of multiple representation. Particularly when the corporation's in house lawyer, regular outside counsel, or outside counsel conducting an internal investigation defends both the company and its employees, prosecutors may not view such counsel as independent, and may even view the common representation as perpetuation of the "scheme" they are investigating. This may make it difficult to negotiate with the prosecutors on settlement or any other matter. In addition, the government may exacerbate the situation by issuing "target letters" indicating that some—but not all—of the employees represented by a single lawyer are targets of the investigation and likely to be indicted. This will require a reshuffling of the representation, with all of the stresses attendant to such an endeavor—including whether the lawyer will be able to cross-examine a former client, can utilize privileged information obtained prior to the reshuffling, or may even face Rule 44(c) disqualification entirely. These considerations make multiple representation potentially unattractive and require a careful examination of the relative legal positions of the affected employees *before* deciding which ones may safely be represented by the same lawyer.

Finally, should the corporation choose to advance the costs of legal representation for its individual employees requiring representation in parallel proceedings, great care should be taken before deciding to discontinue the payments. In particular, an arrangement whereby representation ceases, once an employee chooses to cooperate with the government, may well be viewed as coercive.[198]

H. *Joint Defense Agreements: Benefits, Limits, and Risks*

Where several defense counsel represent multiple parties in criminal or civil proceedings, counsel should be aware of the protection afforded by what

---

were equally culpable); Thomas v. Foltz, 818 F.2d 476, 478 (6th Cir. 1987) (lawyer who persuaded three clients to plead guilty in order to satisfy a prosecutor's "package deal only" policy rendered constitutionally ineffective assistance to an arguably less culpable member of the trio); *see also* Allen, 831 F.2d at 1497 ("[N]o one should be represented by an attorney who is making him the 'fall guy' by design.") (citation omitted). Because of this possibility, it has been recommended that counsel for the corporation represent employees only after interviews and a determination as to potential culpability. Gary G. Lynch & Douglas M. Fuchs, *Conducting Internal Investigations of Possible Corporate Wrongdoing*, 943 PLI/CORP. 615, 628 (June 1996).

198. *See* Pirillo v. Takiff, 341 A.2d 896, 903 (Pa. 1975) (criticizing the Fraternal Order of Police for hiring attorney who would withdraw from representation of police officers once they appeared to be considering cooperation with the government).

is commonly called the joint defense doctrine.[199] The joint defense doctrine is essentially an exception to the rule that no privilege is available for material shared with a third party.[200] It arises most frequently when criminal codefendants agree to coordinate their defenses, but it has been applied to civil litigants as well.[201] As discussed below, joint defense agreements often make partners of unsteady bedfellows. Such agreements necessarily involve communications with lawyers and clients other than one's own. Joint-defense communications therefore must be carefully crafted, with due consideration for the limited boundaries of the privilege.

The joint defense privilege generally reflects a tension between two competing interests: the confidentiality needed to protect the sanctity of the attorney-client relationship, and society's countervailing right to hear "everyman's evidence" to assist the judicial system in its truth-seeking role.[202] In examining the boundaries of the joint defense doctrine, courts attempt to balance these two concerns.[203]

The decisional law on joint defense agreements flows from the seminal case of *Continental Oil Co. v. United States*.[204] In that case, counsel for

---

199. *See* Continental Oil Co. v. United States, 330 F.2d 347 (9th Cir. 1974); Hunydee v. United States, 355 F.2d 183 (9th Cir. 1965); *see also* United States v. Schwimmer, 892 F.2d 237 (2d Cir. 1989); United States v. McPartlin, 595 F.2d 1321 (7th Cir. 1979); *In re* Grand Jury Subpoena Duces Tecum, 406 F. Supp. 381 (S.D.N.Y. 1975). Some courts indicate that the joint defense privilege is "more properly identified as the 'common interest rule.'" *See, e.g.,* Schwimmer, 892 F.2d at 243. Other courts have distinguished between the terms, with the joint defense privilege a specific version of a broader "common interest" privilege. *See* Lugosch v. Congel, 219 F.R.D. 220, 236 n.10 (N.D.N.Y. 2003); *In re* Sealed Case, 29 F.3d 715, 719 (D.C. Cir. 1994).

200. *In re* Regents of the Univ. of Cal., 101 F.3d 1386, 1390-91 (Fed. Cir. 1996); *In re* Grand Jury Subpoenas, 902 F.2d 244, 248-49 (4th Cir. 1990).

201. *See In re* Grand Jury Subpoenas, 902 F.2d at 248-49 (noting extension of joint defense privilege to various situations including co-litigants in civil case; information shared by companies summoned before a grand jury; plaintiffs pursuing lawsuits in different jurisdictions; and defendants sued in separate actions); *see also In re* Regents of the Univ. of Cal., 101 F.3d at 1390-91 (extending privilege to patent prosecution); United States v. DeNardi Corp., 167 F.R.D. 680, 686 (S.D. Cal. 1996) (privilege can apply "whether the jointly interested persons are defendants or plaintiffs, and whether the litigation or potential litigation is civil or criminal") (citations omitted).

202. *In re* Grand Jury, 406 F. Supp. at 386.

203. *See, e.g., In re* Grand Jury Subpoena Duces Tecum, 112 F.3d 910, 918-23 (8th Cir. 1997); Hewlett-Packard Co. v. Bausch & Lomb, Inc., 115 F.R.D. 308, 309 (N.D. Cal. 1987), *aff'd in part and vacated in part on other grounds,* 882 F.2d 1556 (1989); *In re* Grand Jury, 406 F. Supp. at 385-86.

204. 330 F.2d 347 (9th Cir. 1964).

employees of Continental and Standard Oil Companies debriefed their clients after they testified before a grand jury, and then exchanged the information in an effort to discern the nature and scope of the grand jury probe. Upon learning of the memoranda, the government subpoenaed both the companies and their lawyers.[205] The Ninth Circuit rejected the government's argument that any privilege the material might have enjoyed was lost following the exchange among counsel.[206] The court further rejected the government's assertion that a joint defense privilege applies only to post-indictment proceedings.[207]

Subsequently, in *Hunydee v. United States*,[208] the Ninth Circuit spelled out the cornerstone of the doctrine:

> [W]here two or more persons who are subject to possible indictment in connection with the same transactions make confidential statements to their attorneys, these statements, even though they are exchanged between attorneys, should be privileged to the extent that they concern common issues and are intended to facilitate representation in possible subsequent proceedings.[209]

Continental Oil and its progeny define the core elements of the joint defense privilege: (i) the parties (usually co-defendants) must share a *common interest*; (ii) the information must have been exchanged *to facilitate their representation*; and (iii) the material must be *confidential*.[210]

1. Necessity for a Common Interest

This element is the heart of the joint defense doctrine. The parties must be pursuing a common or mutual legal goal in order for the doctrine to apply. It is, however, unlikely that co-defendants or co-litigants will have interests that are identical in every respect. The critical question becomes how diverse and potentially conflicting the parties' interests can be before those interests are no longer "common."

---

205. *Id.*
206. *Id.* at 350.
207. *Id.*
208. 355 F.2d 183 (9th Cir. 1965).
209. *Id.* at 185; *see also* Schwimmer, 892 F.2d at 243-44 (holding that the joint defense privilege "serves to protect the confidentiality of communications passing from one party to the attorney for another party where a joint defense effort or strategy has been decided upon and undertaken").
210. Some cases have stated the third element somewhat differently as "the privilege has not been waived." *See, e.g., In re* Bevill, Bresler & Schulman Asset Management Corp., 805 F.2d 120, 126 (3d Cir. 1986).

Parties seeking the protection of the joint defense privilege can find comfort in the formulation of "common" interest announced by the Seventh Circuit in *United States v. McPartlin*:[211] "[t]he privilege protects pooling of information for any defense purpose common to the participating defendants."[212] The *McPartlin* court found that the defendants' mutual interest in discrediting a government witness constituted a common interest, even though the defendants' various strategies diverged in other respects.[213] Consequently, statements made by one defendant to the investigator[214] for another defendant were protected by the attorney-client privilege, and the defendant could not introduce the co-defendant's confidential statement at their joint trial.[215] The significance of *McPartlin* is its conclusion that some common interest is enough to satisfy the joint defense doctrine—the strategies of the co-defendants need not be uniform to be "common."[216]

Certain courts have found "common" interests, despite recognizing that the co-parties' interests could erupt into litigation in the future.[217] This is so because the inquiry focuses upon the relationship of the parties at the time the material is exchanged, not on subsequent events.[218] As a result, courts have acknowledged that while holders of a joint defense privilege may make for "unsteady bedfellows,"[219] this is not a basis for withholding the privilege.

Indeed, even nonparties to a given litigation may be able to enter into a joint defense agreement with some of the parties, and receive its protections. In *Lugosch v. Congel*, the court noted that "the joint defense privilege should not be so narrowly construed to be limited solely to co-parties as long as the

---

211. 595 F.2d 1321 (7th Cir. 1979).

212. *Id.* at 1337.

213. *Id.* at 1336.

214. The court found that the investigator was the agent of the co-defendant's lawyer, and that communications to the investigator therefore fell within the ambit of the attorney-client privilege. *Id.* at 1337.

215. *Id.*

216. *See also In re* Mortgage Realty & Trust, 212 B.R. 649, 653 (C.D. Cal. Bankr. 1997) (finding common interest between debtor and committee of unsecured creditors); Eisenberg v. Gagnon, 766 F.2d 770, 787-88 (3d Cir. 1985) ("Communications to an attorney to establish a common defense strategy are privileged even though the attorney represents another client with some adverse interests.").

217. *In re* Grand Jury, 406 F. Supp. at 392.

218. *See* John Morrell & Co. v. Local Union 304A, 913 F.2d 544, 555-56 (8th Cir. 1990); *In re* LTV Sec. Litig., 89 F.R.D. 595, 604-05 (N.D. Tex. 1981).

219. *See, e.g., In re* Grand Jury, 406 F. Supp. at 392; *see also* Eisenberg, 766 F.2d at 787; McPartlin, 595 F.2d at 1336.

parties sharing the information have the same reasonable expectation of a shared legal bond and the anticipation of litigation is present."[220]

By contrast, no common interest will be found to exist—and no joint defense privilege is available—if the parties' interests are so antagonistic that they are, in reality, adversaries—such as when counsel for one defendant elicits a confession from a co-defendant, exonerating the first.[221]

2. Exchange of Information to Facilitate Representation

This second requirement of the joint defense doctrine assesses the parties' motives for pooling their confidential information.[222] This requirement is perhaps best phrased in the negative: the information must not have been exchanged "for the purpose of allowing unlimited publication and use, but rather, . . . for the limited purpose of assisting in their common cause."[223] Realistically, the self-interest of co-defendants would seem to make this requirement superfluous. Perhaps all the courts truly seek is an assurance that the cooperation was motivated by legal rather than purely commercial concerns.[224]

---

220. 219 F.R.D. at 238.
221. *See* North River Ins. Co. v. Columbia Cas. Co., No. 90 Civ. 2518 (MJL), 1995 WL 5792, at *4 (S.D.N.Y. Jan. 5, 1995) (communications between parties with antagonistic interests not privileged); *see also* Government of the Virgin Islands v. Joseph, 685 F.2d 857, 862 (3d Cir. 1982) (distinguishing McPartlin on the amount of antagonism present and noting that, unlike Hunydee, the defendant communicated not with his own lawyer but with his co-defendants' counsel); Ferko v. Nat'l Assoc. for Stock Car Auto Racing, Inc., 219 F.R.D. 403, 406 (E.D. Tex. 2003) (finding no common interest between shareholder plaintiff and corporation in shareholder derivative suit).
222. *See, e.g.,* Hunydee, 355 F.2d at 185 (information relating to grand jury proceedings protected by the joint defense doctrine to the extent that it is "intended to facilitate representation in the possible subsequent proceedings").
223. Wilson P. Abraham Constr. Corp. v. Armco Steel Corp., 559 F.2d 250, 253 (5th Cir. 1977); Burton v. R.J. Reynolds Tobacco Co., 167 F.R.D. 134, 139 (D. Kan. 1996) (citation omitted).
224. *See In re* Subpoena Duces Tecum, No. M 8-85 MHD, 1997 WL 599399, at *4 (S.D.N.Y. Sept. 26, 1997) ("it appears that [parties] must possess not merely a common commercial interest, but 'a common legal interest.'") (citations omitted); *see also* United States v. Aramony, 88 F.3d 1369, 1392 (4th Cir. 1996) (privilege not applicable to development of defense for individual defendant that would also protect organization's reputation because "preservation of one's reputation is not a legal matter"); *In re* Diet Drugs Products Liability Litig., MDL Docket No. 1203, 2001 WL 34133955, at *1 (E.D. Pa., April 19, 2001) (rejecting attempt to apply common interest doctrine to three drug makers' efforts to convince federal regulatory authorities to remove drug from controlled-substance list).

Few parties lose the joint defense privilege solely for failing to meet this prong. That is not to say, however, that defendants never lose the privilege for want of this element.[225] When they do, it is often because the parties' communications do not further a shared interest in legal representation in a specific matter. For example, during the Clinton Administration, the Eighth Circuit held that (now Senator) Hillary Clinton and the White House as an institution did not share a common interest in legal representation. While the court found Ms. Clinton's interest in avoiding prosecution sufficient, it rejected the White House's asserted interest in avoiding misunderstandings and information leaks.[226]

Further, courts have not looked favorably on attempts to wrap within the privilege's cloak communications on various subjects over an extended period of time.[227] As the First Circuit has held, "there can be no joint defense agreement when there is no joint defense to pursue."[228]

Accordingly, parties to a joint defense agreement should manifest their intent that the sole purpose for exchanging information is to facilitate their joint interests in obtaining effective legal representation in a discrete litigation, whether pending or anticipated.[229]

3. Requirement of Confidentiality

Because the joint defense doctrine is an application of the attorney-client privilege,[230] the requirement of confidentiality is critical to its success-

---

225. *See, e.g.,* Aramony, 88 F.3d at 1392 (declining to apply privilege because no common interest); United States v. Keplinger, 776 F.2d 678, 701 (7th Cir. 1985) (declining to apply joint defense privilege because defendant failed to meet common interest and confidentiality prongs); Government of the Virgin Islands, 685 F.2d at 862 (same); SCM Corp. v. Xerox Corp., 70 F.R.D. at 513 (declining to apply privilege because no common interest).

226. *In re* Grand Jury Subpoena Duces Tecum, 112 F.3d at 922-23.

227. *See, e.g., In re* Grand Jury Subpoena (Newparent), 274 F.3d 563, 575 (1st Cir. 2001) (rejecting claim by two senior executives and a company that all communications between them and a lawyer over a nine-year period were jointly privileged: "The law will not countenance a 'rolling' joint defense agreement of limitless breadth.").

228. *Id.*

229. *See In re* Grand Jury Subpoena: Under Seal, 415 F.3d 333, 341 (4th Cir. 2005) (denying joint defense privilege between company and employee where the stated purpose of the employee's interview was to gather information); *In re* Santa Fe Int'l Corp., 272 F.3d 705, 710-13 (5th Cir. 2001) (exchanges between competitors for purpose of avoiding antitrust claims, rather than defending against anticipated antitrust claims, not protected by joint defense privilege).

230. While the joint defense privilege is an extension of the attorney-client privilege, it also may be invoked in connection with the work-product doctrine. Haines v. Liggett Group,

ful assertion.[231] Where there is consultation among defense counsel and their respective clients, allied in a common legal cause, it may be reasonably inferred that the discussions and any corollary disclosures are intended to be confidential within the group. If this is the case, and counsel can demonstrate that the disclosures would not have been made except for the purpose of obtaining or advancing legal representation, then it is likely that a claim of privilege will be upheld.[232] As one court stated, a communication will be found privileged "if it is intended to remain confidential and was made under such circumstances that it was reasonably expected and understood to be confidential."[233]

The case law in connection with the confidentiality element shows that the courts engage in two lines of inquiry. The first analysis is subjective and asks whether the co-defendants intended the pooled information to remain confidential. The second line of reasoning looks at the objective circumstances surrounding the materials' purported confidentiality.[234] For a party to succeed on both the subjective and objective prongs, it must demonstrate a "conscious and conscientious joint defense undertaking."[235]

The subjective inquiry into the confidentiality element (i.e., a "conscious" undertaking) is best evidenced by a written joint-defense agreement memorializing the parties' intent that all information exchanged should remain confidential. Perhaps the thornier aspect of the confidentiality requirement is

---

Inc., 975 F.2d 81, 94 (3d Cir. 1992) (citation omitted). Like the attorney-client privilege, the joint defense privilege does not apply in certain instances, *e.g.*, the crime-fraud exception. *Id.* at 94-95.

231. United States v. Bay State Ambulance & Hosp. Rental Serv. Inc., 874 F.2d 20, 28 (1st Cir. 1989) (citations omitted).

232. McPartlin, 595 F.2d at 1335-37 (the defendant's statements to an investigator who was acting as an agent for a co-defendant's lawyer were inadmissible because of joint defense privilege); Hunydee, 355 F.2d at 185 (confidential statements made by two or more persons to their lawyers where such persons are subject to possible indictment in connection with the same transactions should be privileged to the extent that such statements concern common issues and are intended to facilitate representation and possible subsequent proceedings); Continental Oil, 330 F.2d at 350 (exchange of debriefing memoranda between counsel of employees interviewed after their appearance before the grand jury did not destroy the privilege).

233. United States v. Melvin, 650 F.2d 641, 645 (5th Cir. 1981); *see also* Government of Virgin Islands, 685 F.2d at 862 (employing this analysis).

234. *See* Bay State Ambulance, 874 F.2d at 28 ("In addressing whether a given communication was meant to be confidential, what 'the client reasonably understood' is the 'key question.'") (citation omitted, emphasis in original).

235. *In re* Grand Jury, 406 F. Supp. at 391.

the objective manifestations of the parties' intent and the surrounding circumstances as indicia of "conscientiousness." Courts will almost certainly pay more attention to what the co-defendants do than to what they say, regardless of whether they say it in an executed agreement.[236] Courts place significant emphasis on the reasonableness of the parties' beliefs and actions.[237]

Given that parties seeking protection under the joint defense doctrine may make for "unsteady bedfellows,"[238] signatories to joint defense agreements should be aware that if they face co-defendants in a subsequent civil suit, the possibility exists that information previously exchanged pursuant to the doctrine may lose some of its protection from disclosure. It is therefore possible that the pooled information could be used by a co-defendant against a former co-defendant in future civil litigation,[239] even though the information would remain privileged from disclosure to strangers.[240] As one commentator has stated,

> [t]he traditional rule with regard to the joint defense doctrine is that the privilege does not prevent one former joint defendant from disclosing statements made by another former joint defendant in a suit ... between those two parties. The statements remain protected vis-a-vis "strangers"; but they are not protected in a suit between the co-defendants themselves.[241]

Outside this *inter sese* context, the joint defense privilege cannot be waived without the consent of all of its holders.[242] Like any other privilege,

---

236. *See, e.g., In re* Regents of the Univ. of Cal., 101 F.3d at 1390 (finding joint defense privilege despite absence of written agreement to that effect); SIG Swiss Indus. Co. v. Fres-Co Sys., USA, Inc., No. Civ. A. 91-0699, 1993 WL 82286, at *1 (E.D. Pa. Mar. 17, 1993) (same).

237. *See, e.g.,* Sheet Metal Workers Int'l Ass'n v. Sweeney, 29 F.3d 120, 124 (4th Cir. 1994) (no reasonable expectation of confidentiality where defendant's actions were inconsistent with attorney-client relationship, as, for example, when defendant asked his supposed attorney to leave the room during a meeting with the government); *see also* Melvin, 650 F.2d at 645-46 (disclosure of confidential material in the presence of third party who has not joined the "defense team" contravenes reasonable expectation of confidentiality).

238. *In re* Grand Jury, 406 F. Supp. at 392.

239. *See, e.g.,* Ageloff v. Noranda, Inc., 936 F. Supp. 72, 76 (D.R.I. 1996) ("The law is well-settled that a joint defense privilege is waived in a subsequent controversy between the joint defendants.") (citations omitted); United States v. Moscony, 697 F. Supp. 888, 894 (E.D. Pa. 1988), *aff'd,* 927 F.2d 742 (3d Cir. 1991); *In re* Grand Jury, 406 F. Supp. at 389.

240. Query the value of the privilege as against third parties, however, if the material is revealed in open court.

241. John E. Sexton, *A Post–Upjohn Consideration of the Corporate Attorney-Client Privilege,* 57 N.Y.U. L. REV. 443, 512 (1982).

242. *E.g.,* John Morrell & Co., 913 F.2d at 556.

however, conduct inconsistent with a reasonable expectation of confidentiality can be deemed a waiver. In *United States v. LeCroy*, employees asserted that a joint defense agreement prevented their employer from providing the employer's counsel's notes of their internal interviews to the government. The employees, however, had submitted to interviews by company counsel after being advised that the information provided might ultimately be divulged to the government. The court found that these circumstances evinced either a waiver of any joint defense privilege attaching to the interview statements, or a modification permitting the company's disclosure of those statements to the government.[243] Thus, one who would invoke the joint privilege with respect to particular communications would do well to act like those communications are expected to be kept in confidence.

4. Remedies for Breach of Joint Defense Privilege

In *United States v. Melvin*,[244] notwithstanding a pre-trial breach of the joint defense privilege by one defendant, the court concluded that absent prejudice, a breach will not result in the dismissal of the other defendants. In that case, one of the defendants participated in joint meetings with co-defendants and lawyers, after agreeing to become an informant for the prosecution. The defendant provided privileged information to the government prosecution, including tapes of strategy sessions among defense lawyers and their clients. The district court found a violation of the Sixth Amendment and dismissed the indictment. The Fifth Circuit reversed, concluding that the co-defendants were not entitled to any remedy absent a showing of "prejudice." According to the court, even if the co-defendants could demonstrate prejudice, the trial judge should fashion a remedy short of dismissal, such as suppression of the evidence obtained as a result of the breach.[245]

Because of this limited protection, defense counsel should seek ways to prevent, limit, or highlight a breach of the joint defense privilege. If counsel discovers that a co-defendant has become a government witness, it is important to flag this issue immediately. Counsel can seek an order impounding any privileged material in the possession of the co-defendant or the lawyer.

---

243. 348 F. Supp. 2d 375, 386 (E.D. Pa. 2004).
244. 650 F.2d 641 (5th Cir. 1981).
245. *Melvin,* 650 F.2d at 644; *see also* Schwimmer, 892 F.2d at 245 (remanding case and implying that some form of remedy or sanction is available if prejudice is shown).

Counsel can also list all information being shared so that if a breach occurs, an identification of evidence to suppress can be readily identified. Finally, counsel should request a hearing to determine the extent to which privileged information has already been utilized, or may be utilized in a subsequent proceeding.

When a former joint defense participant turns government witness, counsel's joint defense obligations can collide with counsel's ethical responsibility vigorously to defend the client. The resulting conflict of interest may create an ethical obligation to seek withdrawal so that the client may obtain new, unfettered counsel. If the court does not permit withdrawal, counsel's conflict of interest can render any ultimate conviction of the client reversible error.

This is precisely what happened in *United States v. Henke*.[246] In that case, three executives charged with securities fraud were part of a joint defense group until just after jury selection, at which point one of them pled guilty and agreed to testify for the prosecution. Counsel for the remaining defendants wanted to use inconsistencies between the witness' testimony at trial and statements made by the witness during joint defense meetings to impeach the witness, but were warned by the witness' counsel that this would breach their obligation to maintain the confidence of joint defense communications. Counsel moved to withdraw, but the district court denied their motion, after which their clients were tried and convicted. The Ninth Circuit reversed and remanded, holding that "[f]ew aspects of our criminal justice system are more vital to the assurance of fairness than the right to be defended by counsel, and this means counsel not burdened by a conflict of interest."[247]

I. *Keeping the Government-Disclosure Genie in the Bottle*

In the course of parallel proceedings, counsel should remain aware of the possibility that information provided to a government agency either voluntarily or in response to a subpoena, as well as information subpoenaed by a grand jury, could potentially be disclosed to various entities.

---

246. 222 F.3d 633 (9th Cir. 2000).
247. *Id.* at 639. *Henke's* reach may be limited to situations involving conflicting obligations to protect and use joint defense communications. *See* United States v. Stepney, 246 F. Supp. 2d 1069, 1080-84 (N.D. Cal. 2003) (rejecting arguments for withdrawal based on a broader duty of loyalty owed parties to joint defense agreement).

1. Information Provided to Government Agencies

At the beginning of a government agency investigation, the agency will subpoena documents or request the corporation and/or its employees to turn the documents over voluntarily. In deciding whether to challenge the subpoena or disclose documents voluntarily, counsel and corporate officers must consider the freedom with which the agency will share the information with other agencies, private parties, or a grand jury.

As a general matter, information provided to one agency, whether voluntarily or pursuant to summons or subpoena, generally will be made available to other agencies, including state agencies, or to law enforcement agencies such as the DOJ upon request.

It is nearly impossible to obtain agreements from any agency officials that would prevent the transfer of information between law enforcement agencies, or to even require notice to the submitter that a transfer has taken, or will take, place. Certain government agencies have established specific procedures for addressing requests for confidential treatment of submitted information. Counsel should always check the rules and procedures for an agency that requests or subpoenas information and documents. Generally, government agencies are limited by statute in their ability to obtain information. Moreover, in order to enforce any subpoenas, the agency must first file an action in federal district court.

Counsel should also keep in mind that private parties can request agency information under the Freedom of Information Act (FOIA).[248] Federal agencies promulgate regulations implementing procedures under FOIA with respect to granting third parties access to information provided to the agency. The SEC's FOIA regulations are particularly illustrative.[249] The two SEC FOIA provisions that are most important for maintaining the confidentiality of corporate records submitted to a government agency are Exemption 4, covering confidential "commercial or financial information," and Exemption 7, covering "records or information compiled for law enforcement purposes."[250] Counsel should be mindful that the latter exemption ceases to have effect at the conclusion of an investigation,[251] and the former exemption becomes more difficult to assert as time passes. Accordingly, it is always wise to attempt to

---

248. 5 U.S.C. § 552.
249. *See* Confidential Treatment Procedures Under FOIA, 17 C.F.R. § 200.83.
250. 5 U.S.C. §§ 552(b)(4), (b)(7).
251. *In re* Subpoenas Duces Tecum, 738 F.2d 1367, 1374 (D.C. Cir. 1984).

have the agency return materials submitted by the corporation (and any copies that have been made) promptly at the conclusion of the investigation.

Finally, a grand jury can issue a subpoena for government agency material. Subpoenas issued by the grand jury can be broad, and standards of relevance or materiality, which may have some application in civil discovery, do not apply.[252] Consequently, a grand jury can obtain the information and documents in possession of the government agency independently through the use of a subpoena.[253]

An equally important consideration is whether testimony provided in a civil deposition—pursuant to a protective order—can be obtained by the grand jury. The answer, according to the Fourth, Ninth, and Eleventh Circuits, is in the affirmative: a civil protective order cannot be used to shield discovery materials that are sought by a grand jury subpoena.[254] The Second Circuit, however, has declined to adopt this per se rule; instead, it has stated that the government must establish "some extraordinary circumstance or compelling need" to obtain materials subject to an existing protective order.[255] The First Circuit and Third Circuits reject both these approaches in favor of a rule providing that a grand jury subpoena trumps a civil protective order absent exceptional circumstances that clearly favor enforcing the protective order instead of the subpoena.[256]

---

252. *See* United States v. Dionisio, 410 U.S. 1, 9-13 (1973); Branzburg v. Hayes, 408 U.S. 665, 688 (1972).

253. Counsel must be mindful that a failure to continue objections to a grand jury subpoena may result in a court later ruling that materials disclosed pursuant to that subpoena were voluntarily revealed. *See* Westinghouse Elec. Corp. v. Republic of Philippines, 951 F.2d 1414, 1427 n.14 (3d Cir. 1991).

254. *In re* Grand Jury Subpoena, 62 F.3d 1222, 1226 (9th Cir. 1995); *In re* Grand Jury Proceedings, 995 F.2d 1013, 1015 (11th Cir. 1993); *In re* Grand Jury Subpoena (Under Seal), 836 F.2d 1468 (4th Cir. 1988).

255. Martindell v. International Tel. & Tel. Corp., 594 F.2d 291, 296 (2d Cir. 1979). The Second Circuit reaffirmed its approach in *In re* Grand Jury Subpoenas Duces Tecum, 945 F.2d 1221, 1225 (2d Cir. 1991). Relatedly, the Second Circuit has held that an unwilling nonparty witness cannot be forced to testify in reliance on a protective order. Andover Data Servs. v. Statistical Tabulating Corp., 876 F.2d 1080, 1084 (2d Cir. 1989) ("[A] court in a civil action is simply without the means to fashion a sufficiently durable safeguard for the full protection of the fifth amendment rights of a reluctant non-party witness. . . .").

256. *In re* Grand Jury, 286 F.3d 153, 156 (3d Cir. 2002); *In re* Grand Jury Subpoena, 138 F.3d 442, 445 (1st Cir. 1998).

2. Information Obtained by Grand Juries

Another primary concern for corporate counsel is whether information provided to the grand jury will be released to the public or to another federal or state agency. The requirement of grand jury secrecy is embodied in Rule 6(e) of the Federal Rules of Criminal Procedure, which provides that grand jurors and those who work with the grand jury "must not disclose a matter occurring before the grand jury," unless the rules provide otherwise.[257]

In theory, this rule of secrecy makes it very difficult to legitimately transfer grand jury material to administrative agencies. Federal Rule of Criminal Procedure 6(e)(3)(A), however, provides for disclosure to: "(i) an attorney for the government for use in performing that attorney's duty; (ii) any government personnel . . . that an attorney for the government considers necessary to assist in performing that attorney's duty to enforce federal criminal law; or (iii) a person authorized by 18 U.S.C. § 3322."[258] Rule 54(c) defines "attorney for the government" as "the Attorney General, an authorized assistant of the Attorney General, a United States Attorney, [and] an authorized assistant of the United States Attorney. . . ." The Advisory Committee Notes (Notes) make clear that other Justice Department lawyers also are included within this definition.[259]

Pursuant to 1985 amendments to Rule 6(e), the court may authorize disclosure of a grand jury matter to appropriate state or municipal officials for the purpose of enforcement of state criminal statutes "at the request of the government if it shows that the matter may disclose a violation of State . . . criminal law. . . ."[260] The 1985 amendment did away with the standard of "particularized need" previously required of state officials for access to grand

---

257. FED. R. CRIM. P. 6(e)(2).

258. 18 U.S.C. § 3322 permits disclosure of grand jury information to "an attorney for the government for use in enforcing section 951 of the Financial Institutions Reform, Recovery and Enforcement Act of 1989 or for use in connection with any civil forfeiture provision of Federal Law," as well as to certain "identified personnel of a Federal or State financial institution regulatory agency."

259. Note that federal administrative attorneys, including attorneys at the SEC, are not considered "attorneys for the government" under these provisions. Bradley v. Fairfax, 634 F.2d 1126, 1130 (8th Cir. 1980); *In re* Grand Jury Investigation, 414 F. Supp. 74, 76 (S.D.N.Y. 1976).

260. FED. R. CRIM. P. 6(e)(3)(E)(iv).

jury materials.[261] However, according to the Notes to the amendment, it is the policy of the DOJ to seek disclosure on behalf of state officials under Rule 6(e)(3)(E)(iv) only upon approval of the Assistant Attorney General in charge of the Criminal Division. The Notes state: "There is no intention, by virtue of this amendment, to have federal grand juries act as an arm of the state."

Although this amendment relaxes the standards for the release of grand jury materials to state officials pursuing criminal actions, it does not affect access to those materials in civil cases. In *United States v. Sells Engineering, Inc.*,[262] the Supreme Court held that rule 6(e)(3)(A)(i) does not entitle Civil Division lawyers in the DOJ to automatic disclosure of matters occurring before a grand jury for use in a civil suit. The Court in *Sells* upheld the "strong showing of a particularized need" standard enunciated in *Illinois v. Abbott*.[263] The Court concluded that in order to gain access to Rule 6(e) material, the Justice Department lawyers would have to obtain a court order under paragraphs (E)(i) and (F) of the rule after making such a showing.[264]

However, a lawyer who conducts a criminal prosecution may make continued use of materials received as a result of a grand jury investigation during the civil phase of the same dispute without obtaining a court order under Rule 6(e). In *United States v. John Doe, Inc.*,[265] the Supreme Court held that Rule 6(e) forbids only the "disclosure" of material by the government attorney and when the same attorney is involved in civil phase of a dispute, a review of the material does not constitute a disclosure.[266]

With respect to disclosure of grand jury materials to private parties, the Supreme Court has held that the party seeking disclosure must show that (i) the material is needed to avoid a possible injustice in another judicial pro-

---

261. *See* Illinois v. Abbott & Assoc., Inc., 460 U.S. 557 (1983) (district court must weigh whether the need for disclosure to a governmental body is greater than the need for continued secrecy).
262. 463 U.S. 418, 443 (1983).
263. *Id.* at 420; *accord In re* Grand Jury Proceedings, 851 F.2d 860, 865 (6th Cir. 1988); *In re* Sealed Case, 801 F.2d 1379 (D.C. Cir. 1986).
264. Sells, 463 U.S. at 420.
265. 481 U.S. 102 (1987).
266. *Id.* at 107-08; *see* Pilon v. United States, 73 F.3d 1111, 1120 (D.C. Cir. 1996) (emphasizing the limited scope of the holding in John Doe); *see also* DiLeo v. Commissioner, 959 F.2d 16, 21 (2d Cir. 1992) (permitting IRS agent to attend civil trial and citing John Doe for the proposition that "a government employee who has participated in a criminal prosecution may participate in the civil phase of the dispute without obtaining a court order to do so under Rule 6(e)").

ceeding; (ii) the need for disclosure is greater than the need for continued secrecy; and (iii) the request is structured to cover only material so needed.[267] Given the public interest in maintaining the secrecy of grand jury proceedings, this showing must be made regardless of whether the grand jury's operations are ongoing or have terminated.[268] It also should be noted that at least one Circuit has held that the government may "seek release of grand jury materials on behalf of others, including private litigants."[269]

Several Circuits have held that Rule 6(e)'s limitations upon disclosure are not applicable if release of the documents would not reveal what transpired with the grand jury. For example, in *United States v. Stanford*,[270] FBI agents showed interviewees copies of certain documents that previously had been presented to the grand jury. The court held that the disclosure fell outside the scope of Rule 6(e) because the documents had been created for purposes other than the grand jury, and the disclosures were made for legitimate purposes unconnected with the grand jury investigation to persons legitimately connected with the documents.[271] The same result was reached in *United States v. Interstate Dress Carriers, Inc.*[272] In that case, the court upheld the granting of a DOJ application to allow Interstate Commerce Commission representatives to examine records that had been obtained by grand jury subpoena because "testimony or data [was] sought for its own sake—for its intrinsic value in the furtherance of a lawful investigation—rather than to learn what took place before the grand jury. . . ."[273] Courts have noted, however, that the disclosure of grand jury transcripts provides a greater "degree

---

267. *See* Sells, 463 U.S. at 443; Douglas Oil Co. v. Petrol Stops Northwest, 441 U.S. 211, 222 (1979). *But see In re* Grand Jury Proceedings, 813 F. Supp. 1451, 1466 n.11 (D. Colo. 1992) ("[T]here is no indication that Rule 6(e) contemplates disclosure to the public.").

268. Douglas Oil Co., 411 U.S. at 222.

269. United States v. Nix, 21 F.3d 347, 351 (9th Cir. 1994).

270. 589 F.2d 285, 291 (7th Cir. 1978).

271. *Id.* at 291. *See also* United States v. Reiners, 934 F. Supp. 721, 723 (E.D. Va. 1996) (financial records submitted to grand jury could be disclosed to financial institutions seeking to trace payments made to perpetrators of fraud in order to recover from perpetrator's assets, since request was not made for the purpose of determining what took place before the grand jury and disclosure would not reveal any secret aspect of the grand jury's deliberations).

272. 280 F.2d 52, 54 (2d Cir. 1960).

273. *Id.; accord* United States v. Dynavac, Inc., 6 F.3d 1407, 1411-1412 (9th Cir. 1993); Dresser, 628 F.2d at 1369; *see also* DiLeo, 959 F.2d at 19 (reaffirming that Interstate Dress "remains the law in this circuit regarding the proper interpretation of Rule 6(e)"); *In re* Grand Jury Subpoenas Duces Tecum, 904 F.2d 466, 468 (8th Cir. 1990) (permitting release of grand jury materials to Internal Revenue Service for use in tax court proceeding).

of exposure" into the grand jury process than disclosure of the documents divulged to the grand jury would.[274]

As the foregoing discussion illustrates, in determining whether disclosure of grand jury materials is permissible, a court must make the threshold determination that the materials sought to be disclosed are in fact "matters occurring before the grand jury" that come within the purview of the secrecy rule.[275] This question arises whenever a party seeks only documents that were subpoenaed by the grand jury, rather than a transcript of grand jury testimony. Courts have adopted four different approaches. Some courts hold that documents that exist independent of the grand jury process are not "matters occurring before the grand jury" and thus can be disclosed.[276] Other courts hold that documents are always "matters occurring before the grand jury" and can never be disclosed without a showing of particularized need.[277] Still others hold that there is a rebuttable presumption that documents subpoenaed by the grand jury are "matters occurring before the grand jury" and therefore protected.[278] The majority of courts, however, apply an "effects" test, which

---

274. *See, e.g., In re* Grand Jury Proceedings Relative to Perl, 838 F.2d 304, 306 (8th Cir. 1988); *In re* Sealed Case, 801 F.2d at 1381; *cf.* United States v. Weinstein, 511 F.2d 622, 627 n.5 (2d Cir. 1975) ("[I]t is questionable whether Rule 6(e) applies to documents."). Courts have also considered whether to distinguish between a transcript of grand jury testimony and a summary of what a witness divulged to an investigator outside the jury room. *Compare* Anaya v. United States, 815 F.2d 1373, 1378 (10th Cir. 1987) (finding a distinction and permitting the latter to be discovered) *with In re* Potash Antitrust Litig., 896 F. Supp. 916, 918 (D. Minn. 1995) (finding Rule 6(e) applicable to both documents) and United States v. Armco Steel Corp., 458 F. Supp. 784, 790 (W.D. Mo. 1978) (same).

275. *See* In re Special Grand Jury 89-2, 450 F.3d 1159, 1176-77 (10th Cir. 2006) (broadly interpreting 6(e) to encompass "what took place in the grand jury room" or "what was said or ... takes place in the grand jury room.") (citations omitted); *see also* Brian L. Porto, *What Are "Matters Occurring Before Grand Jury" Within Prohibition of Rule 6(e) of the Federal Rules of Civil Procedure,* 154 A.L.R. FED. 385 (1999).

276. *See, e.g.,* Interstate Dress Carriers, 280 F.2d at 54; *see also* United States v. OMT Supermarket, Inc., 995 F. Supp. 526, 532 (E.D. Pa. 1997) (documents that "exist independently of the grand jury process" are not matters occurring before the grand jury for purposes of Rule 6(e)).

277. *See, e.g.,* Texas v. United States Steel Corp., 546 F.2d 626, 629 (5th Cir. 1977).

278. *See, e.g., In re* Grand Jury Proceedings, 851 F.2d at 867 ("The moving party may seek to rebut that presumption by showing that the information is public or was not obtained through coercive means or that disclosure would be otherwise available by civil discovery and would not reveal the nature, scope, or direction of the grand jury inquiry, but it must bear the burden of making that showing, just as it bears the burden of showing that there is a 'particularized need.'").

focuses on whether disclosure will provide a view as to some secret part of the grand jury deliberations.[279]

Once protected material has been revealed in violation of Rule 6(e), it is difficult to devise an adequate remedy. Courts have made efforts to control the damage, usually by attempting to limit further disclosure of the material.[280]

J. The Perils of Parallelism for Government Contractors

Parallel proceedings can have serious economic consequences for corporations that contract with the federal government. Contracts with executive agencies, including the Department of Defense and the General Services Administration, are governed by the Federal Acquisition Regulation (FAR), which includes provisions for suspension and debarment of government contractors.[281] The suspension and debarment provisions of the FAR contain traps for the unwary government contractor and should not be overlooked by counsel guiding a corporation with government contracts through a parallel proceeding.

A government contractor can be suspended from working with the federal government "upon adequate evidence" of certain specified offenses, including "any . . . offense indicating a lack of business integrity or business honesty that seriously and directly affects the present responsibility of a Government contractor or subcontractor."[282] The FAR thus gives government

---

279. *See, e.g, In re* Grand Jury Subpoena (Under Seal), 920 F.2d 235, 241 (4th Cir. 1990); *In re* Grand Jury Proceedings Relative to Perl, 838 F.2d at 306; Senate of Puerto Rico v. United States, 823 F.2d 574, 582 (D.C. Cir. 1987); Anaya, 815 F.2d at 1379; *In re* Special March 1981 Grand Jury, 753 F.2d 575, 578 (7th Cir. 1985); *In re* Grand Jury Matter, 682 F.2d 61, 63 (3d Cir. 1982).

280. *See* Sells, 463 U.S. at 422 n.6 ("We cannot restore the secrecy that has already been lost but we can grant partial relief by preventing further disclosure."); United States v. Smith, 123 F.3d 140, 154 (3d Cir. 1997) ("[E]ven if grand jury secrets are publicly disclosed, they may still be entitled to at least some protection from disclosure."); *see also* Nix, 21 F.3d at 352 (remanding case for a remedy and suggesting possible options); United States v. Coughlan, 842 F.2d 737, 740 (4th Cir. 1988) (indicating that grand jury materials should be suppressed if government cannot demonstrate particularized need for the testimony on remand).

281. *See* 48 C.F.R. subpart 9.4. In addition, some individual agencies have promulgated their own supplemental regulations to implement the FAR. *See, e.g., id.* subpart 209.4 (Department of Defense Supplemental Debarment, Suspension, and Ineligibility Regulations). These supplemental regulations may impose additional burdens on entities facing debarment or suspension proceedings.

282. *Id.* § 9.407-2(a)(7).

officials broad discretion to suspend contractors "pending the completion of investigation or legal proceedings."[283] Moreover, a suspension can apply to all subsidiaries and divisions of a contractor[284] and generally is effective throughout the executive branch of the government.[285] The FAR provides that suspension is to be imposed for a "temporary period pending the completion of investigation and any ensuing legal proceedings,"[286] and cannot extend beyond eighteen months unless legal proceedings have been initiated within that period.[287]

The provisions for debarment of government contractors also can be implicated by a parallel proceeding. A government contractor can be debarred "for a conviction of[[288]] or a civil judgment for" (among other things): fraud in connection with obtaining, attempting to obtain, or performing a public contract; embezzlement, theft, forgery, bribery, falsification or destruction of records, making false statements, tax evasion, or receiving stolen property; or "any other offense indicating a lack of business integrity or business honesty that seriously and directly affects the present responsibility" of the contractor.[289] Like suspension, debarment may apply to all subsidiaries or divisions of a contractor[290] and generally is government-wide, applying throughout the executive branch.[291] The FAR further provides that debarment "shall be for a period commensurate with the seriousness of the cause(s)" and generally should not exceed three years.[292]

In addition to the FAR, a "Common Rule" promulgated by a host of federal agencies (with various modifications by each agency) provides for suspension,

---

283. *Id.* § 9.407-1(b)(1).
284. *See id.* § 9.407-1(c).
285. *See id.* § 9.407-1(d). The suspension also may be extended to any affiliate of the contractor. *See id.* § 9.407-1(c).
286. *See id.* § 9.407-4(a).
287. *See id.* § 9.407-4(b).
288. A criminal conviction constitutes grounds for suspension and debarment regardless of whether it is entered upon a verdict, guilty plea, or plea of nolo contendere. *See id.* § 9.403.
289. *Id.* § 9.406-2(a). Although the FAR gives government officials broad discretion to suspend and debar contractors, *see id.*, the FAR specifically provides that suspension or debarment may be imposed "only in the public interest for the Government's protection and not for purposes of punishment," *id.* § 9.402(b).
290. *See id.* § 9.406-1(b).
291. *See id.* § 9.406-1(c).
292. *Id.* § 9.406-4(a)(1).

debarment, or exclusion from participation in federal *non*-procurement programs and activities.[293] Pursuant to 1995 amendments, suspension and debarment under the Common Rule and the FAR are reciprocal and government-wide.[294] As a result, suspension or debarment from either procurement or non-procurement transactions with one agency means that the entity is suspended or debarred from both non-procurement and procurement transactions with a wide range of agencies. Accordingly, suspension or debarment of an entity in one context can have far-reaching implications for the entity's other business interests.[295]

As one commentator has observed, "[t]he debarment or suspension from government contracting of a major defense contractor is an economic event of catastrophic proportions to the corporation involved."[296] The same can be said

---

293. *See* 53 Fed. Reg. 19,161 (1988) (Common Rule on nonprocurement suspension and debarment); *see, e.g.,* 24 C.F.R. pt. 24 (HUD version of the Common Rule); 40 C.F.R. pt. 32 (EPA version of the Common Rule). Federal nonprocurement programs covered by the Common Rule include grants, cooperative agreements, contracts of assistance, loans, loan guarantees, subsidies, insurance, and other financial and nonfinancial transactions. *See e.g.,* 24 C.F.R. § 24.200(a)(1) (HUD regulation defining "covered transaction" under the Common Rule); 40 C.F.R. § 32.200 (EPA regulation defining "covered transaction").

294. *See* 48 C.F.R. § 9.401 (FAR provision providing for reciprocal, government-wide debarment and suspension); 60 Fed. Reg. 33,037, passim (1995) (amending the Common Rule to provide for reciprocal, government-wide debarment and suspension); *see, e.g.,* 24 C.F.R. § 24.130 (HUD reciprocal provision); 40 C.F.R. § 32.130 (EPA reciprocal provision).

295. Some federal statutes also provide for debarment from contracting with particular agencies as a result of particular kinds of offenses. *See, e.g.,* 10 U.S.C. § 2408(a) (providing for the debarment of individuals convicted of certain felonies arising out of Department of Defense contracts); 41 U.S.C. § 354(a) (ineligibility for future contracts as a result of violations of the Service Contract Act of 1965); 33 U.S.C. § 1368 (providing for debarment for violations of certain provisions of the Clean Water Act); 42 U.S.C. § 7606 (providing for debarment for violations of certain provisions of the Clean Air Act). These statutes typically are very specific and limited in scope. Further, many state and municipal governments also have disqualification procedures comparable to the FAR provisions. *See, e.g.,* FLA. STAT. ANN. § 287.133 (Florida debarment statute); MASS. GEN. L. ANN. ch. 29 § 29F (Massachusetts debarment statute).

296. Frank J. Hughes, *The Fall and Rise of Global Settlements: How Will They Fare in an Age of Voluntary Disclosure?,* ARMY LAW., Jan. 1988, at 4; *accord* Steven D. Gordon, *Suspension and Debarment from Federal Programs,* 23 PUB. CONT. L.J. 573, 604 (1994) (referring to debarment or lengthy suspension as "an economic 'death penalty'"); Michael J. McCarthy, *How One Firm Tracks Ethics Electronically,* WALL ST. J., Oct. 21, 1999, at B1 (quoting a Martin Marietta official as saying that debarment would be "death for this company").

of other enterprises whose business models rely heavily upon government contracts. The reach of the suspension and debarment provisions is extended by the fact that even unauthorized actions of employees, if on behalf of a contractor or with the contractor's knowledge, can be imputed to the entire corporation and result in suspension or debarment.[297] Efforts to challenge the suspension and debarment process in the federal courts generally have not been successful.[298] Counsel retained to represent a corporation in parallel proceedings involving civil fraud allegations or criminal charges should ascertain whether government contracts are at risk. In a society where government is a major consumer of the goods and services supplied by the private sector, defense counsel must be prepared not only to defend against government charges of misconduct, but also against the resulting loss of a client's valuable government contracts.

K. The Gestalt of Parallel-Proceedings Resolution

For counsel representing a corporation facing parallel proceedings, it is often unrealistic to expect complete victory on all fronts. Another theoretical goal might be a "global settlement" that resolves all pending and threatened proceedings on terms acceptable to the client. A leading practitioner (and current federal judge) once defined a global settlement as "one in which the criminal, civil and administrative disposition, with particular regard to sanctions, are

---

297. Gordon, *supra* n.313, at 586-88.

298. These efforts fail largely due to the deferential standard of review that federal courts employ when determining whether a debarment or suspension was warranted. *See* Shane Meat Co. v. United States Dep't of Defense, 800 F.2d 334, 336 (3d Cir. 1986) (explaining that the standard for reviewing a suspension or debarment is whether the decision to suspend or debar was "arbitrary, capricious, an abuse of discretion or otherwise not in accordance with law"); *see, e.g.,* Marshall v. Cuomo, 192 F.3d 473, 480 (4th Cir. 1999) (holding that debarment was not arbitrary or capricious, nor an abuse of discretion); IMCO, Inc. v. United States, 97 F.3d 1422, 1427 (Fed. Cir. 1996) (same); Kisser v. Cisneros, 14 F.3d 615, 618-19, 621-22 (D.C. Cir. 1994) (same); Wellham v. Cheney, 934 F.2d 305, 309 (11th Cir. 1991) (same). However, challenges to suspension or debarment may be successful if the agency failed to follow the proper procedures in reaching the decision to suspend or debar, *see, e.g.,* Humphreys v. DEA, 96 F.3d 658, 664 (3d Cir. 1996) (reversing revocation by DEA because the agency failed to consider defendant's primary defense), or applied the incorrect legal standard in deciding whether the suspension or debarment was warranted under the relevant regulations, *see, e.g.,* Novicki v. Cook, 946 F.2d 938, 942 (D.C. Cir. 1991) (reversing suspension of individual when it appeared that the agency may have applied an incorrect legal standard, and remanding for further proceedings).

negotiated in a single bargain."[299] Although easy to seek in theory, global settlements have proven difficult, if not impossible, to obtain in practice.[300]

In most parallel proceedings situations, the principal impediment to obtaining a global settlement is the autonomy of the various government authorities who are involved (let alone the private parties, whose own interests will be brought to bear).[301] In the context of a criminal investigation, for example, a United States Attorney in one district is not likely to accept language in a plea agreement that could be construed as binding on other districts or other agencies, such as the Internal Revenue Service.[302] In addition, prosecutors may be hesitant to negotiate global settlements because of a "legitimate fear of being charged with improper conduct and abuse of the criminal process."[303]

---

299. Presentation of (now Judge) Paul Friedman titled, "The Law and Tactics of Global Settlements," presented at an American Bar Association program on "Procurement Fraud Prosecutions and Debarment" (Washington, D.C., Feb. 20-21, 1986).

300. Counsel should consider, however, that even seeking to negotiate a global settlement can affect the dynamics of a parallel proceedings case. "By indicating a willingness to negotiate, counsel runs the risk that the government may demand more than it would in separate dispositions, or that the case is perceived to be more significant than otherwise thought, or that information divulged during the course of negotiations may create an unexpected synergism." Stephen Wilson & A. Howard Matz, *Obtaining Evidence for Federal Economic Crime Prosecutions,* excerpted in PARALLEL GRAND JURY AND ADMINISTRATIVE AGENCY INVESTIGATIONS 956 (Neil Kaplan et al. eds., 1981).

301. Agencies also may have policies that deter efforts to achieve a global settlement. For example, the Enforcement Division of the SEC has a policy of not negotiating settlements of civil actions that involve disposition of criminal proceedings. *See* 17 C.F.R. § 202.5(f). Although there are exceptions to this policy, in general, the SEC staff will decline to address potential criminal charges in a civil settlement. *See* Peter Morrison, *SEC Criminal References,* reprinted in Kaplan, *supra* n.300, at 161-163.

302. The Department of Justice "cannot bind independent regulatory agencies, such as [the] SEC, and plea bargains do not exclude possible civil action by those agencies, unless they specifically concur in that agreement." Marvin Pickholz, *Parallel Civil Cases and Global Settlements, excerpted in* Kaplan, *supra* n.300, at 987. *See also* United States v. Killough, 848 F.2d 1523, 1526 (11th Cir. 1988) (promise by assistant U.S. attorney in criminal proceedings not a bar to subsequent False Claims Act case); Johnson v. Lumpkin, 769 F.2d 630, 634 (9th Cir. 1985) (promise by federal prosecutor cannot bind state authorities). *But see* Creel v. Comm'r of Internal Revenue, 419 F.3d 1135, 1141-42 (11th Cir. 2005) (U.S. attorney properly released both criminal and civil liabilities where such liabilities were "inextricably intertwined").

303. *See* Friedman, *supra* n.300 at 2 (*citing* United States v. Litton Systems, Inc., 573 F.2d 195 (4th Cir. 1978)).

Since most complex criminal cases involve conduct occurring in more than one judicial district and subject to enforcement action by more than one federal agency, a settlement with a single authority is not likely to resolve the matter. Similarly, coordinating a settlement involving two or more government agencies with competing policy objectives can be particularly arduous. For example, bringing together DOJ and the Department of Defense to obtain an acceptable global settlement can be a "tortuous task"[304] in which counsel may find themselves "in the awkward position of serving as a 'broker' between the various parts of the government in order to achieve the desired [global settlement] result."[305] The presence of one or more private lawsuits complicates attempts at a global resolution to the point of near impossibility.

Notwithstanding these impediments to a truly "global settlement," there can be no successful global *resolution* of a single corporate crisis without thinking globally. For a major defense contractor, resolving DOJ's investigation by a guilty plea without assurance from the Department of Defense that this will not result in debarment from its procurement programs would be a pyrrhic victory.[306] A settlement with the Enforcement Division of the SEC that does not give the corporation room to deny liability in private contexts (e.g., through language that the corporation "neither admits nor denies" the SEC's allegations) will not be of great benefit to the client who faces issue preclusion in a securities class action based on SEC "findings" accompanying the settlement. Parallel proceedings require a global mindset—not piecemeal, proceeding-specific, reactive defense efforts.

Counsel continually must be focused on the ways in which a corporation's response in one forum will impact its position in others. For example, until December 2006, the practitioner seeking to avoid a corporate criminal prosecution, and thus set the stage for the favorable resolution of parallel proceedings, needed to be prepared for federal prosecutors' frequent demand, with implicit sanction from the Thompson Memorandum, that the corporation waive its attorney-client and work product privileges to avoid criminal prosecution.[307] The recently issued McNulty Memorandum, however, places signif-

---

304. *Id.* at 30.
305. *Id.* at 33.
306. "[A]bsent special circumstances, no defense contractor is likely to enter a guilty plea without the assurance that it will not be debarred." *Id.* at 32.
307. *See* Thompson Memorandum, *supra* n.115, at 7 (stating that prosecutors considering whether to charge corporations should consider a corporation's "willingness to cooperate in the investigation of its agents, including, if necessary, the waiver of the corporate attorney-client and work product privileges"); *see also* Richard Ben-Veniste & Lee H. Rubin, *DOJ*

icant new restrictions on federal prosecutors' flexibility to demand waiver of legal privileges.

First, prosecutors may request waiver only "when there is a legitimate need for the privileged information to fulfill their law enforcement obligations."[308] That obtaining privileged information is "merely desirable or convenient" does not establish "legitimate need." Rather, the prosecutor must balance the "important policy considerations" underlying the legal privileges against the law enforcement needs of the investigation. Notably, in this balance, the prosecutor is to consider, among other things, "the collateral consequences to a corporation of a waiver."[309]

Second, even where a "legitimate need" exists for privileged information, the McNulty Memorandum instructs prosecutors to "seek the least intrusive waiver necessary to conduct a complete and thorough investigation." Prosecutors are to "follow a step-by-step approach," first seeking "purely factual information" (e.g., key document collections, factual chronologies, or interview memoranda).[310] Only in the "rare circumstances" that "purely factual information provides an incomplete basis to conduct a thorough investigation should prosecutors then request that the corporation provide attorney-client communications or non-factual attorney work product."[311]

Third, the McNulty Memorandum imposes significant new up-the-chain requirements on prosecutors seeking privilege waivers. Even where only "purely factual information" that "may or may not be privileged" is sought, the prosecutor must first obtain written authorization from the United States Attorney, who in turn must copy the prosecutor's request to and consult with the Assistant Attorney General for the Criminal Division before granting or denying it.[312] If, after this process is followed, the corporation refuses to provide "purely factual information," the prosecutor may consider that refusal in assessing whether the corporation has cooperated. Moreover, before requesting attorney-client communications or non-factual attorney work product, the

---

Reaffirms and Expands Aggressive Corporate Cooperation Guidelines, 18 No. 25 Andrews Corp. Off. & Directors Liab. Litig. Rep. 18 (2003) (as applied by DOJ, Thompson Memorandum reflects "all but explicit requirement that corporations must waive the protections of the corporate attorney-client privilege and work product doctrine in order to avoid a prosecution of the corporation itself").

308. *See* McNulty Memorandum, *supra* n.115, at 8.
309. *Id.* at 8-9.
310. *Id.* at 9.
311. *Id.* at 10.
312. *Id.* at 9.

United States Attorney must obtain written authorization from the Deputy Attorney General. Even if the authorization is granted, "prosecutors must not consider" a corporation's refusal to provide such privileged information "in making a charging decision"—although "[p]rosecutors may always favorably consider a corporation's acquiescence . . . in determining whether a corporation has cooperated in the government's investigation."[313]

Even with this significant shift in DOJ policy, corporations likely still will face some circumstances in which prosecutors will ask for at least some information that a corporation believes is privileged. Whether information is "purely factual" is often in the eye of the beholder, and the McNulty Memorandum permits prosecutors to consider refusals to provide "purely factual" information in assessing cooperation. And although the McNulty Memorandum clarifies that a corporation's refusal to disclose attorney-client communications or non-factual attorney work product cannot be considered a failure to cooperate, a corporation's voluntary agreement to supply such information to the government will continue to be given credit—perhaps even substantial credit. The economic consequences of a criminal conviction can be so dire that even voluntary waiver of the privilege might seem a small price to pay to settle the matter.

But the real price could be paid in the civil context. Because information typically loses its privilege when disclosed to third parties,[314] the ramifications of waiving the privilege in DOJ's favor can be felt in proceedings not involving DOJ—for example, in civil investigations or proceedings by other government agencies, or even in litigation between private parties. Even if the federal prosecutor might be willing to agree to maintain the confidentiality of privileged information disclosed, the prospects for success in arguing that such an agreement maintains the privileged quality of the information are dubious at best.[315]

---

313. *Id.* at 10. Note that where a corporation agrees to cooperate as part of a plea agreement, the McNulty Memorandum authorizes prosecutors to seek waiver of applicable privileges in order to ensure that the corporation's agreement "is complete and truthful." *Id.* at 19.

314. *See, e.g.,* United States v. El Paso Co., 682 F.2d 530, 540 (5th Cir. 1982).

315. Most courts have held that providing information to the government destroys its confidentiality and, hence, the applicability of the privilege. *See, e.g., In re* Qwest Communications Int'l Inc. Sec. Litig., 450 F.3d 1179, 1192 (10th Cir. 2006) (rejecting selective waiver and collecting cases); *In re* Columbia/HCA Healthcare Corp. Billing Practices Litig., 293 F.3d

Given the many obstacles in the path of a favorable, coordinated overall resolution, often the task becomes one of managing timing and laying groundwork. Even if separate government agencies (let alone private parties) cannot be brought together into a single, comprehensive global settlement, defense counsel may be able to orchestrate a settlement through which an arrangement with one adversary lays the foundation for settlement with another, leading to successful resolution of all proceedings. For example, in a criminal case, negotiating a favorable plea agreement in one judicial district can provide a basis for similar agreements with other districts or agencies.

For another example, a favorable settlement with the SEC, perhaps involving a delicately drafted consent to carefully negotiated regulatory violations that do not include fraud allegations, can serve as the catalyst for an early, favorable settlement of private shareholder litigation. Indeed, Section 308 of the Sarbanes-Oxley Act of 2002 (the so-called "Fair Funds" provision), which the SEC has utilized in several high-profile enforcement cases, provides that civil penalties paid in a SEC enforcement action may be placed in a restitution fund to compensate the alleged victims of the violation.[316] The jury is still out on how effective the SEC will be at distributing funds to investors. Further, available Fair Funds tend to have little impact on negotiations to settle private shareholder class actions, perhaps because plaintiffs' counsel typically cannot include Fair Funds amounts to support their requested fee awards.

There simply are no hard and fast rules that apply in attempting to obtain a favorable overall resolution of the multiple parallel proceedings that almost invariably attend a single corporate crisis. There is no "checklist" for counsel to follow in this area. Instead, defense counsel must be guided by a realistic assessment of the client's exposure (which is usually impossible without a thorough internal investigation), a *gestalt* perspective on "the situation," and a carefully conceived strategic defense plan for optimally resolving all of its parallel manifestations.

289, 303 (6th Cir. 2002) (same); United States v. Massachusetts Inst. of Tech., 129 F.3d 681, 685-86 & n.3 (1st Cir. 1997) (same). *But see generally* Michael H. Dore, *A Matter of Fairness: The Need for a New Look at Selective Waiver in SEC Investigations,* 89 MARQ. L. REV. 761 (Summer 2006).

316. 15 U.S.C. § 7246.

III. CONCLUSION

The authors hope the above discussion provides a helpful overview of some overarching issues that tend to be present in parallel proceedings. The approach to attacking any hydra, however, will vary by the nature of the beast and its associated heads. And in the interest of brevity, even the general issues discussed in this chapter have been given short shrift. For counsel representing corporate counsel in the context of parallel proceedings, there is no adequate substitute for detailed and context-specific knowledge. If this chapter illustrates anything, we hope it is that company counsel must view the many parallel proceedings surrounding any single event as related parts of a single whole.

Disclosure of Results of Internal Investigations to the Government or Other Third Parties

7

Thomas E. Holliday and Charles J. Stevens

I. INTRODUCTION 242
II. REQUIRED DISCLOSURE 243
    A. Common-Law Rule 243
    B. Statutory Disclosure Requirements 245
    C. Problems Arising from Counsel's Knowledge of Criminal Conduct 248
III. VOLUNTARY DISCLOSURE 250
    A. The Benefits 250
    B. The Risks 254
IV. THE MECHANICS OF DISCLOSURE 259
V. CONCLUSION 259

Thomas E. Holliday is a partner in the law firm of Gibson, Dunn & Crutcher in Los Angeles, California, and a member of the firm's Business Crimes and Investigations Group. Mr. Holliday also is a Fellow in the American College of Trial Lawyers. Charles J. Stevens is a founding partner of Stevens & O'Connell LLP in Sacramento, California, and a former United States Attorney for the Eastern District of California. Bradley A. Benbrook and James P. Arguelles of Stevens & O'Connell LLP assisted with the updating of this chapter.

I. INTRODUCTION

A COMPANY CONDUCTING an internal investigation inevitably must decide whether information gathered in the course of the investigation should be disclosed to the government or other third parties. This issue raises two initial questions. First, the company must analyze whether the *nondisclosure* of information evidencing criminal conduct within the company itself constitutes an independent crime or whether an applicable statute or regulation imposes an independent duty to disclose. Second, the company must consider whether, even if there is no affirmative disclosure obligation, disclosure of information gathered in the investigation might nonetheless benefit the company.

Several developments in recent years have substantially complicated this analysis. Among other things, current Justice Department policy has created strong incentives for disclosure of investigation results to the government. Various federal agencies have also established voluntary disclosure programs that offer opportunities for lenient treatment in the event of early disclosure.

When weighing the potential benefits of voluntary disclosure, of course, counsel must also carefully analyze the potential risks. Disclosure of wrongful conduct by company employees never guarantees lenient treatment. Indeed, some argue that disclosure simply "educates" the government and increases the likelihood of prosecution against the company or the individuals involved, or both. Moreover, in light of the proliferation of multi-track civil, criminal, and regulatory proceedings, counsel must consider how a disclosure to criminal authorities would impact the related civil matters, as such disclosures are typically not protected from future discovery, whether because the information disclosed is not privileged or because the disclosure effected a waiver of the attorney-client privilege or the work-product doctrine.

Once a company has decided to disclose, it must also determine the mechanics of the disclosure. Counsel needs to consider who should make the disclosure, to whom it should be made, and whether the disclosure should be oral or written.

In this chapter we explore each of these questions. None has a simple answer, and each depends upon the unique circumstances of the situation confronting counsel and company management. Because disclosure of wrongdoing may have significant ramifications for the company's business and future, senior management should participate in the decision-making process.[1]

---

1. Those involved in such process should, to the maximum extent possible, be free of any involvement in the underlying misconduct.

II. REQUIRED DISCLOSURE

A. *Common-Law Rule*

The threshold question regarding disclosure is whether the company risks criminal liability when it uncovers evidence of criminal conduct but does not report its knowledge to the appropriate authorities. The general rule is that a company is not required to report knowledge of criminal conduct to authorities or to disclose evidence of that conduct voluntarily.[2] For example, the federal misprision of felony statute is violated only if (1) an individual has actual knowledge of the commission of a felony by someone else; (2) the individual fails to notify authorities; and (3) the individual deliberately takes an *affirmative step to conceal the crime*.[3]

In light of the affirmative step requirement, courts have on the one hand held that "'[mere] silence, without some affirmative act, is insufficient evidence' of the crime of misprision of felony," even if there is firsthand knowledge of a crime.[4] On the other hand, the giving of an untruthful statement to investigating authorities is a sufficient act of concealment to sustain a conviction for misprision of felony.[5] It has been held that it is not misprision to disclose some knowledge of a crime to an investigating agent and intentionally withhold other relevant information.[6] However, because *partial* disclosure could in some cases mislead the investigating agents and therefore possibly constitute an act of obstruction or concealment, companies and their counsel should use extreme care in making partial disclosures.

Based upon the rules just described, agents of the company may not actively conceal the wrongdoing from investigators or intentionally mislead them. Indeed, if the affirmative step requirement of the misprision statute is satisfied, criminal liability will likely arise under several other statutes as

---

2. 18 U.S.C. § 4; United States v. Baez, 732 F.2d 780 (10th Cir. 1984); United States v. Sampol, 636 F.2d 621 (D.C. Cir. 1980); United States v. Hodges, 566 F.2d 674 (9th Cir. 1977); Neal v. United States, 102 F.2d 643, 646 (8th Cir. 1939).

3. Neal v. United States, 102 F.2d at 646.

4. United States v. Ciambrone, 750 F.2d 1416, 1418 (9th Cir. 1984); Lancey v. United States, 356 F.2d 407, 410 (9th Cir.), *cert. denied,* 385 U.S. 922 (1966); United States v. Hodges, 566 F.2d 674, 675 (9th Cir. 1977); United States v. Pittman, 527 F.2d 444, 445 (4th Cir. 1975), *cert. denied,* 424 U.S. 923 (1976).

5. *See, e.g.,* Hodges, 566 F.2d at 675; Pittman, 527 F.2d at 445; Lancey, 356 F.2d at 410.

6. Ciambrone, 750 F.2d at 1418 (holding that truthful but partial disclosure of knowledge of a counterfeiting operation is not misprision of a felony because investigating agents could not have been misled by truthful statements and there is no obligation to disclose the information voluntarily).

well.[7] For example, an individual violates the federal accessory-after-the-fact statute if that individual has knowledge that another has committed a crime and proceeds to assist the perpetrator with the purpose of hindering the perpetrator's apprehension.[8] Likewise, impeding certain types of government auditors in their attempt to complete an audit examination or investigation constitutes a crime.[9]

A related question that commonly arises during internal investigations is whether the destruction of company records, not yet subpoenaed, could give rise to liability. Certainly the intentional destruction of documents known to be sought by a grand jury can constitute the crime of obstruction of justice.[10] In addition to the misprision and obstruction concerns, counsel must consider that the federal witness-tampering statute also precludes the destruction of documents (even if the documents were subject to a claim of privilege) if the purpose of the destruction was to impair a judicial proceeding.[11] Note, too, that this statute applies even if a judicial proceeding is not pending at the time of the destruction.

The Sarbanes-Oxley Act has imposed additional document retention requirements that were intended to expand the reach of pre-existing obstruction statutes (and to significantly increase penalties for violations). Specifically, Section 802 of the Act provides for a term of imprisonment of up to twenty years for anyone who knowingly "alters, destroys, mutilates, conceals, covers up, falsifies, or makes a false entry in any matter within the jurisdiction of a federal department or agency. . . ."[12] Likewise, Section 1102 of the Act imposes the same penalty for anyone who corruptly "alters, destroys,

---

7. 18 U.S.C. § 2 (accessory after the fact); 18 U.S.C. § 1503 (obstruction of justice); 18 U.S.C. § 1505 (destruction or concealment of documents to be used in certain administrative proceedings). *See also* 18 U.S.C. § 1512 *and* 18 U.S.C. §§ 1516, 1517. There may also be state statutes implicated by the conduct.

8. United States v. Elkins, 732 F.2d 1280 (6th Cir. 1984) (destruction of contraband while investigators attempting to search for same); United States v. Mills, 597 F.2d 693 (9th Cir. 1979); United States v. Barlow, 470 F.2d 1245 (D.C. Cir. 1972).

9. *See, e.g.,* 18 U.S.C. §§ 1516, 1517.

10. *See, e.g.,* United States v. Quattrone, 441 F.3d 153 (2d. Cir. 2006); United States v. Walasek, 527 F.2d 675 (3d Cir. 1975); United States v. Solow, 138 F. Supp. 812 (S.D.N.Y. 1956). It would also certainly constitute misprision of a felony for an individual to destroy documents or other evidence for the purpose of "covering up" criminal conduct.

11. 18 U.S.C. § 1512. *See* Arthur Andersen LLP v. United States, 544 U.S. 696 (2005) (assessing reach of section 1512). For an analysis of § 1512 and its relationship to other obstruction statutes, see United States v. Kulczyk, 931 F.2d 542 (9th Cir. 1991). For a complete discussion of the witness-tampering statute, see chapter 4, "Perjury and Obstruction of Justice."

12. 18 U.S.C. § 1519.

mutilates, or conceals" a record or document "with the intent to impair the object's integrity or availability for use in an official proceeding," regardless of whether the official proceeding is pending or about to be instituted at the time of the offense."[13]

Yet not every decision to discard incriminating documents constitutes misprision or obstruction. Thus, lawyers conducting internal investigations are frequently asked by management whether the company may discard documents pursuant to the company's policy of periodic document destruction (for example, some companies regularly discard documents after a certain period of time has elapsed from their creation). Allowing document destruction to proceed in the ordinary course (assuming no grand jury subpoena or agency request for documents has been received or is anticipated) is generally acceptable.[14] If, however, the destruction is in any way linked to a concern about future discovery, counsel's safe choice is to advise the client to hold off on the destruction program.

B. *Statutory Disclosure Requirements*

Although federal criminal statutes generally do not compel the disclosure of criminal conduct, various statutes and regulations impose special disclosure requirements.

The Sarbanes-Oxley Act imposed new rules regarding *internal* disclosure of allegations of material violations of certain laws. Specifically, Section 307 of the Act required the SEC to issue rules setting forth the minimum standards of professional conduct for attorneys appearing and practicing before the Commission, including a specific rule requiring attorneys to report evidence of material violations of law "up-the-ladder" within an organization.[15] The SEC responded by adopting what is known as Part 205 Rules, which as initially proposed would have required attorneys to report material violations both within the organization and, in certain circumstances, to "noisily" withdraw from the engagement and "report out."[16] Although the final version of the

---

13. 18 U.S.C. § 1512(c).

14. "A 'knowingly ... corrupt[t] persuade[r]' cannot be someone who persuades others to shred documents under a document retention policy when he does not have in contemplation any particular official proceeding in which those documents might be material." Andersen, 544 U.S. at 707-08 (discussing required "nexus between the 'persuasion' to destroy documents and [a] particular proceeding").

15. 15 U.S.C. § 1547.

16. Implementation of Standards of Professional Conduct for Attorneys, Securities Act Release No. 33-8150 [2002-03 Transfer Binder] Fed. Sec. L. Rep. (CCH) ¶ 86,802 (Nov. 21, 2002).

rules imposed significant new *internal* reporting requirements,[17] it did not include the provision that would have required attorneys to "report out" beyond the organization.[18] While this so-called "noisy withdrawal" requirement was not enacted, the SEC gave notice in its Adopting Regulation that it continues to remain under consideration by the agency.[19]

The federal securities statutes and rules often impose affirmative disclosure obligations on public companies. For example, in each annual report on Form 10-K, an issuer must disclose whether any of its officers or directors is or has been, within the previous five years, "a named subject of a pending criminal proceeding."[20] More generally, the filing of certain registration statements under the Securities Act of 1933 and periodic reports under the Securities Exchange Act of 1934 requires the disclosure of various "material" facts.[21] "Materiality" is an elusive concept for issuers seeking comfort that a decision to refrain from disclosure is safe.[22] Counsel conducting investigations relating to potential environmental problems should take note that the securities laws impose special disclosure obligations relating to environmental proceedings.[23] Given the complexity of the securities laws' disclosure requirements and the pervasive risk of shareholder lawsuits, public companies should consult securities counsel prior to making a disclosure decision with respect to information gathered in an investigation.

---

17. *See generally* 17 C.F.R. § 205.3.

18. 17 C.F.R. § 205.

19. Implementation of Standards of Professional Conduct for Attorneys, Securities Act Release No. 33-8186 [2002-03 Transfer Binder] Fed. Sec. L. Rep. (CCH) ¶ 86,824 (Jan. 29, 2003).

20. *See* 17 C.F.R. Regulations-K, Subpart 229.401(f)(2).

21. *See, e.g.,* 17 C.F.R. Regulations-K, Subpart 303(a)(3)(ii) (MD&A disclosure shall include description of "any known trends or uncertainties that have had or that the registrant reasonably expects will have a material . . . unfavorable impact" on registrant's business).

22. The basic standard for determining "materiality" is whether "there is a substantial likelihood that a reasonable shareholder would consider [the information] important" in deciding how to proceed. TSC Industries, Inc. v. Northway, Inc., 426 U.S. 438, 449 (1976) (applying test to proxy statements); Basic Inc. v. Levinson, 485 U.S. 224 (1988) (applying TSC Industries standard in § 10(b) and Rule 10b-5 context). "[T]o fulfill the materiality requirement 'there must be a substantial likelihood that the disclosure of the omitted fact would have been viewed by the reasonable investor as having significantly altered the "total mix" of information made available.'" Basic, 485 U.S. at 231-32 (quoting TSC Industries, 426 U.S. at 449).

23. *See* 17 C.F.R. Regulations-K, Subpart 101(c)(xii) ("[a]ppropriate disclosure . . . shall be made as to the material effects that compliance with [environmental regulations] may have upon the capital expenditures, earnings and competitive position of the registrant").

Moreover, certain highly regulated industries are subject to special statutory disclosure requirements. For example, the Anti-Kickback Enforcement Act of 1986 requires government contractors to report in writing to the Inspector General of the contracting agency whenever there are "reasonable grounds" to believe that a kickback may have occurred between upper- and lower-tier government contractors.[24] In a similar vein, federally insured banks are subject to provisions that require the submission of a written report to the Office of Comptroller of the Currency if there is cause to believe that the bank has been defrauded.[25] Indeed, regulators of financial institutions generally require outside counsel to conduct an internal investigation of the financial institution and to provide the regulators (e.g., Office of Comptroller of the Currency or Federal Deposit Insurance Corporation) with the report. The financial institution is generally required to sign a Supervisory Agreement providing for the report, or else the institution will be taken over by a conservator or receiver.

Even when disclosure of criminal conduct is not required by statute, a company must still be careful not to commit new crimes by incorporating or acting upon the prior misconduct in the course of its regular business. For example, if a company learns that an employee failed to perform certain product inspections required by a government contract, it would be unlawful for the company to certify in writing that the contract has been fully performed or even to accept payment on the contract where an implicit premise for the payment is full compliance with the agreement.[26] Even keeping records in the company files implying that the inspections were completed can cause additional criminal exposure.[27] Similarly, criminal liability may be premised on the dissemination of documents that incorporate or adopt material statements from earlier documents that are known to be false by the time of the republication.[28]

---

24. 41 U.S.C. § 57. Similarly, states may impose broad disclosure obligations upon government contractors. *See, e.g.,* CAL. PUB. CONT. Code § 10282 (subcontractor or agent or employee of contractor may be guilty of felony for failing to report knowledge of work being performed in violation of government contract).

25. *See, e.g.,* 12 C.F.R. § 21.11 (1989).

26. *See, e.g.,* United States v. Milton-Marks Corp., 240 F.2d 838 (3d Cir. 1957).

27. *See, e.g.,* 18 U.S.C. §§ 1001 and 1516. *See also* United States v. Rutgard, 116 F.3d 1270, 1287-88 (9th Cir. 1997) (affirming conviction under 18 U.S.C. § 1001 of doctor who maintained patient files falsely stating medical necessity of treatment).

28. *See, e.g.,* United States v. Natelli, 527 F.2d 311 (2d Cir. 1975), *cert. denied,* 425 U.S. 934 (1976) (accountants held criminally liable because proxy statement contained materially misleading statements derived from previously prepared financial statements that accountants knew or should have known were false).

Thus, although mere silence regarding previous unlawful conduct does not normally constitute an independent crime, such silence coupled with other conduct may well provide a basis for criminal liability under other statutes.[29] As a consequence, disclosure of past misconduct (at least at some level) may be the only means of avoiding additional future liability.[30]

C. Problems Arising from Counsel's Knowledge of Criminal Conduct

One of the most troubling risks confronting counsel performing an internal investigation is the risk that the lawyer will become involved in what is perceived to be an obstruction of the government's ability to investigate. This problem can arise either in the guise of an obstruction charge[31] or as part of what is alleged to be a conspiracy under the *Klein* doctrine.[32] A *Klein* conspiracy is a conspiracy that impairs, impedes, or obstructs an agency of the United States government from performing its lawful function.

In the modern regulatory state, moreover, it is often difficult to discern the difference between advocacy on behalf of a client that is the subject of investigation, on the one hand, and impairing, impeding, or obstructing an agency in connection with that investigation, on the other. This dilemma is only compounded by Sarbanes-Oxley's provisions permitting—but not requiring—disclosure of facts learned by counsel.[33]

---

29. *See, e.g.,* 18 U.S.C. § 287 (false claim), § 1341 (mail fraud), § 1343 (wire fraud), § 1344 (bank fraud), § 1001 (false statement to government agency).

30. One way of dealing with inaccurate documents that are supposed to be maintained (e.g., test results) is to note on the document that it is inaccurate, and any questions should be directed to counsel or an appropriate person in management.

31. *See, e.g.,* 18 U.S.C. § 1512.

32. 18 U.S.C. § 371; United States v. Klein, 247 F.2d 908 (2d Cir. 1957), *cert. denied,* 355 U.S. 924 (1958). *See also* Haas v. Henkel, 216 U.S. 462 (1910); Hammerschmidt v. United States, 265 U.S. 182 (1924); Tanner v. United States, 483 U.S. 107 (1987).

33. 17 C.F.R. § 205.3(d)(2) provides that any attorney representing an issuer "*may* reveal to the Commission, without the issuer's consent, confidential information related to the representation to the extent the attorney reasonably believes necessary" to "prevent the issuer from committing a material violation likely to cause substantial injury to the financial interest or property of the issuer or investors." In response, the State Bars of Washington and California informed the SEC that this rule conflicts with state professional conduct rules regarding disclosure of client information. The California Bar further advised its members that Rule 205's "financial injury" permissive disclosure provision conflicts with California's Rules of Professional Conduct, which allow an attorney to reveal client confidences only where necessary to prevent a criminal act that could result in either death or serious bodily harm. *See* Ethics Alert, The New SEC Attorney Conduct Rules v. California's Duty of Confidentiality, Calif.

For example, in dealing with regulators in the health care fraud arena, company lawyers frequently find themselves on "the front line" arguing and advocating a particular position against the government's regulators. However, the regulators may perceive that the government has an absolute right to the information it is seeking and may view the advocacy of the lawyer as misleading and obstructionist. For example, if defense counsel responds negatively to a government agent's inquiry as to whether the corporate client has conducted a private audit of alleged overbilling when, in fact, such an audit was performed by the client (and it documented overbilling), the government might accuse counsel of participating in a conspiracy to obstruct when it discovers the private audit. Indeed, in the post-Enron world, prosecutors are increasingly focusing not only on corporate wrongdoers, but on the role played by both internal and outside counsel in the advice and guidance they provide to their corporate clients.[34]

An even more difficult problem arises under the *Klein* doctrine when company employees seek advice from counsel on the company's options after an investigation has uncovered legal problems with potential criminal ramifications. From the lawyer's perspective, a myriad of options for responding to the problem could exist in the abstract and be discussed in that light. Some of these options might, after due consideration, be viewed as improper or illegal and rejected by counsel. But complications arise when employees choose to exercise one of those options rejected by counsel. For example, an employee might destroy documentation of overbilling that falls within the scope of a grand jury subpoena, even after counsel gave advice to the contrary. In such cases, the government will contend that the seeking of advice from counsel in connection with a crime or fraud means the communications between counsel and the client are no longer privileged.[35] This result would obtain even if the lawyer is innocent of any wrongdoing and is an unknowing participant in a discussion that really is intended to further or advance a crime or fraud.[36] At best, the lawyer becomes a chief witness against the company and its employees. At worst, the lawyer becomes a defendant in a criminal prosecution.

Bar Ass'n (http://www.calbar.ca.gov/calbar/pdfs/SEC-ethics-alert.pdf); Corporations Committee of the Business Law Section of the California State Bar, Conflicting Currents: The Obligation to Maintain Inviolate Client Confidences and the New SEC Attorney Conduct Rules, 32 PEPP. L.REV. 89 (2004).

    34. *See generally* Richard M. Strassberg, David B. Pitofsky, Samantha L. Schreiber, *Lawyers on Trial,* N.Y.L.J. (July 18, 2005).

    35. United States v. Hodge & Zweig, 548 F.2d at 1347 (9th Cir. 1977).

    36. *Id.* at 1354.

In sum, it is imperative that counsel weigh every action and reaction carefully while proceeding through the course of an investigation and while dealing with a government agency. If a decision to cooperate has not been finalized, it is far safer to make clear to government representatives at the outset of an internal investigation that company counsel is in an advocate's position with respect to disclosure than to allow the government to believe that counsel intended to fully cooperate with the government's investigation—subsequent events will inevitably demonstrate that this was not the case.

III. VOLUNTARY DISCLOSURE

A. *The Benefits*

Even if a company concludes that it is not legally required to disclose information learned in the course of an internal investigation, the company should consider the potential benefits of voluntarily disclosing the information.[37]

In recent years, the Justice Department has made corporate counsel acutely aware of the potential benefits to their clients of such a disclosure. Under the 2003 revisions to the U.S. Attorneys' Manual through the "Thompson Memorandum," prosecutors may consider, "[i]n determining whether to charge a corporation, that corporation's timely and voluntary disclosure of wrongdoing and its willingness to cooperate with the government's investigation. . . . In gauging the extent of the corporation's cooperation, the prosecutor may consider the corporation's willingness to identify the culprits within the corporation, including senior executives; to make witnesses available; to disclose the complete results of its internal investigation; and to waive attorney-client and work product protection."[38]

A complete discussion of the Thompson Memorandum is beyond the scope of this chapter, but a few observations about its impact on the disclosure calculus are in order. To a number of practitioners, the risks of nondisclosure are so severe that companies have very little choice but to "cooper-

---

37. Care should also be taken, of course, to ensure that the Company is not *prohibited* from disclosing information learned in the course of an investigation. For example, companies often enter into joint defense agreements with individuals or other companies in complex criminal investigations; these agreements typically restrict parties' ability to disseminate information learned in the course of the joint defense. Counsel should further consider whether disclosure implicates any individuals' privacy rights, particularly in the health care arena.

38. Larry D. Thompson, U.S. Department of Justice, Principles of Federal Prosecution of Business Organizations (January 20, 2003).

ate" by disclosing results of internal investigations.[39] There is no question that the Thompson Memorandum has substantially increased the number of "voluntary" disclosures. Still, cooperation through disclosure by no means guarantees a "free pass" on prosecution of the disclosing company. Needless to say, the Thompson Memorandum has come under intense scrutiny and criticism by the defense bar.

Even if the Justice Department's current incentives for disclosure are withdrawn or struck down by a court, counsel will still face the question whether to voluntarily disclose. In some circumstances, voluntary disclosure may increase the likelihood of convincing the government that legal or equitable factors weigh against prosecution or a harsh sentence. Indeed, the primary arguments in favor of disclosure are that disclosure demonstrates the integrity of the company, especially if coupled with prompt and effective corrective action, and that displays of such integrity may persuade the government to decline indictment and focus on less forthright companies.[40]

Voluntary disclosure may, however, afford other potential benefits.[41] It enables a company to bring exculpatory evidence to the prosecutor's attention, to articulate the corresponding legal defenses, and to correct errors or misunderstandings on the part of the investigators reporting to the prosecutor. In complicated investigations, prosecutors commonly overlook defenses and misapprehend facts due, among other reasons, to incomplete or inaccurate investigative reports. Assuming that the disclosure could conceivably preclude an indictment, it is generally beneficial to remedy these problems with a pre-indictment submission. Most successful pre-indictment presentations are premised on these potential benefits, rather than the hope that a company's demonstrated integrity will enable it to avoid indictment.

---

39. For a revealing discussion of the "threat to [companies] inherent in the Thompson Memorandum" and the government's application thereof, see United States v. Stein, 435 F. Supp. 2d 330 (S.D.N.Y. 2006) (dealing with Thompson Memorandum's provision allowing prosecutors to consider advancement of attorneys' fees to individuals as prosecuting factor).

40. Attempting to demonstrate this integrity through disclosure seems particularly important for government contractors; indeed, failing to make disclosures before the government discovers the facts may call into question the contractor's "responsibility" and right to bid on and perform government contracts. And, even if criminal prosecution is inevitable, voluntary disclosure may still help government contractors in administrative debarment or suspension proceedings.

41. One of the less-regularly mentioned benefits is the potential for deterrence. If employees know their company self-discloses criminal conduct, they may well be less likely to engage in wrongdoing in the future.

There also exists the possibility that a company may be able to take advantage of an agency's formal voluntary disclosure program and avoid prosecution entirely. Certain of these disclosure programs represent a commitment by the government to strongly consider a declination of prosecution if the company voluntarily comes forward with incriminating information. The Department of Justice and other agencies, such as the Department of Defense, the Environmental Protection Agency, and the Internal Revenue Service, provide written guidelines for voluntary disclosure in such programs.[42] Each of these programs carries with it a common theme—that the disclosure must be truly voluntary. This means that the disclosure must not in any way be prompted by a fear that the unlawful activity will be discovered.

Not surprisingly, a company considering a formal voluntary disclosure program often doubts whether it will be treated fairly once the disclosure is made. Moreover, once disclosure commences under such a program, there is rarely an opportunity to turn back. And, with rare exceptions,[43] participation by a company does not protect individual employees who committed the wrongdoing; their fate will be determined without regard to the credit given for a voluntary disclosure by the company.[44] Therefore, counsel should engage in careful and thorough analysis with a company prior to participating in a voluntary disclosure program.

Another potential benefit of voluntary disclosure may be found in the federal Sentencing Guidelines for organizations.[45] As discussed in greater detail below, the methodology for calculating fines under the guidelines can

---

42. *See* UNITED STATES ATTORNEY'S MANUAL 9-42.430; Department of Justice Antitrust Division Corporate Leniency Policy (Aug. 10, 1993); "Factors in Decisions on Criminal Prosecutions for Environmental Violations in the Context of Significant Voluntary Compliance or Disclosure Efforts by the Violator," Department of Justice (July 1, 1991); "Incentives for Self-Policing: Discovery, Disclosure, Correction and Prevention of Violations," Environmental Protection Agency (Dec. 22, 1995) (regarding potential civil violations); Environmental Protection Agency Office of Criminal Enforcement, Forensics and Training Memorandum (Oct. 1, 1997) (regarding potential criminal violations); Office of Inspector General "Operation Restore Trust" Voluntary Disclosure Program (May 3, 1995). *See also* United States v. Rockwell, 924 F.2d 928 (9th Cir. 1991).

43. For an example of the risks associated with a good-faith disclosure, see *United States v. Rockwell*, 924 F.2d 928 (9th Cir. 1991).

44. Significantly, the Antitrust Division's Corporate Leniency Policy does provide for the non-prosecution of company employees. *See* Corporate Leniency Policy, Section C; Department of Justice, "The Corporate Leniency Policy: Answers to Recurring Questions" (April 1, 1998).

45. *See* UNITED STATES SENTENCING GUIDELINES, ch. 8.

be dramatically altered based upon a voluntary disclosure by the company. Accordingly, a decision not to disclose carries with it substantial economic risks in the form of a fine, as well as terms and conditions of probation.[46]

As with the sentencing guidelines for individuals, the organizational guidelines establish base penalties—fines in the case of organizations—that are determined by the nature of the offense committed and its economic effect. In order to arrive at a base fine, a sentencing court begins by looking at the guideline tables to determine the offense level of the misconduct in the same manner as for an individual whose conduct led to the corporation's conviction. Under the organizational guidelines, the base fine is then deemed to be the greatest of (1) the amount stated for the crime in the offense-level table just discussed; (2) the organization's pecuniary gain resulting from the criminal conduct; or (3) the pecuniary loss to others caused by the organization "to the extent the loss was caused intentionally, knowingly, or recklessly."[47]

This base fine is then modified by the court by use of a culpability score that takes into account a variety of facts and circumstances. The culpability score determines the multiplier factor that is to be used in adjusting the base fine. A culpability score of 10, for example, requires the sentencing court to multiply the base fine by a multiplier of no less than 2 and no greater than 4. Under these circumstances, a base fine of $10 million would become an actual fine of between $20 million and $40 million (as determined by the sentencing court). On the other hand, a culpability score of 5 reduces the multiple range to between 1 and 2, with a corresponding decrease in the fine exposure.

An organization's voluntary disclosure of wrongdoing tends to reduce its culpability score, and thus its multiplier and actual fine. More specifically, if the organization:

- voluntarily discloses the offense to the government *before disclosure is threatened or a government investigation begins,*

---

46. In 2004, the Sentencing Commission amended the corporate sentencing guideline comments to provide that a corporation that refused to waive the privilege might not be eligible for a reduced sentence if "such waiver is necessary in order to provide timely and thorough disclosure of all pertinent information known to the organization." UNITED STATES SENTENCING GUIDELINES MANUAL, § 8C2.5(g), cmt. 12 (2004). Following the holding of public hearings in early 2006, however, the Sentencing Commission found that Comment 12 "could be misinterpreted to encourage waivers," and voted to remove the language pertaining to a corporation's waiver of the privilege. Latest News, Amendments to the Sentencing Guidelines, Policy Statements and Official Commentary (May 1, 2006), p.29.

47. UNITED STATES SENTENCING COMMISSION, GUIDELINES MANUAL § 8C2.4(a).

- fully cooperates in the subsequent government investigation, and
- clearly recognizes and accepts responsibility for its conduct before trial (i.e., pleads guilty),

then five points will be subtracted from the culpability score.

The effect of this five-point reduction on the multiplier will depend upon where on the culpability score range an organization finds itself, which in turn depends upon the other factors that go into the culpability score calculus.[48] However, as noted above, a reduction in the culpability score from 10 to 5 would result in the court using a multiplier between 1 and 2, rather than between 2 and 4.

Absent the possibility of concrete benefits associated with disclosure through the Sentencing Guidelines or formal agency programs, many defense attorneys still believe that the benefit sof voluntary disclosure are not worth the risks. They contend that any pre-indictment presentation that implicitly concedes guilt serves only to convince the prosecutor that prosecution is warranted.

In sum, given the Thompson Memorandum and the enhanced penalties caused by the Sentencing Guidelines, disclosures of internal investigation results have increased substantially in recent years. In the early stages of an investigation, the company has the argument that it should not be indicted at all given its efforts in bringing the wrongdoing to the attention of the government. If an indictment and conviction should result, the cooperation should prove beneficial to the company with respect to the amount of the fine ultimately imposed at sentencing.

B. *The Risks*

The risks of voluntary disclosure (whether pursuant to a formal program or otherwise) are real and serious. First, the information disclosed might be used directly against the company in a subsequent criminal case, unless a formal voluntary disclosure program or a written agreement precludes this use. There is even some risk that the government may attempt to use representations by defense counsel on the theory that counsel's statements are admissions under Rule 801(d)(2)(C) of the Federal Rules of Evidence.[49]

---

48. These factors include, but are not limited to, the involvement of high-level personnel in the crime and the organization's prior criminal history.

49. *See, e.g.,* United States v. Valencia, 826 F.2d 169 (2d Cir. 1987). For this reason, care should be taken to ensure that the purposes for which the disclosure may be used are expressly agreed upon (e.g., settlement purposes only, pursuant to FED. R. EVID. 408 and 410 or plea negotiations under FED. R. CRIM. P. 11.).

Second, even if not used directly, the information may provide the government with a virtual road map of leads, such as names of witnesses and the existence of documents containing relevant information. Moreover, disclosure may "educate" the government about previously unknown trial issues and defenses, thus permitting the government to explain these problems and counter the defenses, whether in drafting an indictment or at trial.

These risks are further illustrated by the common scenario of a company discovering that an employee has engaged in criminal conduct without the knowledge of anyone in management, and contrary to company policy. Many erroneously believe that this situation does not expose the company itself to criminal prosecution and that the responsible course of conduct is to report the errant employee to the authorities. Under the legal theory of corporate vicarious liability, however, the company is criminally liable for the employee's unlawful act unless that act was outside the scope of the individual's employment—which courts have not often found to be the case.[50] Thus, to disclose unlawful conduct by an employee is often to "serve the company on a platter" to a prosecutor. In many cases, whether the company is indicted will turn purely on the prosecutor's appetite.

Third, it is possible that voluntary disclosure to the government will have a chilling effect on the willingness of employees to disclose knowledge of wrongful conduct. If employees believe their candid responses to the internal company investigators will be disclosed to the government, they may fear criminal liability, or that their employment is at risk.

Finally, factual information provided voluntarily to the government will likely be discoverable by opposing parties in parallel or follow-on civil actions because it is not protected by any privilege and, to the extent the disclosure reveals attorney-client communications or information protected by the work-product doctrine, its provision to the government generally constitutes a waiver of such protections.[51] Indeed, as counsel and companies weigh the risks of disclosure against the potential benefits, concerns about civil plaintiffs' discovery of the information often dominate the discussion.

---

50. *See, e.g.,* United States v. Hilton Hotels Corp., 467 F.2d 1000 (9th Cir. 1972), *cert. denied,* 409 U.S. 1125 (1973); United States v. Basic Construction Co., 711 F.2d 570 (4th Cir.), *cert. denied,* 464 U.S. 956 (1983); United States v. Beusch, 596 F.2d 871 (9th Cir. 1979); Standard Oil Co. of Texas v. United States, 307 F.2d 120 (5th Cir. 1962).

51. For a complete discussion of these issues, see Chapter 2, "Implications of the Attorney-Client Privilege and Work-Product Doctrine."

The issue of whether and to what extent a voluntary disclosure constitutes a waiver of the attorney-client privilege continues to be the subject of litigation, with the general rule being that disclosure of a privilege protected by the attorney-client privilege completely waives the privilege with respect to that communication.[52] Although a few courts have recognized that public policy concerns may argue in favor of allowing a company that has voluntarily conducted an internal investigation to disclose the results of that investigation without completely waiving the attorney-client privilege,[53] this concept of "limited" or "selected" waiver has been rejected by nearly every circuit.[54]

It is not necessarily the case that a complete waiver of the attorney-client privilege also constitutes a waiver of the work product privilege. There are circumstances under which the work product privilege may remain even though the attorney-client privilege has been waived.[55] Because protection of documents under the work product doctrine is based on a different premise than the attorney-client privilege, and because the protection of the doctrine is in some ways broader, the waiver issues with respect to work product are slightly different.

Accordingly, a number of courts have held that not all voluntary disclosures constitute a waiver of the protection afforded by the doctrine. Rather, those courts that have accepted the concept of limited work product waiver look to a number of factors on a case-by-case basis to determine whether work product protection is waived, including whether the party claiming the privilege seeks to use it in a way that is not consistent with the purpose of the privilege, whether waiver of the privilege in the circumstances would tread on

---

52. *See In re* Quest Communications International, Inc., 450 F.3d 1179 (10th Cir. 2006) for a current discussion of the relevant case law in this area.

53. *See, e.g.,* Diversified Industries v. Meredith, 572 F.2d 596, 611 (8th Cir. 1978); *In re* Woolworth Corp., 1996 WL 306576 (S.D.N.Y. 1996).

54. *See, e.g., In re* Quest Communications International, Inc., 450 F.3d 1179, 1192 (10th Cir. 2006); Permian Corp. v. United States, 665 F.2d 1214, 1216-17 (D.C. Cir. 1981); United States v. Mass. Inst. of Technology, 129 F.3d 681, 686 (1st Cir. 1997); *In re* John Doe Corp., 675 F.2d 482, 489 (2d Cir. 1982); Westinghouse Elec. Corp. v. Republic of the Philippines, 951 F.2d 1414, 1422 (3d. Cir. 1991); *In re* Martin Marietta Corp., 856 F.2d 619, 623-24 (4th Cir. 1988); *In re* Columbia/HCA Healthcare Corp. Billing Practices Litigation, 293 F.2d 289 (6th Cir. 2002).

55. United States v. AT&T, 642 F.2d 1285, 1299 (D.C. Cir. 1980).

policy elements inherent in the privilege, whether the party had a reasonable basis for believing that the disclosed materials would be kept confidential by the governmental agency to which disclosure was made, and whether the disclosure was voluntary or involuntary.[56]

Companies occasionally attempt to enter into confidentiality agreements with the government in the hope of protecting disclosed information.[57] While courts had previously looked favorably on the existence of a confidentiality agreement in determining whether to recognize a selective work product privilege waiver,[58] several circuit courts have recently adopted a *per se* rule that all voluntary disclosures to the government waive work product protection, even if the company has entered into a confidentiality agreement with the government.[59]

Given the perceived public policy benefits associated with disclosure, various "fixes" have been proposed to address the risks associated with disclosure. For example, the Advisory Committee on Evidence Rules has approved publishing for public comment proposed new Federal Evidence Rule 502, which would preclude a finding of waiver as to nongovernmental parties when a disclosure of privileged information is made to a federal prosecutor or

---

56. *See, e.g., In re* Martin Marietta Corp., 856 F.2d 619, 625-26 (4th Cir. 1988) (recognizing limited waiver of privilege for "opinion" work product); *In re* Subpoena Duces Tecum, 738 F.2d 1367, 1371-72 (D.C. Cir. 1984); *In re* Steinhardt Partners L.P., 9 F.3d 230, 236 (2d. Cir. 1993); *In re* Leslie Fay Cos. Inc. Sec. Litigation, 161 F.R.D. 274, 280 (S.D.N.Y. 1995); *In re* Kidder Peabody Sec. Litigation, 168 F.R.D. 459, 462-67 (S.D.N.Y. 1996).

57. Any such agreement should provide, in clear terms, that the information disclosed is not to be made available to other government agencies or members of the public without the company's prior consent. To be sure, many agencies will be reluctant to agree to this limitation, and the extent of any agreement will undoubtedly turn upon the specific situation and the relative bargaining power of the parties. (Since there are presumably other advantages that prompt a company to consider voluntary disclosure, the government agency may feel there is no need to grant the company's confidentiality request in order to obtain the materials. Conversely, the government agency may have a particular need for the information and be amenable if an agreement speeds the disclosure.)

58. *See, e.g.,* Permian Corp. v. United States, 665 F.2d 1214, 1219-22 (D.C. Cir. 1981).

59. *See, e.g., In re* Quest Communications International, Inc., 450 F.3d 1179, 1192 (10th Cir. 2006); *In re* Columbia/HCA Healthcare Corp. Billing Practices Litigation, 293 F.2d 289, 307 (6th Cir. 2002); Westinghouse Elec. Corp. v. Republic of the Philippines, 951 F.2d 1414, 1430 (3d. Cir. 1991).

agency.[60] Congress has also turned its attention to these matters; in March of 2006 the House Judiciary Committee's Subcommittee on Crime, Terrorism, and Homeland Security took oral testimony at an oversight hearing on corporate privilege waivers.[61]

Given the uncertainty in the law and the flexibility of tests that courts have applied to waiver issues, it is impossible for company counsel to guarantee that the company's privileged information will remain privileged.[62] And, moreover, the *factual information* provided in a disclosure to the government likely will not be privileged or protected in the first instance. In sum, counsel should operate under the presumption that whatever is provided to the govern-

---

60. The proposed rule would provide as follows:

> Selective Waiver. In a federal or state proceeding, a disclosure of a communication or information covered by the attorney-client privilege or work product protection—when made to a federal public office or agency in the exercise of its regulatory, investigative, or enforcement authority—does not operate as a waiver of the privilege or protection in favor of non-governmental persons or entities. The effect of disclosure to a state or local agency, with respect to non-governmental persons or entities, is governed by applicable state law. Nothing in this rule limits or expands the authority of a government agency to disclose communications or information to other government agencies or as otherwise authorized or required by law.

See Report from Advisory Committee on Ethics Rule to Standing Committee on Rules of Practice and Procedure re Report of the Advisory Committee on Evidence Rules (May 15, 2006). More recently, legislation has been proposed by Senator Arlen Spector that would preclude governmental agencies from conditioning treatment or prosecution/enforcement decisions on a waiver of the attorney-client privilege. This legislation also would permit a voluntary limited waiver in a fashion similar to the proposed amendment to Rule 502. (*See* Attorney-Client Privilege Production Act of 2006, 109th Cong. 2d Sess. 2006.)

61. White Collar Enforcement (Part I): Attorney-Client Privilege and Corporate Waivers: Oversight Hearing Before the H. Comm. on the Judiciary, Subcomm. on Crime, Terrorism, and Homeland Security, 109th Cong. D193 (Mar. 7, 2006).

62. Indeed, given the reluctance of courts to recognize limited waivers, along with the increasing pressure being put on corporations to cooperate, there is a growing trend among outside counsel not to memorialize their interviews and findings in writing. While counsel generally perceive that they will retain more control over the scope of the disclosure by documenting less of their investigation, this practice runs the obvious risk of errors in the reporting of the investigation, not to mention the increased opportunity for disputes to arise over what was stated in the witness interviews.

ment may well wind up in the hands of opposing parties in parallel civil litigation and regulatory proceedings.

IV. THE MECHANICS OF DISCLOSURE

Care should also be exercised with respect to the mechanics of informal disclosure. If the disclosure is made pursuant to one of the recognized voluntary disclosure programs, the mechanics of disclosure should be spelled out in the terms of the program. If, however, the disclosure is not made pursuant to a formal agency program, a number of practical issues arise. First is the question of *who* should make the disclosure—the corporation's counsel, a business representative, or both. Generally, the most prudent course is to effect disclosure through counsel. Counsel is generally in the best position to convey the information in an unemotional manner, and to refrain from saying or doing things that may undermine the effectiveness of a privilege or applicable confidentiality agreement, or narrow its scope. Moreover, most government agencies, especially the Department of Justice, feel more comfortable dealing with lawyers than with individuals who might be viewed as percipient witnesses, or even targets.

The next issue to consider is *when* disclosure should be made. Company management should be very careful not to make any disclosure until the investigation has been completed and all the facts are understood. Credibility is the most valuable asset to a party that voluntarily discloses potentially incriminating information; repeated corrections and additions to previous disclosures will destroy a company's credibility, as well as annoy the government. The piecemeal approach to disclosure has little to commend it.

Finally, a company must decide on the *form* of the disclosure. Should it be written, oral, or both? For a full discussion, see Chapter 10, Report of the Investigation.

V. CONCLUSION

The complexity of decision making for company counsel conducting an internal investigation into alleged wrongdoing by company employees has increased dramatically in light of the government's voluntary disclosure programs, the Sentencing Commission Guidelines, and the increased likelihood that disclosure effects a waiver of the attorney-client privilege or the work-product doctrine, thus making the counsel's investigative work available to hostile third parties. Given this complexity, the most prudent course of action is for company counsel to analyze at the outset the nature and scope of the investigation to be conducted and the course of action that will be taken at the end of the investigation, depending upon the conclusions reached. In other words, before company counsel starts to walk down an investigative path, counsel and the client should clearly understand what the company will do when the end of the path is reached.

The Special Litigation Committee Investigation: No Undertaking for the Faint of Heart

8

Lawrence J. Fox

I. THE SETTING   262
II. THE THEORETICAL FOUNDATION FOR A SPECIAL LITIGATION COMMITTEE   263
III. DERIVATIVE PLAINTIFF'S COUNSEL   265
IV. THE TOTAL CONTEXT   265
V. SELECTION OF COUNSEL   266
VI. THE INDEPENDENCE OF THE COMMITTEE   267
VII. THE DILEMMA INHERENT IN THE COMMITTEE'S WORK   269
VIII. IT IS THE COMMITTEE'S INVESTIGATION   270
IX. COMMITTEE INTERVIEWS   271
X. MINUTES OF COMMITTEE MEETINGS   271
XI. RELATIONSHIP WITH OTHER INSIDE AND OUTSIDE COUNSEL   272
XII. APPEARANCE OF COUNSEL FOR DERIVATIVE PLAINTIFF   273

Lawrence J. Fox is a partner at Drinker, Biddle & Reath. He wishes to acknowledge the able assistance of his former colleagues at Drinker, Biddle & Reath: Joanne Lahner, Sinclair Ziesing, and Bernard Diggins, and his present colleague, Noah Levin.

XIII. PROTECTING THE PRIVILEGE   274
XIV. THE INVESTIGATION   277
XV. CONCLUSION   279

APPENDIX A   280
APPENDIX B   281
APPENDIX C   282

IN THE SPECIAL WORLD of lawyer-conducted investigations, no undertaking calls for more finesse, diplomacy, independence, care, and judgment than acting as counsel for a special litigation committee. Not unlike the raising of mushrooms, the parties must conduct the process in the dark, manage it to inspire confidence that sanitary conditions have been maintained, and produce a perfect product that can withstand the most careful scrutiny of any number of skeptical inspectors. The lawyer who fails to handle it wisely and well can end up not with the sought-after opaque pearlescent mushrooms, but with nothing more than large quantities of mushroom "soil."

I. THE SETTING

How many times have the shouts "Strike suit!," "Plaintiffs' lawyers," or just plain "@#$%*#$ lawyers" reverberated through the corporate board rooms of America? There are few experiences to match that shocking combination of dismay and self-righteous outrage when the titans of our industrial and financial establishment learn that some self-appointed private attorney-general has commenced litigation "on behalf of" the corporation, typically against these very directors. "How dare someone institute litigation over that decision?" "How could anyone suggest that we have acted other than in the best interests of our corporation?" "How are you going to get officers and directors of our stature to serve the corporations of America if frivolous suits like this can be brought at the drop of a hat?"

When the shrill notes are but a lingering echo, the directors will calm down long enough to learn that lawyers not only have created the problem but also can provide, in certain circumstances, an appropriate approach for dealing with the problem—the establishment of a Special Litigation Committee

(SLC, or the Committee) of the board. It is the purpose of this chapter to provide counsel to the SLC with guidelines for the conduct of the SLC's work, particularly the required investigation that lies at the heart of the SLC's responsibilities.

II. THE THEORETICAL FOUNDATION FOR A SPECIAL LITIGATION COMMITTEE

As a general proposition, the decision whether a corporation should proceed with any given litigation matter, like the decision to issue subordinated debentures or to hire a new chief executive officer, is a business decision for the corporation's board.[1] Accordingly, since a derivative action purports to be and, if pressed, is in fact brought on behalf of the corporation, at least in certain instances[2] and as an initial matter,[3] it is the corporation's full board of directors that is entitled to make the decision whether it is in the best interests of the corporation to pursue the derivative claims. As a result, the requirement has been established that, in certain circumstances, a shareholder who wishes to bring a derivative suit must first make a formal demand upon the board of directors that may, as a matter of business judgment, determine that it is not in the best interests of the corporation for the litigation to go forward. Assuming a board with capacity to so decide, if the decision is not to proceed, that is the end of the matter.

---

1. *See, e.g.,* Joy v. North, 692 F.2d 880, 887 (2d Cir. 1982) (decision to bring lawsuit normally corporate business decision for board) (citing United Copper Securities Co. v. Amalgamated Copper Co., 244 U.S. 261 (1917) (same)), *cert. denied,* 460 U.S. 1051 (1983); Spiegel v. Buntrock, 571 A.2d 767, 772-73 (Del. Super. Ct. 1990) (decision to litigate is management decision made by board, not shareholders) (citing Zapata Corp. v. Maldonado, 430 A.2d 779, 782 (Del. Super. Ct. 1981) (same)); American Law Institute, *Principles of Corporate Governance: Analysis and Recommendations* (hereinafter ALI Principles) § 7.05(a) (1994) ("The Board has the authority to dismiss the derivative action as contrary to the best interests of the corporation." (Pennsylvania became the first jurisdiction to adopt the ALI Principles in Cuker v. Mikdauskas, 547 Pa. 600, 692 A.2d 1042 (1997)).

2. Beyond the scope of this chapter is an extensive discussion of when the matter is taken out of the hands of the corporation entirely. *See generally* BLOCK, BARTON & RADIN, *infra* note 8.

3. See the discussion at *infra* note 8 relating to when courts are permitted to second-guess the Committee's judgment.

However, under other circumstances, the courts have held, applying various tests, that the demand requirement is excused as futile.[4] In the demand-excused setting, the full board must recognize an unpleasant fact: because of the nature of the charges and/or the identity of the defendants, the board is disabled from reaching the decision not to proceed with the derivative claim.[5] At that point, the board must either permit the suit to go forward or try to identify from among its members (or even add to its membership) board members who are not so disabled. If the board can find a sufficient number of disinterested directors within its own ranks or if the board can add more directors (with due regard to state corporate law and corporate bylaw requirements as to the number of directors required to act in the name of the board and the method for adding new directors), the board can constitute a special litigation committee of the board.[6] It then becomes the responsibility of the full board to pass an appropriate resolution delegating to the board committee full authority to act in the name of the board with respect to the putative derivative claims. It is important that this resolution clearly provide that final authority rests with the SLC and that the SLC is not simply making a recommendation back to the disabled full board for final action.[7] A typical board resolution is annexed hereto as Appendix A.

---

4. *See, e.g.,* Aronson v. Lewis, 473 A.2d 805, 814 (Del. Super. Ct. 1984) (standard for determining whether demand is futile is reasonable doubt that "directors are disinterested" or that transaction was "a valid exercise of business judgment"); Barr v. Wackman, 329 N.E.2d 180, 188 (1975) (demand excused by allegations of board "participation in and approval of active wrongdoing"); ALI Principles § 7.03 ("Demand on the Board will only be excused if the plaintiff makes a specific showing that irreparable injury to the corporation would otherwise result.") *See also* Kamen v. Kemper Fin. Serv., Inc., 500 U.S. 90, 92 (1991) (rejects "universal demand" requirement under federal common law).

5. Beyond the scope of this chapter is a discussion of when it is desirable to forgo forming an SLC even though enough disinterested directors are available. The decision to pursue an SLC is not always the recommended course of action.

6. *See, e.g.,* Rosengarten v. Buckley, 613 F. Supp. 1493, 1499 (D. Md. 1985) (adopts majority rule that interested board has power to appoint special committee of independent directors to review derivative action (citing Zapata, 430 A.2d at 785 (one shareholder should not have power to incapacitate entire board)); ALI Principles § 7.05(b) ("The Board has the authority to delegate its authority to take any action specified in § 705(a) to a committee of directors or request the court to appoint a special panel in lieu of a committee of directors.") *But see* Miller v. Register and Tribune Syndicate, Inc., 336 N.W.2d 709 (Iowa 1983) (adopts minority rule that when all or nearly all directors are named defendants, no power to add or appoint new directors to special committee).

7. *See, e.g.,* Zapata, 430 A.2d at 786 (express provision of Delaware statute allows for delegation of full board authority to special committee by resolution).

III. DERIVATIVE PLAINTIFF'S COUNSEL

From the beginning, the SLC must guide all its conduct by the overriding expectation that, unless the SLC decides the derivative claim should go forward, plaintiff's counsel will challenge on all available fronts the recommendation of the SLC to terminate litigation. Included will be challenges to the independence of the Committee, the independence of counsel, the adequacy of the investigation, the objectivity of the investigation and, in those jurisdictions where it is available, a challenge that the final decision by the SLC violates the business judgment rule.[8] Thus, counsel must guide the entire SLC investigative process with one eye firmly fixed on the possibility and content of these challenges and the process by which the challenges will be mounted (i.e., likely discovery, anticipated testimony, the contents of the final Committee report).

IV. THE TOTAL CONTEXT

While the Committee is established in the context of a derivative claim pending alone, it is equally likely that the derivative claim will arise as the companion to (or be spawned by) a related class action brought in the name of the shareholders of the corporation against both the putative defendants in the derivative action and the corporation itself. This companion action will allege

---

8. *Id.* at 788-89 (under Delaware approach, court has discretion in demand—excused cases to apply own independent business judgment to special committee's decision not to file suit even after it is found committee is independent, acted in good faith, and conducted reasonable investigation). *See also* D. BLOCK, N. BARTON & S. RADIN, THE BUSINESS JUDGMENT RULE 1695-96 (5th ed. 1998) *(Zapata* approach followed by federal courts construing California, Connecticut, Georgia, Illinois, Maryland, Massachusetts, Michigan, New Jersey, Ohio, Pennsylvania, and Virginia law) [hereinafter BLOCK, BARTON & RADIN]. For an excellent discussion of the continued vitality of *Zapata's* two-step approach to SLC decisions (Was the investigation fair? Is the result reasonable?), *see* G. Varallo, W. McErlean, E.R. Silberglied, *From Kahn to Carlton: Recent Developments in Special Committee Practice,* 53 BUS. LAW. 397 (1998). *But see* Auerbach v. Bennett, 393 N.E.2d 994, 1000-02 (1979) (under New York approach, court inquires into committee's good faith and independence; once found, business judgment rule shields decision of committee from further scrutiny). The American Law Institute, in its *Principles of Corporate Governance,* adopts the *Auerbach* approach except in cases in which the claim is the defendant committed a knowing and culpable violation of law in a control transaction or a tender offer, where the court can determine whether the grounds warrant reliance.

that the same conduct that gave rise in the derivative context to the alleged corporate injury also directly injured the shareholders of the corporation. For example, the situations abound in which a shareholder brings a securities fraud class action alleging a failure to timely disclose some negative information that, when disclosed, resulted in a large drop in the price of a corporation's shares. At the same time, a shareholder might bring a derivative claim against the corporation's officers and directors alleging that their conduct caused the corporation great injury, to wit the need to pay the class significant dollar damages in the class action.

Thus, it is not at all uncommon that as the SLC and its counsel conduct their work, they will have to be mindful of the impact their meetings, deliberations, investigation, decisions, and subsequent report, if any, will have upon companion class-action litigation. Similarly, different counsel will be retained to defend the class-action litigation. Accordingly, the structuring and coordination of the relationship between class-action defense counsel and SLC counsel will require diplomacy and due regard for the often disparate interests or goals of the corporation in each piece of litigation.

V. SELECTION OF COUNSEL

The SLC's first act should be to select counsel to provide legal services to the Committee. While no one should ever select counsel in a casual manner, in this instance, the Committee must look beyond the usual credentials one would seek in counsel (skill, experience, personality, etc.). The Committee must conduct a thorough review of counsel's "independence" and consider whether that independence will withstand the strict scrutiny that will necessarily follow the completion of the Committee's work. It is the job of the Committee members not only to explore that issue, but also to require candidates for the assignment to explore it themselves before "tossing their hats into the ring."

The matters that the Committee should investigate in this context go beyond the usual conflict of interest analysis. Indeed, some possible candidates for the assignment, like present outside corporate counsel, who could "clear the conflict" without even "looking it up," are particularly unsuitable to act as counsel to the SLC simply because they are so involved with the corporation and its present officers and directors that their independence would be subject to substantial challenge.[9] Possible connections between putative counsel's firm colleagues and the defendants in the derivative action that would be irrelevant for conflict purposes (membership in the same clubs, service on common boards, etc.) may have an impact on whether the courts eventually view counsel as independent.[10] Thus, the search for independent counsel may be an arduous one, but one well worth the effort if the courts are to give the work of the Committee full effect. Regardless of the Committee's decision, if counsel is eventually found not to be independent, the Committee's work will be for naught, and the decision whether to pursue the claim will be entirely in the hands of derivative plaintiff and his or her counsel.

VI. THE INDEPENDENCE OF THE COMMITTEE

Once counsel is retained, the Committee should conduct a reciprocal independence analysis of its members. While one would hope that the board thoroughly explored these issues when the Committee was first formed by the board, it is not unusual for the Committee to make these appointments in haste, at a time of frenzy in the corporate board room, on a superficial basis (Jack's not named as a defendant; let's put him on the committee), or for precisely the wrong reason (Mary and I serve on the electric company board; I know I can trust her). In any event, a second check on independence is certainly in order, and, at a minimum, it will give counsel for the Committeean early opportunity to provide the SLC with counsel's own independent

---

9. *See, e.g.,* Kahn v. Tremont, 694 A.2d 422 (Del. 1997) (criticism of lawyer for special litigation committee who was recommended by counsel for the corporation); Maldonado v. Flynn, 485 F. Supp. 274, 283 (S.D.N.Y. 1980) (shareholder challenged independence of committee on basis of appointment of committee member's law firm as special counsel), *aff'd in part, rev'd in part on other grounds,* 671 F.2d 732 (2d Cir. 1982); Einhorn v. Culea, 612 N.W.2d 78, 90 (Wis. 2000) ("Courts should be more likely to find a special litigation committee independent if the committee retains counsel who has not represented individual defendants or the corporation in the past."). *See also* E. BRODSKY & M.P. ADAMSKI, LAW OF CORPORATE OFFICERS AND DIRECTORS; RIGHTS, DUTIES AND LIABILITIES § 9:09, 42 (1984 & Supp. 1989) [hereinafter BRODSKY & ADAMSKI] (special counsel should be without any regular relationship with corporation or management).

10. *See, e.g.,* Kaplan v. Wyatt, 499 A.2d 1184, 1190 (Del. Super. Ct. 1985) (committee's good faith challenged on basis of appointment of special counsel who was former defendant in unrelated litigation prosecuted by shareholder's counsel).

assessment of whether a court will ultimately view the Committee as independent. After all, no special litigation committee is ever free from an attack on the grounds of independence.[11] By definition, the Committee members serve on the board with, or know, the officers or directors who are the defendants in the derivative action because they are directors.

This charge of cronyism is as inevitable as the search by derivative plaintiff's counsel for fees. But it is the other connections, such as those mentioned in the discussion on independence of counsel (Did the president and a member of the special litigation committee room together in college? Is officer A related to SLC member B?), that the Committee and SLC counsel must carefully explore.[12] It is far too late to be surprised by such disclosures when derivative plaintiffs' counsel takes the depositions of the Committee members after the work of the Committee is complete.

Similarly, counsel must warn the Committee in the strongest possible terms to maintain its independence while its investigation is ongoing.[13] The Committee members, as board members, by definition will be meeting with their fellow "interested" board members at the regular meetings of the board. In addition, one can never overstate how nervous the putative derivative action defendants will be regarding the work of the Committee. Reciprocally, the Committee members will want to provide some assurances to their fellow directors if, as, and when it becomes likely that the Committee's work will result in a recommendation to drop the derivative claims. However, the Committee must avoid any of these pre-final report discussions lest plaintiff's

---

11. *See, e.g.,* In re Oracle Oracle Corp. Derivative Litig., 824 A.2d 917 (Del. Ch. 2003) (committee lacked independence merely because SLC members and defendants all had extensive ties to Stanford University).

12. *See, e.g., In re* MAXXAM, No. CIV.A. 12111, 1997 WL 187317 (Del. Ch. Apr. 4, 1997) (questioning independence of committee members); Lewis v. Fugua, 502 A.2d 962, 967 (Del. Ch. 1985) (sole director SLC member "should like Caesar's wife, be above reproach"); Bach v. National Western Life Ins. Co., 810 F.2d 509 (5th Cir. 1967) (plaintiffs challenged independence of SLC members on basis of prior meeting at resort of SLC and defendant director's counsel, among other connections); ALI Principles § 7.09(1)("The board/committee should be composed of two or more persons, no participating member of which was interested in the action, and should as a group be capable of objective judgment in the circumstances.").

13. *See, e.g.,* Abella v. Universal Leaf Tobacco Co., 546 F. Supp. 795, 800 (E.D. Va. 1982) (one factor in holding committee was independent was delegation of full board authority to committee without right of review by board); Spiegel v. Buntrock, 571 A.2d 767, 776 n.18 (Del. Super. Ct. 1990) (formation of committee isolates board from information during investigation and decision-making).

counsel use them at a later date to prove that the Committee either acted too hastily or was otherwise biased or lacked independence. Human nature being what it is, the need to deliver warnings regarding this type of conduct repeatedly and in the strongest terms is manifest.

VII. THE DILEMMA INHERENT IN THE COMMITTEE'S WORK

Once the Committee and counsel are in place, the work of the Committee can progress. As with the selection process itself, the Committee must conduct every phase of its work with great care, under the guidance, but not the control, of outside counsel.

Why such sensitivity? It is because in conducting its work, the Committee is negotiating a minefield, with potential jeopardy to the effectiveness of the Committee's work at every juncture. On the one hand, the Committee wants to conduct a full and independent investigation, including examining privileged materials, interviewing key people, and following leads wherever they may go. On the other, as already noted, it is more common than not that during the investigation, the corporation is a defendant in a class action arising out of the same set of facts. Thus, the Committee and SLC counsel must do everything to ensure that the work of the Committee, if at all possible, does not enhance class-action plaintiffs' case against the corporation by providing plaintiffs' counsel with a road map, waiving the privilege, or otherwise creating a situation where the corporation ends up with a pyrrhic victory—a splendid claim against present or former directors or officers who have few or no assets, coupled with a multimillion-dollar liability for the corporation vis-à-vis its shareholders. The Committee thus must be sure to keep its work as confidential as possible, attempting to protect the attorney-client and attorney work product privileges. Above all, the Committee must make sure its work does not result in greater costs to the corporation than if it had never been formed.[14] For these reasons, not only the guidance of counsel (who are sensitive

---

14. While beyond the scope of this paper, an issue that must be recognized is that there are certain situations in which the creation of an SLC, though technically possible, simply makes no sense because the risks inherent in it are too great to assume. The fact that the Committee conducts an investigation and produces a report always carries with it the possibility that discovery in related litigation will include inquiry into the working of the Committee and disclosure of its work product.

to these issues) but also the participation of counsel (who may provide an attorney work product or attorney-client privilege protection) is essential.

VIII. IT IS THE COMMITTEE'S INVESTIGATION

At the very first meeting, the Committee must decide upon the allocation of responsibility between counsel and Committee. As important as counsel's role is, one thing is certain: The investigation must be that of the Committee, not counsel, if it is to survive scrutiny.[15] Thus, the Committee must establish early some mechanism to meet regularly, perhaps monthly, with counsel. While counsel may make recommendations as to where the investigation should lead, these should be only in the form of suggestions. The Committee members must ratify those suggestions and have ample opportunity to make their own suggestions. If choices are required, those choices must be those of the Committee, not of counsel.

Similarly, while the Committee members presumably do not have the time, inclination, or ability to conduct interviews or search through what are typically thousands of documents, the Committee should establish a mechanism for reporting progress to counsel for evaluating the substance of what is being revealed. There may even be an understanding at this early juncture that, while counsel will do the "grunt work" for the Committee, the Committee itself, before it reaches a final conclusion, will either conduct or observe counsel conducting several key interviews or review key documents that counsel views as pivotal.

The tension here is obvious and inevitable. The more the Committee itself does, the less likely it may be viewed as a privileged undertaking; the less the Committee does, the more likely it is that the investigation will be viewed as a "counsel investigation" and, thus, not entitled to full effect. Good

---

15. *See, e.g.,* Kahn v. Tremont Corp., 694 A.2d at 426 (lack of participation by some members "severely limited the exchange of ideas and prevented special committee as a whole from acquiring critical knowledge of essential aspects of purchase"); *In re* MAXXAM, 1997 WL 187317, at *21 (member of committee cannot recall details, opening position or how many registration meetings were held); Watts v. Des Moines Register & Tribune, 525 F. Supp. 1311, 1328 (S.D. Iowa 1981) (substantial participation of committee members in investigation, though advised by special counsel, supported holding that committee itself made reasonable investigation). *See also* BRODSKY & ADAMSKI, *supra* note 9, § 9:09 at 42 (although special counsel may make recommendations to committee, active involvement and supervision of investigation by committee is essential).

judgment requires that counsel and the Committee, in full recognition of this additional dilemma, reach a balance that makes sense under the circumstances.

IX. COMMITTEE INTERVIEWS

Since the Committee's investigation will inevitably include interviews with employees of the corporation, it is wise for the Committee to adopt a protocol as to how these interviews will be conducted. The role of the special litigation committee and the implications of the investigation it conducts are confusing even to the sophisticated. Because the Committee is a committee of the corporate board, and because counsel are employed by the Committee, interviewees may view counsel as their own lawyer and assume the results are confidential, when in fact just the opposite is the case. Lest any interviewee be misled, counsel should draft a protocol speech similar to the one annexed hereto as Appendix B for the Committee, and the SLC should adopt a resolution stating that no interviews will be conducted without the interviewee first hearing "the speech."

X. MINUTES OF COMMITTEE MEETINGS

The question of recording the work of the Committee is also one that counsel and the Committee must explore at the first meeting. It is best, of course, if only official notes of the Committee meeting exist. Individual handwritten notes that reflect different styles and levels of attention can often be grist for the plaintiffs' counsel's deposition mill when the Committee's work meets its inevitable challenge.

Counsel should prepare the official minutes in the expectation that privilege will not attach to them. The minutes should be written in such a way that Committee members can quickly recall what was discussed, without providing the kind of detail that might come back to haunt all if the court determines the minutes are required to be turned over to plaintiffs' counsel. The minutes ought to reflect the fact that the Committee controlled the investigation, yet the writer should purge the minutes of all tentative conclusions or working hypotheses formed along the way. There will be time and opportunity enough to document the work of the Committee and the reasons for its decision when a final report, if any, is written.

The level of detail the author thinks is appropriate is reflected in the hypothetical Committee meeting minutes attached hereto as Appendix C.

While the minutes tell the reader who attended and how long the meeting lasted, and give a report on past activities, a preview of future activities, a tentative timetable for completion of the work, and a full discussion of all these matters, in the final analysis the minutes contain nothing that would provide fodder for plaintiffs' counsel.

XI. RELATIONSHIP WITH OTHER INSIDE AND OUTSIDE COUNSEL

Once the board launches the investigation, how does counsel begin? The derivative complaint is a start; thus, counsel can identify some early interviewees and relevant documents at the initial meeting. But the first fact of life that counsel for SLC will quickly learn is that they are dependent on the cooperation of inside counsel and, if there is parallel class-action litigation, counsel for the corporate defendant in that matter. Counsel have no subpoena power, no right to take depositions, no entitlement to see privileged documents, though they probably have free rein otherwise over corporate documents. Counsel also do not want to re-invent the wheel. If counsel wish to review relevant documents and lawyers for the class-action corporate defendant are already gathering the same documents for production to class-action plaintiffs' counsel, it does not make sense for the same corporate entity to pay two different firms to undertake this initial canvassing of corporate records. Thus, counsel for the SLC must to some extent coordinate its work with both of these other counsel.

However, there are two other forces at work that complicate this need to coordinate. First, counsel for the SLC must remain independent and also maintain the appearance of independence from other counsel. Counsel for the SLC should never place themselves in a position in which either inside counsel or counsel for class-action defendants are directing or limiting the scope of the investigation. Suggestions, cooperation, and assistance are appropriate, if not required; meddling, direction, and scope limitations are not. In the foregoing example, then, while it was satisfactory to depend on class-action defense counsel to gather the universe of documents, it would be unacceptable for SLC counsel to accept class-action defense counsel's representation that the documents in a given group were the only relevant ones.

Second, inside counsel and counsel for the class-action defendant are vitally interested in the work of the Committee, and frankly hope that the Committee's work will reach a conclusion favorable to incumbent management. These counsel will express their anxiety in many forms; even while recognizing fully that they do not want to sully the independence of the Committee, they will be tempted to intervene.

The Committee and SLC counsel must manage this uneasy alliance with diplomacy. Surely the cooperation of regular outside counsel is a treasured thing; there is no reason not to listen to what they have to say. But the investigation should follow a path mandated by the Committee, not general counsel, and Committee members and counsel should keep confidential reports on the course of the investigation, not share them with nervous general counsel who may be putting intense pressure on SLC counsel.

In this context, SLC counsel may and indeed should share with other counsel matters uncovered in the SLC investigation that directly and significantly impact the class-action litigation. Similarly, SLC counsel should share with class-action defense counsel SLC counsel's views on the credibility of witnesses or the likelihood that any particular defense would prevail. After all, counsel are all seeking to act in the best interests of the corporation, which includes mounting the best possible defense to the plaintiff's class action. If SLC counsel has a second opinion or special insights, the parties should encourage an exchange of this information as entirely consistent with counsel's independent role. And if inside counsel has a special need to get an expedited reading from the SLC on a particular charge or employee because of some pressing business reason (for example, a derivative defendant may be about to be promoted to executive vice president and management is attempting to avoid later embarrassment), the parties should agree to communicate that request to the SLC for it to exercise its independent business judgment in balancing the need for independence and the corporation's need for an early answer.

But at the end of the day, while SLC counsel wants to be able to testify that he received full cooperation from these other lawyers, that the corporation granted complete access to documents, that it arranged all interviews that were required, and that other counsel otherwise provided all necessary assistance, SLC counsel also must be able to testify, under what may be the withering cross-examination of derivative plaintiff's counsel, that the Committee was the sole guide for the investigation.

XII. APPEARANCE OF COUNSEL FOR DERIVATIVE PLAINTIFF

Counsel also must decide with the Committee what role plaintiff's derivative counsel should play in the investigation. After all, it is plaintiff's allegations that are the starting place for the work of the Committee. At a minimum, SLC counsel should invite plaintiff's counsel to submit in writing any presentation plaintiff's counsel wishes the Committee to consider. Though more risky, and perhaps not likely to provide anything more than aesthetics, SLC counsel may invite plaintiff's counsel to meet with SLC counsel or even address the Committee on his or her clients' concerns. The effect of all of this can be quite disarming—it is plaintiff's counsel who may ultimately challenge the Committee's action. Certainly part of that challenge can be blunted if the Committee has considered the views of plaintiff's counsel, and, even more so, if the Committee has followed the leads supplied or suggestions offered by plaintiff's counsel. Moreover, if plaintiff's counsel fails to take advantage of this offer, SLC counsel can feel more comfortable in limiting the investigation to the allegations of the complaint—allegations that are often inartfully crafted and lacking in real substance.

XIII. PROTECTING THE PRIVILEGE

Perhaps the most critical part of the investigation for counsel is dealing with documents that are subject to the attorney-client privilege and attorney work-product doctrine. In the context of an SLC investigation, each of these privileges exists on two different levels. On the first level, there are communications between SLC counsel and the Committee that, if properly handled, qualify for the attorney-client privilege.[16] For example, counsel's opinion to the Committee members on the likelihood of their being deemed independent would come within this doctrine. There is also the work of SLC counsel that—again, if properly handled—should come within the attorney work-product doctrine.[17] Examples of this would include counsel's interview notes, counsel's analyses of documents and counsel's working hypotheses regarding

---

16. *See, e.g,* Dennis J. Block & Nancy E. Barton, *Internal Corporate Investigations: Maintaining the Confidentiality of a Corporate Client's Communications with Investigative Counsel,* 35 Bus. LAW. 5, 9-13 (1979) [hereinafter Block & Barton] (attorney-client privilege extends to communications between client and counsel if purpose for retention is legal advice rather than investigation). *See also* Chapter 2, "Implications of the Attorney-Client Privilege and the Work-Product Doctrine," and Chapter 11, "Report of the Investigation."

17. *See, e.g.,* Block & Barton, *supra* note 15, at 21-23 (work-product doctrine protects documents prepared by counsel in anticipation of litigation absent demonstrated substantial need by plaintiff). *See also In re* LTV Sec. Litig., 89 F.R.D. 595, 620 (N.D. Tex. 1981) (work product of special counsel to audit committee protected because investigation and report required legal acumen and expertise). *But see.* Medinol, Ltd. v. Boston Scientific Corp., 214 F.R.D. 113 (S.D.N.Y. 2002) (defendant's disclosure of the SLC's meeting minutes to auditors waived the protection of the work-product doctrine.)

the possibility that the corporation might have a claim. Because all of this work is conducted in anticipation of litigation (either a motion to have the derivative claim dismissed based on the Committee's work and business judgment or the actual prosecution of a claim on behalf of the corporation), it is not a stretch to argue that the attorney work-product doctrine should apply.

On a second level, there is the review by SLC counsel and the Committee of documents created by other counsel, their experts, or corporate employees that qualify for the attorney-client and/or attorney work product privileges. For example, the SLC counsel may review privileged documents created by general counsel at the time the corporation made an important decision whether to disclose a potentially material fact in filing its report on Form 10-k. Or SLC counsel may review, as part of the SLC investigation, witness notes created by counsel defending the companion class action. Protection of these two privileges is the subject of a separate chapter in this book, and the principles outlined therein apply with equal vigor here. And because counsel for the SLC is simply another counsel for the corporation, SLC counsel's review of the second-level documents subject to the attorney-client and attorney work product privileges should not, if analyzed properly, act as a break or waiver of either.

However, there is one aspect of the SLC investigatory and report process that has special impact on both privileges, at both levels. The Committee must reach a decision. If it is a decision not to proceed with the derivative claim, the SLC must be prepared to demonstrate in some way or other that it reached its decision after a thorough investigation, after numerous interviews, after the review of all relevant documents by an independent committee that met regularly, guided by independent counsel, and, in some jurisdictions, that the decision fits well within the business judgment rule. It also must be prepared to resist an inevitable challenge from the derivative plaintiff's counsel to all of the foregoing. This means that discovery will occur into the work of the Committee and its counsel.

Anticipating the probable scope of this discovery has an inevitable effect on the scope of the Committee's investigation. If the Committee's report mentions a particular document, regardless of its privileged character, derivative plaintiff's counsel certainly will seek and likely receive it in discovery.[18] Similarly,

---

18. *See, e.g., In re* Matter of Continental Illinois Sec. Litig., 732 F.2d 1302, 1314 (7th Cir. 1984) (report prepared by committee to evaluate derivative claims is discoverable, since it was admitted into evidence to support motion to terminate claims) (citing Joy v. North, 692 F.2d 880, 893 (2d Cir. 1982) (committee reports used in adjudicative stages of derivative litigation are discoverable; protected only if confidentiality is maintained)).

if the Committee relies on privileged material to reach its conclusion, the Committee can expect that plaintiff's counsel will succeed in discovering those documents despite their confidential character. However, mere review of privileged material by counsel for the Committee should not have the effect of acting as a waiver. Nonetheless, all of the foregoing suggests that the SLC and its counsel should take care in deciding what to review.

While it might at first appear that the SLC would benefit from appearing to have had its members or counsel review the universe of available documents, there might be situations in the area of privileged documents where it is better to avoid reviewing them—for example, if the Committee or SLC counsel can elicit factual information in a different way. (Why look at counsel's notes of a key interview when the interviewee can be reinterviewed by SLC counsel?) Moreover, while it is clearly helpful, if not necessary, for counsel to have access to underlying privileged documents as well as privileged documents created in connection with the parallel class-action litigation, counsel does not want this access to result in disclosure to derivative plaintiff's counsel. Thus, SLC counsel must make judgments at every step of the way when it comes to privileged documents—whether SLC counsel should review the documents, whether SLC counsel should share the documents with the Committee, whether the documents should play a role in the conclusions reached by the Committee, and whether the final report should reference the documents.

The fine line that must be drawn is exemplified by *Zitin v. Turley*.[19] After the plaintiffs had filed their derivative suit, the corporation created an SLC to investigate their demands. The SLC (with assistance of counsel) produced a report recommending against the action. The company then used the report as a basis for its summary judgment motion.

The plaintiffs thereafter sought drafts of the report, any documents reviewed in preparing the report, and any communications between counsel and the committee. The court held that all of the documents requested were protected by the attorney-client or work product privileges.[20] However, the court held that by disclosing the report, "the Corporation has waived any

---

19. No. Civ. 89-2061-PHX-CAM, 1991 U.S. Dist. LEXIS 10084 (D. Ariz. June 25, 1991).

20. *Id.* at 10-11.

claims of privilege and work product immunity to the extent that counsel communicated the information or documents to the committee."[21]

Farber v. Public Service Co.[22] is also instructive. In preparation for expected derivative suits, the corporation in *Farber* created an SLC, which then produced a report. The report was subsequently filed in one of the pending derivative suits. The plaintiffs then sought the disclosure of all documents reviewed, the notes of the SLC members, and any communications to or from SLC members. Examining the corporation's work product claims, the court held that to permit such broad categories of discovery would militate against common sense and undermine the work-product doctrine.[23] The court permitted disclosure of any documents reviewed, but protected the SLC members' notes and the communications to or from SLC members.[24]

XIV. THE INVESTIGATION

Describing how the actual investigation should be conducted is about as elusive a topic as how to defend litigation. All investigations are fact-specific, and the conscientious and imaginative lawyer must structure and complete the necessary work in an appropriate manner. Nonetheless, there are a few rules that SLC counsel should apply, given the special characteristics of the SLC and the goal of counsel to see the SLC's ultimate decision given full effect.

First, since it is known that plaintiff's counsel will mount an inevitable challenge to the scope of the SLC's investigation in reaching its decision, it may be that counsel will want to extend its work beyond what the normal cost/benefit analysis might suggest was appropriate in other contexts.[25]

While it is almost unavoidable that at least one witness will be left uninterviewed and one box of documents unreviewed, the ability to say that counsel extended the investigation beyond normal limits could be helpful.

---

21. *Id. at* 15.
22. Civ. No. 89-0456 JB/WWD, 1991 U.S. Dist. LEXIS 18051 (D.N.M. Apr. 4, 1991).
23. *Id. at* *3.
24. *Id. at* *3-4.
25. *See, e.g.,* Zapata Corp. v. Maldonado, 430 A.2d 779, 788 (Del. Super. Ct. 1981) (under Delaware approach, corporation must prove "reasonable investigation" conducted before motion to dismiss will be granted); Auerbach v. Bennett, 393 N.E.2d 994, 1000-02 (N.Y. 1979) (under New York approach, court may look at methodologies and procedures of investigation; if restricted in scope, shallow in execution or pro forma, question of good faith raised).

Second, the Committee and SLC counsel should leave no reasonable leads (regardless of their anticipated value) unfollowed. If witness A insists that witness B was a key participant, it is far better to interview B to put that allegation to rest rather than to reject A's suggestion on the basis of other information available to counsel.

The importance of leaving no stone unturned is demonstrated by the court's observations in *Steel Partners II, L.P. v. Aronson, et al.*[26] In *Steel Partners*, the SLC conducted an investigation that lasted more than three months and included document requests and review, numerous interviews, the full-time participation of special counsel, and a 139-page report. Nevertheless, the court found that the SLC had not met its burden of establishing that it had exercised due care in investigating the merits of the litigation.[27] Though the court found that the SLC was independent, it focused on the fact that critical documents were not produced until the week before the SLC report was due. While the court expressed sympathy with respect to the unfortunate situation of the SLC and its counsel where "the material that was the most significant to the Committee's work was not in hand until the final three weeks of the process," it held that the circumstances did not justify a failure to give the material the level of scrutiny that it merited.[28]

Third, the Committee and SLC counsel should thoroughly investigate and evaluate any information supplied by derivative plaintiff's counsel. There is no more likely challenge to the Committee's work than that plaintiffs' counsel's allegations were ignored as part of a "cover-up."

Fourth, if at all possible, the Committee and SLC counsel should interview each derivative claim defendant. Confronting the alleged perpetrators of the injury to the corporation lends a credibility to the investigation that will carry great weight later.

Fifth, SLC counsel should not hesitate to hire an expert to help the Committee evaluate any technical or arcane factual issues that are beyond the expertise of counsel and the Committee members. For example, if the allegation is that pre-release tests should have revealed an inherent defect in a particular product, the SLC should retain an expert to assist with the physics or chemistry in order to enhance its work.[29]

---

26. No. C-101-03 (N.J. Super. Ct. Ch. Div. Mar. 30, 2006).
27. *Id.* at 11 (citing In re PSE & G Shareholder Litigation, 801 A.2d 295 (N.J. 2002).
28. *Id.*
29. Experts should meet the test of independence as well. *See* Kahn v. Tremont, 694 A.2d 422, 426 (Del. 1997) (challenge to an investment adviser to a special transaction committee who had earned fees from affiliates of majority shareholder).

Finally, it should be remembered that in determining whether it is in the best interests of the corporation to pursue derivative litigation, the Committee must evaluate more than the merits of the claim.[30] The Committee also must add into the equation (a) the likely disruption to the corporation that will result from such a suit going forward, and (b) the likely recovery to the corporation if the corporation were successful. With respect to the former, the investigation should focus on the value of the putative defendants to the ongoing operations of the business, the effect of pursuing the litigation on the putative defendants' ability to continue to operate as effective officers or directors, and the effect on other employees' morale of the corporation's suing the putative defendants. With respect to the latter, the investigation must explore the likely cost in legal fees, expert witnesses, and other litigation costs to pursue the claim; the personal wealth of the putative defendants; and the availability of insurance coverage for any of the claims. The Committee or SLC counsel should explore each of these matters independently.

XV. CONCLUSION

The Special Litigation Committee investigation is one of the more challenging and gratifying assignments counsel can be retained to undertake. From start to finish, the tasks involved must be undertaken with conscientious and finely honed skills, ever mindful of the traps for the unwary that lie at every step along the way. If successfully completed, the result will permit the SLC to implement fully its well-considered decision as to how the Corporation should treat a derivative claim whose initial filing was undoubtedly met with a mixture of scorn and dismay. Counsel who fulfill the assignment conscientiously will have empowered the client in a meaningful way, acting in the finest traditions of the profession.

---

30. *See, e.g.,* Auerbach, 393 N.E.2d at 1002 (decision to file suit involves "weighing and balancing legal, ethical, commercial, promotional, public relations, fiscal and other factors familiar to the resolution of ... corporate problems."). *See also* Abella v. Universal Leaf Tobacco Co., 546 F. Supp. 795, 801 n.3 (E.D. Va. 1982) (factors considered in weighing costs against benefits included large attorney's fees, loss of time and energy by management, reduction in morale of employees and management, adverse consequences to insurance coverage, and adverse reaction by customers, banker, and stock market). *Cf.* Joy, 692 F.2d at 892 (court may initially weigh attorney's fees, expenses of litigation, and mandatory indemnification of directors and officers, but may not consider existence of insurance; if court then finds no substantial net return compared to shareholder's equity, court may consider impact to key personnel and lost profits from trial publicity).

APPENDIX A

Resolution Establishing a Special Litigation Committee

WHEREAS a class action has been instituted against the Company, its present and former directors and officers as well as a derivative action on behalf of the Company against the same present and former directors and officers; and

WHEREAS it would be proper for the Board of Directors of the Company to delegate to a Special Litigation Committee the responsibility for determining whether it is in the best interests of the Company to pursue any of the claims alleged in the derivative action;

NOW THEREFORE, the following resolution is adopted by the Board of Directors of the Company:

RESOLVED that, pursuant to the Bylaws of the Company, a Special Litigation Committee shall be appointed by the Executive Committee to be ratified by the full Board of Directors; further, it is

RESOLVED that the Special Litigation Committee is authorized to exercise all lawful authority of the Board of Directors in determining what action, if any, the Company should take with respect to the above-referenced derivative litigation and any similar suits that have been or may be filed on the Company's behalf.

APPENDIX B

Advice to Witnesses

As you may know, litigation has been instituted against the Company by a shareholder purporting to represent a class claiming that the Company overstated earnings in the years 2004 and 2005, thereby allegedly defrauding shareholders who bought the Company's stock in those years. The Company's Board of Directors has now received a demand from a shareholder of the Company requesting that the Company institute litigation against those who were already responsible for the alleged overstatement of earnings. A derivative lawsuit on behalf of the Company has also been filed that makes the same demand to recover from these individuals any damages the Company may be forced to pay in the class action.

Because the decision to institute litigation is, like any other business action, subject to the business judgment of the Board, and because some of the present Board members were on the Board at the time of the allegedly inflated earnings reports, the Board has delegated to a three-member Committee of the Board, all of whom joined the Board since 1986, the decision whether it is in the best interests of the Company to pursue litigation against anyone for any conduct associated with these financial statements.

In reaching its decision, the Committee will investigate the facts and circumstances surrounding the issuance of the financial statements to determine whether those in positions of responsibility properly fulfilled their duties in issuing the financial statements. The Committee, of course, recognizes that disclosures that were made in good faith and involved no actionable conduct may appear incorrect with the benefit of hindsight. On the other hand, it is the responsibility of the Committee to determine whether all concerned acted in a manner consistent with their duties to the corporation and its shareholders.

The Committee, in turn, has retained our law firm to be counsel to the Committee to assist the Committee in the conduct of its investigation. It is in that role that we have asked for an opportunity to interview you. It is important that you understand that our firm neither represents the Company generally nor do we represent you. Our only client is the three-member independent Committee to whom we shall report the results of this, as well as our other interviews, so that the Committee can fulfill its important responsibilities.

APPENDIX C

Confidential Attorney-Client and Attorney Work Product Privilege

Minutes of the Special Litigation Committee Meeting of June 1, 2006.

The Special Litigation Committee of X Corporation met on June 1, 2006. All members of the Special Litigation Committee were present as well as Michael Burns and Bobbi Miller, counsel to the Committee. The Chairman of the Committee asked Mr. Burns to keep the minutes of the meeting.

1. The minutes of the previous meeting were reviewed and approved.

2. Counsel reported on the most recent interviews with the Controller and the Chief Financial Officer of the Company. The Committee discussed whether the Committee ought to meet with the CFO at some future date.

3. A review of the due diligence files of the Company conducted by counsel for the Special Litigation Committee was described.

4. Counsel shared her research into the independence of the members of the Special Litigation Committee.

5. A preliminary investigation by counsel into questions of available coverage under the Company's Directors and Officers Liability policy was discussed.

6. A preliminary chronology of key events was circulated.

7. Counsel provided members of the Committee with a schedule of upcoming interviews as well as an explanation of why counsel had selected this particular order for the interviews.

8. Counsel explained the basis for their fees for the last month and a budget for completing counsel's work was discussed.

The next meeting of the Committee was scheduled for July 17, 2006.

Unique Problems Associated with Internal Investigations in Environmental Cases

9

James Chen and Michele C. Coyle

I. INTRODUCTION 284
II. REACTIVE INVESTIGATIONS 285
    A. Search Warrants 285
    B. Agency Demands to Review and Photocopy Documents 288
    C. Notices of Violations 289
    D. Conducting a Reactive Internal Investigation 289
III. VOLUNTARY ENVIRONMENTAL INTERNAL INVESTIGATIONS 291
    A. Reasons for Environmental Compliance Audits 291
    B. Importance of Periodic Audits by Outside Consultants 292
    C. Problems Posed by Audits 293
    D. Electronic Records 294
    E. Audit Privilege Law 294

James Chen is a partner with the Washington, D.C.-based firm of Crowell & Moring, LLP, where he practices environmental and safety regulatory law. The views expressed in this article are entirely his own and do not necessarily represent those of the firm or any of his clients. Michele C. Coyle is Campus Counsel, University of California, Riverside, California. The views she expresses in this article are her personal views and are not to be attributed to the Regents of the University of California.

IV. CONCLUSION   295

APPENDIX A   296

I. INTRODUCTION

INTERNAL CORPORATE investigations in the environmental area often begin in response to contact by a government agent or agency. Service of a search warrant on company employees is becoming a frequent occurrence, and one that triggers an internal investigation in less than ideal circumstances.

Most companies in these instances are shocked by the appearance of government agents, sometimes in great numbers, executing a search warrant. This is especially disconcerting to many companies, since company managers usually have no idea that there are any environmental problems within the company. Investigators may seize documents or attempt to make unannounced interviews—all of which are likely to take company officers or employees by surprise. Sometimes government agents arrive unannounced at a company with a demand to review and photocopy documents that relate to environmental permits held by the company. In other instances, a company may simply receive a notice of violation or some other type of citation, receipt of which should warn the company it may have problems. In all of these circumstances, the government contacts usually prompt a reactive internal company investigation.

With greater emphasis on corporate accountability, especially in light of legislation like Sarbanes-Oxley, more and more companies are conducting voluntary internal investigations, often called "environmental audits." Larger companies have even begun putting into place policies and procedures for conducting these audits on a routine basis. Because many companies have various government permits, which are necessary to carry on their business, environmental audits are seen as a prudent way to ensure the company is in compliance with its permits. Voluntary environmental audits, however, present problems different in some respects from those encountered in a reactive internal investigation.

This chapter first discusses some of the unique aspects of reactive investigations, particularly those triggered by government action, and provides suggestions in conducting such investigations. The second part of this chapter focuses on voluntary environmental audits. Many companies now conduct voluntary internal investigations. Therefore, the discussion of voluntary, proactive investigations focuses on the advantages and disadvantages of these investigations, some of the unique problems they present, rather than on the nuts and bolts of conducting them.

II. REACTIVE INVESTIGATIONS

Reactive investigations are those triggered by some defining event, such as an industrial accident, chemical release, a pollution incident, or the announcement of a government investigation of the company. This type of investigation is more difficult than the routine internal investigation because the company must deal not only with often complex underlying technical issues, but also with internal and external pressure to resolve the matter quickly, the crisis atmosphere that usually develops within the company, the siege mentality that usually develops relative to those outside the company, and, often, issues of internal company politics and career preservation. In short, the company must cope with a technical problem and, simultaneously, the collateral issues flowing from the ramifications of the incident.

A. *Search Warrants*

One of the most difficult types of reactive investigations for a company to respond to is that triggered by the execution of an administrative or criminal search warrant at the company. Unfortunately, search warrants are commonly used by investigators in the environmental area. In the environmental context, investigators tend to believe that search warants are essential and more beneficial than subpoenas. Environmental investigators can be expected to take samples during the execution of a search warrant, as well as to seize all documents relating to environmental procedures before evidence can be altered or destroyed.

Environmental search warrants are often executed by a SWAT team of numerous law enforcement officers. Some of these officers are dressed in "moonsuits" and take samples during the search. Other officers are assigned to go through all the company's documents and confiscate everything that is reasonably responsive to the search warrant, which is typically very broad in scope. And some officers will attempt to segregate employees into offices and interview them in an isolated and intimidating atmosphere. These tactics can have an intimidating and overwhelming effect on management and other personnel present at the time the warrant is executed. Obviously, the manner in which the company deals with a search warrant is part of, and will be essential to, the subsequent internal investigation that will immediately follow.

A few simple steps can minimize disruption and potential harm of the search and enhance any subsequent internal investigation.[1] All companies should designate a senior person to serve as the contact with government

---

1. Attached as Appendix A is a short checklist of things to do in response to a search warrant.

investigators. If law enforcement agents appear on the premises and announce their intention to execute a search warrant, the pre-designated person should talk to the officers, identify which agent is heading the search warrant or subpeona, and read it carefully. Normally, valid objections during the course of a search warrant arise only if the agents go beyond the scope of the warrant. Otherwise, the company must cooperate with the search or risk possible allegations of obstruction of justice.

The responsible corporate official should always ask the agents executing the warrant if they could either return after business hours to avoid disrupting the business or at least wait until its attorney arrives. Not surprisingly, the agents may object to the delay. For this reason, it is important that the pre-designated senior employee be familiar with counsel experienced with search warrant and criminal matters, so the company can contact its outside counsel immediately. The presence of an experienced lawyer will protect against inadvertent waivers of constitutional rights and procedural protections. The company should advise the lawyer of all details of the warrant, including the regulatory agencies involved, the areas to be searched under the provisions of the warrant, and the types of evidence to be seized.

If the agents insist on proceeding with the search warrant, the company representative should inform them that, due to the disruption, conducting business will be impossible and therefore employees will be sent home. The agents may object, but a search warrant for documents and tangible evidence should not authorize the detainment of employees at the company beyond the brief time necessary to secure the premises and conduct the search.[2] An exception may exist for employees with material knowledge of the subject of the search warrant. In that case, certain employees may be required to remain available to agents.

If members of the news media are present, politely and firmly ask them to leave. Do not engage in any behavior that would make a bad impression, such as ducking, hiding, blocking cameras, or using force to move them. Portrayal of this conduct in newspapers or on television could prejudice prospective jurors and harm the company's reputation in the community.

Do not consent to a warrantless search or to a search beyond the scope of the warrant. Even though the company may have nothing to hide, there is

---

2. *See e.g.,* Michigan v. Summers, 452 U.S. 692, 702-03 (1981); Daniel v. Taylor, 808 F.2d 1401, 1403-05 (11th Cir. 1986); United States v. Rowe, 694 F. Supp. 1420, 1423-25 (N.D. Cal. 1988); United States v. Stevens, 543 F. Supp. 929, 942-43 (N.D. Ill. 1982) (distinguishing the detaining of individuals pursuant to a search warrant for contraband as opposed to a search warrant for documents and evidence).

little gained by giving government investigators carte blanche to rummage through company records in an attempt to conjure up damaging evidence. The terms of a search warrant must clearly outline the scope of the search permitted. Any search beyond the scope of the warrant is not authorized and may be inadmissible in a subsequent court proceeding.

Likewise, because search warrants are often executed in a circus atmosphere, which can terrify company employees, interviews conducted under intimidating circumstances can lead to inaccurate statements that must be clarified at a later date. Accordingly, it is prudent to advise employees that they do not have to talk to the investigators, that it is entirely their decision to talk to anyone, and that if they choose to speak with investigators, the company will make counsel available prior to the interview if they so desire. Do not, however, instruct the employees not to cooperate. This could lead to allegations of obstruction of justice. In other words, companies should advise employees that they do not have to talk to investigating officers unless they so choose, but the company should not develop a policy or make statements prohibiting employees from talking to the investigators. In addition, any written statements made by investigators about representations made by employees during interviews should be reviewed and signed off upon by the employee in order to ensure accuracy. A copy of any such statements should be retained by the company.

The company should monitor the search to ensure that it is proceeding within the proper scope. If the investigators insist on interviewing employees on company premises during the execution of the search warrant, the company should object to interviews being conducted on company time and company premises, at least until the employees can be advised of their rights with regard to the interviews and counsel can be provided. A representative of the company should follow the investigators and note carefully what the investigators take. The company will receive at the end of the search a detailed receipt of the property seized, but the receipt can be confusing and not particularly helpful. Therefore, a detailed list of seized documents prepared by a company employee is normally more helpful in conducting a subsequent internal investigation.

The company representative also should observe whether any physical items are seized and whether any soil or other samples are taken. If the agents take samples, the company should request "split" samples right away. Certain chemicals must be tested within limited time periods to ensure the validity of the results. Also, if photographs or videotapes are taken, the company will want copies. If employees are interviewed, someone should list all employees interviewed so the company can follow up in its own investigation.

The company also should make arrangements with the investigators to obtain copies of all seized documents as quickly as possible. During the subsequent internal investigation, the company will want to know precisely what the investigators have in their possession. It is also essential to get an environmental consultant involved quickly. Indeed, in addition to the company's attorney, it is desirable to get the consultant to the premises during the course of the search warrant, if possible. The consultant can then observe the agents taking samples and the manner in which they are taken. Of course, one of the most serious problems for the investigating agency is the failure of the agents during the seizure of evidence to follow required procedures for the taking of samples. Improper sampling as well as improper testing of those samples may result in fatal flaws to the investigator's case.[3]

Finally, a search warrant should cause a company to believe it may have serious problems. A search warrant is obtained by going to a court with an affidavit showing sufficient cause to permit the court to sign off on the search warrant. It is a serious matter for investigators and should be treated accordingly by the company. Consequently, as soon as the officers leave the premises, the company should begin its own internal investigation. If the suggestions above have been followed, the internal investigation should run smoothly regarding the circumstances or incidents at issue.

B. *Agency Demands to Review and Photocopy Documents*

Often an agency that has an ongoing regulatory inspection function at a company will arrive and demand to view and photocopy documents pursuant to a permit or other license issued to the company. This procedure can also cause confusion. Although it is not as confrontational as the execution of a search warrant, a government demand for documents provides the requesting agency with just as much information in terms of volume and detail as a wide-ranging search warrant. Unless such inspections are a condition of the permit or license, agency demands for documents should serve as a high-level warning that the company may have environmental problems. Presumably, the regulatory agency is there to review and photocopy documents in the civil context, not as part of a criminal investigation. A criminal investigation requires a search warrant.[4]

---

3. *See e.g.,* People v. Mobil Oil Corp., 143 Cal. App. 3d 261 (1983).

4. *See, e.g.,* United States v Utedit, 238 F.3d 882, 886-87 (7th Cir. 2001); People v. Todd Shipyards Corp., 192 Cal. App. 3d Supp. 20, 238 Cal. Rptr. 761 (1987); Los Angeles Chem. Co. v. Superior Ct., 226 Cal. App. 3d 703, 276 Cal. Rptr. 647 (1990) (interpreting federal search and seizure law).

In response to a demand to review and photocopy documents, the company should read the request carefully. Again, it is advisable to consult experienced counsel. The company representative should be present at all times to observe what is being reviewed and photocopied. The company representative should take notes of what occurs during the regulatory agents' visit, and should request copies of all documents the regulatory agency photocopies. The prudent company will perceive this investigation to be a very serious matter and will conduct an ensuing investigation of its own.

C. Notices of Violations

A notice of violation, citation, or other document indicating a problem with the facility may be served on any of a range of employees from upper management to a lower-level employee. Companies should set up in-house procedures that ensure a notice of violation or similar document (e.g., "show-cause" letter, notice of warning, intent to inspect, civil administrative complaint, or demand for penalty) is reported immediately to appropriate management.

In the past, companies have often allowed lower-level employees to handle these notices with the agencies, only to find themselves later embroiled in civil or criminal litigation with the agency. The notice or citation should state on its face the problem perceived by the agency. However, the absence of a criminal warning on the citation itself does not mean the investigation will not someday turn into a criminal enforcement action. In a time of increasing public pressure for environmental compliance and of increased use of the government's criminal enforcement power, these notices should be treated seriously by the company—both because of the immediate administrative problems and because of the potential civil or criminal enforcement actions. Usually, an attorney and/or consultant should be called in immediately and an internal investigation should begin.

D. Conducting a Reactive Internal Investigation

One of the most unique aspects of conducting an internal investigation in the environmental area is the importance of an expert or consultant. Technical issues, such as the improper taking or testing of samples, can be critically fatal to the prosecutor's criminal case. Even in a civil dispute with a regulatory agency, technical problems with data can often force the regulatory agency to reach a more beneficial settlement in favor of the company. Finally, an outside consultant brings to the investigation the benefit of a fresh perspective and the objectivity of being independent of the company. Therefore, it is a tremendous advantage for the company to have an experienced engineer or specific consultant on its team.[5]

The company's outside counsel and the consultant should execute a written agreement as soon as possible. Oftentimes, attorneys specializing in environmental law have worked in such attorney/consultant relationships in the past and may be able to advise companies as to appropriate consultants they may wish to approach. By having the attorney and consultant enter into a written agreement, the company establishes that the consultant is an agent of, works with, and reports to the lawyer. This procedure protects the consultant's work on attorney-client privilege and work product theories.[6]

The consultant can also serve an essential role during the interviews of company employees due to the importance of technical issues in these cases. The consultant may attend some of the employees' interviews with the lawyer to help explore and clarify these critical issues.

Many of the aspects of an internal environmental corporate investigation—interviewing employees, preparing interview memoranda, advising employees of their rights, and reporting to management—are conducted in much the same manner as described above and in other chapters of this book. One significant difference, however, may be the speed at which it is often necessary to conduct an internal environmental investigation. This is partly due to concerns that the company could be hit quickly with a parallel administrative proceeding where both a civil and criminal investigation and/or prosecution is conducted simultaneously.

Although the EPA generally does not favor parallel proceedings, at the state level they are very common. For example, when a company is served with a warrant or notice of violation regarding effluent to the sewer, a criminal investigation typically has already been or soon will be referred to a prosecutor, who could take several months to prepare a case and determine if criminal prosecution is appropriate. On the other hand, if there is a problem with effluent to the sewer line, the agency that has issued a sewer permit to the company probably will order the company to appear in the near future at

---

5. Although investigators and regulatory agencies are steadily improving in their technical expertise, it should be noted that very few of the regulatory or investigative agents are engineers or Ph.Ds.

6. This "privilege" aspect of an internal investigation is discussed in detail in Chapter 2 of this book and therefore will not be belabored here.

a hearing to show why the sewer line should not be severed. If the sewer line is severed, it could put the company out of business. Thus, the company is caught in an unpleasant squeeze between trying to keep the sewer line open and avoiding admissions that might damage the defense of a subsequent criminal case. Therefore, reactive internal investigations should be conducted soon after government action such as service of a search warrant or a notice of violation so that strategic decisions can be made as quickly as possible.

III. VOLUNTARY ENVIRONMENTAL INTERNAL INVESTIGATIONS

Voluntary environmental internal investigations typically are performed for one of two reasons: (1) to ascertain the status of the company's compliance with the environmental statutes and regulations to which the company is subject, and/or (2) to investigate conditions existing on property or at a facility the company contemplates selling or acquiring. The latter is part and parcel of environmental due diligence investigations undertaken by both parties to a real estate transaction or corporate rearrangement, and can be more fully addressed in a treatise focusing on these transactions. Therefore, the following material focuses on compliance audits.

A. *Reasons for Environmental Compliance Audits*

The need for environmental compliance audits is triggered by the fact that many companies and industries are regulated by environmental laws to varying degrees. At minimum, many companies have permits or licenses that are provided by one or more agencies and that are necessary to conduct business. These permits not only authorize the agencies to visit and inspect the company periodically, but also to prepare and submit reports and other technical documents to the agencies. In this growing arena of required permits and documentation, many companies now deem it prudent to conduct internal environmental audits to ensure compliance with all the regulatory requirements.

Internal audits of environmental documentation are becoming more critical as regulatory agencies and prosecutorial offices proceed against companies failing to maintain required documentation. Many permit violations are now misdemeanors carrying strict liability. Others are simply civil violations, which carry no criminal penalties per se, but can cost the company significantly in the form of civil penalties. For example, many of the core federal environmental statutes allow for penalties of up to $33,500 per violation, after adjusting for inflation, with each incident constituting a separate violation.[7] The result can be penalties into the millions, if not billions, of dollars. In this atmosphere, the regulated community has ever-greater incentives to routinely conduct their own audits.

In addition to audits of environmental permits and documentation, other factors encourage companies to conduct voluntary internal investigations. Audits can be conducted facility-by-facility and building-by-building to survey all environmental issues. Internal audits can review the company's discharge, storage, and disposal practices, and can examine disposal equipment, printouts, and other technical aspects of the facility to ensure that there are no hidden equipment or operational deficiencies. Also, audits can look at the potential exposure of employees to harmful substances and reveal whether all proper safeguards are in place and that required disclosures are being made to employees. Companies should not underestimate the OSHA implications of operations subject to environmental regulation, especially now that OSHA matters are being enforced in their own right.[8]

Environmental audits can also be beneficial in discovering and deterring possible criminal prosecutions based on illegal disposals by rogue employees. For example, in large companies, one department may be in charge of all incoming materials; a different department may be in charge of manifesting hazardous waste and hauling it off. If a rogue employee is illegally disposing of hazardous waste, the company may be caught in a situation where the left hand does not know what the right hand is doing. In other words, no one will realize that, given the materials coming into the company and the manufacturing process, much more hazardous waste should be manifested and sent to a permitted treatment, storage, or disposal facility. An environmental audit looking at the big picture will likely discover this problem.

B. *Importance of Periodic Audits by Outside Consultants*

Although most routine audits are conducted by the company's own staff, periodic audits conducted by independent technical experts or consultants

---

7. *See, e.g.,* the Clean Air Act, 42 U.S.C. § 7413(d)(1); the Clean Water Act, 33 U.S.C. § 1319(d); the Resource Conservation and Recovery Act, 42 U.S.C. § 6928(g); the Toxic Substances Control Act, 42 U.S.C. § 2615(a).

8. For example, the district attorney for the County of Los Angeles, California, has a department titled Environmental Crimes MHA Division.

together with lawyers should be considered by companies. The consultant can identify the areas of vulnerability for the company, such as whether the focus should be on air issues, discharges to sewers or waterways, underground tanks, asbestos, or a host of other potential concerns. This work, however, should be done under a lawyer's supervision, and for the purpose of providing legal advice to the company, to attempt to protect the work from disclosure absent a state audit privilege statute.

C. Problems Posed by Audits

Environmental audits should not be conducted cavalierly. At first blush, it seems that an environmental audit is always desirable; however, there are serious problems that can be presented by an internal investigation. For example, what if the environmental audit discovers unknown problems on the premises? Many cases of spills require immediate reporting. If an audit uncovers a recent spill that was not reported to management, it would open the door to problems with regulatory agencies. An audit might also discover a historic problem that did not trigger immediate reporting requirements. Nevertheless, a historic problem would have to be reported at a sale of the property. If the discovered contamination in any way affects groundwater, the company might have to advise a regulatory agency. Once the regulatory agency is advised of a problem, costly preliminary sampling, reports, and subsequently expensive remediation could be required. Although these concerns do not commend an avoidance of auditing, the company should be aware of ramifications that might flow from the result of the audit, and be committed to taking corrective measures if problems are discovered.

Another serious concern presented by an environmental audit is the possible necessity to disclose the findings at a subsequent date. For example, if the company ends up in civil or criminal litigation over environmental issues, the opposing party probably will serve a document request or subpoena *duces tecum* demanding any and all environmental audits conducted by the company. While the company will attempt to protect these documents under various arguments of privilege, including any statutory privilege under state law, a voluntary environmental audit may be more difficult to protect than a consultant's investigation pursuant to a reactive internal company investigation. It is very difficult to persuade a court that a voluntary environmental audit was done in anticipation of litigation and is therefore work product. With regard to attorney-client privilege, it is also difficult to protect pure facts contained in an audit report. The company should therefore realize at the outset that a voluntary environmental audit does not have absolute protection from disclosure.

As a final thought, it should be noted that the Department of Justice continues to evaluate the issue of how to exercise prosecutorial discretion when the violator company has conducted an environmental audit or has disclosed the violations to the government. In short, an environmental audit is perceived by the Department of Justice as an important mitigating factor in favor of the company, especially if all necessary corrective action recommended by the audit has been implemented by the company.[9]

D. *Electronic Records*

Records maintained on electronic media such as disks, hard drives, flash drives, or similar devices used to store company information pose a particular problem to companies. As this new technology evolves and more and more companies utilize these convenient, space-saving methods of information storage, new legal issues are being raised about the ability of government agencies and other regulatory bodies to seize such information. In particular, the prevalence of the use of electronic mail or instant messaging between company employees and contractors is creating a whole new spectrum of records and information potentially subject to government seizure. In fact, courts have taken the view that e-mail and IM messages sent and received on company e-mail systems may be considered "business records" and as such, subject to discovery and production in an investigation or during litigation.[10] As a result, companies must be sure to establish strict policies regarding the use of e-mail and employ comprehensive electronic records management (ERM) systems. Such strategies must recognize that not only must ERM systems address the maintenance, storage, and disposal of electronic records, but also deviations from such practices, as sloppy ERM heightens the risk for civil or criminal liability for improper destruction of records.

E. *Audit Privilege Law*

In order to address some of the uncertainties related to auditing, more then twenty states have enacted environmental audit privilege or immunity laws.[11] Most state laws provide a privilege for an environmental audit report

---

9. *See, e.g.,* June 3, 1991 Memorandum of U.S. Dept. of Justice from Richard B. Stewart, Asst. Attorney General, to all U.S. Attorneys.

10. *See, e.g.,* Andersen v. United States, 544 U.S. 696 (2005).

11. At this time, the following states have enacted such laws: Alaska, Arkansas, Colorado, Idaho, Illinois, Indiana, Iowa, Kansas, Kentucky, Michigan, Minnesota, Mississippi, Montana, Nebraska, Nevada, New Hampshire, New Jersey, Ohio, Oregon, Rhode Island, South Carolina, South Dakota, Texas, Utah, Virginia, and Wyoming.

under certain circumstances, and usually require any environmental violation to be corrected in order for the privilege to apply. In addition, many state laws also provide qualified penalty immunity for voluntary disclosures of violations discovered during an environmental audit. These laws significantly limit the risk of performing environmental audits and then disclosing violations to the regulatory agency. However, as each state's law has different requirements and different benefits, companies should carefully review the state laws to which they are subject in order to best determine how such laws may benefit the company.

Companies also should be careful when using state privilege and immunity laws, since EPA believes it is not bound by these laws and it is possible that a violation that is voluntarily disclosed under a state law may still be subject to enforcement actions by EPA. Companies may also want to consider using EPA's audit policy when disclosing violations of environmental laws, although the policy does not provide a privilege for audit reports and provides limited penalty immunity.[12]

IV. CONCLUSION

In a quickly changing world, all companies that have any exposure to environmental issues should be keenly aware of the increasing role of regulatory agencies and prosecutorial offices in environmental compliance. Companies should have procedures in place to react quickly to any aggressive move by an agency, such as a search warrant, demand to review documents, or notices of violation. The company's quick response to initial indications of environmental problems will greatly enhance a subsequent internal investigation. To avoid environmental problems with regulatory agencies and prosecutorial offices, companies are turning more and more to internal environmental audits. Although there are positive and worthwhile reasons to conduct environmental audits and, indeed, companies should be encouraged to do so, certain areas of concern may arise from unfavorable findings in an environmental audit. Nevertheless, as criminal and civil prosecution by regulatory agencies increases and private-party litigation over contamination escalates, prophylactic environmental audits will undoubtedly increase in importance.

---

12. Incentives for Self-Policing: Discovery, Disclosure, Correction and Prevention of Violations, 65 Fed. Reg. 19,618, (Apr. 11, 2000).

APPENDIX A

U.S. Environmental Protection Agency Inspector Tip List

The U.S. Environmental Protection Agency (EPA) has broad authority to conduct inspections, but that authority varies somewhat statute by statute. Inspections may be routine, based on a tip by an employee or a competitor, or part of an enforcement initiative. EPA may conduct unannounced "surprise" inspections, but most inspections are announced in advance to facilitate scheduling.

Pre-Inspection Preparation. There are a number of steps a facility can take before the inspector arrives to help ensure that the inspection goes smoothly. Indeed, these steps should be taken even before the inspector calls to schedule a visit of the facility:

- **Designate a Point Person.** The facility should designate an employee familiar with environmental matters as well as facility operations (e.g., the environmental manager) as the "Point Person" to accompany the inspector around the facility. It is generally best to identify two Point Persons, in case one is absent or EPA sends more than one inspector to the facility. The names of the Point Persons should be put on a list and given to personnel at reception areas and security gates. The Point Persons should receive some training by counsel regarding appropriate procedures for handling EPA inspections.

- **Establish Procedures for Inspections.** Let employees know what to do when an inspector arrives, whom to notify, and under what conditions the inspector should be provided access to documents and property. This includes advising the Point Person of the circumstances under which the facility will require EPA to obtain a warrant before inspecting the facility. (Warrantless administrative inspections have been upheld by the courts where certain conditions are met.) Facility employees should be instructed to be courteous and truthful, but not to speculate in response to an inspector's questions. Some facilities include written procedures for handling EPA inspections in their environmental training programs.

- **Consider Whether Counsel Should Be Present.** Unless counsel is readily available, most facilities do not ask counsel to be present for announced, routine environmental inspections. However, it is generally advisable for counsel to be present where (a) the inspection is non-routine or unannounced, (b) an EPA or state enforcement action is already threatened or pending, or (c) there are indications that EPA is investigating allegations of criminal activity. Even where it has been decided that counsel need not be present, counsel should always be forewarned of an impending inspection so that arrangements can be made to contact counsel by telephone in case questions arise as to the scope of the inspection and access to company records or employees.

- **Pump the Inspector for Information.** When the inspector calls to schedule the inspection, find out as much as possible about the inspection, including: (a) the statutory authority under which the inspection will be conducted; (b) the portions of the facility that will be inspected; (c) how long the inspection will last; (d) what prompted the inspection; (e) whether the inspection is part of a new enforcement initiative; (f) how many inspectors will be coming; and (g) whether the inspector intends to collect samples. Document the discussion, perhaps with a confirming letter to the inspector.

- **Review Recordkeeping.** Recordkeeping violations are a favorite target of EPA inspectors. At a minimum, relevant employees should refresh their recollections as to where key documents (hazardous waste manifests, spill contingency plans, permits) are kept, and be sure records are maintained in an orderly fashion. Good recordkeeping makes a very positive impression on an inspector. On the other hand, fumbling around for key documents will raise suspicions that the facility does not take environmental requirements seriously.

Prior to the inspection is also a good time to determine which of the facility's records will be off limits to inspectors (such as attorney-client correspondence or environmental audits) and which will be made available to inspectors but claimed as "confidential business information" (CBI) (e.g., trade secrets). These materials should be segregated and properly labeled prior to the inspection.

- **Take Corrective Actions.** Be sure that items noted in previous inspections have been corrected. If time permits, consult the relevant EPA inspection manual to determine areas of likely interest. Do a quick compliance check and fix what you can. Clean up messy operations, even if they are not violations.

- **Define Scope of Physical Access.** Decide which areas, if any, may be off limits to the EPA inspector due to safety or other requirements. Be sure to follow food safety and worker health and safety requirements (goggles, hard hats) where applicable.
- **Notify Employees.** Inform employees of the impending inspection and remind them of facility procedures for inspections.

During the Inspection. Once the inspector arrives, the inspector should be met by the Point Person. The Point Person should check the inspector's credentials, review any warrants, and be sure that the warrant is limited to the agreed-upon scope. This is also the time to review and confirm any previously agreed-upon procedures. If possible, the Point Person should attempt to establish an order for the inspection, explain the facility's operations, and identify any trade secret concerns.

During the inspection:

- **Do as the Inspector Does.** The Point Person should accompany the inspector at all times. If the inspector takes notes or photos, the Point Person should as well. If the inspector wants a copy of certain records, make one for the facility as well. If the inspector takes a sample, the facility should seek to obtain a split sample. Also, the Point Person should obtain receipts for any samples or original documents taken.
- **Cooperate, but Don't Speculate.** Federal law prohibits knowingly and willfully falsifying or concealing material facts from, or making false or fraudulent statements of material facts to, the United States. Accordingly, it is important to answer the inspector's questions truthfully. The Point Person should promise to get back to the inspector when the answer to the inspector's question is not known, and then do so in a timely matter. To the extent possible, the Point Person should seek to limit the inspector's questioning of other facility employees.
- **Identify the Inspector.** Make sure all employees know that the inspector is an EPA employee evaluating the facility's environmental compliance (not "the EPA person"—which could mean an in-house environmental expert). If the inspector wants to formally interview specific individuals, legal counsel should be notified immediately.
- **Claim CBI If Applicable.** If EPA copies records that contain trade secrets, make sure that the facility notifies EPA that it is claiming the

records as CBI. Failure to claim CBI at this point may waive the facility's claim.

- **Request an Exit Conference.** Although most inspectors will ultimately send an inspection report to the inspected facility, this may take many months, by which time the Point Person's recollection of the inspection may be unclear. Accordingly, the Point Person should request an exit interview and learn as much as possible about the inspector's findings in the interview. Sometimes it is possible to get the inspector to share his or her completed inspection checklist at the exit interview. Discuss the inspector's conclusions and make sure that they are not based on inadequate information or a misunderstanding.

Post Inspection Follow-up. Following the inspection:

- Correct whatever violations or potential violations you can, as quickly as possible. This not only demonstrates a cooperative attitude to EPA, but cuts off additional "per day" penalties.
- If additional information was promised to the inspector, provide it as promptly as possible.
- Have the Point Person prepare a memorandum summarizing the inspection and the exit conference. Appropriate facility management should be informed of the results of the inspection. If possible violations were noted, counsel should be contacted to evaluate proper next steps.
- Obtain the inspection report, either from the inspector directly or by requesting it through the Freedom of Information Act. Notify the Agency of any errors in the report, promptly and in writing.

Report of the Investigation

10

Edwin G. Schallert and Natalie R. Williams

I. INTRODUCTION 302
II. DISCOVERABILITY OF THE INTERNAL INVESTIGATIVE REPORT 304
   A. Attorney-Client Privilege 305
   B. Work-Product Doctrine: A More Certain Refuge 308
   C. Expanding the Privilege of Self-Criticism 310
III. PROTECTING THE REPORT: SHAREHOLDER ACTIONS AND DISCLOSURE TO GOVERNMENT AGENCIES 312
   A. Shareholder Actions 312
   B. Disclosure to Government Agencies 315
IV. LIBEL 319
   A. Written Reports May Invite Libel Claims 319
   B. Example of Libel Claims against Counsel 321
   C. Opinion and Qualified Interest Privileges 322
   D. Strategies for Minimizing Liability for Defamation 329

Edwin G. Schallert is a partner at Debevoise & Plimpton in New York, New York. Natalie R. Williams is Chief of the Civil Rights Bureau of the Office of the New York State Attorney General in New York, New York.

V. CONCLUSION 331
   A. Summary 331
   B. Minimizing Risks 331

I. INTRODUCTION

AT FIRST GLANCE, a written investigative report may seem an indispensable conclusion to an internal corporate investigation. One might conclude, for example, that there is no better way to persuade corporate officials of the necessity of remedial action, or government lawyers of the legality of your position, than a well-reasoned, comprehensive statement in writing. To some, a written report is preferable to purely oral discussions between counsel and client for any of the following reasons:

- Often providing detailed information about questionable business activities and their legal implications, the report can be a valuable aid for corporate management in deciding what steps, if any, to take in addressing the matter.
- If wrongdoing is identified, a report offers tangible evidence that an internal corporate investigation has been performed and that corrective action is under way. This may forestall a more intrusive government investigation and can be used in settlement negotiations with government agencies.
- Government agencies may require the preparation of a written report and access to it, or at least a summary of the report.
- When not required by government counsel, a detailed report of fact and law may be an important tool in persuading government lawyers that misconduct did not occur and that criminal or civil proceedings should not be brought.
- In the context of a derivative action, a written report may be used as evidence in support of a motion by the board of directors to terminate a lawsuit.

Yet these benefits are accompanied by a variety of risks, all quite serious.

- A written report may contain "smoking-gun" evidence that, if discovered in later litigation, may spawn or strengthen lawsuits against the client that commissioned the report.
- Production of a report to a government agency may result in the loss of all legal privileges associated with preparing the report, opening up virtually all underlying files in the agency investigation, as well as later, related private litigation.

- Production to government lawyers may result in the affirmative use by the agency and possibly civil litigants of any "admissions" within the report, under Federal Rule of Evidence 801(d)(2).
- The conceptual inconsistencies that surround application of established privileges can make these documents susceptible to discovery by a host of adverse parties. Consider several actual examples:
  - Shareholders in a securities fraud action were granted discovery of an internal investigative report prepared by company counsel pursuant to a consent decree with the Securities and Exchange Commission.[1]
  - An internal investigative report commissioned by a company to investigate allegations of fraudulent business dealings on the part of corporate employees was initially held to be not exempt from disclosure to a civil litigant.[2]
  - Third parties were granted access to internal investigative reports that had been voluntarily disclosed to government agencies.[3]
  - On the basis of an internal investigative report prepared while a lawyer in private practice, a former Attorney General was sued for libel by an employee identified in the report as having knowingly assisted in the orchestration of a multimillion-dollar check-kiting scheme.[4]
  - Lawyers conducting an internal investigation found that when the allegations underlying the investigation later resulted in a lawsuit, they were unable to act as trial counsel because opposing counsel designated them as fact witnesses at trial.[5]

In short, internal investigative reports can cause disputes as well as resolve them. And, not infrequently, lawyers and clients have wished the reports had never been prepared.

In light of the serious risks that attend its preparation, a written report should be avoided where possible in favor of an oral report presented to select corporate officers, special committees, or members of the board of directors.

---

1. Osterneck v. E.T. Barwick Indus., 82 F.R.D. 81, 87 (N.D. Ga. 1979).

2. Spectrum Sys. Int'l Corp. v. Chemical Bank, 157 A.D.2d 444, 558 N.Y.S.2d 486 (1st Dept., 1990), *rev'd*, 78 N.Y.2d 371, N.E.2d 1055, 575 N.Y.S.2d 809 (1991).

3. *In re* Subpoena Duces Tecum (Fulbright & Jaworski), 738 F.2d 1367 (D.C. Cir. 1984) (disclosure to SEC implied waiver of both attorney-client and work-product privileges); *In re* Sealed Case, 676 F.2d 793, 818 (D.C. Cir. 1982) ("selective disclosure for tactical purposes waives the privilege"); Permian Corp. v. United States, 665 F.2d 1214 (D.C. Cir. 1981).

4. Pearce v. E.F. Hutton Group, 664 F. Supp. 1490 (D.D.C. 1987).

5. *See* Burton, *Baxter Fails to Quell Questions on Its Role in the Israeli Boycott*, WALL ST. J., Apr. 25, 1991, at A10.

The oral report minimizes many, though not all, of the risks associated with conducting an investigation, since the primary documents used in making the presentation, counsel's notes, are afforded virtual absolute protection under the work-product doctrine.[6] An oral report provides needed flexibility to investigative counsel if ever compelled to testify about the investigation and its findings. Conversely, a written report necessarily confines later testimony to the expressed statement of facts, opinions, and conclusions found within the report. Furthermore, without a written analysis, adverse parties have no Rule 801(d)(2) admissions and no road map on which to rely later.

In instances when a written report is considered essential, either as a means of dissuading government action or of spurring remedial action within the company, the issue then becomes how best to structure the report and the underlying internal investigation to minimize the risks of discovery and liability for counsel.

This chapter focuses on the most significant problems surrounding the written internal investigative report and suggests methods for minimizing those problems. First, the chapter examines the courts' application of the attorney-client and work-product doctrines in the context of the internal investigative report. Next, the issue of libel liability for counsel preparing the report is addressed, analyzing the applicability of the "opinion" and common-law qualified, "interest-related" privileges to the written report. Finally, the chapter recommends strategies for structuring the investigation and reporting to the company, whether orally or in writing.

II. DISCOVERABILITY OF THE INTERNAL INVESTIGATIVE REPORT

The attorney-client privilege and the work-product doctrine have been the principal legal devices used to protect corporate internal investigative reports and their underlying documentation from discovery. The protection afforded to investigative reports by these privileges has been neither complete nor wholly predictable.[7]

---

6. Counsel's notes and other investigative information are generally characterized as "opinion work product." *See infra* notes 25-29 and accompanying text. *See also* Upjohn Co. v. United States, 449 U.S. 383, 399 (1980) ("[f]orcing an attorney to disclose notes and memoranda of witnesses' oral statements is particularly disfavored because it tends to reveal the attorney's mental processes").

7. The discussion of the attorney-client privilege and work-product doctrine within this chapter is not intended as a comprehensive treatment of the law in this area; instead, it is provided to remind the lawyer conducting the investigation that the inadvertent discovery of a

A. Attorney-Client Privilege

The attorney-client privilege exists to "encourage full and frank communication between attorneys and their clients ... [since] sound legal advice or advocacy serves public ends and ... depends upon the lawyer's being fully informed."[8] Because the privilege is concerned with protecting the relationship between the lawyer and the client,[9] a critical element of a successful claim of privilege is that the contested communications be for the purpose of securing legal advice.

1. Ensuring Privilege Entails Rendering Legal Advice

If the lawyer conducting an internal investigation was hired to render legal advice and the report in fact reflects this advice, it should be privileged. Some courts, however, take the narrow view that a lawyer's investigation of the facts makes the lawyer more like a private eye than a lawyer and the report is not privileged. This view confuses the state of the law and undercuts a lawyer's rightful function.

Most courts have examined both the context of the internal investigation and the resulting report to determine whether a lawyer was employed to render legal advice or mere investigative services.[10] Courts have considered the circumstances of the lawyers' initial engagement in the matter, the tasks performed during the course of the investigation, and the content of the investigative report, focusing on whether the document contained "legal" opinions or "business" recommendations. The mere fact that lawyers were employed to conduct the investigation has not guaranteed a successful claim of privilege under the attorney-client doctrine.[11]

One court has concluded that the participation of lawyers in an internal investigation provided prima facie evidence that the purpose of the communications was to secure legal advice.[12] *Diversified Industries* involved an internal investigation into an alleged "slush fund" maintained by the company allegedly to bribe purchasing agents, including the plaintiff. The board of directors of Diversified commissioned outside counsel to conduct an internal

---

written report can likely be avoided when counsel keeps uppermost in mind basic principles of privilege. For a complete discussion of these legal doctrines, see Chapter 2.

8. Upjohn v. United States, 449 U.S. 383, 389 (1981).
9. United States v. United Shoe Mach. Corp., 89 F. Supp. 357 (D. Mass. 1950).
10. *See In re* Grand Jury Subpoena Duces Tecum, 731 F.2d 1032, 1037-38 (2d Cir. 1984).
11. *See In re* Grand Jury Subpoena, 599 F.2d 504, 511 (2d Cir. 1979) ("[p]articipation of the general counsel does not automatically cloak the investigation with legal garb").
12. Diversified Indus., Inc. v. Meredith, 572 F.2d 596 (8th Cir. 1977) (en banc).

investigation into the matter. After a preliminary review, outside counsel prepared a memorandum stating that it would examine relevant records and recommend that the corporation engage an independent accounting firm to assist in the investigation. The final report, which the plaintiff sought through discovery, included the substance of statements made by interviewees, the findings of the accountants, and recommendations by both the firm and the accountants. While a panel of the court originally determined that outside counsel "was employed solely for the purpose of making an investigation of facts and to make business recommendations with respect to the future conduct of Diversified" and that the work done by outside counsel "could have been performed just as readily by non-lawyers aided to the extent necessary by a firm of public accountants," the Court of Appeals for the Eighth Circuit sitting en banc reasoned that, while accountants and lay investigators could have just as easily interviewed the employees, "neither would have had the training, skills, and background necessary to make the independent analysis and recommendations which the Board felt essential to the future welfare of the corporation."[13] The en banc court further observed that "the application of the attorney-client privilege to this matter and others like it will encourage corporations to seek out and correct wrongdoing in their own house and to do so with lawyers who are obligated by the Code of Professional Responsibility to conduct the inquiry in an independent and ethical manner."[14]

Other courts have reacted differently. Noting that a lawyer's particular expertise in interviewing witnesses and compiling and evaluating data makes the lawyer an ideal candidate for performing an internal investigation, courts have often reasoned that the use of such skills in an internal investigation does not mean that the lawyer was employed for his legal expertise or for the purpose of securing legal advice.[15]

For example, in *Spectrum Systems Int'l Co. v. Chemical Bank*,[16] an internal investigative report prepared by an outside law firm to examine allegations of fraudulent business dealings between certain bank employees and the company's outside vendors was sought in a civil suit. An intermediate appellate court held that the report was not exempt from disclosure to the civil liti-

---

13. *Id.* at 608, 610.
14. *Id.*
15. Osterneck v. E. T. Barwick Indus., 82 F.R.D. at 85; *see also In re* Grand Jury Subpoena, 599 F.2d at 510-11 (documents resulting from an internal investigation conducted by senior management and general counsel into alleged foreign bribes were not within scope of attorney-client privilege).
16. 78 N.Y.2d 371, 581 N.E.2d 1055, 575 N.Y.S.2d 809 (1991).

gant in a suit for nonpayment of consulting services. The court reasoned that outside counsel's role was that of investigator as opposed to legal advisor.[17] On appeal, New York's highest court reversed, concluding that the report was made primarily to give legal advice.[18]

2. Required Report May Not Be Privileged

Courts have also considered the "voluntariness" of the corporation's decision to conduct an internal investigation. In *Osterneck v. E. T. Barwick Industries*,[19] an internal investigative report prepared by outside counsel was held discoverable by shareholders in an action alleging securities fraud. The court reasoned that the lack of "voluntariness" in the corporation's decision to conduct the investigation—the internal investigation was commissioned pursuant to a consent decree with the SEC—indicated that counsel engaged to perform the investigation had been employed solely "to investigate and report."[20] The court specifically stated that it could take notice of the fact that "the decision to set up the [Special Review Committee] and hire special counsel was not reached independently or voluntarily." Another court reached a different result, recognizing a "hybrid" privilege in connection with investigations by special counsel hired pursuant to an SEC consent decree.[21]

3. The Better Rule

The assessment in these cases of the lawyer's role in the internal corporate investigation is questionable. First, because the lawyer's task often involves compiling relevant facts to form a legal opinion, the distinction between investigative and legal activities suggested in these cases is typically blurred. Second, in the corporate context, the demarcation between business advice and legal advice is especially fuzzy. The corporate lawyer's role is often to ascertain how, within the constraints of relevant legal obligations, the corporation should structure its business to achieve desired objectives. Moreover, in the context of the internal investigation, it is the suspected violation

---

17. 157 A.D. 2d 444, 588 N.Y.S.2d 486 (1st Dept. 1990). The court also noted that no standard legal tasks, such as legal research, had been performed by the lawyers in course of the investigation.

18. 78 N.Y.2d 371, 581 N.E.2d 1055, 575 N.Y.S.2d 809. Investigative reports prepared by inside counsel have been subjected to even greater scrutiny because these individuals often provide business as well as legal advice. *See In re* Grand Jury Subpoena, 599 F.2d at 510-11.

19. 82 F.R.D. 81 (N.D. Ga. 1979).

20. *Id.* at 85.

21. *See In re* LTV Civ. Litig., 89 F.R.D. 595, 618-22 (N.D. Tex. 1981).

of a *legal* obligation that typically triggers the investigation. In these instances, the strands of business and legal advice cannot be easily disentangled.

Some courts also fail to consider perhaps the most important policy behind maintaining confidentiality of the internal investigative report: the promotion of corporate self-policing.[22] Uncertainty as to whether the internal investigative report is protected by the attorney-client privilege can only serve as a disincentive to corporations deciding whether to commission an internal investigation.

B. *Work-Product Doctrine: A More Certain Refuge*

The purpose of the work-product doctrine is to promote the adversarial system by protecting a lawyer's preparation on behalf of his or her client from discovery. Codifying the doctrine set forth in *Hickman v. Taylor*,[23] Rule 26(b)(3) delineates the elements of the work product protection for the federal courts and provides that documents or tangible things, prepared in anticipation of litigation or for trial, by or for another party or by or for that party's representative, are protected against discovery unless the party seeking disclosure can demonstrate substantial need, and that it would experience undue hardship about discovery.

1. Internal Investigations "in Anticipation of Litigation"

The "in anticipation of litigation" requirement has not posed a significant barrier to the protection of internal investigative reports from discovery. Most courts have recognized that once the suspicion of wrongdoing rises to the level where an internal investigation is commissioned, litigation is virtually inevitable, particularly where the investigation confirms wrongdoing. This recognition applies to a variety of actions, whether brought by shareholders, governmental agencies, or other parties.[24]

---

22. However, the suspicion that "many internal probes are really velvet-coated cover-ups" may cause courts to be skeptical of invocations of this policy. One article notes that many legislators believe that after "the company's lawyers have framed the issues and defined the events, [the] written report can serve as a road map to help corporate officials orient their stories." Strasser, *Dicey Dilemmas: Corporate Probe Use Expanding,* NAT'L L.J., Jan. 9, 1989, at 1.

23. 329 U.S. 495 (1947).

24. *See In re* Grand Jury Investigation, 599 F.2d 1224, 1228-30 (3d Cir. 1979) (when internal investigation was prompted by suspected criminal violations, "litigation of some sort was almost inevitable"); *In re* LTV Sec. Litig., 89 F.R.D. 595, 612 (N.D. Tex. 1981) ("[i]nvestigation by a federal agency presents more than a 'remote prospect' of future litigation and gives grounds for anticipating litigation sufficient for the work product rule to apply"); United States v. Lipshy, 492 F. Supp. 35, 44 (N.D. Tex. 1979) (bribery allegations and a simultaneous

2. Reports That Receive Protection from Discovery

The qualified work-product doctrine can be overcome in some circumstances by a showing of substantial need and undue hardship. Opinion work product, defined as material that reveals the lawyer's opinions, conclusions, and mental impressions, receives near-absolute protection.[25] By contrast, ordinary work product, inherently factual in nature and not reflective of the lawyer's mental processes, is provided markedly less protection.[26]

The concept of opinion work product offers substantial assistance in efforts to protect internal investigative reports from discovery: the more the report reflects the lawyer's evaluative tasks, as opposed to mere factual findings, the greater the likelihood that the report, or substantial portions of it, will be characterized as opinion work product.[27] Indeed, some statements,

---

IRS investigation "rendered the prospect of litigation sufficiently likely"); *but see* Litton Sys., Inc. v. American Tel. & Tel. Co., 27 Fed. R. Serv. 2d 819, 821 (S.D.N.Y. 1979) (internal investigation concerning allegedly illegal activity by employees suggested only a "remote possibility" of litigation, insufficient to trigger work product immunity). *See also* cases cited *infra* at 48-49.

25. Parties seeking disclosure of documents defined as opinion work product must make a showing of extraordinary need. As the Supreme Court noted in *Upjohn*, "a far stronger showing of necessity and unavailability . . . would be necessary to compel disclosure" of opinion work product. 449 U.S. at 402. The Court, however, declined to decide whether such materials were entitled to absolute protection. Some lower courts, however, have held that opinion work product is afforded absolute protection. *In re* Echostar Comm. Corp., 448 F.3d 1294, 1302 (Fed. Cir. 2006) (courts are "require[d]" to "protect against the disclosure of mental impressions, conclusions, opinions or legal theories of an attorney"). *In re* Martin-Marietta Corp., 856 F.2d 619, 626 (4th Cir. 1988), *cert. denied,* 109 S. Ct. 1655 (1989) ("First and most generally, opinion work product is to be accorded great protection by the courts. While certainly actual disclosure of pure mental impressions may be deemed waiver, and while conceivably there may be indirect waiver in extreme circumstances, we think generally such work product is not subject to discovery."). *In re* Grand Jury Investigation (Sturgis), 412 F. Supp. 943, 949 (1976) ("[interview notes] are so much a product of the lawyer's thinking and so little probative of the witness's actual words that they are absolutely protected from disclosure."); *In re* Grand Jury Proceedings (Duffy), 473 F.2d 840, 848 (8th Cir. 1973) (while "statements prepared or signed by the interviewee" may be discovered upon a showing of good cause, "attorney's personal recollections, notes, and memoranda" may not).

26. Though the determination of whether the particular circumstances merit discovery of ordinary work product is made on a case-by-case basis, courts have considered the nature of the materials requested, the effort entailed in compiling the information, the availability of alternative sources of information, the relevance of the materials to the issues presented, and the procedural posture in which the claim arises in making this evaluation.

27. Often, in analyzing claims of privilege under the work-product doctrine, the courts will perform an in camera review of the documents in order to better evaluate the requesting party's need or undue hardship. If the requesting party carries its burden of demonstrating substantial need and undue hardship, the in camera review will enable the courts to excise those parts constituting opinion work product.

seemingly factual in nature, may be protected as opinion work product if by discovery the adverse party would be able to ascertain counsel's thought processes or line of reasoning. Consequently, where the report is written in a way that minimizes verbatim statements by interviewees and provides as much of the information as possible in the form of opinion or evaluation, the report is more likely to receive near-total protection from discovery.[28] One should keep clearly in mind, however, that the greater the reliance on subjective opinion and mental impressions, the greater the harm should the report be discovered through inadvertent waiver.

While the foregoing doctrines offer substantial assistance to clients desiring to protect internal investigative reports from discovery, a more tailored framework in which to evaluate these claims would be the privilege of self-critical analysis.[29]

C. *Expanding the Privilege of Self-Criticism*

Although the self-criticism privilege has generally protected only corporate materials prepared for required government reports, the rationale behind this privilege is consistent with that favoring protection of internal investigative reports of corporate wrongdoing from discovery: promoting the public interest in encouraging institutional self-policing. As a result, the self-criticism privilege offers perhaps a more appropriate analytical framework than either the attorney-client privilege or work-product doctrine.

1. Self-Criticism Privilege Encourages Open Exchange

First fashioned in *Bredice v. Doctor; Hospital, Inc.*,[30] the privilege of self-criticism was held to protect from discovery in a malpractice suit the minutes and reports of a hospital investigative committee charged with the task of improving hospital care. The *Bredice* court reasoned that since confidentiality was critical to the committee's evaluative task, disclosure would

---

28. In some cases, however, the court has granted discovery of opinion work product where it was impossible to redact the contested documents "in such a way as to allow production of the needed facts without disclosing a lawyer's mental impression, opinions, or legal theories." *See* AMERICAN BAR ASSOCIATION, THE ATTORNEY-CLIENT PRIVILEGE AND WORK-PRODUCT DOCTRINE, at 109 (1989), *discussing* Xerox Corp. v. Int'l Bus. Mach. Co., 64 F.R.D. 367 (S.D.N.Y. 1974).

29. As one commentator noted, if the goal of courts analyzing discovery attempts of internal investigative reports and underlying documentation was to encourage corporate self-investigation, the selection of the "attorney-client privilege and work product immunity as the vehicles for protecti[on]" was not the best. Note, *Discovery of Internal Corporate Investigations,* 32 STAN. L. REV. 1163, 1177 (1980).

30. 50 F.R.D. 249 (D.D.C. 1970), *aff'd,* 479 F.2d 920 (D.C. Cir. 1973).

greatly diminish the frank and open exchange necessary for effective internal review; the important public interest in health care required that these discussions be encouraged. Balancing the public interest in improved health care against the individual's need for discovery, the court denied discovery of the committee minutes.

2. Self-Criticism Privilege Offers Uncertain Haven

In the corporate context, the self-criticism privilege, rooted in the *Bredice* public interest rationale, has protected internal corporate reports examining equal employment opportunity practices, consultants' evaluation of sexual harassment and assault prevention policies, and information on intracompany complaints.[31] Though no clear guidelines have been articulated, documents qualifying for protection under the self-criticism privilege have satisfied the following criteria: (1) the document has resulted from a critical self-analysis undertaken by the party desiring protection; (2) the public has a strong interest in maintaining the free flow of information of the type sought; and (3) the information is of the type whose flow would be stifled without protection.[32] Courts in some jurisdictions also require a showing that the information was prepared with the expectation that it would be kept confidential.[33] Some courts have defined the scope of the privilege in terms of subjective or evaluative materials reminiscent of a distinction found in the context of the work-product doctrine.[34] The self-criticism privilege has also been held inapplicable against government entities.[35]

Despite the broad range of documents ostensibly meeting these criteria, the courts have been hesitant to grant the privilege broad application given its

---

31. *See* Reid v. Lockheed Martin Aeronautics Co., 199 F.R.D. 379 (N.D. Ga. 2001); McAllister v. Royal Caribbean Cruises, Ltd., No. Civ. A. 02-2393, 2004 WL 2216487, at *1 (E.D. Pa. Oct. 4, 2004); O'Connor v. Chrysler Corp., 86 F.R.D. 211 (D. Mass. 1980). While a number of courts have expressly rejected the self-criticism privilege, *see* Friermuth v. PPG Indus., Inc., 218 F.R.D. 694, 697 (N.D. Ala. 2003), some courts have approved its rationale. *See* Note, *Criticizing the Self-Criticism Privilege,* 1987 ILL. L. REV. 675, 679-80 (1984).

32. Note, *The Privilege of Self-Critical Analysis,* 96 HARV. L. REV. 1083, 1086 (1983).

33. *See e.g.,* Hobley v. Burge, No. 03 C3678, 2006 WL 1460028, at *2 (N.D. Ill. May 24, 2006); E.B. v. New York City Bd. of Educ., 233 F.R.D. 289, 296 (E.D.N.Y. 2005).

34. Lloyd v. Cessna Aircraft Co., 74 F.R.D. 518 (E.D. Tenn. 1977) (product list not protected); O'Connor v. Chrysler Corp., 86 F.R.D. 211, 218 (D. Mass. 1980) (facts upon which self-evaluative report is based are discoverable); Roberts v. National Detroit Corp., 87 F.R.D. 30, 32 (E.D. Mich. 1980) (while statistical information is discoverable, evaluation of institutional goals is not); Wright v. Patrolmen's Benevolent Ass'n, 72 F.R.D. 161, 164 (S.D.N.Y. 1976) (witnesses' names and statements are not protected).

35. Federal Trade Comm'n. v. TRW, 628 F.2d 207, 211 (D.C. Cir. 1980); United States v. Noall, 587 F.2d 123, 126 (2d Cir. 1978), *cert. denied,* 441 U.S. 923 (1979).

undefined scope.[36] The Court of Appeals for the Seventh Circuit, for example, has expressly declined to recognize a privilege of self-critical analysis for internal corporate investigations examining suspected corporate improprieties.[37] In a case implicating not the self-criticism privilege but rather its principal rationale—the encouragement of free, frank evaluations concerning matters in which the public has an interest—the Supreme Court refused to recognize a qualified privilege shielding tenure peer review materials from disclosure, reasoning, in part, that the "chilling effect" on frank evaluation of academics by their colleagues caused by the absence of such a privilege, was, at best, speculative.[38] Judicial apprehension about a broad self-criticism privilege may stem from the Supreme Court's admonitions against the expansion of existing, and the creation of new, privilege doctrines.[39]

III. PROTECTING THE REPORT: SHAREHOLDER ACTIONS AND DISCLOSURE TO GOVERNMENT AGENCIES

A. *Shareholder Actions*

Shareholder suits, whether derivative or stockholder class actions, present a conceptual dilemma for the attorney-client privilege due to the fiduciary relationship that exists between the corporation and its shareholders. Because

---

36. Rule 501 of the Federal Rules of Evidence leaves the formulation of new privileges to the courts. It states, in relevant part:

> Except as otherwise required by the Constitution of the United States or provided by Act of Congress or in rules prescribed by the Supreme Court . . . the privilege of a witness . . . shall be governed by the principles of the common law as they may be interpreted by the courts of the United States in the light of reason and experience.

FED. R. EVID. 501.

37. *In re* Continental Illinois Sec. Litig., 732 F.2d 1302, 1315 (7th Cir. 1984) ("There is no general privilege, analogous to the fifth amendment's protection against self-incrimination, that protects against disclosure of information that may lead to civil liability.").

38. University of Penn. v. EEOC, 110 S. Ct. 577, 587-88 (1990). Reasoning that the asserted injury to the academic freedom was "speculative," the Court stated: "Although it is possible that some evaluators may become less candid as the possibility of disclosure increases, others may simply ground their evaluations in specific examples and illustrations in order to deflect potential claims of bias or unfairness."

39. *See, e.g.,* University of Penn. v. EEOC, 110 S. Ct. at 588 (Supreme Court is reluctant to recognize constitutional privileges of uncertain scope and application); Wei v. Bodner, 127 F.R.D. 91, 100 (D.N.J. 1989) (*Bredice* rationale is "questionable" in light of Supreme Court decisions in United States v. Nixon, 418 U.S. 683, 710 (1974) (stating "these exceptions to the demand for every man's evidence are not lightly created nor expansively construed, for they are in derogation of the search for truth"), and Herbert v. Lando, 441 U.S. 153, 175 (1979) (stating that "[e]videntiary privileges in litigation are not favored")).

the corporation exists for the benefit of the shareholders, allowing the corporation free rein to assert the privilege against these same shareholders appears anomalous. On the other hand, the corporation will need to seek legal advice free from fear of disclosure to individual shareholders who may not represent the best interests of the majority of stockholders.

1. Company May Not Own the Privilege or Report

To strike an appropriate balance between the interests of shareholders and those of the corporation, several courts have incorporated a "good-cause" exception into the attorney-client privilege. The good-cause exception holds that the corporation maintains the right to assert the privilege in a shareholder suit "subject to the right of the stockholders to show cause why it should not be invoked in the particular instance."[40]

---

40. Garner v. Wolfinbarger, 430 F.2d 1093, 1104 (5th Cir. 1970), *cert. denied,* 401 U.S. 974 (1971). The following factors were deemed relevant in making the "good cause" assessment:

> [T]he number of shareholders and the percentage of stock they represent; the bona fides of the shareholders; the nature of the shareholders' claim and whether it is obviously colorable; the apparent necessity or desirability of the shareholders having the information and the availability of it from other sources; whether, if the shareholders' claim is of wrongful action by the corporation, it is of action criminal, or illegal but not criminal, or of doubtful legality; whether the communication related to past or to prospective actions; whether the communication is of advice concerning the litigation itself; the extent to which the communication is identified versus the extent to which the shareholders are blindly fishing; the risk of revelation of trade secrets or other information in whose confidentiality the corporation has an interest for independent reasons.

Garner has been an influential decision, with some courts extending its rationale to fiduciary relationships outside the shareholder derivative context, as well as situations where the fiduciary relationship did not exist at the time of the communication. *See, e.g.,* Quintel Corp. v. Citibank, 567 F. Supp. 1357 (S.D.N.Y. 1983) (*Garner* applied to fiduciary relationship between bank and its client in context of a real estate transaction); Cohen v. Uniroyal, 80 F.R.D. 480, 484 (E.D. Pa. 1978) (*Garner* applied although no fiduciary relationship existed at the time communications were made). In light of these expansions of the *Garner* doctrine and their concomitant effect on the corporation's ability to assert the attorney-client privilege, some courts have criticized *Garner*'s logic and attempted narrowly to confine its scope. *See, e.g.,* Shirvani v. Capital Investing Corp., Inc., 112 F.R.D. 389, 390-91 (D. Conn. 1986) ("[t]he *Garner* problem is perhaps that the shareholder or other owed a duty of trust becomes too readily and artificially recognized as the 'client' for purpose of privilege."); Weil v. Investment/Indicators Research & Mgmt., Inc., 647 F.2d 18 (9th Cir. 1981) (refusing to extend *Garner* outside the context of shareholder derivative actions); Ward v. Succession of Freeman, 854 F.2d 780, 785 (5th Cir. 1988) ("clear that *Garner* did not establish an absolute exception to the attorney-client privilege rule"); *but see In re* Int'l Sys. & Controls Corp. Sec. Litig., 693 F.2d 1235, 1239 n.1 (5th Cir. 1982) (rejecting Ninth Circuit's limitation of the *Garner* doctrine solely to shareholder derivative actions).

If discoverable by shareholders, the internal investigative report could provide damning evidence of corporate wrongdoing, thereby laying the foundation for shareholders' claims. Moreover, facts revealed in the internal investigative report could spawn lawsuits not previously contemplated. Given the threat of these consequences, corporations may be less likely to undertake internal investigations and to document those findings in a written report.

Recognizing the "great injury to the corporate interest in self investigation,"[41] courts have imposed a temporal limitation on the application of the good-cause exception. The exception has been held not to apply to "after-the-fact" communications concerning offenses already completed."[42] This distinction stems from a recognition that, after wrongdoing is complete, management will need to seek assistance from counsel. The internal investigative report, generally a post-event examination and evaluation of allegedly improper corporate practices, seems to fall within this category of protected post-event communications.

Whatever the status of the corporation's attorney-client privilege against its own shareholders, the work product protection should be available. It exists to protect information in the context of anticipated or pending litigation—exactly when shareholders seek information. Rejecting the application of the *Garner* good-cause exception in the context of the work-product doctrine, the Fifth Circuit, in *In re International Systems & Controls Corp.*,[43] reasoned that once there was a sufficient anticipation of litigation to trigger work product immunity, the "mutuality of interest" upon which the *Garner* exception is predicated is destroyed.

2. Affirmative Use Requires Production to Dissident Shareholders

The internal investigative report commissioned by a special litigation committee to evaluate the merits of a shareholder derivative action is in a

---

41. *In re* LTV Sec. Litig., 89 F.R.D. 595, 608 (N.D. Tex. 1981).
42. *Id.* at 607.
43. 693 F.2d 1235, 1239 (5th Cir. 1982). In that case, the corporation, desiring to enroll in the SEC's voluntary disclosure program, appointed a special audit committee to commission an internal investigation that was conducted by an outside law firm, assisted by independent accountants. Subsequently, a consent decree was negotiated with the SEC. A derivative action shortly followed, and the stockholders sought access to certain information found in the accountants' binders. The court held that the *Garner* doctrine should not be extended to the work-product doctrine, because once the threshold of "anticipation of litigation" sufficient to trigger work product immunity has been reached, the "mutuality of interest" between corporation and shareholders no longer exists.

different class. If the report is being used to support a motion by the board of directors to dismiss the action, courts have held that it is freely discoverable by shareholders and other third parties. In *Joy v. North*,[44] the Second Circuit ruled that the corporation could not use the attorney-client privilege to shield its investigative report from shareholders when it sought to assert the report as evidence in support of its motion to terminate. In *In re Continental Illinois Securities Litigation*,[45] a newspaper covering a shareholder suit was granted access to an internal investigative report that had been placed into evidence to support a motion to terminate the derivative action.[46]

B. *Disclosure to Government Agencies*

Disclosure of the internal investigative report to government agencies[47] may be beneficial, particularly if the internal investigation has uncovered evidence of wrongdoing. Providing government lawyers with a written analysis of fact and law may be, in counsel's mind, the only realistic means available of avoiding prosecution. By submitting the report to government agencies, the corporation may forestall a disruptive agency investigation and perhaps negotiate a favorable settlement. Despite these advantages, disclosure of the report to government entities may constitute a waiver of the privilege for a potentially damaging document, as well as all underlying documentation, to other agencies and to third parties.

1. "Limited" Waiver Usually Total Waiver

In accordance with a principal objective of both the work product and attorney-client privileges, the maintenance of confidentiality, disclosure of privileged documents or communications generally constitutes a waiver of

---

44. 692 F.2d 880, 894 (2d Cir. 1982), *cert. denied*, 460 U.S. 1051 (1983).
45. 732 F.2d 1302 (7th Cir. 1984).
46. 732 F.2d at 1314. Noting the Second Circuit's decision in *North* holding that disclosure of an investigative report in support of a motion to dismiss waived the privilege, the court reasoned that although it would not go so far as to rule the privilege waived upon disclosure, it nonetheless "attach[ed] less weight to the public interest in the attorney-client privilege and work product immunity . . . than in a case where absolute confidentiality had been maintained."
47. This topic—Disclosure to Government Agencies—is treated at length in Chapter 7. Here, the authors discuss it briefly because of its obvious relevance to the present topic. Not infrequently, written reports are prepared for the very purpose of dissuading government action, and thus counsel may choose to provide the report to government lawyers, in whole or in summary.

the privilege.[48] However, in the context of voluntary corporate disclosures of internal investigative findings to government agencies, very few courts have protected documents from discovery in subsequent proceedings under the concept of "limited" waiver.[49] First articulated in *Diversified*, the limited waiver theory recognizes the potential "chilling effects" a doctrine of total waiver would have on corporate cooperation in voluntary government disclosure programs and holds that disclosure of documents to a government

---

48. Under the attorney-client privilege, voluntary disclosure waives the privilege. United States v. American Tel. & Tel., 642 F.2d 1285, 1299 (D.C. Cir. 1980). In contrast, under the work-product doctrine, disclosure to parties "with common interests on a particular issue against a common adversary" generally does not constitute a waiver. *Id.* Indeed, some courts have suggested that disclosure of work product to a governmental agency under a confidentiality agreement *may* protect the contested work product. *See In re* Subpoena Duces Tecum, 738 F.2d at 1372-74 (reasoning that parties "did not have any proper expectations of confidentiality which might mitigate" fairness considerations raised by disclosure). *In re* Sealed Case, 676 F.2d at 823 ("[c]orporations may protect their privileges . . . simply by being forthright with their regulators and identifying material as to which they claim privilege at the time they submit their voluntary disclosure reports."); *see also* Teachers Ins. & Annuity Ass'n v. Shamrock Broadcasting Co., 521 F. Supp. 638, 644-45 (S.D.N.Y. 1981) ("Disclosure to the SEC should be deemed a complete waiver of the attorney-client privilege unless the right to assert the privilege in subsequent proceedings is specifically reserved at the time disclosure is made.").

49. *See Diversified Indus.*, 572 F.2d at 611, 606 (since the company disclosed contested documents "in a separate and nonpublic SEC agency investigation, only a limited waiver of the privilege occurred"); *In re* LTV, 89 F.R.D. at 620-21 ("The voluntary disclosure of information to an agency, as part of an agency enforcement proceeding, often is viewed as only a partial waiver of the attorney-client privilege."); Byrnes v. IDS Realty Trust Co., 85 F.R.D. 679, 687-89 (S.D.N.Y. 1983) (supporting *Diversified's* "limited waiver" theory); Saito v. McKesson HBOC, Inc., No. Civ. A. 18553, 2002 WL 31657622, at *11 (Del. Ch. Nov. 13, 2002) ("[B]ecause . . . it is in the best interests of shareholders to encourage corporate compliance, and because law enforcement agencies are designed by our legislatures as the first line of defense for such shareholders" the Court "adopt[ed] a selective waiver rule for disclosures made to law enforcement agencies pursuant to a confidentiality agreement." The Court reasoned that "[t]he selective waiver rule encourages cooperation with law enforcement agencies without any negative cost to society or to private plaintiffs."); *but cf.* United States v. Bergonzi, 216 F.R.D. 487, 497 (N.D. Cal. 2003) ("With all due respect to the *Saito* court" the United States District Court rejected the selective waiver doctrine, finding that the company had waived work product protection, by sharing with the government an investigative report prepared by outside counsel, because "[i]t is inherently unfair to permit an entity to choose to disclose materials to one outsider while withholding them from another on the grounds of privilege."); McKesson HBOC, Inc. v. Superior Court, 115 Cal. App. 4th Supp. 1229, 1241 (2004) (considering the decisions in both *Saito* and *Bergonzi,* and finding that under California law production to the government of an investigative report and related interview memoranda—all prepared by outside counsel—resulted in waiver of the privilege).

agency does not effect a complete waiver of the privilege. This notion of "limited waiver" has encountered sharp criticism in both legal and academic circles.[50] Because the doctrine creates risks of encouraging tactical selective disclosure by corporations while offering speculative benefits,[51] a vast majority of courts have rejected the limited waiver theory with respect to both the attorney-client and work product privileges, holding that disclosure of internal investigative reports and related documentation to government agencies waives the privilege in subsequent proceedings.[52]

On May 15, 2006, the Advisory Committee on Evidence Rules presented to the Standing Committee on Rules of Practice and Procedure, Proposed

---

50. *See, e.g.*, Note, *Discovery of Internal Corporate Investigations*, 32 STAN. L. REV. 1163 (1980); Note, *The Limited Waiver Rule: Creation of an SEC-Corporation Privilege*, 36 STAN. L. REV. 789 (1984).

51. *See Permian Corp.*, 665 F.2d at 1221, n.13 ("We cannot see how the developing procedure of corporations to employ independent outside counsel to investigate and advise them would be thwarted by telling a corporation that it cannot disclose the resulting reports to the SEC if it wishes to maintain their confidentiality.").

52. *See In re* Qwest Communications Int'l Inc., 450 F.3d 1179 (10th Cir. 2006) (rejecting the selective waiver doctrine in the context of production to the government, despite the existence of a confidentiality agreement); *In re* Columbia/HCA Healthcare Corp., 293 F.3d 289, 302-03 (6th Cir. 2002) ("[A]ny form of selective waiver, even that which stems from a confidentiality agreement, transforms the attorney-client privilege into 'merely another brush on an attorney's palette, utilized and manipulated to gain tactical or strategic advantage.' Once 'the privacy for the sake of which the privilege was created [is] gone by the [client's] own consent, . . . the privilege does not remain in such circumstances for the mere sake of giving the client an additional weapon to use or not at his choice.'") (internal citations omitted); United States v. Mass. Inst. of Tech., 129 F.3d 681, 685 (1st Cir. 1997) (While acknowledging that the "search for truth will not be much advanced" if the target of an investigation "limits or recasts its disclosures" as a result of courts' refusal to embrace the selective waiver doctrine, "the general principle that disclosure normally negates the privilege is worth maintaining. To maintain it here makes the law more predictable and certainly eases its administration."). *See In re* Subpoena Duces Tecum (Fulbright & Jaworski), 738 F.2d at 1370 ("[f]or the purposes of the attorney-client privilege, there is nothing special about another federal agency in the role of potential adversary as compared to private party litigants acting as adversaries"); *In re* Sealed Case, 676 F.2d at 822-23 (while recognizing that the purposes of the work-product doctrine were not inconsistent with selective disclosure, concluded that a corporation that decides that the benefits of participation in voluntary disclosure program outweigh the benefits of confidentiality "forgoes traditional protections of the adversary system . . . to avoid some of the traditional burdens"); Permian Corp. v. United States, 665 F.2d at 1221 ("client cannot be permitted to pick and choose among his opponents, waiving the privilege for some and resurrecting the claim of confidentiality to obstruct others, or to invoke the privilege as to communications whose confidentiality he has already compromised for his own benefit . . . the attorney client privilege is not designed for such tactical employment.").

Federal Rule of Evidence 502, "Waiver of Attorney-Client Privilege and Work Product."[53] Subdivision (c) provides:

> In a federal or state proceeding, a disclosure of a communication or information covered by the attorney-client privilege or work product protection—when made to a federal public office or agency in the exercise of its regulatory, investigative, or enforcement authority—does not operate as a waiver of the privilege or protection in favor of non-governmental persons or agencies."[54]

The proposed rule adds, however that "[t]he effect of disclosure to a state or local government agency, with respect to non-governmental persons or entities, is governed by applicable state law." Thus, if the proposed rule is implemented, the target of an investigation risks waiver when producing information to state or local authorities. It should be noted that in its report to the Standing Committee, the Advisory Committee indicated its tentativeness in advancing the proposal. The Committee further noted that while Subdivision (c) "should be included in any proposed rule released for public comment . . . the Committee has not determined whether a provision on selective waiver should be sent to Congress."[55] At the time of publication, the proposed rule has not yet been considered by Congress.

2. Disclosure May Waive Protection of All Papers

Disclosure of the internal investigative report to government agencies presents the further problem of waiving the privilege for the report's underlying documentation. In *In re Sealed Case*, a grand jury sought information that had not been disclosed to the SEC when the company submitted its final report to the agency. Rejecting the corporation's argument that disclosure would thwart voluntary corporate cooperation with the government, the court upheld the grand jury's subpoena for the documents, giving special consideration to the following factors: (1) the final report had emphasized that it was based on a review of all relevant files; (2) the corporation had misrepresented the completeness of the file when it granted the SEC access to the records;

---

53. Gregory P. Joseph, *Privilege Waiver: Proposed Federal Rule of Evidence 502*, in Ethics in Context Summer 2006, at 263 (PLI N.Y. Practice Skills, Course Handbook Series No. 8698, 2006).

54. *Id.* at 272.

55. Letter from Hon. David F. Levi, Chair, Standing Comm. on R. of Practice and Procedure to Hon. Jerry E. Smith, Chair, Advisory Comm. on Evid. R. at 3 (May 14, 2006, revised June 30, 2006) *available at* http://www.uscourts.gov/rules/reports/EV05-2006/pdf.

and (3) the documents were particularly significant because they shed doubt on the truth of the final report.[56] Similarly, in *In re Martin Marietta Corp.*,[57] the court held that the corporation had waived the attorney-client privilege for materials that formed the basis for information disclosed to the U.S. Attorney.

These cases illustrate that where courts sense that a corporation is trying to deceive or manipulate the government, they will not tolerate the use of a privilege as both a shield and a sword.

IV. LIBEL

A. *Written Reports May Invite Libel Claims*

In order for the written report to be a useful tool in ferreting out and addressing wrongdoing, it must be both meticulous and frank. Candor usually requires that the responsible parties be identified and their allegedly "questionable" activities be detailed. These descriptions may be tantamount to the accusation of a crime, or at least of dishonesty and untrustworthiness. Assessments may have a devastating impact on the professional and personal lives of the individuals so identified.[58] Consequently, the written investigative report, pitting the individual's reputational interest[59] against the corporation's interest in self-policing, provides fertile ground for possible libel actions.

---

56. 676 F.2d at 817-22.

57. 856 F.2d at 623-24. The *Marietta* court, noting that the Fourth Circuit had not adopted *Diversified's* "limited waiver" concept, reasoned that since the contested material or its underlying documentation had already been disclosed to the government, attorney-client privilege protection was lost.

58. As one commentator noted:

> Very few defamatory statements carry more potential for devastating harm to the victim than false and defamatory evaluations of an employee's work performance. Careers may turn on such evaluations and courts are thus faced with a power conflict between protecting the substantial social interest in candid and honest appraisals of an employee's competence and the equally substantial interest in safeguarding the employee from undeserved injury.

R. Smolla, *Law of Defamation* 8-27 (1986) [hereinafter *Law of Defamation*].

59. As the Supreme Court noted in Rosenblatt v. Baer, "[s]ociety has a pervasive and strong interest in preventing and redressing attacks upon reputation." 383 U.S. 75, 86 (1966). Given society's significant interest in addressing attacks on reputation, the law of defamation is "aimed at preventing wrongful disruption of the relational interest that an individual has in maintaining personal esteem in the eyes of others." *See Law of Defamation, supra* note 58, at 1-15 (1986). In the pre-*New York Times* v. Sullivan era, defamation law's recognition of this interest consisted largely of strict liability tort rules highly favorable to the plaintiff.

Defamation generally consists of unprivileged false statements of fact, of and concerning the plaintiff, that are defamatory and published to third parties.[60] In some jurisdictions, the construction of the term "publication" may allow the internal investigative report to fall outside the boundaries of defamation liability altogether. Predicated on agency principles, a significant minority of jurisdictions has held that wholly intra-corporate communications among employees within the scope of their employment do not constitute publication. Under this view, such communication is "simply the corporation talking to itself."[61] However, most jurisdictions have not recognized this exception for corporate actors, reasoning that the "no publication" view rests upon a confusion of the publication issue with the existence of a common-law privilege.[62]

Nonetheless, other avenues of protection exist for defamatory statements contained in the investigative report. Modem defamation law is characterized by an array of constitutional and common-law doctrines designed to balance competing reputational and free speech interests. Countervailing free speech interests have been given legal significance in part through the doctrine of privileged communications.[63] Both absolute and qualified privileges have been

---

60. *See* RESTATEMENT (SECOND) OF TORTS § 558 (1977).

61. Luttrell v. United Tel. Sys., Inc., 683 P.2d 1292, 9 Kan. App. 2d 620 (Kan. App. 1984), *aff'd*, 695 P.2d 1279, 236 Kan. 710 (Kan. 1985); *see, e.g.,* Johnson v. Delchamps, 715 F. Supp. 1345 (D. La. 1989) (no publication where results of a polygraph test that resulted in plaintiff employee's dismissal were only disseminated among employees during termination decision); Wilson v. Southern Med. Ass'n, 547 So. 2d 510 (Ala. 1989) (no publication occurred, since memorandum containing allegedly defamatory statements was read only by executive director's secretary, plaintiff, and plaintiff's supervisor); Washington v. Thomas, 778 S.W.2d 792 (Mo. App. 1989).

62. *See Law of Defamation, supra* note 58, at 15-7 to 15-8; Loughry v. Lincoln Bank, 67 N.Y.2d 369, 377, 502 N.Y.S.2d 965 (Ct. App. 1986) (rejecting defendant corporation's "no publication" claim, reasoning that it was "clear that a false and malicious utterance by one employee to another c[ould] be actionable"); Heselton v. Wilder, 496 A.2d 1063 (Me. 1985) (communication by plaintiff's supervisor to loss-prevention department may have been privileged but still constituted publication); Cashio v. Holt, 425 So. 2d 820 (L.A. App. 1982) (publication of plaintiff's termination occurred when copies were provided to six principal managers); Bander v. Metropolitan Life Ins. Co., 313 Mass. 337, 47 N.E.2d 595 (Mass. 1943) (no good reason exists to immunize defamation communicated by one corporate agent to another); Arsenault v. Allegheny Airlines, Inc., 485 F. Supp. 1373, *aff'd,* 636 F.2d 1199 (1st Ch. 1981), *cert. denied,* 454 U.S. 821 (1981) (Massachusetts rejects the proposition that there can be no publication of an intracorporate communication); Jones v. Britt Airways, Inc., 622 F. Supp. 389 (N.D. Ill. 1985) (discussions between managerial employees and several low-level employees constituted publication where statements revealed that investigation as to allegations that plaintiff had embezzled corporate funds had been commenced, and where low-level employees were outside the scope of such investigation).

63. Constitutional fault standards have also been developed to promote the public interest in robust, rich public debate.

developed to immunize otherwise actionable defamatory statements because of the type of speech involved, the status of the speaker, the forum in which the speech occurs, or the relationship between the publisher and third parties.[64]

The privileges of particular import for the investigative report are the "opinion" and the common-law "interest-related" privileges. However, these privileges are mired in uncertainty, with reviewing courts employing different standards to determine their contours and applicability. As a result, defamation liability, as well as the costs associated with defending these actions, should be a source of concern for both investigative counsel and the client.

B. *Example of Libel Claims against Counsel*

Vividly illustrating the investigative report's "libel potential" is the case of *Pearce v. E.F. Hutton Group*.[65] *Pearce* involved a libel suit against former Attorney General Griffin Bell and the Hutton Group on the basis of an internal investigative report prepared by Bell while a lawyer in private practice. The Hutton report concluded that the plaintiff had participated knowingly in an unlawful check-kiting scheme. At issue in the suit were Bell's assessments that "no reasonable person could have believed that this conduct was proper," "[plaintiff's conduct was] so aggressive and egregious as to warrant sanctions," and "[plaintiff had] actually engaged in wrongdoing" and was "a moving force in improprieties."[66] Bell sought to protect the statements through the invocation of various constitutional and common-law doctrines, including the absolute opinion privilege, the common-law interest-related privileges, the fair-comment privilege, and the constitutional "actual malice" fault standard.

Applying the "totality of the circumstances test" articulated in *Ollman v. Evans*,[67] one of several different tests used to distinguish "opinion" from "fact,"[68] the court in *Pearce* ruled that the alleged defamatory statements were not sheltered by the absolute opinion privilege.[69] The court further declined to find that a qualified "interest-related" privilege even initially attached to the statements.[70] The court rejected the notion that the standard of fault should be "actual malice"—a knowing or reckless falsehood—and applied a negligence

---

64. *See generally* R. SACK, LIBEL, SLANDER & RELATED PROBLEMS 267-339 (1980).
65. 664 F. Supp. 1490 (D.D.C. 1987).
66. *Id.* at 1501.
67. 750 F.2d 970, 974-75 (D.C. Cir. 1984).
68. *See infra* notes 76-83 and accompanying text.
69. 664 F. Supp. at 1500-03.
70. *Id.* at 1504-06. The court reasoned that "there [was] little likelihood that [refusing to recognize a qualified privilege would] have a chilling effect on speech. Future investigative reports are unlikely to be deterred as they are motivated by profit."

standard.[71] The case was then sent to the jury on the issue of compensatory damages, where Bell and Hutton ultimately prevailed.[72]

This case highlights the risks presented by the written report and the uncertainty surrounding judicial application of the relevant privileges. Investigative counsel's task therefore becomes the fine art of drafting the document in a manner that places the report as securely as possible within the scope of these somewhat confused doctrines.

C. *Opinion and Qualified Interest Privileges*
1. Opinion Privilege

With the pronouncement that "there is no such thing as a false idea," the Supreme Court, in *Gertz v. Robert Welch, Inc.*,[73] appeared to elevate the well-established, common-law fact-opinion distinction, which found its expression under the aegis of the fair comment privilege,[74] to constitutional stature.[75] However, by failing to articulate an approach to be employed in making the all crucial fact-opinion distinction, *Gertz* spawned the development of a flurry of tests by the lower courts.

---

71. The plaintiff's claims for punitive damages were dismissed because the court deemed sufficient evidence had not been adduced to support a finding that counsel had published the report knowing that it was false or with reckless disregard as to its truth or falsity. 664 F. Supp. at 1509-19. This portion of the court's holding reflected the rule established in *Gertz v. Robert Welch Inc.*, 418 U.S. 323, 349 (1974) (discussed *infra* note 99), where the Supreme Court held that "states may not permit recovery of presumed or punitive damages, at least when liability is not based on a showing of knowledge of falsity or reckless disregard for the truth."

72. Ladd, *Bell Suit Fallout: Outside Probers Want Protection*, LEGAL TIMES, June 27, 1988, at 8.

73. 418 U.S. 323, 339 (1974).

74. The fair comment privilege protected only statements of opinion; as should have been anticipated, distinguishing between fact and opinion was an exceptionally arduous, if not impossible, task that led to a hodgepodge of results. *See* Note, *The Fact-Opinion Distinction in First Amendment Law: The Need for a Bright-Line Rule,* 72 GEO L.J. 1817, 1820 (1984).

75. Specifically the Court stated:

> We begin with the common ground. Under the First Amendment there is no such thing as a false idea. However pernicious an opinion may seem, we depend for its correction not on the conscience of judges and juries but on the competition of other ideas. But there is no constitutional value in false statements of fact.

Lower courts and the RESTATEMENT (SECOND) OF TORTS had interpreted this language as requiring absolute protection for statements of opinion. *See, e.g.*, Ollman v. Evans, 713 F.2d 838, 840-41 (D.C. Cir. 1983) (Robinson, C.J., concurring); Bose Corp. v. Consumers Union of United States, Inc., 692 F.2d 189, 193-94 (1st Cir. 1982); Church of Scientology of Cali-

2. Applicable Tests for Libel

Some courts have chosen a "provable as false" standard to determine whether a statement is protected.[76] Several courts, adopting a "reasonable reader" standard as the inquiry's focal point, have deemed privileged statements depicted as "rhetorical hyperbole" such that no reasonable reader could perceive as fact.[77] Others have adopted the *Restatement (Second) of Torts* method, which focuses on the adequacy of the factual presentation made by the author.[78] Premised upon the common-law rationale that stated facts provide a basis upon which the reader can evaluate the soundness of the opinion, the *Restatement* approach protects a statement if it "does not imply the existence of undisclosed defamatory facts."[79] Some courts have employed

---

fornia v. Cazares, 638 F.2d 1272, 1286 (5th Cir. 1981); Avins v. White, 627 F.2d 637, 642 (3d Cir. 1980), *cert. denied,* 449 U.S. 982 (1980); RESTATEMENT (SECOND) OF TORTS § 566 (1977), stating defamation actions for "pure" expressions of opinion are unconstitutional in light of *Gertz*. However, the Supreme Court's opinion in Milkovich v. Lorain Journal Co., 110 S. Ct. 2695, 2707 (1990), held that no "additional separate constitutional privilege for 'opinion' is required to ensure the freedom of expression guaranteed by the First Amendment." This case has been interpreted as rejecting only the notion that *Gertz* established an absolute privilege for statements of opinion, limiting opinion protection to those statements not provable as false and those that cannot be reasonably interpreted as assertions of fact. *See The Supreme Court—Leading Cases: Libel Law-Opinion Privilege,* 104 HARV. L. REV. 219 (1990).

76. *See, e.g.,* Liberty Lobby, Inc. v. Anderson, 746 F.2d 1563, 1572 (D.C. Cir. 1984), *vacated and remanded on other grounds,* 477 U.S. 242 (1986); Buckley v. Littell, 539 F.2d 882, 895 (2d Cir. 1976), *cert. denied,* 429 U.S. 1062 (1977). *See also* Milkovich v. Lorain Journal Co., 110 S. Ct. 2695, 2701-07 (1990), discussed *infra* notes 80-89 and accompanying text.

77. Pring v. Penthouse Int'l Ltd., 695 F.2d 438, 443 (10th Cir. 1983), *cert. denied,* 462 U.S. 1132 (1983); Pease v. Telegraph Publishing, Inc., 121 N.H. 62, 65, 426A.2d 463, 465 (N.H. 1981).

78. Avins v. White, 627 F.2d 637 (3d Cir. 1980), *cert. denied,* 449 U.S. 982 (1980); Bruno v. New York News, Inc., 89 A.D.2d 260, 264, 456 N.Y.S.2d 837, 840 (3d Dept. 1982); Holy Spirit Ass'n for Unification of World Christianity v. Sequoia Elsevier Publishing Co., 75 A.D.2d 523, 426 N.Y.S.2d 759, 760 (1st Dept. 1980); Braig v. Field Communications, 456 A.2d 1366, 310 Pa. Super. 569 (Pa. Super. 1983).

79. *The Fact-Opinion Distinction, supra* note 74, at 1826. Although the common law never resolved the fundamental problem of how to discern whether a statement implies defamatory facts, this approach was adopted by the RESTATEMENT (SECOND) OF TORTS, which subdivided "opinions" into two categories: pure opinion, based upon stated facts or "clearly" based on facts known or assumed by the audience, and mixed opinion, not based on stated or assumed facts, therefore implying the existence of undisclosed defamatory facts. Under the RESTATEMENT view, expressions of pure opinion are absolutely protected, while expressions of "mixed opinion" may be actionable. Though the RESTATEMENT offers clarifying examples, these hypotheticals fail to grapple with the critical question, especially trying in the usual complex factual background found in fact-opinion cases: *how* to decide *when* a statement implies no undisclosed defamatory facts.

contextual analyses in making the determination. The "totality of the circumstances" test assesses "all relevant factors including: the surrounding words, any cautionary language, and the surrounding circumstances such as the medium used and the audience addressed."[80] Despite the wealth of choice, each of these tests suffers from problems of vagueness and ambiguity. In "reasonable reader" jurisdictions, no guidance is offered as to how to measure the "reasonable reader's" perceptions.[81]

The mechanical *Restatement* test, with its full disclosure requirement, fails to define what constitutes a "fact" and to offer any clear method of ascertaining when a statement implies undisclosed facts.[82] The contextual approaches, similar to the "reasonable reader" test, place the prospective defendant in the position of determining what circumstances will be deemed legally significant.[83]

3. Supreme Court's Decision Provides Little Clarity

The Supreme Court's decision in *Milkovich v. Lorain Journal Co.*[84] did little to bring clarity to this area. Rejecting a categorical absolute privilege for "opinion," the *Milkovich* Court held that statements not susceptible of being proved as false are protected opinion, thereby making only those statements that may reasonably be interpreted as asserting a verifiable fact capable of forming the basis for a defamation action.[85] Despite this attempt to define protectible "opinion," the Court's articulation of the "provable as false" standard essentially reiterates the principal thrust of the tests applied by the lower courts for years.

The continued viability of the test most favorable to the investigative report, the *Restatement* test, is more doubtful in light of dicta in the majority

---

80. Comment, *Statement of Facts, Statements of Opinion and the First Amendment*, 74 CALIF. L. REV. 1001, 1015 (1984); *see, e.g.,* Lewis v. Time, Inc., 710 F.2d 549 (9th Cir. 1983); Information Control Corp. v. Genesis One Computer Corp., 611 F.2d 781, 784 (9th Cir. 1980); Gregory v. McDonnell-Douglas Corp., 17 Cal. 3d 596, 601-03, 552 P.2d 425, 428-29 (1970).
81. *The Fact-Opinion Distinction, supra* note 74, at 1831-32.
82. *Id.* at 1827-29.
83. *Id.* at 1836-39.
84. 110 S. Ct. 2695 (1990).
85. 110 S. Ct. at 2701-07.

opinion. Writing for the *Milkovich* majority, Justice Rehnquist posed the following hypothetical:

> If a speaker says, "In my opinion John Jones is a liar," he implies a knowledge of facts which lead to the conclusion that Jones told an untruth. Even if the speaker states the facts upon which he bases his opinion, if those facts are either incorrect or incomplete, or if his assessment of them is erroneous, the statement may still imply a false assertion of fact.[86]

The investigative report, presenting conclusions based upon the investigation's factual findings, provides a classic example of "deductive opinion."[87] Fully disclosing the underlying factual basis for its "opinion," the investigative report would be nonactionable, even if false, under the *Restatement* test. The language in *Milkovich*, however, suggests that a statement will be actionable, though it does not imply the existence of defamatory facts, if the author's conclusion as to the meaning of those facts is erroneous.[88]

Consequently, the post-*Milkovich* "opinion" privilege is not a sure "safe haven" for the investigative report. The uncertainty surrounding *Milkovich*'s "provable as false" and "reasonable reader" standards is highlighted by the divergent outcomes reached by the majority and the dissent in their respective applications of the tests.[89] Similarly, as illustrated in *Pearce*, the contextual

---

86. 110 S. Ct. at 2705-06.

87. "An opinion is deductive if it implies or deduces misconduct or a disparaging fact about the plaintiff on the basis of true information supplied to the public or already generally known to the public." *Law of Defamation, supra* note 58, at 6-19, discussing the opinion classifications set forth in W. PROSSER & W. KEETON, THE LAW OF TORTS § 113 A, 813-14 (5th ed. 1981).

88. *Leading Cases, supra* note 75, at 226, n.72. *See also* Goodale, *Milkovich: Modest Loss for the Press,* NEW YORK L.J., June 27, 1990, at 1, stating that "[a]fter *Milkovich* there will be liability for statements of opinion complicating facts about public officials or public figures when made recklessly or without knowledge that the facts are false."

89. The majority found the statement, "Anyone who attended the meet ... knows in his heart that Milkovich and Scott lied at the hearing after each having given his solemn oath to tell the truth," implied that Milkovich committed perjury and was "sufficiently factual to be susceptible of being proved true or false." 110 S. Ct. at 2707. In contrast, Justice Brennan in dissent declared that, assessing the column in context, "[n]o reasonable reader could understand [the reporter] to be implied asserting—as fact that Milkovich lied." Milkovich v. Lorain Journal Co., 110 S. Ct. at 2711-12 (Brennan, J., dissenting).

analysis tends to favor a finding of fact, not opinion, when examining an investigative report.[90]

Although *Milkovich* rejected the existence of an absolute "opinion" privilege under the First Amendment, state courts, invoking state constitutional law, may still afford expressions of "opinion" heightened protection.[91] The New York Court of Appeals, reconsidering a pre-*Milkovich* case on remand from the Supreme Court, affirmed its decision that the statements at issue were protected "opinion" on both federal and independent state law grounds.[92] Noting the "expansive language" of the state's constitutional guarantee of freedom of expression, manifested in its "exceptional history and rich tradition" of jurisprudence in that area, the court of appeals concluded that it was appropriate to decide the matter on independent state law grounds as well as on federal First Amendment bases.[93] In light of the diminished significance of

---

90. In *Pearce,* a case expressly involving a libel claim based on an internal investigative report, the court, employing the *Ollman* test, deemed the opinion privilege inapplicable. In its analysis of the four factors, the court reasoned that the professional nature of the report, the purpose of the underlying investigation, the content of the contested statements, and the surrounding context of the internal investigation led to the conclusion that the statements were assertions of fact and not opinion. The final two prongs of the inquiry, the immediate and broader social context queries, posed particular problems for the report. The court found that both elements suggested the Hutton investigative report was factual rather than opinion-based. The report's use of cautionary language, such as "we conclude" or "we think" was deemed inconclusive, as the context of this particular report made the language seem "more akin to a summary of facts than a subjective analysis of them." 664 F. Supp. at 1502. Incorporating the RESTATEMENT test into the immediate context inquiry, the court found that because "the challenged statements set forth plaintiff's culpability, they impl[ied] the existence of damaging, undisclosed facts beyond the mere description of the chaining and overdrafting activities given in more detailed sections of the Hutton report." *Id.* Without much discussion, the Pearce court found that the broader social context an investigative report into illegal corporate activities prepared by independent counsel who was a former attorney general and federal judge— "would cause the reasonable person to view [the statements] as fact, not opinion." *Id.*

91. *See Goodale, Modest Loss, supra* note 88.

92. Immuno v. Jan-Moor Jankowski, No. 264 (N.Y. Jan. 15, 1991) (LEXIS, N.Y. library, *Cases* file).

93. The court of appeals reasoned that the Supreme Court in *Milkovich* applied an analysis similar to the *Ollman* contextual inquiry, differing primarily on the construction of the last two prongs of the *Ollman* test—the immediate and broader social context inquiries. The court reasoned that these inquiries focused on the "type of speech" at issue, and that the Supreme Court ostensibly intended absolute protection to apply only to "loose, figurative hyperbolic language"; in contrast, "statements that contain[ed] or impl[ied] assertions of provably false fact w[ould] likely be actionable." Concluding that its decision could rest on state constitutional law, the court expressed its "concern[ ] that if indeed the type of speech is to be construed narrowly—insufficient protection may be accorded to the central values protected by the law of this State."

the constitutional opinion privilege in the context of the written investigative report, the qualified or conditional common-law privileges assume greater importance.

4. Qualified Interest-Related Privileges

In recognition of the need for frank communication regarding matters in which the parties have an interest or duty, qualified privileges exist to immunize otherwise actionable statements. These privileges have been recognized for statements made in the interests of the publisher, the recipient, third parties, the public, and persons sharing a common interest.[94]

The qualified privilege does not sanction all defamatory statements cloaked with the requisite interest. Critical to the successful invocation of this doctrinal shield is the publisher's "good faith," evidenced by the publisher's motivations in making the statements, the nexus between the statement's content and the proffered purpose, and the degree to which "malice," "ill-will," or "spite" played a factor in publication. The qualified privilege is thus subject to loss for "abuse."

The employer's traditional qualified privilege for critical statements concerning former and current employees communicated to persons having a corresponding interest or duty provides a particularly apt analytical framework for shielding written investigative reports from defamation liability. This privilege initially attaches to communications made by employers[95] or agents such as private investigators hired to make employee evaluations.[96] This is of great assistance since in many instances, as demonstrated by *Pearce*, the defamation plaintiff will be an employee criticized in the report.[97]

---

94. B. SANFORD, LIBEL & PRIVACY: THE PREVENTION AND DEFENSE OF LITIGATION 413-24 (1985).

95. Note, *Employer Defamation: The Role of Qualified Privilege,* 30 WM. & M. L. REV. 469, 471 (1989), citing RESTATEMENT (SECOND) OF TORTS § 595 (1977) and 50 AM. JUR. 2D, *Libel and Slander* § 275 (1970).

96. Campbell v. Willmark Serv. Sys., 123 F.2d 204 (3d Cir. 1941); Roscoe v. Schoolitz, 105 Ariz. 310, 464 P.2d 333 (1970); Freeman v. Mills, 97 Cal. App. 2d 161, 217 P.2d 687 (Cal. App. 19-50); Dierson v. Robert Griffin Investigations, 92 Nev. 605, 555 P.2d 843 (Nev. 1976).

97. Even if the plaintiff is not an employee, a qualified privilege, based either on self-interest, common interest, or the furtherance of another's interest, should still apply. Moreover, if the plaintiff is a public figure, as may occur, e.g., in the context of an investigative report examining alleged violations of the Foreign Corrupt Practices Act, the report may enjoy the enhanced protection of the "actual malice" constitutional standard.

Some confusion arises as to when the privilege is lost through abuse. The employer's qualified privilege may be forfeited by a showing of "excessive publication," publication for purposes other than those giving rise to the privilege, malice in both its common law and constitutional sense, bad faith, recklessness, and negligence.[98] Clearly, excessive publication and publication for purposes unrelated to those giving rise to the privilege will lose the qualified privilege. However, it is unclear what standard of fault—negligence or a more culpable standard—is necessary to overcome the privilege.

Since negligence is already a minimum constitutional standard for fault liability,[99] a determination that a showing of negligence defeats the qualified privilege renders the privilege meaningless. The negligence "abuse" standard

---

98. *Employer Defamation, supra* note 95, at 488.

99. Constitutionalizing much of modern defamation law, New York Times Co. v. Sullivan, 376 U.S. 254 (1964), and its progeny established the principle that the First Amendment requires a finding of fault, ranging from "actual malice" in public figure cases to negligence in private-figure cases involving "matters of public concern," be made before liability is imposed for libel. Curtis Publ'g Co. v. Butts, 388 U.S. 130 (1967) ("actual malice" standard governs public figures); Associated Press v. Walker, 389 U.S. 997 (1967) ("actual malice" governs public figures); Gertz v. Robert Welch, Inc., 418 U.S. 323 (1974) (no liability without fault); Dun & Bradstreet, Inc. v. Greenmoss Builders, Inc., 105 S. Ct. 2939 (1985) (presumed and punitive damages restricted to cases that "do not involve matters of public concern"). Predicated on the status of the plaintiff and the type of speech involved, these fault standards operate in much the same fashion as privileges, providing varying safe harbors for speech in which the public has an interest.

In *Gertz,* the Court reaffirmed *New York Times Co.* v. Sullivan's holding that public officials and public figures were required to demonstrate actual malice and ruled that with respect to private figure plaintiffs, states could devise their own standard of liability as long as no liability was imposed without a showing of fault. 418 U.S. at 348. *Gertz* appeared to require a showing of at least negligence in all defamation actions, and lower courts accordingly interpreted *Gertz's* fault requirement as establishing a minimum culpability standard of negligence. However, in a dramatic retreat from *Gertz,* the Court in *Dun & Bradstreet* ruled that *Gertz's* restriction of punitive and presumed damage awards to cases in which actual malice is shown does not apply to defamatory statements that "do not involve matters of public concern." The task of discerning what constitutes "public concern" has been left largely to the lower courts; the *Dun & Bradstreet* plurality opinion articulated no clear guidelines or benchmarks, simply stating that "whether . . . speech addresses a matter of public concern must be determined by [the statement's] content, form, and context . . . as revealed by the whole record"—basically holding that courts must consider everything.

Dun & Bradstreet thus called into question at least some aspect of the applicability of the *Gertz* "no liability without fault" rule for speech not involving matters of public concern. This decision potentially permits the states to revitalize early strict liability standards for their defamation actions involving private figure plaintiffs and no public issues.

Consequently, three standards of fault negligence, actual malice, and strict liability conceivably govern modern defamation law, turning on the status of the plaintiff and the subject matter at issue. The vast majority of jurisdictions tend to follow the "negligence" rule for priis the minority rule,[100] with most jurisdictions opting for some standard of malice, either in its constitutional or common-law forms.[101] Thus, the employer's qualified privilege should provide substantial protection for the investigative report, provided the report is disclosed only to essential parties and the prior investigation is thorough and complete.

D. Strategies for Minimizing Liability for Defamation

1. Emphasize Opinions

While the "opinion" privilege is of limited value for the investigative report, investigative counsel should still attempt to use the protections of this privilege to the greatest extent possible by explicitly detailing the factual basis for the report's conclusions about individual culpability. Cautionary language, though possessing no automatic power to turn factual statements into protected opinion, should be used when practicable.

2. Avoid Overstatement and Loosely Formed Conclusions

Because the most important vehicle of protection will be the qualified privilege and particularly the employer's qualified privilege, both the investigation and the report should be carefully done. To ensure the report is not negligently prepared[102] and that it is not "knowingly" or "recklessly false,"

---

vate figure plaintiff cases, while a few states have adopted an actual malice standard. Other states, notably New York, have developed some intermediate standard for private figure plaintiffs. *See Law of Defamation, supra* note 58, at 3-28.

100. *See, e.g.*, Schneider v. Pay'N Save Corp., 723 P.2d 619 (Alaska 1986).

101. Actual malice is defined as "knowledge of falsity or reckless disregard for the truth," Dun & Bradstreet, 105 S. Ct. at 2941, while common-law malice envisions actual "spite" or "ill-will." *See Law of Defamation, supra* note 58, at 3-28. *See, e.g.*, Lewis v. Equitable Life Assurance Soc'y, 389 N.W.2d 876, 891 (Minn. 1986) (common-law malice); Stuempages v. Parke, Davis & Co., 297 N.W.2d 252, 257 (Minn. 1980) (common-law malice); Hoesl v. United States, 451 F. Supp. 1170, 1179 (N.D. Cal. 1978) (actual malice); Marchesi v. Franchino, 283 Md. 131, 387 A.2d 1129 (Md. App. 1978) (actual malice); Roemer v. Retail Credit Co., 3 Cal. App. 3d 368, 83 Cal. Rptr. 540 (Cal. App. 1978) (actual malice).

102. The reasonable person standard governs the negligence inquiry. In making this determination, courts generally will examine such issues as "the cost of further investigation and further delay in publishing, and the importance of the interests being promoted by the speech measured against the probability of foreseeable harm to the plaintiff's reputation, including the reliability of sources ... the seriousness of the defamatory charges, and their inherent plausibility." *Law of Defamation, supra* note 58, at 3-73. Negligence problems can arise as a result of the lawyer's "failure to pursue further investigation; unreasonable reliance on sources; unreasonable formulation of conclusions, inferences or interpretations; errors in note-taking and quotation of sources; misuse of legal terminology; mechanical or typographical errors; unreasonable screening or checking procedures; and the failure to follow established internal practices and policies." *Id.* at 3-75.

the underlying investigation should be thorough, supporting facts and sources should be verified, and the conclusions drawn should be reasonably justified by the facts. Lawyers should refrain from the use of caustic, hyperbolic, and otherwise colorful language.

3. Avoid Unnecessary Publication

Since excessive publication will negate the common-law privilege, lawyers and the corporation should be especially careful in disseminating the report. Disclosure of the report pursuant to a corporation's participation in a voluntary disclosure program should not be fatal since the government agency, in all probability, would be deemed a party with a corresponding interest in the communication. Likewise, disclosure of the report to the direct supervisors of the persons named in the report should not constitute excessive publication. Outside this audience, however, disclosure of the report should be curtailed. As *Pearce* demonstrates, widespread disclosures (a public news conference in that case) are hazardous and may prompt reviewing courts to refuse to recognize even the existence of the privilege.[103]

4. Consider Indemnification

Finally, investigative counsel should consider including an indemnification clause within the engagement contract. While the qualified privilege generally will safeguard both counsel and the corporation from liability, the costs of defending defamation actions are quite substantial.[104] Given that in most instances of suspected corporate wrongdoing, an internal investigation and concluding report will be in the corporation's best interest, indemnification clauses should not pose any substantial threat to the internal investigation practice area.[105]

---

103. The unusual circumstances surrounding the Hutton report, most notably the fact that the investigation was commissioned after settlement had been reached with the Department of Justice and was designed to calm public furor generated by the settlement agreement, appeared to play a pivotal role in the court's decision, particularly on the qualified privilege issue. *See Pearce,* 449 F. Supp. at 1504-06.

104. *See Bell Suit Fallout: Outside Probers Want Protection, supra* note 72, discussing the indemnification debate among lawyers specializing in internal corporate investigations in the aftermath of the Bell suit. Many practitioners in the field, including Bell, have decided to ask for indemnification clauses in their engagement contracts. Others believe that such a condition may be seen as compromising the impartiality and independence of investigative counsel, and have chosen not to seek it.

105. As one lawyer noted: "Most of these companies won't be in a position to decide against an investigation simply because they are going to have to assume a contingent liability." *Id.*

V. CONCLUSION

A. *Summary*

As must be clear by now, the preparation of a written report of the internal investigation is fraught with danger. It may subject the author to a lawsuit in which exemplary damages are sought; it may be turned against the client by the very agency counsel is seeking to appease; it may be disclosed in later litigation and admissions within; it may prove quite harmful; and its disclosure, intended or not, may result in disclosure of all underlying records.

Given the range of uncertainties accompanying the preparation of a report, one might well conclude that *no* good reason exists to create a written document. As this chapter suggests, oral reports are far preferable to a written record. More fundamentally, one might ask whether the reasons arguing against the creation of a written report argue just as strongly that no investigation take place at all. Whether the ultimate product of the investigation—the report—is oral or written, the fact remains that in the course of the investigation considerable information is collected by counsel; and some of that information, perhaps much, will damage the company once disclosed.

Yet, the option of beginning an investigation, or of rendering only an oral report, may not always be available to counsel. The client may insist on the investigation and insist on the preparation of a thorough, detailed written analysis, believing that nothing short of that will accomplish its purposes. Or, the lawyer may conclude that a well-reasoned statement of fact and law is essential to dissuading government lawyers from prosecution. Finally, the preparation of the report—indeed the convening of the investigation itself—may be imposed by government regulation or made a predicate to settlement.

B. *Minimizing Risks*

In view of these competing considerations, how can counsel best minimize the many risks associated with undertaking the corporate investigation, while still fully probing into the conduct giving rise to the investigation in the first place? This is not an easy task, but the following guidelines may be helpful in walking this fine line.

1. Strictly Observe Legal Privileges

While the privilege of self-criticism would provide a more appropriate protection for the internal investigative report than the attorney-client or work product protections, courts have been reluctant to accept it. Hence, a lawyer preparing a report should structure both the investigation and written report to obtain the full protection of the established privileges. It is certainly more prudent to attempt to keep the protection of the privileges so the client will have the option of waiving them rather than to lose them by inadvertence. In this regard, counsel must never forget that *any* disclosure of the report beyond the company may result in some degree of waiver, whether complete or partial, of both the contents of the report and of underlying work papers. By understanding this distinct possibility—in a sense, expecting the worst—counsel can more intelligently go about the task of accumulating the facts and reporting the results.

2. Begin with Clear Engagement Letter

Since the analysis of the attorney-client privilege depends on content, the initial engagement letter between the corporation and its counsel should frame the representation in accordance with the Supreme Court's decision in *Upjohn*[106] and should explicitly state that counsel is being engaged for the purpose of securing legal advice. Where possible, the report should recite that the investigation is undertaken in anticipation of litigation. Moreover, using outside rather than inside counsel increases the chances for protection because it avoids the argument that in-house lawyers often provide business advice. It will be a more difficult task, in the event of a discovery dispute, to demonstrate that inside counsel acted solely in its "legal capacity" in the course of the investigation. Finally, counsel may wish to include an indemnification clause.

3. Enlist Independent Audit Committee or Outside Directors

If the various "self-policing" rationales are to have any force, appearance must be a critical concern in every aspect of the internal investigation. To convey credibility, the supervisory body, as well as the investigators and the investigation, must possess a significant degree of independence. Particu-

---

106. According to *Upjohn*, to come within the privilege, the following circumstances must be present: (1) the communications by employees to corporate counsel are to secure legal advice for the company; (2) the employees are cooperating with corporate counsel at the direction of corporate superiors; (3) the communications concern matters within the employees' scope of employment; and (4) the information is not available from upper-echelon management. Upjohn Co. v. United States, 449 U.S. 383 (1981).

larly in matters involving complex and wide-ranging schemes, where a colorable claim of high-level knowledge and participation can be made, the corporate board of directors should not be in charge of supervising the investigation. In most cases, an independent audit committee of the board of directors or a specially appointed committee comprising outside directors should be assigned this task.[107] In certain circumstances, for example, investigations triggered by suspicions of wrongdoing by low-level employees, supervisory authority exercised by executive management or the board is appropriate.

In all instances, however, the role played by corporate personnel in structuring the investigation, including the persons interviewed, the documents reviewed, and the avenues pursued, should be strictly advisory and facilitative, not decisive. Investigative counsel alone should be in charge of the investigation, though its scope should be articulated and ostensibly formulated by the board of directors or senior management in the initial engagement letter.

4. Act as Legal Counsel

Courts have denied claims of privilege and protection to those reports in which counsel provided investigative services only, or rendered business advice alone. Thus, the report should plainly indicate that the lawyer was hired to provide legal advice with respect to certain matters and explain what the lawyer did to provide the advice. To ensure coverage by both the attorney-client and work product privileges, the lawyer's analysis of the factual findings and their legal implications should be reflected throughout the document. The actual investigative report should consist of a statement of the objective of the investigation, the investigation's factual findings, the lawyer's analysis of these findings, and a list of recommendations. The lawyer's recitation of the facts should be structured so as to reveal the reasoning. Furthermore, the statements of persons interviewed and other primarily factual information should be summarized in order to fall more comfortably under the rubric of opinion work product and to avoid the problem of legal "admissions." The report should indicate that it is the lawyer's views of the witnesses' statements that enable conclusions to be drawn.

---

107. *See* Mueller, *Practical Considerations in Conducting an Internal Business Investigation*, in PLI, THE ROLE OF OUTSIDE COUNSEL IN THE BUSINESS INVESTIGATION, No. 279, 163, 170-71 (1985).

5. Express Limitations

Both for purposes of accuracy and protection in the event of subsequent disclosure, the report should make clear its limitations. Frequently, a discussion of methodology and procedures followed will help achieve this. Where recollections or documents are ambiguous or in conflict, they should be conveyed. Where assumptions have been made, they should be stated. A report that presents a balanced appraisal of events will best serve the client and its authors.

6. Match Conclusions with Facts

Finally, to maximize the protections afforded by constitutional and common-law privilege against libel suits, the report should be distributed to a limited, relevant audience; should carefully explain the factual bases for its conclusions; and should attempt to characterize its ultimate conclusions as subjective opinions and recommendations.

Internal Investigations for Government Contractors

11

Michael Waldman

I. WHO ARE GOVERNMENT CONTRACTORS? 336
   A. Suppliers to the Federal Government 337
   B. Health Care 338
   C. Other Government Contractors 338
II. BEGINNING OF THE INVESTIGATION 339
   A. Subpoenas 340
   B. Internal Discovery 342
   C. The Qui Tam Telephone Call 342
III. RESPONDING TO A FRAUD INVESTIGATION: BASIC PRINCIPLES FOR GOVERNMENT CONTRACTORS 344
   A. Unique Features of Fraud Investigations Faced by Government Contractors 344
IV. CONCLUSION 350

Michael Waldman is a partner at the firm of Fried, Frank, Harris, Shriver & Jacobson in Washington, D.C. He specializes in representing clients in internal investigations, civil fraud, False Claims Act, and white-collar criminal defense matters.

THE U.S. GOVERNMENT is the world's largest purchaser of goods and services. Numerous businesses rely heavily on their contracts with the government, ranging from the neighborhood doctor providing medical services to Medicare/Medicaid patients to the large defense contractor supplying multi-million-dollar weapons systems to the U.S. military. For all government contractors regardless of size, internal corporate investigations are especially important. Unlike other commercial businesses, government contractors cannot simply treat a potential criminal or civil problem in isolation. Rather, the government contractor has a more complex task: the contractor must ensure that it continues to maintain the confidence and good favor of its government customer throughout the investigatory process. In addition, the detailed statutory and regulatory framework in which government contractors operate greatly complicates any internal investigation. While the techniques used by the lawyer for identifying the potential legal problem, gathering documents, and interviewing witnesses are generally common to all internal investigations, this chapter highlights some of the special considerations that must be analyzed when conducting an internal corporate investigation for a government contractor.[1]

I. WHO ARE GOVERNMENT CONTRACTORS?

It is important for a lawyer to determine early on whether the client is a government contractor, since this will likely affect the subsequent approach to the internal investigation. Recognizing that the client is a government contractor is not always easy. Because of the pervasive role of the federal government, many companies have ties to the government that one would not expect. Along with being cognizant of the client's direct contracts with the plethora of government agencies and departments, a lawyer also needs to be watchful for the company being the supplier of parts or services to a customer who, in turn, is providing an end-product to the U.S. government. In these circumstances, the subcontractor also is generally subject to the statutory and regulatory rules applicable to the prime contractor.

---

1. This chapter does not attempt to address the basic techniques and procedures for conducting internal corporate investigations, which are set out elsewhere at length in this book.

A. Suppliers to the Federal Government[2]

When one typically thinks of government contractors, major military suppliers such as Lockheed Martin, Northrop Grumman, and Raytheon immediately come to mind. The U.S. government, however, purchases much more than B-2 bombers, aircraft carriers, and Patriot missiles. There is almost no product that the U.S. government does not purchase in substantial quantities—in almost all instances it is the largest purchaser in the world.[3] The General Services Administration maintains a vast schedule from which government offices around the country can purchase wastepaper baskets, furniture, office supplies, and the like. Government agencies also contract out (or, in the popular parlance, "outsource") broad varieties of services, from fixing equipment to maintaining parks and grounds to the running of certain prisons. Highway projects and other public works projects remain a staple of government contracting in numerous localities. The Department of Homeland Security has become a major new source of government spending. Lawyers must be aware that no matter how mundane or unusual the company's product or service, the U.S. government may be a major customer.

For example, computer hardware and software have been among the largest and fastest-growing areas of federal government procurements in recent years. Like private businesses, the federal government is attempting to increase productivity through technology innovations. Almost every major department

---

2. This chapter will focus on suppliers to the federal government. It should be noted that the same issues and problems generally apply at the state and local government levels. In fact, many states have enacted their own false claims statutes. *See, e.g.,* John T. Boese, *Civil False Claims and Qui Tam Actions,* ASPEN LAW & BUSINESS 3d ed., ch. 6 and Appendices I-Z (collecting false claims statutes for various states). The move toward passing state statutes akin to the federal False Claims Act is expected to increase markedly in the coming years. Congress included a provision in the Deficit Reduction Act of 2005 that provided strong incentives for states to enact Medicaid false claims laws with *qui tam* enforcement provisions similar to the federal FCA. Specifically, the provision offers to states a 10 percent reduction in the federal government's share of the state's recovery of Medicaid funds under the state's qualifying false claims statute if the state enacts a Medicaid false claims statute that is "at least as effective in rewarding and facilitating *qui tam* actions" as the federal Act.

3. One distinguished government contracts lawyer tells the story, perhaps an apocryphal, of his representation of a maker of musical instruments. This attorney asserted that, through the numerous military bands, the U.S. Department of Defense was the world's largest single purchaser of musical instruments.

and agency is regularly purchasing new computers or upgrading its present capacity. The government also is continually pouring billions of dollars into integration and software services. As a result, like numerous other industries, counsel for companies involved in the various aspects of the information technology industry need to be mindful of these government 'entanglements' when contemplating how to respond to a potential issue that might require an internal investigation.

B. *Health Care*

The increasing role of government funding is nowhere more obvious than in the health care area. The passage of Medicare and Medicaid in 1965 has led to the U.S. government playing a major role in the health care industry.[4] The new prescription drug benefits created by the Medicare Prescription Drug, Improvement and Modernization Act of 2003 increased further the scope of government health care coverage. The federal government spends countless billions of dollars annually on Medicare and Medicaid spending. Few hospitals, nursing homes, home health companies, or laboratories can function without some Medicare and Medicaid patient funding. Pharmaceutical companies, medical device companies, and other suppliers of health care products and services derive significant revenues from government health care programs. Individual doctors also are frequently dependent on the payment from patients covered by these federal programs. While many criticize the complex regulations and burdensome paperwork involved in Medicare and Medicaid, few health care providers can stay in business without participating in these programs. Stamping out fraud in these federal health care programs has become the top priority of federal law enforcement. As a result, when conducting an internal investigation of a health care provider, a lawyer should consider as a matter of course the potential liabilities to the United States.

C. *Other Government Contractors*

There also exist other companies that have significant dealings with the federal government, yet in more unconventional ways. For example, there have been a number of false claims lawsuits against the major oil and gas

---

4. Medicare is codified primarily at 42 U.S.C. §§ 1395-139511. Medicaid is codified primarily at 42 U.S.C. §§ 1396-1396p.

companies based on alleged violations of their federal land leases.[5] In other instances, the United States or its whistle-blower proxy has filed civil false claims actions against tugboat operators for improper waste dumping[6] and against a well-known clothing retailer for allegedly false customs declarations.[7] While not strictly government contractors, these companies perform in a regulatory framework that subjects their businesses to many of the same onerous fines and penalties as government contractors. As one judge wrote:

> In this day of pervasive government regulation of both public and private conduct, it is impossible even to estimate the number of times each day, each month, or each year that private citizens create or submit some type of document required by the government or subject to government review or the number of times that such a document, if not completely accurate, could lead to the filing of a False Claims Act case.[8]

II. BEGINNING OF THE INVESTIGATION

When a lawyer is considering performing an internal investigation of a government contractor, he or she needs to understand the basic history and peculiarities of the specific business in question. Defending Lockheed Martin presents very different issues than representing a local ambulance company. Each operates against a different regulatory background, and each will be faced with different government strategies to combat fraud. Nevertheless, there are certain fundamental similarities that implicate and organize the internal investigation of all government contractors.

The lawyer may first learn of the potential problem in a myriad of ways. The first appearance of trouble may be the typical type of notice of a government criminal investigation: the grand jury subpoena for documents, the FBI agent interviewing employees, the search warrant. The issues raised by learning of the existence of a government criminal investigation, and the possible responses, are addressed elsewhere in this book and need not be repeated

---

5. *See, e.g.,* United States *ex rel.* Johnson v. Shell Oil Co. et al., 183 F.R.D. 204 (E.D. Tex. 1998).

6. Pickens v. Kanawha River Towing, 916 F. Supp. 702 (S.D. Ohio 1996).

7. United States *ex rel.* American Textile Mfrs. Inst., Inc. v. The Limited, Inc., Case No. C2-97-776, 1997 U.S. Dist. LEXIS 18142 (S.D. Ohio Nov. 13, 1997).

8. *Id.* at 26. Although that court rejected such an expansive view of False Claims Act liability, there is no doubt that such false statements made in a regulatory context subject the company or individual to criminal liability under 18 U.S.C. §1001 as well as possible administrative sanction.

here. It is important to recognize, however, that several government investigative tools are unique to government contractors.

A. *Subpoenas*

1. Inspector General Subpoena

The inspector general (IG) subpoena is an administrative subpoena that may be used by investigators from federal agencies to require the production of information, documents, reports, answers, records, accounts, papers, and other data and documentary evidence necessary for the performance of the Inspector General's duties.[9] The Inspectors General of federal departments or agencies are charged with fighting "fraud, waste and abuse" related to that department or agency. Although the IG subpoena has historically been documentary only, the Inspector General of the Department of Health and Human Services (HHS) has recently used this subpoena to take oral testimony as well as collect documentary evidence. However, counsel may be present for an oral interview made pursuant to an IG subpoena, and a court order must be obtained to compel its enforcement. The evidentiary threshold that must be met before an IG subpoena may be served is equivalent to a grand jury subpoena—"nothing more than official curiosity" is enough to justify its enforcement against a contractor.[10] Additionally, the IG subpoena lacks the secrecy requirement found in Rule 6(e) of the federal grand jury, thereby providing IG investigators with increased flexibility.[11] As a result, the government—especially HHS in health care investigations—makes frequent use of the IG subpoena. IG subpoenas tend to be used by the Government in its civil and administrative investigations.

2. Civil Investigative Demand

A civil investigative demand (CID) is another specialized tool that allows the Attorney General to obtain information crucial to a fraud investigation without the necessity of seeking a grand jury subpoena.[12] Like a grand jury subpoena, a CID may be used to obtain oral testimony, in addition to

---

9. *See* 5 U.S.C. app. 3, 6(a).
10. *See, e.g.,* United States v. Morton Salt Co., 338 U.S. 632, 643, 652 (1950) ("Even if one were to regard the request for information in this case as caused by nothing more than official curiosity, nevertheless law enforcing agencies have a legitimate right to satisfy themselves that corporate behavior is consistent with the law and the public interest.").
11. *See* Pamela Bucy, *Health Care Fraud*, LAW JOURNAL SEMINARS PRESS, 1998, at ¶ 6.04.
12. *See* 28 U.S.C. § 3733.

documentary materials and written interrogatory answers. Congress has only authorized the issuance of CIDs for specific violations of the law, and a CID cannot be issued after the commencement by the government of a civil suit. The information obtained with a CID usually can only be disclosed to government agents within the scope of the authorized inquiry, and ordinarily cannot be disclosed to a qui tam relator suing under the False Claims Act[13] or to law enforcement agencies.[14] Moreover, the person authorized to issue a CID, usually the Attorney General, cannot delegate that authority. Like an IG subpoena, a person who receives a CID may refuse to comply in the first instance—a CID does not carry contempt sanctions, and the Attorney General must obtain a separate court order to compel enforcement of a CID.[15] The Justice Department frequently uses CIDs to gather documents and testimony to assist in determining whether to intervene in a qui tam complaint or (if no such qui tam action has been filed) to file its own lawsuit.

3. DCAA Request

The Defense Contract Audit Agency (DCAA) is the Department of Defense's (DoD) auditor and has extensive audit rights over virtually all DoD contracts. Congress granted DCAA the power to subpoena those records it already has a contractual right to review, but that a contractor has refused to turn over. Congress's grant of this limited subpoena power was not meant to expand the scope of DCAA's authority to review documents, and in most circumstances the power amounts to the right to compel disclosure of a contractor's cost and pricing data. However, companies must be cognizant of the fact that a DCAA request can indicate that the agency has identified a problem with a specific aspect of a contractor's accounting.

4. Medicare Fiscal Intermediary Request

The fiscal intermediaries (FIs) are private companies that process Medicare claims for the federal government. As part of this task, the government has directed these FIs to actively seek to root out fraud by those Medicare providers submitting bills to the FI. Accordingly, one must be aware

---

13. *See* 31 U.S.C. §§ 3729 *et seq.*
14. *See id.*
15. CIDs have been authorized for investigations concerning the Racketeer Influenced and Corrupt Organizations Act, antitrust violations, false claims investigations, and certain enumerated violations of the health care laws. *See* 18 U.S.C. § 1968 (RICO); 15 U.S.C. § 1312 (antitrust); 31 U.S.C. § 3733 (false claims).

that on occasion the FIs' specific requests for information may relate to possible mischarging allegations.

B. *Internal Discovery*

A company may also learn of a potential problem through internal means. All responsible government contractors, as well as virtually all other public companies in the post-Sarbanes-Oxley world, now have internal "hotlines" to handle complaints by employees. Some employees may call these hotlines anonymously to report fraudulent activities by coworkers. Other employees may come forward to their supervisor or the legal department with possible problems. In addition, internal audits may reveal anomalies that demand further investigation. The need for internal investigations in these circumstances is readily apparent. However, a key difference exists concerning what government contractors and non-government contractors may choose to do with the results of such an internal investigation. Government contractors generally have the option of applying for admission to the formal voluntary disclosure programs at the Department of Defense and the Department of Health and Human Services. There are advantages and disadvantages in engaging in such a voluntary disclosure. While it is beyond the scope of this chapter to discuss the calculus that must go into any voluntary disclosure decision, it is important that an attorney recognize from the outset that a voluntary disclosure is a possible strategy, and in some cases may be an obligation,[16] when faced with a possible fraud discovered internally and of which the government has no knowledge.

C. *The Qui Tam Telephone Call*

A government contractor also may first learn of a fraud allegation by receiving a telephone call from a lawyer from the Department of Justice or the U.S. Attorney's Office. In these telephone calls, the government attorney informs the contractor that a civil false claims action has been filed by a qui tam relator against the contractor under seal, that the United States intends to or is seriously considering joining the lawsuit, and that the United States is willing to hear arguments from the contractor or consider settlement. This type of a telephone call is unique to government contractors.

The Civil False Claims Act (FCA) is perhaps the government's oldest, yet one of the most powerful, weapons against government fraud.[17] Originally enacted in the Civil War, the FCA allows the government or a private party

---

16. For example, government contractors are required by law to report violations of the Anti-Kickback Act, 41 U.S.C. § 51 *et seq.*

17. 31 U.S.C. § 3729 *et seq.*; originally codified at Ch. 67, 12 Stat. 696-98.

on behalf of the United States to bring suit against any persons or companies who present a false claim to the government. The FCA provides for the United States to recover treble damages as well as penalties of $5,500 to $11,000 per false claim. In many government contracts, the number of false claims can seem virtually limitless to the contractor. This statute also contains a qui tam provision, which allows the whistle-blower suing on behalf of the United States to share in the recovery awarded the United States, up to 30 percent. The whistle-blower or qui tam relator also can pursue the lawsuit even if the government does not wish to intervene in the litigation. The qui tam relator must initially file his or her lawsuit under seal and without serving the defendant in order to give the United States an opportunity to investigate the allegations in secret and determine whether to join the relator in the lawsuit. Through the FCA and its qui tam provisions, the United States has recovered staggering amounts in damages and penalties in recent years.[18]

Because qui tam lawsuits must be filed under seal, the government contractor may not become aware that a qui tam claim has been filed against it until well after both the relator and the government have completed significant investigation. In fact, because of the under-seal provisions, the contractor's first indication that it is the subject of an FCA claim may not occur until the Department of Justice (DOJ) contacts the contractor "to discuss" the qui tam complaint. The common practice is that the DOJ will first obtain a court order for a "partial unsealing" of the qui tam complaint to allow the department to disclose the existence and nature of the complaint to the defendant. The government attorney in charge of the investigation will then telephone the defendant, inform it of the complaint, and offer it an opportunity to address the allegations.

At that point, the contractor generally has two options: 1) try to convince the United States that the case is without merit and that it should not intervene in the lawsuit, or 2) begin settlement discussions to resolve the matter. The government lawyer may indicate directly or indirectly whether the first option is a realistic possibility at this point in the government's review. In many instances, the government has already reached its decision to intervene and does not even profess to still being open-minded on this issue. It may be that, given the government's firmly held view as to liability or the results of the company's own investigation, the contractor may wish to pursue settlement.

---

18. The Justice Department reports that since 1986, it has recovered more than $15 billion in settlements and recoveries. This includes settlements of approximately $900 million from Tenet Healthcare Corp., $880 million from HCA Inc., $567 million from Serono, S.A., and $569 million from TAP Pharmaceuticals Products, Inc.

A settlement reached prior to the formal unsealing may allow the client to suffer only a one-time hit of bad publicity relating to the fraud.

If the contractor has a strong defense, however, defense counsel may wish to explain to the government why it should not waste government resources in joining the relator in a losing lawsuit. This presentation may take the form of an oral presentation to the government attorney handling the case or a formal written response with extensive citation to legal authority. This initial presentation may be the most important of the case. The government's intervention in a qui tam claim should be avoided if at all possible. Unlike most relators, the United States boasts significant resources and institutional expertise in these matters. In addition, the prestige of the United States has an impact on both judges and juries. Persuading the government to stay out of the case will sometimes be followed by a quick capitulation by relator's counsel unwilling to bear the time and expense of litigating alone. Moreover, even if the government should ultimately elect to intervene, an effective presentation by the company as to the problems with the government's theory may set the stage for reasonable settlement demands by the government and/or narrow the issues for discovery and trial.

In some cases, the contractor does not receive a phone call from the government attorney, but first learns of the qui tam complaint when it is served by the relator. This direct service of the complaint occurs when the United States decides not to intervene while the case is under seal. In those instances, the government's review concludes the qui tam allegations lacked sufficient merit to warrant government participation in prosecuting the lawsuit. The government's declination is a positive sign for the contractor. Nevertheless, the relator can continue to litigate the action against the contractor without the United States and, as with any lawsuit, it will be important for the contractor's counsel to investigate quickly and thoroughly the allegations in order to defend the litigation.

III. RESPONDING TO A FRAUD INVESTIGATION: BASIC PRINCIPLES FOR GOVERNMENT CONTRACTORS

A. *Unique Features of Fraud Investigations Faced by Government Contractors*

1. The Qui Tam Suit

As the previous section makes clear, one of the unique features with which legal counsel for a government contractor must contend is the qui tam lawsuit. The qui tam provisions of the False Claims Act—whereby a private party (the relator) stands in the shoes of the United States and sues government contractors for fraud on behalf of the United States in return for a percentage of the recovery—raise a host of unusual and distinctive issues. The False Claims Act has special provisions or case law addressing virtually every aspect of litigation, from the procedure for the initial filing by the qui tam relator under seal to the procedures for settling of the lawsuit by the United States and/or relator. It is essential for the attorney for government contractors to be knowledgeable about this unique body of law and to take it into account in identifying issues and conducting any internal investigation.[19]

2. Complex Structure of Parties

In any fraud investigation by the United States against a government contractor, there will typically be at least two, and often three, distinct and separate "parties" on the government side. One is the Justice Department or U.S. Attorney's Office, which is the government's law firm responsible for running the investigation and legal action. The other is the government agency that contracted with the company and that arguably was defrauded. This government agency is, in theory, the "client/victim" of the Justice Department. In the case of qui tam lawsuits, there is a third party on the government side, since the relator has a financial interest and a statutory right to participate as a party to the litigation against the government contractor.[20] Quite obviously, this unusual proliferation of parties has the potential to create a dynamic and complex interrelationship between the various interests.

The relationship among these parties on the government side will change as the suit progresses, but at any given moment they may well have differing, and even conflicting, views of the case. The relator may wish to litigate aggressively, either in the hope of seeking to win a big payday or due to personal animus arising from the whistle-blower's often former employment with the contractor.

The government agency that is supposedly the victim may have a very different view, and is often more sympathetic to the contractor. Many times the government contractor has a longstanding and ongoing relationship performing services for the government agency, which makes the agency reluctant to seek harsh measures against the company. It is not unheard of, for instance, for employees of the contractor's customer to testify favorably for the defendant.

---

19. For the definitive treatise on the subject, *see* JOHN T. BOESE, CIVIL FALSE CLAIMS AND *QUI TAM* ACTIONS (ASPEN LAW & BUSINESS 2d ed.).

20. 31 U.S.C. § 3730(c) & (d).

The Justice Department, on the other hand, often finds itself in the middle between the wishes of its client, the "defrauded" government agency, and the relator's desire for a large monetary settlement. In addition, the Justice Department itself is often conflicted between its institutional imperative of enforcing the laws and ensuring that the United States receives the largest damages and fines possible and, in contrast, its need to balance the broader policy impact and precedent created by any single case.

The key point is that there are a number of interested parties on the government side of any investigation or lawsuit against a government contractor. The different interests on the other side present problems and opportunities for the company's attorney. At every stage, the attorney for the government contractor must keep all these stakeholders in mind and conduct his or her work accordingly, taking advantage of the different vantage points and interests on the government side wherever possible.

3. Regulations and Oversight

A government contractor, unlike many commercial concerns, is always subject to an intricate web of detailed regulations and elaborate performance verification and oversight. These rules will likely consist of highly specific statutes, regulations, or contracts governing interactions with the relevant government agency. For example, many investigations involve fraud or wrongdoing in obtaining government contracts, so the rules governing private companies in such federal procurements would be the lengthy and highly technical Federal Acquisition Regulation (FAR). Similar comprehensive regulatory schemes control a contractor's dealings with virtually every agency or department of the government, whether DoD, HHS, EPA, GSA, or another government agency. These regulations will invariably be very complicated—and potentially very helpful. In the event that a contractor's lawyer becomes aware of the existence of a fraud investigation, whether qui tam or government initiated, it will be necessary to gain a thorough understanding of the applicable regulations as quickly as possible.

It is impossible to overstate the importance of finding and learning the applicable regulations. Government contracts fraud cases frequently turn on the interpretation of the complicated regulatory scheme. In many instances, the lawyers handling the investigation from the Justice Department or U.S. Attorney's Office are not expert in the specialized fields, such as defense contracting or billing for health care services, and government contractors can succeed in having investigations ended or cases dropped by educating the government about its own arcane and technical rules. Learning the applicable regulatory scheme better than the government is essential to any internal investigation for government contractors.

By understanding the regulatory scheme, the lawyer also will be in a better position to find and know the controlling documents. In a case based on a government procurement or grant, one should find, and then study, the contract or grant documents. In a health care case, identify and review the key patient or billing records or physician agreements. These documents will often solve the case for the contractor or, at least, clarify the issues and frame the internal investigation. Also, the attorney for the government contractor should search for documents or testimony showing that individuals from the government agency involved in the contract approved, or at least knew of, the contractor's contested conduct. Government investigations and lawsuits can often be derailed by demonstrating that government officials reviewed and acquiesced in the contractor's actions. Although "government knowledge" is not an absolute defense, it goes far to demonstrating good faith and lack of wrongful intent on the part of the contractor;[21] as a practical matter, it goes far toward ending the United States' interest in a matter.

4. Parallel Criminal Proceedings

Whenever the government is pursuing a civil fraud investigation, it should be assumed that the government also will be conducting a parallel criminal investigation into any allegations of wrongdoing. Because of the numerous quasi-criminal investigators from the IG and other law enforcement groups involved in government contracts matters, and because of the priority given to health care fraud and other government contracts fraud among the "Public Integrity" units at the Justice Department and U.S. Attorney's Offices, there is a high probability that any allegations against a government contractor will be reviewed for possible criminal prosecution.

While such a parallel criminal investigation does not always ensue, the lawyer for a government contractor faced with allegations of possible wrongdoing is best advised to always assume that there may be a parallel criminal investigation.

---

21. 18. *See, e.g.,* Wang v. FMC Corp., 975 F.2d 1412, 1420 (9th Cir. 1992); United States *ex rel.* Butler v. Hughes Helicopter Co., 1993 U.S. Dist. LEXIS 17844, *41 (C.D. Cal. Aug. 25, 1993), *aff'd,* 71 F.3d 321 (9th Cir. 1995).

5. Waiver of Privilege

As discussed above, one of the key differences between government contractors and non-government contractors is that the government contractor may elect to avail itself of a formal voluntary disclosure program offered by the government agency or department with which the company contracted.[22] Voluntary disclosure of possible wrongdoing should be carefully considered by all companies in light of the obligations imposed under Sarbanes-Oxley and the benefits of cooperation in prosecutors' charging decisions and sentencing. This approach may be especially beneficial to a government contractor because, along with allowing the company to avoid some of the harsher criminal or administrative punishments by demonstrating the contractor's good faith and cooperation, voluntary disclosure may allow the contractor to maintain ongoing good relations with the government agency for which it works and receives contracts.

As part of demonstrating the contractor's good faith and cooperation, however, the government may urge or essentially require that the contractor waive its attorney-client and work product privileges in connection with the subject matter of the disclosure.[23] Therefore, while conducting any internal investigation of potential government fraud, lawyers for the government contractor should be aware that there may well be some form of voluntary disclosure of their own activities and work product. Attorneys for the government contractor must perform their internal investigation with the recognition that their own communications and work product may ultimately end up with the Justice Department and may even become available to the general public.

Even where the contractor does not make a voluntary disclosure, the lawyer should be prepared to have the government obtain his or her privileged materials. Often the contractor's best chance to escape indictment or the government's intervention in a qui tam lawsuit is to make a fulsome presentation to the government attorneys as to why the allegations against the contractor are incorrect. To be successful, this presentation will necessarily draw upon the results of the contractor's internal investigation. Thus, a significant collateral effect of making such a presentation to the government is the potential waiver of both the attorney-client privilege and the work-product doctrine.[24]

---

22. *See supra*, Section II.B.
23. *See* Section V of Chapter 2, "Implications of the Attorney-Client Privilege and Work-Product Doctrine."
24. It has been argued, and one court has adopted the position, that disclosure to the United States in this situation should not result in a general waiver of either privilege. *See* Diversified Indus., Inc. v. Meredith, 572 F.2d 596, 610 (8th Cir. 1977). Other courts have

The contractor's attorney should attempt to obtain a confidentiality or a non-disclosure agreement with the Department of Justice in which it agrees not to deem such a presentation to be a waiver and not to disclose to the relator any materials obtained from the report or the presentation. The Justice Department may or may not be willing to enter into such an agreement. Although some courts have upheld a particular confidentiality agreement, many courts have not found their existence dispositive of the waiver issue.[25] The most effective way to mitigate this potential consequence of a waiver of privilege is to presume its inevitability and to plan your internal investigation from the outset with such a possible waiver in mind.

6. Suspension and Debarment

Avoiding the administrative sanction of debarment[26] (i.e., no longer being eligible for additional government contracts) is often the first and foremost goal for a government contractor. Even a brief suspension of a company's ability to obtain government contracts can have a devastating impact. For many companies who rely heavily on government contracts, any prolonged suspension or debarment is the equivalent of the corporate death penalty.

The federal government imposes suspension or debarment of a contractor to protect the government from engaging in business relations with dishonest, unethical, or otherwise irresponsible persons. Suspension or debarment is primarily imposed for a conviction or civil judgment for commission of a fraud, antitrust violation, or other offense indicating a lack of business integrity or honesty. Depending on the nature and severity of the crime, debarment may be statutorily mandated.[27] However, most suspensions and debarment are discretionary. One of primary factors considered by a debarring official is whether the contractor has fully investigated the circumstances concerning the cause of the possible debarment and, if so, whether it made the investigation's results

---

specifically rejected this argument, however, and the law in this area remains unsettled. *See* Westinghouse Elec. Corp. v. Republic of the Philippines, 951 F.2d 1414 (3d Cir. 1991); Permian Corp. v. United States, 665 F.2d 1214 (D.C. Cir. 1981).

25. *See* Westinghouse Electric Corp. v. Republic of the Philippines, 951 F.2d 1414, 1427 (3d Cir. 1991) ("Even though the DOJ apparently agreed not to disclose the information, under traditional waiver doctrine a voluntary disclosure to a third party waives the attorney-client privilege even if the third party agrees not to disclose the communications to anyone else.").

26. In the Medicare and Medicaid context, suspension or debarment from participating in these government programs is generally referred to as "exclusion." 42 U.S.C. 1320a-7.

27. *See, e.g.,* 42 U.S.C. 1320a-7.

available to the debarring official.[28] As a result, conducting a thorough internal investigation and making a fulsome voluntary disclosure to the government agency can be critical to avoiding this administrative sanction. Debarment officials also will look to cooperation with the government investigation, restitution, and discipline of responsible employees as other key factors in evaluating the company's present responsibility. Where serious criminal or fraudulent activity is alleged, attorneys conducting internal investigations should be mindful of the possibility (and likely deleterious impact) of suspension or debarment as well as the advisability of approaching the relevant debarment authorities earlier, rather than later, in the investigative process.

IV. CONCLUSION

In many respects, the principal objectives in conducting an internal investigation for a government contractor are the same as for any other corporate client. First, one wants to be in a position to convince the ultimate finder of fact—whether it be a civil jury or a U.S. Attorney deciding whether to indict—of the strength of the company's position. In the government contractor context, there often is a special wrinkle because of the False Claims Act's procedure whereby whistle-blowers file qui tam lawsuits under seal and the Justice Department then decides whether to intervene. As a result, lawyers for government contractors often find themselves conducting investigations aimed toward convincing the DOJ lawyers why the whistle-blower is mistaken and why intervention in the qui tam lawsuit is not warranted.

The other objective common to all internal investigations is to follow the maxim of the medical profession:[29] "do no harm." The response to the government investigation should not cause the company to be in deeper trouble than before. For attorneys, this usually entails preventing the company employees from destroying documents, lying to investigators, or otherwise obstructing justice.[30] Retaliating against the suspected whistle-blower is another common temptation that must be resisted by government contractors. In addition, the lawyer should not create new evidence that can be used against the company—a concern where the waiver of attorney-client and attorney work product privileges is a real possibility.

---

28. FAR 9-406-1.
29. *See* In re Qwest Communications International Inc. Sec. Litig., CV No. 06-1070 (10th Cir., June 19, 2006) (and cases cited therein).
30. *See supra* Chapter 4, "Perjury and Obstruction of Justice."

In one important respect, the government contractor has a very different objective. In addition to being the putative plaintiff against the company, the government also is a valuable customer. For this reason, the government contractor strives to remain on good terms with its customer throughout any litigation. In addition to the primary objective of avoiding criminal and civil liability, the lawyer for the government contractor must also conduct his or her activities with a view toward mitigating or eliminating any potential damage to the company's ongoing relationship with the government department or agency with which it does business. In this context, a scorched earth litigation strategy is rarely in the contractor's best interest. Rather, understanding the regulatory scheme and convincing the government agency and Justice Department lawyers of the contractor's good faith are usually more useful approaches for the attorney conducting an internal investigation for a government contractor.

No Security: Internal Investigations into Violations of the Securities Laws

12

Michael J. Shepard and Robert B. Buehler

I. OVERVIEW OF SECURITIES VIOLATIONS 354
II. DUTIES—AND PRESSURE—TO UNCOVER, INVESTIGATE, AND REPORT VIOLATIONS 360
    A. Publicly Traded Companies 360
    B. Brokers and Dealers 381
III. CONDUCTING INTERNAL INVESTIGATIONS AND DEALING WITH RELATED ISSUES IN THE CONDUCT OF PARALLEL PROCEEDINGS 384
    A. Ensuring an Independent Investigation 386
    B. The (Largely) Insoluble Problem of Using the Investigation to Assist in Dealing with the Government without Waiving the Privilege 389

Michael J. Shepard and Robert B. Buehler are shareholders at Heller Ehrman LLP. The authors thank Heller Ehrman associates Erin McMurray-Killelea and Zachary Taylor, as well as Samantha Choe, a 2006 Heller Ehrman summer associate, without whom many good thoughts would be missing and in place of many citations would be only the phrase "find cite."

C. Fifth Amendment Assertions: The Difficult Choices Faced by Individuals in Internal Investigations, and the Potential Impact of Those Choices on the Company 406
D. Stays of Parallel Civil and SEC Proceedings 413
E. Auditors' Involvement in Internal Investigations 417
IV. CONCLUDING LESSONS 420

A<small>NY INTERNAL INVESTIGATION</small> calls upon the lawyer to negotiate between Scylla and Charybdis: the risks of exposing the corporation to increased liability by failing to inquire sufficiently into possible wrongdoing, and the risks of exposing the company to increased liability by developing evidence of that wrongdoing (and possibly additional wrongdoing) that can later be used against the corporation and against valuable employees, officers, and directors, either criminally, in civil litigation, or both. Internal investigations into violations of the securities laws add several additional twists that heighten the challenge: the complexities created by various obligations to disclose wrongdoing; the pressures generated by the likelihood of parallel proceedings; the delicate interaction between the company and the accounting firms involved in the conduct under investigation; and the new burdens placed on public companies by the Sarbanes-Oxley Act. The existence of these twists means that internal investigations into potential violations of the securities laws put a premium on the speed, accuracy, and judgment that is desirable in all internal investigations.

This chapter begins by briefly identifying the most typical securities violations that generate internal investigations. It then describes the duties to investigate and to disclose those violations, as well as the risks of parallel proceedings inherent in such violations, and then offers some principles to assist in making the challenging decisions inherent in such investigations.

I. OVERVIEW OF SECURITIES VIOLATIONS

Securities violations that might prompt an internal investigation come in many forms. For publicly traded companies, the most common violations are financial frauds, such as misstatements of earnings or failure to disclose adequately some material news—a result of a range of conduct from the more traditional "cooking of the books" as a way of inflating revenues[1] to the more current stock option backdating,[2] resulting in understated expenses;[3] violations of the Foreign Corrupt Practices Act;[4] and insider trading.[5]

---

1. Starting in the late 1990s, "book-cooking" at companies such as Enron, WorldCom, Cendant, and McKesson resulted in dozens of indictments and prison sentences as well as billions of dollars in civil suits. For more on the criminal cases, see U.S. v. Fastow, No. 02 Cr. 00889 *(W.D. Tx., indicted Oct. 31, 2002);* U.S. v. Ebbers, No. 02 Cr. 001144 (S.D.N.Y., indicted March 1, 2004); U.S. v. Scrushy, No. 03 Cr. 00530 (N.D. Al., indicted Oct. 26, 2005). *See, e.g., Crime and Consequences Still Weigh on Corporate World; Four Years Later, Enron's Shadow Lingers as Change Comes Slowly,* N.Y. TIMES, Jan. 5, 2006, at C1; *Quattrone Walks,* WALL ST. J., Aug. 23, 2006, at A10; *Bernie Ebbers Told to Start 25 Years in Prison on September 26,* WASH. POST, Sept. 8, 2006, at D3; *McKesson Agrees to Settle an Accounting Fraud Suit,* N.Y. TIMES, Jan. 13, 2005, at C2; *Fastow a Key for Plaintiffs in Bank Suits,* N.Y. TIMES, Oct. 2, 2006, at C1; *Lay, Skilling Pursued by U.S. for $183 Million,* WALL ST. J., July 1, 2006, at A1. *Clean Sweep: HealthSouth's Scrushy is Acquitted—Outcome Shows Challenges for Sarbanes-Oxley Act; SEC Suit Still Ahead—No Job Offer from Company,* WALL ST. J., June 29, 2005, at A1; *Acquittal Casts Cloud Over Sarbanes-Oxley in Its First Test;* WALL ST. J., June 29, 2005, at A8; *Former Chief of HealthSouth Acquitted in $2.7 Billion Fraud,* N.Y. TIMES, June 29, 2005, at A1; *McKesson Ex-Official Is Cleared,* WALL ST. J., July 12, 2005, at C4; *Symbol of an Era: Lay, Skilling Are Convicted of Fraud—Jurors Reject Defense Claim That Enron Was Clean; Question of Credibility—Two "Very Controlling People,"* WALL ST. J., May 26, 2006, at A1; *The Enron Verdicts: Trial Fails to Answer Many Questions About a Spectacular Collapse,* WALL ST. J., May 26, 2006, at A9.

2. As of November 2006, at least 120 companies were being investigated by the SEC and/or Justice Department, have had executive/director departures, or have issued restatements because of matters related to options backdating. Indictments have been returned in two cases, against executives from Brocade Communications Systems, Inc., and Comverse Technology, Inc. *Ex-Brocade Executives Are Indicted,* WALL ST. J., Aug. 11, 2006, at A6; *A Fugitive's Haven in Africa Turned Out to Be Anything But: Kobi Alexander Is Arrested in Namibia; the Tip-Off Was Hefty Bank Transfer,* WALL ST. J., Sept. 28, 2006, at A1. The Wall Street Journal has been keeping a daily tally of developments. *Perfect Payday Options Scorecard,* WALL ST. J., Oct. 2, 2006, *available at* http://online.wsj.com/public/resources/documents/info-optionsscore06-full.html.

3. Section 10(b) of the Securities Exchange Act of 1934, 15 U.S.C. § 78j(b); *In the Matter of Sensormatic Electronics Corp.,* Rel. No. 33-7518 (misstated earnings); S.E.C. v. Fries et al., Lit. Rel. No. 14263, Rel. No. AE-604 (materially overstated results of operations); S.E.C. v. Time Energy Systems, Lit. Rel. No. 11106, Rel. No. AE-99 (misstated net and retained earnings).

4. Section 13(b)(2) of the 1934 Act, 15 U.S.C. § 78m(b)(2); Exchange Rules 13b2-1 and 13b2-2, 17 C.F.R. §§ 240.13b2-1 and 240.13b2-2; S.E.C. v. Moskowitz et al., Lit. Rel. No. 11849 (misleading statements to auditors); S.E.C. v. Cali Computer Systems, Inc., et al., Lit. Rel. No. 11733, Rel. No. AE-190 (false and misleading statements to auditors concerning performance of its franchise contract obligations and opening of franchise centers using its products); S.E.C. v. Hermetite Corp., et al., Lit. Rel. No. 9756 (violation of books and records, and internal control provisions of the FCPA).

5. Under the "classical" theory of insider trading, a corporate insider who trades in the securities of his corporation on the basis of material, nonpublic information violates Section

Corporations generally are held responsible for employees who engage in these financial frauds and corrupt practices.[6] Insider trading can be unique because a corporation is liable for a civil penalty for the insider trading of an employee only if the corporation "knew or recklessly disregarded the fact" that the employee was likely to engage in insider trading and "failed to take appropriate steps to prevent such act or acts before they occurred."[7] While these limits may affect the need for and conduct of an internal investigation,[8] they do not free the corporation from all liability. For example, a lesser standard applies to the imposition of liability other than civil penalties, ranging from disgorgement to injunctive relief and from private civil damage remedies to delisting.[9] There also are stock exchange rules broad enough to permit

---

10(b) of the 1934 Act and Rule 10b-5, 17 C.F.R. § 240.10b-5. United States v. O'Hagan, 117 S. Ct. 2199, 2207 (1997). Under the misappropriation theory of insider trading, a person who misappropriates confidential information and trades on the basis of that information, in breach of a duty owed to the source of the information, violates § 10(b) and Rule 10b-5. *Id.* While the classical theory is based on the insider's breach of a fiduciary duty owed to the corporation's shareholders, the misappropriation theory is based on the trader's deception of those who entrusted him with access to the confidential information. *Id.*

6. A corporation may be liable for the violations of its employees under theories of respondeat superior. Hollinger v. Titan Capital Corp., 914 F.2d 1564, 1576-78 (9th Cir. 1990). In addition, under the controlling person standard of § 20(a) of the 1934 Act, 15 U.S.C. § 78t(a), the defendant bears the burden of proving that it acted in good faith and did not induce the violation by the controlled person. *Id.* at 1575.

7. *See* Section 21A(b)(1)(A) of the Securities Exchange Act of 1934, 15 U.S.C. § 78u-1(b)(1)(A). This provision specifies the standard for corporate liability for a civil penalty as a "controlling person" of an inside trader. *See* Section 21A(a)(1), 15 U.S.C. § 78u-1(a)(1) (civil penalty may be imposed on a person who "directly or indirectly controlled the person who committed the violation"). Liability, would, of course attach if the trading was conducted for the benefit of the corporation.

Section 21A(b)(2), 15 U.S.C. § 78u-1(b)(2), further specifies that a penalty may not be imposed on an employer on the basis of respondeat superior and that the controlling person standards of Section 21A(b)(1) must be met.

8. *See* Section II.(A).(1).(c).

9. Section 21A(b)(2) provides that the general controlling person standard set forth in Section 20(a) of the 1934 Act, 15 U.S.C. § 78t(a), does not apply to actions *for civil penalties* for insider trading under Section 21A(a). However, Section 21A does not specify the standard for liability of a controlling person for an employee's insider trading in other contexts, such as SEC actions for disgorgement or private actions for damages. In these contexts, the general standard for controlling person liability set forth in Section 20(a) of the 1934 Act, 15 U.S.C. § 78t(a), still applies. Under Section 20(a), "[e]very person who, directly or indirectly, controls any person liable under any provision of this chapter or of any rule or regulation thereunder" is jointly and severally liable for the controlled person's violation, "unless the controlling person acted in good faith and did not directly or indirectly induce the act or acts constituting the violation or cause of action." Section 21A(b)(2).

the delisting or expulsion of an issuer for the insider trading of its employees, but it does not appear that either the NYSE or the NASD has ever taken such action against an ongoing, established business.[10]

Brokers and dealers[11] face an even wider range of potential liability in the event their registered or unregistered employees defraud customers, breach any fiduciary duties owed to customers (for example, by recommending unsuitable securities to a customer),[12] trade excessively in a customer's account for

---

10. Although no reported cases against major firms exist, NYSE Rule 801.00, which superseded Rule 499 on May 5, 2005, provides that: "Securities admitted to the list may be suspended from dealings or removed from the list at any time." Rule 802.01 states that the numerical criteria (such as number of publicly held shares and aggregate market value of publicly held shares) for listing on the NYSE are not exclusive criteria and that the NYSE may consider other factors, such as "the failure of a company to make timely, adequate, and accurate disclosures of information to its shareholders and the investing public; failure to observe good accounting practices in reporting of earnings and financial position; other conduct not in keeping with sound public policy; unsatisfactory financial conditions and/or operating results; most recent independent public accountant's opinion on the financial statements contains a qualified opinion, adverse opinion, disclaimer opinion, or unqualified opinion with a "going concern" emphasis; inability to meet current debt obligations or to adequately finance operations; abnormally low selling price or volume of trading; unwarranted use of company funds for the repurchase of its equity securities; any other event or condition which may exist or occur that makes further dealings or listing of the securities on the Exchange inadvisable or unwarranted in the opinion of the Exchange."

Similarly, NASD Rule 4300 provides that Nasdaq "may deny initial inclusion or apply additional or more stringent criteria for the initial or continued inclusion of particular securities or suspend or terminate the inclusion of particular securities based on any event, condition, or circumstance which exists or occurs that makes initial or continued inclusion of the securities in Nasdaq inadvisable or unwarranted in the opinion of Nasdaq, even though the securities meet all enumerated criteria for initial or continued inclusion in Nasdaq." NASD Rule 4330 provides that Nasdaq may "deny inclusion or apply additional or more stringent criteria for the initial or continued inclusion of particular securities or suspend or terminate the inclusion of an otherwise qualified security if: . . . (3) Nasdaq deems it necessary to prevent fraudulent and manipulative acts and practices, to promote just and equitable principles of trade, or to protect investors and the public interest."

11. The term "broker" is defined in Section 3(a)(4) of the Securities Exchange Act of 1934 to mean "any person engaged in the business of effecting transactions in securities for the account of others. . . ." The term "dealer" is defined in Section 3(a)(5) of the Securities Exchange Act of 1934 to mean "any person engaged in the business of buying and selling securities for his own account, through a broker or otherwise . . . or any person insofar as he buys or sells securities for his own account, either individually or in some fiduciary capacity, but not as a part of regular business."

This article refers to brokers and dealers collectively as "broker-dealers."

12. *In re* Hampton, Exchange Act Rel. No. 35,570 (Apr. 5, 1995); *In re* Grosby, Exchange Act Rel. No. 34,805 (Oct. 7, 1994); *In re* Sela, Exchange Act Rel. No. 33, 789 (Mar. 21, 1994).

the purpose of generating commissions,[13] or manipulate the market through activity such as frontrunning.[14] The SEC has sought to impose liability on firms and individuals based on the failure to provide reasonable supervision over the actions of their employees. The SEC and self-regulatory organizations (SROs) have increasingly sought to impose such liability,[15] which can

---

13. *In re* Parodi, Exchange Act Rel. No. 27,299, 44 S.E.C. Docket (CCH) 1111 (Sept. 27, 1989) (broker churned accounts); Mihara v. Dean Witter & Co., Inc., 614 F.2d 814, 820 (9th Cir. 1980) (churning is when "a securities broker engages in excessive trading in disregard of his customer's investment objectives for the purpose of generating commission business. . . .").

14. A broker or dealer front-runs when he or she trades in anticipation of a large block transaction of one of his or her customers. The broker or dealer benefits from the price change in the security expected to follow the block transaction. *See, e.g., In re* NYSE Specialists Securities Litigation, 405 F. Supp. 2d 281 (S.D.N.Y. 2005). *See also* NASD MANUAL & NOTICES TO MEMBERS, Conduct Rules, IM-2110-3; *'Squawk Box' Figure Is Aiding Federal Probe,* WALL ST. J., Mar. 14, 2005, at C1 (describing investigation of traders using access to confidential communications among Wall Street firms to front-run trades by mutual funds and other institutional investors).

15. *S.E.C. v. Citron, et al.,* Civil Action No. SA CV 96-0074 AHS (E. Ex.) (C.D. Cal.), Lit. Rel. No. 14792 (Jan. 24, 1996); *In the Matter of Credit Suisse First Boston Corporation, Jerry Nowlin and Douglas Montague,* 1998 WL 30378 (S.E.C.), Rel. No. 34-39595, 66 S.E.C. Docket 807. *See also John H. Gutfreund,* Exchange Act Rel. No. 31554, 52 S.E.C. 2849 (Dec. 3, 1992) (sanctions imposed on Salomon Brothers executives based on their failure to take any action upon learning that the head of the firm's Government Trading Desk had committed what amounted to a criminal act by purposely submitting a false $3.15 billion bid for U.S. Treasury securities); *see also Patricia A. Johnson,* Exchange Act Rel. No. 35698, 59 S.E.C. 618 (May 10, 1995) (branch manager ignored numerous warning signs that broker was misappropriating customer funds and committing other fraudulent acts); *Dan A. Druz,* Exchange Act Rel. No. 35203, 58 S.E.C. 1526 (Jan. 9, 1995) (branch office manager ignored repeated indications that broker was defrauding customers by executing unauthorized trades); *Prudential Bache Securities,* Exchange Act Rel. No. 35698, 59 S.E.C. 618 (May 10, 1995) (sanctions imposed on a branch manager for failure to follow numerous supervisory and compliance procedures designed to detect and prevent violations of the law); *Frank J. Custable,* Exchange Act Rel. No. 33324, 55 S.E.C. 1794 (Dec. 10, 1993) (manager failed to follow firm's compliance procedures, including maintaining customer contact log, and reviewing employee's customer book); *Nicolas A. Boccella,* Exchange Act Rel. No. 26574, 42 S.E.C. 1388 (Feb. 27, 1989) (manager failed to "police compliance" with firm procedures relating to hand delivery of checks to customers by sales brokers and identification and proper designation of employee-related accounts); *Steven P. Sanders and Daniel M. Porush,* Exchange Act Rel. No. 34-40600, 68 S.E.C. Docket 745 (Oct. 26, 1998) (head trader employed by broker-dealer engaged in excessive and fraudulent markups; SEC sustained sanctions imposed by NASD against president of broker-dealer for president's failure to supervise head trader); *Stuart K. Patrick,* Exchange Act Rel. No. 34-32314, 51 S.E.C. 419 (May 17, 1993) (floor trader employed by broker-dealer committed violations in connection with trades in firm's proprietary account; SEC sustained NYSE's sanctions against Patrick, the chief executive officer and president of the firm, where Patrick failed to establish systems and procedures and failed to provide supervision over trader).

be avoided by proof that: (1) there were established procedures to prevent and detect the violation; and (2) the broker or dealer implemented the procedures without cause to believe that they were not being followed.[16]

Insider trading issues for brokerage firms are even more complex. While not automatically liable for insider trading of their employees, brokerage firms can be responsible for such trading on a lesser standard than a corporation: liability may arise from the firm's failure to have in place and enforce written policies and procedures reasonably designed to prevent insider trading violations.[17] This concern is highlighted by the ability of integrated firms to offer a range of financial services from investment banking to retail sales, which results in the presence of insider information in one portion of the firm

---

16. Securities Exchange Act Section 15(b)(4)(E); 15 U.S.C. § 78o(b)(4)(E).

Section 15(b)(4)(E) is a "safe harbor" provision, and a broker-dealer may comply with it and avoid sanctions for failure to supervise by having and enforcing procedures as specified in that Section. See In re Lehman Bros., Inc., Rel. No. 34-37673, 1996 WL 519914, *7 n.11 (Sept. 12, 1996); In re Goldman, Sachs & Co., Rel. No. 34-33576, 1994 WL 29479, *6 (Feb. 3, 1994).

Section 15(b)(4)(E) does not specify that establishing and following such procedures is the *only* way that a firm can satisfy its supervision obligations. However, several SEC opinions have emphasized the importance of formal written procedures, especially for large firms, and have indicated that, if violations occur, the absence of adequate procedures is likely to result in a finding that the firm did not provide reasonable supervision. See In re Smith Barney, Inc., Rel. No. 34-39118, 1997 WL 583802, *5 (Sept. 23, 1997) ("The responsibility of broker dealers to supervise their employees by means of effective, established procedures is a critical component in the federal investor protection scheme regulating the securities market."; firm liable for failure to supervise because absence of written procedures "or other institutionally-recognized practice" resulted in failure to detect violations by firm's municipal derivatives banker) (citations omitted); In re Lehman Bros., Inc., Rel. No. 37673, 1996 WL 519914, *8 (Sept. 12, 1996) (firm liable for failure to supervise where firm had insufficient policies or procedures designed to prevent excessive markups); In re Goldman, Sachs & Co., Rel. No. 34-33576, 1994 WL 29479, *6 (Feb. 3, 1994) ("It is essential . . . not only that a system of controls adequate to meet the problems inherent in a large and scattered organization be established but also that such controls be effectively enforced by those in authority;" firm was not entitled to protection of safe harbor provision where firm had general policy regarding execution of trades to realize tax losses, but policy was not committed to writing, firm did not articulate criteria explaining general rule, and firm had no procedures for detecting violations of policy) (citations omitted); In re Smith Barney, Harris Upham & Co., Rel. No. 21813, 1985 WL 61318, *7 (Mar. 5, 1985) ("Broker-dealers must not only adopt effective procedures but also ensure that their branch managers and compliance personnel fully understand and follow their job requirements and firm compliance procedures."; firm had inadequate procedures for detecting improper sales of uncovered options).

17. S.E.C. v. First Boston Corp., Lit. Rel. No. 11092 [1986-1987 Transfer Binder] CCH Fed. Sec. L. Rep. ¶ 92,712 (S.D.N.Y. May 5, 1986); S.E.C. v. Kidder, Peabody & Co., Lit. Rel. No. 11452, 38 S.E.C. Docket 647 (S.D.N.Y. June 4, 1987).

and a special need to ensure that trading decisions are not made by employees in possession of material nonpublic information.[18]

II. DUTIES—AND PRESSURES—TO UNCOVER, INVESTIGATE, AND REPORT VIOLATIONS

Publicly traded companies and broker-dealers involved in potential violations of the securities laws must assess not only their own liability for such violations, but also the extent to which they have an obligation to report the violation in a public filing or to a stock exchange, or to investigate the violation for purposes of making a report. The existence of these obligations impacts the necessity for conducting an investigation and the decision whether to disclose the results to prosecutors and/or the SEC. In addition, these obligations affect the process of conducting the investigation, and particularly the process of protecting any written report or memoranda of the investigation. The Sarbanes-Oxley Act has added to the obligations of publicly traded companies to investigate possible wrongdoing.

This section describes the obligations of and pressures on publicly traded companies and of brokers and dealers to investigate and report wrongdoing; the next section addresses the issues created by such investigations and reports in the context of parallel proceedings, where the results of investigations and reports can be turned against the corporation or firm.

A. *Publicly Traded Companies*

For publicly traded companies, a body of law has developed about what material a company is obligated to disclose to the public; flowing in part

---

Section 21A(b)(1)(B) of the 1934 Act provides that a civil penalty may be imposed on a broker or dealer or investment adviser who "knowingly or recklessly failed to establish, maintain, or enforce any policy or procedure required under Section 78o(f) of this title [Section 15(f) of the Exchange Act] or Section 80b-4a of this title [Section 204A of the Investment Advisers Act of 1940] and such failure substantially contributed to or permitted the occurrence of the act or acts constituting the violation." Section 15(f) of the Exchange Act and Section 204A of the Investment Advisers Act of 1940, referenced in Section 21A(b)(1)(B), require brokers, dealers, and investment advisers to establish "written policies and procedures reasonably designed" to prevent insider trading violations.

18. Rule 14e-3(b) creates a "safe harbor" by acknowledging the use of "Ethical walls" and restricted trading lists as effective defenses to firm liability for insider trading by firm employees. "Ethical walls" typically consist of written policies restricting the dissemination of material, nonpublic information within the firm. Restricted lists prohibit trading in the identified security while material, nonpublic information exists within the firm about the security. *In re* Merrill, Lynch, Pierce, Fenner & Smith, Exchange Act Rel. No. 8459 [1967-1969 Transfer Binder] CCH Fed. Sec. L. Rep. ¶ 77,629 at 83,350.

from those obligations and, in part, from other sources such as the Sarbanes-Oxley legislation and rules promulgated thereunder, standards are being created governing when investigations are required. Described in Part A.1 below, these disclosure and investigation obligations are, as a general matter, limited to material information, but the utility of that limitation is suspect given the development of the concept of "qualitative" materiality discussed in Part A.2 below. In any event, it appears that what is actually happening in the field is outpacing the development of legal standards: based in part on public relations issues and on a desire to limit government sanctions in the event the alleged wrongdoing later becomes known to the government, many companies are promptly initiating internal investigations as soon as they get wind of possible wrongdoing, without pausing to parse their legal obligations to do so.

1. Duties of Disclosure

While a corporation need not disclose information of wrongdoing unless there is a specific duty to do so,[19] there are at least two types of situations in the securities laws in which a specific duty to disclose information exists.[20] For information that is material: (1) a corporation must disclose it when required by a specific SEC rule; and, (2) even in the absence of a specific SEC rule, when a corporation discloses information, it must also disclose such further information as is necessary to ensure that its disclosure is not inaccurate, incomplete, or misleading. *Roeder*, 814 F.2d at 27; *Yeaman*, 987 F. Supp. at 377-78.

---

19. *See, e.g., Roeder v. Alpha Industries, Inc.*, 814 F.2d 22, 27 (1st Cir. 1987) (no general affirmative duty to disclose material information where "there is no insider trading, no statute or regulation requiring disclosure, and no inaccurate, incomplete, or misleading prior disclosures"); United States v. Yeaman, 987 F. Supp. 373, 377-78 (E.D. Pa. 1997) (same), cited in Securities Release No. ID-247, 2004 WL 407490 (March 4, 2004) (SEC revoked registration of company's common stock after it failed to file annual and quarterly reports); United States Securities & Exchange Comm'n v. Fehn, 97 F.3d 1276, 1289 (9th Cir. 1996) (Section 10b-5 imposes liability only for misstatements or omissions that are misleading; "'in the case of an omission [of material fact], '"silence, absent a duty to disclose, is not misleading'") (quoting *McCormick v. Fund American Cos.,* 26 F.3d 869, 875 (9th Cir. 1994) (quoting Basic, Inc. v. Levinson, 485 U.S. 224, 239 n.17 (1988))). There are relatively few specific violations of law that themselves contain an affirmative obligation to disclose the wrongdoing. One example is the Comprehensive Environmental Response, Compensation and Liability Act (CERCLA), which criminalizes the failure to report the known release of a hazardous substance into the environment and the failure to notify the EPA of the existence of an unpermitted site where hazardous substances are treated disposed, or stored. 42 U.S.C. § 9603(b) (1994).

20. In addition, anyone who trades on inside information must disclose that information to persons with whom he trades or abstain from trading. *See* Chiarella v. United States, 445

a. SEC Rules Requiring Specific Disclosures of Actual or Potential Wrongdoing.

The SEC's Regulation S-K, 17 C.F.R. Part 229, sets forth specific information that must be disclosed in the periodic and other reports filed with the SEC by publicly traded companies. See generally 17 C.F.R. Part 229; United States v. Crop Growers Corp., 954 F. Supp. 335, 347 (D.D.C. 1997). Regulation S-K includes three provisions that may require a corporation to disclose specific information about actual or potential wrongdoing by the corporation or its directors or officers: (1) Item 103, 17 C.F.R. § 229.103, governing the disclosure of legal proceedings involving the corporation; (2) Item 401(f), 17 C.F.R. § 229.401(f), governing the disclosure of legal proceedings involving directors, nominees to become directors, and executive officers; and (3) Item 303, 17 C.F.R. § 229.303, concerning management's discussion and analysis of the corporation's financial condition and results of operations. After Sarbanes-Oxley, the SEC came close to adding another form of a disclosure requirement when it promulgated 17 C.F.R. § 205.3.

1. Item 103: Legal Proceedings Involving the Corporation. Item 103 requires public disclosure of certain pending legal proceedings.[21] It does not on its face require disclosure of matters that are under investigation, either by the government or internally. Rather, Item 103 requires disclosure only of legal proceedings that are actually pending or that are "known to be contemplated by governmental authorities."[22]

Accordingly, the mere knowledge of possible securities violations (or other wrongdoing) does not require public disclosure. See Bolger v. First State Financial Services, 759 F. Supp. 182, 194 (D.N.J. 1991) (in the context of proxy disclosures under SEC Rule 14a-9, 17 C.F.R. § 240.14a-9, corpora-

---

U.S. 222, 227-29 (1980). *See also* SEC v. Park, 99 F. Supp. 2d 889, 889-900 (N.D. Ill. 2000) (SEC properly alleged its claim regarding online information provider under *Chiarella* because provider had relationship of trust and confidence with plaintiffs).

21. § 229.103 (Item 103) provides:

> Describe briefly any material pending legal proceedings, other than ordinary routine litigation incidental to the business, to which the registrant or any of its subsidiaries is a party or of which any of their property is the subject. Include the name of the court or agency in which the proceedings are pending, the date instituted, the principal parties thereto, a description of the factual basis alleged to underlie the proceeding and the relief sought. Include similar information as to any such proceedings known to be contemplated by governmental authorities.

22. For SEC investigations, it is not clear whether proceedings are "known to be contemplated" when the SEC requests a Wells submission, when the Commission actually authorizes an action against the corporation, or at some other point.

tion was not required to disclose mere allegations of illegal conduct and mismanagement by officers and directors); *Estate of Flake ex rel.* Flake v. Hoskins, 124 F. Supp. 2d 666 (D. Kan. 2000) (upholding *Bolger*); Levine v. NL Industries, Inc., 717 F. Supp. 252, 255 (S.D.N.Y. 1989) (where corporation had knowledge of possible violations of environmental statutes and knowledge that such violations could *possibly* result in legal proceedings by state regulators, but no information that regulators were actually contemplating such proceedings, Item 103 did not require disclosure of this knowledge on a Form 10-K). Neither Item 103, nor its instructions, nor subsequent judicial decisions specify at what point beyond the existence of mere allegations it can be said that a corporation *knows* that legal proceedings are contemplated. While its holding is suspect, one court has stated that Item 103 does not require disclosure even if the corporation has received a target letter. *See Crop Growers,* 954 F. Supp. at 347 (citing *In re Browning-Ferris Indus., Inc. Shareholder Derivative Litig.,* 830 F. Supp. 361, 369 (S.D. Tex. 1993), *aff'd mem.,* 20 F.3d 465 (5th Cir. 1994)).[23] Moreover, a company may initiate an investigation into the allegations without automatically triggering a disclosure

In addition to the cases discussed in the text, two SEC releases have discussed this issue. The first, Securities Act Release No. 33-5949, *Uniform and Integrated Reporting Requirements* (July 28, 1978), which extended the obligation to disclose proceedings "known to be contemplated by government authorities" to quarterly reports on Form 10Q, was of little help. Commentators argued that extending the obligation in this fashion "would increase costs and risks of error because companies would be required to determine on a more or less continuous basis what the government was contemplating." *Id.* The SEC responded to this argument by stating that "only 'material' proceedings 'known' by the registrant to be contemplated need be reported. It appears to the Commission that these qualifications sufficiently assure the reasonableness of the requirement." *Id.*

Second, in *In re* Occidental Petroleum Corp., Exchange Act Release No. 16950 (July 2, 1980), the government had informed a subsidiary of Occidental that a criminal action against the subsidiary for environmental violations was likely, but negotiations between the subsidiary and the government were still continuing. The SEC stated that Occidental should have disclosed this matter as a proceeding "known to be contemplated" by the government. *Id.*

23. *Crop Growers* cites *Browning-Ferris* as holding that receipt of a target letter is insufficient to trigger a disclosure obligation under Item 103. *See Crop Growers,* 954 F. Supp. at 347. However, *Browning-Ferris* held that receipt of a target letter by a director nominee did not trigger a disclosure obligation under Item 401(f), which governs disclosure of legal proceedings involving directors, officers, and director nominees, rather than under Item 103. *Browning-Ferris,* 830 F. Supp. at 368-70. Moreover, *Browning-Ferris* did not address whether a target letter received in a currently pending investigation would trigger a duty of disclosure. In *Browning-Ferris,* the court held that the corporation was not obligated to disclose in a proxy statement a target letter received by the director nominee three years earlier, in connection with an investigation that did not result in an indictment and that was no longer pending at the time the proxy statement was issued. *Id.*

obligation. In *Bolger*, the court held that, because the corporation was not obligated to disclose mere allegations of wrongdoing, it also was not obligated to disclose "whatever preliminary steps it took in response to those allegations." *Id.*

(2) Item 401(f): Legal Proceedings Involving Directors, Director Nominees, or Executive Officers

Item 401(f), 17 C.F.R. § 229.401(f), governs the obligation to disclose information about legal proceedings involving directors, persons nominated to become directors, or executive officers of the corporation. Like Item 103, Item 401(f) is also focused on more advanced stages of proceedings than the start of a government or internal investigation.[24]

By all accounts, Item 401(f) does not require disclosure of uncharged criminal conduct. *See, e.g., United States v. Matthews*, 787 F.2d 38, 43-44, 47 (2d Cir. 1986) (Item 401(f) only required disclosure of convictions and pending criminal proceedings and did not require disclosure of fact that director was the named subject of a criminal investigation); *Crop Growers*, 954 F. Supp. at 347 (Item 401(f) did not require disclosure of uncharged criminal conduct); *Browning-Ferris*, 830 F. Supp. at 369 (Item 401(f) did not require disclosure of the fact that a target letter was sent to director nominee in an investigation that was no longer pending).

(3) Item 303: Management's Discussion and Analysis (MD&A)

Item 303 of Regulation S-K is potentially the broadest and the least easily defined disclosure provision. It requires a public company to provide management's discussion and analysis (MD&A) of the company's "financial condition, changes in financial condition, and results of operations." 17 C.F.R. § 229.303. Comment 3 to Item 303(a) requires the corporation to discuss "material events and uncertainties known to management that would cause reported financial information not to be necessarily indicative of future

---

24. With respect to civil violations of federal or state securities laws or federal commodities laws, Item 401(f) requires disclosure only after a court or the SEC or CFTC has actually made a finding that the director, nominee, or executive officer committed a violation. *See* 17 C.F.R. § 229.401(f)(5) and (6). With respect to criminal proceedings, Item 401(f) requires disclosure only when the director, nominee, or executive officer was "convicted in a criminal proceeding" or "is a named subject of a pending criminal proceeding." *See* 17 C.F.R. § 229.401(f)(2). Item 401(f) requires public companies to: "Describe any of the following events that occurred during the past five years and that are material to an evaluation of the ability or integrity of any director, person nominated to become a director or executive officer of the registrant: . . . (2) Such person was convicted in a criminal proceeding or is a named

operating results or of future financial condition. This would include descriptions and amounts of (A) matters that would have an impact on future operations and have not had an impact in the past, and (B) matters that have had an impact on reported operations and are not expected to have an impact on future operations." Interpreting this requirement, the SEC stated in an August 1988 Release that government *inquiries* into questionable conduct must be disclosed if the issuer reasonably expects the investigation to have a material impact on the company's business practices or financial condition.[25]

The SEC has interpreted the financial disclosure provisions of Rule 303 as requiring a corporation to disclose illegal conduct that has a material impact on its financial condition *and* to disclose the *cessation* of illegal conduct when the cessation has a material impact on the corporation's financial condition. For example, in *In re E.F. Hutton & Co.,* Litigation Release No. 10915 (1985), the SEC charged E.F. Hutton (Hutton) with improperly failing to disclose illegal conduct in the MD&A sections of two Forms 10-K. In 1985, Hutton pleaded guilty to 2,000 counts of mail and wire fraud in connection with checking account practices allegedly designed to obtain interest-free use of bank funds. *Id.* at *1. The SEC filed and settled a complaint charging Hutton with, among other things, improperly failing to discuss this misconduct in the MD&A sections of its 1981 and 1982 Forms 10-K. *Id.* at *3-4. In the complaint, the SEC contended that Hutton should have disclosed that the increased use of the illegal practices in 1981 was a material cause of the material increase in Hutton's net interest income from 1980 to 1981 and that the decreased use of such practices in 1982 was a material cause of the material decrease in Hutton's net interest income from 1981 to 1982. *Id.*

(4) 17 C.F.R. § 205.3 (Sarbanes-Oxley Standards of Professional Conduct)

The Sarbanes-Oxley Act, legislation enacted in 2002 largely as a response to several high-profile cases of corporate fraud and investor losses,[26] almost produced a rule provision specifically requiring an oblique form of

---

subject of a pending criminal proceeding (excluding traffic violations and other minor offenses)." Item 401(f) also requires disclosure if a director, nominee, or executive officer was found by a court in a civil action, or by the SEC or CFTC, to have violated federal or state securities laws or federal commodities laws, and such finding has not been reversed, suspended, or vacated. *See* 17 C.F.R. § 229.401(f)(5) and (6).

25. Exchange Act Rel. No. 34-25951 (Aug. 1, 1988).

26. *See, e.g. In re* Worldcom, Inc. Sec. Litig., No. 02 Civ. 3288, 2003 WL 21488087, at *7 (S.D.N.Y. June 24, 2003); *In re* Enron Corp. Secs., Derivative & ERISA Litig., 235 F.

public disclosure of material violations of securities laws, breaches of fiduciary duty, and "similar violations by the company or any agent thereof." Instead, after public comment, in addition to certification requirements and other provisions that might cause those making the certifications to be more vigilant about following up on any issues that might bear on the accuracy of financial statements, Sarbanes-Oxley produced an internal disclosure requirement that of necessity will trigger internal investigations. *See* subsection II.A.2(a) below.

Part of Congress' direction to the SEC "in the public interest and for the protection of investors" to set forth "minimum standards of professional conduct for attorneys appearing and practicing before the SEC,"[27] the SEC rules called for by the Act initially contained a mandatory reporting-out provision, which would have required an attorney to report to the SEC if he or she did not believe that the company had adopted an appropriate response to a report of a material violation. Specifically, this proposed rule required an attorney to withdraw from the representation of the company and to notify the SEC of his or her withdrawal.[28] This controversial provision came to be known as the "noisy withdrawal" rule, and was bitterly attacked by the legal profession. In January 2003, when the SEC issued its final rules pursuant to Sarbanes-Oxley, it deferred adoption of the noisy withdrawal rule.[29] Instead, the SEC adopted a far milder and entirely discretionary version of the reporting-out rules.[30] Pursuant to the rule issued by the SEC, an attorney may, but is not required to, reveal to the SEC, without the company's consent, confidential information related to the representation of the company to the extent the attorney reasonably believes is necessary to protect the company in one of three ways.[31] According to the SEC, the mandatory noisy withdrawal provi-

---

Supp. 2d 549, 587 (S.D. Tex. 2003). The statute was intended to "protect investors by improving the accuracy and reliability of corporate disclosures made pursuant to the securities laws, and for other purposes." Sarbanes-Oxley Act of 2002, Pub. L. No. 107-204, 116 Stat. 745.

27. 15 U.S.C.A. § 7245 (2002).

28. Securities Act Release No. 8150 at 86, 539-40.

29. Implementation of Standards of Professional Conduct for Attorneys, Securities Act Release No. 33-8186, (Jan. 29, 2003), *available at* http://sec.gov/rules/proposed/33-8186.htm.

30. 17 C.F.R. § 205.3 (b)-(c).

31. 17 C.F.R. § 205.3(d)(2). The three ways are (1) to prevent the issuer from committing a material violation likely to cause substantial injury; (2) to prevent the issuer from committing or suborning perjury or violating 18 U.S.C § 1001 in a Commission investigation or administrative proceeding, and (3) to rectify the consequences of a material violation by the issuer that caused or may cause substantial injury. In addition to considering whether disclosure is prohibited under state ethics codes, *see* infra note 33, an attorney contemplating disclosure must also evaluate whether the SEC's grant of permission might become a basis for civil

sion is still under consideration while the SEC observes how the up-the-ladder rules and other provisions work out.[32]

At least as of November 2006, the disclosure *obligations* imposed by the new SEC rules on lawyers practicing before the Commission—as opposed to the limited permission granted by the SEC to make discretionary disclosure to the Commission—are limited to disclosures within the company. The Act mandated, and the SEC issued, rules that required attorneys "to report evidence of a material violation of securities law or breach of fiduciary duty or similar violation by the company or any agent thereof" to the general counsel or chief executive officer of the company in the first instance, and then to the audit committee, a special committee made up of independent directors, or the full board of directors if the general counsel or the CEO did not appropriately respond to the attorney's report.[33]

(5) Form 8-K Reporting Obligations, and Amendments to Form 8-K Implementing Section 409 of the Sarbanes-Oxley Act

Form 8-K, the Exchange Act form used by public companies since 1936 to file current reports disclosing important corporate events, has long provided for certain mandatory disclosures as well as voluntary disclosure of information that companies consider important to investors; in 2004, the SEC adopted amendments to the form.[34] These amendments implement Section 409 of the Sarbanes-Oxley Act, which requires a public company to

---

liability in the event the attorney remains silent and people suffer injury as a result. *See, e.g.,* Tarasoff v. Regents of the University of California, 17 Cal. 3d 425 (Cal. 1976) (psychotherapist has duty to disclose information to protect a patient's potential victim where principles of ethics allowed disclosure of confidences when necessary to protect the welfare of the community).

32. In considering whether to report a material violation to the SEC, attorneys must still be mindful of their state ethical obligations. While the ABA amended its Model Rules in 2003 to mirror the discretionary reporting-out provision adopted by the SEC, AMERICAN BAR ASSOCIATION MODEL RULES OF PROF'L CONDUCT R. 1.13 (2003), many states have not adopted these amendments. Significantly, the SEC rules state that they preempt any conflicting state standards. 17 C.F.R. § 205.1. A minority of states, however, have explicitly warned their lawyers not to disclose information to the SEC unless the disclosure is also allowed by the state's own professional conduct rules. *See, e.g.* Wash. R.P.C. 1.6 (1990). *See also Letter Regarding Washington State Bar Association's Proposed Opinion on the Effect of the SEC's Attorney Conduct Rules* (July 23, 2003), *available at* http://www.sec.gov/news/speech/spch072303gpp.htm.

33. 15 U.S.C. § 7245 (2002).

34. *See* Additional Form 8-K Disclosure Requirements and Acceleration of Filing Date, Securities Act Release No. 8400, Exchange Act Release No. 49,424, 82 SEC Docket 147 (Mar. 16, 2004) ("2004 8-K Amendments").

disclose "on a rapid and current basis" information concerning material changes in the company's financial condition or operations that the SEC determines, by rule, is necessary or useful for the protection of investors and in the public interest.[35] Prior to the adoption of the 2004 amendments, six categories of events triggered the requirement to file Form 8-K: a change in control of the company, the acquisition or disposal of a significant amount of assets, bankruptcy, a change in the company's auditors, the resignation of a director, and a change in the fiscal year.[36] Having determined that under this procedure, "companies were required to report very few significant corporate events,"[37] the SEC in the 2004 amendments provided a list of additional events that trigger disclosure requirements.[38]

Even after the 2004 Amendments, internal investigations are not expressly included on the list of items that must be reported on a Form 8-K. Nonetheless, in the flood of stock option backdating investigations, many companies have disclosed their investigations.[39] This may be a reflection of a trend in favor of greater disclosure, or it may merely reflect that option backdating issues generally consume so much time to unravel that delayed financial filings (and resulting disclosures) are inevitable, so the company might as well get the news out sooner rather than later.

---

35. 15 U.S.C. § 78m(l) (2002).

36. *See* Additional Form 8-K Disclosure Requirements and Acceleration of Filing Date, Securities Act Release No. 8106, Exchange Act Release No. 46,084, 67 Fed. Reg. 42914-01, 42914 (proposed June 25, 2002).

37. 2004 8-K Amendments at *3.

38. Twelve events were introduced or modified by the 2004 amendments: eight are new, two were transferred from public companies' disclosure requirements for periodic reports, and another two expanded items already on the list. The new triggering events are: (i) entry into or amendment of a material non-ordinary course agreement; (ii) termination of a material non-ordinary course agreement; (iii) creation of a material direct financial obligation or an obligation under an off-balance sheet arrangement; (iv) triggering events that accelerate or increase a material direct financial obligation or a material obligation under an off-balance sheet arrangement; (v) material costs incurred in connection with exit or disposal activities; (vi) material impairments; (vii) notice of delisting, failure to satisfy a continued listing rule or standard, or transfer of listing; and (viii) non-reliance on previously issued financial statements or a related audit report or completed interim review. The two events transferred from periodic reports are: (i) unregistered sales of equity securities; and (ii) material modifications to the rights of security holders. Finally, the two expanded items are: (i) the departure of directors or principal officers, election of directors, or appointment of principal officers; and (ii) amendments to the company's articles of incorporation or bylaws, or change in fiscal year. Generally, reporting is required within four days of the triggering event.

39. *See, e.g.,* McAfee, Inc., Form 8-K (filed June 9, 2006), *available at* http://phx.corporate-ir.net/phoenix.zhtml?c=104920&p=irol-sec&secCat01.2_rs=31&secCat01.2_rc=10; Home Depot, Inc., Form 8-K (filed June 23, 2006), *available at* http://ir.homedepot.com/edgar.cfm?PageNum=12&DocType=&SortOrder=Date%20Descending&Year=.

b) Rules 10b-5 and 12b-20: The Duty to Disclose Information Necessary to Ensure That Prior Disclosures Are Not Misleading

Even if none of the SEC's specific disclosure rules require a corporation or any individual to disclose a particular item of information pertaining to corporate or managerial wrongdoing, the corporation may still be required to disclose the information in order to ensure that any prior disclosures it has made are not misleading under Rule 10b-5[40] and Rule 12b-20.[41]

Rules 10b-5 and 12b-20 permit the imposition of liability for failure to disclose information about corporate or managerial wrongdoing. For example, in *Securities & Exchange Comm'n v. Fehn*, 97 F.3d 1276, 1280 (9th Cir. 1996), a corporation and the individual who served as its president and CEO committed securities violations in connection with the corporation's initial public offering. The corporation subsequently filed several Forms 10Q that did not mention contingent liabilities stemming from the prior securities violations. *Id.* at 1281. The Ninth Circuit held that, because the Forms 10Q included required financial information supplied by the corporation's accountants, the failure to disclose contingent liabilities stemming from the prior securities violations rendered the required financial information misleading. *Id.* at 1289-90.

A second example is *Par Pharmaceuticals*, 733 F. Supp. at 672-74, in which the defendants allegedly bribed FDA officials to obtain FDA approvals

---

40. Rule 10b-5 requires the disclosure of information necessary to ensure that any disclosure, whether it was mandatory or voluntary, is not misleading. *See, e.g.* Securities & Exchange Comm'n v. Fehn, 97 F.3d 1276, 1290 n.12 (9th Cir. 1996); *In re* Par Pharmaceuticals, Inc. Securities Litigation, 733 F. Supp. 668, 675 (S.D.N.Y. 1990) ("Under [Rule 10b-5], even though no duty to make a statement on a particular matter has arisen, once corporate officers undertake to make statements, they are obligated to speak truthfully and to make such additional disclosures as are necessary to avoid rendering the statements made misleading."). A statement is misleading if "a reasonable investor, in the exercise of due care, would have received a false impression from the statement." *Par Pharmaceuticals,* 733 F. Supp. at 677; *see Levine v. NL Industries, Inc.,* 717 F. Supp. 252, 254 (S.D.N.Y. 1989), *aff'd,* 926 F.2d 199 (2d Cir. 1991). *See also In re* Citigroup Securities Litigation, 333 F. Supp. 2d 367, 378 (S.D.N.Y. 2004) (limiting applicability of *Par Pharmaceuticals* to situations where defendants made specific projections of continued success based on purported expertise in obtaining approvals from the Food and Drug Administration, while knowing that the success was attributable to bribery).

41. Rule 12b-20, 17 C.F.R. § 240.12b-20, provides: "In addition to the information expressly required to be included in a statement or report, there shall be added such further material information, if any, as may be necessary to make the required statements, in the light of the circumstances under which they are made not misleading."

for drug products and subsequently made claims in Forms 10K and 10Q and other public documents about their ability to obtain speedy FDA approvals. Rejecting in part a motion to dismiss in a civil case, the court held that a jury could find these disclosures misleading under Rule 10b-5 because the disclosures gave investors the false impression that the defendants' success in obtaining FDA approvals stemmed not from bribery but from expertise constituting a legitimate competitive advantage. *Id.* at 678; *see also Yeaman*, 987 F. Supp. at 380 (where Form 10K provided incomplete and misleading information about defendant's prior securities violation, Rule 12b-20 required the inclusion of corrective information in the 10K); Ballan v. Wilfred American Educational Corp., 720 F. Supp. 241, 249 (E.D.N.Y. 1989) (where educational corporation allegedly violated federal student aid regulations and then made disclosures about its financial condition without disclosing facts about the alleged violations that might materially affect the corporation's financial condition, jury could find such disclosures materially misleading under Rule 10b-5).[42]

2. Duty to Investigate

In the current climate of aggressive governmental investigation and prosecution of corporate criminal conduct, there appear to be few allegations of significant corporate wrongdoing that do not lead to internal investigations; this trend is largely the result of a desire to minimize adverse consequences in the event the conduct later becomes known to the government—in other words, a result of a (correct) perception of the government's expectations—as well as a desire to hold the highest available ground for public relations purposes. As more and more companies conduct internal investigations post-Enron, and as the government has more and more success in "outsourcing" its investigative work to the companies themselves, the pressure to conduct investigations increases because of the fear that, if the conduct is later discov-

---

42. There is a dispute over whether this general disclosure duty is sufficient to support *criminal* liability for nondisclosure of uncharged criminal conduct. Two cases hold that the due process clause limits the government's ability to impose criminal liability for failing to disclose uncharged prior criminal conduct. *See Matthews,* 787 F.2d at 49 (holding that "at least so long as uncharged criminal conduct is not required to be disclosed by any rule lawfully promulgated by the SEC, nondisclosure of such conduct cannot be the basis of a criminal prosecution" and noting "the obvious due process implications that would arise from permitting a conviction to stand in the absence of clearer notice as to what disclosures are required in this uncertain area"); *Crop Growers,* 954 F. Supp. at 346 (due process dictates that, if defendant does not receive fair notice that specific conduct is prohibited, that conduct cannot be prosecuted; rejecting application of general requirements of Item 303 and Rule 12b-20 as bases for criminal liability). In addition, *Matthews,* which involved an individual

ered, the government will impose more severe punishment on a company that eschewed conducting an investigation in order to make an example of it.[43]

In this climate, "private attorneys can effectively be commissioned into government service" to conduct an evaluation into whatever issues the government chooses, at whatever cost to the company,[44] without the need for the government to make a specific request or for the company to parse its legal obligations to conduct the investigation. Put differently, the *in terrorem* effect of the government's ease in establishing corporate criminal liability and the severe consequences that flow from a criminal charge against a corporation

---

defendant, stated that its holding was "buttressed by concerns about the self-incrimination implications" of permitting imposition of criminal liability for failure to confess uncharged criminal conduct. *Matthews,* 787 F.2d at 49. But it is generally not an excuse in civil cases to rely on the Fifth Amendment to justify a non-disclosure, *see, e.g., Fehn,* 97 F.3d at 1293; *Par Pharmaceuticals,* 773 F. Supp. at 675 n.8; other courts have distinguished *Matthews* and *Crop Growers* even in criminal cases. In *Yeaman,* a criminal case, the court held that Rule 12b-20 can be the basis for the imposition of criminal liability for the failure to disclose wrongdoing. The *Yeaman* court stated that *Crop Growers* had rejected the application of Rule 12b-20 "because that rule cannot, in the first instance, impose a duty to speak where none otherwise existed" but held that, where Regulation S-K specifically requires particular disclosures, Rule 12b-20 requires the disclosure of additional information necessary to render the disclosed information not misleading. *Yeaman,* 987 F. Supp. at 381 n.7. In *Fehn,* a civil case, the Ninth Circuit noted that *Matthews* involved the disclosure requirements for proxy statements under Rule 14a-9, 17 C.F.R. § 240.14a-9, rather than Rule 10b-5, and stated that Rule 10b-5 imposes liability for failure to make corrective disclosures even where no specific regulation requires disclosure of the omitted information. *Fehn,* 97 F.3d at 1290 n.12.

One case has applied similar due process principles to prohibit criminal prosecution for nondisclosure even when the nondisclosure is based on more specific obligations such as Item 303. In *Crop Growers,* 954 F. Supp. at 347-48, the court held that Item 303's requirement to disclose "any known trend or uncertainty" likely to influence the registrant's liquidity or operational results did "not provide sufficient notice that a particular disclosure is required to allow criminal liability for the alleged non-disclosure." *Id.* at 348. No case has applied the principles of *Crop Growers* outside the context in which the government is seeking to prosecute the nondisclosure criminally.

43. Because the government is able to outsource without cost to itself, it can and does effectively require investigations even when the likelihood of finding a violation is low and the cost is high. McLucas, Shapiro & Song, "The Decline of the Attorney-Client Privilege in the Corporate Setting," 96 J. Crim. L. & Criminology 621, 639 n.69 (2006). One firm reported that among recently revealed government investigations into violations of The Foreign Corrupt Practices Act—a relatively hard crime for the government to uncover given that the victim is unaware of the activity and the conduct generally takes place abroad—fully 85 percent were the result of self-reported internal investigations. *See* D. Newcomb, (Shearman & Sterling LLP), Digest of Cases and Review Releases Relating to Bribes to Foreign Officials Under the Foreign Corrupt Practices Act of 1977 (as of October 2, 2006), at 7.

44. *Id.*

means that, for better or worse, many corporations conduct internal investigations that they may not be legally required to conduct. Nonetheless, rules and developing precedents also lend some support to the quick trigger companies are pulling in the initiation of internal investigations.

a) Sarbanes-Oxley and Other Developments Potentially Creating a Duty to Investigate

In the event an attorney reports evidence of a material violation of securities law or breach of fiduciary duty or similar violation, the Sarbanes-Oxley Act and the SEC rules promulgated thereunder essentially impose an affirmative duty on the company to investigate the attorney's report of wrongdoing.[45] No such duty had previously been imposed by the SEC's rules. Following such a report, the recipient of the report—who could be the Chief Legal Officer, or the Chief Executive Officer, or, failing appropriate action by those individuals, the audit committee, a special committee, the full Board of Directors, or a Qualified Legal Compliance Committee[46]—is required to adopt an "appropriate response" to the report of evidence of a material violation[47] unless the recipient reasonably believes no material violation has occurred.

Absent a conclusion that it is already aware of all the facts and that those facts as a matter of law could not rise to the level of a material violation of the securities laws, breach of fiduciary duty, or the like, it would be hard for any recipient to formulate an "appropriate response" without learning the facts through an investigation of some kind.[48] This is especially true in light of Sec-

---

45. 15 U.S.C. § 7245 (2002); 17 C.F.R. § 205.3(b). Under the rule initially proposed by the SEC in November 2002, the attorney would need to report as follows: "Evidence of a material violation means information that would lead an attorney reasonably to believe that a material violation has occurred, is occurring, or is about to occur." Implementation of Standards of Professional Conduct for Attorneys, Securities Act Release No. 33-8150 (Nov. 21, 2002). This proposed standard was relatively simple to apply, but it was attacked for, among other things, potentially setting the bar too low. *See, e.g.*, John C. Coffee, *The Latest Sarbanes-Oxley Controversy: Section 307*, N.Y.L.J., Nov. 21, 2002, at 5 (expressing disappointment in the SEC's bar-protective stance in that it permitted a lawyer to rationalize his or her silence by claiming that he or she had no reasonable belief that a violation had occurred). As a result, the SEC later revised the standard. The final rule now states that evidence of a material violation "means credible evidence based on which it would be unreasonable, under the circumstances, for a prudent and competent attorney not to conclude that it is reasonably likely that a material violation has occurred, is ongoing, or is about to occur." 17 C.F.R. § 205.2(e). Needless to say, this double-negative laden provision is awkwardly phrased and hard to interpret.

The procedure for reporting is set forth in 17 C.F.R. §§ 205.3(b)(1), (3).

46. *See* 17 C.F.R. §§ 205.3(b)(1), (3), 205.3(c)(2).

47. C.F.R. § 205.3(b)(3).

48. The SEC rules do not require that a reporting attorney maintain any records of his or her conduct. However, for any number of reasons, it seems prudent for an attorney making

tions 302 and 906 of the Act,[49] which require top officers of public companies to certify that the corporation's financial statements are fairly presented.

Other provisions of the Act, recent legislation, and a longstanding cause of action in corporate litigation add still other triggers for investigative duties. Within the Act, Section 404's imposition of a requirement on management to assess internal controls[50] has created a whirlwind of activity, some of which has generated issues that led to internal obligations.

Similar to the company's obligation to adopt an appropriate response when an attorney raises issues of wrongdoing, the outside auditor who becomes aware of information "indicating that an illegal act ... has or may have occurred" is obligated under Section 10A of the 1934 Act to inform itself, advise the company, and satisfy itself that the company has remedied the act appropriately.[51] Under Statement on Accounting Standards No. 99 (SAS 99),[52] which establishes guidelines for compliance with Section 10A,[53] auditors are required to exercise professional skepticism during an audit and to gather evidence, including making inquiries "about the existence or suspicion of fraud" of any company employee.[54] These inquiries can lead the auditors to insist that the company investigate possible wrongdoing—and to keep the auditors informed of the results.[55]

---

such a report to create and maintain records of what he or she did, i.e., by retaining all e-mails or writing memoranda to the file memorializing conversations with the CLO or CEO. Such records will be important if the company does not respond properly to the report and the attorney is later questioned about his or her conduct and compliance with the SEC rules. Significantly, under the SEC rules, a reporting attorney is permitted to reveal the material violation report "or the contemporaneous record thereof" in any proceeding in which the attorney's compliance with Sarbanes-Oxley is in issue. 17 C.F.R. § 205.3(d)(1). This is commonly referred to as an attorney self-defense disclosure, and is a permissible exception to the attorney-client privilege under the SEC rules and many state disciplinary rules as well.

49. 15 U.S.C. § 7241 (2002).
50. 15 U.S.C. § 7262 (2002).
51. 15 U.S.C. 78j-1(b) (2000).
52. Statements on Accounting Standards are promulgated by the Auditing Standards Board of the American Institute of Certified Public Accountants (AICPA). The Statements help auditors meet GAAS.
53. AICPA Professional Standards, AU § 316, *Consideration of Fraud in a Financial Statement Audit* (2002).
54. *Id.* at § 316.20-26. Section 10A is modeled after an early incarnation of SAS 99 which requires auditors to "obtain reasonable assurances about whether the financial statements are free of material misstatements, whether caused by error or fraud." AICPA Professional Standards, AU § 316.
55. The issues created by any demand by the auditors to be kept informed of the investigation are addressed in Section III.E. below.

Another increasingly common trigger for investigations is shareholder derivative actions. With intense media focus on allegations of corporate wrongdoing, in some instances—the article about stock option backdating being a prime example—the company learns of its possible wrongdoing at the same time that the wrongdoing is reported to the public and is then seized upon by derivative plaintiffs. The company's internal investigation in these circumstances is conducted partly with an eye toward its use in dealing with the government, but also with an eye toward its potential use by a Special Litigation Committee to address whether claims should be brought by the company against individual wrongdoers.

b) A Judicially-Imposed Duty to Investigate

Apart from the SEC's Sarbanes-Oxley rules and related obligations, principles developed in civil cases also impose a duty to investigate under certain circumstances. For instance, numerous civil cases have held that a failure to investigate signs of illegal conduct by employees may constitute recklessness and subject a corporation to liability for failure to disclose those violations. *See* Hollinger v. Titan Capital Corp., 914 F.2d 1564, 1569-70 (9th Cir. 1990) (recklessness requires a "highly unreasonable omission" constituting an "extreme departure from the standards of ordinary care, and which presents a danger of misleading buyers and sellers that is either known to the defendant or is so obvious that the actor must have been aware of it"; broker-dealer did not act recklessly in failing to disclose registered representative's eleven-year-old forgery conviction) (citations omitted); *distinguished by* Asplund v. Selected Investments in Financial Equities, Inc., 103 Cal. Rptr. 2d 34, 44-45 (Cal. App. 1st 2000) (*Hollinger* distinguished where registered representative was not acting in his capacity as a representative, where his authority to market did not emanate from the defendant broker-dealer, and the representative did not meet with investors in the broker-dealer's office). The failure to investigate adequately and the resulting failure to uncover wrongdoing can constitute recklessness if the defendant ignored clear warning signs. *See, e.g., In re* Leslie Fay Companies, Inc., 871 F. Supp. 686, 698 (S.D.N.Y. 1995) (if, as complaint alleged, accountants recklessly ignored "red flags" indicating that issuer's employees were falsifying issuer's books, accountants could be held liable under Rule 10b-5; accountants' alleged conduct supported inference that accountants acted with intent and deliberately disregarded warning signs to avoid antagonizing issuer).

No court has yet imposed a duty to conduct an internal investigation per se, but the Delaware Chancery Court took a giant step down that road in *In re Caremark International Inc. Derivative Litigation*, 698 A.2d 959, 970 (Del. Chan. Ct. 1996), a case that anticipated some of the issues encompassed by the SEC's Sarbanes-Oxley rules. By imposing an obligation to create "information and reporting systems to keep track of the corporation's compliance with law," *Caremark* not only emphasized the corporation's duty to keep informed, but also required the creation of a system that will identify allegations of wrongdoing and effectively compel the corporation to investigate them or face charges that it recklessly avoided learning about the misconduct.[56]

The obligation implied by *Caremark* to investigate allegations of wrongdoing also follows from other disclosure obligations imposed by the SEC's rules; the company's obligation to disclose matters covered by Item 303, for example, implies the existence of some duty of gather—or at least not to ignore—potential matters to be disclosed.

A remaining question, which has yet to be squarely addressed, is whether there are any limits on the corporation's need to address any possibility of wrongdoing by conducting an internal investigation. An interesting example

---

56. Most of the litigation interpreting *Caremark's* holding has focused less on whether there is a requirement to conduct an internal investigation once potential wrongdoing is known and more on the sufficiency of monitoring information in order to learn of such alleged wrongdoing. On these monitoring issues, the *Caremark* court itself recognized that a claim for failure to monitor "is possibly the most difficult theory in corporation law upon which a plaintiff might hope to win a judgment." *Id.* at 967. For this reason, many *Caremark* claims do not survive a motion to dismiss. Several courts have heard *Caremark* claims with varying results. *See, e.g.,* Dellastatious v. Williams, 242 F.3d 191, 197 (4th Cir. 2001) (court held that the company's directors could not be held liable under *Caremark* because the company had a system for drafting and reviewing offering documents); *In re Cray Inc. Derivative Litigation,* 431 F. Supp. 2d 1114, 1124 (W.D. Wash. 2006) (allegations that defendant was "virtually devoid of internal controls, processes and procedures in every area of the finance and accounting departments" not sufficiently particular to sustain *Caremark* claim); Sachs v. Sprague, 401 F. Supp. 2d 159, 164-65 (D. Mass. 2005) (plaintiffs' claim that there is a reasonable doubt concerning a majority of the board's disinterest based upon each director's failure to fulfill his obligation to supervise corporate conduct not sustainable under *Caremark*). It is important to note, however, that despite *Caremark's* heavy pleading burden, a few cases have survived a motion to dismiss or have led to liability. Generally, these cases involve allegations of an absence of any corporate monitoring or egregious behavior by corporate directors. *See, e.g.,* Pereira v. Cogan, 294 B.R. 449, 529-30 (Bankr. S.D.N.Y. 2003) (directors found liable for a failure to monitor, due to the fact that no system was in place to supervise or control the making of loans to insiders), *vacated and remanded on other grounds,* Pereira v. Farace, 413 F.3d 330 (2d Cir. 2005).

is presented by the stock option backdating investigations, the most significant of which dealt primarily with conduct that was several years old,[57] and were triggered by a journalist's mention of companies that had either backdated or had overcome incredible odds in frequently finding the low-price date of a quarter on which to grant options.[58] Suppose there is a company, the management of which has changed since the likely time of any possible wrongdoing, and also suppose that the company is not mentioned in any article suggesting that its options dating overcame incredible odds. Is that company obligated to investigate? Is it obligated to at least run the same statistical analysis that the journalist published, in order to see if its grants beat incredible odds? Or, reasoning broadly from the SEC's rewrite of the lawyer reporting-up provision in the Sarbanes-Oxley Act, can it safely do nothing, despite the carnage of other companies around it, absent credible evidence of a likely violation, or at least some basis to believe that the company engaged in a material violation? As a matter of law, it can be argued that no obligation to investigate exists on such facts. But, judging from the host of companies conducting internal investigations into stock option backdating, it appears that few companies are willing to test the government's or the market's tolerance of a failure to inquire, and as a result the legal limits on a corporation's obligation to investigate possible wrongdoing may remain undefined.

3. Materiality

All of the theories imposing liability for a corporation's failure to disclose wrongdoing in its SEC filings require that the information be material. Levine v. NL Industries, Inc., 926 F.2d 199, 202 (2d Cir. 1991). An omitted fact is material if there is a substantial likelihood that a reasonable investor would consider it important in making an investment decision. *See* Basic, Inc. v. Levinson, 485 U.S. 224, 231-32 (1988). There must be a "substantial likelihood that the disclosure of the omitted fact would have been viewed by the

---

57. Much but not all backdating ceased after the implementation of the Sarbanes-Oxley Act, which included a provision requiring prompt reporting of the issuance of options to certain officers. 15 U.S.C. § 16(c). Prompt reporting made it virtually impossible to backdate. While much backdating of options occurred with rank-and-file employees as well as officers, at many companies Sarbanes-Oxley led to the implementation of new option granting procedures that precluded backdating and applied to rank-and-file employees as well.

58. C. Forelle & J. Bandler, "*The Perfect Payday—Some CEOs Reap Millions By Landing Stock Options When They Are Most Valuable; Luck—Or Something Else?,*" WALL ST. J. March 18, 2006, at A1 (based in part on Professor Lie). *See also* R. Heron & E. Lie, *What Fraction of Stock Option Grants to Top Executive Have Been Backdated or Manipulated* (July 14, 2006) http://www.issproxy.com/optionsbackdating/index.jsp.

reasonable investor as having significantly altered the total mix of information made available." *Id.* (quoting TSC Industries, Inc. v. Northway, Inc., 426 U.S. 438 (1976)). The materiality of an event that is "contingent or speculative" in nature "will depend at any given time upon a balancing of both the indicated probability that the event will occur and the anticipated magnitude of the event in light of the totality of the company activity." *Basic*, 485 U.S. at 238 (quoting SEC v. Texas Gulf Sulphur Co., 401 F.2d 833, 849 (2d Cir. 1968) (en banc)).[59]

Avoiding disclosure based on an asserted lack of materiality is a risky proposition. Not only is such a determination "peculiarly one[] for the trier of fact," *Basic*, 485 U.S. at 231-32, but the assessments are "delicate." *Id.* While there are cases holding that mere allegations of wrongdoing are not automatically material, *see* Bolger v. First State Financial Services, 759 F. Supp. 182, 194 (D.N.J. 1991); GAF Corp. v. Heyman, 724 F.2d 727, 739 (2d Cir. 1983), the case law is mixed at best. Because materiality is a fact-intensive inquiry, courts are reluctant to decide as a matter of law that the failure to disclose certain information about corporate misconduct was not material. *E.g., Ballan*, 720 F. Supp. at 249-50 (declining to dismiss complaint alleging that defendants failed to disclose policies that violated federal regulations).

In judging the likelihood that the event will occur—that alleged corporate wrongdoing will result in harm to the corporation—most courts appear to give the corporations some room, recognizing that the "outcome of legal proceedings is inevitably uncertain," *Ballan*, 720 F. Supp. at 248, and not requiring

---

59. The SEC's disclosure rules, such as Items 103 and 401(f), also incorporate the requirement of materiality. Under Item 103, pending legal proceedings involving the corporation need not be disclosed if they are "routine" and "incidental to the business" of the corporation. *See* 17 C.F.R. § 229.103; *id.,* Instruction 1; *Bolger,* 759 F. Supp. at 194. In addition, proceedings that "involve[] primarily a claim for damages" need not be disclosed if the amount involved does not exceed ten percent of the current assets of the corporation and its subsidiaries. *See* 17 C.F.R. § 229.103, Instruction 2. If several actions that are pending or known to be contemplated involve the same legal and factual issues, the amounts involved in those proceedings must be added together in computing the percentage under Instruction 2. *See* 17 C.F.R. § 229.103, Instruction 2.

Under Item 401(f), the corporation is only required to disclose criminal convictions or charges that occurred within the last five years and that are "material to an evaluation of the ability or integrity" of the director, nominee, or executive officer. The SEC has stated that the five-year period specified in Item 401(f) is intended only as a "guide" and that "events occurring outside this period should be disclosed." *See* Securities Act Release No. 5949, 1978 WL 14845, *8 (July 28, 1978); Securities Act Release No. 5758, 1976 WL 15989, *2 (Nov. 2, 1976). One court, however, has rejected the SEC's interpretation as inconsistent with the plain language of Item 401(f), holding that Item 401(f) requires disclosure only of events occurring within the last five years. United States v. Yeaman, 987 F. Supp. 373, 384 (E.D. Pa. 1997).

management to "characterize its behavior in a pejorative manner." *Id.* at 249; *see* Amalgamated Clothing and Textile Workers Union, *AFL-CIO*, 475 F. Supp. 328, 330-31 (S.D.N.Y. 1979), *vacated as moot*, 638 F.2d 7 (2d Cir. 1980) (per curiam) (rejecting contention that proxy solicitation was fraudulent where it disclosed specific labor litigation in which the corporation was involved and specific findings of labor violations but did not disclose that nominees for directorships "had participated in a concerted effort to thwart the labor laws of this country"). In addition to harm resulting from the imposition of legal proceedings, corporations also must consider the harm resulting from the cessation of the activities. *See In re* E.F. Hutton & Co., Lit. Rel. No. 10915, 1985 WL 61025 (1985) (SEC charged that firm should have disclosed fact that reduced use of illegal checking account practices was a material cause of a material decrease in firm's interest income). In either case, while not necessarily requiring disclosure of the fact of an investigation, some courts have required disclosure of "facts showing that [the corporation's] management or employees committed specific acts or permitted specific practices that an informed investor would consider as potentially endangering its future financial performance." *Ballan*, 720 F. Supp. at 249.

In judging the "magnitude of the event," there is authority establishing that wrongdoing with little or no impact on earnings need not be disclosed. *See, e.g.*, Levine v. NL Industries, 717 F. Supp. 252, 253 (S.D.N.Y. 1989), *aff'd*, 926 F.2d 199 (2d Cir. 1991) (where defendant corporation was contractually entitled to indemnification for all expenses incurred in complying with environmental laws, corporation's environmental violations could have no effect on corporation's financial condition and were therefore immaterial and did not have to be disclosed). At the same time, any conduct that could undermine a corporation's license to do business, Securities & Exchange Comm'n v. Joseph Schlitz Brewing Co., 452 F. Supp. 824, 830 (E.D. Wis. 1978), or its ability to obtain government contracts, Cooke v. Teleprompter Corp., 334 F. Supp. 467, 470-71 (S.D.N.Y. 1971), may have a sufficient impact on earnings to require disclosure no matter how small an amount of money may initially be implicated.

These cases, described by commentators as "quantitative materiality" cases, present a standard that, while difficult, has been applied with some predictability. *See, e.g., Schlitz*, 452 F. Supp. at 830 (alleged bribes to retailers, although relatively small in amount, were material because they posed a threat to the company's ability to retain its licenses to sell beer, which were essential to the company's continued operations and prosperity). But for quite some time, other courts have added a second concept requiring disclosure: "qualitative materiality." "Qualitative materiality" rests on the notion that acts of wrongdoing that in and of themselves are insignificant to the corporation's bottom line could still have "vast economic implications" in that they might call into question the "competency of management" in putting the corporation at risk, or might otherwise undermine the integrity of management, making the corporation less attractive to investors. *See Roeder*, 814 F.2d at 25-26 (bribes paid by corporation to obtain subcontracts created risk that corporation could lose its ability to obtain future government contracts).

This principle is potentially boundless, but, at least when it first began to appear, not all courts read it expansively. In determining when "qualitative" disclosures regarding the integrity of management are required, courts held that management misconduct is not material if it does not involve self-dealing and does not affect the corporation's financial condition. In *Gaines v. Haughton*, 645 F.2d 761, 776-79 (9th Cir. 1981), *overruled in part on other grounds*, *In re McLinn*, 739 F.2d 1395, 1397 (9th Cir. 1984), the court held that the corporation was not required to disclose in a proxy statement its payments to foreign officials, which payments had been made prior to the enactment of the Foreign Corrupt Practices Act. The court drew "a sharp distinction . . . between allegations of director misconduct involving breach of trust or self-dealing, the nondisclosure of which is presumptively material, and allegations of simple breach of fiduciary duty/waste of corporate assets, the nondisclosure of which is never material for § 14(a) purposes." *Id.* at 776-77; *see* Maldonado v. Flynn, 597 F.2d 789, 796 (2d Cir. 1979) (finding that alleged self-dealing by corporate directors could be material under proxy solicitation disclosure rules, as "the circumstances surrounding corporate transactions in which directors have a personal interest are directly relevant to a determination of whether they are qualified to exercise stewardship of the company"). A few cases went even farther and rejected the theory that "qualitative" materiality requires disclosure of matters bearing on management ethics and integrity, stating that courts "almost universally have rejected efforts to require that management make qualitative disclosures that were not at least implicit in the Commission's rules." 787 F.2d at 48.

Since the qualitative aspect was first inserted into the definition of materiality, the American Institute of Certified Public Accountants (AICPA) and the SEC have opined on what constitutes "qualitative materiality." The AICPA's Statement on Auditing Standards No. 85, issued in 1997, replaced SAS No. 19 and provides guidance on what must be stated in a management representation letter.[60] SAS 85 proved to be a key element in the increased reliance upon, and expanded definition of, qualitative materiality, a trend that appears to have been gaining momentum since SAS 85 was adopted. After adopting SAS 85, the AICPA clarified its position in a 1998 article, which advised that a client and auditor should be aware that certain representations not directly related to amounts included in financial statements should not be subject to materiality limits.[61]

In Staff Accounting Bulletin No. 99 (SAB No. 99), the SEC added more fuel to the increasing use and breadth of qualitative materiality by setting forth the views of its staff that misstatements are not immaterial merely because they fall beneath a numerical threshold.[62] SAS No. 99 did not object to companies using a "rule of thumb" approach to preparing financial statements, i.e., that the misstatement or omission of an item falling beneath a 5 percent threshold is immaterial in the absence of egregious circumstances, but noted that such an approach was only the beginning of an analysis of materiality.[63] The SEC has been increasingly aggressive in finding materiality based on qualitative materiality,[64] and even though the case law has been

---

60. Explanation of SAS No. 85 available on the AICPA website at http://www.aicpa.org/members/div/practmon/recover/appenda.htm. These representations include management's acknowledgment of its responsibility for the financial statements and the availability of financial records and information regarding fraud involving management and employees significantly involved in internal controls.

61. Kim M. Gibson, C.P.A. & James S. Gerson, C.P.A., *Talking with the Auditor*, available at http://www.aicpa.org/pubs/jofa/mar98/gibson.htm.

62. Securities Exchange Commission, *Staff Accounting Bulletin No. 99*, Aug. 12, 1999, available at http://www.sec.gov/interps/account/sab99.htm.

63. *Id.* The SEC added that the materiality of a misstatement may turn on where it appears in financial statements and suggested that, in assessing the materiality of a misstatement, registrants and auditors should consider the size of the misstatement and also the significance of the misstated segment to the statement taken as a whole. *Id.*

64. *Id.* Recently, the SEC settled a civil enforcement action that alleged that Huntington Bancshares's CEO, CFO, and Controller engaged in fraud. In determining the materiality of the accounting improprieties, the SEC focused on qualitative materiality factors: although the increased reported earnings stemming from improper accounting were negligible, they were material because they enabled the company to meet or exceed analysts' estimates. It is important to note that the alleged improper accounting occurred even though the company and its management had a due diligence and disclosure process in place. *See In the Matter of Huntington Bancshares, Inc., et al.*, Release No. 8579 (June 2, 2005); Release No. 51781 (June 2, 2005); Release No. 2252 (June 2, 2005); Administrative Proceeding File No. 3-11940. There are few recent court cases addressing "qualitative materiality," and those that do so do not present challenging facts. *See, e.g., Takara Trust v. Molex, Inc.*, 429 F. Supp. 2d 960, 979 (N.D. Ill. 2006) (qualitative materiality demonstrated by the fact that the defendants knew of

slower in addressing and adopting this now-expanded theory, the auditors have embraced it. In an era in which most companies cannot afford the adverse publicity from a resignation by their auditor and in which the auditing firms, having been burned with huge liabilities, are increasingly willing to use this leverage whenever they see risk, the principle of qualitative materiality appears to be far more accepted in practice than the case law might suggest.

B. *Brokers and Dealers*

Brokers and dealers face additional reporting requirements to their exchanges. In certain circumstances, these requirements go so far as to compel reports of the details of, progress of, and results of internal investigations. While the penalties have not necessarily been severe, proceedings have been brought to sanction violators.

Both the New York Stock Exchange (NYSE)[65] and the National Association of Securities Dealers (NASD)[66] require members to report violations of

---

the error and failed to inform its auditors or the public for five months, failed to disclose their reversal of two accruals to offset an error adjustment, and committed several additional GAAP violations to smooth over the errors).

65. NYSE Rule 351(a)(1) requires that members or member organizations report to the Exchange whenever they or any of their employees has "violated any provision of any securities law or regulation, or any agreement with or rule or standards of conduct of any governmental agency, self-regulatory organization, or business or professional organization, or engaged in conduct which is inconsistent with just and equitable principles of trade or detrimental to the interests or welfare of the Exchange." Rule 351(a)(1). The remaining provisions of Rule 351(a) require members and member organizations to report customer complaints of theft or forgery, proceedings against the member or its employees for violations of the securities laws, settlement of civil actions, criminal indictments and convictions, and other information. Rule 351(a). Rule 351(b) requires that each member associated with a member organization and each employee of a member or member organization report the same information "to the member or member organization with which such person is associated."

66. NASD Rule 3070(a)(1) requires each member to report to the NASD whenever the member or a person associated with the member "has been found to have violated any provision of any securities law or regulation, any rule or standards of conduct of any governmental agency, self-regulatory organization, or financial business or professional organization, or engaged in conduct which is inconsistent with just and equitable principles of trade; and the member knows or should have known that any of the aforementioned events have occurred." Rule 3070(a)(1). Like NYSE Rule 351(a), the balance of NASD Rule 3070(a) requires disclosure of customer complaints of theft or forgery, proceedings against the member or its employees for violations of the securities laws, settlement of civil actions, criminal indictments and convictions, and other information. Rule 3070(b) requires each person associated with a member to report the same information to the member. Rule 3070(b). However, any "member subject to substantially similar reporting requirements of another self-regulatory organization of which it is a member is exempt from the provisions of" Rule 3070. Rule 3070(e).

the securities laws committed by them or by their employees.[67] The NYSE Rules also require each member to review securities trades effected for the account of the member ("proprietary trades") or its employees ("employee trades"), to investigate any trades that may be in violation of the securities laws or regulations or Exchange rules, and report to the Exchange the results of its reviews and investigations.[68] Each quarter, members and member organizations must either report that there is no cause to believe a violation occurred, or provide details of any questionable trades and the internal investigations into them.[69]

The NASD does not have a similar rule specifically requiring reviews and/or investigations of proprietary and employee trades to identify trades that may violate securities laws and exchange rules pertaining to insider trading and manipulative and deceptive devices. However, NASD Rule 3010, which specifies the supervisory responsibilities of NASD members, contains a more general provision requiring NASD members to conduct annual internal inspections that are "reasonably designed to assist in detecting and preventing violations of and achieving compliance with applicable securities laws and regulations, and with the Rules of [the NASD]."[70]

---

67. If an event is reportable, the member must file a Disclosure Reporting Page (DRP) with the Central Registration Depository (CRD), a computer system operated by NASD that maintains registration information regarding broker-dealers and their registered personnel. *See generally Broker-Dealer Registration and Reporting,* Release No. 34-31660, 1992 WL 395541, *1-3 (Dec. 28, 1992). The DRP becomes part of the broker-dealer's or registered employee's record in the CRD. The event reported to the CRD may become the subject of an investigation, and possibly an enforcement action, by the SEC or by one or more SROs.

68. NYSE Rule 342.21 requires members and member organizations to:

"(a) Subject trades in NYSE listed securities and in related financial instruments which are effected for the account of the member or member organization or for the accounts of members, allied members or employees of the member or member organization and their family members (including trades reported by other members pursuant to Rule 407) to review procedures that the member or member organization determines to be reasonably designed to identify trades that may violate the provisions of the Securities Exchange Act of 1934, the rules under that act or the rules of the Exchange prohibiting insider trading and manipulative and deceptive devices, and

(b) Conduct promptly an internal investigation into any such trade that appears that it may have violated those laws and rules in order to determine whether it did violate those laws and rules."

69. NYSE Rule 351(e).
70. NASD Rule 3010(c) provides:

Each member shall conduct a review, at least annually, of the businesses in which it engages, which review shall be reasonably designed to assist in detecting and

The NYSE has brought actions against brokers and dealers for failure to report violations required to be reported under its rules. For example, in *Sutro & Co., Inc.*, 1997 WL 594193, *1 (N.Y.S.E.) (Exchange Hearing Panel Decision 97-105) (1997), an Exchange Hearing Panel approved a Stipulation of Facts and Consent to Penalty entered into by the NYSE's Division of Enforcement and the securities firm Sutro. The stipulation stated that Sutro had violated Rule 351(a) by failing to report at least 80 reportable events and failing to promptly report at least 74 reportable events. *Id.* at *2-3. The unreported events included customer complaints, settlements, and arbitration awards. *Id.* The stipulation further provided that Sutro violated Exchange Rule 342 by failing to "maintain appropriate procedures of supervision and control, and a system of follow-up and review, with respect to its obligation to promptly report matters to the Exchange as required by Exchange rules." *Id.* at *4. Sutro consented to a censure, a $115,000 fine, and an undertaking to have a review done of its reporting system and procedures by "a person or entity not unacceptable to the Exchange." *Id.* at *6.[71] Likewise, the NASD has sought to discipline brokers and dealers under Rule 3070, which sets forth members'

---

preventing violations of and achieving compliance with applicable securities laws and regulations, and with the Rules of this Association. Each member shall review the activities of each office, which shall include the periodic examination of customer accounts to detect and prevent irregularities or abuses and at least an annual inspection of each office of supervisory jurisdiction. Each branch office of the member shall be inspected according to a cycle which shall be set forth in the firm's written supervisory and inspection procedures. In establishing such cycle, the firm shall give consideration to the nature and complexity of the securities activities for which the location is responsible, the volume of business done, and the number of associated persons assigned to the location. Each member shall retain a written record of the dates upon which each review and inspection is conducted.

71. In other cases, the NYSE has imposed penalties on firms that violated Rule 351 by failing to file reports or by filing late reports. *See, e.g., Smith Barney, Inc.*, 1997 WL 431496 (N.Y.S.E.) (Exchange Hearing Panel Decision 97-73) (1997) (approving stipulation and consent providing that Smith Barney violated Exchange rules by filing numerous late reports pertaining to the termination of registered employees and the initiation and settlement of customer complaints and arbitrations; firm consented to censure, $125,000 fine, and requirement to maintain centralized tracking system for reportable events); *Oppenheimer & Co., Inc.*, 1997 WL 219814 (N.Y.S.E.) (Exchange Hearing Panel Decision 97-32) (1997) (firm violated Rule 351(a) and other rules by failing to promptly report information pertaining to registered employees, customer complaints, commencement of arbitrations, and dispositions of matters including settlements, awards, and dismissals; firm violated Rule 342 by failing to maintain adequate supervisory systems to ensure compliance with reporting requirements; NYSE imposed censure, $60,000 fine, and required review of firm's procedures designed to ensure compliance with reporting requirements).

reporting requirements.[72] Most recently, the NASD disciplined a member firm and its President/CEO for failure to report customer complaints.[73] The NASD ultimately barred the President/CEO, expelled the member firm, and ordered both to pay restitution and costs to the customers.

III. CONDUCTING INTERNAL INVESTIGATIONS AND DEALING WITH RELATED ISSUES IN THE CONDUCT OF PARALLEL PROCEEDINGS

Of all the types of cases in which internal investigations are conducted, violations of the securities laws are perhaps the most likely to lead to parallel proceedings. In addition to the active plaintiffs' securities bar, any willful violation of the securities laws is a crime,[74] and the SEC possesses and exercises considerable jurisdiction to review violations.[75]

The SEC's enforcement powers were codified in 1990 with the passage of the Remedies Act and recently supplemented by the Sarbanes-Oxley Act.[76] The SEC may seek civil money penalties in enforcement actions in federal district court and in administrative actions,[77] cease and desist orders restraining

---

72. National Association of Securities Dealers, Rule 3070, *available at* http://nasd.complinet.com/nasd/display/index.html.

73. *In the Matter of Department of Market Regulation Complainant, Yankee Financial Group, Inc. and Richard F. Kresge,* Complaint No. CMS030182 (Aug. 4, 2006). "Complaint" includes "any written grievance by a customer involving the member or person associated with a member." NASD Conduct Rule 3070(c). A firm's president is responsible for the firm's compliance with Rule 3070 unless and until he reasonably delegates responsibility for that obligation and neither knows nor has reason to know that such person's performance is deficient. Dep't of Enforcement v. Fox & Co. Invs., Inc., Complaint No. C3A030017, 2005 NASD Discip. LEXIS 5, at *36 (NAC Feb. 24, 2005) (holding that a firm president violated Rule 3070(a)), *aff'd,* Exchange Act Rel. No. 52697, 2005 SEC LEXIS 2822 (Oct. 28, 2005).

74. *See* 15 U.S.C. § 77x (Securities Act of 1933); 15 U.S.C. § 78ff (Securities Exchange Act of 1934); 15 U.S.C. § 80b-17 (Investment Advisers Act of 1940); 15 U.S.C. § 80a-48 (Investment Company Act of 1940).

75. *See* 15 U.S.C. § 77v; 15 U.S.C. § 78aa; 15 U.S.C. § 80b-14; 15 U.S.C. § 80a-43.

76. The Securities Enforcement Remedies and Penny Stock Reform Act of 1990, Pub. L. No. 101-429, 104 Stat. 931 (codified in various Sections of 15 U.S.C.); Sarbanes-Oxley Act of 2002, Pub. L. No. 107-204, 116 Stat. 745. The SEC may pursue administrative proceedings against regulated entities, 15 U.S.C. §§ 80a-9(d), 80a-42(e), 80(b)-3(i), and 80(b)-9(e), or may pursue actions in federal district court, 15 U.S.C. §§ 77t, 78u, 78u-1. The SEC has broad authority to investigate past, ongoing, or potential violations and to order the production of documents and appearance of witnesses regarding the subject of its investigation. 15 U.S.C.A. §§ 78u, 77t, 77u, 80b-9, 80a-41.

77. 15 U.S.C. §§ 77t(d), 78u(d)(3), 77u-1, 80a-41(e), 80b-9(e), 78u-2.

violation of the securities laws,[78] and bars from service as officers or directors of publicly traded companies.[79] The expanded powers under the Remedies Act and Sarbanes-Oxley have increased the complexity and duration of case investigations, settlement negotiations, and other case dispositions.[80]

Brokers and dealers are subject to the same sanctions from the SEC as others who violate the securities laws, such as injunctions, disgorgement, and civil penalties. In addition, as persons subject to licensing and registration requirements, brokers and dealers are subject to sanctions imposed administratively by the Commission, which include monetary penalties[81] and restrictions on acting as brokers or dealers.[82]

---

78. 15 U.S.C. §78u-3. The SEC may order the corporation to take specific steps to come into compliance within a set period of time, and may initiate proceedings to extract a civil penalty if the corporation does not comply. *See* 15 U.S.C. § 78u(d)(3)(A).

79. 15 U.S.C. §77t-(e) and 78u(d).

80. *See generally* Arthur B. Laby & W. Hardy Callcott, *Patterns of SEC Enforcement Under the 1990 Remedies Act: Civil Money Penalties,* 58 ALB. L. REV. 5 (1994); *Committee on Federal Regulation of Securities, Report of the Task Force on SEC Settlements,* 47 BUS. LAW. 1083 (1992). Furthermore, there is arguably, at least for some claims, no limited time frame under which the SEC must pursue actions. Many courts have ruled that no statute of limitations applies to certain SEC civil enforcement actions. *See, e.g.,* SEC v. Rind, 991 F.2d 1486 (9th Cir. 1993) (no statute of limitations bars Commission's enforcement proceedings seeking injunctive relief under the Securities Act or Exchange Act, though court could consider remoteness of violations in deciding whether to grant equitable relief); SEC v. Lorin, 869 F. Supp. 1117 (S.D.N.Y. 1994) (citing other decisions). *But see* Johnson v. SEC, 87 F.3d 484 (D.C. Cir. 1996) (imposing five-year statute of limitations on Commission-initiated proceedings where penalties are sought). *See also* Matthew Scott Morris, *The Securities Enforcement Remedies and Penny Stock Reform Act of 1990: By Keeping Up with the Joneses, the SEC's Enforcement Arsenal Is Modernized,* 7 ADMIN. L.J. AM. U. 151, 195-196 (Spring, 1993) (noting that the Remedies Act does not contain a provision for the automatic termination of a cease-and-desist order issued without prior notice, and that the order may remain in effect indefinitely).

81. Section 21B(a) of the 1934 Act, 15 U.S.C. § 78u-2(a), authorizes the SEC to impose a civil penalty on a broker-dealer in an administrative proceeding if the SEC finds that such a penalty is in the public interest and that the broker-dealer: (1) willfully violated a provision of the federal securities laws or regulations; (2) willfully aided, abetted, counseled, commanded, induced, or procured such a violation by any other person; (3) willfully made a false or misleading statement in an application or report required to be filed with the SEC or certain other regulatory agencies, or omitted to state a material fact required to be stated therein; or (4) failed reasonably to supervise, with a view to preventing violations of the securities laws and regulations, another person who commits such a violation, if such other person is subject to the broker-dealer's supervision.

82. Section 15(b)(4) of the 1934 Act empowers the Commission to censure, place limitations on the activities of, deny, suspend, or revoke the registration of a broker or dealer. The ultimate sanction the Commission may administratively impose is an order barring the individual for life from associating with any registered broker or dealer. Sub-Sections (A) through

While many SEC offices now ask a company to respond informally to allegations of wrongdoing, often within weeks or sometimes within days of the events, more formal inquiries often still proceed on a somewhat slower track. After the passage of the Private Securities Litigation Reform Act of 1995, the plaintiffs' securities bar has been waiting longer—and perhaps conducting longer investigations themselves—before filing suit in shareholder class actions;[83] such delays are uncommon, however, in derivative actions.

As a result, at least for shareholder class actions, there can be a narrow window within which the corporation can conduct its internal investigation before parallel proceedings begin and make that investigation more difficult to conduct. Such intervening events can include subpoenas to or interviews of individuals that cause them to retain separate and potentially uncooperative counsel, or seizures of documents necessary to prepare a defense or conduct an investigation. But while the internal investigation must therefore be conducted swiftly, it also must be conducted with an eye toward a series of issues that are likely to arise as parallel proceedings develop and progress: ensuring the independence of the investigation; maintaining work product and other privileges protecting the information gathered in the investigation, either from the government or, more likely, from third-party plaintiffs; managing the risk of potential assertions by employees of their Fifth Amendment privilege; assessing the possibility of staying either the SEC investigation and/or the private securities action; and dealing with the involvement of outside auditors who demand to participate or at least be kept apprised of the status of the internal investigation.

A. *Ensuring an Independent Investigation*

Until the past few years, outside counsel for internal investigations was often selected because he or she was a partner in the company's regular outside corporate law firm. This rote selection process is now far less common,

---

(F) of Section 15(b)(4) enumerate the grounds on which the Commission may impose such sanctions. Section 15(b)(4)(D) is a catch-all that allows the Commission to revoke or suspend a broker's license if he or she violates any of the statutes under the Commission's jurisdiction.

83. Joseph A. Grundfest & Michael A. Perino, *Ten Things We Know and Ten Things We Don't Know About the Private Securities Litigation Reform Act of 1995*, 1015 PLI/CORP 1015, 1090 (September, 1997); Joseph A. Grundfest & Michael A. Perino, *Securities Litigation Reform: The First Year's Experience,* 1015 PLI/CORP 955, 959-966 (September, 1997); Joseph A. Grundfest & Michael A. Perino, et al., *Securities Class Action Litigation in Q1 1998: A Report to NASDAQ from the Stanford Law School Securities Class Action Clearinghouse,* 1070 PLI/CORP 69, 74 (September-October, 1998).

and rightly so. The shift in thinking was substantially advanced by the negative press and commentary generated by the work of Enron's regular outside counsel in the weeks before that company's collapse. *See In re Enron Corp. Sec. Derivative & ERISA Litigation*, 235 F. Supp. 2d 549, 665-68 n. 103 (S.D. Tex. 2002) (questioning appropriateness of law firm undertaking internal investigation when company was firm's "biggest client" and firm had "excessive involvement" in transactions to be reviewed).

While the SEC has not yet prescribed any criteria, let alone rules, for the selection of independent counsel, it has increasingly stressed the importance of independence. *See* Cynthia A. Glassman, SEC Commissioner, Remarks before the European Corporate Governance Summit: The Post-Sarbanes-Oxley Environment for Foreign Issuers, Mar. 2, 2005[84] ("I would suggest that the company consider conducting an independent internal investigation—and I stress the term "independent," in definition as well as spirit.").[85]

The SEC's encouragement has gone beyond mere jawboning and entered the world of potential sanctions. *See* Stephen Cutler, SEC Enforcement Director, Remarks at the UCLA School of Law (Sept. 20, 2004) ("We are also considering actions against lawyers, both in-house and outside counsel. . . . One area of particular focus for us is the role of lawyers in internal investigations of their clients or companies. We are concerned that, in some instances, lawyers may have conducted investigations in such a manner as to help hide

---

84. *Available at* http://www.sec.gov/news/speech/spch030205cag.htm.

85. In the Seaboard report, the SEC explained that the reasons for not taking regulatory action against the company included the fact that the company hired "an outside law firm to conduct a thorough inquiry," indicating a preference for outside lawyers over in-house counsel for the choice of investigative counsel. *See* Commission Statement on the Relationship of Cooperation to Agency Enforcement Decisions, Exchange Act Release No. 44969 (Oct. 23, 2001) ("21(a) Report"). *Available at* http://www.sec.gov/litigation/investreport/34-44969.htm. The SEC further wrote that it would consider the following questions in deciding whether to take action in future cases:

> Did management, the board or committees consisting solely of outside directors oversee the review? Did company employees or outside persons perform the review? If outside persons, had they done other work for the company? *Where the review was conducted by outside counsel, had management previously engaged such counsel?* Were scope of limitations placed on the review? If so, what were they?

21(a) Report (emphasis added). In the context of the Investment Company Act of 1940, the SEC has spoken more definitively. In a 2001 release, the Commission stated its belief that "a lawyer whose firm simultaneously represents the fund's advisor and independent directors in connection with areas of conflict between the fund and its advisor, is [not] an 'independent legal counsel.'" 66 Fed. Reg. 3734 (Jan. 16, 2001) (codified at 17 C.F.R. parts 239, 240, 270, and 274).

ongoing fraud, or may have taken actions to actively obstruct such investigations."). True to this warning, the SEC reportedly sent a Wells notice to a partner in a major law firm in 2004 who conducted an internal investigation on behalf of Endocare, a corporate client of the firm. *See SEC May Sue Lawyer in Endocare Probe*, L.A. TIMES, Dec. 7, 2004.

Although no public proceeding has been brought against the partner, the rumors associated with his receipt of a Wells notice—that the SEC believed that the internal investigation he conducted failed to find material wrongdoing that later was revealed, and that the SEC associated the alleged failure of the investigation to find the wrongdoing with the lack of independence of the partner and his firm—had the effect of cementing the change that gained momentum after Enron: a movement away from the selection of regular outside counsel to conduct an internal investigation, at least if that firm had any involvement in the conduct under investigation or if it has any personal or business connection with any of the officers, directors, or employees who may come within the ambit of the investigation.

Even stricter standards may be appropriate if the internal investigation is anticipated to be used as part of the process of responding to derivative litigation and the company seeks to use the investigation as work that may be properly relied upon by a Special Litigation Committee. The selection of independent outside counsel is regularly cited as a factor in an evaluation of whether a Special Litigation Committee is sufficiently independent to be allowed to terminate a derivative action. *See, e.g., In re* PSE & G Shareholder Litigation, 173 N.J. 258, 300 (2002) (Stein, J., concurring); Strougo v. Bassini, 112 F. Supp. 2d 355 (S.D.N.Y. 2000); Garfman v. Century Broadcasting Corp., 762 F. Supp. 215, 220 (N.D. Ill. 1991); Lichtenberg v. Zinn, 663 N.Y.S.2d 452 (N.Y. App. Div. 1997); Strougo v. Padegs, 27 F. Supp. 2d 442 (S.D.N.Y. 1998); Einhorn v. Culea, 612 N.W.2d 78 (Wis. 2000). Historically the use of the company's regular outside counsel—or even a director or officer's regular outside counsel or his or her own firm—was not disqualifying, *see, e.g.*, Maldonado v. Flynn, 485 F. Supp. 274 (S.D.N.Y. 1980), *aff'd in part* and *rev'd in part* on other grounds, 671 F.2d 729, 732 (2d Cir. 1982); Levit v. Rowe, 1992 U.S. Dist. LEXIS 15036, at *17-18 & n. 3, 1992 WL 277997, at *6, 13 n.3 (E.D. Pa. 1992) (upholding choice by a General Electric special litigation committee of a law firm that represented GE "in significant matters" but that received "less than one percent of the money GE paid for outside legal services" and that derived no more than one half of one percent of its total annual revenues from GE in part on the ground that there were few firms capable of supervising the investigation that did not have some contact with GE or its directors), *In re* Consumers Power Co. Derivative Litig., 132 F.R.D. 455, 478-79 (E.D. Mich. 1990) (dismissing action pursuant to the recommendation of an advisory committee where counsel to the committee also was counsel to the corporation in related litigation). But more recent cases have begun to take the opposite view. *See*, *e.g.*, *In re* Oracle Sec. Litig., 829 F. Supp. 1176, 1187-90 (N.D. Cal. 1993) (refusing to approve settlement pursuant to the recommendation of a committee of nondefendant directors because the committee was advised by the corporation's general counsel rather than independent counsel), *subsequent proceedings*, 852 F. Supp. 1437, 1440-45 (N.D. Cal. 1994) (approving same settlement on the basis of a recommendation by a newly constituted special litigation committee acting with the advice of independent counsel). With the SEC pushing in the same direction, it is likely that increasingly strict standards will be used to judge the independence of counsel used by Special Litigation Committees.

Independence and balance in the conduct of internal investigations may prove to be difficult concepts to calibrate and maintain. Fueled by rumors that the SEC is maintaining a spreadsheet that tracks the performance of law firms conducting internal investigations in stock option backdating cases, it is possible to question whether "independent" law firms now have an incentive to throw their "clients" under the proverbial bus in order to build or preserve the firm's reputation with the regulators (and potentially the prosecutors as well). Consistent with this concern, in the field there are numerous tales of "scorched earth" internal investigations that permanently disrupt relationships within the company, or are so costly as to bankrupt the company. Much as was the case with the old independent counsel statute, one byproduct of independence in the conduct of investigations outsourced by the government is the lack of the sort of governing standards and review procedures that would exist if the government were conducting the investigation. As a result, one lasting question generated by the current regime is whether the necessary and appropriate focus on independence will lead to a lack of balance and fairness in the conduct of internal investigations.

B. *The (Largely) Insoluble Problem of Using the Investigation to Assist in Dealing with the Government without Waiving the Privilege*

One dilemma repeatedly presented in parallel proceedings is the tension between using the internal investigation to obtain a favorable result in negotiations with the government and maintaining the privilege for reports or other records of the internal investigation so that those materials do not end up in the hands of private plaintiffs. There are many potential advantages to the corporation in disclosing the results of or information from an internal investigation to federal prosecutors or to the SEC. Such disclosures may facilitate an earlier settlement; especially absent a report, the government is traditionally unwilling to settle promptly out of a fear that by doing so it will miss a material aspect of the wrongdoing, and a disclosure of an internal investigation can speed the government's ability to obtain a full understanding of the events. Disclosure also serves the purpose of demonstrating proper corporate governance to the market. In cases with the potential for criminal prosecution, disclosures provide the benefit of supporting an argument that the corporation should not be charged in light of its corrective actions and in light of the impact on innocent shareholders; even if this argument fails, disclosure may allow the corporation to seek the increasingly common deferred prosecution agreement,[86] or at worst a reduced punishment under the sentencing guidelines.[87] These arguments are often needed given the relative ease with which corporations can be found liable for the wrongdoing of their employees.[88] In any event, even if it were not often beneficial to the corporation to supply its internal investigation to the government, prosecutors have increasingly demanded the waiver of privileges and the production of reports as a precondition to settlement or a declination of prosecution.

This trend has led to what many observers call a "culture of waiver" in both criminal prosecutions and civil enforcement actions by the SEC.[89] In recent years, both the Department of Justice and the SEC issued detailed guidelines for their attorneys to follow in prosecuting corporations that place

---

86. *See, e.g., U.S. v. KPMG, LLP,* 05-CR-0903 (LAP) (S.D.N.Y. Aug. 29, 2005); Press Release, U.S. Dep't of Justice, *The Bank of New York Resolves Parallel Criminal Investigations Through Non-Prosecution Agreement with the United States* (Nov. 8, 2005), *available at* http://www.usdoj.gov/usao/nys/PressReleases/November05/BankofNYNonpros.AgreementPR.pdf. *See also A Corporate Nanny Turns Assertive,* N.Y. TIMES, Sept. 19, 2006, at C1 (discussing the increasing use by the government of deferred-prosecution agreements).

87. *See* United States Sentencing Guidelines (U.S.S.G.) § 8C2.5(g).

88. *See* supra note 7.

89. *See, e.g.,* Marcia Coyle, *Lawyers Fear a DOJ "Culture of Waiver": Corporate Investigations Rely Too Often on Waiving Privilege, Attorneys Say,* NAT'L L. J., Mar. 24, 2006, at 13; Colin P. Marks, *Corporate Investigations, Attorney-Client Privilege, and Selective Waiver: Is a Half-Privilege Worth Having At All?,* 30 SEATTLE U. L. REV. 155, 175 (2006); AM. CHEMISTRY COUNCIL ET AL., *The Decline of the Attorney-Client Privilege in the Corporate Context: Survey Results* 3 (2006).

great emphasis on cooperation by the corporation in any investigation.[90] In particular, a series of memoranda from Deputy Attorney Generals of the Justice Department, starting with Eric Holder, and continuing with Larry Thompson and Paul McNulty (and the aggressiveness with which those memoranda have sometimes been utilized by prosecutors), put significant pressure on corporations to waive their attorney-client privilege and provide the government with otherwise privileged materials from their internal investigations.[91] Both

---

90. Principles of Federal Prosecution of Business Organizations, Deputy Attorney General Larry Thompson, Jan. 20, 2003 ("Thompson Memorandum"); Report of Investigation Pursuant to Section 21(a) of the Securities Exchange Act of 1934 and Commission Statement on the Relationship of Cooperation to Agency Enforcement Decisions, Securities Act Release No. 44969 (Oct. 23, 2001) ("Seaboard Report"), *available at* http://www.sec.gov/litigation/investreport/34-44969.htm.

91. In an effort to set federal guidelines for the prosecution of business organizations, the Thompson Memorandum was issued in January 2003 by then-Deputy Attorney General Larry Thompson, who had recently been named the chairman of the newly-formed President's Corporate Fraud Task Force. The Thompson Memorandum directed federal prosecutors to consider a series of factors in deciding whether, and to what extent, the government would prosecute corporations and other entities. Among other criteria, the Thompson Memorandum listed as a factor "the corporation's timely and voluntary disclosure of its wrongdoing and its willingness to cooperate in the investigation of its agents, including, if necessary, the waiver of corporate attorney-client and work-product protection." The Thompson Memorandum updated a similar memorandum issued in 1999 by a previous Deputy Attorney General. *See* Eric H. Holder, Jr., Bringing Criminal Charges Against Corporations (June 16, 1999), *available at* http://www.usdoj.gov/criminal/fraud/policy/Chargingcorps.html.

In an October 21, 2005, memorandum, the Department of Justice directed prosecutors to "establish a written waiver review process for their district or component." Memorandum from Robert D. McCallum, Jr., Acting Deputing Attorney General, *available at* http://www.usdoj.gov/usao/eousa/foia_reading_room/usam/title9/crm00163.htm. Portrayed as a means of creating standards for the extraction of waivers, the memorandum was criticized on the ground that it ensured that each district or component would "be ready to strike with a demand for a privilege waiver" and that there would be no uniform standard—"an issue that is particularly troublesome for corporations doing business in a global marketplace." McLucas, Shapiro & Song, *The Decline of the Attorney-Client Privilege in the Corporate Setting*, 96 J. CRIM. L. & CRIMINOLOGY 621, 639 n.69 (2006).

The Seaboard Report is the SEC's version of and precursor to the Thompson Memorandum. It lists the factors the SEC will consider when deciding "whether, and how much, to credit self-policing, self-reporting, remediation, and cooperation." Like the Thompson Memorandum, the Seaboard Report lists as a factor the nature and extent of the company's cooperation and contemplates that the company will, among other things, share the results of its internal investigation with the SEC, produce a written report, and secure the cooperation of employees with the staff of the SEC. In the process, the Seaboard Report states that the SEC recognizes that the attorney-client and work-product protections "serve important social interests." On its face, the Seaboard Report comes across as more reasonable with regard to the waiver of the corporate attorney-client privilege. Indeed, in an attempt to cushion the effect of

the Justice Department's memoranda and the SEC's somewhat analogous Seaboard Report listed the waiver of a corporation's attorney-client and work-product protections as a significant factor in determining whether a corporation should receive favorable or lenient treatment from the government. Seeking to ward off potentially disastrous indictments and SEC enforcement actions, corporate counsel have become almost as well versed in these guidelines as their government counterparts. Not surprisingly, corporations facing an investigation now feel considerable pressure to waive their attorney-client privilege as a matter of course.

So considerable has been the pressure that it has begun to generate adverse political reaction, including criticism and other activity from the bar,[92] the

---

such a waiver and thereby acknowledging some of the dangers of waiving the privilege in this context, the Report also pointed out that the SEC had filed an amicus brief arguing that providing privileged information to the Commission staff pursuant to a confidentiality agreement did not necessarily waive the privilege as to third parties, and that, in certain circumstances, the staff has agreed that production of privileged information would not constitute a subject-matter waiver that would entitle the staff to receive further privileged information. As discussed below, however, on the basis of recent precedent in this area, there is real doubt that the selective waiver of the privilege is a viable option for corporations. *See* infra notes 118 & 119 and accompanying text.

In early 2006, the Commission reaffirmed its expectation and encouragement of privilege waivers when it announced its long-awaited policy on the imposition of penalties against corporations. Its two primary factors were the presence or absence of a direct benefit to the corporation as a result of the violation and the degree to which the penalty will recompense or further harm the injured shareholders. Significantly, among the other factors the Commission said it would consider was the corporation's cooperation with law enforcement authorities. *See* Statement of the U.S. Securities & Exchange Commission Concerning Financial Penalties (Jan. 4, 2006), *available at* http://www.sec.gov/news/press/2006-4.htm.

92. The ABA vehemently criticized those portions of the Thompson Memorandum that it viewed as impinging on the attorney-client privilege of either the corporation or a corporation's individual employees. In August 2005, the ABA Task Force on the Attorney-Client Privilege presented the ABA House of Delegates with Recommendation 111 opposing the government's practice of trying to obtain a waiver of that privilege. The ABA approved the Recommendation unanimously. *Report by Task Force on Attorney Client Privilege,* Aug. 8, 2005, *available at* https://www.abanet.org/buslaw/attorneyclient/materials/hod/0806_report.pdf. The ABA engaged in similar activism at its Annual Meeting in 2006, when it approved the recommendation of its Attorney-Client Task Force (which was created to educate policymakers and the general public on the importance of preserving the attorney-client privilege) opposing the government's policy of considering the corporation's payment of employees' legal fees in determining whether the corporation has cooperated with the government. American Bar Association Task Force on Attorney-Client Privilege Recommendation 303 and Related Report (Aug. 8, 2006) ("ABA Recommendation and Report"), *available at* www.abanet.org/buslaw/attorneyclient/materials/hod/emprights_report_adopted.pdf.

Sentencing Commission,[93] the courts,[94] and Congress.[95] In response to this criticism, Deputy U.S. Attorney General Paul McNulty issued a memorandum in December 2006 setting forth revised guidelines for federal prosecutors to follow when deciding whether to charge a corporation or other business organization.[96] While the McNulty Memorandum confirms many of the principles articulated in the Thompson Memorandum, the new guidance departs from its predecessor in two important respects. First, the McNulty Memorandum establishes a process by which prosecutors must obtain written approval within the Department of Justice before requesting waiver of the attorney-client privilege.[97] Second, the new guidelines state that a prosecutor "generally" should

---

93. While not directly critical, in November, 2006 the Sentencing Commission deleted from the sentencing guidelines the reference to privilege waiver as a factor in assessing cooperation credit. *See* U.S.S.G. § 8C2.5, comment 12.

94. *See* infra note 100 and accompanying text.

95. On December 8, 2006, Senator Arlen Specter (R-Pa.) introduced a bill called the Attorney-Client Privilege Protection Act of 2006, which would prohibit any agent or attorney of the United States from requesting that a corporation waive the privilege. S. 30, 109th Cong. § 3 (2006). In addition, the legislation would prohibit government lawyers from conditioning a civil or criminal charging decision on a corporation's assertion of the attorney-client privilege or work-product protection, provision of legal defense fees to its employees, or entry into a joint-defense arrangement with its employees. *Id.* The bill's findings characterized the pressure exerted by the Department of Justice and other agencies to encourage waiver as "undermin[ing] the adversarial system of justice" and "encroaching on the constitutional rights and other legal protections of employees." *Id.* § 2. *See also* Statement of Sen. Patrick Leahy, Hearing on "The Thompson Memorandum's Effect on the Right to Counsel in Corporate Investigations" (Sept. 12, 2006), *available at* http://leahy.senate.gov/press/200609/091206.html ("Many critics worry that the Thompson Memorandum is yet another example of this Administration's tendency to overreach in asserting executive power without regard for the Constitution, the laws, and basic fairness.").

96. Deputy Attorney General Paul J. McNulty, Principles of Federal Prosecution of Business Organizations (Dec. 12, 2006), *available at* http://www.usdoj.gov/dag/speech/2006/mcnulty_memo.pdf ("McNulty Memorandum"). *See also* Prepared Remarks of Deputy Attorney General Paul J. McNulty at the Lawyers for Civil Justice Membership Conference Regarding the Department's Charging Guidelines in Corporate Fraud Prosecutions (Dec. 12, 2006), *available at* http://www.usdoj.gov/dag/speech/2006/dag_speech_061212.htm ("McNulty Remarks").

97. McNulty Memorandum at 8-11. Pursuant to the McNulty Memorandum, prosecutors may seek a waiver only where they have "a legitimate need" for the privileged information. Whether a legitimate need exists depends on the following four factors: (1) the likelihood and degree to which the privileged information will benefit the government's investigation; (2) whether the information sought can be obtained in a timely and complete fashion by using alternative means that do not require waiver; (3) the completeness of the voluntary disclosure already provided; and (4) the collateral consequences to a corporation of waiver.

not take into account whether a corporation is advancing attorneys' fees to its employees who are under investigation, noting the existence of state law and contractual obligations and concluding that a corporation's compliance with governing state law and its contractual obligations cannot be considered a failure to cooperate.[98] These changes may signal a retreat by the Department of Justice from its increasingly aggressive posture in recent years.

While Deputy Attorney General McNulty has described the new guidelines as "very protective of the attorney-client privilege" and sufficient to assuage concerns about a "culture of waiver,"[99] critics have identified several shortcomings in the new approach. One objection is that the McNulty Memorandum merely requires high-level Department of Justice approval of waiver

---

In addition, the McNulty Memorandum distinguishes between two types of putatively privileged information: purely factual information relating to the underlying misconduct, including legal advice that: (i) is contemporaneous to the underlying misconduct when the corporation or one of its employees is relying on an advice-of-counsel defense, or (ii) comes within the crime-fraud exception to the attorney-client privilege ("Category I"); and attorney-client communications and non-factual attorney work product containing counsel's mental impressions and conclusions, legal determinations reached as a result of an internal investigation, and legal advice given to the corporation ("Category II"). Prosecutors may seek only Category I information in the first instance; Category II information "should only be sought in rare circumstances" where "purely factual information provides an incomplete basis to conduct a thorough investigation. Before seeking waiver of Category I information, line prosecutors must request authorization from their U.S. Attorney, who must in turn consult with the Assistant Attorney General for the Criminal Division before granting or denying the request. Both the request and the authorization, if granted, must be in writing. Furthermore, if authorization is granted, the U.S. Attorney must communicate the waiver request to the corporation in writing. Before seeking waiver of Category II information, the U.S. Attorney must obtain written authorization from the Deputy Attorney General. A waiver request with respect to Category II information must also be communicated to the corporation in writing. Although prosecutors may not consider a corporation's refusal to waive Category II information in making a charging decision, they may favorably consider a corporation's acquiescence. As to a request for Category I information, a prosecutor may consider both a corporation's willingness to provide the requested information as well as its refusal to do so. *Id.* at 9.

98. *Id.* at 11. In *United States v. Stein,* Judge Lewis Kaplan of the U.S. District Court for the Southern District of New York held that the Thompson Memorandum, and the manner in which the government implemented it, violated the Fifth and Sixth Amendments to the Constitution insofar as it interfered with an individual employee's right to obtain counsel and mount an effective defense. 435 F. Supp. 2d 330, 356-69 (S.D.N.Y. 2006) ("*Stein I*"). Specifically, the court held that the Thompson Memorandum, by its reference to "the advancing of attorneys' fees" as a factor in assessing a company's cooperation, violated the individual employees' substantive due process rights under the Fifth Amendment to be free from government interference with their ability to defend themselves. *Id.* at 364-65.

99. McNulty Remarks, supra note 98.

requests and provides little or no substantive protection of the privilege itself.[100] In addition, observers note that the guidelines are merely an internal policy, and no remedy exists if a prosecutor fails to follow them.[101] Finally, and most significantly, the McNulty Memorandum addresses only the most visible manifestation of the government's outsourcing and waiver-generating machine— the express demand for privileged materials—and leaves the rest of the regime intact. As a result, most experienced practitioners are likely to continue to waive the privilege even if they are not requested to do so, with the recognition that they can obtain a benefit by waiving the privilege.[102] This incentive remains even on the fact of the McNulty memorandum itself: although prosecutors may not consider a refusal to provide information, they may favorably consider its production. Put differently, while the stick has at least in name been eliminated, the carrot remains. And under the McNulty Memorandum, prosecutors may continue to consider negatively a corporation's refusal to turn over its factual attorney work product, which in practice is a subject in the vast majority of waiver requests.

While the McNulty Memorandum may be a harbinger of a shift in emphasis, its more likely use in the short term is for public relations in the Justice Department's potential face-off with Congress, the American Bar Association, and some federal courts. The government may be reducing its use of its most heavy-handed tool to coerce waivers, but the Memorandum leaves unchanged the basic incentives encouraging a corporation to waive its privilege. Except perhaps in a few cases on the margin where corporations more concerned about their civil liabilities will rely on the McNulty Memorandum to delay or perhaps refuse voluntary waivers, the government's outsourcing machine can be expected to speed on using most if not all of its cylinders.

With strong benefits and encouragement remaining in effect for a corporation that waives its privilege and produces internal investigation material to the government, a decision to do so nonetheless carries with it a series of potential disadvantages. Disclosure may result in the government learning

---

100. *DOJ Revises Thompson Memorandum to Limit Consideration of Privilege Waivers*, 75 LAW WK. 2355 (Dec. 19, 2006) (quoting Karen Mathis, president of the American Bar Association); *see also* ASS'N OF CORPORATE COUNSEL, *What Does the DOJ's Issuance of the "McNulty Memorandum" Mean for You and Your Client* (Dec. 13, 2006), *available at* http://www.acc.com/resource/v7741.

101. *See* Marcia Coyle, *The "McNulty Memo": Real Change, or Retreat?*, NAT'L L. J., December 21, 2006, at 25.

102. *Id.*

of and prosecuting wrongdoing of which it otherwise would have been unaware,[103] and disclosure inherently places the corporation in a position adverse to individual employees who may face career-threatening penalties or even jail as a result of the disclosures.[104]

Another potentially significant disadvantage to consider in evaluating whether to make a disclosure to the government is that it may waive the attorney-client and/or work-product privilege and as a result impair the corporation's ability to defend itself against shareholder suits, derivative actions, or other civil cases. Many have tried but few have succeeded in trying to cooperate with the government—which invariably requires production of at least some of the information generated by and results of the investigation—while keeping that information out of the hands of private plaintiffs who would use it to the company's detriment.

One approach to cooperation without losing the privilege, which found some initial but not lasting success, was to create a principle of law that the attorney-client privilege and work product protection can be waived selectively for information disclosed to the government for the purpose of assisting the government's investigation. At first, there was a modicum of support for a principle of selective waiver, or for creating a new privilege, sometimes called the self-evaluative privilege, either of which would have made the information immune from disclosure to third parties despite its production to the government. But with rare exceptions,[105] prevailing authority refuses to recognize the

---

103. It is also possible that a report to the government, especially if protected by some sort of settlement privilege may mean that the investigation will be viewed as a contemplated legal proceeding for purposes of Item 103. *See* supra note 23 and accompanying text.

104. 15 U.S.C. §77t-(e) and 78u(d) (prohibiting persons from serving as officers or directors); 15 U.S.C. §§77x, 78ff, §80b-17, and 80a-48, and U.S.S.G. § 2F1.1 (penalty and sentencing provisions).

105. *See* Diversified Industries v. Meredith, 572 F.2d 596 (8th Cir. 1977) (*en banc*); United States v. Shyres, 898 F.2d 647, 657 (8th Cir. 1990); *In re LTV,* 89 F.R.D., 595, 615 n. 13 (N.D. Tex. 1981); *In re* Grand Jury Subpoena dated July 13, 1979, 478 F. Supp. 368, 372-73 (E.D. Wis. 1979); Byrnes v. IDS Realty Trust, 85 F.R.D. 679, 685-89 (S.D.N.Y. 1980); The Triax Co. v. United States, 11 Cl. Ct. 130, 133 (1986); M & L Business Machine Company, Inc. v. Bank of Boulder, 161 B.R. 689, 697 (D. Colo. 1993). *See also* Anne C. Flannery & Katherine M. Polk, *Between a Rock and a Hard Place: Internal Corporate Investigations and the Attorney-Client Privilege,* 963 PLI/CORP. 585 (October/November 1996); Anne C. Flannery & Jennifer S. Milano, *The Confusion Continues: Protection of Internal Corporate Investigation Materials Under the Attorney-Client Privilege and Work Product Doctrine, Revisited,* 1023 PLI/CORP. 519 (November 1997); Attorney-Client Privilege Protection Act of 2006 §3, supra note 97 (bill providing that disclosure of privileged information to the government shall not constitute a general waiver).

viability of the selective waiver doctrine[106] or to accept the existence of any self-evaluative privilege,[107] other creative approaches such as calling the information a hypothetical proffer, seeking the protection provided for settlement

---

106. See Permian Corp. v. United States, 665 F.2d 1214 (D.C. Cir. 1981); *In re* Martin Marietta Corp. 856 F.2d 619 (4th Cir. 1988); Westinghouse Electric Corp. v. Republic of Philippines, 951 F.2d 1414 (3d Cir. 1991); Neal v. Honeywell, Inc., 1995 U.S. Dist. Lexis 14488 (N.D. Ill. 1995); *In re* Kidder Peabody Securities Litigation, 168 F.R.D. 459 (S.D.N.Y. 1996); Genentech, Inc. v. United States Internat'l Trade Comm'n, 122 F.3d 1409, 1417 (Fed. Cir. 1997); *In re* Steinhardt Partners, *L.P.,* 9 F.3d 230, 235 (2d Cir. 1993); McMorgan & Co. v. First California Mortgage Co., 931 F. Supp. 703 (N.D. Cal. 1996). It should be noted, however, that many of these decisions are premised on the voluntary nature of the disclosure. *See In re Subpoenas Duces Tecum,* 738 F.2d 1367, 1373 (D.C. Cir. 1984) ("there may be less reason to find waiver in circumstances of involuntary disclosure..."); *Bank of Boulder,* 161 B.R. at 696-97 (limited waiver where bank's cooperation with U.S. Attorney was in compliance with mandatory duties under Federal Reserve System procedures, unlike SEC's voluntary disclosure program); *Westinghouse,* 951 F.2d at 1427 n. 14 (Westinghouse's disclosure to the DOJ was voluntary even though it was prompted by a grand jury subpoena because Westinghouse withdrew its motion to quash the subpoena and produced documents pursuant to a confidentiality agreement); Boston Auction Company, Ltd. v. Western Farm Credit Bank, 925 F. Supp. 1478 (D. Haw. 1996) (bank's disclosures to the FCA not voluntary because FCA has federal authority to access all files). In 2006, the Tenth Circuit became the latest court to reject the theory of selective waiver of the privilege. In *In re* Qwest Communications, Inc., 450 F.3d 1179, 1200 (10th Cir. 2006), the court granted the motion of the shareholder plaintiffs in a class action suit to compel the production of documents the defendant corporation had submitted to the SEC and DOJ, despite the fact that the defendants claimed the documents were protected by the attorney-client privilege.

107. The "self-evaluative" privilege, designed to encourage self-criticism by protecting self-evaluative materials, initially seemed to be a promising basis on which a corporation could withhold internal reports. *See, e.g.,* Allen & Hazelwood, *Preserving the Confidentiality of Internal Corporate Investigations,* 12 J. CORP. L. 355 (1987); Crisman & Mathews, *Limited Waiver of Attorney-Client Privilege and Work-Product Doctrine in Internal Corporate Investigations: An Emerging Corporate 'Self-Evaluative' Privilege,* 21 AM. CRIM. L. REV. 123 (1983); *Note, Discovery of Internal Corporate Investigations,* 32 STAN. L. REV. 1163 (1980). However, there has been much confusion about the privilege and it has been applied only seldom and in limited contexts. *See* Dowling v. American Hawaii Cruises, Inc., 971 F.2d 423, 426 n. 1 (9th Cir. 1990). The application in the context of internal corporate investigations is rare. *See, e.g.,* FTC v. TRW, Inc., 628 F.2d 207, 210-11 (D.C. Cir. 1980). Furthermore, courts have refused its application where documents are sought by a government agency, *see* United States v. Dexter, 132 F.R.D. 8, 9 (D. Conn. 1990), or by a grand jury, *In re* Grand Jury Proceedings, 861 F. Supp. 386 (D. Md. 1994), while many find no self-evaluative privilege under federal law at all, Spencer Savings Bank v. Excell Mortgage Corp., 960 F. Supp. 835 (D.N.J. 1997). However, the public policy reasons that supported the privilege are now frequently weighed by courts in deciding whether a corporation has waived the attorney-client or work product privilege by providing internal investigations to third parties like government agencies.

discussions in Federal Rule of Evidence 408, or asserting a common interest privilege, have generally met a similar fate.[108]

While the courts have not readily embraced the selective waiver doctrine or the self-analysis privilege, the benefits to the government of voluntary waiver by corporations and others during the course of an investigation have been widely recognized.[109] As a result, there is currently an amendment proposed to the Federal Rules of Evidence that would adopt the principle of selective waiver that has been largely rejected by the courts.[110] In addition, Section 607 of the Regulatory Relief Act of 2006, which was enacted into law in October 2006, applies the doctrine of selective waiver to disclosures of oth-

---

See, e.g., In re Kidder Peabody Secs Litigation, 168 F.R.D. 459 (S.D.N.Y. 1996); *In re* Woolworth Corp. Secs. Class Action, No. 94 Civ. 2217, 1996 WL 306576 (S.D.N.Y. June 7, 1996); Picard Chemical Inc. Profit Sharing Plan v. Perrigo Company, 951 F. Supp. 679 (W.D. Mich. 1996).

108. In the event that the government suggests that proceedings are not far enough advanced to be "settled" under Rule 408, then it might be amenable to agreeing that the corporation is not yet an adversary, so that an exception to the waiver analysis in *Steinhardt* is available. Especially given the SEC's unwillingness to advise anyone whether they are a subject or a target, this approach might be stretched into an argument that the corporation and the SEC have common interests in corporate governance and therefore fall within a common interest privilege. *Steinhardt,* 9 F.3d at 236, citing *In re* Sealed Case, 676 F.2d 793, 817 (D.C. Cir. 1982) and *In re* LTV Securities Litigation, 89 F.R.D. at 614-15. But this argument appears to have gained little acceptance: as *Steinhardt* itself indicates, the fact that production of a report to the SEC is voluntary and that formal enforcement proceedings have not begun is not enough to make the SEC and the corporation "non-adversaries" so that the common interest privilege applies. *Steinhardt,* 9 F.3d at 234. *See also In re* Subpoenas Duces Tecum, 738 F.2d at 1372 (no common interest between law firm and SEC as to materials provided as part of voluntary disclosure program). *Cf. Bank of Boulder,* 161 B.R. at 694 (bank's and U.S. Attorney's "purported joint interest in prosecuting federal banking crimes is too abstract to permit the Bank to benefit from the common interest exception"). The common interest privilege was squarely rejected in United States v. Bergonzi, 216 F.R.D. 487 (N.D. Cal. 2003). *But see In re* Cardinal Health Securities Litigation, 2/9/07 N.Y.L.J. 25 (S.D.N.Y.) (work product not waived by production to SEC and DOJ of material generated during internal investigation on behalf of Audit Committee, because Audit Committee and the SEC "shared a common interest in developing legal theories and analyzing information concerning potential financial irregularities)."

109. *See, e.g.,* Diversified Industries v. Meredith, 572 F.2d 596, 611 (8th Cir. 1977); Schnell v. Schnall, 550 F. Supp. 650, 653 (S.D.N.Y. 1982) (public policy considerations encouraging voluntary cooperation with the SEC "are paramount").

110. The Advisory Committee's Proposed Rule 502 states that disclosures of privileged materials to federal regulatory, investigative, and enforcement authorities do not operate as a waiver of the privilege as to third parties. FED. R. EVID., PROPOSED R. 502(c) (2006). The Proposed Rule also imposes a fairness analysis on subject matter waiver. FED. R. EVID., PROPOSED R. 502(a) (2006). This concern has also been echoed in Congress. The then Chairman of the House Committee on the Judiciary requested the Judicial Conference to initiate the rulemaking process to address the litigation costs and burdens created by the current law on waiver of attorney-client privilege and work product protection. Letter from Chairman of the House Committee on the Judiciary to the Judicial Conference, Jan. 23, 2006.

erwise privileged materials to a variety of authorities that regulate banks and credit unions.[111]

Without the availability of a principle of law that would automatically protect the results of an internal investigation, the next battleground has been over whether the information can be produced to the government on terms that would allow it still to be withheld from private plaintiffs. A leading case describing steps that might allow a corporation to produce information to the government and still maintain privilege is *In re Steinhardt Partners, LP*, 9 F.3d 230 (2d Cir. 1993). The SEC had asked Steinhardt for documents relating to allegations of wrongdoing in the securities markets, and later asked for a memorandum addressing legal theories applicable to the facts of the case. Steinhardt supplied the information, adding the "confidential treatment requested" stamp common to SEC productions.[112] As is typical, the SEC did not respond to or acknowledge the request. Later, civil suits were filed and the plaintiffs asked for all documents previously produced to the government. Steinhardt refused to produce its memorandum, but the district court granted the plaintiffs' motion to compel.

The Second Circuit's affirmation explicitly recognized the "Hobson's choice" between disclosing information in an effort to avoid an SEC sanction on the one hand, and protecting the privilege against private litigants on the other, but addressed on the notion that *voluntary* disclosure of work product (or attorney-client privileged material) to an *adversary* waived the privilege. Underscoring the significance of those circumstances, the court explained that waiver might not occur where "the SEC and the disclosing party have entered into an explicit agreement that the SEC will maintain the confidentiality of the disclosed materials." *Id.* at 236.

This decision suggests several steps that can be taken to increase the chance that disclosure of a report to the government will not result in waiver of the privilege.[113] While none of these steps guarantee protection, proposing

---

111. 12 U.S.C. § 1828 (2006) ("The submission by any person of any information to any federal. . ., state, or foreign banking authority for any purpose in the course of any supervisory or regulatory process of such agency . . . shall not be construed as waiving, destroying, or otherwise affecting any privilege such person may claim with respect to such information under Federal or State law as to any person or entity other than such agency, supervisor, or authority.").

112. This legend, based on 17 C.F.R. § 200.83, seeks protection from disclosure under the Freedom of Information Act.

113. While auditors can lend considerable credibility and support to an investigation, the use of a company's regular outside auditors—as opposed to independent consultants hired by lawyers—should be approached with caution. Auditors generally have duties not to disclose the confidential information of their clients. *See, e.g.,* Checkosky v. SEC, 23 F.3d 452 (D.C.

them has little downside risk. First, especially when it will not undermine an attempt to claim the benefits of voluntary disclosure, a subpoena can be requested.[114] Second, a confidentiality agreement can be sought. While there is growing authority that a protective order in a civil case cannot trump a

---

Cir. 1994). However, there are several situations in which information discovered by or disclosed to an auditor must or may be disclosed to other parties. Most significantly, the 1995 Reform Act implemented procedures for reporting the discovery of potential illegal acts. 15 U.S.C. § 78j-1. If an independent public accountant determines that an illegal act may have occurred, the accountant must make certain findings and report such findings to the audit committee or board of directors, unless the illegal act is clearly inconsequential; if the accountant concludes that there is a failure to take remedial action, it must report its conclusions to the board of directors. *Id.* The issuer whose board of directors receives such a report must immediately inform the Commission of the report. If the accountant does not receive confirmation that such notice has been given, the accountant must resign from the engagement, or furnish the Commission with documentation of its report; even if the auditor resigns, it must furnish to the Commission a copy of its report. *Id. See generally* Andrew W. Reiss, *Powered by More Than GAAS: Section 10A of the Private Securities Litigation Reform Act Takes the Accounting Profession for a New Ride,* 25 HOFSTRA L. REV. 1261 (1997). Additionally, even apart from these provisions in the Reform Act, parties in litigation may have access to information about corporations generated by or in the possession of accountants because there is no confidential accountant-client privilege under federal law. *See* United States v. Arthur Young & Co., 465 U.S. 805, 817 (1984) (ordering production of accountants' tax accrual workpapers). The relationship of a client with an auditor does not give rise to the same privileges as does the relationship with an attorney because "the independent auditor assumes a public responsibility transcending any employment relationship with the client." *Id.* at 817-18. An exception to this rule arises where information is disclosed to an accountant for the purpose of obtaining legal advice from a lawyer. *See* United States v. Kovel, 296 F.2d 918, 922 (2d Cir. 1961) (privilege applies where the client first consults with a lawyer who retains an accountant, or if the client consults a lawyer with his own accountant present, but not where the client communicates first to his accountant, even though the client later consults an attorney on the same matter); Grand Jury Proceedings Under Seal v. U.S., 947 F.2d 1188, 1190-91 (4th Cir. 1991) (same). However, statements to accountants that are not related to the corporation's seeking of legal advice are not privileged. *See, e.g.,* John Doe Corporation v. United States, 675 F.2d 482, 488 (2d Cir. 1982). *See also In re* Subpoena Duces Tecum Served on Willkie, Farr & Gallagher, No. M8-85(JSM), 1997 WL 118369 (S.D.N.Y. 1997) (documents generated during an internal investigation were no longer protected under the attorney-client privilege once they were revealed to company's outside auditors).

See generally First Fed'l Savings Bank of Hegewisch v. United States, 55 Fed. Cl. 263, 265 (2003) ("*Hegewisch II*") (While disclosure of board minutes to KPMG during the course of a "special accounting procedure" as a part of an internal investigation was held not to have waived the attorney-client privilege, subsequent disclosure of the same board minutes to KPMG in the course of its regular annual audit was held to have waived the privilege because the latter had no legal or investigative purpose.).

114. As noted above, both the McNulty Memorandum and the SEC's Seaboard Report make a corporation's willingness to cooperate with the government's investigation a key factor in determining whether, and to what extent, to charge a corporation. In some cases, claiming such benefits while still requesting a subpoena might be accomplished by making a more informal, unwritten voluntary disclosure in advance of the production of the report.

grand jury subpoena,[115] at a minimum a protective order can be of utility in opposing a civil discovery request.[116]

These approaches depend on support from or agreement by the government, and as a result rest on the ability to convince the government to assist in helping to maintain the privilege.[117] In urging this position on the government, the now-rejected arguments in favor of the critical self-analysis privilege can come in handy: the government's task can be made easier, and corporations can be encouraged to police wrongdoing and assist the government, if doing so does not lay the corporation bare to the claims of private plaintiffs, who will be seeking further recovery on top of the punishment that the government deemed appropriate under the circumstances. While prosecutors and regulators are usually sympathetic to these arguments, they face potentially dispositive limitations in their ability to grant unlimited confidentiality: most notably, prosecutors cannot, consistent with *Brady v. Maryland*, 373 U.S. 83 (1963), and its progeny agree not to produce to criminal defendants any exculpatory material in their possession. *See United States v. Bergonzi*, 216 F.R.D.

---

115. *In re* Grand Jury Subpoena, 836 F.2d 1468 (4th Cir. 1988); *In re* Grand Jury Subpoena, 62 F.3d 1222 (9th Cir. 1995); *In re* Grand Jury Proceedings, 995 F.2d 1013 (11th Cir. 1993). However, some circuits hold that a protective order prevents disclosure notwithstanding a grand jury subpoena, under certain circumstances. *See In re* Grand Jury Subpoena Duces Tecum Dated April 19, 1991, 945 F.2d 1221 (2d Cir. 1991); *In re* Grand Jury Subpoena, 138 F.3d 442 (1st Cir. 1998). Courts indicate that a mere confidentiality agreement is less compelling than a protective order entered by the court. *See, e.g., In re* Grand Jury Subpoena Duces Tecum Dated October 29, 1992 v. Doe, 1 F.3d 87, 94 n. 4 (2d Cir. 1993); *In re* Grand Jury Subpoena Duces Tecum Dated April 19, 1991, 945 F.2d at 1225; *In re* Grand Jury Subpoena, 836 F.2d at 1474.

116. *See, e.g.,* Florida State Board of Administration v. Waste Management Inc., No. 98 L 6034 (Circuit Court of Cook County, Illinois, April 2, 1999) (in an unreported opinion, Illinois trial court upheld confidentiality agreement between company and SEC relating to internal investigation report, without prejudice to civil plaintiffs' opportunity to seek the material later in the case).

117. No such approval can be granted by the SEC for a so-called Wells procedure, which provides a process allowing for a party facing potential charges to submit a written argument to the Commissioners setting forth the reasons why charges should not be filed. The Wells procedure does not permit confidentiality. *See* 17 C.F.R. § 200.83 (specifying that parties submitting information to the SEC may request confidential treatment under the Freedom of Information Act but that such a request does not affect the SEC's right or obligation to disclose information in any other context). There are cases in which the SEC has agreed to notify a party before disclosure. Permian v. United States, 665 F.2d 1214, 1215-16 (D.C. Cir. 1981). The government's ability to consent to nondisclosure may be limited by obligations such as those under Brady v. Maryland, 373 U.S. 83 (1963). However, as noted above, in the Seaboard Report, the SEC at least noted a willingness to support a corporation's position that the disclosure of privileged information to the SEC pursuant to a confidentiality agreement did not necessarily waive the privilege as to third parties.

487, 497 (N.D. Cal. 2003) (compelling production of internal investigation material to criminal defendants, finding protection as waived in part because the government's confidentiality agreement was not unconditional).

Nonetheless, in response to this urging, the SEC has agreed to enter into confidentiality agreements: an affidavit from the Commission's Associate Director of the Division of Enforcement submitted in an amicus brief supporting a confidentiality agreement challenged by civil plaintiffs reported that the SEC agreed to something fewer than ten confidentiality agreements between 1996 and 1999. These agreements, which provide that the SEC will not disclose the documents to third parties except in certain limited circumstances (generally disclosures required by federal law or in furtherance of the Commission's discharge of its duties and responsibilities), were based on the corporation's agreement to turn over work product and the SEC's determination that the work product was reliable, would significantly benefit the SEC's investigation, and could not otherwise be obtained. See Affidavit of Thomas C. Newkirk in Support of the Brief of United States Securities and Exchange Commission as Amicus Curiae, *Florida State Board of Administration v. Waste Management, Inc.* No. 98L6034 (Circuit Court of Cook County, Illinois, March 30, 1999). The SEC is continuing to enter into confidentiality agreements and to seek to protect the disclosed materials from production to third parties, but without much success.[118]

---

118. In 2004, the SEC filed an amicus brief in the *McKesson* matter. Brief of The Securities and Exchange Commission as Amicus Curiae in Support of McKesson Corporation and Supporting Reversal, McKesson Corp. v. McCall (9th Cir. 2005) (No. 03-10511), *available at* http://www.sec.gov/litigation/briefs/mckesson.htm.

In that case, McKesson investigated irregularities in its financial statements, and ultimately signed two confidentiality agreements with the Commission. Through that process, McKesson produced to the Commission a report that included an internal audit report and back-up materials that McKesson deemed privileged. This report enabled the Commission to file a series of enforcement actions in an expedited fashion. In addition, innumerable civil cases were brought and a series of indictments were returned; the prosecutors too used McKesson's materials. In the criminal proceedings, two defendants moved to compel the production of the report, which the district court granted. See United States v. Bergonzi, 216 F.R.D. 487 (N.D. Cal. 2003). In the civil proceedings, a different judge of the same court refused to order production in those proceedings, reasoning that disclosure to a public entity pursuant to a confidentiality agreement—even one with exceptions—should fall within an exception to the rules establishing waiver of work product protections. *See Order Sustaining Defendant's Objection to Magistrate Judge's Denial of Protective Order, In re McKesson HBOC Inc. Securities Litigation,* No. C-99-20743 RMW (N.D. Cal. March 31, 2005) (unpublished order). Adding to the inconsistency in parallel state civil cases brought by large individ-

Despite the possibility that the SEC might later agree to confidentiality and a court might uphold the agreement, the potentially severe consequences of the disclosure to private plaintiffs of internal investigation materials counsel the use of a third approach: to carefully examine and limit the amount of written material that is created in the investigation. A complete written record of an internal investigation should not always be viewed as an inevitable part of the assignment. With rare exceptions, some material must be created. Because the bargain with the government is at its heart trading a pass for the company in exchange for assistance in prosecuting the company's employees,[119] what the government most wants from the deal are memoranda of the interviews of the allegedly culpable employees, which frequently are created at a time when the employees do not have a lawyer and do not have the benefit of seeing the array of potential evidence against them, as they would before they have an opportunity to speak on their own behalf at a criminal trial. As a result, production of interview memoranda—also potentially cloaked, at least initially, with work product protection—is a key deliverable to the government. As, of course, are the documents that evidence the underlying activity, which would be subject to discovery in civil litigation anyway.

The same is not necessarily true of a comprehensive written report of the investigation. Management or the Board of Directors may view a written

---

ual investors or funds that were coordinated for discovery, the state court ordered production of the same material. *See* McKesson HBOC Inc. v. Superior Court, 115 Cal. App. 4th 1229 (2004).

In its amicus brief on McKesson's behalf, the Commission discussed a number of opinions regarding the effect of such confidentiality agreements and noted that some state court cases involving confidentiality agreements with the Commission have held (without written opinions) that producing work product to the Commission under such a confidentiality agreement does not otherwise waive work product protection: State ex. rel. Oregon Public Employees Retirement Board v. McKesson HBOC, Inc., 2003 WL 23315698 (Cal. Sup. June 16, 2003); Shirvanian v. Waste Management, Inc., No. 2000 00211 (Tex. Dist. Ct. March 1, 2002); Florida State Board of Administration v. Waste Management, Inc., No. 98 L 6034 (Ill. Cir. Ct. April 2, 1999). Conversely, the SEC pointed out, other state court cases have held that the company waived work product protection: Merrill Lynch Fundamental Growth Fund, Inc. v. McKesson HBOC, Inc., No. CGC 02 405792 (San Francisco County, Cal. June 16, 2003), *petition for review granted,* No. S117911 (Cal. Oct. 15, 2003) (transferred to Cal. Ct. App.); McKesson Corp. v. Green, 279 Ga. 95 (Ga. 2005) (order compelling production of audit documents affirmed), 266 Ga. App. 157 (2004).

119. *See* Howard W. Goldstein, *Corporate Crime: The Thompson Memorandum,* N.Y.L.J. Online, March 6, 2003, at 5, *available at* http://www.nylj.com (the DOJ is more likely under the Thompson Memorandum to "listen to arguments that individual prosecution obviate the need for corporate prosecutions").

report as necessary for the discharge of their responsibilities[120] and the government may regard the written report as a useful step in the corporation's acceptance of responsibility. But where management, the Board, and the government do not require a written report, the benefits of eliminating the risk of disclosure to civil plaintiffs should not be ignored.

Any written material should be drafted to take full advantage of work product protection,[121] but whether argued as attorney-client privilege, work product protection, or both, few devices have succeeded in keeping internal investigation materials given to the government out of the hands of plaintiffs. Not circulating the report has had little or no success,[122] and most attempts to limit

---

120. *Cf. In re* Caremark International Inc. Derivative Litigation, 698 A.2d 959, 970 (Del. Chan. Ct. 1996). In *Caremark,* following the company's guilty plea, the court evaluated whether corporate directors violated their duty of care and were thus responsible for the corporation's noncompliance with applicable legal standards. The court held that to satisfy their obligations to be reasonably informed about the corporation, corporate boards must "assur[e] themselves that information and reporting systems exist in the organization that are reasonably designed to provide to senior management and to the board itself timely, accurate information sufficient to allow management and the board, each within its scope, to reach informed judgments concerning both the corporation's compliance with law and its business performance."

121. The work product should include not just the assertion that the memoranda contain mental impressions but also that the selection of what to omit and what to include in the memoranda is also work product. Although some cases have rejected the work-product doctrine as a way to protect internal investigation materials on the theory that the investigation was conducted primarily for reasons other than to assist in pending or impending litigation, *see* First Pacific Networks, Inc. v. Atlantic Mut. Ins. Co., 163 F.R.D. 574, 582 (N.D. Cal. 1995) (If documents "would have been prepared independent of any anticipation of use in litigation (i.e., because some other purpose or obligation was sufficient to cause them to be prepared), no work product protection can attach."). *See, e.g., In re* Subpoena Duces Tecum Served on Willkie Farr & Gallagher, 1997 WL 118369 (S.D.N.Y. March 14, 1997); *In re* Leslie Fay Cos. Sec. Litig., 171 F.R.D. 274, 1280-81 (S.D.N.Y. 1995); *In re* Kidder Peabody Sec. Litig., 1996 WL 263030 (S.D.N.Y. May 16, 1996); *In re* Columbia/HCA, 293 F.3d 289 (6th Cir. 2002). But *see In re* Woolworth Corp. Sec. Class Action Litig., 1996 WL 306576 (S.D.N.Y. June 7, 1996); *In re* McKesson HBOC Inc. Securities Litigation, C-99-20743 RMW (N.D. Cal. Mar. 31, 2005); see generally *In re* White, Weld & Russell, 1 SEC 574 (1936) (an investigation "is simply a preliminary inquiry conducted by the Commission to enable it to determine whether grounds exist for the institution of formal proceedings . . . it is not in any sense an adversary proceeding."). In other cases, the argument has failed because production to the government—almost by definition as a potential adversary given that the purpose of the production is to avoid a potential prosecution—waives the privilege. *See, e. g.*, United States v. Bergonzi, 216 F.R.D. 487, 498 (N.D. Cal. 2004).

122. Another sometimes-tried option is for the corporation to generate a written report and keep it in counsel's possession. However, if the court were to find a waiver of the attorney-client privilege, this act alone would probably not be sufficient to protect the document.

the waiver when a report has been provided to the government have been unsuccessful.[123] No cases yet have squarely addressed the issue whether the fact that a *disclosure* is required for the reasons set forth in Section II above means that the protection of investigation *materials* provided by the attorney-client privilege and the work-product doctrine will inevitably be lost.[124] While the attorney-client privilege in other contexts has been limited when the client instead understands that the material will be revealed to others in reports or disclosures,[125] even this principle has been distinguished and the privilege has been maintained in cases more analogous to internal investigations, in which the

---

Cf. Fisher v. United States, 425 U.S. 391, 403 (1976) ("This Court and the lower courts have thus uniformly held that pre-existing documents which could have been obtained by court process from the client when he was in possession may also be obtained from the attorney by similar process following transfer by the client in order to obtain more informed legal advice.")

123. Once a court finds the privilege for an investigative report has been waived, there is a danger that it will also find a waiver as to the materials underlying the report. *See, e.g., In re* The Leslie Fay Companies, Inc. Secs. Litig., 161 F.R.D. 274, 283 (S.D.N.Y. 1995) (production of report to public and use in litigation waived privilege as to documents underlying the report); Neal v. Honeywell, Inc., 1995 U.S. Dist. Lexis 14488 (N.D. Ill. 1995) (upholding magistrate judge's opinion that production of report to government agency constituted subject matter waiver, but noting that Seventh Circuit had not ruled on the issue); *In re* Kidder Peabody Securities Litigation, 168 F.R.D. 459 (S.D.N.Y. 1996) (ordering Kidder to produce factual summaries of witness statements and other documents that formed the basis of a report given to the SEC and the public). *But see* Judge Whyte's order in the *McKesson* case, which maintained that McKesson was not required to produce a report to plaintiffs in an ERISA litigation. 5:99-CV-20743, order entered Apr. 4, 2005.

124. One court held that no privilege exists when a report was required pursuant to a consent decree with the SEC. Osterneck v. E.T. Barwick Industries, 82 F.R.D. 81 (N.D. Fl. 1979). *But see In re LTV Civ. Litig.*, 89 F.R.D. 595, 618-22 (N.D. Tex. 1981).

125. *See In re* Grand Jury Investigation, 557 F. Supp. 1053, 1056 (E.D. Pa. 1983); United States v. (Under Seal), 748 F.2d 871 (4th Cir. 1984) (privilege held not to protect any information disclosed with the understanding that it will be revealed to others and applying holding also to "the details underlying the data which was to be published," including the communications relating the data, any document to be published containing the data, all preliminary drafts of the document, attorney's notes containing material necessary to the preparation of the document, and even copies of other documents, the contents of which were necessary to the preparation of the published document). Accordingly, courts have held that if a client communicates information to an attorney with the understanding that the information will be revealed to others in reports or disclosures, the information is not protected by the attorney-client privilege. *See, e.g.,* United States v. Lawless, 709 F.2d 485, 487-88 (7th Cir. 1983) (information transmitted for use on tax return); United States v. Oloyede, 982 F.2d 133, 141 (4th Cir. 1993) (information for use in filing citizenship application); *Grand Jury Investigation,* 557 F. Supp. at 1056-57 (information on attorney's accident report sheets, that "will, in almost all circumstances, have been either disclosed to third parties, a matter of public record, or intended by the client to be disclosed by the attorney in filing claims, instituting litigation, or investigating the accident").

information is communicated with the understanding that the attorney has discretion about whether to include the information in a report to be made public.[126]

Ultimately, disclosure of internal investigation materials is made to the government not because of any reliable belief that some device can keep the information away from the plaintiffs, but rather because the government's sanctions usually bring a greater wallop and the production is necessary to avoid those consequences; the lesser consequences from the resulting required production of the material in the civil cases is merely part of the price to be paid. But identifying this as the rationale for the creation and production of internal investigation materials puts a premium on an evaluation of the relative risks of the potential government actions compared to the civil claims (so that a different choice can be made in the rare case in which the civil claims bring a more severe sanction), as well as on evaluating exactly how little material can be provided to the government while still ensuring the desired disposition of criminal and regulatory investigations and satisfying any obligations of the Board. Taken together, the continued production of substantial internal investigation materials under these circumstances is a testament to the government's power to coerce cooperation and to its success in outsourcing its investigative work: that power is sufficient to convince companies to spend substantial sums of money, to do so even in the absence of a strict legal requirement, to turn on its key employees, and to inflict damage on itself in civil litigation, all to avoid criminal and regulatory sanctions.

C. *Fifth Amendment Assertions: The Difficult Choices Faced by Individuals in Internal Investigations, and the Potential Impact of Those Choices on the Company*

Individuals, especially current employees of the company, who are asked to respond to questions in an internal investigation face a difficult choice, one that in some ways parallels the choices that companies face in deciding

---

126. This is a significant limitation given that, even when disclosure is required, what is required to be disclosed is likely to be far less than the report and all the supporting documentation created by counsel. *See generally* United States v. Threlkeld, 241 F. Supp. 326 (W.D. Tenn. 1965) (some privilege maintained for information provided to attorney in course of preparation of tax return); *see also In re* Grand Jury Subpoena (Dorokee Co.), 697 F.2d 277, 280 (10th Cir. 1983). Moreover, in United States v. (Under Seal), 748 F.2d 871, 875-76 (4th Cir. 1984), the Fourth Circuit held that, if a client communicates information to an attorney not

whether to investigate (and later disclose) alleged wrongdoing. Those individuals can decline to speak and risk termination of their employment and the opprobrium that might result, or they can speak and run the risk that their words might come back to haunt them in the event they ever are prosecuted for their conduct. For those current employees who may become subjects or targets of government investigations, this choice can be especially difficult because it is usually made in virtually a complete vacuum of information about what evidence exists—and occasionally even about what the subject of the investigation is.

Most investigators decline to share information with individuals who are to be questioned, especially in advance of their interview, and most refuse to accept any limitation—such as some sort of joint defense agreement[127]—covering any information provided by the individuals. While it can be of considerable benefit to the company to learn information even through a joint defense agreement—among other things the employee may have leads or other information vital to the company's ability to learn the facts and defend itself—a restriction on disclosure can crimp any presentation to the government and cause the government to conclude that the company's cooperation has been less than full. In fact, like the Thompson Memorandum, the McNulty Memorandum provides that in deciding whether to reward a corporation for its cooperation, the Justice Department will view with disfavor the corporation's decision to support its culpable employees by "providing information to the employees about the government's investigation pursuant to a joint defense agreement."[128] As the ABA Task Force on Attorney-Client Privilege has found, this provision has been interpreted broadly, with the result that "organizations have been discouraged from entering into agreements of this sort."[129]

Of course, asserting the Fifth Amendment privilege is an option only available to individuals, because corporations possess no such privilege. But even individuals can face restrictions on and sanctions for their exercise of the

---

so that the attorney can file a public document but so that the attorney can research the *possibility* of filing a public document, such information remains privileged unless the information actually is disclosed. See also United States v. Schlegel, 313 F. Supp. 177, 179 (D. Neb. 1970) (waiver limited to whatever is finally sent to the government).

127. *See, e.g., In re* Grand Jury Subpoenas, 902 F.2d 244, 248 (4th Cir. 1990).
128. McNulty Memorandum at 11; Thompson Memorandum at 8.
129. ABA Recommendation and Related Report at Section (IV).

privilege: for example, an individual can suffer civil sanctions, such as termination, as a result of asserting the privilege.[130] In addition, the privilege is inapplicable to requests to brokers and dealers for records they are required to maintain by the SEC.[131]

Frequently individuals will lose some of the benefit of asserting the privilege by agreeing to answer the company's questions at the outset of an internal investigation and then seeing the company volunteer that information to the government (or, in some instances with broker-dealers, tender the information to the exchange as required—and thereby, in turn hand it over to the government). While this does not mean that the individual has waived the privilege in the subsequent SEC or grand jury investigations,[132] the individual will have impaired her ability in any subsequent criminal case to keep her defense a secret until after seeing the government's case, and may have created impeaching material in the event she chooses to testify at trial. Moreover, if it chooses to do so, the government can introduce the individual's statement at trial as admissions of a party-opponent.

Until 2006, no court had any problem with the difficult and coercive position in which current employees are put, either in the company's own

---

130. This is especially true for brokers and dealers. Rule 8210 of the National Association of Securities Dealers (NASD) Procedural Rules require any person associated with a member firm, or subject to NASD jurisdiction, to testify under oath when requested by the NASD for the purpose of an investigation, complaint, examination, or proceeding. NASD Manual Rule 8210, p. 7241. Similarly, the rules of the New York Stock Exchange provide that members and employees are required to cooperate with investigators and may be expelled, suspended, fined, or barred for failure to comply with a request by the NYSE for documents, testimony, or other information. Rule 476(a) of the New York Stock Exchange, Inc. Disciplinary Rules. The imposition of such sanctions has been upheld. *In the Matter of the Application of Frank W. Leoneseio,* Exchange Act Release No. 34-23524 (Aug. 11, 1986), 36 SEC. Dkt. 328, 331; *In the Matter of the Application of Daniel C. Adams,* Exchange Act Release No. 34-19915 (June 27, 1983), 28 SEC Dkt. 245 (refusal to provide information based on assertion of privilege against self-incrimination "[w]ould not affect the right of a self-regulatory organization, such as the NASD, to sanction [the broker] for that refusal, since such organizations are not part of the government.").

131. Production of other documents may be compelled under the fifth amendment's "required records" exception, if: (1) the government's inquiry is essentially regulatory rather than criminal; (2) the requested records contain information the party ordinarily would keep; and (3) the documents have assumed public aspects analogous to public documents. *See, e.g., Grosso v. United States,* 390 U.S. 62, 67-68 (1968); *Smith v. Richert,* 35 F.3d 300 (7th Cir. 1994). Objections to producing such records based on not betraying confidences to customers, *McMann v. SEC,* 87 F.2d 377 (2d Cir. 1937), and the disruption such production would cause to the business, *SEC v. Brigadoon Scotch Distributing Co.,* 480 F.2d 1047 (2d Cir. 1973), have been rejected.

132. *See, e.g., United States v. Housand,* 550 F.2d 818, 821 n.3 (2d Cir. 1977).

internal investigation or in the government's investigation, in which the company might pressure its employees to cooperate. But in an extreme case involving the government's prosecution of several former employees of KPMG for their role in allegedly abusive tax shelters, Judge Kaplan of the Southern District of New York found that the relationship between the Justice Department and the entity under investigation was sufficiently close, and the government's tactics sufficiently coercive, that statements made by individuals to the government during the government's investigation should be suppressed.[133] Specifically, the court suppressed statements of two defendants who had been employed by KPMG, finding that, under pressure from the government to cooperate, KPMG had in turn pressured the defendants (the employees of KPMG) to be interviewed by the government pre-indictment and, in the process, threatened to stop payment of legal fees if the employees did not agree to be interviewed. The court ultimately suppressed the statements on the ground that the government, through its aggressive application of the Thompson Memorandum, was responsible for the pressure that KPMG exerted on its employees and that, as a result, KPMG's conduct was "fairly attributable" to the government so as to constitute the government action required to support the defendants' suppression claim.[134]

Given the extent to which Judge Kaplan's decision breaks new ground, and given a set of factual findings that may be difficult to replicate in other cases,[135] predicting the extent to which Judge Kaplan's decision will be followed in other cases is an uncertain venture. Will the decision be only the start of increased protection for individuals in internal investigations and of limitations on corporate adherence to the urgings of the government's guidelines for charging corporations, now set forth in the McNulty Memorandum? For example, will the principle that the employer's conduct was "fairly attributable" to the government be extended to the coercion the company itself places on its employees in its own investigation? Some support for this extension may come from cases in which prosecutors have begun to explore the

---

133. United States v. Stein, 440 F. Supp. 2d 315, 333-35 (S.D.N.Y. 2006) (*"Stein II"*).
134. *Id.* at 334.
135. In *Stein,* Judge Kaplan found that the government expressly alluded to the Thompson Memo in its initial discussions with KPMG's counsel and later pushed KPMG to dissuade its employees from obtaining their own counsel. *Stein I,* 435 F. Supp. 2d at 341-46; *Stein II,* 440 F. Supp. 2d at 320. The U.S. Attorney's Office engaged in several other intimidation tactics: it urged KPMG to tell its employees to be "totally open . . . even if that [meant admitting] criminal wrongdoing" and also threatened KPMG that it would look at the payment of its employees' legal fees that KPMG was not legally obliged to pay "under a microscope." *Stein I,* 435 F. Supp. 2d at 344.

theory that false statements to a company's internal investigators violate the federal statute prohibiting false statements "in any matter within the jurisdiction of the executive, legislative or judicial branch of the Government of the United States," 18 USC § 1001(a).[136]

The likely impact of the decision appears to be in two forms, one readily apparent and a second beneath the surface. After the decision, the Department of Justice revised a portion of the Thompson Memorandum, and now "generally" prohibits prosecutors from considering whether a corporation is advancing attorneys' fees to its employees under investigation. Beneath the surface, the *Stein* decision may result only in increasing the subtlety with which the government pressures corporations to turn against their employees who are under investigation, and in giving prosecutors greater cover with which to defend against future claims that they applied excessive coercion.[137]

---

136. In 2004, the United States Attorney for the Eastern District of New York brought securities fraud and obstruction charges against three former executives of software giant, Computer Associates International, Inc. based on statements made to internal investigators. *See* Information, United States v. Zar, No. 04-331 (ILG) E.D.N.Y. Apr. 2004); Information, United States v. Kaplan, No. 04-330 (ILG) (E.D.N.Y. Apr. 2004); Information, United States v. Rivard, No. 04-329 (ILG) (E.D.N.Y. Apr. 2004), *available at* http://www.usdoj.gov/dag/cftf/cases_a_c.htm. The government alleged that the defendants not only misled internal investigators, but did so knowing and intending that the company's attorneys "would present false and misleading justifications to the United States Attorney's Office, the SEC and the FBI," which "would have the effect of obstructing and impeding the Government investigations." *See* Information, *Zar,* No, 04-331 (ILG); Information, *Kaplan,* No. 04-330 (ILG); Information, *Rivard,* No 04-329 (ILG). The three executives pled guilty. *See* Alex Berenson, *3 Plead Guilty in Computer Associates Case,* N.Y. TIMES, Apr. 9, 2004, at C1. Two years later, this theory of prosecution was used in an indictment of a natural gas trader for El Paso Corporation. *See* Indictment, United States v. Singleton, No. H-04-514-SS (S.D. Tex. Mar. 8, 2006). The indictment alleges that during an interview with outside counsel, Singleton did not "disclose, falsely denied, and otherwise concealed that he had provided false information to trade publications" and that Singleton "believed that El Paso's Outside Lawyers would inform government agencies of his statements during the interview." *Id.*

137. The McNulty Memorandum will make less likely any future findings, as in *Stein I,* that the Department of Justice infringed individual employees' right to counsel by pressuring their employers to cut off the advancement of attorneys' fees. However, other guidance relating to prosecutors' assessment of the extent and value of a corporation's cooperation remains unchanged. For instance, like its predecessor, the McNulty Memorandum encourages prosecutors to look askance at joint defense agreements, insofar as they allow corporations to pass information concerning the government's investigation to their culpable employees. *See* Thompson Memorandum at 8; McNulty Memorandum at 11 ("[W]hile cases will differ depending on the circumstances, a corporation's promise of support to culpable employees and agents, *e.g.,* through . . . providing information to the employees about the government's investigation pursuant to a joint defense agreement, may be considered by the prosecutor."). Similarly, both memoranda pressure corporations to direct their employees to cooperate with the government's investigation. *See* Thompson Memorandum at 8; McNulty Memorandum at 12.

Once the company survives any hurdles created by Fifth Amendment assertions in its own investigation, the problems for the company may only get worse if the employees persist in their assertion of the privilege. In civil cases, the trier of fact will be asked to draw adverse inferences against the *employer* on the basis of an *employee's* or former *employee's* assertion of the privilege against self-incrimination in that civil proceeding. In determining whether to draw adverse inferences from a nonparty's assertion of the Fifth Amendment privilege, courts may consider the circumstances of the particular case. In *LiButti v. United States*, 107 F.3d 110, 123-24 (2d Cir. 1997), the Second Circuit identified nonexclusive factors to guide a trial court in making this determination: (1) the nature of the relationship between the party and the nonparty; (2) the degree of control of the party over the nonparty witness; (3) the compatibility of the interests of the party and the nonparty witness in the outcome of the litigation; and (4) the role of the nonparty witness in the litigation. In evaluating these and other relevant factors, the "overarching concern is fundamentally whether the adverse inference is trustworthy under all of the circumstances and will advance the search for the truth." *Id.* at 124.

There are substantial arguments against drawing the inference. First, the employee's assertion of the privilege provides little basis to conclude that the employee, let alone the employer, engaged in criminal wrongdoing.[138] Second, especially in the current world of high employee mobility, some employees—and many former employees—are disgruntled enough not to mind that their assertion of the privilege discredits the employer, *see, e.g., FDIC*, 45 F.3d 969, 978, thereby undermining the premise on which drawing an adverse inference is based: that "an employee's self-interest would counsel him to exculpate the employer if possible." RAD Servs., Inc. v. Aetna Casualty & Surety Co., 808 F.2d 271, 275 (3d Cir. 1986).

Nonetheless, the inference is often allowed. *See, e.g., Brink's, Inc. v. City of New York*, 717 F.2d 700, 707-10 (2d Cir. 1983) (when corporate plaintiff's former employees asserted Fifth Amendment privilege in response to questions about whether they stole parking meter revenues, jury was properly instructed that it could draw adverse inferences against plaintiff); *RAD Servs., Inc.*, 808 F.2d at 275-77 (trial court properly permitted jury to draw adverse

---

138. *See, e.g.,* Slochhower v. Board of Higher Education, 350 U.S. 551, 557 (1956) ("[W]e must condemn the practice of imputing a sinister meaning to the exercise of a person's constitutional right under the Fifth Amendment."); State Farm Life Ins. Co., v. Gutternman, 896 F.2d 116, 119 (5th Cir. 1990) ("the assertion of the privilege, particularly on the advice of counsel, is an ambiguous response"); *In re* Stelweck, 86 B.R. 833, 850-51 (Bkrtcy). E.D. Pa. 1988), *aff'd* 108 B.R. 488 (E.D. Pa. 1989).

inference against plaintiff when current or former employees of plaintiff asserted the Fifth Amendment in response to questions about environmental violations; it was uncertain whether witnesses were current or former employees because witnesses asserted Fifth Amendment privilege when asked that question).

Indeed, some courts have stated that the employee-employer relationship presents the strongest case for drawing adverse inferences against a party based on a nonparty's assertion of the Fifth Amendment privilege. In *RAD*, 808 F.2d at 275, the court stated that the rationale for admitting statements of employees as vicarious admissions of a corporation under Federal Rule of Evidence 801(d)(2)(D) also justifies informing the trier of fact when the corporation's agent invokes the Fifth Amendment privilege. In addition to reasoning that the employee would want to exculpate the employer, the court explained that the employer "could rebut any adverse inference that might attend the employee's silence, by producing contrary testimonial or documentary evidence." *Id.; see also* Federal Deposit Ins. Corp. v. Fidelity & Deposit Co. of Maryland *("FDIC")*, 45 F.3d 969, 978 n.4 (5th Cir. 1995) ("The fact of present employment serves primarily to reduce the chance that the employee will falsely claim to have engaged in criminal conduct for which the defendant employer is liable.").

Even assertions of the privilege by former employees or other nonparties have been used in some cases against the employer. *See, e.g., Brink's*, 717 F.2d at 707-10 (former employees); *RAD*, 808 F.2d at 275-77 (former employees). In *FDIC*, the court held that it was permissible for the trier of fact to draw adverse inferences against a loan officer on the basis of Fifth Amendment assertions by loan recipients with whom the officer dealt. 45 F.3d at 978. In reaching this conclusion, the court discussed the propriety of drawing adverse inferences against a party based on Fifth Amendment assertions by former employees. *Id.* Acknowledging that not all former employees would remain loyal, the court stated that any "factors suggesting that a former employee retains some loyalty to his former employer—such as the fact that the employer is paying for his attorney—" would reduce the chance that the former employee would falsely cast blame on the former employer and justify use of the adverse inference.[139] But at least one case has read *LiButti* to counsel caution before allowing an adverse inference against an employer whose former senior vice president and general counsel had asserted the privilege;

---

139. *Id.* at 978 n.4. This reasoning is curious given that the corporation may be paying the fees solely as a result of a legal obligation to do so. *See, e.g.,* California Labor Code § 2802.

the court reasoned that it needed more information about the compatibility of the parties' interests and the degree of control the corporation had over the officer. Wechsler v. Hunt Health Systems, Ltd., No. 94-9294, 2003 WL 21998980, *1 (S.D.N.Y. August 22, 2003). And the implications of Judge Kaplan's rulings in the *Stein* opinions—which show the differing interests between an entity and its current and later former employees, as well as the limits on the entity's ability to pressure those individuals—can lend additional support at least for making a more refined analysis of whether an inference can be drawn, if not also reducing the number of cases in which such an inference is allowed.

D. *Stays of Parallel Civil and SEC Proceedings*

It is now well settled that the due process clause does not require the government to choose between proceeding criminally and civilly,[140] and the SEC and federal prosecutors often investigate the same case[141]—sometimes in a coordinated fashion and sometimes not.[142] In addition, private plaintiffs frequently have causes of action parallel to those of the SEC.

In the event that parallel proceedings develop and a corporation addresses the prospect of a stay of civil proceedings, the corporation must first decide whether it would be benefited by discovery or whether the protections of a stay would be desirable, and then evaluate its ability to win either the right to take discovery or the protection of a stay in the event the government or other parties take a contrary position.

While in some instances it will be in the interests of a corporation, as well as in the interests of its individual employees, to stay civil discovery in the face of a criminal investigation, there may be some cases in which the corporation or its employees would achieve a net gain by engaging in discovery.

---

140. United States v. Kordel, 397 U.S. 1 (1970).

141. The only exception, rarely if ever found to exist but perhaps used as a basis to seek limited discovery, is if the civil proceeding was designed solely to gather evidence for the criminal case. *See, e.g.,* United States v. LaSalle National Bank, 437 U.S. 298 (1978); United States v. Gel-Spice Co., Inc., 773 F.2d 427 (2d Cir. 1985); United States v. Cahill, 920 F.2d 421 (7th Cir. 1990); United States v. Aero-Mayflower Transit Co., 831 F.2d 1142 (D.C. Cir. 1987).

142. Coordination, including full access for prosecutors to SEC files, is permitted at the discretion of SEC supervisors. *See* 17 C.F.R. § 200. 30-4(A)(7). Investigations that proceed on an uncoordinated basis allow opportunity for informal discovery. For example, when the SEC sends a Wells notice, 17 C.F.R. § 202.5(c), the staff in response to a request will often describe the evidence it has gathered, even if by doing so it reveals matters that prosecutors conducting a grand jury investigation have not yet disclosed. Alternatively, prosecutors are often willing to address at the outset what is being investigated, while the SEC may be refusing to respond to similar inquiries.

Among the factors impacting this balance are the relative significance of the criminal case compared to any civil matters; the extent of discovery already gained by the government; and the existence of pivotal adverse witnesses (such as cooperators or confidential informants utilized by the government during an investigation) whom the company would otherwise not have an opportunity to question before they appear as prosecution witnesses in a criminal case. When the potential civil liability is relatively small, the government has already questioned most or all of the company's employees, and the pivotal prosecution witnesses refuse to be interviewed, the balance could tip in favor of pursuing discovery, even if doing so exposes the corporation and its employees to the adverse inferences in subsequent civil proceedings resulting from the assertion of a Fifth Amendment privilege by employees.[143] But for the most part, from the corporation's perspective, the knowledge and tactical assistance gained through discovery will be outweighed by the costs, the difficulties of deciding on a defense and on whether to exercise Fifth Amendment privileges before the government's case is fully known, and by the benefits to the government of additional discovery from the corporation.

For individuals with a serious criminal risk, the balance may be different. Given the limited discovery to which a criminal defendant is entitled, *see, e.g.,* FED. R. CRIM. P. 16; 18 U.S.C § 3500, the opportunity to depose potential government witnesses in a civil proceeding could have considerable value (even though some of them may assert their own Fifth Amendment privilege). If the risk of criminal sanction is of more concern than a civil damage judgment—or if the defendant may later be allowed both by the court and the timing of the two proceedings to undo the privilege assertion and testify once his criminal exposure is resolved[144]—then the individual may be better served by opposing any stay.

If a stay is sought, the law of stays in parallel proceedings is difficult to reconcile except based on the notion that the government usually, but not always, gets what it wants. The traditional factors considered by courts in deciding stay motions are the effect on the plaintiff's interest,[145] the effect on

---

143. *See, e.g.,* SEC v. Chestman, 861 F.2d 49 (2d Cir. 1988); *In re Boesky,* 128 F.R.D. 47 (S.D.N.Y. 1989).

144. *See, e.g.,* United States v. Snyder, 233 F. Supp. 2d 293 (D. Conn. 2002).

145. Typical interests in prompt resolution for plaintiffs are fading memories of witnesses, loss or destruction of evidence, and dissipation of assets. *See, e.g.,* Connecticut v. BPS Petroleum Distribution, 1991 U.S. Dist. Lexis 13951 (D. Conn. 1991).

the defendant's interests,[146] the convenience to the courts,[147] and the public interest.[148] In the event that the defense seeks a stay and that request is contested by the government, the stay is usually denied on the theory that "effective enforcement of the securities laws requires that the SEC and Justice be able to investigate possible violations simultaneously,"[149] and that "the public's interest in the integrity of the stock market" is advanced by swift resolution of SEC complaints.[150]

No case has ever stayed a criminal investigation or proceeding. There is language suggesting that civil cases, including those brought by the SEC, can be stayed until the end of the companion criminal proceeding based on "special circumstances"[151] but such special circumstances are rarely found when it is the defendant who makes the request.[152] An argument based on special circumstances would start with the burdens placed upon the defendant by parallel discovery and attempt to magnify them based on the facts of the case. Among these burdens are undermining the Fifth Amendment privilege of the individuals by forcing them to choose between the privilege and protecting themselves in civil proceedings; expanding discovery available to the prosecution beyond that permitted by Federal Rule of Criminal Procedure 16; and prematurely disclosing theories of defense.[153] Another possibility is that adverse

---

146. *See* discussion below.

147. This factor usually translates into judicial economy: avoiding duplication by staying a civil case that might be resolved or limited substantially by the disposition of a criminal case. Some courts have discounted this factor when no criminal case is pending. *See In re* Mid-Atlantic Toyota Antitrust Litigation, 92 F.R.D. 358, 359 (D. Md. 1981).

148. One case distinguished a large group of individuals—beneficiaries of a pension plan—from the general public. Brock v. Tolkov, 109 F.R.D. 116, 120-21 (E.D.N.Y. 1985).

149. *See, e.g.*, United States v. Kordel, 397 U.S. 1 at 12, n.27 (1970).

150. *See, e.g.*, SEC v. Grossman, Fed. Sec. L. Rep. ¶ 93, 184 (S.D.N.Y. 1987); *see* Connecticut v. BPS Petroleum Distribution Inc., 1991 U.S. Dist. LEXIS 13951 (D. Conn. 1991)

151. SEC v. Dresser Industries, Inc., 628 F.2d 1368, 1375 (D.C. Cir. 1980). The authority for a stay appears to be based on the All Writs Act, 28 U.S.C. § 1651(a). *See* United States v. Birrell, 276 F. Supp. 798, 812 (S.D.N.Y. 1967).

152. *See, e.g.* Arden Way Assoc. v. Boesky, 660 F. Supp. 1494, 1497 (S.D.N.Y. 1987) ("[I]t is plainly ludicrous for Mr. Boesky to argue that it is 'unfair' to compel him to face the civil lawsuits against him which are the creations of his own alleged misconduct."). Outside the securities context, there are a few cases staying parallel proceedings, but these opinions turn on the perceived lack of public interest in prompt resolution of the civil case, a perception unlikely to be applicable to an SEC proceeding. *See, e.g.* Brock v. Toklow, 109 F.R.D. 116 (E.D.N.Y. 1985).

153. *Dresser,* 628 F.2d at 1376.

publicity from a civil trial (as opposed to the discovery, which can be conducted under a protective order) would deprive the defendant of a fair trial in the criminal case and therefore require a stay.[154]

The timing of the various proceedings appears to have an effect on how the stay motion is received. When the defendant is actually under indictment, the burdens of parallel proceedings on the Fifth Amendment and discovery are magnified.[155] When a defendant is under indictment, there are cases in which discovery has been stayed when the defendant requests it and the SEC is not a party. *See, e.g., Perry v. McGuire*, 36 F.R.D. 272 (S.D.N.Y. 1964). By contrast, where there is no known criminal investigation, there is no chance to obtain a stay.

In the event that the government seeks a stay when the defense tries to avail itself of civil discovery, the same traditional factors are generally turned against the defendant. The defendant's interest in obtaining discovery—and in being able to supply a prompt and vigorous defense to allegations filed against him—is generally found to be outweighed by the "public interest." It could be argued that the public interest in a speedy disposition is unaffected by who asks for a stay, and that in seeking a stay the government is not advancing the public interest and is instead advancing a tactical litigation advantage, but this argument is generally not accepted.[156] The argument seems even stronger in cases where federal prosecutors seek to stay a case brought by the SEC, a request to which the SEC often consents. This situation raises the question, absent a statute of limitations issue, of why the SEC brought the case at all at a time it was willing to stay it; it is hard to envision the public interest in allowing the SEC to make a public—and often highly publicized—allegation, and then join in an effort to keep the defendant from having a chance to respond promptly to the charges.[157]

---

154. *Dresser Industries, Inc.*, 628 F.2d at 1375;. *See also* United States v. Birrell, 276 F. Supp. 798, 812 (S.D.N.Y. 1962).

155. *See* DeVita v. Sills, 422 F.2d 1172 (3d Cir. 1970).

156. Courts more commonly resolve this argument by viewing the defendant as attempting to "get around" the limits of federal criminal discovery.

157. In an oral statement explaining a denial of the prosecutor's motion to stay a parallel SEC case arising out of stock option backdating, one court adopted the same analysis set forth in the text above: "When the SEC decides they want to charge people with a violation of the securities laws . . . they invite the defense, of course, to respond; and the defendant has a right to respond in civil litigation, and so I don't understand the logic if the SEC is filing charges against people and then saying, 'Oh, by the way, don't do any discovery, we'll wait a year or so.' . . . What I am saying is that I don't appreciate the fundamental fairness of that approach." United States v. Reyes, No. CR-06-0556 CRB (N.D. Cal. October 4, 2006).

Nonetheless, the "public interest" is allowed by many courts to be determined by "a government policy determination of priority." *See* Campbell v. Eastland, 307 F.2d 478, 487 (5th Cir. 1962). There have been, however, a few cases outside of securities violations that have accepted the argument and denied a stay of discovery sought by the government, *see, e.g.,* United States v. Banco Cafetero Int'l, 107 F.R.D. 361, 366 (S.D.N.Y. 1986), *aff'd on other grounds,* 797 F.2d 1154 (2d Cir. 1986), and some judges are beginning to apply these same principles in securities cases: for example, an alliance of class action plaintiffs and individuals who were both civil and criminal securities fraud defendants defeated a stay motion in the McKesson securities litigation.[158]

E. Auditors' Involvement in Internal Investigations

Like lawyers, auditors have had their work subjected to increased scrutiny in the wake of the accounting scandals of 2001, and the SEC has recently listed auditors alongside lawyers as the "gatekeepers" of capital markets.[159] Section 10A of the 1934 Act requires auditors to employ procedures in accordance with generally accepted auditing standards (GAAS) to provide "reasonable assurance of detecting illegal acts that would have a material effect on the financial statements."[160] As with attorneys subject to the requirements of Sarbanes-Oxley, an auditor who becomes aware of information "indicating that an illegal act . . . has or may have occurred" must take steps to inform itself, advise the company, and satisfy itself that the company has remedied the act appropriately.[161]

When companies receive such information from auditors, they typically commence internal investigations with outside legal counsel at the helm. In such instances, not only would the company conduct an investigation in order to stay on the government's good side, but also to stay on the good side of the

---

158. *See Order Granting the United States' Motion to Intervene and Denying Without Prejudice Its Motion to Stay Certain Discovery, Aronson, et al. v. McKesson HBOC, Inc., et al,* No. 99 CV 40743 (N.D. Cal., entered Oct. 21, 2004); United States v. Reyes, No. CR-06-0556 CRB (N.D. Cal. October 4, 2006).

159. Stephen M. Cutler, Director of the Division of Enforcement at the SEC, Remarks at UCLA School of Law, September 20, 2004 (*available at* http://www.sec.gov/news/speech/spch092004smc.htm).

160. 15 U.S.C. 78j-1(a).

161. 15 U.S.C. 78j-1(b).

accounting firm—which might otherwise threaten to resign[162] and thereby create considerable problems for the company, especially public companies, by generating adverse publicity and by delaying required financial filings while a new auditing firm gets up to speed. The internal investigations that grow out of information initiated by the accounting firms will generate extensive attorney-client and work product communications to which auditors may ultimately seek access in their quest to comply with Section 10A and industry standards. In fact, some accounting firms under these circumstances—if not also others—have begun to insist, based on their obligations under Section 10A, not only that they get access to the investigation materials but also that they be allowed to look over the shoulders of the investigators themselves as they review documents and conduct interviews; engagement letters from independent accounting firms may now set forth expectations that the auditors will be present in internal investigations. Necessarily, such auditor involvement will severely limit an attorney's ability to preserve the privilege of the corporation.[163]

---

162. While there does not appear to have been a significant number of resignations on this basis, in the wake of Section 10A and Sarbanes-Oxley, auditing firms and their clients are parting ways at an alarming rate (for the Big Four, almost three times the rate of 2002). Rather than comply with the new regulations for existing clients, auditing firms are electing to drop clients entirely. These dropped clients tend to be smaller companies potentially not worth the extra time and effort of compliance. Similarly, some companies are switching auditors because of steep increases in audit fees. This process is undoubtedly extremely disruptive to public companies as they must also comply with the Securities Act and Sarbanes-Oxley. *See Sorry, the Auditor Said, But We Want a Divorce,* N.Y. TIMES, Feb. 6, 2005, Section 3.

163. Courts generally hold that disclosure of attorney-client communications to auditors, as independent third parties, constitutes a waiver of the privilege. *In re Pfizer Inc. Sec. Litig.,* No. 90 Civ. 1260 (NRB), 1993 U.S. Dist. Lexis 18215, at *22 (S.D.N.Y. 1993) ("[d]isclosure of documents to an outside auditor destroys the confidentiality seal required of communications protected by the attorney-client privilege, notwithstanding that the federal securities laws require an independent audit"); *In re* Subpoena Duces Tecum Served on Willkie, Farr & Gallagher, No. M8-85 (JSM), 1997 U.S. Dist. LEXIS 2927, at *8 (S.D.N.Y. Mar. 14, 1997) (disclosure by investigative counsel of paraphrased statements from employee interviews and its assessment as to employees' credibility to company auditors to obtain an unqualified audit opinion waived the attorney-client privilege as to specific items disclosed to auditors). Courts have also held that an auditor's presence at an interview prevents privilege from attaching in the first place. *See, e.g.,* Ampa, Ltd. v. Kentfield Capital LLC, No. 00 Civ. 0508, 2000 WL 1156860, at *1 (S.D.N.Y. Aug. 16, 2000) (privilege for Board minutes waived when accountant, unrelated to the legal issue discussed, was present).

State law is a bit less settled: fifteen states that have enacted statutes to protect accountant-client communications are listed below. Of these, seven states (in bold) have extended the privilege, either by statute or judicial ruling, to independent auditors. ARIZONA, ARIZ. REV. STAT. § 32-749; **Colorado,** COLO. REV. STAT. § 13-90-107; Florida, FLA. STAT. ANN. § 90.5055;

There is no developed law on whether the accountants are justified in relying on Section 10A and insisting on being present at internal investigations. The Statement on Auditing Standards No. 99 (SAS 99),[164] which establishes guidelines for compliance with Section 10A,[165] requires auditors to exercise professional skepticism during an audit and requires auditors to gather evidence regarding the presence of a fraud.[166] This evidence-gathering includes making inquires "about the existence or suspicion of fraud" of any company employee.[167] While SAS 99 does not explicitly require auditors to be present at or participate in internal investigations, at a minimum its language encourages increased vigilance. In a 2003 report, the SEC concluded that "audit failures most often arise from auditors accepting management representations without verification, truncating analytical and substantive procedures, and failing to gain sufficient evidence to support the numbers in financial statements."[168]

Georgia, GA. CODE ANN. § 43-3-32; Idaho, IDAHO CODE § 9-203A and IDAHO ST. REV., Rule 515; **Illinois**, 225 ILL. COMP. STAT. 450/27; Indiana, IND. CODE. § 34-46-2-18; **Kansas**, KS. STAT. ANN. § 1-401; Louisiana, LA. CODE EVID. ANN. art. 515; **Maryland**, MD. CODE ANN., Cts. & Jud. Proc. § 9-110; **Michigan**, Mich. Comp. Laws § 339.732; Missouri, Mo. REV. STAT. § 326.322; **New Mexico**, N.M. STAT. ANN. § 38-6-6; Pennsylvania, PA. STAT. ANN. tit. 63 § 9.11; and Tennessee, TENN. CODE ANN. § 62-1-116.

The *Kovel* doctrine—that accountants retained to perform special services may qualify as agents of an attorney and resulting communications may be considered privileged if such communications assist the attorney in the provision of legal advice—is likely inapplicable in the context of independent auditors. *See, e.g., In re* Horowitz, 482 F.2d 72 (2d Cir. 1973) (attorney-client privilege waived where privileged communications disclosed to an accountant for a purpose other than to secure legal advice).

164. Statements on Accounting Standards are promulgated by the Auditing Standards Board of the American Institute of Certified Public Accountants (AICPA). The Statements help auditors comply with GAAS.

165. AICPA Professional Standards, AU § 316, *Consideration of Fraud in a Financial Statement Audit* (2002). It is notable that Section 10A has a "reporting-out" requirement that exposes auditors to SEC sanctions for noncompliance.

166. *Id.* at § 316.20-26. Section 10A is modeled after an early incarnation of SAS 99 that required auditors to "obtain reasonable assurances about whether the financial statements are free of material misstatements, whether caused by error or fraud." AICPA Professional Standards, AU § 316.

167. *Id.*

168. SEC Report Pursuant to Section 704 of the Sarbanes-Oxley Act of 2002 (Jan. 24, 2003). *Available at* http://www.sec.gov/news/studies/sox704report.pdf. The SEC's Deputy Chief Accountant has opined that if a company's outside counsel is unwilling or unable to provide its expert views, the auditor should consider whether sufficient alternate procedures can actually be performed to allow the audit to be completed. *See* Scott Taub, Comments by the SEC's Deputy Chief Accountant at the University of Southern California Leventhal School of Accounting, *available at* http://www.sec.gov/news/speech/spch052704sat.htm.

Regardless of whether the demand to be present is justified by Section 10A or by any other provision, the company may be in no position to argue, at least in the short term. It faces the risk of an auditor resignation and all its attendant consequences over the issue of protecting a privilege that it may soon be forced to relinquish at the government's behest anyway. Over the long term, however, as companies and their auditors negotiate about the terms of new engagements, and especially if companies and their lawyers make some headway with the prosecutors about how frequently waivers will be required or if a legislative solution permitting selective waiver is obtained, the insistence by auditors upon conduct that likely punctures the company's attorney-client privilege could become a significant source of controversy. Auditors and attorneys have historically cooperated to protect the respective goals of the bar and the accounting profession: protection of the attorney-client privilege on the one hand and precise auditing on the other.[169] Pitting maintenance of the privilege against precise auditing may encourage conflict, rather than cooperation, between attorneys and auditors, and may undermine the goal of corporate transparency sought by Section 10A and Sarbanes-Oxley. Ultimately, this controversy may need to be addressed in the same way that the ABA and AICPA reached a treaty over audit letter requests in 1975 to see if a protocol can be created through which, for example, the auditor can receive enough information to satisfy its needs but that information is provided in some form that does not waive any privilege.

IV. CONCLUDING LESSONS

The space between Scylla and Charybdis, especially for investigations into violations of the securities laws, seems to be shrinking. The Seaboard Report and the various iterations of what is now called the McNulty Memorandum

---

("If a company's outside counsel is unwilling or unable to provide its expert views, the auditor should consider whether sufficient alternate procedures can actually be performed to allow the audit to be completed.").

169. The 1975 "Treaty" between auditors and lawyers balanced the public interest in promoting confidence in capital markets through reliable financial reporting and in encouraging companies to confide in counsel. The "Treaty" was adopted by the ABA and consented to by the AICPA. *American Bar Association, Statement of Policy Regarding Lawyers' Responses to Auditors' Requests for Information* (1975), *available at* http://www.abanet.org/buslaw/catalog/5070426i/secure.html.

have increased the pressure to conduct internal investigations, the law governing disclosures and assessing material is moving in the direction of requiring more disclosure, no reliable solution has yet been found for the issue of limiting privilege waivers when producing internal investigation materials to the government, and auditing firms may make preserving the privilege even more difficult. Absent a legislative solution or a swing of the political pendulum in favor of corporations that may have engaged in wrongdoing—hardly a particularly sympathetic group—corporations facing allegations of potential wrongdoing are likely to be presented with increasingly difficult choices and little by way of helpful precedent that can aid in the task.

As Odysseus chose to risk Scylla at the cost of some of his crew rather than lose his whole ship to Charybdis,[170] so too have most companies chosen to sacrifice some employees in order to soften the blow to the company as a whole. Still, even a company cooperating with the government continues to face serious risk on the civil side as a result of its disclosures, as well as the potential for costly pretrial diversion or sometimes even more serious criminal consequences. It may not be possible to escape unscathed, but with speed and good judgment about what needs to be investigated and recorded, the downside risks can be mitigated. At a minimum, in the current environment, companies can be confident that they are not alone in trying to make it past these difficult obstacles.

---

170. HOMER'S ODYSSEY, Book XII. Mike's wife will be proud that he has cited to something literary. Plus being able to politely refer to the government as a six-headed monster has to be viewed as some sort of a coup.

Internal Investigations in Health Care: Unique Enforcement Environment and the Dilemma of Disclosure

13

Stacy L. Brainin and Bill Morrison

I. INTRODUCTION   424
II. HEALTH CARE ENFORCEMENT ENVIRONMENT   424
   A. Civil and Administrative Enforcement   425
   B. Criminal Enforcement   425
III. CORPORATE COMPLIANCE PROGRAMS   427
   A. Federal Sentencing Guidelines   427
   B. The OIG Model Plans   428
   C. Corporate Integrity Agreements   430
IV. SELF-REPORTING: MANDATORY OR VOLUNTARY   431
   A. Relevant Statutes   432
   B. Corporate Integrity Agreements and the OIG Model Plans   433

Stacy L. Brainin and Bill Morrison are with Haynes and Boone LLP in Dallas, Texas.

C. The OIG's Provider Self-Disclosure Protocol   434
D. Risks and Benefits of Voluntary Disclosure   436
V. CONCLUSION   439

I. INTRODUCTION

INVESTIGATIVE COUNSEL FACE TRULY unique challenges in conducting internal audits of health care providers. The whirlwind of enforcement activity within this industry has complicated the role of legal counsel immensely, and created a set of challenges rarely found in more traditional audits. The Health Insurance Portability and Accountability Act of 1996 (HIPAA), which created so-called "health care fraud crimes," recently celebrated its ten-year anniversary. Since its passage, prosecuting health care fraud has become a top enforcement priority. Enhanced funding and manpower are committed to investigating and prosecuting health care fraud and formulating new enforcement strategies. Beyond public enforcement, the False Claims Act allows qui tam actions by private citizens on the government's behalf. Corporate compliance programs are common among providers, and corporate integrity agreements are routinely imposed in any settlement of government claims. These compliance programs and the information they generate in turn pose troublesome issues of mandatory or voluntary disclosure.

To be sure, internal audits of health care providers proceed much like legal audits in many other industries. Familiarity with applicable privileges, employee rights, and interview techniques is essential. This chapter will not revisit these more familiar topics, but will instead focus on the complex statutory environment in which health care providers operate, the prominent role of corporate compliance programs within the industry, and the thorny issue of mandatory or voluntary disclosure.

II. HEALTH CARE ENFORCEMENT ENVIRONMENT

Over the years, federal enforcers have punished health care fraud under a wide variety of federal administrative, civil, and criminal statutes. With the enactment of HIPAA came legislative manifestation of the initiative to end health care fraud. The act created a new category of crimes called "health care fraud crimes." What follows is an overview of the laws that affect health care providers and a review of some of the important provisions of HIPAA.

A. Civil and Administrative Enforcement

In the civil context, the Civil False Claims Act is particularly dangerous to health care providers because, in addition to treble damages, a fine up to $11,000 per false claim may be imposed.[1] Because health care providers typically generate huge volumes of small claims, this statute carries potentially astronomical sanctions. Perhaps the most devastating sanction of all is an administrative sanction—exclusion from Medicare. Title 42 requires mandatory exclusion from the Medicare program of any provider convicted of a crime related to delivery of an item or service or neglect or abuse of patients.[2] The same statute also contains permissive exclusion provisions under which a provider may be excluded for various grounds. Finally, Title 42 also authorizes imposition of civil monetary penalties and places limitations on certain physician referrals.[3]

Recent years have seen a steady increase in health care fraud investigations conducted by state agencies. Eleven states have false claims act laws with qui tam enforcement provisions. More states will be enacting false claims laws because of economic incentives from the federal government to states who enact state false claims acts patterned after the federal FCA.[4] Section 6031 of the Deficient Reduction Act provides states that enact false claims acts an extra 10 percent of the federal Medicare share of any funds recouped in a Medicare fraud case. In order to be eligible for the financial incentive, the state law must contain (i) equivalent qui tam provisions that reward whistleblowers; (ii) a requirement for filing the action under seal for 60 days for review by the State Attorney General; and (iii) a provision imposing civil penalties no less than those imposed under the federal FCA.

B. Criminal Enforcement

In the criminal context, the Anti-Kickback Statute prohibits illegal remuneration arrangements based on referrals under Medicare or state health care programs.[5] In addition to existing criminal and administrative penalties, the

---

1. *See* 31 U.S.C. § 3729(a); 28 C.F.R. § 85.3(9) (2003). FCA penalties of between $5,000 and $10,000 are provided in the statute, but these penalties were adjusted for inflation to between $5,500 and $11,000 for conduct occurring after September 29, 1999.

2. *See* 42 U.S.C. § 1320a-7.

3. *See* 42 U.S.C. §§ 1320a-7a; 1395nn.

4. *See* Deficient Reduction Act of 2005, Pub. L. No. 109-171 § 6031 (2006) (to be codified in amendments to the Social Security Act, 42 U.S.C. § 1909(a)).

5. *See* 42 U.S.C. § 1320a-7b(b).

Balanced Budget Act of 1997 amended section 1320a-7a to create a civil monetary penalty for anti-kickback violations.[6] Title 42 also prohibits the intentional making of a false statement in order to qualify for Medicare or Medicaid; the intentional charging or acceptance of excess Medicaid payments; and the intentional violation of participating physician or supplier agreements in the Medicare program.[7]

HIPAA changed the landscape in the government's fight against health care fraud. By creating comprehensive new laws and broadening old ones, the act expanded the government's power to investigate and prosecute health care fraud beyond public programs to fraud affecting private plans. The act provided for increased funding for investigating health care fraud, new investigative tools for the Department of Justice, rewards to individuals who report Medicare fraud, and expanded Medicare exclusions.[8]

Under HIPAA, there are five federal crimes specifically directed at health care fraud. Importantly, criminal penalties now extend beyond federal programs to private insurers as well. HIPAA prohibits knowingly and willfully executing or attempting to execute a scheme or artifice to defraud any "health care benefit program."[9] HIPAA also prohibits false statements relating to health care matters.[10] Other statutes under HIPAA prohibit theft or embezzle-

---

6. The Office of Inspector General has the authority to impose civil monetary penalties (CMPs) of up to $15,000 for each service billed in *knowing* violation of the physician self-referral law and $50,000 for each kickback plus an assessment up to three times the total amount of remuneration offered, paid, solicited, or received. 42 U.S.C. § 1395nn(g)(3); 42 U.S.C. § 1320a-7a(a)(7).

7. *See* 42 U.S.C. §§ 1320a-7b(a), (c), (d), (e). In addition to these Title 42 crimes, the government still uses various Title 18 criminal statutes, when applicable, to prosecute health care providers. These include mail fraud (§ 1341), wire fraud (§ 1343), conspiracy to defraud (§ 371), money laundering (§§ 1956, 1957), obstruction of justice (§ 1505), RICO (§§ 1961-1968), aiding and abetting (§ 2), forgery (§ 494), misprision of felony (§ 4), false claims (§ 287), conspiracy to defraud by false claims (§ 286), theft or bribery concerning federally funded programs (§ 666), and fraud or false statements (§ 1001).

8. HIPAA also contains comprehensive and complex rules regarding the privacy of patient information. 65 Fed. Reg. 82,461-82,829 (Dec. 28, 2000). Although it is beyond the scope of this chapter, counsel conducting an internal investigation involving patient information must be familiar with these restrictions, which may affect the provider's ability to disclose covered information.

9. 18 U.S.C. § 1347. A "health care benefit program" is defined as: "[A]ny public or private plan or contract, affecting commerce, under which any medical benefit, item, or service is provided to any individual, and includes any individual or entity who is providing a medical benefit, item, or service for which payment may be made under the plan or contract." 18 U.S.C. § 24(b).

10. 18 U.S.C. § 1035.

ment in connection with health care; obstruction of criminal investigations of health care offenses; and disposing of assets in order to qualify for Medicaid.[11]

The Attorney General has significant investigative and enforcement powers. HIPAA authorizes the Attorney General to: (1) seek injunctive relief to stop ongoing federal health care offenses or prevent prospective ones; (2) bring suits to freeze assets; and (3) seek forfeiture of property that constitutes or is derived from the proceeds of the commission of a federal health care offense.[12] In addition, under the act there is an investigative demand procedure for use in "any investigation relating to any act or activity involving a Federal health care offense."[13] Accordingly, the DOJ has administrative subpoena authority to require the production of documents and records and the testimony of their custodians in health care fraud investigations.

III. CORPORATE COMPLIANCE PROGRAMS

As the above discussion illustrates, health care providers face an array of civil and criminal statutes that can impact the provider's ability to conduct business. In the face of these laws and their harsh consequences, health care providers have increasingly turned to corporate compliance programs. This trend has been spurred by three realities facing health care providers: (1) the Federal Sentencing Guidelines and their incentives to adopt compliance programs; (2) the OIG's Model Plans for the health care industry; and (3) Corporate Integrity Agreements, often required when settling governmental actions.

A. *Federal Sentencing Guidelines*

The Federal Sentencing Guidelines unequivocally laud the benefits of corporate compliance programs.[14] Generally, the Guidelines require an organization to exercise due diligence to prevent and detect criminal conduct and promote a corporate culture that encourages ethical conduct.[15] However, by mandating seven requirements for an "effective" compliance program, the

---

11. 18 U.S.C. § 669; 18 U.S.C. § 1518; 42 U.S.C. § 1320a-7b(a)(6).
12. 18 U.S.C. §§ 1345(a)(1); 1345(a)(2); 982(a)(7).
13. 18 U.S.C. § 3486.
14. A three-point reduction in culpability level is available if "the offense occurred despite an effective program to prevent and detect violations of law." U.S. SENTENCING COMMISSION GUIDELINES MANUAL (USSG), § 8C2.5(f)(1) (Nov. 2005).
15. *See* USSG § 8B2.1(a).

guidelines all but prescribe failure.[16] To make matters worse, these requirements are vague and strict, and a failure to meet even one may eliminate any benefit whatsoever. And even when all seven requirements are met, a reduction in fine can be obtained only if additional conditions exist. A company may receive no credit for its compliance program if any "high-level personnel participated in, condoned, or was willfully ignorant of the offense" or if it failed to report violations without "unreasonable delay."[17] To many, these exceptions swallow any potential benefit. As discussed below, self-reporting or voluntary disclosure is a thorny dilemma.

In short, the guidelines speak aspirationally of effective compliance programs and consequent benefits. Experienced counsel may well recommend the implementation of such programs, but in doing so will likely look to the obvious value of detection and self-correction rather than to any reduction in sentence.

B. *The OIG Model Plans*

The most valuable source of information on the characteristics of an effective compliance program are the model compliance plans issued by the Department of Health and Human Services, Office of Inspector General

---

16. According to the guidelines, at a minimum, the corporation must meet seven requirements to claim due diligence:
    - The corporation should establish "standards and procedures" to prevent and detect criminal conduct.
    - The corporation's governing authority should be knowledgeable about the content and operation of the compliance and ethics program. Specific individuals within the corporation should be delegated to oversee the day-to-day operation of the program.
    - The corporation should not delegate substantial discretionary authority to someone who it knows or should know has a propensity to engage in illegal activities.
    - The corporation should take steps to communicate effectively its standards and procedures to its employees and agents.
    - The corporation should take reasonable steps to insure that its compliance program is followed such as utilizing reasonably designed "monitoring and auditing systems" and establishing and "publicizing a reporting system" that eliminates fear of retaliation.
    - The corporation should consistently enforce the standards through appropriate incentive and disciplinary mechanisms.
    - After criminal conduct has been detected, the corporation should take reasonable steps to respond appropriately and prevent similar criminal conduct.

    See USSG § 8A1.2(k).

17. USSG § 8C2.5(f)(2).

(OIG). These Model Plans or "Compliance Program Guidance," are important not only because they apply specifically to the health care industry, but also because they constitute the OIG's opinion of what is required for an "effective" program. The OIG has issued Compliance Program Guidance for Clinical Laboratories; Hospitals; Home Health Agencies; Third-Party Medical Billing Companies; Durable Medical Equipment, Prosthetics, Orthotics, and Supply Industry; Hospices; Nursing Facilities; Medicare+Choice Organizations; Individual Physicians and Small Group Practices; Ambulance Suppliers, and Pharmaceutical Manufacturers. The model plans are posted on the OIG's Web site at www.oig.hhs.gov/fraud/complianceguidance.html and published in the *Federal Register.*

The Model Plans are more detailed renditions of the Sentencing Guidelines' seven requirements, adapted for particular segments of the health care industry. The Model Plans specifically disclaim that they are model compliance programs, but rather guidelines to be considered when developing and implementing a new compliance program. The OIG Model Plans identify specific conduct that the OIG considers necessary to maintaining an effective compliance program in the health care industry.

For example, the OIG's Compliance Program Guidance for Hospitals and Supplemental Compliance Program Guidance provide specific guidance on investigating and reporting detected violations.[18] According to the OIG, whenever there is a report or reasonable indication of suspected noncompliance, the compliance officer "should initiate prompt steps to investigate the conduct" to determine whether there has been a material violation of applicable law or the requirements of the compliance program.[19] The compliance officer should also take appropriate steps to prevent the destruction of documents or other evidence and should keep records of the investigation, including documentation of the alleged violation, a description of the investigative process, copies of interview notes and key documents reviewed, and the results of the

---

18. *See* Compliance Program Guidance for Hospitals, Department of Health and Human Services, Office of Inspector General (Compliance Guidance for Hospitals), 63 Fed. Reg. 8987, 8997-98 (Feb. 23, 1998) and Supplemental Compliance Program Guidance for Hospitals, Department of Health and Human Services, Office of Inspector General, 70 Fed. Reg. 4858, 4858-4876 (Jan. 31, 2005).

19. Depending on the circumstances, such steps may include an immediate referral to criminal and/or civil law enforcement authorities, a corrective action plan, a report to the government, and the submission of any overpayments. *See* Compliance Guidance for Hospitals, 63 Fed. Reg. at 8997.

investigation.[20] In addition, if there is reason to believe that the integrity of the investigation may be affected by the presence of certain employees under investigation, those employees should be removed from their current work activity until the investigation is completed.

A properly functioning compliance program will likely generate damaging allegations, true or false, that may ultimately serve as a road map for adversaries, public or private. Although techniques for protecting such information are beyond the scope of this chapter, it is worth noting that some steps that might seem intuitive in another setting may have unforeseen implications in the context of the OIG's Compliance Program Guidance. As only one example, while it might seem advisable to install in-house counsel as the gatekeeper of the compliance process, the OIG's Compliance Guidance for Hospitals specifically advises against this.[21]

C. *Corporate Integrity Agreements*

Corporate Integrity Agreements (CIAs) are an almost unavoidable component of settlement agreements with the government and thus serve as a useful resource for internal compliance programs.[22] While these agreements are not formally published, copies of recent CIAs are available on the OIG's website at www.oig.hhs.gov/fraud/cia.index.html; others can be requested through the Freedom of Information Act. Procedures for making such a request and a

---

20. The OIG acknowledges that "some hospitals should consider engaging outside counsel, auditors, or health care experts" to assist with the investigation. Compliance Guidance for Hospitals, 63 Fed. Reg. at 8997.

21. The OIG believes that having a compliance process subordinate to the hospital's general counsel undercuts the independence and objectivity of the process. It is the OIG's view that, by separating the compliance function from the general counsel, a system of checks and balances is established to more effectively achieve the goals of the compliance program. *See* Compliance Guidance for Hospitals, 63 Fed. Reg. at 8993 n.35.

22. *See* Open Letter to Health Care Providers, Department of Health and Human Services, Office of Inspector General, November 20, 2001, www.org.hhs.gov/fraud/openletters.htm. The OIG set forth the following criteria to determine whether a CIA should be required: (1) whether the provider self-disclosed the alleged misconduct; (2) the monetary damage to the federal health care programs; (3) whether the case involves successor liability; (4) whether the provider is still participating in the federal health care programs or in the line of business that gave rise to the fraudulent conduct; (5) whether the alleged conduct is capable of repetition; (6) the age of the conduct; (7) whether the provider has an effective compliance program and would agree to limited compliance or integrity measures and would annually certify such compliance to the OIG; and (8) other circumstances, as appropriate.

list of health care providers who are currently subject to these agreements are available on the OIG's Web site at www.oig.hhs.gov/fraud/cia.index.html. In some cases where the provider has independently enacted a compliance program, the OIG will enter into a Certification of Compliance Agreement (CCA) in lieu of a CIA. CCAs require providers to certify that they will continue to operate their compliance programs for a period of time, usually three years, and agree to certain compliance obligations, including reporting overpayments, reportable events, and ongoing investigative and legal proceedings and providing annual reports detailing the providers' compliance activities.

Though mandatory compliance programs implemented through these agreements are similar in form and substance to the guidance found in the Sentencing Guidelines and in the OIG's Model Plans, there are several key differences. The first concerns the audit team itself. Under mandatory programs, much of the monitoring and auditing must be performed by independent professionals or the government itself. Additionally, often the agreements provide that the settling company must allow the OIG to examine its records and evaluate its compliance program. Finally, mandatory programs require self-reporting of "material violations" and require annual reporting to the OIG. Thus, these agreements, once entered into, necessarily predetermine such crucial judgments as when to conduct an internal investigation, how to define the investigative team, and whether to agree in advance to self-report the results.

IV. SELF-REPORTING: MANDATORY OR VOLUNTARY

Effective compliance programs routinely generate allegations of misconduct, and those allegations will ordinarily be reviewed by investigative counsel.[23] Because of unique disclosure issues faced by health care providers, careful consideration of the potential obligation to disclose the results of the investigation must be taken into account *before* commencing the inquiry. Because self-reporting has historically been contrary to almost every instinct and because the risks of voluntary disclosure may outweigh possible benefits, experienced counsel seldom chose this route in the past. Developments within the

---

23. This discussion addresses the disclosure issues when wrongdoing is uncovered in an internal investigation. In the absence of fraud or other violations, repayment issues are ordinarily resolved with the carrier or intermediary.

law enforcement community, however, suggest that investigative counsel is wise to undertake a more critical analysis of this issue when representing a health care provider. Considerations that must now be taken into account include: (1) relevant health care statutes; (2) mandatory disclosure provisions of Corporate Integrity Agreements and the OIG Model Plans; and (3) the OIG's Provider Self-Disclosure Protocol.

A. *Relevant Statutes*

As a general rule, companies are under no legal obligation to report past misconduct to enforcement authorities. No one would seriously suggest that company counsel is legally obligated to report, for example, past price-fixing behavior within a client organization. However, under the Medicare Fraud and Abuse Statute, it is a felony for anyone "having knowledge of the occurrence of an event affecting his initial or continued right to any benefit or payment" to "conceal or fail to disclose that event."[24] It should be noted that while there are no reported cases interpreting this statute, it remains in the government's enforcement arsenal.

Despite this warning, there are sound reasons to question such far-reaching interpretations. First, section 1320a-7b(a)(3) was transposed, in its entirety, from the Social Security Act that makes illegal an entirely different type of conduct (keeping a Social Security check to which one is not entitled). There is no legislative history indicating its purpose or meaning in the Medicare context. The statute provides no procedure for disclosure and does not state to whom any disclosure should be made. Further, the statute requires that the failure to disclose be coupled with a criminal intent, "an intent fraudulently to secure benefit or payment either in a greater amount or quantity than is due or when no such benefit or payment is authorized."[25] Additionally, courts interpreting nearly identical statutes in other Title 42 sections have held that the government must prove "that the defendant knew that he was legally obligated to disclose" the information or event in question.[26] Finally, courts have held that the due process clause prohibits punishment of wholly passive con-

---

24. 42 U.S.C. § 1320a-7b(a)(3). In the Compliance Program Guidance for Hospitals, the OIG warns that failure to repay "overpayments" within a reasonable time may be interpreted as an intentional attempt to conceal the overpayment and may thereby establish an independent basis for criminal liability. This warning would apply not only to a hospital, but also to any involved individual. *See* Compliance Guidance for Hospitals, 63 Fed. Reg. at 8998.

25. 42 U.S.C. § 1320a-7b(a)(3).

26. *See* United States v. Phillips, 600 F.2d 535, 536 (5th Cir. 1979).

duct.[27] Thus, it would seem that simple knowledge of past misconduct without more would not be seen as criminal.

Another statute counsel should consider on the issue of disclosure is 18 U.S.C. § 1035. Under this HIPAA provision, it is a felony if a provider "in any matter involving a health care benefit program . . . knowingly and willfully falsifies, conceals, or *covers up* a material fact."[28] Although a failure to disclose prior "misconduct" stands in sharp contrast to any practical interpretation of "cover-up," this statute must not be overlooked by the health care practitioner. It is useful to note that the language of section 1035 parallels other Title 18 "false statement" statutes (sections 1001 et seq.), and that it is generally thought that, to establish a false statement violation, federal prosecutors must prove an affirmative act by which a material fact was actively concealed.[29]

B. *Corporate Integrity Agreements and the OIG Model Plans*

As discussed above, if a provider is operating under a Corporate Integrity Agreement pursuant to a settlement with the government, certain disclosures may be mandatory under the terms of that agreement.

Also as discussed above, the OIG's Compliance Program Guidance for Hospitals (so-called Model Plan) states that once there is reason to believe there may have been a violation of criminal, civil, or administrative law, the hospital should promptly report[30] the misconduct to the appropriate governmental authority and provide all evidence relevant to the alleged violation and potential

---

27. *See* Lambert v. California, 355 U.S. 225, 228 (1957).
28. 18 U.S.C. § 1035.
29. *See* United States v. Ford, 797 F.2d 1329, 1334 (5th Cir. 1986); United States v. London, 550 F.2d 206, 212-13 (5th Cir. 1977). Other statutes that could possibly be implicated by a failure to disclose overpayments or refund monies include the HIPAA health care conversion statute (18 U.S.C. § 669) and the federal money laundering statute (18 U.S.C. § 1956(c)(7)(F)). At least one U.S. attorney has taken the position that the failure to refund overpayments constitutes HIPAA criminal health care fraud and theft or embezzlement in connection with a health care benefit program under 18 U.S.C. §§ 1347 and 669. In January 2007, a medical practice of 42 cardiologists entered into a criminal pretrial diversion agreement, separate civil settlements with the federal and state governments, and a five-year Corporate Integrity Agreement with HHS OIG to settle criminal charges brought by the United States Attorney for the Eastern District of Tennessee.
30. The misconduct must be reported within a reasonable period, but not more than sixty days after determining that there is credible evidence of a violation. *See* Compliance Guidance for Hospitals, 63 Fed. Reg. at 8998.

cost impact.[31] The decision to make a voluntary disclosure and the mechanics of that disclosure depend on the totality of the facts and circumstances.[32]

C. *The OIG's Provider Self-Disclosure Protocol*

The OIG's voluntary disclosure program is called the Provider Self-Disclosure Protocol (Protocol).[33] The Protocol is open to all health care providers nationwide, including providers making good-faith disclosures related to matters already the subject of government inquiry.[34] The Protocol does not require participants to apply for admission or submit pre-acceptance disclosures.

The Protocol basically operates in four steps. First, a provider initiates the process by making a written, certified Voluntary Disclosure Submission to the OIG.[35] This initial disclosure should include basic but detailed information about the disclosing provider and the misconduct being reported. Second, the disclosing health care provider is expected to conduct an internal investi-

---

31. According to the OIG, the prompt reporting of misconduct "will be considered a mitigating factor in determining administrative sanctions (e.g., penalties, assessments, and exclusion), if the reporting provider becomes the target of an OIG investigation." Compliance Guidance for Hospitals, 63 Fed. Reg. at 8998.

32. For example, if the particular incident of noncompliance is merely an unintentional overbilling, disclosure should be made in the form of an overpayment refund to the carrier or fiscal intermediary. The OIG recognizes that "where potential fraud or False Claims Act liability is not involved . . . HCFA regulations and contractor guidelines already include procedures for returning overpayments as they are discovered." Compliance Guidance for Hospitals, 63 Fed. Reg. at 8997. On the other hand, "the OIG believes that some violations are so serious that they warrant immediate notification to government authorities," even prior to commencing an internal investigation. These include any conduct that: (1) is a clear violation of criminal law; (2) has a significant adverse effect on the quality of care provided to program beneficiaries; or (3) indicates a systematic failure to comply with applicable laws, an existing corporate integrity agreement, or other standards of conduct. *See* Compliance Guidance for Hospitals, 63 Fed. Reg. at 8998 n.58.

33. *See* Provider Self-Disclosure Protocol, Department of Health and Human Services, Office of Inspector General (Protocol), 63 Fed. Reg. 58,399 (Oct. 30, 1998); www.oig.hhs.gov/authorities/docs/selfdisclosure.pdf.

34. The Protocol is intended only for matters that are potentially violative of federal criminal, civil, or administrative laws. It is consistent with the Compliance Guidance for Hospitals in suggesting that matters involving overpayments or simple billing errors should be brought to the attention of the appropriate carrier or intermediary. *See* Protocol, 63 Fed. Reg. at 58,400.

35. Unfortunately, the Protocol requires that all submissions, including the initial disclosure, internal investigation report, and financial self-assessment, contain a certification that the report is truthful "to the best of the individual's knowledge." Protocol, 63 Fed. Reg. 58,399. These requested certifications create additional risk for participating providers.

gation and internal financial assessment and report its findings to the OIG.[36] The Protocol contains Internal Investigation Guidelines requiring the provider to collect and submit specific categories of information identifying and describing the nature and extent of the improper practice and the discovery of and response to it. The Protocol also contains Self-Assessment Guidelines requiring the provider to estimate the monetary impact of the disclosed matter and describing acceptable approaches to the self-assessment process.[37] Third, the OIG must verify the information disclosed. The Protocol is vague regarding the verification process but states that the "OIG must have access to all audit work papers and other supporting documents without assertion of privileges or limitations on the information produced."[38] Once a provider decides to enter the Protocol, it is imperative that its disclosures be clear and complete. Otherwise, any matters discovered during the verification process unrelated to the matters disclosed will be treated as new matters, and thus outside the Protocol.[39] Fourth, the disclosing health care provider must make appropriate payments. Generally, the OIG will not accept reimbursement of presumed overpayments until verification is completed.[40] Even after verification and

---

36. However, when an ongoing fraud scheme is discovered, the Protocol dictates that the provider should contact the OIG immediately, before investigating further, to avoid compromising any subsequent investigation by the government. *See* Protocol, 63 Fed. Reg. at 58,400. While the OIG's position is understandable, it is never prudent to cut short an internal review at the risk of reporting unfounded allegations.

37. A provider can either review all the claims affected or calculate the loss through statistical sampling. However the financial assessment is made, the disclosing provider must submit to OIG a work plan describing the self-assessment process. *See* Protocol, 63 Fed. Reg. at 58,402-03.

38. According to the Protocol, verification will not normally impact the attorney-client privilege but may require production of documents or other materials covered by the work-product doctrine. *See* Protocol, 63 Fed. Reg. at 58,403.

39. Once a provider enters the Protocol, it is too late to turn back and dangerous to withhold cooperation. "If a provider fails to work in good faith with OIG to resolve the disclosed matter, the lack of cooperation will be considered an aggravating factor when OIG assesses the appropriate resolution of the matter. Similarly, the intentional submission of false or otherwise untruthful information, as well as the intentional omission of relevant information, will be referred to DOJ or other Federal agencies and could, in itself, result in criminal and/or civil sanctions, as well as exclusion from participation in the Federal health care programs." *See* Protocol, 63 Fed. Reg. at 58,403.

40. If the OIG does consent to such a payment, the disclosing provider must agree in writing that acceptance of the payment does not constitute the government's agreement as to the amount of losses suffered or affect the government's ability to pursue criminal, civil, or administrative remedies. *See* Protocol, 63 Fed. Reg. at 58,403.

payment, it is unclear how a provider is formally removed from the Protocol or what removal means.[41]

In April 2006, HHS OIG Inspector General Daniel Levinson announced a new initiative designed to expand the use of the Protocol to resolve conduct that may result in liability under the OIG's CMP authority for physician self-referral and anti-kickback violations.[42] In the Open Letter the Inspector General points out that it will continue to consult with the DOJ before it accepts any provider into the Protocol, but the OIG makes no guarantee on DOJ's action with respect to the self report of self-referral and kickback violations. However, the April 2006 Open Letter states that once a provider is accepted into the Protocol, the OIG will generally settle the matter for an amount on the low end of the continuance of potential penalties and be less inclined to impose harsh compliance requirements.

D. *Risks and Benefits of Voluntary Disclosure*
1. Risks

The Protocol suffers from many of the weaknesses inherent in any voluntary disclosure program. First, because there is no amnesty from criminal prosecution or waiver of damages in return for disclosure, the consequences of disclosure are still uncertain.[43] The Protocol makes it clear that the "OIG is not bound by any findings made by the disclosing provider under the Provider Self-Disclosure Protocol and is not obligated to resolve the matter in any particular manner . . . [and] upon review of the provider's disclosure submission and/or reports, the OIG may conclude that the disclosed matter warrants a referral to DOJ for consideration under its civil and/or criminal authorities."[44] Second, regardless of the government's response, the program offers a

---

41. Under the pilot program, a provider was not removed from the program until the OIG decided what criminal or civil action should be brought and what administrative sanctions should be imposed and until the provider received written notice that the matter was officially closed. *See* Medicare Compliance Alert Special Document Service: OIG Procedures for PilotVoluntary Disclosure Program (June 19, 1995).

42. *See* Open Letter to Health Care Providers, Department of Health and Human Services, Office of Inspector General, April 24, 2006, www.oig.hhs.gov/fraud/openletters.html.

43. The OIG has published specific criteria setting forth the factors taken into consideration in determining whether it is appropriate to exclude a health care provider under 42 U.S.C. § 1320a-7(b)(7). *See* Criteria for Implementing Permissive Exclusion Authority Under Section 1128(b)(7) of the Social Security Act, Department of Health and Human Services, Office of Inspector General, 62 Fed. Reg. 67,392 (Dec. 24, 1997).

44. Protocol, 63 Fed. Reg. at 58,401.

volunteer no protection whatsoever against spinoff litigation[45] or against the possibility of waiver of the attorney client privilege or work-product doctrine in subsequent civil litigation as a result of the required disclosure to the government.

2. Benefits

While disclosure under the Protocol requires a certain amount of faith, undoubtedly there is a strong incentive for the government to treat participants fairly and make it less likely that a criminal prosecution will result. In an open letter to the health care community in 2000, the OIG identified several ways it would consider lessening the normally rigorous nature of corporate integrity agreements in appropriate self-disclosure cases.[46] Indeed, the OIG went so far as to state that "if a self-disclosing provider has demonstrated that its compliance program is effective and agrees to maintain its compliance program as part of a False Claims Act settlement, the OIG may not even require a corporate integrity agreement."[47] In a subsequent open letter to providers in 2006, the OIG reiterated that "a provider's self-disclosure

---

45. Disclosure may encourage both private claims and qui tam suits. One step that companies making disclosures can take to avoid qui tam suits is to also make a public disclosure. Once the facts are public knowledge, qui tam actions are jurisdictionally barred. One way for the government to eliminate the disclosure disincentive created by the possibility of a qui tam suit would be to implement a procedure whereby an administrative monetary penalty action is filed in conjunction with every disclosure. False Claims Act § 3730(e)(3) bars actions based on allegations or transactions that are the subject of a civil suit or administrative proceeding in which the government is already a party. Therefore, the government could preempt qui tam suits by filing a formal complaint with a provisional settlement. The OIG, however, has been unwilling to consider such a policy, claiming that it would be improper for it to intentionally undermine the qui tam provision and that it does not have the authority to grant immunity.

46. *See* Open Letter to Health Care Community Urging Providers to Self-Disclose Improper Conduct, Department of Health and Human Services, Office of Inspector General (Open Letter) (March 9, 2000); www.oig.hhs.gov/fraud/docs/openletters/openletter.htm. In particular, the open letter stated that while typically all Corporate Integrity Agreements include a provision to exclude a provider from participation in the federal health care programs if there is a material breach of the agreement, the OIG may forgo the exclusion remedy in appropriate cases where the provider demonstrates "sufficient trustworthiness." The OIG may also consider alternatives to standard auditing requirements and permit a self-disclosing provider to perform some or all of the billing audits internally. *See* Open Letter (March 9, 2000).

47. Open Letter (March 9, 2000); *see* Open Letter (November 20, 2001).

of conduct continues to be an important factor in determining whether a CCA is appropriate, because detection and prompt disclosure of potential fraud are evidence of an effective compliance program."[48]

In addition, there are tangible statutory "benefits" that may be gained from voluntary disclosure. The Federal Sentencing Guidelines have already been addressed above, and counsel must have a clear understanding of the "benefits" of disclosure.[49] Additionally, the False Claims Act includes voluntary disclosure provisions that can reduce the judgment imposed on an offending party.[50]

There are other considerations as well. Voluntary disclosure may well appeal to the considerable discretion of federal prosecutors and trial judges. For example, voluntary disclosure may encourage the Department of Justice to look favorably upon the company, and not insist upon treble damages or civil penalties under the False Claims Act. Disclosure may also encourage civil settlement and reduce the likelihood that criminal charges will be brought in a particular situation. Because exclusion from federal reimbursement programs can be ruinous, voluntary disclosure may assist the provider who seeks to avoid exclusion from Medicare or other federal programs, or at least limit its duration. Finally, voluntary disclosure allows a corporation to *control* the time, place, and manner of disclosing prior misconduct.

---

48. Open Letter (April 24, 2006).

49. Just as a corporation may earn a three-point reduction in its culpability score for having an effective compliance program, it may earn an additional five-point reduction if it voluntarily and promptly discloses a particular offense to the government, cooperates with the investigation, and accepts responsibility for its conduct. *See* USSG § 8C2.5(g). Moreover, if the corporation does not disclose, it may lose the three-point credit attributable to its compliance program. *See* USSG § 8C2.5(f). Therefore, the decision on disclosure can result in an eight-point swing in the corporation's culpability score.

50. Under the False Claims Act, corporations found liable are subject not only to treble damages but also to a civil penalty of between $5,500 and $11,000 per false claim. *See* 31 U.S.C. § 3729(a). If certain disclosure criteria are met, however, the court may reduce a provider's liability to double damages. *Id..* The basic thrust of the criteria is that there must be a timely, complete, and truly "voluntary" disclosure, rather than simply a belated attempt to mitigate the results of an already ongoing government investigation. The specific criteria are as follows: (1) the disclosure was made to the DOJ; (2) the disclosure was made within 30 days after the information was obtained; (3) the corporation fully cooperated with any government investigation; and (4) at the time the information was furnished to the government, no criminal, civil, or administrative action had commenced with respect to the violation, and the corporation had no knowledge of the existence of an investigation of the violation. *See* 31 U.S.C. § 3729(a).

V. CONCLUSION

Internal investigations in the health care industry are complicated by the complex enforcement environment, the prevalence of compliance programs that generate issues to investigate, and the unique dilemma of self-disclosure. A clear understanding of the risks and benefits of an internal investigation is critical at the outset.

An Overview of Internal Investigations from the In-House Perspective

14

H. Lowell Brown

I. INTRODUCTION   441
II. WHEN SHOULD AN INTERNAL INVESTIGATION BE UNDERTAKEN?   449
III. WHO SHOULD CONDUCT THE INVESTIGATION?   450
IV. INITIATING THE INVESTIGATION   452
V. STRUCTURING THE INVESTIGATION   453
   A. Assembling the Investigative Team   453
   B. The Investigative Plan   453
VI. REPORTING THE RESULTS OF THE INVESTIGATION   463
VII. CONCLUSION   464

I. INTRODUCTION

THE INTENT OF THIS CHAPTER is to provide observations (mostly personal) concerning corporate internal investigations from the perspective of in-house counsel. Other chapters address

---

H. Lowell Brown is the former Assistant General Counsel for Compliance at Northrop Grumman Corporation and now practices law in Washington, D.C., where he is counsel to the law firm of Cadwalader, Wickersham and Taft LLP.

in detail the significant, substantive legal issues that arise in conducting internal investigations. In contrast, the discussion here attempts a broader view of the considerations that go into structuring an internal investigation: why a corporation should undertake an internal investigation; when an investigation should be undertaken and who should conduct it; how the investigation should be organized; and finally, how the results of the investigation should be reported.

In the present day of frequent litigation and government oversight, in-house counsel must be vigilant in investigating allegations of illegal behavior and serious misconduct by corporate employees. The requirements of the Sarbanes-Oxley Act[1] of certification by the Chief Executive Officer and the Chief Financial Officer of the truthfulness and accuracy of material facts in company reports[2] as well as discussion in those reports of the existence and effectiveness of internal controls[3] and the adoption of a code of ethics applicable to senior management,[4] have established new benchmarks for corporate disclosure. The need for corporate management to be fully informed of questionable corporate conduct has grown commensurately with these requirements. However, even before the enactment of Sarbanes-Oxley, the decision of the Delaware Chancery Court in the case of *In re: Caremark International, Inc. Derivative Litigation*,[5] had underscored the importance of corporate management, both directors and officers, informing themselves of violations of law that may adversely affect the operation of the corporation's business.[6] The Court of Chancery concluded that a rational director "attempting in good faith to meet an organizational governance responsibility" should take account of the compliance program provisions in the Federal Sentencing Guidelines for

---

1. Sarbanes-Oxley Act, P.L. 107-204, 116 Stat. 745 (2002), 15 U.S.C.A. §§ 7201 *et seq.* (2006).
2. Sarbanes-Oxley Act, § 302, 15 U.S.C.A. § 7241(a) (2006).
3. Sarbanes-Oxley Act, § 404, 15 U.S.C.A. § 7262 (2006).
4. Sarbanes-Oxley Act § 406, 15 U.S.C.A. § 7264 (2006).
5. 698 A.2d 959 (Del. Ch. 1996).
6. Following indictments by grand juries in Minnesota and Ohio, Caremark International, Inc., a provider of patient care and managed health care services, pleaded guilty to mail fraud in connection with payments of "referral fees: and other monetary inducements to physicians. Caremark agreed to pay civil and criminal fines and to make reimbursements to insurers totaling $250 million. Five shareholder derivative actions were filed against Caremark's directors alleging a breach of the director's duty of care by failing to supervise the conduct of Caremark's employees or to otherwise take correctives measures, thereby exposing Caremark to significant criminal and civil liability. A settlement agreement was reached and was submitted to the Delaware Chancery Court for approval. Based on the actions taken by the directors and management to address the issues under investigation, including termination of past practices, issuance of revised policies and procedures, compliance reviews by the internal audit organi-

organizations[7] and should ensure that the corporation has in place an "information and reporting system" that is adequate to ensure that information concerning legal compliance comes to its attention in a timely manner.[8] The court went so far as to suggest that these obligations were elements of a director's duty of care.[9]

---

zation, review of the control structure by independent auditors, training, and appointment of the chief financial officer as compliance officer, the court concluded that "there is a low probability that it would be determined that the directors of Caremark breached any duty to appropriately monitor and supervise the enterprise. 698 A.2d at 968-972.

7. *See* "Sentencing of Organizations," Federal Sentencing Guidelines Manual (1995) (Guidelines). Under those guidelines, a corporation can reduce the applicable fine by having in place "an effective program to prevent and detect violations of law" § 8C2.5(f). The fine can also be reduced by self-reporting, cooperating, and accepting responsibility pursuant to §8C2.5(g). In order to qualify as having an "effective program to prevent and detect violations of law," the corporation must have "exercised due diligence in seeking to prevent and detect criminal conduct by its employees and other agents" including, inter alia, "utilizing monitoring and auditing systems reasonably designed to detect criminal conduct by its employees and other agents. . . ." § 8A1.2 Application Note 3(k). Additionally, the fine can be increased if there is evidence that "high-level personnel" within the corporation "condoned" or were "willfully ignorant of the offense." § 8C2.5(b). Such a person will be considered to have been "willfully ignorant" of the criminal conduct "if the individual did not investigate the possible occurrence of unlawful conduct despite knowledge of circumstances that would lead a reasonable person to investigate whether unlawful conduct had occurred." § 8A1.2 Application Note 3(j). Thus, as Chancellor Allen noted in *Caremark,* the sentencing guidelines for organizations "offer powerful incentives for corporations today to have in place compliance programs to detect violations of law, promptly to report violations to appropriate public officials when discovered, and to take prompt, voluntary remedial efforts," and in light of those incentives, "[a]ny rational person attempting in good faith to meet an organizational governance responsibility would be bound to take into account this development and the enhanced penalties and the opportunities for reduced sanctions that it offers." 698 A.2d at 969.

8. In the chancellor's view, it would be a "mistake" for directors to conclude that "the obligation to be reasonably informed" could be satisfied "without assuring themselves that information and reporting systems exist in the organization that are reasonably designed to provide to senior management and to the board itself timely, accurate information sufficient to allow management and the board, each within its scope, to reach informed judgments concerning both the corporation's compliance with law and its business performance." 698 A.2d at 970. Thus, the chancellor considered it "important that the board exercise a good faith judgment that the corporation's information reporting system is in concept and design adequate to assure the board that appropriate information will come to its attention in a timely manner as a matter of ordinary operations, so that it may satisfy its responsibility. 698 A.2d at 970.

9. As the chancellor stated, "I am of the view that a director's obligation includes a duty to attempt in good faith to assure that a corporate information and reporting system, which the board concludes is adequate, exists, and that failure to do so under some circumstances may, in theory at least, render a director liable for losses caused by non-compliance with applicable legal standards." 698 A.2d at 970. In the earlier case of Hoye v. Meek, 795 F.2d at 893 (10th Cir. 1986), the court of appeals observed that "where suspicions are aroused, or should be aroused, it is the director's duty to make necessary inquiries." 795 F.2d at 896.

Even had *Caremark* not been decided, corporate self-policing, as part of an overall program of compliance, makes good business sense. Prompt investigation of alleged misconduct allows the corporation to correct errors and to mitigate their effects before a problem worsens. Prompt investigation and appropriate discipline also send a powerful message to employees that violations of law and company policy will not be condoned.

There are also significant incentives for the corporation to investigate misconduct that may result in exposure to criminal liability. In general, the law permits corporations to be held liable for crimes an employee committed within the scope of the employee's duties with at least some intent to benefit the corporation.[10] Although several courts have suggested that an employee's actions in contravention of established, and rigorously enforced, company policy will not subject the corporate employer to vicarious criminal liability,[11] this is not the majority view.[12] Moreover, because both the intent[13] and collective knowledge[14] of the corporation's employees will be imputed to the corporate employer, there are circumstances in which the corporation may be held liable when none of its employees would be held individually respon-

---

10. This has been the law for the better part of a century. *See* New York Central & Hudson River R.R. Co. v. United States, 212 U.S. 481, 494 (1909); United States v. Adams Express Co., 229 U.S. 381, 390 (1913) (joint stock companies); United States v. A.P. Trucking Co., 358 U.S. 121, 124 (1958) (partnerships). "It is," as Learned Hand observed in 1918, "a question upon which the law has always tended towards larger and larger liability." United States v. Nearing, 252 F. 223, 231 (S.D.N.Y. 1918).

11. *See,* e.g., Holland Furnace Co. v. United States, 158 F.2d 2 (6th Cir. 1946); United States *ex rel..* Porter v. Kroger Grocery & Baking Co., 163 F.2d 168 (7th Cir. 1947); Nobile v. United States, 284 Fed. 253 (3d Cir. 1922); John Gund Brewing Co. v. United States, 204 Fed. 17 (8th Cir.), *modified,* 206 Fed. 386 (8th Cir. 1913).

12. *See* United States v. Basic Construction Co., 711 F.2d 570, 573 (4th Cir.), *cert. denied,.* 464 U.S. 956 (1983); United States v. Beusch, 596 F.2d 871, 878 (9th Cir. 1979); United States *ex rel.* Porter v. Kroger Grocery & Baking Co., 163 F.2d 168 (7th Cir. 1947); Holland Furnace Co. v. United States, 158 F.2d 2, 5 (6th Cir. 1946); Nobile v. United States, 284 Fed. 253, 255 (3d Cir 1922); John Gund Brewing Co. v. United States, 204 Fed. 17, 23 (8th Cir.), *modified,.* 206 Fed. 386 (8th Cir. 1913).

13. United States v. Portac, Inc., 869 F.2d 1288 (9th Cir. 1989), *cert. denied,* 498 U.S. 845 (1990); United States v. Automated Med. Labs. Inc. 770 F.2d 399 (4th. Cir. 1985); United States v. Cadillac Overall Supply Co., 568 F.2d 1078 (5th Cir. 1978); United States v. Hilton Hotel Corp., 467 F.2d 1000 (9th Cir. 1972), *cert. denied,.* 409 U.S. 1125 (1973); United States v. Harry L. Young & Sons, Inc., 464 F.2d 1295 (10th Cir. 1972); Standard Oil Co. v. United States, 307 F.2d 120 (5th Cir. 1962); Dollar S.S. Co. v. United States, 101 F.2d 638 (9th Cir. 1939); United States v. Wilson, 59 F.2d 97 (W.D. Wash. 1932).

14. A corporation may be held liable for "knowing" violations of law based on the knowledge of one or more of its employees. For example, in Apex Oil Co. v. United States, 530

sible.[15] Thus, because the corporation's vicarious criminal liability is often strict liability, a corporation, faced with the real possibility of criminal liability, must act expeditiously to analyze its exposure and to frame an appropriate response.

The corporation's prompt response to alleged misconduct can mitigate the consequences to the corporation. For example, the corporation may seek

---

F.2d 1291 (8th Cir. 1976), a corporation was liable under the Water Pollution Control Act, 22 U.S.C. § 1321(b)(5), for failing to report a "known oil spill." Although it was acknowledged that "no officer or director of the corporation had knowledge of the spill prior to the determination by the Coast Guard of the spill's origin," the court nevertheless held that "the knowledge of the employees is the knowledge of the corporation." 530 F.2d at 1295. Similarly, in Steere Tank Lines, Inc. v. United States, 330 F.2d 719, 723 n.3 (5th Cir. 1964), Judge Bell observed that "Knowledge affecting the corporation, which has been gained by any officer, agent or employees thereof in the course of his work for the company is attributed to the corporation, and this includes subordinate employees, such as truck drivers." Knowledge of employees has been attributed to the corporate employer in a variety of circumstances. *See e.g.,* United States v. Miller, 676 F.2d 359, 362 (9th Cir. 1982) (employees' knowledge of a fraudulent real estate financing scheme was imputed to the lender); United States v. Andreadis, 366 F.2d 423 (2d Cir. 1966) (corporation convicted of fraud in connection with advertising claims that manager knew to be false), *cert. denied,* 385 U.S. 1001 (1967); United States v. Chicago Express, Inc., 273 F.2d 751 (7th Cir. 1960) (truck driver's knowledge that truck did not display required dangerous cargo warnings attributed to corporate employer).

15. For example, in United States v. Bank of New England, 821 F.2d 844 (1st. Cir.), *cert. denied,* 484 U.S. 943 (1987), the bank was convicted of 31 counts of violating the Currency Reporting Act, 31 U.S.C. §§ 5311–5322, for failing to report cash withdrawals in excess of $10,000 by one of its customers. These withdrawals were effected on 31 occasions between May and July 1983 by the simultaneous presentation of a series of checks, each under $10,000, to a single teller. The bank's argument that it should not be held liable when "one part of the corporation has half the information making up [the total], and another part of the entity has the other half" was rejected. Instead, the court held that:

> Corporations compartmentalize knowledge, subdividing the elements of specific duties and operations into smaller components. The aggregate of those components constitutes the corporation's knowledge of a particular operation. It is irrelevant whether employees administering one component of an operation know the specific activities of employees administering another aspect of the operation.

821 F.2d at 856. *Accord.* United States v. T.I.M.E. – D.C., Inc. 381 F. Supp. 730, 738 (W.D. Va 1974) ("knowledge acquired by employees, within the scope of their employment is imputed to the corporation. In consequence, a corporation cannot plead innocence by asserting that the information obtained by several employees was not acquired by any one individual employee who then would have comprehended its full import. Rather, the corporation is considered to have acquired the collective knowledge of its employees and is held responsible for their failure to act accordingly."); *see also* United States v. LBS Bank-New York, Inc., 757 F. Supp 496 , 501 n.7 (E.D. Pa. 1990) ("[k]nowledge possessed by employees is aggregated so that a corporate defendant is considered to have the collective knowledge of its employees.")

entry into a voluntary disclosure program administered by any of several federal agencies.[16] Admission to a voluntary disclosure program often results in an agreement by the government not to prosecute the corporation criminally.[17] Admission to such programs ordinarily requires that the disclosure be made before a government investigation has commenced.[18] In the event that the corporation is already the subject of a government investigation, an informal disclosure to the prosecutor may be made in an effort to convince the prosecutor that, in the exercise of prosecutorial discretion, the corporation should not be prosecuted.[19]

Both the Department of Justice and the Securities and Exchange Commission have stated that voluntary disclosure of corporate wrongdoing is a factor in their determination whether to bring an enforcement action against a corporation. The Department of Justice policy is set forth in what has become known as the "Thompson Memorandum," which states that "In determining whether to charge a corporation, that corporation's timely and voluntary disclosure of wrongdoing and its willingness to cooperate with the government's investigation may be relevant factors."[20] The report of the Securities and Exchange Commission pursuant to Section 21(a) of the Securities Exchange Act of 1934 in regard to Seaboard Corporation similarly emphasized that in

---

16. For example, the U.S. Department of State has adopted a voluntary disclosure program for violations of the Arms Export Control Act, 22 U.S.C. §§ 2751 *et seq.* (1968) and the International Traffic In Arms Regulations, 22 C.F.R. §§ 120 *et seq..* (2005). The U.S. Department of Justice, Antitrust Division has also instituted an amnesty program, U.S. Department of Justice, Antitrust Division, Corporate Leniency Policy (Aug. 10, 1993). The Justice Department and the U.S. Department of Defense jointly administer a voluntary disclosure program for defense contractors to report instances of fraud, waste, and abuse. Inspector General, Department of Defense, The Department of Defense, The Department of Defense Voluntary Disclosure Program (April 1990).

17. This subject deserves a more thorough treatment than contemplated within this chapter.

18. *See, e.g.,* The Department of Defense Voluntary Disclosure Program, *supra* n.16, at 5 ("[a] matter will be preliminarily accepted to the DoD Voluntary Disclosure Program" if it is determined that "the disclosure was not triggered by the contractor's recognition that the potential criminal or civil fraud matter or the underlying facts were about to be discovered by the government through audit, investigation, contract administration efforts, or reported to the government by third parties. One factor in determining whether the requirement has been met is whether the government had prior knowledge of the matter(s) disclosed").

19. *See* Justice Department Manual, Principles of Federal Prosecution, § 230 at 9-505 to 9-506 (voluntary disclosure as factors in the decision whether to pursue criminal charges).

20. Memorandum dated January 20, 2003 from Larry D. Thompson, Deputy Attorney General to Heads of Department Components and United States Attorneys, 6.

evaluating whether to bring an enforcement action, the Commission would take into consideration whether a company conducted a prompt and thorough investigation of wrongdoing and whether the results of that investigation were disclosed to the Commission.[21]

Moreover, even if the corporation does not escape criminal prosecution altogether, a company's prompt response to allegations of criminal misconduct can be beneficial. As was noted in *Caremark*, the Federal Sentencing Guidelines for organizational defendants[22] offer "powerful incentives" for organizations to implement what the guidelines refer to as an "effective program to prevent and detect violations of law."[23] An essential element of such a program is the investigation of wrongdoing resulting in prompt remediation, including appropriate discipline.[24] The guidelines also recognize timely self-reporting of violations as a mitigating factor in determining punishment.[25]

Additionally, for corporations in regulated industries, disqualification from conducting business as a result of conviction may be a greater punishment than

---

21. Report of Investigation pursuant to Section 21(a) of the Securities Exchange Act of 1934 and Commission Statement on the Relationship of Cooperation to Agency Enforcement Decisions, Exchange Act Release No. 44969, Accounting and Auditing Enforcement Release No. 1470 (Oct. 23, 2001). Among the criteria identified by the Commission as bearing on whether to bring an enforcement action and the basis on which an action would be resolved were: "Did the company commit to learn the truth, fully and expeditiously? Did it do a thorough review of the nature, extent, origins and consequences of the conduct and related behavior?"; and "Did the company promptly make available to our staff the results of its review and provide sufficient documentation reflecting its response to the situation?" *Id.*

22. *Supra* note 7.

23. 698 A.2d at 969.

24. According to the guidelines, the "hallmark" of an effective program is that the organization exercised due diligence in seeking to prevent and detect criminal conduct by its employee and other agents. Guidelines, *supra* note 3, § 8A1.2 application Note (3)(k). Among the steps required by this due diligence is that "[t]he organization must have taken reasonable steps to achieve compliance with its standards [of conduct] ... by utilizing monitoring and auditing systems reasonably designed to detect criminal conduct by its employees and other agents ..." *Id.* Another element of due diligence under the Guidelines is that:

> The standards must have been consistently enforced through appropriate disciplinary mechanisms, including, as appropriate, discipline of individuals responsible for failure to detect an offense. Adequate discipline of individuals responsible for an offense is a necessary component of enforcement; however, the form of discipline that will be appropriate will be case specific.

Id.

25. Guidelines, *supra* note 7, § 8C2.5(g). The guidelines contemplate "that the organization will be allowed a reasonable period of time to conduct an internal investigation." *Id.* § 8C2.5 application note 10.

the fine or probationary term imposed under the sentencing guidelines. For example, corporations doing business with the U.S. government are subject to immediate suspension from contracting with the government if indicted and may be debarred from contracting for up to three years if convicted of offenses reflecting a lack of "present responsibility."[26] Prompt and comprehensive corrective action can position the corporation to argue that it is "presently responsible" to continue government contracting notwithstanding the criminal conviction.

Thus, there are significant benefits to the corporation from timely response to employee misconduct. However, in order to obtain those benefits, the corporation must be able to respond quickly to reports of misconduct by aggressively investigating such reports, analyzing the legal consequences, and formulating an appropriate response.

Nevertheless, it must also be recognized that an internal investigation can have significant adverse effects on the organization. The presence of lawyers, the formality of the interview process, and the gathering of documents unavoidably signal to employees that the corporation believes there may be something wrong in the workplace. Employees who may have been involved, however innocently, in the conduct under investigation may feel that they have been singled out and are under suspicion. These employees and their management may fear, often with reason, that investigation of their actions will adversely affect their careers.

Further, disclosure of the results of an internal investigation may result in a waiver of the attorney-client privilege and the work-product doctrine, even if the disclosure is made pursuant to a confidentiality agreement with the government agency.[27] Such a waiver can have substantial adverse affects in collateral civic litigation with third parties.

---

26. *See, e.g.,* 48 C.F.R. § 9.406 (2005); Joseph Construction Co. v. Veterans Admin., 595 F. Supp. 448 (N.D. Ill. 1984) (criminal conduct of company's president and sole shareholder was sufficient grounds to warrant debarment of the company).

27. *See, e.g., In re:* Columbia/HCA Healthcare Corporation Billing Practices Litigation, 293 F.3d 289 (6th Cir. 2002); *In re* Massachusetts Institute of Technology, 129 F.3d 681, 685 (1st Cir. 1997); *In re* Westinghouse Electric Corporation v. Republic of the Philippines, 951 F.2d 1414 (3d Cir. 1991); United States v. Bergonzi, 216 F.R.D. 481 (N.D. Cal. 2003), *app. dismissed as moot,* 403 F.3d 1048 (9th Cir. 2005); *compare In re* Steinhardt Partners, 9 F.3d 230, 236 (2d Cir. 1993); *In re* Leslie Fay Companies Inc. Securities Litigation, 161 F.R.D. 274, 284 (S.D.N.Y. 1995), to the effect that disclosure pursuant to a confidentiality agreement preserved the work-product doctrine. There is also an issue whether the waiver extends only to the contents of the disclosure or whether there is a broader subject matter waiver. *see In re* Grand Jury Proceedings (John Doe v. United States, 350 F.3d 299, (2d Cir. 2003); *In re* Von

None of this diminishes the importance of internal investigations, which are essential to responsible corporate self-governance. But in planning and executing internal investigations, in-house counsel must be mindful of the short- and long-term effects the investigation may have on the corporation, its employees, and its culture.

II. WHEN SHOULD AN INTERNAL INVESTIGATION BE UNDERTAKEN?

An internal investigation should be conducted whenever there is a credible indication of a violation of law or established company policy. These indications may come from a variety of sources, and the corporation's response will depend on the nature and gravity of the violation.

If the corporation has established a mechanism for employees to report possible misconduct without fear of retaliation[28] (e.g., "hotlines" or ombudsmen), all such reports should be followed up. Other sources of information include internal audits, exit interviews with departing employees, reports by outside auditors, press reports or inquiries, and allegations made in employment actions and civil litigation.

In some instances the corporation must react to a government investigation that is already under way. Search warrants, grand jury subpoenas, administrative subpoenas, and civil investigative demands are increasingly becoming common "investigative tools" by government prosecutors. Once it learns of a government investigation, the corporation must move swiftly to identify and analyze relevant documents; to interview percipient witnesses; to assess the corporation's rights, obligations, and potential liability; and to report conclusions to senior management and the board of directors.

As a general rule, all credible reports of misconduct should be investigated. Obviously, however, not all such reports require the level of investigation described in previous chapters. Once it is decided that an internal investigation should be initiated, the next critical question is who should have responsibility for conducting the investigation.

Bulow, 828 F.2d 94, 103 (2d Cir. 1987); XYZ Corporation v. United States, 348 F.3d 16 (1st Cir. 2003).

28. See Guidelines, *supra* note 7, § 8A1.2 application note 3(k)(5) (among the "reasonable steps to achieve compliance" with the corporation's standards of conduct is "having in place and publicizing a reporting system whereby employees and other agents could report criminal conduct by others within the organization without fear of retribution").

III. WHO SHOULD CONDUCT THE INVESTIGATION?

As an initial matter, it must be decided who will be responsible for conducting the internal investigation. To a great extent, this will depend on the nature and circumstances of the alleged wrongdoing. Allegations of theft, or long lunch hours and other isolated incidents of erroneous time charging can be appropriately responded to by the corporation's human resources or security organizations. On the other hand, violations of law or significant corporate policy that expose the corporation to criminal or civil liability should be conducted under the direction of lawyers in order to obtain the protections of the attorney-client privilege and work-product doctrine against compelled disclosure to third parties. An internal investigation in response to a government inquiry should be conducted under counsel's auspices for the same reason.

Having determined that a matter should be investigated on a privileged basis by counsel, it must then be determined whether to rely on in-house counsel to conduct the investigation or to engage outside counsel. It has been recognized, since the Supreme Court's decision in *Upjohn Company v. United States*,[29] that attorney-client privilege and work-product doctrine apply to corporate internal investigations.[30] It is also settled that these protections against forced disclosures attach equally to investigations by both in-house and outside counsel.[31]

Unless the corporation has had a longstanding relationship with a law firm, in-house counsel are usually more familiar with the nature of the company's business. In-house counsel generally have a greater understanding of the corporate culture and organization than their counterparts in private law practice. In-house counsel are also more familiar with the corporation's

---

29. 449 U.S. 383 (1981).
30. *See.* United States v. Rowe, 96 F.3d 1294, 1297 (9th Cir. 1996); United States v. Shyres, 898 F.2d 647, 655 (8th Cir. 1990); *In re,* Grand Jury Subpoena Dated December 19, 1978, 599 F.2d 504, 510 (2d Cir. 1979); Diversified Indus, Inc. v. Meredith, 572 F.2d 596, 610 (8th Cir. 1979) (en banc); *In re* Woolworth Corp. Sec. Class Action Litig., 1996 U.S. Dist. LEXIS 7773 (S.D.N.Y. 1996); *In re* Leslie Fay Companies, Inc. Sec Litig. 161 F.R.D. 274, 282 (S.D.N.Y. 1995); *In re* LTV Sec. Litig., 89 F.R.D. 595, 601 (N.D. Tex. 1981).
31. *See In re* Sealed Case, 737 F.2d 94, 99 (D.C. Cir. 1984); Natta v. Hogan 392 F.2d 686, 692 (9th Cir. 1968); *In re* LTV Sec. Litig., 89 F.R.D. at 601; O'Brien v. Board of Educ., 86 F.R.D. 548, 549 (S.D.N.Y. 1980); Valiente v. PepsiCo., Inc. 68 F.R.D. 361, 367 (D. Del. 1975); Malco Mfg. Co. v. Elco Corp., 45 F.R.D. 24, 26 (D. Minn 1968); 8-in-1 Pet Products, Inc. v. Swift & Co., 218 F. Supp. 253 (S.D.N.Y. 1963); Georgia-Pacific Plywood Co. v. United States Plywood Corp., 18 F.R.D. 463, 464 (S.D.N.Y. 1956); United States v. United Shoe Mach. Corp., 89 F. Supp. 357, 360 (D. Mass 1950).

processes and procedures. In-house counsel may be better prepared to evaluate the significance of documents, or their absence, than counsel from outside the corporation. Finally, in-house counsel may know, at least by reputation, the personalities of the people involved in the matter.

On the other hand, because outside counsel are not "captive" employees of the corporation, they enjoy a greater perception of being independent.[32] Further, because outside counsel are generally not as directly involved in providing business as well as legal advice, there is a stronger presumption that their work for the corporation is within the attorney-client privilege and work-product doctrine.[33] Outside counsel are likely to be more familiar with local practices, particularly if in-house counsel is located in a distant city, and may enjoy better relationships with local prosecutors. Outside counsel may also have greater resources and expertise in specialized areas of the law relevant to the investigation.

The choice between in-house counsel and outside counsel may by determined by reasons of economy. There may not be sufficient resources for in-house counsel to conduct an internal investigation. Likewise, in-house counsel may lack the background or expertise necessary to conduct internal investigations effectively. Of course, cost is always a consideration, and the corporation may be unwilling to accept the expense of an investigation conducted by someone outside the corporation. There may also be circumstances in which the investigation should be undertaken by someone outside the corporation, as when the conduct of senior management is directly implicated.

In most instances, the most effective approach has proved to be a teaming of in-house and outside counsel. By joining the two, the benefits that both

---

32. Interestingly, in the Seaboard Corporation Section 21(a) Report, the S.E.C. indicated that in evaluating a corporation's internal investigation, the Commission would inquire whether "where the review was conducted by outside counsel, had management previously engaged such counsel?" This suggests that even the independence of outside counsel will be questioned if counsel has provided other legal services to the corporation.

33. *See, e.g.,* United States v. Chevron Corp., 1996 U.S. Dist. LEXIS 4154 (N.D. Cal. 1996) ("[s]ome courts have applied a presumption that all communications to outside counsel are primarily related to legal advice. . . . In this context, the presumption is logical, since outside counsel would not ordinarily be involved in the business decisions of a corporation. However, the . . . presumption cannot be applied to in-house counsel because in-house counsel are frequently involved in the business decisions of a company. While an attorney's status as in-house counsel does not dilute the attorney-client privilege . . . a corporation must make a clear showing that in-house counsel's advice was given in a professional legal capacity.") (citations omitted).

in-house and outside counsel bring to the investigation can be obtained. Additionally, the participation of in-house counsel can facilitate communication with management, who may expect in-house counsel to be involved, as well as with employees, who may be reluctant to confide in "outsiders."

After counsel has been designated to conduct the investigation, there are formalities that should be observed, and issues that should be addressed at the outset of the investigation.

IV. INITIATING THE INVESTIGATION

In order to establish and document the basis for asserting the attorney-client privilege with regard to the internal investigation, it is advisable to recognize certain formalities. The first of these is a formal request by corporate management that counsel undertake the investigation of a specific matter for the purpose of providing legal counsel to the management concerning the corporation's rights and obligations. Such a request is often referred to as an "*Upjohn* letter."

This request should describe the subject matter of the investigation with reasonable specificity and should be addressed to the senior in-house lawyer. The recipient of the request may then delegate authority to other counsel to carry out the investigation. Counsel receiving the original request may wish to acknowledge the assignment in a separate document.

Next, the manager requesting the investigation should issue a directive to the employees who may be contacted by counsel during the investigation. This document should inform the employees that counsel has been requested by management to conduct an inquiry and to provide legal advice to the corporation, and that they may be contacted by counsel as part of this inquiry. The employees should be further instructed that they are to provide counsel with any information requested by counsel concerning the performance of the employees' duties and assignments. The purpose of this document is to evidence that counsel is acting at the request of the corporation's management, as set forth in the *Upjohn* letter, and that the information sought and received is in furtherance of that request.

Finally, if outside counsel is to participate in the internal investigation, it is advisable to engage counsel in writing. The letter retaining counsel should also reference management's request as set forth in the *Upjohn* letter. This correspondence will further evidence that counsel is acting pursuant to management's request for legal advice.

V. STRUCTURING THE INVESTIGATION

In addition to the formalities that should be observed at the time the investigation is initiated, a number of important decisions should be made at or near the outset concerning how the investigation is to be conducted. These decisions pertain to the resources necessary to conduct the investigation, the investigative plan, the legal representation of individual employees, and document control and organization.

A. *Assembling the Investigative Team*

Once the composition of the legal team has been established, thought should be given to the additional resources that will be necessary to analyze the facts gathered during the investigation. Auditors and forensic accountants may be needed to analyze financial records and data. Engineers, architects, and systems designers may be needed for technical or quality issues. Chemists, hydrologists, and other technicians may be needed in environmental investigations.

Often these resources can be found within the corporation. Indeed, the expertise of operations personnel is in most instances essential to understanding processes and analyzing relevant documents. Similarly, the assistance of internal auditors who are familiar with company practices and procedures is invaluable.

When the necessary expertise cannot be found in the corporation, outside consultants must be engaged. These experts should be brought in as early as possible so that they can assist in structuring and refining the investigation. In some instances, even when the necessary expertise exists within the corporation, it may be advisable to retain an outside expert either to assist in a presentation to the government prosecutor or to provide expert testimony should civil or criminal litigation ensue.

In order to preserve the privileges applicable to these experts' work, it should be documented that this nonlegal assistance is being rendered at the request and under the direction of counsel. If resources outside the corporation are being used they should be retained by outside counsel. If in-house personnel are being used, they should be formally tasked to work at the direction and under the supervision of counsel.

B. *The Investigative Plan*

Once the team has been assembled, it is essential that an investigative plan be developed and agreed upon. The plan should include a clear understanding of the objectives of the investigation as well as the means to be employed in achieving those objectives. The plan should define the specific responsibilities of the individual members of the team and should establish the work product for which each member of the team will be responsible. The plan should also establish a budget for accomplishing each of the principal tasks.

1. Objectives

The plan should identify what it is that the investigation seeks to accomplish. The objective may be as simple as determining whether a discrete allegation of misconduct is well-founded. In contrast, the objective may be as complex as evaluating the legality and effect of a widespread company procedure and, if the procedure is deficient, proposing corrective measures.

An internal investigation can take on a life of its own. Issues may arise that were not anticipated, and leads may develop that must be pursued. For these reasons, it is critical that the objectives of the investigation be understood so that focus is not lost as the investigation unfolds. At the same time, the plan needs to be flexible enough to enable counsel conducting the investigation to adapt to new facts, new leads, and new issues. In formulating the investigative plan and in formulating the objectives, care should taken to ensure that the objective of the investigation is consistent with the preservation of the attorney-client privilege and work-product doctrine. For example, unless there is a compelling business reason to the contrary, the decision whether to disclose the results of the investigation to third parties should be reserved until the investigation has been completed. Otherwise, an announcement that the results of the investigation will be reported to the government or the public threatens to compromise attorney-client and work-product protections.[34]

2. Communication with Management

It is essential that corporate management and the board of directors be kept apprised of significant investigations. Indeed, the purpose of an internal investigation is to gather information in order to provide legal advice to

---

34. *See, e.g.,* United States v. Bergonzi, 216 F.R.D. 287, 293 (N.D. Cal. 2003); *app. dismissed as moot,* 403 F.3d 1048 (9th Cir. 2005); *In re* Kidder Peabody Sec. Litig., 168 F.R.D. 459 (S.D.N.Y. 1996) (company's stated intent to disclose the report of an internal investigation to the Securities and Exchange Commission and to the public was evidence that the report was not intended to be confidential and had not been prepared in anticipation of litigation and therefore the attorney-client privilege and the work-product doctrine did not apply).

the corporation. However, the level of detail that is communicated while the investigation is ongoing is a matter of some delicacy and should be appropriate to the recipient's "need to know." As part of the structuring of the investigation, a mechanism must be established for briefing responsible management periodically during the investigation.

a. The Board of Directors. If the investigation directly implicates the continued viability of the corporation (the so-called "bet-the-company problem"), the board must be actively involved. If the investigation concerns the actions of senior management, the board itself (acting through the independent directors) should oversee the investigation, which in this instance should be conducted by outside counsel engaged by the board.[35] In other serious but not life-threatening matters, the board of directors should be regularly apprised of the status of the investigation.

The corporation's chief legal officer (i.e., the general counsel) is the appropriate person to advise the board of directors of the progress of internal investigations. The general counsel should also keep the board advised on the status of government investigations. This can be accomplished as part of the general counsel's regular briefing of significant legal matters.

b. Chief Executive Officer. Similarly, the general counsel should keep the CEO regularly apprised of the progress of significant investigations. However, in providing information to the CEO, it is important to advise restraint (not something that comes naturally to most CEOs) so that the investigation can run its course. There may be intense pressure from the board or the CEO to put the problem "behind us," and the challenge to the general counsel in those instances is to forestall action until the matter has been investigated and fully analyzed.

c. Operations Management.[36] Understandably, operations management will also demand to be informed of investigations involving their areas of responsibility. The success of the investigation—that is, the ability to gather

---

35. Discussed above in this chapter.
36. As used here, "Operations Management" includes those managers directly involved in the conduct of the company's business (in contrast to overall management), such as division or sector general managers and program managers. These managers may feel that they have the most at stake as the investigation concerns conduct alleged to have occurred in their area of responsibility.

relevant, reliable information quickly—will depend to a great extent on the cooperation of operations management. However, because operations managers are often "can-do" people who thrive on problem solving, extra care and diplomacy must be exercised in providing information concerning the investigation.

Operations managers may become witnesses in a government investigation, and care must therefore be taken not to "educate" potential witnesses about information learned in the course of the investigation that was not otherwise known to them. In this connection, it is extremely important to explain the operation of the attorney-client privilege and to preface every briefing with a reminder of the applicability of the privilege and the need for confidentiality.

Equally important, operations managers will often try to "get to the bottom" of the problem. In so doing, unprivileged documents, some of which may be quite damaging to the company's best interest, may be created. The investigators must be attentive to such activities and attempt, insofar as possible, to avoid or truncate them. Good communication, and confidence building between the investigators and the managers, can go a long way in avoiding the problem.

The degree of detail provided to each of these groups must be carefully considered. Any disclosure creates the risk of waiver of the attorney-client privilege or work-product doctrine. Further, some of these people, particularly at the operations level, may have a motive to alter or destroy documents because of the investigation. Thus, counsel must exercise good judgment to ensure that the level of information imparted to employees is appropriate under the circumstances.

3. Communication Outside the Corporation

There may be occasions when it is necessary or advisable to communicate with persons outside the corporation concerning the investigation. Obviously, these communications create the greatest risk of waiver of the attorney-client privilege or work-product doctrine. Accordingly, a mechanism for effecting these communications should be established as well.

a. The Government. If the corporation does business in a regulated industry, it is often advisable to make contact with the licensing authority at an early stage in an investigation, particularly if the corporate investigation parallels a government investigation. Early contact with the licensing authority may avoid precipitous action by the licensing authority and will provide a predicate for establishing the corporation's "present responsibility" necessary to prevent or mitigate suspension or debarment from the regulated activity.

Additionally, regulatory agencies may require corporations to report investigations of misconduct. Publicly traded companies that are targets of grand jury investigations may be obliged to disclose the pendency of such investigations in filings with the U.S. Securities and Exchange Commission if indictment would have a material adverse impact on their operations.[37] In like fashion, bank regulatory authorities require financial institutions to make reports of "known or suspected criminal activity."[38]

If the corporate internal investigation is in response to a government investigation, it is also generally advisable to establish communication with the prosecutor assigned to the case. It is usually necessary to negotiate the scope of grand jury subpoenas as well as a schedule for producing responsive documents. Early informal communication with the prosecutor can help refine the issues under investigation (thereby avoiding time-consuming and expensive tangents) and can provide insight into the government's specific concerns. Corporate management will also take some comfort from the knowledge that the company's lawyers are engaged in dialogue with the government.

b. Third Parties. There are also a variety of nongovernmental third parties who will seek information concerning the corporation's investigation. Depending on the circumstances, there may be substantial business reasons for communicating with them.

First among these third parties are the corporation's independent auditors. The auditors will request a representation concerning potential "loss contingencies," in accordance with Statement of Financial Accounting Standards No. 5 issued by the Financial Accounting Standards Board, as part of their annual audit of the corporation's financial records. The American Bar Association has provided guidance to counsel responding to such requests.[39] Nevertheless, there are significant risks of waiver of the attorney-client privilege

---

37. *See* Item 103, SEC Reg. S-K, 17 C.F.R. § 229.103 (2006).

38. See 12 C.F.R. §§ 21.11 et seq. (2006) (requiring national banks to report known or suspected criminal violations or transactions related to money-laundering activity or violations of the Bank Secrecy Act); 12 C.F.R. §§ 353.1 et seq. (2006) (imposing the same requirements on FDIC-insured state banks).

39. American Bar Association, Auditors Letter Handbook (1976).

and work-product doctrine in providing otherwise privileged information in response to these requests.[40]

If the government's investigation has attracted public notice, counsel should anticipate that there will be requests for information concerning the investigation from other third parties as well. Investment bankers and commercial lenders may seek assurances, as may institutional investors and other shareholders. Customers and suppliers may also seek to be assured that ongoing commercial relationships will not be disrupted. The financial press, and even the general press, may cover the investigation. Coordination with the corporation's public affairs, banking, and shareholder relations organizations is especially important in responding, if at all, to these requests.

4. Employee Interviews

There should be a clear understanding on the part of the investigators and the company in regard to several issues that routinely arise when employees are interviewed. These issues involve the rights and obligations of employees—first when the employee is interviewed by the company, and second when the government seeks to interview the company's employees.

When the company interviews its own employees as part of an internal investigation, there is often a question whether an employee will be permitted to be accompanied by a representative during the interview. If the employee is covered by a collective-bargaining agreement, the terms of the agreement may control whether a representative can be present. Similarly, if the employee is involved in litigation with the corporation, the subject matter of which is related to the transaction under investigation, company counsel may be ethically constrained from interviewing the employee without the employee's counsel being present. Absent such considerations, it is discretionary whether the company will allow the employee to be represented during an interview by the company's counsel, there being no general right to counsel at a company interview.[41]

---

40. *See, e.g.,* Medinol, Ltd. v. Boston Scientific Corporation, 214 F.R.D. 113, 115 (S.D.N.Y. 2002) (disclosure of specific litigation committee minutes to the outside auditors waived the protections of the work-product doctrine); *In re* Subpoena Duces Tecum Issued to Wilkie Farr & Gallagher, 1997 U.S. Dist. LEXIS 2927 (S.D.N.Y. 1997) (disclosure of a report to an internal investigation to the outside auditors was a waiver of the attorney-client privilege).

41. *See* United States v. Calhoon, 859 F. Supp. 1496,1498 (M.D. Ga. 1994); TRW, Inc. v. Superior Court of Los Angeles County, 25 Cal. App. 4th 1834, 31 Cal. Rptr. 2d 460 (1994).

A second issue that arises when employees are interviewed in a corporate internal investigation is whether the employee will be subject to adverse personnel action for refusing to cooperate with the investigation. Most, if not all, companies take the position that an element of the employer/employee relationship is the obligation to provide information concerning matters within the scope of employment. Indeed, the memorandum from management to employees advising them of the investigation, discussed earlier, is intended to document management's directive that employees provide information to the investigators pursuant to this employment obligation.

If an employee refuses to cooperate, the company must determine whether to take disciplinary action. Many companies have a policy that failure to cooperate with company counsel is grounds for termination (a so-called "talk or walk" policy). Other companies provide for a range of possible disciplinary actions. In any event, the investigators and the company should agree on the approach to be taken in the event of noncooperation. If it is decided that discipline will result from a failure to cooperate, that discipline should be imposed consistently and uniformly.

Very different considerations apply when it is the government that seeks to interview the corporation's employees. First, the employee has a constitutional privilege against self-incrimination that entitles the employee, if he or she chooses, to decline to be interviewed, even though the corporation itself is cooperating with the government's investigation. Second, the corporation must decide whether to advance the fees for the legal representation of the employees interviewed by the government.

There is a tendency among many companies to have company counsel (in-house or outside) represent employees at interviews with government agents, largely for reasons of cost. Although there are circumstances in which representation by company counsel is completely appropriate, it is often a false economy to have the same counsel represent both the corporation and its employees.[42] There is the risk that a conflict of interest can develop between one employee and another or between one or more employees and the company.[43]

---

42. Discussed above in this chapter.
43. *See, e.g.,* Wood v. Georgia, 450 U.S. 261, 271-272 (1981) ("petitioners were represented by their employer's lawyer who may not have pursued their interest single-mindedly."); United States v. Talad, 222 F.3d 1133, 1140 (9th Cir. 2000) (conflicts arose when employee determined to give information concerning corporation's criminal conduct). Such a conflict may arise in later litigation between the company and the employee. *See* Montgomery Academy v. Kohn, 50 F. Supp. 2d 344, 353 (D.N.J. 1999).

In that event, counsel would be bound to withdraw from the representation and could face possible disqualification at a critical juncture in the investigation.[44]

Counsel representing one or more individuals often interacts with government investigators differently from company counsel. Counsel for an individual properly may instruct the individual not to be interviewed or, even during an interview, not to answer particular questions. Company counsel cannot give either instruction while at the same time maintaining that the company is cooperating with the government's investigation. Similarly, an individual's counsel may negotiate immunity when company counsel could not.

Alternatively, the corporation may be obliged to make individual counsel available to employees who may become involved in a government investigation. For example, under California state law, an employer is required to indemnify employees for expenses incurred as a consequence of the discharge of the employees' duties.[45] In these circumstances, the corporation should refrain from requiring that the employee choose a particular lawyer.

When the corporation advances fees for an individual's counsel, it may be necessary to require the individual employee to execute an undertaking that the fees and expenses advanced will be repaid if it is determined that the individual was not entitled to indemnification. Such an undertaking may be required by law,[46] or may be warranted by sound corporate governance.

---

44. *See* DR5-105 (ABA 1981); Model Rule 17(a) (ABA 1989); United States v. Moscony, 927 F.2d 742, 748 (3d Cir. 1991). In this connection, great care must be taken by company counsel at the outset of an interview with an employee to make clear that counsel represents the corporation, not the employee. Counsel should also explain the applicability of the attorney-client privilege to the matters discussed during the interview and should emphasize the importance of maintaining confidentiality. Counsel must also make clear, however, that the privilege belongs to the corporation, not the employee, and that the corporation may waive the privilege and disclose the matters discussed in the interview at a future time.

45. CAL. LABOR CODE § 2802 provides:

> An employer shall indemnify his employee for all that the employee necessarily expends or loses in direct consequences of the discharge of his duties as such, or of his disobedience to the directions of the employer, even though unlawful, unless the employee, at the time of obeying such directions, believed them to be unlawful.

Similarly, CAL. CORP. CODE § 317(d) provides:

> To the extent that an agent of a corporation has been successful on the merits in defense of any proceedings . . . or in defense of any claim, issue or matter therein, the agent shall be indemnified against expenses actually and reasonably incurred by the agent in connection therewith.

46. For example, Delaware corporation law establishes a corporation's authority to indemnify persons acting on behalf of the corporation (i.e., directors, officers, employees, or agents) against attorney's fees and expenses in connection with a civil, criminal, administrative, or investigative matter if the individual "acted in good faith and in a manner he reason-

Employees are often confused when confronted with such an undertaking. They are concerned that the corporation, which had just assured them that counsel would be provided, is now saying that they may have to repay the fees at a later time. As a result, both company counsel and the individual's counsel should each endeavor to explain the import of the undertaking to the individual employee.

Finally, when one or more counsel are engaged to represent individuals, it may be in the best interests of all concerned to enter into an information-sharing and confidentiality agreement. These agreements are also known as "joint defense agreements." Some government agents and prosecutors have been critical of, if not overtly hostile to, joint defense agreements and for that reason, companies have been reluctant to enter into formal agreements out of concern that the government will not view the companies as being cooperative with the government if they have entered into joint defense agreements. However, so long as the independence and loyalty of the attorneys and their clients are recognized and respected, information-sharing agreements are a legitimate response to a government investigation. Nevertheless, any disclosure of confidential information risks a subsequent finding that the attorney-client privilege and work-product doctrine have been waived. Similarly, there may be circumstances in which the corporation may decide that it is inappropriate to ally itself closely with others. Thus, while there are clear benefits to information-sharing agreements, company counsel should carefully consider the disadvantages before entering into such agreements.

5. Maintaining Control Over Documents

Concurrent with and sometimes prior to the interview of knowledgeable employees, documents relevant to the investigation must be identified and analyzed. If the government has made a formal request for the production of documents, by means of subpoena, civil investigative demand, or other

---

ably believed to be in or not opposed to the best interests of the corporation, and, with respect to any criminal action or proceeding, had no reasonable cause to believe his conduct was unlawful." DEL. CORP. LAW § 145 (a) and (b).

Delaware law further provides:

> Expenses incurred by an officer or director in defending a civil or criminal action, suit or proceeding may be paid by the corporation in advance of the final disposition of such action, suit or proceeding upon receipt of an undertaking by or on behalf of such director or officer to repay such amount if it shall ultimately be determined that he is not entitled to be indemnified by the corporation as authorized in this Section.

DEL. CORP. LAW § 145(e).

administrative process, the corporation must act promptly to preserve responsive documents so that they can be collected, reviewed, and produced. Additionally, even before a formal request has been made, it is prudent for the corporation to take the steps necessary to preserve relevant documents once the subject matter of the government's investigation is known in order to avoid a later claim of spoliation of evidence, and the attendant negative interference.[47]

If the corporation has an established document retention program, the destruction of potentially relevant documents must be halted immediately. Employees who reasonably may be expected to have relevant, responsive documents should be given notice of the government's document request and should be specifically instructed to preserve documents. Members of the investigative team should meet with these employees and their supervisors to emphasize the importance of retaining documents and to explain the procedures that will be followed. Frequent monitoring is necessary to ensure that counsel's directives are being followed and that the procedures are being implemented.

As early as possible in the process, a document custodian should be designated to oversee the gathering and production of responsive documents. The document custodian should be familiar with the types of responsive documents that are created by the corporation in the ordinary course of business and with their location. The document custodian should bear principal responsibility for conducting the corporation's search for documents.

On the other hand, company counsel must be responsible for the determination of responsiveness and privilege. Counsel should be assisted in determining what documents are responsive by operations personnel. Thus, when assembling the investigative team, it is often helpful to include persons from the operations who can interpret the relevant documents.

Lastly, a document control center should be established for housing the documents relevant to the subject matter of the investigation, regardless of whether the documents are responsive to the document request or are privileged. The document control center should be under the control of the docu-

---

47. *See, e.g.,* CAL. EVID. CODE § 412 ("[i]f weaker less satisfactory evidence is offered when it was within the power of the party to produce stronger and more satisfactory evidence, the evidence offered should be viewed with distrust") and § 413 ("[i]n determining what inferences to draw from the evidence or facts in the case against a party, the trier of fact may consider, among other things, the party's failure to explain or to deny by his testimony such evidence or facts in the case against him or his willful suppression of evidence relating thereto, if such be the case").

ment custodian. If warranted, use of scanning technology will allow the transaction of the documents at the control center to electronic images accessible by members of the investigative team at remote locations, obviating the need for team members to come to the center to review the documents.

VI. REPORTING THE RESULTS OF THE INVESTIGATION

Once the investigation has been completed, it must be determined what is to be done with the results. Of course, appropriate management, including the board of directors, must be advised of counsel's findings, conclusions, and advice. This information can be given in a series of oral briefings tailored to the manager's need to know or through a written report. However, great care must be exercised in reporting counsel's conclusion to preserve applicable privileges and to avoid possible claims of defamation.

Also, the corporation must decide whether to disclose the results of the investigation to the government. Such a disclosure may be in the form of a formal voluntary disclosure under the auspices of an established voluntary disclosure program.[48] The disclosure may also be made less formally to the prosecutor in an effort to persuade the prosecutor to decline prosecution. In either event, the disclosure can result in the waiver of the waiver of the attorney-client privilege and work-product doctrine, at least as to the report itself.[49] The consequences of such a waiver, particularly in regard to third-party civil liability, must be carefully weighed.

Management will expect that the investigation will also result in proposed remedial actions to mitigate any damage that may have resulted. It will also

---

48. *See supra* note 16.
49. *See In re* Columbia/HCA Healthcare Corporation Billing Practices Litigation, 293 F.3d 289 (6th Cir. 2002) (disclosure to Department of Justice); *In re* Steinhardt Partners, L.P., 9 F.3d 230, 236 (2d Cir. 1993) (disclosure to the SEC); Westinghouse Elec. Corp. v. Republic of the Philippines, 951 F.2d 1414, 1427-29 (3d Cir. 1991) (disclosure to the SEC and Department of Justice); *In re* Martin Marietta Corp., 856 F.2d 619, 623-24 (4th Cir. 1988) (disclosure to the U.S. Attorney's Office), *cert. denied,* 109 S. Ct. 1655 (1989); *In re.* Subpoena Duces Tecum (Fulbright & Jaworski), 738 F.2d 1367, 1370-75 (D.C. Cir. 1984) (disclosure to the SEC); *In re* Sealed Case, 676 F.2d 793, 817 (D.C. Cir. 1981) (disclosure to the SEC); United States v. Bergonzi, 216 F.R.D. 487, 493 (N.D. Cal. 2003) (disclosure to the SEC); *In re* Kidder Peabody Sec Litig., 168 F.R.D. 459 (S.D.N.Y. 1996); (disclosure to the SEC); Isaacson v. Keck, Mahin & Cate, 875 F. Supp. 478, 48 (N.D. Ill. 1994) (disclosure to the SEC and attorney disciplinary committee); *In re* Leslie Fay Co. Sec. Litig., 152 F.R.D. 42 (S.D.N.Y 1993) (disclosure to the SEC and the U.S. Attorney's Office); United States v. Mierzwicki, 500 F. Supp. 1331, 1334 (D. Md 1980) (disclosure to the Department of Justice).

be expected that corrective actions will be proposed to prevent recurrence of similar misconduct in the future.

If recommendations are made, they must be practical and realistically achievable by the corporation. It must also be impressed on management that if the recommendations are adopted, they must be implemented. Otherwise, if they are not, there is the risk that the government will later point to the corporation's failure to follow through as evidence of the corporation's indifference to legal compliance and its intent to violate the law.

VII. CONCLUSION

Although there are clear benefits to the corporation from conducting internal investigations of suspected wrongdoing, the manner in which investigations are conducted can have a decidedly negative effect within the corporation. The role of in-house counsel is critical both to achieve these benefits and to minimize the negative effects of the investigation itself.

Thus, the successful investigation not only gathers and analyzes facts quickly and efficiently, but also responds effectively to the concerns within the corporation. Obviously, that does not mean that individual responsibility for misconduct should not be established without fear or favor. Rather, in structuring and carrying out the investigation along the lines discussed in the previous chapters, it is important that the investigation have clear objectives, that the investigation follow a plan established at the outset, that efforts be made not to disrupt the operation of the company unnecessarily, and that both management and the board of directors be kept advised of the progress and status of the investigation.

Internal Investigations in Antitrust Matters 15

Jacqueline K. Shipchandler

I. OVERVIEW OF APPLICABLE LAWS AND ENFORCEMENT LANDSCAPE   467
   A. Federal Enforcement   467
   B. State Enforcement   468
   C. Foreign Enforcement   468
II. UNIQUE CONSIDERATIONS IN ANTITRUST INTERNAL INVESTIGATIONS   469
   A. Identifying Your Client   469
   B. Investigative Steps   470
   C. Privilege Waiver Issues   471
   D. Reporting Process   471
   E. Relations with Counsel for Other Investigated Parties   472
III. CRIMINAL INVESTIGATIONS—WHAT EVERY PRACTITIONER AND CLIENT MUST KNOW   472
   A. Increasingly High Stakes   473
   B. Investigative Tools   475

Ms. Shipchandler practices in the area of antitrust and white collar defense at Haynes and Boone LLP, in Dallas, Texas. Christopher Rogers, an associate in the Antitrust, Securities Litigation, and White Collar Criminal Defense Practice Group at Haynes and Boone, LLP, assisted in the preparation of this chapter.

C. Amnesty Under the Corporate Leniency Policy   478
D. Value of Cooperation When Amnesty Is Not Available   485
E. Assessing Whether Individual Employees Need Separate Counsel   486
F. Making a Proffer and Preparing for Interviews and Testimony   487
IV. RELATED LITIGATION   488
   A. Types of Civil Actions   488
   B. Parallel Litigation Concerns   489
   C. Benefits in Private Litigation from Amnesty Participation   490
V. CONCLUSION   490

WITH ANY INTERNAL INVESTIGATION, time is of the essence. This mantra takes on heightened significance for counsel and clients embarking on an internal investigation involving potential antitrust violations, particularly when the risk of criminal liability is present. When facing a criminal antitrust probe, companies often vie for first place in the "race for amnesty," hoping to qualify for admission into the Corporate Leniency Program run by the Antitrust Division of the United States Department of Justice and thereby avoid the sanction—including stiff fines and incarceration—that can accompany criminal prosecutions. Because amnesty is available only to the first company to self-report and to meet the Antitrust Division's qualification requirements, the speed with which a company conducts its internal investigation and, in particular, its initial assessment of liability becomes even more important in antitrust matters when compared to other types of internal investigations.

Aside from the crucial timing issues, there are several other distinct considerations to keep in mind when conducting an internal antitrust investigation. This chapter highlights these considerations, including: (I) an overview of the antitrust enforcement landscape; (II) factors that tend to set antitrust investigations apart from other types of internal investigations; (III) key considerations when investigating potential criminal antitrust violations; and (IV) potential concerns relating to parallel litigation.

I. OVERVIEW OF APPLICABLE LAWS AND ENFORCEMENT LANDSCAPE

At the outset of an internal investigation into possible antitrust violations, counsel must be prepared to navigate and advise clients on the overlapping enforcement regimes in the United States and abroad, any or all of which may take an interest in the subject matter and results of the investigation.[1]

A. *Federal Enforcement*

The Antitrust Division of the United States Department of Justice (the Antitrust Division) and the Federal Trade Commission (the Commission) share jurisdiction for federal enforcement of the U.S antitrust laws. At the federal level, three major statutes govern U.S. competition laws: the Sherman Antitrust Act (the Sherman Act),[2] the Clayton Act,[3] and the Federal Trade Commission Act (the FTC Act).[4]

Section 1 of the Sherman Act prohibits all contracts, combinations and conspiracies that restrain interstate trade or trade with foreign nations, including price-fixing, bid-rigging, and market or customer allocation agreements among competitors.[5] Section 2 of the Sherman Act outlaws monopolization and attempted monopolization.[6] Sherman Act violations can be enforced both criminally and civilly;[7] however, the Antitrust Division has exclusive jurisdiction to bring criminal prosecutions under the Act. This chapter will focus on investigations involving potential criminal liability.

---

1. In the post–Sarbanes-Oxley world, publicly traded companies conducting antitrust investigations should also consider potential securities law reporting obligations associated with their findings. *See* Chapter 11.
2. 15 U.S.C. §§ 1-7.
3. 15 U.S.C. §§ 12-27.
4. 15 U.S.C. §§ 41-51.
5. 15 U.S.C. § 1.
6. 15 U.S.C. § 2.
7. While Section 2 violations can, under the language of the Sherman Act, constitute felony offenses, *see* 15 U.S.C. § 2, the Antitrust Division typically reserves criminal prosecutions for Section 1 violations.

The Clayton Act prohibits, among other practices, mergers or acquisitions that are likely to cause a substantial lessening of competition, or that tend to create a monopoly in the affected market. Unlike the Sherman Act, the Clayton Act is a civil statute and carries no criminal penalties. Both the Antitrust Division and the Commission have jurisdiction to review mergers under the Clayton Act.

The FTC Act gives the Commission authority to bring civil enforcement actions against unfair methods of competition in interstate commerce, including monopolization and attempted monopolization, as well as conspiracies in restraint of trade. As noted, the Antitrust Division handles all federal criminal enforcement. In civil matters in which the Commission and the Antitrust Division have concurrent jurisdiction, the agencies typically avoid duplicative enforcement actions by consulting before opening a new case.

B. *State Enforcement*

In addition to potential enforcement of the federal antitrust laws by the Antitrust Division and the Commission, companies may also face investigations and enforcement actions by state officials, which can be brought under either state or federal law. Most states have enacted their own antitrust laws, many of which allow the state Attorney General to challenge anticompetitive practices, often as a representative of the state and its agencies or as *parens patriae* on behalf of individuals.[8] States are also empowered to seek relief under the federal antitrust laws in a variety of circumstances.[9]

C. *Foreign Enforcement*

Counsel must also be cognizant of applicable foreign antitrust laws and enforcement regimes. An in-depth discussion of foreign antitrust enforcement falls outside the scope of this chapter, but, at a minimum, counsel must understand that global antitrust enforcement has been on the rise in recent years, triggered in no small part by efforts of the Antitrust Division to foster cooperation with foreign antitrust authorities in its crusade against international car-

---

8. For a discussion of the various states' antitrust laws, *see* ABA SECTION OF ANTITRUST LAW, MONOGRAPH NO. 15, ANTITRUST FEDERALISM: THE ROLE OF STATE LAW (1988).

9. For example, federal antitrust laws consider states to be "persons" within the meaning of Section 4 of the Clayton Act, and state Attorneys General are entitled to represent the proprietary interests of the state and state agencies in federal cases seeking civil damages or injunctive relief. 15 U.S.C. §§ 15, 26; Hawaii v. Standard Oil Co., 405 U.S. 251 (1972). States may also be able to bring federal parens patriae actions on behalf of state residents. 15 U.S.C. § 15c.

tels and to promote enactment and vigorous enforcement of foreign antitrust laws. As the Antitrust Division's Deputy Assistant Attorney General for Criminal Enforcement stated in 2006:

> Antitrust authorities around the world have become increasingly aggressive in investigating and sanctioning cartels that victimize their consumers. Seemingly with each passing day, the antitrust community learns of a foreign government that has enacted a new antitrust law, created a new cartel investigative unit, or obtained a record antitrust penalty.[10]

As a result of the rise in antitrust enforcement on a global level, counsel must assess not only the risks of liability in the United States, but also the potential for enforcement actions in foreign jurisdictions. Perhaps even more importantly, counsel must simultaneously assess the risks of foreign enforcement and coordinate strategies for dealing with the competition authorities in the affected jurisdictions. The global reach of antitrust enforcement means that the U.S. investigation cannot take place in a vacuum. If counsel is considering seeking amnesty in the U.S., it must likewise assess the merits of seeking leniency in, for example, the European Union. Cooperation between foreign enforcement agencies, confidentiality concerns, and document discovery issues are just a few of the considerations that counsel will need to assess as part of the investigation.

II. UNIQUE CONSIDERATIONS IN ANTITRUST INTERNAL INVESTIGATIONS

In many ways, conducting an internal antitrust investigation will mirror that of any other internal corporate investigation. This chapter will not address basic principles but instead will highlight aspects of the antitrust internal investigation that may set it apart from other internal corporate investigations.

A. *Identifying Your Client*

Counsel must determine early on who the client is and come to an agreement on lines of reporting and supervision, including whether counsel will report to in-house attorneys, senior management, the board of directors, or some combination thereof. Typically, in antitrust internal investigations, outside

---

10. Scott D. Hammond, Charting New Waters in International Cartel Prosecutions, at 3, Speech Before the Twentieth Annual National Institute on White Collar Crime (Mar. 2, 2006), *available at* http://www.usdoj.gov/atr/public/speeches/214861.htm.

counsel is retained by management to represent the corporation. It is therefore unusual that counsel in an antitrust investigation would report to or be supervised by the direct supervision of the Board of Directors. Rather, the more typical course is to report to in-house litigation counsel and/or senior management.

B. *Investigative Steps*

Antitrust investigations have much in common with other forms of internal inquiries with one huge exception. That exception: the time pressure associated with deciding whether to seek protection under the Antitrust Division's Corporate Leniency Program and, if so, compiling the necessary evidence to make an application before one of the corporation's competitors does so. The investigative steps taken in the initial days of an investigation can make the difference between qualifying for amnesty and essentially receiving a "get out of jail free" card from the Antitrust Division, or facing significant monetary fines for the corporation and jail time for culpable executives.

While the basic interviewing techniques may not vary greatly, there are specific facts that counsel will want to understand early on, all directed to a better understanding of the competitive landscape. First and foremost, counsel must collect basic information about the corporation's operations and locations, including: the identity of sellers and purchasers in the affected markets; whether sellers operate worldwide or only in certain regions; the dollar sales and market shares of the participants, worldwide and regionally; the length of time that each participant has been in the market; and a description of regional markets (by seller and purchaser). Counsel must also understand the key in-house players. For each market, this means finding out the employees within the corporation who participate in sales and marketing decisions, reviewing organizational charts, and ascertaining quickly who in the corporation has authority over pricing and production decisions and who is most likely to have had contacts with competitors. Finally, counsel must understand the sales and pricing process for the relevant markets, such as how the client approaches sales and pricing decisions and the fundamentals of how industry/market sales are structured (e.g., open or closed bid; annual price quotes; order-by-order pricing; etc.). Counsel will also want to touch upon any related products, particularly those handled by the same sales and marketing staff. This list is by no means exhaustive, but it provides an overview of the basic building blocks that counsel will need as the investigation develops.

C. Privilege Waiver Issues

Waiver of attorney-client privilege in the context of cooperation with government investigations continues to be a topic of debate among enforcement officials and practitioners. *See* Chapter 2, Implications of the Attorney-Client Privilege and Work-Product Doctrine. Despite the concerns that have been raised in recent years that the Department of Justice and SEC have taken steps to erode the protections of the attorney-client privilege by increasingly requiring waiver as a prerequisite to cooperation, the same trends have not been observed with respect to antitrust probes by the DOJ's Antitrust Division.

In fact, the Antitrust Division has expressly acknowledged that waiver of the attorney-client privilege is not required as part of the cooperation expected of amnesty applicants under the Division's Corporate Leniency Program.[11] And, even outside the context of the amnesty process, antitrust practitioners and their clients have not been confronted with privilege waiver requests as part of plea agreement cooperation obligations.

D. Reporting Process

Written reports are not the norm in antitrust investigations, especially in situations where the government has already begun its inquiry and issued a subpoena. In that setting, the focus of the interviews is to gather information as expeditiously as possible and to obtain a sense of each employee's knowledge *before* the government seeks to interview them or the window of opportunity for amnesty passes.

Moreover, in instances where a company or an individual is interested in seeking protection from prosecution in the United States, either under the

---

11. Gary R. Spratling, The Corporate Leniency Policy: Answers to Recurring Questions (hereinafter "Answers to Recurring Questions"), at 17-18, Speech Before the American Bar Association's Antitrust Section 1998 Spring Meeting (Apr. 1, 1998), *available at* http://www.usdoj.gov/atr/public/speeches/1626.htm (stating that "... the Division will not consider disclosures made by counsel in furtherance of the amnesty application to constitute a waiver of the attorney-client privilege or the work-product privilege."). The model amnesty letter includes language commemorating this position. *See* Spratling, Making Companies an Offer They Shouldn't Refuse, The Antitrust Division's Corporate Leniency Policy—An Update (hereinafter, "Making Companies an Offer"), at 20-21, Speech Before the Bar Association of the District of Columbia's 35th. Annual Symposium on Associations and Antitrust (Feb. 16, 1999), *available at* http://www.usdoj.gov/atr/public/speeches/2247.htm (attaching copy of the model amnesty letter).

Antitrust Division's Leniency Program, or through some other nonprosecution agreement, the Antitrust Division will accept oral proffers of information, which are often accompanied by interviews of knowledgeable employees and production of pre-existing corporate documents.[12] This negates the need for a written submission to the U.S. authorities and minimizes concerns that government submissions will be discoverable in ensuing private litigation.[13]

E. *Relations with Counsel for Other Investigated Parties*

Criminal antitrust investigations into cartel activity by their very nature will implicate one or more of your client's competitors in the investigated market. Accordingly, counsel should assess the merits of making contact with counsel for other competitors and whether it makes sense to enter into a joint defense arrangement, either during the course of the government investigation or in the context of follow-on civil litigation.

III. CRIMINAL INVESTIGATIONS—WHAT EVERY PRACTITIONER AND CLIENT MUST KNOW

Criminal antitrust investigations typically involve hard-core cartel offenses, such as price-fixing, bid-rigging, and market or customer allocation. These are considered the most serious of antitrust offenses and are per se illegal, meaning that they are deemed unlawful without any inquiry into their actual anticompetitive effect. The Antitrust Division has devoted consider-

---

12. Spratling, D. Jarrett Arp and Alexandra J. Shepard, *Making the Decision: What to Do When Faced with International Cartel Exposure—Developments Impacting the Decision in 2006,* at 68, Presented at the American Bar Association's Section of Antitrust Law and International Bar Association 2006 International Cartel Workshop (Feb. 2006) (pointing out that "In the U.S. and Canada, experienced practitioners make all 'submissions' on behalf of amnesty applicants as oral presentations and typically provide knowledgeable witnesses for interviews by government prosecutors."). *See* Section III.F. of this chapter for further discussion of the proffer process.

13. Likewise, following conflicting decisions from U.S. courts regarding the discoverability of written leniency applications by private plaintiffs, the European Commission shifted to a policy of allowing leniency applicants to make oral presentations, rather than written submissions. *See* Bertus van Barlingen, *A View from the Inside: The European Commission's 2002 Leniency Notice After One Year of Operation,* 17 ANTITRUST No. 2 at 84 (Spring 2003). This policy is in the process of being formalized through a proposed amendment to the 2002 Commission Notice on Immunity from fines and reduction of fines in cartel cases (the "Leniency Notice"), *available at* http://ec.europa.eu/comm/competition/antitrust/legislation/leniency.html.

able resources to the detection and prosecution of cartels, with a particular focus on international cartel enforcement in the past decade.[14]

A. *Increasingly High Stakes*

As the Antitrust Division's emphasis on cartel prosecution has increased in recent years, so too have the accompanying penalties for criminal antitrust violations. Along with stiff monetary penalties for violations, the Antitrust Division has increased its reliance on incarceration. From the Antitrust Division's perspective, "nothing in our enforcement arsenal has as great an effect as the threat of substantial incarceration in a United States prison—nothing is a greater deterrent and nothing is a greater incentive for a cartelist, once exposed, to cooperate in the investigation of his co-conspirators."[15]

The Antitrust Criminal Penalty Enhancement and Reform Act of 2004 (ACPERA)[16] significantly increased the monetary penalties and prison sentences associated with antitrust offenses. Under ACPERA, the maximum jail time available for Sherman Act offenses increased more than threefold from three years to ten years,[17] bringing them in line with the criminal penalties for other types of serious white-collar offenses. The statute also imposed significantly higher monetary fines, increasing the maximum individual fine from $350,000 to $1 million[18] and the maximum corporate fine from $10 million

---

14. *See, e.g.*, Hammond, An Update on the Antitrust Division's Criminal Enforcement Program, at 2, Remarks Before the American Bar Association's Section of Antitrust Law Fall Forum, Cartel Enforcement Roundtable (Nov. 16, 2005), *available at* http://www.usdoj.gov/atr/public/speeches/213247.htm ("The detection, prosecution, and deterrence of cartel offenses continue to be the highest priority of the Antitrust Division. The Division places a particular emphasis on combating international cartels that target U.S. markets because of the breadth and magnitude of the harm that they inflict on American businesses and consumers."); R. Hewitt Pate, Securing the Benefits of Global Competition, at 6, Remarks before the Tokyo American Center (September 10, 2004), *available at* http://www.usdoj.gov/atr/public/speeches/205389.htm (speech by then-Assistant Attorney General for Antitrust, describing the Antitrust Division's hierarchy of enforcement priorities and stating that "[a]t the top of this hierarchy is enforcement against cartels, conduct that is devoid of any efficiency justification and inflicts tremendous harm on our economy. Our Supreme Court, in its recent *Trinko* decision, described collusive behavior as 'the supreme evil of antitrust.' Obviously, this is our core priority at the Antitrust Division.").

15. Thomas O. Barnett, Seven Steps to Better Cartel Enforcement, at 5, Presented to the Eleventh Annual Competition Law & Policy Workshop (June 2, 2006), *available at* http://www.usdoj.gov/atr/public/speeches/216453.htm.

16. Pub. L. No. 108-237, § 215(a), 118 Stat. 661, 668 (Jun. 22, 2004) (codified at 15 U.S.C. § 1-3).

17. *Id.*

18. *Id.*

to $100 million.[19] In addition to the changes heralded by ACPERA, the United States Sentencing Commission increased the penalties allowed under its antitrust guideline, § 2R1.1, in November 2005.[20] The changes to the Sentencing Guidelines, which are not mandatory but must be taken into consideration during sentencing,[21] were designed to take "into account both the revised Sherman Act maximum jail sentence and recent experience with the enormous volumes of commerce affected by international cartels."[22]

The Antitrust Division has taken steps to make these heightened penalties as potent as possible. The statutory penalties are higher, and the Antitrust Division regards cartels as serious crimes. To that end, the Antitrust Division has shifted to a policy of increasing the number of high-level culpable executives who are "carved out" of corporate plea arrangements and forced to face individual prosecution for their involvement in cartel activities and has moved toward insisting on jail time as part of any individual plea deal.[23] For the antitrust counselor, these enhanced penalties provide a stark illustration of the risks associated with antitrust violations.

The risk of prosecution is not limited to potential antitrust violations. In antitrust investigations, the Division will seek to enforce related offenses,

---

19. *Id.* Higher fines may still be available under the alternative fines provision of the United States Sentencing Guidelines (the "Guidelines"), which provides for a maximum fine of twice the gain or twice the loss resulting from the anticompetitive conduct. 18 U.S.C. § 3571(d).

20. The changes to § 2R1.1 of the Guidelines increased the base offense level to Level 12, and increased the sentencing range for antitrust offenses from 24-30 months to 78-97 months.

21. United States v. Booker, 543 U.S. 220, 245-46 (2005).

22. Barnett, Seven Steps, at 6. *See also* United States Sentencing Commission, News Release: Emergency Guideline Amendments on Obstruction of Justice and Intellectual Property Crimes Take Effect; Aggravated Identity Theft and Antitrust Amendments Also Become Effective (Nov. 1, 2005), *available at* http://www.ussc.gov/PRESS/rel110105.htm (stating that "[t]he amendment to the antitrust guideline responds to the Antitrust Criminal Penalty Enhancement and Reform Act of 2004, which increased the statutory maximum term of imprisonment for Sherman Act violations from three years to ten years. The amendment provides heightened penalties for antitrust offenses and includes a new 'volume of commerce' table. This new table recognizes the depreciation in the value of the dollar since the table was last revised in 1991, responds to data indicating that the financial magnitude of antitrust offenses has increased significantly, and provides greater deterrence to large-scale price-fixing crimes.").

23. Hammond, Charting New Waters in International Cartel Prosecutions, at 16-18, Speech Before the Twentieth Annual National Institute on White Collar Crime (Mar. 2, 2006), *available at* http://www.usdoj.gov/atr/public/speeches/214861.htm.

such as mail fraud and wire fraud, where applicable.[24] The Division will also prosecute companies and individuals that interfere with the investigative process.[25]

B. *Investigative Tools*

Counsel and clients also must factor the Antitrust Division's enhanced focus on cartel enforcement into their analysis when conducting—and deciding whether to report to the government—internal antitrust investigations that raise the specter of criminal liability. The likelihood of cartel activity going undetected decreases with each passing year, as the Antitrust Division acquires news methods of detecting cartels and tracking down their participants for prosecution—both domestically and abroad. As the penalties for cartel participation increase, the antitrust counselor faces a heightened burden of ensuring that the client is aware of the pros and cons associated with self-reporting and cooperation versus rolling the dice and adopting a noncooperation stance.

The Antitrust Division has long relied upon investigative techniques such as the federal subpoena power, drop-in interviews, and the execution of

---

24. For example, in January 2006, the Antitrust Division successfully indicted four people for participating in self-dealing schemes involving kickbacks and embezzlement and netting more than $2 million while acting as executives and purchasing agents for the Archdiocese of New York. The indictment included charges of mail fraud, false statements, conspiracy to commit mail fraud, conspiracy to defraud the IRS, tax evasion, and obstruction, but did not include any Sherman Act antitrust violations. United States Department of Justice, News Release: Four New York Archdiocese Purchasing Representatives Indicted on Fraud, Tax, and Obstruction of Justice Charges (Jan. 5, 2006), *available at* http://www.usdoj.gov/atr/public/press_releases/2006/214014.htm).

25. In January 2006, the Antitrust Division announced the fourth in a series of indictments arising out of a joint investigation into a kickback scheme in Puerto Rico. The charges included obstruction of justice and conspiracy to obstruct justice. United States Department of Justice, News Release: Puerto Rico Attorney Charged with Obstruction of Justice (Jan. 11, 2006) *available at* http://www.usdoj.gov/atr/public/press_releases/2006/releases/2006/214082.htm. Obstruction charges can include the following: (1) false statements to federal officials (under 18 U.S.C. § 1001, subject to penalties of fines and up to five years in prison); (2) witness tampering (under 18 U.S.C. § 1512 (b), anyone who causes another person to withhold testimony or to destroy documents can be prosecuted and subject to penalties of fines and up to ten years in prison); (3) document destruction (under 18 U.S.C. §§ 1512 (c) and 1519, anyone who destroys, conceals, or tampers with documents can be prosecuted and subject to penalties of fines and up to twenty years in prison); and (4) perjury (under 18 U.S.C. §§ 1621-1623, perjury and subornation of perjury are punishable by fines and up to five years in prison).

search warrants. They have also relied upon cooperating witnesses to conduct consensual electronic surveillance of cartel activities. These existing techniques have been supplemented in recent years by increased cooperation with foreign authorities, which has manifested itself in coordinated raids, assistance with gathering foreign-located evidence, and other efforts to promote cartel enforcement in the United States and around the world.

In March 2006, the Antitrust Division expanded its domestic enforcement capabilities with passage of amendments to the USA Patriot Act that added antitrust violations to the list of predicate offenses eligible for wiretapping and other forms of electronic surveillance.[26] The change was spurred at least in part by concerns that the "inability to obtain wiretaps unquestionably severely handicaps the detection and prevention of [antitrust] conspiracies;" that the "secret nature" of cartels makes it harder to detect antitrust offenses than other types of fraudulent conduct; and that "[a] properly issued wiretap, therefore, is even more necessary to detect criminal antitrust conspiracies than other white collar offenses."[27] Attorneys conducting internal investigations must therefore counsel their clients that the government may be relying upon electronic surveillance to monitor the activities of employees and their contacts with competitors. As part of the investigation, counsel must, now more than ever before, take steps to understand the scope and context of such communications in order to properly advise their clients on both the risks of criminal liability and the merits of self-reporting to the government.[28]

It seems clear that the existence of the wiretapping capability will provide the Antitrust Division with access to stronger, more conclusive evidence of ongoing cartel activities. This, in turn, could impact the ability of companies to qualify for amnesty under the Antitrust Division's alternative amnesty policy after an investigation has already started. As discussed below, in order to qualify for alternative amnesty after an investigation has commenced, a corporation must come forward before the Antitrust Division has collected evidence likely to result in a sustainable conviction.[29] With the availability of nonconsensual wiretapping, companies interested in amnesty need to consider

---

26. USA Patriot Improvement and Reauthorization Act of 2005, Pub. L. No. 109-177 § 113 (2006) (amending 18 U.S.C. § 2516(1)).

27. 250 Cong. Rec. S11850 (daily ed. Oct 25, 2005) (statement of Sen. Kohl).

28. *See* Mark A. Racanelli, *Bugs in the Boardroom? Congress Is Poised to Allow Wiretapping in Federal Antitrust Investigations,* THE ANTITRUST SOURCE (January 2006), *available at* http://www.abanet.org/antitrust/at-source/06/01/Jan06-Racanelli1=26f.pdf (providing an overview of factors that counsel should consider).

29. *See* Section III.C.i.

the possibility that the Antitrust Division may now be able to access the information it needs without the assistance of an amnesty applicant. This possibility puts even greater pressure on companies to decide quickly whether to come forward. Similarly, the wiretapping statute may make it even more difficult for companies that come in after the amnesty applicant to strike advantageous plea deals. Whereas in the past, there could be substantial benefits to being the company that is second-in to cooperate with the Antitrust Division, wiretapping may make it less likely that the second-in company will be able to provide new information that would assist it in obtaining a favorable plea deal.

Clients operating outside the United States should also be made aware that the Antitrust Division's arsenal of investigative tools includes several means for tracking down foreign nationals for prosecution. In addition to enhanced cooperation and coordination with foreign authorities,[30] these tools include border watches in the United States, and detention when foreign witnesses and defendants travel to the United States.[31] The Antitrust Division has also touted its success in apprehending fugitive defendants by placing them on INTERPOL's Red Notice list, which operates as an international "wanted"

---

30. Hammond, An Update on the Antitrust Division's Criminal Enforcement Program, at 4-7, Remarks Before the American Bar Association's Section of Antitrust Law Fall Forum, Cartel Enforcement Roundtable (Nov. 16, 2005), *available at* http://www.usdoj.gov/atr/public/speeches/213247.htm. The U.S. has developed several tools for increased international cooperation in antitrust investigations. For example, the U.S. has entered into antitrust cooperation agreements with several foreign governments (Australia; Brazil; Canada; EU; Germany; Israel; Japan; and Mexico). *Id.* These agreements promote enhanced cooperation with these governments in all aspects of antitrust enforcement, including international cartel investigations. In addition, the U.S. has entered into Mutual Legal Assistance Treaties (MLATs), which are designed to foster cooperation between foreign governments on criminal investigations. *Id.* In 2001, the U.S. and the U.K. removed a limitation on the existing MLAT, opening the door for cooperation between the two governments on antitrust matters, which had previously been excluded. The U.S. has also International Antitrust Enforcement Assistance Agreement between Australia and the U.S. (1999). The Agreement is a "comprehensive mutual legal assistance agreement," which permits Australia and the U.S. to exchange evidence and to assist each other in investigations. *Id.* at 6. Finally, in 2005, the Organization for Economic Development's (OECD) Competition Law and Policy Committee adopted *Best Practices for the Formal Exchange of Information Between Competition Authorities in Hard Core Cartel Investigations, available at* http://www.oecd.org/dataoecd/1/33/35590548.pdf, detailing recommended strategies for member countries to consider implementing pertaining to information sharing in cartel matters.

31. Hammond, Charting New Waters in International Cartel Prosecutions, at 7-8, Speech Before the Twentieth Annual National Institute on White Collar Crime (Mar. 2, 2006), *available at* http://www.usdoj.gov/atr/public/speeches/214861.htm.

list and serves as an arrest request in many of INTERPOL's member nations.[32] In addition, the Antitrust Division has recently stepped up efforts to use extradition as a tool to force foreign nationals to face U.S. prosecution.[33]

C. Amnesty Under the Corporate Leniency Policy

Perhaps the most unique enforcement tool at the Antitrust Division's disposal is its Corporate Leniency Policy (Leniency Policy),[34] under which companies can qualify for complete amnesty from prosecution by being the first to self-report and to cooperate with the Antitrust Division in its investigation into criminal antitrust violations. In a nutshell, the benefit of participating in the amnesty program is that both the company and its employees can qualify for immunity from prosecution, thereby eliminating the possibility of facing the significant criminal fines and penalties discussed above.[35]

1. Overview of the Policy

The Antitrust Division has repeatedly stressed that the benefits and protections of amnesty are only available to the first company to come forward and qualify.[36] This dynamic creates a time-pressured atmosphere for counsel and clients. Since a company must terminate its participation in the unlawful activities in order to qualify for amnesty, other cartel participants

---

32. *See, e.g., id.,* at 9; Hammond, An Update on the Antitrust Division's Criminal Enforcement Program, at 3-4; Hammond, An Overview of Recent Developments in the Antitrust Division's Criminal Enforcement Program, at 3, Remarks Before the American Bar Association Midwinter Leadership Meeting (Jan. 10, 2005), *available at* http://www.usdoj.gov/atr/public/speeches/207226.htm.

33. The Antitrust Division moved in 2004 to extradite Ian Norris, an indicted British national, to the United States to face criminal charges in connection with its investigation into price-fixing in the carbon products industry. In June 2005, a British magistrate court ruled in favor of extradition, and the United Kingdom's Home Secretary ordered extradition in September 2005. Hammond, Charting New Waters, at 10-12. Mr. Norris's appeal was rejected by the British High Court in January 2007, and he is seeking further consideration before the House of Lords. Nikki Tait, *Price-Fixing Case "of General Importance,"* FINANCIAL TIMES, at 4 (Mar. 14, 2007).

34. United States Department of Justice, Antitrust Division, Corporate Leniency Policy (Aug. 10, 1993) (hereinafter "Leniency Policy"), *available at* http://www.usdoj.gov/atr/public/guidelines/0091.htm.

35. Amnesty applicants may also be eligible for protections in damages actions brought by civil plaintiffs. *See* Section IV.C., *supra.*

36. *See, e.g.,* Hammond, An Update on the Antitrust Division's Criminal Enforcement Program, at 10.

may become suspicious when one of their co-conspirators ceases communication—thus triggering a wave of potential interest in getting to the government first. Delay of just a few days (or even hours) could mean the difference between receiving amnesty or facing the severe penalties associated with a cartel prosecution.[37] This dynamic often puts companies in the position of having to make the decision whether to seek amnesty *before* they have completed their internal investigation. This highlights the importance of structuring the investigation so as to best uncover potential anticompetitive conduct early on in the investigation. Waiting until the investigation has substantially progressed before interviewing the key executives with control over pricing and production decisions is simply not an option once the amnesty stopwatch is running.

The Antitrust Division first introduced the Leniency Policy in 1978, and revised it in 1993 to include three key incentives. First, amnesty will be granted automatically if there is no pre-existing investigation at the time of the application. This means that a company that discovers, investigates, and is the first to self-report violations to the Antitrust Division *before* the Division has instigated an investigation is eligible for amnesty with no questions asked. To qualify, the corporate applicant must still satisfy certain prerequisites:

1. "At the time the corporation comes forward to report the illegal activity, the Division has not received information about the illegal activity being reported from any other source;
2. The corporation, upon its discovery of the illegal activity being reported, took prompt and effective action to terminate its part in the activity;
3. The corporation reports the wrongdoing with candor and completeness and provides full, continuing and complete cooperation to the Division throughout the investigation;
4. The confession of wrongdoing is truly a corporate act, as opposed to isolated confessions of individual executives or officials;
5. Where possible, the corporation makes restitution to injured parties; and
6. The corporation did not coerce another party to participate in the illegal activity and clearly was not the leader in, or originator of, the activity."[38]

---

37. *Id.*
38. *Id.*, Part A.

Second, if a corporation is unable to satisfy the foregoing requirements, or the Antitrust Division already has an investigation underway when the corporation decides to come forward and cooperate, amnesty may still be available under the alternative amnesty provisions introduced as part of the 1993 revisions. To qualify for alternative amnesty, a corporation must satisfy the following conditions:

1. "The corporation is the first one to come forward and qualify for leniency with respect to the illegal activity being reported;
2. The Division, at the time the corporation comes in, does not yet have evidence against the company that is likely to result in a sustainable conviction;
3. The corporation, upon its discovery of the illegal activity being reported, took prompt and effective action to terminate its part in the activity;
4. The corporation reports the wrongdoing with candor and completeness and provides full, continuing and complete cooperation that advances the Division in its investigation;
5. The confession of wrongdoing is truly a corporate act, as opposed to isolated confessions of individual executives or officials;
6. Where possible, the corporation makes restitution to injured parties; and
7. The Division determines that granting leniency would not be unfair to others, considering the nature of the illegal activity, the confessing corporation's role in it, and when the corporation comes forward."[39]

The Leniency Policy provides that, when applying this last condition, the two primary considerations will be: first, how early in the course of the investigation the corporation comes forward to self-report and, second, what role the corporation played in the conspiracy. As to the first, a corporation will face a lower burden at the inception of an investigation than it will if it does not come forward until after the Antitrust Division has amassed substantial evidence that could likely support a sustainable conviction. As to the second, the Antitrust Division will consider whether the corporation "coerced another party to participate in the illegal activity or clearly was the leader in, or originator of, the activity."[40]

---

39. *Id.,* Part B.
40. *Id.*

The third key incentive included in the 1993 revisions to the Leniency Policy is that, under automatic amnesty, cooperating officers, directors, and employees of the corporation who admit their wrongdoing as part of the corporation's confession will also automatically be covered under the corporation's application and will receive immunity from prosecution, so long as they "admit their wrongdoing with candor and completeness and continue to assist the Division throughout the investigation."[41]

The changes included in the 1993 revisions were designed to limit prosecutorial discretion, increase the transparency of the program, and provide applicants with more predictability about the outcome of their application.[42] Along with a series of clarifications that the Antitrust Division has issued about the policy in the years since the revisions were introduced, these changes contributed to a surge in interest in the program; applications increased from approximately one per year between 1978 and 1993 to two per month since the 1993 revisions.[43]

2. Placing a Marker

Timing is everything during the race for amnesty. One option that may be available to a company that is interested in applying for amnesty is to "place a marker" with the Antitrust Division to hold its place in line while it completes its internal investigation. Typically, prosecutors will give a potential applicant a certain period of time within which it must complete its investigation and report back with the findings. If it does so and satisfies the requisite criteria, the corporation will receive amnesty. If it does not complete its investigation in time—or is unable to muster sufficient evidence to satisfy the

---

41. *Id.,* Part C. If a corporation does not qualify for automatic amnesty, employees, officers, and directors who come forward with the corporation will be considered for immunity from criminal prosecution on the same basis as if they had approached the Division individually. *Id. See also* United States Department of Justice, Antitrust Division, Individual Leniency Policy (Aug. 10, 1994), *available at* http://www.usdoj.gov/atr/public/guidelines/0092.htm.

42. *See* Pate, International Anti-Cartel Enforcement, at 6. Presented to the 2004 ICN Cartels Workshop (Nov. 21, 2004), *available at* http://www.usdoj.gov/atr/public/speeches/206428.htm. In contrast, under the previous incarnation of the program, there was no written policy, there was no automatic qualification criteria, and amnesty was completely unavailable once the Antitrust Division had begun its investigation.

43. *Id. See also* Spratling, et al., *Making the Decision,* at 49-53. Counsel seeking additional information about the Leniency Policy and its application are encouraged to visit the Criminal Enforcement section of the Antitrust Division's website, http://www.usdoj.gov/atr/public/criminal.htm.

conditions for amnesty—the corporation loses its place and the amnesty opportunity shifts to the next company waiting in line to apply. While placing a marker does not entirely relieve the company of the time pressure, it can provide a little breathing room to fully assess the situation before perfecting the application.[44]

3. Cooperation Obligations Under the Amnesty Program

Acceptance into the amnesty program carries with it substantial obligations that every corporation should fully consider before making its application. As noted above, the Antitrust Division expects that amnesty applicants will, where possible, make restitution for the wrongful activity. In addition, the cooperation obligations under the Leniency Policy should not be taken lightly. Counsel should stress that cooperation is not a one-shot deal, but rather an ongoing commitment that will last for the duration of the government's investigation and any ensuing prosecutions. Not only will the company be expected to provide the government with copies of documentation relating to the cartel activities and related conduct, it will need to make key employees, directors, and officers available for in-depth interviews by the prosecuting attorneys. Often there will be follow-up requests for additional information and interviews as the investigation progresses. In addition, if the government's case against other participants moves forward, it is likely that certain employees will be required to testify before the grand jury and ultimately at trial. From a legal perspective, the company can expect to expend considerable resources piecing together the many pieces of evidence within the company that relate to the conduct, including phone records, documents, and employee interviews, all with an eye to compiling a coherent explanation for the government. From a business perspective, the company will want to factor in the costs associated with these efforts and the related distractions from company business. The assessment of whether a company is willing to undertake these obligations must, of course, be weighed against the costs associated with defending—and potentially losing—a government prosecution for the conduct in question.

The Leniency Policy expressly states that key elements of cooperation include full disclosure *and* the complete cessation of the unlawful conduct.[45]

---

44. Hammond, When Calculating the Costs and Benefits of Applying for Corporate Amnesty, How Do You Put a Price Tag on an Individual's Freedom, at 3-4. Presented to the Fifteenth Annual National Institute on White Collar Crime (Mar. 8, 2001), *available at* http://www.usdoj.gov/atr/public/speeches/7647.pdf.

45. *See* Leniency Policy, Parts A and B. *See also* Spratling, Answers to Recurring Questions, at 6-8 (clarifying what is required to effectively terminate the activity).

A grant of amnesty is conditional until the Division determines that the conditions for amnesty have been satisfied.[46] In one notable example, the Antitrust Division recently sought to revoke a conditional grant of amnesty, based on concerns that the applicant, Stolt-Nielsen, did not terminate its involvement in the conspiracy at the time that it said it had and that the applicant failed to fully disclose material information about its ongoing participation in the conspiracy. When applying for amnesty, Stolt-Nielsen represented to the government that it took prompt and effective action to terminate its part in the anticompetitive activity being reported to the government.[47] The DOJ warned Stolt-Nielsen that it would not be accepted into the amnesty program if the company had only pretended to withdraw from the conspiracy.[48]

Stolt-Nielsen cooperated with government investigators for several months under the amnesty program. Eventually, however, the government concluded that Stolt-Nielsen failed to disclose that it had not ceased participating in the conspiracy at the time it asserted that it had implemented its early remedial measures. Based on this conclusion, the government informed Stolt-Nielsen that its amnesty would be revoked. Stolt-Nielsen then applied to federal court for an injunction to enjoin its indictment, which the court granted, focusing on the fact that the government had enjoyed the benefit of its bargain with Stolt-Nielsen.[49] On appeal, without discussing the merits, the Third Circuit held that except in certain limited contexts not present in the *Stolt-Nielsen* case (e.g., First Amendment violations), federal courts do not have authority to enjoin the executive branch from filing an indictment.[50] Following the Third Circuit's decision, the district court dissolved the injunction, and, in September 2006, the Antitrust Division obtained indictments against Stolt-Nielsen

---

46. *See.* Spratling, Making Companies an Offer, at 20-21 (attaching copy of Model Amnesty Letter).

47. Specifically, the company pointed to internal controls and an antitrust policy adopted at the time it discovered the conspiracy as evidence of its remedial measures. Stolt-Nielsen, S.A. v. United States, 352 F. Supp. 2d 553, 557-58 (E.D. Pa. 2005), *rev'd,*. 442 F.3d 177 (3d Cir. 2006).

48. The government learned of Stolt-Nielsen's potential violation by allegations contained in a lawsuit filed by its former general counsel, the details of which were published in the *Wall Street Journal.* Stolt-Nielsen, 352 F. Supp. 2d at 557; *see also* J. Bandler & J. McKinnon, *Stolt-Nielsen Is Probed for Traffic with Iran,* WALL ST.. J., Nov. 22, 2002, at A3.

49. Stolt-Nielsen, 352 F. Supp. 2d at 561-62.

50. Stolt-Nielsen, S.A. v. United States, 442 F.3d 177, 181-82 (3d Cir. 2006), *petition for cert. filed,* 75 USLW 3035 (U.S. Jul 20, 2006) (NO. 06-97). The Third Circuit also indicated that Stolt-Nielsen may be able to assert its leniency agreement in a pre-trial motion as an affirmative defense to conviction.

and certain of its subsidiaries and key executives.[51] The case stands as a stark reminder that applicants must take the amnesty agreement's cooperation requirements seriously and must take decisive steps to ensure that employees terminate any and all unlawful conduct.[52]

4. Amnesty Plus and Penalty Plus

Any corporation that seeks protection under the Leniency Policy must also be aware of the Division's "Amnesty Plus" and "Penalty Plus" policies. Under the Amnesty Plus policy, a corporation that is under investigation for cartel activities in one market, but does not qualify for amnesty in that market, may qualify for a fine reduction if it discloses cartel activity in another market. In addition to the fine reduction relating to the first investigation, the company may also be eligible for amnesty in that second market. This policy is designed to provide investigated companies with an incentive to fully disclose any and all antitrust violations.[53]

The corollary to the Amnesty Plus program is the Antitrust Division's "Penalty Plus" policy, under which the Antitrust Division will seek to impose tougher sentencing penalties against a company that has knowledge of a second offense and decides not to report it. If the Antitrust Division subsequently discovers and prosecutes the company for its participation in the second offense, the Division will ask the sentencing court to consider the failure to voluntarily report the violation as an aggravating factor at sentencing.[54] In addition, the Division will seek fines and sentencing at the upper end of the range permitted under the Sentencing Guidelines and may seek harsher sentencing based on prior criminal history.[55]

These two policies operate together to provide an inducement for companies to come forward and report the full scope of unlawful conduct, while simultaneously increasing the risk that the company will face severe consequences for not doing so. For the antitrust counselor, they heighten the need to conduct a thorough internal investigation, so that the client may make an

---

51. United States Department of Justice, News Release: Stolt-Nielsen S.A. Indicted on Customer Allocation, Price Fixing, and Bid Rigging Charges for Its Role in an International Parcel Tanker Shipping Cartel (Sep. 6, 2006), *available at* http://www.usdoj.gov/atr/public/press_releases/2006/218199.pdf.

52. *See* Jim Walden and Christopher Dawes, *The Curious Case of Stolt-Nielsen SA v. United States,* THE ANTITRUST SOURCE. 1, 8-11 (Mar. 2005), *available at* http://www.abanet.org/antitrust/at-source/05/03/02-mar05-walddawe323.pdf.

53. *See* Spratling, Making Companies an Offer, at 7-8.

54. *See* Hammond, When Calculating the Costs, at 6.

55. *Id.*

informed decision whether to go forward and, if so, what information to report.

5. Confidentiality Considerations

The Antitrust Division's stated policy is to maintain the confidentiality of the amnesty applicant and the information that it obtains from the applicant. Under this policy, the Antitrust Division will not release the identity of the applicant either publicly or to foreign enforcement authorities unless (1) ordered to do so by a court or (2) given permission to do so by the applicant.[56] Counsel should advise clients, however, that in international cartel investigations, the Antitrust Division may request a waiver to share the amnesty applicant's information with antitrust enforcement officials in other jurisdictions.[57] This highlights the importance of coordinating the company's investigative and defense strategies in investigations that implicate multiple jurisdictions. Although the Antitrust Division will not reveal the identity of the amnesty applicant, it will typically let other companies under investigation know whether amnesty is still available, which can be important information for a company determining whether to cooperate with the government's investigation.

D. *Value of Cooperation When Amnesty Is Not Available*

Once the Antitrust Division has the benefit of a cooperating amnesty applicant, the risks of prosecution for other participants in the cartel activity significantly increase. With the emphasis that prosecutors place on the benefits of being the first company to come forward and qualify for protection under the Corporate Leniency Program, companies and their counsel may ask whether it makes sense to self-report the findings of an internal investigation when amnesty is no longer available. Unlike the amnesty recipient, there are no guarantees as to the type of treatment that a company will receive for being "second in the door."[58] Instead, the Antitrust Division has indicated that the rewards for being second-in will vary depending on the circumstances of a particular case, considering a variety of factors, such as:

- Whether the information will significantly advance the Antitrust Division's investigation or is merely cumulative of information already collected in the investigation;

---

56. Hammond, An Overview of Recent Developments, at 11.
57. *Id.*
58. Hammond, Measuring the Value of Second-In Cooperation in Corporate Plea Negotiations, Remarks before the 54th Annual Bar Association, Section of Antitrust Law, Spring Meeting (Mar. 29, 2006), *available at* http://www.usdoj.gov/atr/public/speeches/215514.htm.

- Whether the company comes forward early on in the investigation, or only after the Antitrust Division has developed evidence through its work with the amnesty applicant and other investigative strategies;
- Whether the company comes forward voluntarily or only after the Division has notified it that it is a target or that indictment is likely; and
- Whether the company can provide information about other anticompetitive behavior under the Amnesty Plus program.[59]

While treatment will vary on a case-by-case basis, the Antitrust Division has enumerated several potential benefits that companies should consider when determining whether to cooperate with the Division when amnesty is no longer available.[60] These can include (1) a "cooperation discount" or downward departure in the recommended sentencing fine, often ranging from 30 to 35 percent off the bottom of the Guidelines range; (2) a reduction in the scope of commerce used to calculate sentencing fines, if the company provides information revealing that the conspiracy was broader than the Antitrust Division had suspected; (3) eligibility for a low starting point under the Sentencing Guidelines for application of the cooperation discount, unless the company played a significant leadership role in the conspiracy or failed to report pursuant to the Division's Penalty Plus program; (4) enhanced ability to obtain favorable treatment for culpable executives (although the company should still expect that its most senior culpable executives will be carved out for individual prosecution); and (5) potential amnesty qualification for other cartel offenses that it reports.[61]

E. *Assessing Whether Individual Employees Need Separate Counsel*

As with any internal investigation, attorneys conducting antitrust investigations need to consider whether there are any employees who need separate counsel and cannot properly be represented by company counsel. Often in antitrust investigations, the company has a heightened interest in maintaining alignment with executives who may have participated in culpable activities. They are typically in the best position to help the company develop evidence it needs to create its amnesty application (which, under Part A of the Leniency

---

59. *Id.* at 2.
60. *Id.* at 3-11.
61. *Id.*

Policy, can potentially cover the executives as well) or to qualify for substantial assistance in plea negotiations. Depending on the circumstances, the company's counsel may be able to negotiate protections for culpable executives as part of its corporate plea discussions. If an executive is willing to cooperate in the company's internal investigation and, if necessary, concede wrongdoing, it can be beneficial for company counsel and the individual's counsel to collaborate in their investigation and defense strategies.

F. *Making a Proffer and Preparing for Interviews and Testimony*

If the corporation decides to cooperate with the Antitrust Division, it will typically present evidence through a hypothetical proffer, followed by more detailed follow-up discussions and, eventually, interviews of relevant employees. As noted above, this information will typically be supplemented with documentary evidence. Ultimately, the company can expect that employees may be called to testify before the grand jury or at trial as part of the government's prosecution.

Developing the Proffer. A proffer essentially allows companies to give the Antitrust Division a preview of the type of information they can provide. It gives the Antitrust Division an opportunity to assess the value of the information so that the terms of cooperation can be worked out before the company actually brings its employees forward for interviews. For that reason, the proffer is typically couched as a hypothetical description of the information that relevant employees will be able to provide the Antitrust Division, with an emphasis on the type of conduct involved, the scope of the conspiracy, the nature of the competitor contacts, the frequency of meetings, and the impact on the competitive process. Because of the uncertainty of the process, the proffer will not disclose the identities of the participants until sufficient assurances by the Division. The proffer process is typically a give and take between counsel and the Antitrust Division—after counsel's initial description of the conduct, the Antitrust Division will often ask for more detailed follow up on certain points, sometimes revealing information that it has collected through other avenues of investigation. The goal of the proffer process is to provide the Antitrust Division with a window into the type of information that the company can provide.

Interviews and Testimony. If the corporation is cooperating with the government's investigation, it is likely that employees will be made available—often multiple times—for interviews with Division attorneys. It is crucial that counsel for the company or for the witness arrange for the necessary witness protections before presenting the witness for an interview or testimony. In some cases, the Antitrust Division will enter into what is commonly referred to as a "Queen for a Day" agreement, pursuant to which a witness provides information and documents in exchange for the government's agreement not to make direct or indirect use of the information against the witness in the related antitrust investigation. In other instances, the Antitrust Division will seek to conduct the interview subject to a cooperation and nonprosecution agreement, which provides similar protections, subject to revocation if the witness does not comply with the cooperation obligations set forth by the government.

Counsel should also be aware of and prepare the witness for what the Antitrust Division terms its "Omnibus Question." This refers to whether the witness has knowledge not just about price-fixing in the industry or the product under investigation, but any information about cartel activity in other markets as well.[62]

IV. RELATED LITIGATION

Private litigation invariably trails government cartel prosecutions. In the U.S., this can often be more time-consuming, costly, and burdensome than the initial criminal matter. The U.S. antitrust laws permit private antitrust plaintiffs to sue for treble damages and injunctive relief.[63] In addition, antitrust defendants are subject to joint and several liability in private civil litigation. Courts often allow plaintiffs to seek extensive discovery, permitting access to documents and materials outside the relevant limitations period if the requested materials are relevant to the pattern and effects of the alleged conspiracy. Typically, these cases can take several years to resolve, continuing long after the original criminal investigation has concluded.

A. *Types of Civil Actions*

There are several categories of potential plaintiffs in private antitrust actions. The federal antitrust laws generally limit the right to sue to "direct purchasers" and, except in a few limited circumstances, do not allow indirect purchasers to sue for damages that have been "passed on" to them by direct purchasers.[64] Indirect purchaser plaintiffs allege damages on the

---

62. Hammond, Cornerstones of an Effective Leniency Program, at 16. Presented Before the ICN Workshop on Leniency Programs (Nov. 22-23, 2004), *available at* http://www.usdoj.gov/atr/public/speeches/206611.htm.
63. Clayton Act, § 4, 15 U.S.C. § 15; Clayton Act, § 16, 15 U.S.C. § 26.
64. *See, e.g.,* Illinois Brick Co. v. Illinois, 431 U.S. 720 (1977).

grounds that all or part of a defendant's unlawful overcharge for a product was passed on to them. While indirect purchasers are typically barred from filing federal court actions under the Supreme Court's decision in *Illinois Brick*,[65] courts have recognized limited exceptions, such as suits for federal injunctive relief and cases involving pre-existing cost-plus contracts.[66] Despite the federal bar, numerous states allow some form of indirect purchaser actions.[67] Finally, because many direct and indirect purchaser actions are filed as class action lawsuits, counsel should prepare the client for negotiations with plaintiffs that opt-out of these actions.

Foreign purchasers often seek recourse under the U.S. antitrust laws. Under the Foreign Trade and Antitrust Improvements Act of 1982,[68] foreign purchasers must show that the conduct had an effect on domestic commerce, and that the effect on competition in the United States in fact gave rise to their particular claims. The Supreme Court addressed the reach of the FTAIA in *F. Hoffman-La Roche, Ltd. v. Empagran S.A.*,[69] in which it held that the antitrust laws do not permit claims based on foreign harm if the domestic effects were independent of and did not help bring about the foreign injury. However, the precise contours of the FTAIA continue to be litigated.[70]

B. *Parallel Litigation Concerns*

The potential risks of parallel civil litigation and enforcement actions are myriad. Counsel must structure and conduct the initial internal investigation with an eye to how each investigative step impacts not only the Antitrust Division's investigation, but also these other potential actions. As noted above, the decision whether to seek amnesty in the U.S. must also factor in whether to seek leniency in other jurisdictions. When making information proffers and document productions to the U.S. government (or other enforcement authorities), counsel must consider potential discoverability issues related to

---

65. *Id.*

66. *See, e.g.,* Kansas v. UtiliCorp United, Inc., 497 U.S. 199, 204, 217 (1990) (addressing cost-plus contracts) *and* Dickson v. Microsoft Corp., 309 F.3d 193, 214 n.24 (4th Cir. 2002) (holding that "*Illinois Brick*'s indirect purchaser rule, when applicable, bars only compensatory damages and does not apply to injunctive relief.").

67. *See* Kevin J. O'Connor, *Is the* Illinois Brick *Wall Crumbling?*, 15 ANTITRUST 34, 34 (2001), for a discussion of state indirect purchaser laws. While state indirect purchaser cases have historically been litigated predominantly in state court, the Class Action Fairness Act of 2005 has important ramifications for federal court removal. Pub. L. 109-2, 119 Stat. 4 (2005).

68. 15 U.S.C. § 6a.

69. 542 U.S. 155 (2004).

70. *See, e.g.,* Empagran S.A. v. F. Hoffman-LaRoche, Ltd., 417 F.3d 1267 (D.C. Cir. 2005); United States v. LSL Biotechnologies, 379 F.3d 672 (9th Cir. 2004).

the follow-on civil litigation. Likewise, if private civil litigation proceeds to discovery while the government's criminal action is still pending, counsel will need to consider whether there are risks associated with witnesses providing testimony in civil matters.

C. Benefits in Private Litigation from Amnesty Participation

In addition to the benefits of participation in the amnesty program discussed above, the Antitrust Criminal Penalty Enhancement and Reform Act of 2004 (ACPERA) places limits on the damages that private plaintiffs can recover from amnesty applicants in civil litigation.[71] ACPERA limits the amount of damages recoverable from an amnesty participant to actual damages thereby potentially eliminating the risk of treble damages and joint and several liability in private U.S. litigation. To qualify for this limitation on recovery, however, the amnesty applicant must provide "satisfactory cooperation" to the private plaintiff, which the statute defines to include providing a "full account" of all known facts potentially relevant to the civil action, furnishing all potentially relevant documents, and making employees available for interviews, depositions, and testimony in the civil litigation.[72] The court in which the civil case is pending will determine whether the amnesty applicant has satisfied the cooperation requirements and is entitled to the benefit of ACPERA's limitations on civil recovery.

V. CONCLUSION

Conducting an antitrust internal investigation presents unique challenges for both counsel and client. The Antitrust Division's Corporate Leniency Policy provides companies with an opportunity not found in other types of white-collar investigations to reap immeasurable benefits—in the form of a free pass from prosecution—for conducting a prompt and thorough investigation targeted at uncovering problematic conduct. While these rewards can be great, the penalty for not moving fast enough stands in stark comparison, amply illustrated by the enhanced criminal sanctions currently available to the Antitrust Division. The stakes involved in antitrust prosecutions highlight the importance of counsel's role in crafting and implementing a successful investigative strategy.

---

71. Pub. L. No. 108-237, § 213, 118 Stat. 661, 666-67 (Jun. 22, 2004) (codified at 15 U.S.C. § 1-3).
72. *Id.* at § 213(b).

SOX It to Me: Internal Investigations in a Sarbanes-Oxley World

16

Gregory J. Weingart & J. Martin Willhite

I. INTRODUCTION   492
II. BACKGROUND OF THE ACT   493
III. THE ACT'S IMPLICATIONS FOR INTERNAL CORPORATE INVESTIGATIONS   496
   A. Provisions of the Act Contributing to the Increase of Investigations   496
   B. Preliminary Considerations at the Commencement of the Investigation   499
   C. Dealing with the Company's Outside Auditors   505
   D. Disclosure to the Market   509
   E. Remedial Steps   510
IV. CONCLUSION   511

Gregory J. Weingart and J. Martin Willhite are partners at Munger, Tolles & Olson LLP in Los Angeles, California.

I. INTRODUCTION

When the Sarbanes-Oxley Act of 2002[1] was signed into law on July 30, 2002, the United States had just suffered a flood of colossal corporate governance failures in the form of Enron, WorldCom, Tyco International, Adelphia Communications, and others. President Bush's remarks on that occasion, bristling with fury and a rhetoric of raised expectations and swift justice, announced a new American corporate morality:

> This law says to every dishonest corporate leader: you will be exposed and punished; the era of low standards and false profits is over; no boardroom in America is above or beyond the law.[2]

The Sarbanes-Oxley Act (the Act) itself represented federal preemption of areas that had traditionally been left to the several states, self-regulatory organizations, and industry best practices or standards. To date, the Act has spawned vast quantities of legal commentary and a corresponding amount of anxiety in public company executive suites and boardrooms. The Act has also had a significant and far-reaching impact on the conduct of corporations and those who serve as corporate gatekeepers such as auditors and lawyers, and regulators.

In fact, because internal corporate investigations occur at the point where the Act's provisions intersect with so-called "bad conduct," the Act has affected the investigative process in many important ways. It has institutionalized the use of internal corporate investigations to review and reform corporate conduct, and created mechanisms that encourage the frequency, the independence, and the breadth of those investigations. It has effectively conscripted attorneys and others involved in conducting investigations into agents for those outside the company, including government regulators and company auditors, in a way that presents complex issues ranging from ethics questions such as the duty of loyalty to preservation of attorney-client privilege. Finally, it has upped the ante on those accountable for ensuring the proper conduct of an internal investigation.

---

1. Sarbanes-Oxley Act of 2002, 116 Stat. 745 (2002).
2. *President Bush Signs Corporate Corruption Bill,* Transcript, July 30, 2002 (http://www.whitehouse.gov/news/releases/2002/07/20020730.html).

II. BACKGROUND OF THE ACT

Although readers doubtlessly are already familiar with the general structure of the Act, it is helpful to keep its general approach and goals in mind when assessing the Act's impact on internal investigations. Simply stated, the Act sought to restore investor confidence in America's financial markets through a series of specific reforms and new initiatives. Despite all of the rhetoric about cleaning up public company boardrooms, the Act did not impose any new burdens on boards of directors as a body or on individual directors. Instead, Congress focused on executive officers, auditors, audit committees, research analysts, attorneys, and the actual content of corporate disclosure for the Act's specific reforms. With regard to its effect on internal corporate investigations, the following major philosophical goals of the Act should be considered:

- improving the volume and quality of corporate disclosure;
- increasing management responsibility for such disclosures, and the imposition of penalties for the failure to do so;
- enhancing the independence of corporate audits;
- bolstering the authority and obligations of corporate gatekeepers; and
- strengthening the Securities and Exchange Commission (SEC).

Improving Corporate Disclosure: At its heart, the Act is a fundamental reworking of several aspects of the federal securities disclosure framework. The Act increases the mix of publicly available information about each issuer by expanding the matters covered by each issuer's periodic public reports required by the integrated disclosure system of the Securities Act of 1934,[3] while simultaneously introducing the concept of "real-time issuer disclo-

---

3. The Securities Exchange Act of 1934 advances a series of periodic reports pursuant to which issuers of publicly traded securities communicate important business and financial information to the investing public. Under certain circumstances, these periodic reports may be incorporated by reference into "short-form" registration statements under the Securities Act of 1933. Both the integrated disclosure system and the Sarbanes-Oxley Act depend upon the "efficient market" hypothesis that the market prices of publicly traded securities reflect the market's opinion of all publicly available information about the issuer, and that more and accurate information will result in better pricing. However, this hypothesis has been subjected to fierce academic skepticism in recent years, with evidence that financial markets often react disproportionately to news, especially bad news. *See,* Cornell, Bradford and Rutten, James, "Market Efficiency, Crashes and Securities Litigation" (December 2005) (http://ssrn.com/abstract=871106).

sures."[4] Specifically, the Act focuses on many perceived areas of abuse in the corporate fraud cases considered by Congress:

- off-balance sheet transactions (Section 401(a));
- non-GAAP financial measures (Section 401(b)); and
- reports of insider stock sales (Section 403(a)).

Increasing Management Responsibility/Penalties: The Act singles out chief executive officers (CEOs) and chief financial officers (CFOs) for special attention. CEOs and CFOs must certify the accuracy of their company's quarterly and annual periodic reports and must assure that appropriate systems of disclosure controls, and internal controls over financial reporting, exist to gather the information necessary for inclusion in those periodic reports.[5] Civil and criminal penalties await CEOs and CFOs who submit knowingly false certifications. For obvious self-preservation reasons, this senior officer certification requirement has produced elaborate certification rituals to make sure all "material" information flows from the bottom to the top of each public reporting company. The Act also strengthens the SEC's power to force wrongdoers to disgorge compensation in the event of a financial restatement.

Enhancing Auditor Independence: One of the most significant structural refinements of the Act was the creation of the first quasi-governmental body to regulate auditors and auditing standards: the Public Company Accounting Oversight Board (the PCAOB). All public accounting firms (whether foreign or domestic) who audit public reporting companies must register with the PCAOB. The PCAOB, in turn, is vested with the authority to establish all audit and other related standards, and investigate and impose sanctions on these public accounting firms, in every case subject to supervision by the SEC.

---

4. *See* Section 409 of the Act: Real Time Issuer Disclosures: "Each issuer reporting under Section 13(a) or 15(d) shall disclose to the public on a rapid and current basis such additional information concerning material changes in the financial condition or operations of the issuer, in plain English, which may include trend and qualitative information and graphical presentations, as the Commission determines, by rule, is necessary or useful for the protection of investors and the public interest." Sarbanes-Oxley Act § 409.

Section 409 led to much SEC rulemaking, including the increase of the categories of information reportable on Form 8-K and shortening the applicable filing deadline to four business days. *See* Final Rule: Additional Form 8-K Disclosure Requirements and Acceleration of Filing Date, 17 C.F.R. 228-230, 239-240, 249 (2004) Release Nos. 33-8400; 34-49424) (effective August 23, 2004) (http://www.sec.gov/rules/final/33-8400.htm). Also, although not mandated by the Act, but certainly in keeping with its philosophy, the SEC has required that a class of accelerated filers must file their Forms 10-K within sixty days after their fiscal year end (rather than the previous ninety days) and their forms 10-Q within thirty-five days after the relevant fiscal quarter end (rather than the previous forty-five days).

5. Sarbanes-Oxley Act §§ 302, 404, 906.

Beyond creation of the PCAOB, the Act redrew the relationship between auditors and their clients by forbidding the audit firms from providing so-called "non-audit" services "contemporaneously with the audit." The Act also prohibits the destruction of "audit or review papers" and makes criminal the improper influence of any audit or auditor.

Strengthening Authority and Duties of Corporate "Gatekeepers": The Act attempts to force improved compliance with the law by regulating the conduct of groups other than the board of directors itself. It expands the role of audit committees, taking away management's control over the audit process and placing it with the audit committee. The SEC's rules under Section 301 require that audit committee members be independent. They alone are responsible for the appointment, compensation, retention, and oversight of a company's outside auditor, and the auditor must report directly to the audit committee. The audit committee also has authority to establish the level of funding necessary to fulfill its duties, including, if necessary, the retention of independent counsel and other advisors.

Another of the Act's major concepts was Section 307, which instructed the SEC to establish minimum standards of professional conduct for lawyers who practice before the SEC, including rules requiring lawyers to report evidence of a "material violation" of securities laws or a breach of fiduciary duty to the company's chief legal officer or CEO. This actual reporting duty itself might not have been so important on its own, but the Act also directed the SEC to require the lawyer to report up to the audit committee or the full board if the lawyer is not satisfied that the chief legal officer or CEO has made an appropriate response to such evidence.

In January 2003, the SEC promulgated the lawyer conduct rules required by the Act,[6] as well as a very controversial set of proposed rules suggesting that if the lawyer is not ultimately satisfied with the company's response to his or her proffered evidence, then the lawyer must, in certain cases, make a "noisy withdrawal" of his or her representation of the client.[7] The "noisy withdrawal" rules have not been adopted so far, but Section 307 of the Act and the SEC's lawyer conduct rules have profoundly shifted how lawyers investigate and communicate possible corporate wrongdoing.

---

6. *See* Final Rule: Implementation of Standards of Professional Conduct for Attorneys, Release Nos. 33-8185; 34-47276 (effective August 5, 2003) 17 CFR Pt. 205 (2003) p. 126 (http://www.sec.gov/rules/final/33-8185.htm).

7. *See* Proposed Rule: Implementation of Standards of Professional Conduct for Attorneys, Release Nos. 33-8186; 34-47282 (August 5, 2003) (http://www.sec.gov/rules/proposed/33-8186.htm).

* * * * *

The Act, and the associated rule-making from the SEC has cast a widespread net across the entirety of corporate conduct, and began regulating it in new and more vigorous ways. By declaring certain categories of financial and operating information "material" *per se* and then requiring executive certification of company reports, the Act intentionally puts incredible pressure on the quality of each company's public disclosure process. Furthermore, by changing the obligations of audit committees, auditors, lawyers, and research analysts (e.g., people who have both the most to lose and the least to gain by countenancing any inappropriate corporate behavior), the Act effectively deputized these groups into the SEC's compliance function. These facts and circumstances have strongly impacted the carrying out of internal corporate investigations.

III. THE ACT'S IMPLICATIONS FOR INTERNAL CORPORATE INVESTIGATIONS

French writer/critic Jean-Baptiste Alphonse Karr wrote: "The more things change, the more they remain the same."[8] What was true in France 150 years ago is also largely true of the Act's influence on the internal corporate investigative process today. While the Act has changed certain points of emphasis, and raised the stakes for all involved, the basic issues that one must confront and think through when undertaking an internal investigation remain largely the same after the Act as they did before the Act. The Act's most direct impact on the investigative process has been threefold: (1) a sharp increase in the circumstances that will likely necessitate an internal corporate investigation, (2) a more complicated analysis relating to who should conduct the investigation and what its proper scope should be, and (3) an expansion of the various constituencies whom an investigation may need to satisfy.

A. *Provisions of the Act Contributing to the Increase of Investigations*

1. Whistleblower Provisions

The Act seeks to root out misconduct and force full and adequate disclosure of all material facts to the investing public. An obvious manifesta-

---

8. "Plus ça change, plus c'est la même chose." Alphonse Karr (1808–1890), French journalist, novelist. Les Guêpes (Paris, Jan. 31, 1849).

tion of the former focus appears in Section 301 of the Act (Public Company Audit Committees), which requires audit committees to establish procedures for:

> "(A) the receipt, retention, and treatment of complaints received by the issuer regarding accounting, internal accounting controls, or auditing matters;
> (B) the confidential, anonymous submission by employees of the issuer of concerns regarding questionable accounting or auditing matters."

This "whistleblower" provision forced issuers subject to the Act to review their internal procedures and their audit committee charters. Consequently, many companies implemented hotline systems (either telephonic or web-based) through which employees and others may anonymously communicate concerns about company behavior. To bolster the feeling of anonymity, some companies have completely outsourced their hotline function to third-party service providers who receive the hotline complaints and then communicate them on a "no-names" basis back to appropriate contacts at the company.

Merely collecting hotline data is insufficient to satisfy Section 301's mandate that each company's whistleblower procedures cover the "treatment" of complaints. Because audit committees typically do not have their own staff and administrative support, the process of receiving and reviewing hotline complaints has generally devolved to the company's internal audit group, inside or outside legal counsel, or some other appropriate party. Yet, the Act puts the ultimate responsibility for these whistleblower procedures with the audit committee, so well functioning audit committees should receive every complaint submitted (or at least a detailed summary of such) through the company's whistleblower system, and then review those complaints with company management, to then determine what steps, if any, are necessary or advisable to respond to the legitimate complaints. At some time, each audit committee will likely instigate an internal investigation in response to complaints received through its hotline process.

2. Executive Officer Code of Ethics Provisions

SEC rulemaking pursuant to Section 406 of the Act requires publicly traded companies to disclose whether they have adopted a code of ethics for their senior financial officers.[9] These rules, along with the scores of SEC

---

9. *See* Final Rule, Disclosure Required by Sections 406 and 407 of the Sarbanes-Oxley Act of 2002 (Release Nos. 33-8177; 34-47235) (http://www.sec.gov/rules/final/33-8177.htm) (http://www.sec.gov/rules/final/33-8177a.htm).

enforcement actions, are the SEC's attempt to improve the "tone at the top." Furthermore, the SEC requires that companies file an internal control report with their annual report outlining management's responsibilities for establishing and maintaining adequate internal controls as well as its conclusions about the effectiveness of those controls. The company's auditor must attest to management's evaluation. These codes of ethics properly raise the baseline of proper corporate behavior from mere compliance with the law to a higher standard. A corollary result, however, is that the variety of conduct allegedly at odds with these codes of ethics, and thus subject to investigation, has been expanded.

3. Executive Officer Certifications

The Act's provisions requiring that the company's CEO and CFO certify both the accuracy of financial statements and the adequacy of internal controls also helps to compel internal investigations. Before the CEO and CFO make the required certifications of their company's periodic reports, it has become commonplace for elaborate internal certification processes to occur. During these processes, successive layers of employees certify the accuracy of their respective inputs to the public and financial reporting regimes to their superiors to guarantee either that all "material" information flows from the bottom to the top or that there is an unbroken chain of deniability. However, if an employee is unable or unwilling to certify unconditionally with respect to their respective reporting area, or if allegations of wrongdoing are made that in any way might impact these certifications, alarm bells go off, as they should. The company then needs to verify the legitimacy of those allegations quickly—before its next quarterly filing containing the Act's required certifications.

4. Chief Legal Officer Requirements

As noted above, Section 307 of the Act requires the company's chief legal officer to investigate evidence of material violations that are reported up to him by in-house or outside counsel. Because the duties owed by each of these reporting counsel are only discharged once the chief legal officer (CLO) makes an "appropriate response," the type and quality of the CLO's response will be under close scrutiny. The practical impact of the Act is that any non-facially ridiculous report of a potentially material violation requires some type of internal investigatory process to satisfy the demands of the reporting counsel and to provide needed solace to the CLO.

5. SEC and DOJ Requirements

Around the same time as the adoption of the Act, the SEC and the United States Department of Justice (DOJ) both adopted policy memos setting forth their guidelines for weighing whether and how to prosecute corporate misconduct. In its October 2001 Section 21(a) report in the Seaboard matter, the SEC explained that a prompt and thorough internal investigation is a key factor in assessing whether it will bring regulatory action against a company.[10] Similarly, DOJ guidelines for prosecuting corporate entities issued in a January 2003 internal memorandum (known as the Thompson Memo) also stressed the importance of an effective internal investigation in determining whether a company should face criminal charges.[11] Later revisions to the principles governing federal prosecution of business organizations continue to state that a factor in whether to charge a corporation is the value of its cooperation, and that "the Department, in conjunction with regulatory agencies and other executive branch departments, encourages corporations, as part of their compliance programs, to conduct internal investigations and disclose their findings to the appropriate authorities."[12]

B. *Preliminary Considerations at the Commencement of the Investigation*

When presented with a reported material violation or an allegation of wrongdoing, a public company's chief legal officer and/or audit committee

---

10. *See* Report of Investigation Pursuant to Section 21(a) of the Securities Exchange Act of 1934 and Commission Statement on the Relationship of Cooperation to Agency Enforcement Decisions; Securities and Exchange Lit. Release No. 4496, Accounting and Auditing Enforcement Release No. 1470 (Oct. 23, 2001). The SEC recently released guidance regarding penalties that should be imposed against corporate wrongdoers, and noted that one factor is whether the corporation promptly self-reports securities laws violations and cooperates with the investigation and remediation. Statement of the SEC Concerning Financial Penalties, Release 2006-4. This recent statement, however, does not provide any guidance on the factors considered by the SEC in determining whether a corporation cooperated with an investigation.

11. In this regard, the Thompson Memo reiterated the position of DOJ set forth in a June 16, 1999, memorandum from Deputy Attorney General Eric Holder setting forth what factors federal prosecutors should consider in deciding whether to bring criminal charges against a corporation. The Holder Memorandum made clear that one important factor is the timely, complete, and voluntary disclosure of wrongdoing, and the memo encouraged corporations "to conduct internal investigations and to disclose their findings to appropriate authorities."

12. Memorandum from Deputy Attorney General Paul McNulty, Principles of Federal Prosecution of Business Organizations (2006).

must make at least four initial determinations in order to satisfy the public reporting and professional responsibility pressures created by the Act:

- What kind of an internal investigation should be commenced?
- Who should perform that investigation?
- To whom should the investigators report?
- What should be the scope of the investigation, and when can it be considered complete?

The Act's provisions present specific considerations to be weighed when making these decisions. These considerations are discussed below.

1. What Kind of Investigation Is Appropriate, and Who Should Conduct It?

When the CLO or the audit committee receives a report or allegation of wrongdoing, they must respond to it appropriately or face the risk that the person making the report will go "up the ladder" and create a more highly charged situation. But an appropriate response need not always be an internal investigation, for it is impractical to launch a full-blown internal investigation into every single anonymous complaint, no matter how trivial. Audit committees, CLOs, and their counselors must exercise judgment about the credibility of the specific complaint, and the appropriate response to it. However, no allegation should be ignored. It is not unheard of for people to find themselves in unpleasant situations by ignoring the first few pieces of evidence of what later turns out to have been a major problem. Still, depending on the initially perceived level of seriousness and credibility, the investigation of some allegations may best be left to the company's internal audit function. Others can be handled by in-house counsel or by regular outside counsel. Some (and we would argue increasingly more since the Act became law) necessitate the audit committee, or a special committee of the board, engaging counsel with no prior relationship with the company to perform an independent review. Nevertheless, at all points in any such investigation, care must be given, and oversight maintained, to determine whether or not the appropriate investigatory scrutiny and independence is being dedicated.

Deciding what type of investigative response is appropriate is a highly fact-specific inquiry about which the Act provides essentially no guidance whatsoever. Factors that should be considered include the level of detail contained in the complaint, whether the alleged wrongdoing is pervasive or isolated, how senior the employees alleged to be involved are, whether the alleged misconduct has the potential to impact materially the company's financial statements, or whether the alleged misconduct may result in potential criminal liability regardless of its relative economic materiality to the company. Making sure the investigation is cost effective, and completed with appropriate dispatch, must also be considered because the next round of public certifications by the CEO and CFO are always no more than four months away, and often far less. Inside counsel, or regular outside counsel, are often able to investigate quickly and efficiently because they are familiar with the company's history, its area of business and operations, and its personnel. However, the very familiarity that these attorneys have with the company may conversely be perceived as a lack of appropriate independence by those that ultimately review the results of the investigation. If independent outside counsel is not engaged, that decision should be periodically reevaluated as the investigation progresses, and more is learned about the scope and seriousness of the alleged problems.

As a general rule, the more pervasive or criminal the alleged misconduct, the higher it goes in the organization, and the more material it is to the company's financials, the more desirable it is to engage independent outside counsel to conduct the investigation. As the seriousness of alleged misconduct escalates, so do the number of audiences interested in the results of the internal investigation. These audiences include not only the company's management and board, but its shareholders, the business press and analysts, company auditors, and government regulators. It is vitally important that the persons chosen to conduct the investigation have the necessary independence and credibility for these various audiences to have faith in its results.[13]

2. Reporting Structure

Another fundamental point to be considered at the outset of the investigation is to whom the investigators should report. The Act suggests three primary options—the CLO, the audit committee, or a special committee of the board established for purposes of the investigation. Prior to the Act, outside counsel hired to perform an internal investigation were typically engaged by the company itself. The Act's focus on the audit committee, and its independence, have increasingly led to the audit committee supervising the investigation and

---

13. For example, the initial internal investigation at Enron was conducted by the same firm that had provided legal advice on some of the transactions at issue. *See* D. Ackman, *Enron's Lawyers: Eyes Wide Shut?*, FORBES, Jan. 28, 2002. After that and similar incidents, prosecutors became increasingly skeptical not only of narrowly constrained internal investigations, but also of any investigation performed by lawyers whose firms had a prior and long-standing relationship with the corporation.

hiring its own counsel to assist it in doing so. In addition to respecting the Act's emphasis on audit committee independence, this oversight structure typically limits the potential for claimed conflicts of interest in the investigation. For example, if the alleged wrongdoing involves the most senior management of the company, to whom the CLO reports, or the CLO is a witness, having investigators report to the CLO is not advisable. By placing the supervision of the investigation with independent, nonemployee directors, the independence of the investigation is much more assured.

For particularly serious matters, the board should consider the creation of a special committee of independent directors to oversee the investigation, with the special committee retaining independent counsel to assist it. In this way, both the investigating board committee and its counsel are "independent." If members of the board themselves are implicated in potential wrongdoing, any such board members should be screened from supervising the investigation.

Regardless of the ultimate reporting structure, counsel should consider documenting it in a written retainer agreement that explains who is retaining counsel, what that counsel has been retained to do, and to whom that counsel is reporting. Counsel retained to do an independent investigation must also consider the limits of their representation. For example, if counsel has been retained by a special committee to perform an independent investigation, it may be inappropriate for that same counsel to represent the company in any related government investigation or in civil litigation. In the eyes of government investigators, the results of what is supposed to be an evenhanded report of what happened may lack credibility if they are delivered by counsel who are also vigorously advocating their client's position before the government, or in civil litigation. This, of course, can result in multiple and overlapping sets of counsel for the company and its board members, which can be both cumbersome and costly. In other circumstances, however, government attorneys may be familiar with counsel and trust that they are giving them the unvarnished truth, and this type of division of responsibility may not be necessary. In any event, careful thought should be given to the issue as to who will represent the company in what capacity.

3. Scope of the Investigation, or When Does It Ever End?

For any internal investigation to have the credibility and effectiveness necessary to satisfy the company and its interested observers (including the outside auditors), its scope must be robust. At the same time, the scope must be defined so that expectations are clear, and privilege is protected. In nearly every internal investigation, there are usually additional issues that come up in the course of the investigation—a witness brings forth a new allegation, or an e-mail turns up with troubling content unrelated to the matter then being investigated. One always needs to determine what to do with those additional issues, but the Act's provisions place special requirements on investigators to do so. As noted above, Section 307 requires attorneys to report evidence of a "material violation" of securities laws or a breach of fiduciary duty to the company's CLO or CEO. Moreover, the lawyer must report "up the ladder" to the audit committee or the full board if the lawyer is not satisfied that the CLO or CEO has made an appropriate response.

These responsibilities should not be taken lightly. The SEC has not read the Act's focus on gatekeepers as ending with inside counsel, but extending to those outside the company conducting internal investigations. SEC enforcement staff have spoken publicly of concern that lawyers hired to investigate signs of fraud may not have pursued investigations with sufficient vigor.[14] In one reported instance, the SEC staff notified an outside attorney that the staff was considering recommending taking action against him for his role in conducting an internal investigation after it was announced that the probe he conducted found no intentional wrongdoing by management.[15]

The reporting-up requirements, along with the SEC's vigorous oversight of those requirements, injects an interesting tension into the internal investigatory process: the outside investigator who turns up a lead of potential wrongdoing outside the scope of the investigation will feel compelled by his or her professional responsibility obligations to report it and insist upon an "appropriate response." The company, on the other hand, may want that investigator to finish the original investigation and make a report, with the additional allegations to be investigated thereafter, or by someone other than the outside investigator—for example, if the company views the additional allegations as less serious, it may wish to have them reviewed in-house instead of by the outside investigators. That outside investigator, however, may not be willing to close the original investigation until the "appropriate response" has

---

14. "One area of particular focus for us is the role of lawyers in internal investigations of their clients or companies. We are concerned that, in some instances, lawyers may have conducted investigations in such a manner as to help hide ongoing fraud, or may have taken actions to actively obstruct such investigations." Speech by SEC Director of Enforcement Stephen Cutler on "The Themes of Sarbanes-Oxley as Reflected in the Commission's Enforcement Program," (Sept. 20, 2004), http://www.sec.gov/news/speech/spch092004smc.htm.

15. O. Bilodeau, "SEC Threatens Ex-Brobeck Lawyer Over Client's Probe, People Say," Bloomberg, Dec. 6, 2004, http://www.bloomberg.com/applnews.

run its course, or unless he or she can personally investigate the additional allegations.

4. Increased Focus on Obstruction of Justice

At the time the Act was adopted, the document destruction by Arthur Andersen in connection with Enron was headline news. Since that time, prosecutors have brought a number of high-profile cases against Martha Stewart, Frank Quattrone, and others focusing on alleged obstruction of justice. In cases where proving complicity in a complex fraud would be long and arduous, prosecutors instead may seize on allegations that individuals have misled investigators or destroyed or tampered with evidence.

The Act contains specific provisions addressing document destruction. In any internal investigation, appropriate steps should be taken to preserve potentially relevant evidence. The Act raises the stakes in this regard by broadening the definitions of obstruction of justice to include the destruction of documents with the intent to impair the document's availability for use in any future official proceeding,[16] and the destruction or falsification of records with the intent to obstruct not only pending investigations, but contemplated investigations.[17] As one can reasonably contemplate a federal investigation following an internal investigation (if in fact one is not already proceeding in parallel), counsel—whether they be counsel for the audit committee, the company, individuals, or anyone else involved—should make certain that appropriate steps are taken to preserve evidence, and that those steps are documented.

The emphasis that the Act places on internal investigations and disclosure has also created a new twist on obstruction, which the internal investigator should keep in mind. Often, the statements that witnesses make to investigators during the internal investigation are shared, in some form or another, with the government. In a case involving the company Computer Associates, three former executives were charged with obstruction of justice based not on any direct lie to the government, but rather on the theory that they lied to the outside counsel conducting an internal investigation into possible wrongdoing at the company. The government's theory was that these lies to outside counsel constituted obstruction of justice because the witnesses knew and intended that counsel would pass those lies on to the government as part of the corpo-

---

16. 18 U.S.C. § 1512(c). An official proceeding need not be pending or about to be instituted, nor does the record, document, or other object need to be admissible in evidence or free of a claim of privilege. 18 U.S.C. § 1512(f).

17. 18 U.S.C. § 1519.

ration's cooperation with regulators, and thereby mislead the government about the alleged wrongdoing.[18]

In response to the Computer Associates matter, some counsel have expressed the view that consideration should be given to expanding the admonition at the beginning of interviews to include a warning that false or misleading statements may lead to potential criminal charges.[19] In any event, outside counsel must consider the possibility that they may become witnesses in later government proceedings regarding witness interviews or other subjects of investigation.

C. *Dealing with the Company's Outside Auditors*

As discussed previously, the Act places increased emphasis on corporate disclosure. There are at least three categories of disclosure that should be considered in connection with an internal investigation—disclosure to the company's outside auditors, disclosure to the government, and disclosure to the market. Disclosure to the government, and the disclosure obligations of public companies, are dealt with in more depth elsewhere in this book, and the points made there (which apply with equal force to public companies subject to the Act) will not be reiterated here.[20]

The Act did, however, work significant changes in the oversight role of auditors—particularly with regard to internal investigations. With the creation of the PCAOB, and increased oversight by the SEC of auditing firms' compliance with Generally Accepted Auditing Standards, outside auditors now demand greater involvement and participation in internal investigations to discharge their obligations under Section 10A(b)(1) of the Securities Exchange Act of 1934.[21] Under Section 10A, which was enacted in 1995, an outside auditor who discovers information indicating that an illegal act may have occurred is required to determine whether it is "likely" that the illegal act has

---

18. See DOJ press release, "Former Computer Associates Executives Indicted on Securities Fraud, Obstruction Charges," (Sept. 22, 2004), http://www.usdoj.gov/opa/pr/2004/September/04_crm_642.htm.

19. *E.g.*, J. Farrell & J. Suiter, *The Cooperation Conundrum,* WALL STREET LAWYER (Vol. 8, No. 2, July 2004). As the authors note, the negative consequences of giving such an admonition can include discouraging employees from consenting to interviews, and bolstering the scienter element that was apparently crucial to the Computer Associates prosecutions. *Id.*

20. *See* T. Holliday & C. Stevens, *Disclosure of Results of Internal Investigations to the Government or Other Third Parties* (Chapter 8), and M. Shepard, *No Security: Internal Investigations into Violations of the Securities Laws* (Chapter 13).

21. 15 U.S.C. § 78j-1.

in fact occurred. If the auditor concludes that it is "likely" that the illegal act occurred, he or she must: (1) determine the possible effect of the illegal act on the financial statements; and (2) inform management and the Audit Committee of the Board of Directors, as soon as practicable, of the illegal act, unless the act "is clearly inconsequential."

If, after informing the company's audit committee, the auditor concludes that the illegal act has a material effect on the financial statements, the company has not taken "timely and appropriate remedial actions," and the failure to take remedial actions is reasonably expected to warrant departure from a standard report of the auditor, or warrant resignation from the audit engagement, the auditor must, as soon as practicable, report his or her conclusion directly to the board. Upon receiving such a report, the board has one business day to inform the SEC that it received the report and give the auditor notice that it has informed the SEC. An auditor who does not receive such notice must either resign from the engagement or furnish the SEC with a copy of its report.

Since the creation of the Act, outside auditors are frequently the key constituency to whom the results of an internal investigation are communicated. In light of the high-stakes created by the Act, auditors will not sign off on a company's financial statements until they are 100 percent satisfied that any potential wrongdoing has been run to ground, if not further. As the auditors hold the keys to the company making timely quarterly filings of financial information, and can withhold their sign-off until satisfied, they have tremendous power to influence the scope and depth of any internal investigation. This need to satisfy the auditors creates tremendous pressure to complete the investigation swiftly so as to avoid any unnecessary delay in quarterly filings.

Delayed public reporting due to the auditors' unwillingness to sign off on the financial information or the executive officers' unwillingness to certify the financials has the potential to lead to a nuclear meltdown at the company. The consequences stretch beyond a drop in the company's stock price, which usually follows a failure to make timely filings. For instance, nearly every indenture (a detailed contract between an issuer and investors) will contain a covenant requiring the issuer to file its periodic reports with the SEC on time, and then to deliver that information to the bondholder within a relatively short period of time. If the auditors are not satisfied that a pending internal investigation has run its course, and are therefore unwilling to sign off on the financials such that the company cannot file its periodic report with the SEC on time, then covenant defaults under these bond indentures happen. Those defaults will result in actual or threatened accelerations of the debt subject to such indentures. At the end of the day, the company can find itself facing bondholders able to accelerate hundreds of millions or billions of dollars of indebtedness unless their demands (usually only seeking cash payments) are met.[22] Of course, this is all happening at a time when the company attempts to deal with the crisis that begat the original internal investigation, so it is commonplace for the company and its management to be distracted from the actual operation of the business. As one can imagine, this leads to further erosion of the business and the downward spiral continues.

The potential for this nightmare scenario, which has unfolded all too frequently, requires counsel to bring the auditors into the investigative process early, to reach common understandings about the investigation and its scope, how privilege can be preserved while still providing auditors the information they require, and a timetable for completion. The major auditing firms have internal sign-off procedures that take time, and the last thing a company wants or needs is to find out on the eve of a quarterly or yearly filing that additional investigation is necessary before the auditors will sign off.

Because of the Act's restrictions on auditors performing other services for their audit clients, auditors are constrained from using their own forensic auditing units to conduct their own independent investigation. The result often is a "shadow" investigation, where the auditors essentially audit the internal investigation. Auditors will want early on to understand the issues being investigated, and the investigative plan to address those issues. They may request that the proposed scope or workplan of the investigation be expanded, that they participate directly in investigative interviews, or that e-mail searches or other document review be expanded beyond that originally contemplated. They also may request access to e-mails and other documents to audit whether proper searches were conducted, and responsive documents found. Additionally, in the course of the investigation, the auditors may ask counsel for legal

---

22. See, Peter Lattman and Karen Richardson, "*Hedge Funds Play Hardball with Firms Filing Late Financials,*" August 29, 2006, WALL STREET JOURNAL and Caroline Salas, "*Options Scam Lets Citadel, Whitebox Hedge Funds, Exploit Bonds,*" September 12, 2006, Bloomberg http://bloomberg.com/apps/news. Frank "Grange" Johnson, who runs the $300 million LaGrange Capital Management hedge fund, went on record in the above-cited Bloomberg article saying, "You're taking advantage of a loophole in the system. You're trying to send a company to jail for jaywalking. You have this options scandal, and there is incredible pressure on boards and management not to file false financials." According to the same Bloomberg article, this "loophole" may put as much as $36 billion of bonds at risk of acceleration or other bondholder activism based on the more than hundreds of internal investigations into stock option backdating. The scrutiny of stock option issues and the length of time required to complete the required internal investigations have clearly been influenced by the Sarbanes-Oxley Act.

opinions regarding certain transactions, and issues regarding those transactions that are pertinent to the accounting treatment of those transactions.[23]

Sharing information with the auditors—including things such as the auditors' participation in interviews, or the sharing of the content of interviews with auditors—can raise conflict and privilege waiver issues that must be thought through carefully. Companies must be transparent with their auditors. However, if auditors were aware of certain matters under investigation, or participated in discussions with management about how to properly account for transactions under investigation, care should be taken to structure the auditors' participation in the investigation so there is no appearance that they are in some way influencing the investigation. With regard to privilege, if the investigation is subject to the attorney-client and work product privileges, care must be taken in reporting the results (either interim or final) of the investigation in a way that does not create waiver issues. Courts generally hold that the disclosure of attorney-client communications to auditors waives the attorney-client privilege.[24] With regard to work product, however, there is authority stating that disclosure of attorney work product to auditors does not constitute a waiver with regard to litigation adversaries.[25] Other courts, however, have

---

23. For example, the SEC's Deputy Chief Accountant has suggested that auditors should seek this information in support of audits of loss contingency accruals under FAS 5. SEC Deputy Chief Accountant Scott Traub, Remarks at the USC Leventhal School of Accounting SEC and Financial Reporting Conference (May 27, 2004), http://www.sec.gov/news/speech/spch052704sat.htm ("If a company's outside counsel is unwilling or unable to provide its expert views, the auditor should consider whether sufficient alternate procedures can actually be performed to allow the audit to be completed.").

24. *E.g.*, SEC v. Brady, __ F.R.D. __, 2006 WL 2880444, at *8 (N.D. Tex., Oct. 5, 2006) ("Federal case law makes it clear that disclosure of confidential communications or documents to auditors for purposes other than seeking legal advice destroys confidentiality and with it, the right to claim the attorney-client privilege."); Gutter v. E.I. Dupont De Nemours & Co., No. 95-CV-2152 1998 WL 2017926, at *4 (S.D. Fla. May 18, 1998) ("[d]isclosure to outside accountants waives the attorney-client privilege"); *In re* Pfizer Inc. Securities Litig., No. 90 Civ 1269 1993 WL 561125, *7 (S.D.N.Y. Dec. 23, 1993) ("Disclosure of documents to an outside accountant destroys the confidentiality seal required of communications protected by the attorney-client privilege, notwithstanding that the federal securities laws require an independent audit."). Some states, by statute, have recognized a privilege that protects the confidentiality of communications between accountants and their clients. *E.g.*, Ariz. Rev. Stat. § 32-749; Fla. Stat. Ann. § 90.5055; 225 Ill. Comp. Stat. 450/27; Pa. Stat. Ann. Tit. 63 § 9.11. The majority of states, however, have not. Other jurisdictions, including perhaps most importantly the federal courts, have not recognized any such privilege. *See* Couch v. United States, 409 U.S. 322, 335 (1973) ("no confidential accountant-client privilege exists under federal law, and no state created privilege has been recognized in federal cases").

25. *See, e.g.*, United States v. Aldman, 134 F.3d 1194, 1200 (2d Cir. 1998) (litigation report could still be work product protected even though shared with a company's outside auditors); *In re* JDS Uniphase Corp. Sec. Litig., No. C-02-1486 2006 WL 2850049 (N.D. Cal.,

come to the opposite conclusion.[26] Given the uncertainties, the prudent practitioner should expect that waiver may result from the sharing of any work product with outside auditors.

Auditors are typically sensitive to this concern when it is raised with them, and will not seek to create unnecessary waivers. Most often, what auditors are interested in are the facts—what happened, and who knew what when. These underlying facts are not protected by the attorney-client or attorney work product privileges, and when divorced from any attorney interpretation of those facts, can be shared in a way that minimizes the risk of waiver.

D. *Disclosure to the Market*

While the analysis of public company disclosure obligations is beyond the scope of this chapter, it is important that all persons involved in a public company internal investigation rigorously continue to assess whether there are any material facts that should be disclosed to the market. The Act, as well as the 1934 Act and other laws and regulations, require public companies to make prompt disclosure of material facts. Close coordination with disclosure counsel is essential to ensure that appropriate and accurate disclosure is made. The timing of disclosure must also be assessed. Tardy disclosure is obviously problematic—if material facts become known before the investigation is completed, they need to be disclosed. However, disclosure before key facts are understood can lead to inaccurate disclosure, or the need to make supplemental disclosures because the initial disclosure was too cramped or incomplete in light of later developments, or just plain wrong. The Act's focus on "real time" disclosures can make this a difficult balance to strike, and requires that

---

Oct. 5, 2006) (board minutes protected work protect despite disclosure to auditors); Lawrence E. Jaffe Pension Plan v. Household Int'l, Inc., 237 F.R.D. 176, 183-84 (N.D. Ill. 2006) (audit letter responses protected work product); Int'l Design Concepts, Inc. v. Saks Inc., No. 05-Civ 4754 2006 WL 1564684 (S.D.N.Y., June 6, 2006) (internal investigative report disclosed to auditors protected by attorney work-product doctrine); Merrill Lynch & Co. v. Allegheny Energy, Inc., 229 F.R.D. 441 (S.D.N.Y. 2004) (same); *In re* Honeywell, Int'l, Inc. Sec. Litig., 230 F.R.D. 293 (S.D.N.Y. 2003); *In re* Pfizer, Inc. Sec. Litig., 1993 WL 561125 at *6 (S.D.N.Y., Dec. 23, 1993).

26. *E.g.*, Medinol, Ltd. v. Boston Scientific Group, 214 F.R.D. 113 (S.D.N.Y. 2002). In *Medinol*, the court reasoned that work-product protection exists for parties that share common interests in litigation. *Id.* at 116-17. As auditors have a public watchdog function that requires their independence from clients, the court found that they do not share common interests and the sharing of work product information with auditors thus waives its protection. *Id.* at 116. *See also In re* Diasonics Sec. Litig., No. C-83-4584 1986 WL 53402 at *1 (N.D. Cal. June 15, 1986) (documents disclosed to an accounting firm acting as a public auditor were not entitled to work product protection and even if entitled to such protection, the protection was waived by disclosure to the accountants).

counsel conducting the investigation work closely with disclosure counsel, and update them frequently, to address these issues and concerns.

E. *Remedial Steps*

Given that the Act requires CEO and CFO certification of the adequacy of internal controls, any internal investigation in a company subject to the Act should include an assessment of the adequacy of the internal controls implicated by the alleged wrongdoing, whether changes in existing controls should be made, and whether additional controls should be instituted. These questions must be considered and addressed so that when company officers make future certifications regarding internal controls, they are truthful and accurate.

The necessity of employee discipline is another action item typically addressed after an internal investigation. Here, the Act created new criminal and civil standards that must be kept in mind in connection with any contemplated disciplinary action. The Act makes it a crime to knowingly take any action, with the intent to retaliate, that is harmful to any employee, including interference with the employment or livelihood of the employee, for providing to a law enforcement officer any truthful information relating to the possible commission of any federal offense.[27]

The Act further created a civil right of action for employees of publicly traded companies who claim retaliation for "blowing the whistle." Specifically, the Act made it illegal to discharge, demote, or otherwise retaliate against an employee for providing information or otherwise assisting in an investigation regarding any conduct that the employee reasonably believes constitutes a violation of federal securities laws.[28] Some courts have gone further and said that this includes complaining about internal controls.[29]

---

27. 18 U.S.C. § 1513(e).

28. 18 U.S.C. § 1514A; *see also* Procedures for the Handling of Discrimination Complaints Under Section 806 of the Corporate and Criminal Fraud Accountability Act of 2002, Title VIII of the Sarbanes-Oxley Act of 2002, 29 C.F.R. Part 1980 (2004). Under this statute, the aggrieved employee must first file a complaint with the Secretary of Labor. If the Secretary does not issue a final decision within 180 days thereafter, the employee can bring suit in federal district court. *Id.* at § 1514A(b)(1)(B). The statute reaches only employers who are publicly traded companies. Brady v. Calyon Securities (USA), 406 F. Supp. 2d 307, 317-18 (S.D.N.Y. 2005). The First Circuit recently held that this provision does not apply to employees located outside the United States. Carnero v. Boston Scientific, 433 F.3d 1 (1st Cir. 2006). Actions brought pursuant to this provision are governed by the burdens of proof set forth in 49 U.S.C. § 42121. *See* 18 U.S.C. § 1514A(b)(2)(C). To prevail, a complaining employee must show by a preponderance of the evidence that (1) s/he engaged in protected activity; (2) the employer knew of the protected activity; (3) s/he suffered an unfavorable personnel action; and (4) circumstances exist to suggest that the protected activity was a contributing

While these provisions appear fairly straightforward and noncontroversial, they can raise complicated questions when the whistleblower himself or herself is both complicit in wrongdoing, and at the same time has provided truthful information about wrongdoing. Care must be taken to document properly the reasons for disciplinary action, and to communicate properly the thinking behind the decision, so as not to potentially run afoul of these provisions. Appropriate steps should also be taken to make sure that whistleblowers are not retaliated against by fellow employees.

IV. CONCLUSION

As described above, the Act has influenced the investigative process in three important ways: (1) increasing the circumstances that will result in an internal corporate investigation, (2) making more complicated the analysis about who should conduct the investigation and what its scope should be, and

---

factor to the unfavorable action. *E.g.*, Collins v. Beazer Homes USA, Inc., 334 F. Supp. 2d 1365, 1375 (N.D. Ga. 2004) (citations omitted); Klopfenstein v. PCC Flow Technologies Holdings, DOL Arb. Case No. 04-149, ALJ Case No. 04-SOX-11 2006 DOL Ad. Rev. Bd. Lexis 50 at *27 (May 31, 2006). If the employee carries this burden, the employer can still avoid liability if it can demonstrate by clear and convincing evidence that it "would have taken the same unfavorable personnel action in the absence of the protected activity." *Id.*

29. *See* Morefield v. Exelon Servs., Inc., Dep't of Labor ALJ No 2004-SOX-2 slip op. at 3, 2-8 (ALJ Jan. 28, 2004), granting whistleblower protection for reported manipulations of financial information even though the manipulations occurred only in "internal and interim" reports to the parent company and not the investing public. The ALJ wrote, "by blowing the whistle, [individuals] may anticipate the deception buried in a draft report or internal document, which if not corrected, could eventually taint the public disclosure." See also Collins v. Beazer Homes USA, Inc., 334 F. Supp. 2d 1365, 1368 (N.D. Ga. 2004), allowing an employee to prosecute a claim under the Act despite the alleged wrongdoing relating only to internal accounting controls, rather than conduct that might result in material fraud against shareholders. Finally, *see also,* Platone v. FLYi, ARB Case No. 04-153, 2006 DOL Ad. Rev. Bd. Lexis, 89 at *28, 32 (Sept. 29, 2006), in which the Department of Labor's Administrative Review Board provided the following guidance on protected whistleblower activity under the Act: (1) the Act protects activity that one reasonably believes to be a violation of the securities laws, but also the federal criminal mail, wire, and bank fraud statutes, but only to the extent such allegation of mail or wire fraud would be "at least of a type that would be adverse to investors' interests," (2) the protected activity "must relate 'definitively and specifically' to the subject matter of the particular statute under which protection is afforded" (e.g., the Act does not "provide whistleblower protection for all employee complaints about how a public company spends its money or pays it bills") and (3) the materiality of the potential loss from the alleged wrongdoing is significant." This statement by the Administrative Review Board that materiality of the potential loss is a necessary element for whistleblower protection contrasts starkly with the Department of Labor holdings described above that materiality is irrelevant to Sarbanes-Oxley whistleblower claims.

(3) deputizing some groups as internal investigators for the government while simultaneously adding to the various constituencies whom an investigation may need to satisfy (i.e., the external auditors). The Act has not so much affected a substantive rethinking of why and how to conduct an internal investigation or even the issues present during that process. Rather, the somewhat counterintuitive result has been both to make very obvious when a company should *start* an investigation into alleged wrongdoing and to make very unclear when, if ever, the investigation can ever be permitted to *conclude*. Of course, all along the way the investigator and the company will be faced with a combination of high-stakes disclosure, process, and third-party management issues. It would not seem out of place for a company caught in the vice between an internal investigation and the Act to utter the title of Tom Petty and the Heartbreakers' underrated 1987 album: *Let Me Up (I've Had Enough)*.

Index

A
ABA Model Rules of Professional Conduct
  Rule 1.3, 367 n.32
  Rule 1.3(f), 38
  Rule 1.7(b), 212–213
  Rule 4.1(a), 106–107
  Rule 4.2, 41, 200, 203, 204–205, 206 n.158, 207, 208
Accountants. *See* Auditors
Advice by counsel
  and attorney-client privilege, 21, 24, 26, 27–32, 305–307
  discovery of, shareholder actions, 83–84
  employee requests for, 115
  existence of, 27–32
  investigative report statements, 333
  privilege waiver by reliance on, 66–67
Agents of counsel, privilege for, 25–26
AICPA (American Institute of Certified Public Accountants), 379–380
American Bar Association (ABA). *See also* ABA Model Rules of Professional Conduct
  Code of Professional Responsibility, 40–41
  Disciplinary Rules DR 7-104, 41–42, 43, 200, 201
  Standing Committee on Ethics and Professional Responsibility, 207
  third party requests for information concerning internal investigation, 457–458
American Institute of Certified Public Accountants (AICPA), 379–380

Amnesty, antitrust matters, 97, 473, 478–488
Anti-Kickback Enforcement Act (1986), 107, 247, 425–426
Anticipation of litigation, work-product doctrine, 48–54, 109, 308
Antitrust Criminal Penalty Enhancement and Reform Act (ACPERA) (2004), 474–475, 492
Antitrust matters
  criminal investigations, 472–489
  enforcement of, 467–469
  internal investigations, 469–472
  overview of, 466
  parallel proceedings, 489–490
  private litigation, 488–490
Arthur Andersen, 133, 134, 141
Attorney-client privilege, 17–44
  advice requirement, 21, 24, 26, 27–32, 305–307
  antitrust matters, 471
  application to internal investigations, 10–11
  attorney requirement, 25–27
  auditors, 508
  burden of establishing, 20
  client requirement, 22–24
  communication requirement, 32–35
  confidentiality in, 35–36
  crime/fraud exception, 78–80
  definition of, 19–21
  elements of, 21–36
  employee communications, 22–24
  and employee interviews, 36–44
  government contractor investigations, 348–349
  and inadvertent disclosures, 69–71

513

Attorney-client privilege, *continued*
  investigative report discoverability, 305–308
  and joint defense agreements, 73–74
  limited waiver of, 315–318
  and non-waiver stipulations, 72–73
  and shareholder litigation, 82–86, 313–314, 315
  Special Litigation Committee protection, 274–277
  and testimony of client, 67–68
  and voluntary disclosure, 61–65
  waiver of, 5, 7, 60–74, 86–87, 89–90, 161–162, 237–238, 256–257, 348–349, 473, 508
  vs. work-product doctrine, 19
Attorney General
  civil investigative demand, 340–341
  communication with employees, 43, 202, 203
  DR 7-104, 43
  HIPAA enforcement powers, 427
Attorneys. *See* Counsel
Audit committees, 151–152, 332–333, 495, 501–502, 506
Audit privilege law, environmental, 294–295
Auditors
  internal control reports, 498
  recordkeeping requirements under Section 1520, 144–145
  requests for information on potential "loss contingencies," 457–458
  role in internal investigations, 417–421, 505–508
  Sarbanes-Oxley standards, 494–495
Audits, environmental. *See* Environmental audits

B

Balanced Budget Act (1997), 425–426
Banks, 247, 458
Bar codes, 157
Bates stamping, 157

Boards of directors
  compliance programs, responsibility for, 442–443
  and internal investigations, 151–152, 333, 455, 502
  legal proceedings involving, disclosure requirements, 364
  special litigation committees, establishment, 263–264
Brokerage firms, insider trading liability, 359–360
Brokers
  liability of, 357–358
  reporting requirements, 381–384
  SEC sanctions, 385

C

Cartels. *See* Antitrust matters
Cendant, 355 n.1
Chief executive officers (CEOs), 4, 7, 455, 494, 498
Chief financial officers (CFOs), 4, 494, 497–498
Chief legal officers (CLOs), 498
Citizen's Protection Act (1998), 203, 209
Civil actions, stays of, 178–185, 413–417
Civil False Claims Act (FCA), 200, 339, 342–343, 345, 424–425, 437, 438
Civil investigative demand (CID), 340–341
Class-action litigation, 265–266, 269, 272, 386
Clayton Act, 467, 468
Clients, 22–24. *See also* Attorney-client privilege; Communication with client
Codes of conduct, 4
Collateral estoppel, 193–197
Commodity Futures Trading Commission (CFTC), 192
Common-interest privilege, 217–219

Common-law rule, for disclosure of
   information, 243–245
Common Rule, 232–233
Communication with client
   by adversary, 40–44, 99
   "control group" test, 22–23, 24, 205
   former employees, 39–44, 116,
      207–208
   lower-level employees, 22–23, 99
   scope of privilege, 32–35
   senior management, 22
   transmitted to third party, 36
Computer Associates, 114, 410 n.136,
   504–505
Confidentiality agreements
   between companies and government,
      63, 257, 349, 400, 402
   types of, 168–169
Confidentiality of information. *See also*
   Attorney-client privilege;
   Disclosure of information; Work-
   product doctrine
   and attorney-client privilege, 35–36
   employee interviews, 13, 104, 111
   joint defense, 220–223
Conflicts of interest
   joint-defense agreements, 212–214,
      459–460
   Special Litigation Committee counsel,
      266–267
   warnings in employee interviews,
      37–39, 103–107, 110–111,
      139–140
Constitution. *See* United States
   Constitution
Consultants, 153, 288, 289–290,
   292–293
Contractors. *See* Government
   contractors
"Cooking the books," 355
Cooperation of employees, 24, 101, 102,
   105, 115
Corporate and Criminal Fraud
   Accountability Act, 133

Corporate compliance programs,
   427–431
Corporate Integrity Agreements (CIA),
   430–431, 433
Corporate Leniency Policy, 478–485
   Amnesty Plus policy, 484
   and attorney-client privilege, 471
   confidentiality, 485
   cooperation under, 482–484
   damages, limitation, 490
   overview of, 478–481
   Penalty Plus policy, 484
   placing a marker, 481–482
Corporations
   as client, 22–24
   liability of, 255, 444–445
   misconduct by, 198
Counsel. *See also* Advice by counsel;
   Attorney-client privilege
   bar membership, 25
   communication with agents and
      subordinates, 25–27
   companies' provision for employees,
      210–215
   duty to report securities law violation,
      112, 503
   employees' right to, 106, 201, 208,
      214, 458
   fees paid for employees, 210–211
   files, 35
   in-house vs. outside, 12
   independence of, 12
   initial engagement letter, 332, 452
   on investigative team, 11–12,
      152–153
   joint or multiple representation,
      73–74, 212–215
   knowledge of criminal conduct,
      248–250
   libel claims against, 321–322
   mental impressions, protection of,
      57–60
   professional conduct rules (SOX),
      245, 365–367, 495

Counsel, *continued*
  role in internal investigations, 6–7, 11–12, 305–307, 387–388, 502, 503
  selection of, 386–389, 450–452
  for Special Litigation Committee, 266–267, 272–273, 388–389
Crime/fraud exception
  attorney-client privilege, 78–80
  internal investigation application, 82
  work-product doctrine, 80–81
Criminal convictions, 194–195
Criminal investigations, 14–15, 472–488. *See also* Parallel proceedings

D

Databases, 159–160
DCAA (Defense Contract Audit Agency), 341
Dealers
  liability of, 357–358
  reporting requirements, 381–384
  SEC sanctions, 385
Debarment proceedings, 177, 232–234, 349–350
Defamation, 14, 320–321. *See also* Libel
Defense Contract Audit Agency (DCAA), 341
Deficit Reduction Act (2005), 337 n.2
Department of Defense (DoD), 231, 252, 341, 342
Department of Health and Human Services (HHS), 340, 342, 436
Department of Homeland Security, 337
Department of Justice (DOJ). *See also* Antitrust matters
  attorney-client privilege, 89–91
  confidentiality agreement with, 349
  environmental audits, 294
  false statement prosecutions, 133
  federal securities law enforcement, 88–89
  fraud investigations against government contractors, 345, 346
  health care fraud investigations, 427
  joint-defense agreements, 212
  McNulty Memorandum, 2, 5–6, 89–90, 210–211, 212, 236–238, 394–395, 407
  prosecution of witnesses for misleading statements, 114
  qui tam suits, 342–344
  Thompson Memorandum, 5, 100, 210, 211, 236, 250–251, 407, 410, 499
  Thornburgh Memorandum, 200–204
  voluntary disclosure program, 86–87, 250–254
Derivative suits, 84–85, 264, 374. *See also* Special Litigation Committees (SLCs)
Directors. *See* Boards of directors
Discipline, of employees, 197–200, 459, 510
Disclosure of information. *See also* Publicly traded companies, disclosure requirements; Voluntary disclosure of information; Waiver of privilege
  affirmative obligation of, 361 n.19
  and attorney-client privilege, 32
  common-law rule, 243–245
  counsel's knowledge of criminal conduct, 248–250
  to employees, 38
  to government authorities, 61–65, 97–98, 224–231, 315–319
  to grand juries, 227–231
  inadvertent or unwanted, 10, 13, 69–71
  overview of, 242
  prior crimes, 9
  requirements, 243–250
  Sarbanes-Oxley's impact on, 493–494
  statutory requirements, 245–248
Documentation. *See* Records and record keeping
Documents
  coding, 159–160, 174
  computer imaging, 160

control over, 461–463
copies, 157–158, 288–289
criminal investigations, 15
destruction of, 133, 140–145,
  167–168, 244–245, 504
electronic documents, 155–156
at employee interviews, 101
environmental audits, 287–289
gathering process, 153–156
"hot," 149, 162–164
indexing, 155, 159–160, 173
initial organizational meeting,
  150–152
investigative team for review of,
  153–156, 158
numbering, 155, 157
on-sight inspections, 153
processing, 156–162
retention and preservation, 152,
  244–245, 462
review process, 98–99, 158, 170–171
summaries, 164
waiver of privilege, inadvertent,
  161–162
DoD (Department of Defense), 231,
  252, 341, 342
DOJ. *See* Department of Justice (DOJ)
Double Jeopardy Clause protection,
  188–193
Dual representation, 73–74, 212–224

E

E-mail, 142, 152, 154, 294, 507
Electronic documents and data
  computer-imaged, 160
  environmental audits, 294
  experts hired to review, 153
  gathering, 154, 155–156
Electronic records management (ERM)
  system, 294
Employee hotlines, 449, 497
Employee interviews. *See also*
  Obstruction of justice; Perjury
  by adversary, 40–44, 99
  antitrust matters, 487–488

and attorney-client privilege, 36–44,
  104, 105, 106–107
conditional requirements by
  employee, 115–116
confidentiality, 13, 104, 111
counsel's notes and memoranda from,
  64–65, 403
employees' refusal to cooperate, 459
environmental audits, 287
Fifth Amendment invocation,
  185–188, 406–413
former employees, 39–44, 116,
  207–208
goal of, 107
by government, 99, 102, 200–209
importance of, 94
legal advice request during, 115
legal representation, 210–215,
  459–460, 486–487
mechanics of, 96, 102–103, 107–108
notification of, 101–102, 452
and obstruction of justice, 112–114
preparation for, 95–102
record of, 108–111
reluctant employees, 115
risk, 94
Sarbanes-Oxley requirements,
  111–112
setting for, 103
by Special Litigation Committee, 271
time sequence, 98–100
transcripts, 102–103
union representatives present
  during, 458
warnings given in, 37–39, 103–107,
  110–111, 139–140
and work-product protection, 105
Employees. *See also* Employee
  interviews; Former employees
  communications with counsel
    protected under attorney-client
    privilege, 22–24
  cooperation of, 24, 101, 102, 105, 115
  counsel, right to, 106, 201, 208,
    214, 458

Employees, *continued*
  disciplining for misconduct, 197–200, 459, 510
  duty of loyalty, 106
  and in-house counsel, 12
  internal communication among, 320
  lower-level, 22–23, 24, 99, 151, 289
  materials prepared by, 56
  misconduct, 9
  notification of, 101–102
  preparation for criminal investigations, 15
  reluctant, 115
  self-incrimination, privilege against, 137–138, 166–167, 179, 185–188, 411, 459
  termination for failure to cooperate, 407, 408
  whistle-blowers, protection of, 200, 343, 496–497, 510
Enron scandal, 87, 118, 133, 134, 141, 355 n.1
Environmental audits, 283–299
  audit privilege law, 294–295
  disclosure requirements, 246
  document review and copy demand, 288–289
  electronic records, 294
  EPA inspection tips, 296–299
  internal investigations, 289–295
  notices of violations, 289
  overview of, 284
  parallel proceedings, 290–291
  periodic audits by outside consultants, 292–293
  problems posed by, 293–294
  reactive investigations, 285–291
  reasons for internal audits, 291–292
  search warrants, 284, 285–288
  seizure of documents, 287–288
  voluntary internal investigations, 291–295
Environmental Protection Agency (EPA), 252, 290, 295, 296–299

ERM (electronic records management) systems, 294
Estoppel, collateral, 193–197
Ex parte communication, 41
Experts
  internal environmental audits, 289–290, 292–293
  on investigative team, 453
  privilege for, 26–27

F
Fair Funds provision, 239
False Claims Act (FCA), 200, 339, 342–343, 345, 424–425, 437, 438
False statements
  obstruction of justice laws, 131–135
  perjury laws, 119–121
FASB (Financial Accounting Standards Board), 457
Federal Acquisition Regulation (FAR), 231–233, 346
Federal Deposit Insurance Corporation (FDIC), 192
Federal prosecutors, ex parte interviews by, 200–209
Federal Rules of Civil Procedure
  Rule 26(b)(3), 46, 49, 50–51, 55, 56, 58, 77–78, 308
  Rule 34(b), 164
Federal Rules of Criminal Procedure
  Rule 6(e), 227–228, 229, 340
  Rule 16, 415
  Rule 16(b), 179–180
  Rule 16(b)(2), 44–45
  Rule 44(c), 214, 215
Federal Rules of Evidence
  Rule 403, 188
  Rule 408, 398
  Rule 501, 20
  Rule 502, 257, 318
  Rule 503, 20
  Rule 612, 77
  Rule 801(d)(2), 303, 304
  Rule 801(d)(2)(C), 254

Federal Sentencing Guidelines.
　See Sentencing Guidelines
Federal Trade Commission Act,
　467, 468
Federal Trade Commission (FTC), 469
Fifth Amendment, 138, 166–167, 180,
　185–188, 406–413, 414, 415, 416
Financial Accounting Standards Board
　(FASB), 457
Financial Institution Reform, Recovery,
　and Enforcement Act (FIRREA)
　(1989), 131
Financial institutions, disclosure
　requirements, 247, 457
Financial statements, 4, 419, 494,
　498, 506
First Amendment, 326, 485
Fiscal intermediaries (FIs), 341–342
Food Stamp Act, 192
Foreign antitrust laws, 470–471
Foreign Corrupt Practices Act (1977),
　355, 379
Foreign Trade and Antitrust
　Improvements Act (FTAIA)
　(1982), 489
Forensic auditing services, 507
Former employees
　adversary's communication with,
　　40–44
　counsel's communication with,
　　39–40
　Fifth Amendment invocation,
　　187–188
　interviewing, 39–44, 116, 207–208
Fraud
　attorney-client privilege exception
　　for, 78–80
　financial, 354–355
　qui tam suits, 342–345
　responding to allegations, 344–350
　securities, 89
　Statement on Auditing Standards
　　No. 99, 419
　work-product exception for, 80–81

Freedom of Information Act (FOIA),
　225, 299, 401 n.117, 430
Frontrunning, 358

G
Garner rule, 82–84, 86
General Services Administration,
　231, 337
Generic Drug Enforcement Act, 192
Global settlement, 234–239
Government authorities
　communication with, 456–457
　disclosure of information to, 61–65,
　　97–98, 224–231, 315–319
　employee interviews by, 99, 102
　fraud investigations against
　　government contractors,
　　345–346
　global settlements with, 234–239
Government contractors
　commencement of investigation,
　　339–344
　companies considered, 336–339
　health care providers as, 338
　internal discovery, 342
　kickbacks, 247
　parallel proceedings, 231–234, 347
　qui tam suits, 342–345
　regulations and oversight, 346–347
　responding to allegations, 344–350
　subpoenas to, 340–342
　suppliers as, 337–338
　suspension or debarment, 231–234,
　　349–350
　waiver of privilege, 348–349
Government investigations, 14–15
Grand jury proceedings
　civil deposition access, 226
　disclosure of information,
　　227–231
　perjury, 118, 124–126
　secrecy rule, 227
　subpoenas by, 226
Guilty pleas, 194–195

H

Health and Human Services (HHS)
    Department, 340, 342, 436
Health care companies
    compliance programs, 427–431
    counsel's knowledge of, 249
    document review, 347
    as government contractors, 338
    laws governing, 424–427, 432–433
    self-reporting, 431–438
Health Insurance Portability and
    Accountability Act (HIPAA)
    (1996), 424, 426–427, 433
Homeland Security Department, 337
"Hot" documents, 149, 162–164

I

IM messages, 294
Immunity, qualified, 56–57
Immunity law, environmental, 294–295
In-house counsel, 12, 25, 64, 272–273,
    450–452
Indemnification clauses, 330
Informants, 42
Initial meeting, 7–14
Insider trading, 355, 356, 359–360
Inspections, 247
Inspector general (IG) subpoena, 340
Internal investigations. *See*
    Investigations, internal
Internal Revenue Service (IRS),
    192, 252
INTERPOL, Red Notice list, 477–488
Interviews, witness. *See* Employee
    interviews
Investigations, internal
    advantages of, 8–9, 444–448
    adverse effects on company, 448
    antitrust matters, 469–472
    attorney-client privilege, 10–11
    auditors involved in, 417–421,
        457–458, 505–508
    client identification, 7–8, 469–470
    communication outside corporation,
        456–458
    communication with management,
        454–456
    in connection with government
        investigation, 88–89
    counsel selection, 386–389,
        450–452, 501
    crime/fraud exception, 82
    criminal inquiries, 14–15
    decision to conduct, 8–9, 449, 500
    document control, 461–463
    document review, 152–153
    Garner doctrine, 86
    government contractors, 342
    initial meeting, 7–14
    initiation of, 452
    and McNulty Memo, 5–6
    objectives of, 454
    plan for, 453–463
    publicly traded companies, 370–376
    reporting and supervision, 12–13,
        501–502
    risk anticipation, 13–14
    Sarbanes-Oxley's impact on, 3–5,
        496–511
    scope of, 9–10, 502–504
    SEC requirements, 386–389
    structure of, 453–463, 470
    types of, 6–7, 96–97, 500–501
    and work-product protection
        doctrine, 11
Investigative record, 18
Investigative team
    document review, 152–153
    establishment of, 11–12, 453
Investment bankers, 458
IRS (Internal Revenue Service),
    192, 252
Issue preclusion (collateral estoppel),
    193–197

J

Joint defense doctrine
    common interest requirement,
        217–219
    confidentiality requirement, 220–223

definition of, 215–216
government authorities' view of, 461
information exchange, 219–220
remedies for breach of, 223–224
and waiver privilege, 83–86
Joint representation
and attorney-client privilege, 73–74
risks and benefits of, 212–224
Judicial proceedings, definition of, 131–132
Justice Department. *See* Department of Justice (DOJ)

K

Kennedy factors, 190–191
Klein conspiracy, 248–249

L

Legal advice. *See* Advice by counsel
Leniency Policy. *See* Corporate Leniency Policy
Libel, 319–330
  claims against counsel, 321–322
  minimizing liability for, 329–330
  opinion privilege, 322, 324–327, 329
  tests for, 323–324
  written reports as basis for, 319–321
Litigation support companies, 156
Lower-level employees, 22–23, 24, 99, 151, 289
Loyalty, duty of, 106

M

Management's discussion and analysis (MD&A), 364–365
McDade Amendment, 203
McKesson, 355 n.1, 402–403 n.118
McNulty Memorandum, 2, 5–6, 89–90, 210–211, 212, 236–238, 394–395, 407
Media, 286, 458
Medicaid, 337 n.2, 338, 426
Medicare, 338, 341–342, 425, 426, 432
Medicare fiscal intermediaries (FIs), 341–342

Medicare Fraud and Abuse Statute, 432
Medicare Prescription Drug, Improvement and Modernization Act (2003), 338
Meetings
  corporate, privilege for, 34–35
  initial meeting for document review, 150–152
  initial meeting for internal investigation, 7–14
  minutes, 271–272, 282
Memorandums, of employee interviews, 108–111
Misleading conduct, 113, 136–138
Misprision of felony, 118, 130 n.55, 243, 245

N

National Association of Securities Dealers (NASD), 381, 382, 383–384, 408 n.130
Negligence, 328–329
New York Stock Exchange (NYSE), 381–382, 383
No-contact rule, 200, 205–206, 208–209
Nolo contendere pleas, 195
Non-waiver stipulations, 72–73

O

Obstruction of justice
  dangers for counsel, 112–114, 248–250
  dangers for witnesses, 114
  document destruction, 140–145
  document production abuses, 167
  false statements, 131–135
  Sarbanes-Oxley provisions, 504–505
  witness tampering, 135–140
Occupational Safety and Health Administration (OSHA), 192, 292
Office of Inspector General (OIG)
  model compliance plans, 428–430, 433–434
  Provider Self-Disclosure Protocol, 434–438

Office of the Comptroller of the
    Currency (OCC), 189, 191, 247
Official proceedings, definition of, 133
Operations managers, 455–456
Opinion privilege, 322, 324–327, 329
Outside counsel, 12, 151, 272–273, 332,
    451–452

P

Parallel proceedings, 175–240
  antitrust matters, 489–490
  civil actions, stays of, 178–185,
    413–417
  collateral estoppel, 193–197
  and companies' provision of legal
    representation for employees,
    210–215
  debarment proceedings, 177,
    232–234, 349–350
  disciplining employees for
    misconduct, 197–200
  disclosure protection, 224–231
  Double Jeopardy Clause protection,
    188–193
  environmental, 290–291
  Fifth Amendment invocations by
    employees, 185–188, 406–413
  global settlements of, 234–239
  government contractors, 231–234, 347
  government lawyers' ex parte
    interviews of employees, 200–209
  joint defense agreements, 212–224
  overview of, 176–178
  privilege protection, 389–406
  securities violations, 384–420
  suspension proceedings, 177,
    231–234, 349–350
Patriot Act (2006), 476
PCAOB (Public Company Accounting
    Oversight Board), 494–495, 505
Perjury, 118–130
  ambiguous questions, 122–124
  burden of proof, 121–122
  false statements, willful, 119–121
  grand jury proceedings, 118, 124–126

  misleading answers, 123–124
  Section 1621 provisions, 118,
    119–124
  Section 1622 provisions, 118,
    126–127
  Section 1623 provisions, 118,
    124–126
  subornation of, 126–130
  true answers, 122–124
  two witness rule, 121–122, 125
Preparation of documents
  anticipation of litigation, work-
    product doctrine, 48–54
  by corporate employees, 56
  subsequent litigation, work-product
    doctrine, 54–56
Privacy, 57–58
Private Securities Litigation Reform Act
    (1995), 386
Privilege. *See also* Attorney-client
    privilege; Joint defense doctrine;
    Waiver of privilege; Work-product
    doctrine
  common-interest privilege, 217–219
  opinion, 322, 324–327, 329
  qualified interest-related, 327–329
  self-criticism, 18 n.1, 310–312,
    331, 398
Production of documents
  abuses in, 164, 167
  business records, 166–167
  complete set of documents, 165–166
  destruction of documents, 133,
    140–145, 167–168, 244–245, 504
  extraordinary measures, 164
  narrowing scope of request, 165
  on-site inspection, 165–166
  ordinary course, 164
  overloading opposition with, 165
  personal records, 166–167
Proffers, 489
Protective orders, 184–185, 226,
    400–401
Provider Self-Disclosure Protocol,
    434–436

Public Company Accounting Oversight
  Board (PCAOB), 494–495, 505
Public domain, 161
Publication, 219, 320, 327, 328, 330
Publicly traded companies, disclosure
    requirements
  investigation obligations, 370–376
  legal proceedings, 362–364
  management's discussion and analysis
    (MD&A), 364–365
  materiality requirement, 376–381
  specific duties, 361–370
  timing, 509–510

Q

Qualified immunity, 56–57
Qualified interest-related privilege,
    327–329
Questionnaires, 59, 60, 63, 64
Qui tam suits, 342–345

R

Records and record keeping
  auditors, 144–145
  business vs. personal, 166–167
  employee interviews, 108–111
  purpose of retention of investigative
    counsel, 32
Regulatory Relief Act (2006), 398
Report of investigation, 301–334
  antitrust matters, 471–472
  attorney-client privilege, 305–308,
    331–332
  disclosure to government agencies,
    63, 315–319, 406, 463
  discoverability of, 304–308
  libel claims from, 319–330
  minimizing risks, 331–334
  oral reports, benefits, 303–304
  privilege protection, 403–406
  qualified interest-related privileges,
    327–329
  remedial actions, recommendations,
    463–464
  self-criticism privilege, 310–312

shareholder actions, 312–315
who receives, 12–13
work-product doctrine, 308–310,
    331–332
written reports, 302–303, 319–321,
    403–404
Research, 100–101
Restatement (Second) of Torts,
    323–324, 325
Restitution funds, 239
Reverse Jencks rule, 103, 110

S

Sarbanes-Oxley Act (SOX) (2002)
  and attorney-client privilege, 86–88
  audit committees, 495
  auditors' obligations, 494–495,
    505–508
  certification of financial statements,
    442, 498
  chief legal officer requirements, 498
  code of ethics for senior financial
    officers, 497–498
  counsel conduct, 111–112, 245, 248,
    365–367, 495
  disclosure requirements, 4, 248,
    367–368, 493–494, 509–510
  document destruction, 133, 142–145,
    168, 504
  document retention requirements,
    244–245
  Fair Funds provision, 239
  impact of, 3–5, 492
  internal reporting, 245
  investigation obligations, 3–5,
    372–374, 496–511
  obstruction of justice provisions,
    504–505
  overview of, 493–496
  remedial steps, 510–511
  SEC enforcement powers,
    384–385
  Title VIII, 133, 142
  whistleblower provisions, 496–497
Seaboard Report, 87, 392, 446–447, 499

Search warrants
 antitrust matters, 476
 environmental audits, 284, 285–288
 expanded use of, 15
Securities Act (1933), 246
Securities and Exchange Act (1934)
 disclosure of information, 246, 493
 Section 10A, 418–420, 505–506
Securities and Exchange Commission (SEC)
 attorney-client privilege, 87–91
 civil penalties, 192, 239
 enforcement powers, 87–88, 384–385
 federal securities law enforcement, 88–89
 FOIA provisions, 225
 Form 8-K, 367–368
 investigative reports to, 76
 noisy withdrawal rule, 366–367
 Part 205 Rules, 245–246
 proposed rules of attorney professional conduct, 88 n.328
 Regulation S-K, 362–368
 Rule 10b-5, 369–370
 Rule 12b-20, 369–370
 Rule 205, 112
 Seaboard Report, 87, 392, 446–447, 499
 voluntary disclosure program, 86–87
Securities Enforcement Remedies and Penny Stock Reform Act (1990), 384–385
Securities law, 88–91, 112, 246
Securities violations
 auditors in internal investigations, 417–421
 broker obligations, 381–384
 dealer obligations, 381–384
 disclosure, duty of, 361–370
 Fifth Amendment invocation, 406–413
 materiality of, 376–381
 obligations to uncover, investigate, and report, 360–385
 parallel proceedings, 384–420

 privilege protection, 389–406
 publicly traded company obligations, 360–381
 stays of proceedings, 413–417
 types of, 354–360
Selective waiver doctrine, 397–399
Self-critical/self-evaluative privilege, 18 n.1, 310–312, 331, 398
Self-incrimination
 corporate rights, 166, 187
 employee rights, 137–138, 166–167, 179, 185–188, 411, 459
Self-regulatory organizations (SROs), 358–359
Sentencing Guidelines
 attorney-client privilege waiver, 91
 corporate compliance program provisions, 427–428, 442–443
 fine calculation and voluntary disclosure, 252–254
Settlement, global, 234–239
Sexual harassment, 41, 311
Shareholder litigation. *See also* Special Litigation Committees (SLCs)
 and attorney-client privilege, 82–86, 315
 class-action litigation, 265–266, 269, 272, 386
 derivative suits, 84–85, 264, 374
 investigative report discoverability, 312–315
 work-product doctrine, 84, 314
Sherman Antitrust Act, 467, 473–474
Sixth Amendment, 208, 211, 214, 223
SLCs. *See* Special Litigation Committees (SLCs)
Social Security Act, 432
SOX. *See* Sarbanes-Oxley Act (SOX) (2002)
Special Litigation Committees (SLCs), 261–282
 advice to witnesses, sample, 281
 and class-action litigation, 265–266
 counsel, selection of, 266–267, 388–389

dilemma of, 269–270
independence of, 267–269
interviews by, 271
investigation by, 277–279
meeting minutes, 271–272, 282
plaintiff's counsel, 265, 273–274
privilege protection, 274–277
relationship with other counsel, 272–273
resolution establishing, 280
responsibility of Committee vs. counsel, 270
setting for, 262–263
theoretical foundation for, 263–264
SROs (self-regulatory organizations), 358–359
State law
    antitrust enforcement, 468
    attorney fees, 5
    corporate misconduct, 178
    disclosure to state or local government agency, 319
    environmental audits, 294–295
    health care fraud, 425
    opinion privilege under, 326
    privilege under, 20–21, 46, 293, 294
    work-product protection, 11
Statement on Auditing Standards No. 99, 419
Stock exchange delisting or expulsion, 356–357
Stock option backdating, 355, 376, 389
Subornation of perjury, 126–130
Subpoenas
    antitrust matters, 475
    civil investigatory demands, 340–341
    DCAA requests, 341
    disclosure considerations before challenging or cooperating with, 225–226
    of documents, 167
    to employees, 96
    to government contractors, 340–342
    grand jury, 8, 226, 230, 249, 339

inspector general, 340
Medicare fiscal intermediaries, 341–342
Summaries, of documents, 164
Suppliers, 337–338
Supremacy Clause, 43
Suspension proceedings, 177, 231–234, 349–350

T

Team, investigative, 11–12, 152–153, 453
Testimony, and attorney-client privilege, 67–68
Third parties, 36, 40, 74, 157, 457–458
Thompson Memorandum, 5, 100, 210, 211, 236, 250–251, 407, 410, 499
Thornburgh Memorandum, 200–204

U

Union representatives, at employee interviews, 458
United States Constitution
    Double Jeopardy Clause, 188–193
    Eighth Amendment, 193
    Fifth Amendment, 138, 166–167, 180, 185–188, 406–413, 414, 415, 416
    First Amendment, 326, 485
    Sixth Amendment, 208, 211, 214, 223
Upjohn letters, 452
USA Patriot Act (2006), 476

V

Vicarious liability, 255, 444–445
Victim and Witness Protection Act (1982), 131, 135, 140, 200
Voluntary disclosure of information
    attorney-client privilege, effect on, 61–65, 255–256
    benefits of, 242, 250–254, 446–447
    government contractors, 342, 348–349
    health care companies, 431–438
    and libel liability, 330

Voluntary disclosure of information, *continued*
  mechanics of, 259
  non-waiver agreements, 72–73
  risks of, 242, 254–259
  SEC program, 86–87
  work-product doctrine, effecton, 256

W

Waiver of privilege. *See also* Disclosure of information
  attorney-client privilege, 5, 7, 60–74, 86–87, 89–90, 161–162, 237–238, 256–257, 348–349, 471, 508
  by government contractors, 348–349
  by joint defense agreements, 83–86
  limited, 315–318
  non-waiver stipulations, 72–73
  privileged information, 5
  with securities violations, 389–406
  selective waiver doctrine, 397–399
  Wigmore rule, 70
  work-product doctrine, 75–78, 89–90, 161–162, 237–238, 256, 257, 348–349, 508–509
Wells notice, 388
Whistle-blowers
  legal protection of, 200
  qui tam suits, 343
  Sarbanes-Oxley provisions, 496–497, 510
Wigmore rule, 70
Wiretapping, 476–477
Witness interviews. *See* Employee interviews
Witness tampering, 133, 135–140, 244

Work-product doctrine, 44–60
  anticipation of litigation, 11, 48–54, 109, 308
  vs. attorney-client privilege, 19
  auditors, 508–509
  corporate employees, materials prepared by, 56
  crime/fraud exception, 80–81
  definition of, 44–46
  elements of, 47–56
  employee interviews, 105, 109
  factual work product, 46–47, 56, 58–59, 77, 80, 309
  government contractor investigations, 348–349
  investigative report discoverability, 308–310
  lawyer's mental impressions protection, 57–60
  limited waiver of, 315–318
  opinion work product, 46–47, 56, 58–60, 77, 81, 309–310
  qualified immunity, overcoming, 56–57
  shareholder litigation protection, 84, 314
  Special Litigation Committee protection, 274–277
  subsequent litigation, 54–56
  substantial need test, 35, 47, 56, 58, 84
  undue hardship test, 35, 47, 56, 58, 84
  waiver of, 75–78, 89–90, 161–162, 237–238, 256, 257, 348–349, 508–509
WorldCom, 355 n.1